THE
DYNAMICS
OF MODERNIZATION
AND
SOCIAL CHANGE:
A READER

George S. Masannat
Western Kentucky University

Goodyear Publishing Company, Inc.
Pacific Palisades, California

K

Copyright © 1973
GOODYEAR PUBLISHING COMPANY, INC.
Pacific Palisades, California

Current Printing (last digit):
10 9 8 7 6 5 4 3 2 1
ISBN: 0-87620-209-1   73-3594
Library of Congress Catalog Card Number: 78-190510
Y- 2091-0
Printed in the United States of America

To My Mother — with much love

CONTENTS

iv

PART SIX

PART SEVEN

PREFACE

The main objective of this book is to explore the nature and magnitude of socio-economic and political problems that developing nations face in the transitional process from traditionalism to modernity. Since World War II the withdrawal of imperial powers from Asia and Africa has resulted in the creation of about 80 states and the transfer of political power to native leaders. Many of the developing nations of Africa, Asia and Latin America face, in varying degrees, crises of political integration, personal identity, and social unity. They differ in political culture, political structures, economic systems, natural resources, literacy rate, per capita income, and levels of development. Therefore, we should bear in mind, that any generalization about developing states must be qualified. Each state confronts particular problems. Even with a given geographic region such as the Middle East, Africa South of the Sahara, and Latin America we find variation between states such as between Yemen and Turkey in the Middle East, Ethiopia and the Republic of South Africa in Sub-Sahara Africa and between Bolivia and Columbia in Latin America. On the other hand, we should avoid considering each developing country as unique. It is therefore, the task of the social scientist to identify and analyze similarities and differences between developing states.

The articles in this volume present a set of scholarly, probing essays that will provide a conceptual framework of understanding the dynamic process of political development and its relationship to other societal transformations. In addition, these essays will give the student of developing nations a greater insight into the various aspects of political development and nation-building. Since only a fraction of the large body of relevant literature on modernization and political development can be reproduced in a collection of this type, I urge the student to explore his specific interests by reading some of the books noted at the end of each part of this text. Although the readings are hardly exhaustive, I have deliberately included selections that will sharpen the reader's curiosity, interest, and understanding in the field of politics of developing countries.

The readings are divided into seven parts: (1) Approaches to the Study of Comparative Political Systems; (2) The Meaning of Political Development; (3) Dilemmas of Traditional and Transitional Societies; (4) Nation-Building: Modernization and Political Integration; (5) Economic Development and Social Change; (6) Ideologies and Political Development; and (7) The Elites, Parties, Military, and Bureaucracy and Political Development. Each part opens with a brief introduction that supplies the political and analytical context for the readings and identifies their salient aspects.

Creating a book of this kind while immersed in the vast sea of literature on political modernization and political development led to difficult decisions by the editor. I am fully aware that many outstanding essays on modernization and political development have been omitted. The omission is not the result of an oversight but rather because of space limitations. Also, opinions may differ about the relevance and utility of the selections included, but this is to be expected. I am hopeful that what I have assembled in this volume will meet the needs of both students and instructors in the field of modernization and political development.

I want to express my deep appreciation to the authors and publishers who were kind enough to grant permission for reproduction of their materials. Also, I am grateful to Mrs. Ann Boggs, Department of Government secretary, for her cheerful and competent assistance; and, of course, to my wife for her inspiration and understanding. Finally, I am indebted to Western Kentucky University for the use of its library facilities in the reproduction of the essays in this book.

George S. Masannat

PART ONE

approaches
to the study
of comparative
political
systems

During the past two decades much of the work of political scientists has been concerned with the processes of modernization, social change, and institution formation in new states. In fact, the dominant concern in the field of comparative politics for methodological rigor and theoretical explication on the one hand and the study of modernization and political development on the other have been the most important themes in political science. The interest in the study of the politics of the "emergent," "developing," and "non-Western" nations of Afro-Asia and Latin America for the first time suggests the possibility of a global study of comparative politics.

Political scientists studying the new nations have used many models of theorizing about political development and the characteristics of the non-Western political processes. These models include: first, the legal administrative approach which explains development in terms of constitutional forms and administrative capacity to maintain law and order, efficiency, rationality, and neutrality. Second, the functional-system model as formulated by such social theorists as Talcott Parsons,

1

Marion Levy, R.K. Merton, and A.R. Radcliffe-Brown, to
mention a few, emphasizes interdependence, social stability,
and equilibrium. Perhaps the best known work in the function-
alist school is *The Politics of the Developing Areas* by Gabriel
A. Almond and James S. Coleman (eds.). In his introductory
chapter Almond writes: "This book is the first effort to compare the political systems of the 'developing' areas, and to
compare them systematically according to a common set of
categories."[1] The value of the Almond model is in the unified
way in which he selected and categorized the "universal"
political functions.

One of the main aspects of the functional model of political
development is the concern for the functional requisites of all
political systems. These requisites include the input functions of
political socialization and recruitment, interest articulation,
interest aggregation, and political communication on the one
hand, and the output functions which include rule making, rule
application, and rule adjudication on the other.

The third model of political development is the economic
approach which has, until recently, been based on the assumption that adequate capital formation and economic intrastruc-
tures are essential for sustained political development and stable
or viable democracies. The best known works dealing with this
economic approach to political development are W.W. Rostow's
The Stages of Economic Growth: A Non-Communist Manifesto
(Cambridge: Cambridge Univeristy Press, 1960) and Max F.
Millikan and W.W. Rostow's *A Proposal: Key to an Effective
Foreign Policy.* (New York: Harper, 1957) This model has been
criticized by many students of political development. Many
scholars, including economists, feel that in the developmental
process of the emerging nations, *political* factors are more
important than purely economic ones. Moreover, economic
modernization is only one of the many variables or determinants shaping political institutions and behavior in the new
states.[2]

A fourth model of political development is the elite model
which is represented in the work of Edward Shils' *Political
Development in the New States.* Shils points out that the main
task of the ruling elites in new states is the closing of the gap
between the aspirations of the intellectuals who are the few and
the masses who are the many. The closing of the gap Shils
writes, "is the prerequisite of the creation of a political society,

of a society which is modern not only in its economy and administration but in its moral order as well."[3] The ruling elites must be able to cope with the crisis of values as their societies move from traditionalism to modernity, and must be able to manipulate social change, set goals, and maintain their legitimacy.

Another model of political development is the communications approach. Perhaps the best known works in the communication models are Karl W. Deutsch's *Nationalism and Social Communication* (Cambridge: MIT Press, 1953) and Daniel Lerner's *The Passing of Traditional Society.* (Glencoe, Ill.: Free Press, 1958) The communication models emphasize mobilization or participation, rationalization, national integration and differentiation, and democratization.

Furthermore, there is the institutional model which examines the capacity of social organizations to adapt to change in the face of economic and political crisis. Political institutionalists such as Samuel P. Huntington and S.N. Eisenstadt assert that modernizing as well as modern states can change by losing capabilities as well as by gaining them. Huntington states that a theory of political development must, therefore, be considered along with a theory of political decay. Institutionally oriented social scientists such as Leonard Binder, William J. Foltz, Lloyd Fallers, and Seymour Martin Lipset have addressed themselves to political discontinuities, institutional change, and political integration and have viewed socio-political change as a problematic process that must be faced by ruling elites.[4]

In the following three articles in this chapter we will examine the classification of political systems, the major characteristics of the non-Western political processes, and finally, the various approaches to the study of political development.

Almond discusses the classification of political systems and uses sociological concepts (Weber-Parsons-Shils) to point out the differences between political systems. For instance, he defines such concepts as political system and role and states that these sociological concepts "can only be a beginning of a conceptual model of the political system." The concept of a political system implies that roles are interdependent and any significant change in one role affects changes in other roles. Almond points out that the distinguishing feature of the political system is the legitimate monopoly of force over a given people and territory. He discusses the meaning of orientation to

3

political action or political culture and turns his attention to a detailed examination of his fourfold classification of political systems.

Almond's classifications include: First, the Anglo-American political systems which are characterized by a secular and homogeneous political culture. He vividly points out the meaning of homogeneous and secular political culture and the role structure in the Anglo-American systems. Second, the pre-industrial political systems are mixed political cultures and mixed political systems. Mixed political cultures present the most serious problems of coordination and communication. Moreover, they face the problems of instability and unpredictability. These political systems are characterized by a low degree of structural differentiation, a lack of a stable and clear role structure, and a mixture of political role structures. Third, the totalitarian political culture is a controlled system which tends to be non-consensual. Orientation towards authority tends to be a combination of apathy and conformity. There are two distinctive aspects of the totalitarian role structure: (1) the predominance of the coercive roles and (2) the functional instability of the power roles—party, army, secret police, and bureaucracy. Fourth, the continental European political systems are characterized by a fragmented political culture. Almond discusses the various subcultures of the continental European systems and their general characteristics.

In the second article Lucian W. Pye discusses the dominant and distinctive characteristics of the non-Western political process. He points out that (1) in the non-Western countries the political sphere is not clearly differentiated from the spheres of social and personal relations. Political behavior is strongly colored by considerations of communal identification; (2) political parties in non-Western societies tend to adopt a world view and represent a way of life; (3) the political process is characterized by a prevalence of personal cliques; (4) the leadership of political groups enjoys a high degree of freedom in determining matters of strategy and tactics and this is because of the nature of political loyalty in non-Western societies; (5) opposition parties and counter-elites tend to appear as revolutionary movements; (6) the non-Western political process lacks integration among the participants and this situation is a function of a unified communications system; (7) the non-Western political process is characterized by a constant increase in

4

recruitment of new elements to political process. This aspect is attributed to the rapid rise in the urban population which has increased the number of people who have cognitive orientation towards national politics; (8) the non-Western process is characterized by sharp differences in the political orientation of the generation; (9) in non-Western societies there is little consensus as to the legitimate ends and means of political action; (10) in non-Western societies there is little relationship between the scope of political discussion and political decision making; (11) in non-Western political process there is a high degree of substitutability of roles; (12) in non-Western societies there are relatively few explicitly organized interest groups with clearly differentiated functions of roles. Interest groups act as protective associations and do not openly seek to influence the formation of public policy; (13) in non-Western societies the national leadership must appeal to an undifferentiated public; (14) the unstructured character of the non-Western political process encourages national leaders to adopt more clearly defined positions on international issues than on domestic issues. The international process is more clearly structured than the domestic political scene; (15) in non-Western societies the affective aspect of politics tends to override the problem-solving aspect of politics; (16) charismatic leaders tend to prevail in non-Western politics; and (17) the non-Western political process functions without the benefit of political "brokers."

Robert A. Packenham examines the various approaches to the study of political development, including: (1) the legal-formal, (2) economic, (3) administrative, (4) social system, and (5) political culture. The legal-formal approach conceives the conditions of political development in terms of constitutional forms. However, there is a movement away from this approach to the administrative, socio-economic, and psychological factors approach as explanatory variables of political development. The administrative approach to political development emphasizes administrative capacity to maintain law and order and rational, efficient, and effective organization. The danger of this approach may be that by stressing the need for achievement it may give inadequate attention to the problem of democratic political development.

Another approach is the idea that political development is mainly a function of a social system that facilitates popular participation in the political processes. This approach is ex-

5

pressed in terms of social correlates of democracy, social communication, group approach to politics, and structure-function analysis. Finally, political development is viewed primarily as a function of political culture. Packenham surveys the various works dealing with political development and political culture and states that it would be possible to add still other approaches such as the geographic approach and a seventh that might deal with stages of modernization over time.

NOTES

1. Gabriel A. Almond, "Introduction: A Functional Approach To Comparative Politics," in *The Politics of The Developing Areas*, ed. Gabriel A. Almond and James S. Coleman (Princeton: Princeton University Press, 1960), p. 3.

2. Almond and Coleman, *The Developing Areas*, pp. 538-44.

3. Edward Shils, *Political Development In The New States* (The Hague: Mouton, 1968), p. 87.

4. For a critique of the current models of political development see Chong-Do Hah and Jeanne Schneider, "A Critique of Current Studies on Political Development and Modernization," *Social Research* 35, no. 1 (Spring 1968): 130-58.

COMPARATIVE POLITICAL SYSTEMS

Gabriel Almond

What I propose to do in this brief paper is to suggest how the application of certain sociological and anthropological concepts may facilitate systematic comparison among the major types of political systems operative in the world today.

At the risk of saying the obvious, I am not suggesting to my colleagues in the field of comparative government that social theory is a conceptual cure-all for the ailments of the discipline. There are many ways of laboring in the vineyard of the Lord, and I am quite prepared to concede that there are more musical forms of psalmody that sociological jargon. I suppose the test of the sociological approach that is discussed here is whether or not it enables us to solve certain persistent problems in the field more effectively than we now are able to solve them.

Our expectations of the field of comparative government have changed in at least two ways in the last decades. In the first place as American interests have broadened to include literally the whole world, our course offerings have expanded to include the many areas outside of Western Europe—Asia, the Middle East, Africa, and Latin America. Secondly, as our international interests have expanded and become more urgent, our requirements in knowledge have become more exacting. We can no longer view political crises in France with detached curiosity or view countries such as Indo-China and Indonesia as interesting political pathologies. We are led to extend our discipline and intensify it simultaneously.

It would simply be untrue to say that the discipline of comparative government has not begun to meet both of these challenges. As rapidly as it has been possible to train the personnel, new areas have been opened up to teaching and research; and there has been substantial encouragement to those who have been tempted to explore new aspects of the political

From Gabriel Almond, "Comparative Political Systems," *Journal of Politics* 18 (August 1956): 391-409. Reprinted by permission of the author and the publisher.

7

process both here and abroad and to employ new methods in such research. It is precisely because of the eagerness and energy with which these challenges have been met that the field is now confronted with the problem of systematic cumulation and comparison. What appears to be required in view of the rapid expansion of the field are more comparative efforts in the tradition of Finer and Friedrich, if we are to gain the maximum in insight and knowledge from this large-scale research effort.

The problem to which this paper is a tentative and provisional answer is the following. With the proliferation of courses and special studies of specific "governments" and groupings of governments on an area or other bases, is it possible to set up and justify a preliminary classification into which most of the political systems which we study today can be assigned? The classifications which we now employ are particularistic (e.g., American Government, British Government, the Soviet Union, and the like); regional (e.g., Government and Politics of the Far East, Latin America, and the like); or political (e.g., the British Commonwealth, Colonial Government, and the like); or functional (e.g., the comprehensive comparative efforts limited to the European-American area, such as Finer and Friedrich, and the specific institutional comparisons such as comparative parties, and comparative administration).

Anyone concerned with this general problem of classification of political systems will find that all of the existing bases of classification leave something to be desired. Dealing with governments particularistically is no classification at all. A regional classification is based not on the properties of the political systems, but on their contiguity in space. The existing structural classifications, such as democracy-dictatorship, parliamentary-presidential systems, two-party and multi-party systems, often turn out to miss the point, particularly when they are used in the strikingly different political systems of the pre-industrial areas. There may be a certain use therefore in exploring the possibilities of other ways of classifying political systems. What is proposed here is just one of these ways, and because of the uneven state of our knowledge is necessarily crude and provisional.

In my own efforts to stand far off, so to speak, and make the grossest discriminations between types of empirical political systems operative in the world today, I have found a fourfold classification to be most useful: the Anglo-American (including some members of the Commonwealth), the Continental European (exclusive of the Scandinavian and Low Countries, which combine some of the features of the Continental European and the Anglo-American), the pre-industrial, or partially industrial, political systems outside the European-American area, and the totalitarian political systems. This classification will not include all the political systems in existence today, but it comes close to doing so. It will serve the purpose of today's discussion, which is not that of testing the inclusiveness of this classification but rather the usefulness of sociological concepts in bringing out the essential differences between these political systems.

The terms which I shall use in discriminating the essential properties of these classes have emerged out of the Weber-Parsons tradition in social theory.[1] I shall try to suggest why I find some of these concepts useful. First, a political system is a system of *action*. What this means is that the student of political systems is concerned with empirically observable behavior. He is concerned with norms or institutions in so far as they affect behavior. Emphasizing "action" merely means that the description of a political system can never be satisfied by a simple description of its legal or ethical norms. In other words, political institutions or persons performing political roles are viewed in terms of what it is that they do, why they do it, and how what they do is related to and affects what others do. The term *system*[2] satisfies the need for an inclusive concept which covers all of the patterned actions relevant to the making of political decisions. Most political scientists use the term *political process* for these purposes. The difficulty with the term *process* is that it means any patterning of action through time. In contrast to process, the concept of *system* implies a *totality* of relevant units, an interdependence between the interactions of units, and a certain stability in the interaction of these units (perhaps best described as a changing equilibrium).

The unit of the political system is the role. The role, according to Parsons and Shils, ". . . is that organized sector of an actor's orientation which constitutes and defines his participation in an interactive process."[3] It involves a set of complementary expectations concerning his own actions and those of others with whom he interacts. Thus a political system may be defined as a set of interacting roles, or as a structure of roles, if we understand by *structure* a patterning of interactions. The advantage of the concept of *role* as compared with such terms as *institutions*, *organizations*, or *groups*, is that it is a more inclusive and more open concept. It can include formal offices, informal offices, families, electorates, mobs, casual as well as persistent groupings, and the like, in so far as they enter into and affect the political system. The use of other concepts such as those indicated above involves ambiguity, forced definitions (such as groups) or residual categories. Like the concept of system it does not prejudice our choice of units but rather enables us to nominate them on the basis of empirical investigation.

While there appear to be certain advantages in these concepts of political system and role for our purposes, they confront the political scientist with a serious problem. While he intends the concept to have a general application, Parsons appears to have had before him in elaborating the concept the model of the primary group—family, friendship, and the like—and not complex social systems, the units of which are collectivities and not individual actors. In this sense the sociological concept of system and of role can only be a beginning of a conceptual model of the political system. The job of developing additional concepts necessary to handle macrocosmic social systems such as political systems—national and international—is still to be done.

9

My own conception of the distinguishing properties of the political system proceeds from Weber's definition—the legitimate monopoly of physical coercion over a given territory and population.[4] The political systems with which most political scientists concern themselves are all characterized by a specialized apparatus which possesses this legitimate monopoly, and the political system consists of those interacting roles which affect its employment. There are, of course, simpler societies in which this function of maintenance of order through coercion is diffuse and unspecialized; it is combined with other functions in the family and other groupings. While these systems are also properly the subject matter of political science, there are few political scientists indeed with the specialized equipment necessary to study them.

It may be useful to add a few comments about this definition of politics and the political in order to avoid misunderstanding. To define politics as having this distinguishing property of monopolizing legitimate coercion in a given territory is not the same thing as saying that this is *all* that government does. It is the thing that government does and that other social systems ordinarily may not do legitimately. Other social systems may employ other forms of compulsion than physical coercion. Some indeed may legitimately employ physical coercion on a limited scale. But the employment of *ultimate, comprehensive,* and *legitimate* physical coercion is the monopoly of states, and the political system is uniquely concerned with the scope, the direction, and the conditions affecting the employment of this physical coercion. It is, of course, clear that political systems protect freedoms and provide welfare, as well as impose order backed up by physical compulsion, but even their protection of freedom and their provision of welfare is characteristically backed up by the threat of physical compulsion. Hence it seems appropriate to define the political system as the patterned interaction of roles affecting decisions backed up by the threat of physical compulsion.

The task of describing a political system consists in characterizing all the patterned interactions which take place within it. It takes us beyond the legal system into all the roles which occur and involves our defining these roles in action or behavioral terms. The concept of system implies that these roles are interdependent and that a significant change in any one role affects changes in the others, and thereby changes the system as a whole. Thus the emergence of pressure groups in the present century produced certain changes in the party system and in the administrative and legislative processes. The rapid expansion of executive bureaucracy was one of the factors that triggered off the development of legislative bureaucracy and pressure group bureaucracy. Changes in the role of political communication have transformed the electoral process, the behavior of parties, the legislature, the executive. The concepts of system and of interdependence lead us to look for these changes when any specific role changes significantly. It suggests the usefulness of thinking at the level of the system and its interdependence rather than in terms of

10

discrete phenomena or only limited bilateral relationships, or relationships occurring only within the formal-legal role structure.

The fourth concept is *orientation to political action.* Every political system is embedded in a set of meanings and purposes. We speak of "attitudes toward politics," "political values," "ideologies," "national character," "cultural ethos." The difficulty with all these terms is that their meanings are diffuse and ambiguous. The concepts of orientation to action and of the pattern variables are useful since they at least attempt logical distinctness and comprehensiveness. It is not essential for my purposes to go into the modes of orientation of action, or into the "pattern variables" in detail. Parsons and Shils tell us that any orientation to politics involves three components: the first is perception, or *cognition;* the second is preference, involvement, or affect (*cathexis*); the third is evaluation or choice through the application of standards or values to the cognitive and affective components. By *cognition* is meant the knowledge and discrimination of the objects, events, actions, issues, and the like. By *cathexis* is meant the investment of objects, issues, etc., with emotional significance, or affect. By *evaluation* is meant the manner in which individuals organize and select their perceptions, preferences, and values in the process of establishing a position *vis-a-vis political action.*[5]

Every political system is embedded in a particular pattern of orientations to political action. I have found it useful to refer to this as the *political culture.* There are two points to be made regarding the concept of political culture. First, it does not coincide with a given political system or society. Patterns of orientation to politics may, and usually do, extend beyond the boundaries of political systems. The second point is that the political culture is not the same thing as the general culture, although it is related to it. Because political orientation involves cognition, intellection, and adaptation to external situations, as well as the standards and values of the general culture, it is a differentiated part of the culture and has a certain autonomy. Indeed, it is the failure to give proper weight to the cognitive and evaluative factors, and to the consequent autonomy of political culture, that has been responsible for the exaggerations and over-simplificatons of the "national character" literature of recent years.

The usefulness of the concept of political culture and its meaning may perhaps be conveyed more effectively through illustration. I would argue that the United States, England, and several of the Commonwealth countries have a common political culture, but are separate and different kinds of political systems. And I would argue that the typical countries of continental Western Europe, while constituting individual political systems, include several different political cultures which extend beyond their borders. In other words, they are political systems with fragmented political cultures.

In an effort to overcome understandable resistances to the introduction of a new term, I should like to suggest why I find the concept of political culture more useful than the terms we now employ, such as *ideology* or

11

political party. As I understand the term *ideology,* it means the systematic and explicit formulation of a general orientation to politics. We need this term to describe such political phenomena as these and should not reduce its specificity by broadening it to include not only the explicit doctrinal structure characteristically borne by a minority of *militants,* but also the vaguer and more implicit orientations which generally characterize political followings. The term *political party* also cannot serve our purpose, for we are here dealing with a formal organization which may or may not be a manifestation of a political culture. Indeed, we will be gravely misled if we try to force the concept of party to mean political culture. Thus the commonly used distinctions between one-party, two-party, and multi-party systems simply get nowhere in distinguishing the essential properties of the totalitarian, the Anglo-American, and the Continental European political systems. For the structure we call *party* in the totalitarian system is not a party at all; the two parties of the Anglo-American system are organized manifestations of a homogeneous political culture; and the multi-parties of Continental European political systems in some cases are and in some cases are not the organized manifestations of different political cultures.

But the actual test of the usefulness of this conceptual scheme can only come from a more detailed application of it in developing the special properties of the classes of political systems to which we earlier referred.

THE ANGLO-AMERICAN POLITICAL SYSTEMS

The Anglo-American political systems are characterized by a *homogeneous, secular* political culture. By a secular political culture I mean a multivalued political culture, a rational-calculating, bargaining, and experimental political culture. It is a homogeneous culture in the sense that there is a sharing of political ends and means. The great majority of the actors in the political system accept as the ultimate goals of the political system some combination of the values of freedom, mass welfare, and security. There are groups which stress one value at the expense of the others; there are times when one value is stressed by all groups; but by and large the tendency is for all these values to be shared, and for no one of them to be completely repressed. To a Continental European this kind of political culture often looks sloppy. It has no logic, no clarity. This is probably correct in an intellectual sense, since this balancing of competing values occurs below the surface among most people and is not explicated in any very elegant way. Actually the logic is complex and is constantly referred to reality in an inductive process. It avoids the kind of logical simplism which characterizes much of the Continental European ideological polemic.

12

A secularized political system involves an individuation of and a measure of autonomy among the various roles. Each one of the roles sets itself up autonomously in political business, so to speak. There tends to be an arms-length bargaining relationship among the roles. The political system is saturated with the atmosphere of the market. Groups of electors come to the political market with votes to sell in exchange for policies. Holders of offices in the formal-legal role structure tend to be viewed as agents and instrumentalities, or as brokers occupying points in the bargaining process. The secularized political process has some of the characteristics of a laboratory; that is, policies offered by candidates are viewed as hypotheses, and the consequences of legislation are rapidly communicated within the system and constitute a crude form of testing hypotheses. Finally, because the political culture tends to be homogeneous and pragmatic, it takes on some of the atmosphere of a game. A game is a good game when the outcome is in doubt and when the stakes are not too high. When the stakes are too high, the tone changes from excitement to anxiety. While "fun" is frequently an aspect of Anglo-American politics, it is rarely a manifestation of Continental European politics; and, unless one stretches the definition, it never occurs at all in totalitarian politics.

ROLE STRUCTURE IN THE ANGLO-AMERICAN POLITICAL SYSTEMS

The role structure in this group of political systems is (1) highly differentiated, (2) manifest, organized, and bureaucratized, (3) characterized by a high degree of stability in the functions of the roles, and (4) likely to have a diffusion of power and influence within the political system as a whole.

With regard to the first point, each one of the units—formal governmental agencies, political parties, pressure groups and other kinds of voluntary associations, the media of communication, and "publics" of various kinds—pursues specialized purposes and performs specialized functions in the system. As was already pointed out, each one of these entities is more or less autonomous—interdependent, but autonomous. Certainly there are striking differences in this respect as between the United States and the United Kingdom, but their similarity becomes clear in contrast to the other major types of systems which will be described below. Secondly, this role structure is manifest and on the surface. Most of the potential "interests" have been organized and possess bureaucracies. Thirdly, there is in contrast to some of the other systems a relatively high degree of stability of function in the various parts of the structure. Bureaucracies function as bureaucracies, armies as armies, parliaments as parliaments. The functions are not ordinarily substitutable as among these various institutions and organizations, in contrast to some of the other

13

systems. This is another way of saying that the political division of labor is more complex, more explicit, and more stable. There are, of course, striking differences between the British and American versions in these respects. For the American system is at the same time more complex and less stable than the British. There are, for example, many more pressure groups and types of pressure groups in the United States for reasons of size, economic complexity, and ethnic and religious heterogeneity. Furthermore there is more substitutability of function in the American system, more policy making by pressure groups and the media of communication, more intervention in policy making through the transient impact of "public moods." But again if we are comparing the Anglo-American system with, for example, the pre-industrial or partially industrial systems, the British and American systems will stand out by virture of their similarities on the score of complexity, manifestness, and stability of role structure.

Finally the Anglo-American type of political system is one in which there is a diffusion of power and influence. This is only partially expressed in the formal legal phraseology of a democratic suffrage and representative government. There is an effective as well as a legal diffusion of power, resulting from a system of mass communications, mass education, and representation by interest groups. Here again the British and American versions differ sharply in terms of formal governmental structure, the relations between parties and pressure groups, and the system of communication and education. The net result is a more centralized, predictable role structure in Britain than in the United States.

THE PRE-INDUSTRIAL
POLITICAL SYSTEMS

The political systems which fall under this very general category are the least well-known of all four of the classes discussed here. But despite our relative ignorance in this area and our inability to elaborate the many subtypes which no doubt exist, a discussion of this kind of political system is analytically useful since it presents such a striking contrast to the homogeneous, secular political culture, and the complex and relatively stable role structure of the Anglo-American political system.

The pre-industrial—or partially industrialized and Westernized—political systems may be best described as mixed political cultures and mixed political systems. Nowhere does the need for additional vocabulary become clearer than in the analysis of these systems; for here parliaments tend to be something other than parliaments, parties and pressure groups behave in unusual ways, bureaucracies and armies often dominate the political system, and there is an atmosphere of unpredictability and gunpowder surrounding the political system as a whole.

Some clarity is introduced into the understanding of these systems if one recognizes that they are embedded in mixed political cultures. What this means is that as a minimum we have two political cultures, the Western system with its parliament, its electoral system, its bureaucracy and the like, and the pre-Western system or systems. In countries such as India there are many traditional political cultures which intermingle with the Western system. What kind of amalgam emerges from this impingement of different political cultures will depend on at least five factors: (1) the type of traditional cultures which are involved; (2) the auspices under which Westernization has been introduced (e.g., Western colonial powers, or native elites); (3) the functions of the society which have been Westernized; (4) the tempo and tactics of the Westernization process; (5) the type of Western cultural products which have been introduced. As a consequence of this impingement of the Western and traditional political cultures, there is a third type of political culture which frequently emerges in this type of system; what in Max Weber's language may be called a charismatic political culture. It often happens as a consequence of the erosion of a traditional political culture that powerful forces are released—anxieties over the violation of sacred customs and relationships, feelings of rootlessness and directionlessness because of the rejection of habitual routines. The impact of the Western rational system on the traditional system or systems often creates a large potential for violence. One of the typical manifestations of this conflict of political cultures is the charismatic nationalism which occurs so frequently in these areas and which may be in part understood as being a movement toward accepting a new system of political norms, or a movement toward reaffirming the older traditional ones, often both in peculiar combinations. To overcome the resistance of habitual routines backed up by supernatural sanctions, the new form of legitimacy must represent a powerful affirmation capable of breaking up deeply ingrained habits and replacing earlier loyalties. Thus, at the minimum, we must have in these political systems the old or the traditional political culture, or cultures, the new or the Western-rational political culture, and transitional or resultant political phenomena of one kind or another. Needless to say, this typical mixture of political cultures presents the most serious problems of communication and coordination. We are dealing with a political system in which large groups have fundamentally different "cognitive maps" of politics and apply different norms to political action. Instability and unpredictability are not to be viewed as pathologies but as inescapable consequences of this type of mixture of political cultures.

ROLE STRUCTURE IN THE
PRE-INDUSTRIAL POLITICAL SYSTEMS

These characteristics of the pre-industrial political systems may be brought out more clearly and systematically in an analysis of the political role structure which is more or less characteristic.

15

There is first a relatively low degree of structural differentiation. Political interest often tends to be latent and when it emerges into politics often takes the form of spontaneous, violent action. Political parties are unstable; they fragment and consolidate, appear and disappear. There is ordinarily only a rudimentary specialized system of communication. Unless there is a bureaucracy left by a Western colonial power, the bureaucratic structure may be only partially developed.

Secondly, because of the absence of a stable and explicit role structure, there is likely to be a high degree of *substitutability* of roles. Thus bureaucracies may take over the legislative function, and armies may and often do the same. A political party may preempt the policy-making function, or a mob may emerge and take the center of the policy-making stage for a brief interval. In other words, in contrast to the Anglo-American political systems, there is no stable division of political labor.

A third and most important aspect of these political systems is the mixing of political role structures. Thus there may be a parliament formally based on a set of legal norms and regulations; but operating within it may be a powerful family, a religious sect, a group of tribal chieftains, or some combination of these. These are elements of the traditional role structure operating according to their own traditional norms. The student of these political systems would be greatly misled if he followed Western norms and expectations in describing such a decision making system. What would be corruption in a Western parliament would be normatively oriented conduct in a "mixed parliament" of the kind often found in the regions outside of the Western-European American area.

Thus such concepts as mixed political culture and mixed political role structures may prepare the field researcher more adequately than the accepted political science theory and terminology; for in going to Indonesia or Thailand he will not have in mind the Western conception of political process and system and a conception of the appropriate roles of legislatures, bureaucracies, parties, pressure groups, and public opinion, but will rather look for the particular pattern of amalgamation of these roles with the traditional roles. His intellectual apparatus would enable him to grapple more quickly and more adequately with political phenomena which he might otherwise overlook, or treat as pathologies.

TOTALITARIAN POLITICAL SYSTEMS

The totalitarian political culture gives the appearance of being homogeneous, but the homogeneity is synthetic. Since there are no voluntary associations, and political communication is controlled from the center, it is impossible to judge in any accurate way the extent to which there is a positive acceptance of the totalitarian order. One can only say that in view of the thorough-going penetration of the society by a centrally controlled system of organizations and communications, and the special way in which coercion or its threat is applied, the totalitarian system, in contrast to the others, tends to be non-consensual. This is not to say that it is completely non-consensual. A completely coercive political system is unthinkable. But if one were to place the totalitarian system on a continuum of consensual-non-consensual it would be located rather more at the non-consensual end of the continuum than the others described here. Unlike the other systems where some form of legitimacy—whether traditional, rational-legal, or charismatic—underlies the acquiescence of the individual in the political system, in the totalitarian order the characteristic orientation to authority tends to be some combination of conformity and apathy. This type of political system has become possible only in modern times, since it depends on the modern technology of communication, on modern types of organization, and on the modern technology of violence. Historic tyrannies have no doubt sought this kind of dominion but were limited in the effectiveness of their means. Totalitarianism is tyranny with a rational bureaucracy, a monopoly of the modern technology of communication, and a monopoly of the modern technology of violence.

ROLE STRUCTURE IN
TOTALITARIAN POLITICAL SYSTEMS

I believe Franz Neumann in his *Behemoth*[6] was one of the first students of totalitarianism who rejected the *monocratic* model as being useful in understanding these systems. He spoke of the peculiar shapelessness of the Nazi regime, of the fact that there was no stable delegation of power among the bureaucracy, party, the army, the organizations of big business, and the like. He concluded, as you recall, that there was no state under the Nazis. I believe what he meant to say was that there was no *legitimate* state. Later students of totalitarianism such as Hannah Arendt,[7] Merle Fainsod,[8] Carl Friedrich,[9] Alex Inkeles,[10] and Barrington Moore, Jr.,[11] have been led to similar conclusions about totalitarianism in general, or about Soviet totalitarianism. Hannah Arendt has painted the most extreme picture, which, while an exaggeration, is useful analytically. She argues that the "isolation of atomized individuals provides not only the mass basis for totalitarian rule, but is carried through at the very top of the whole structure." The aim of this process of atomization is to destroy solidarity at any point in the system and to avoid all stable delegations of power which might reduce the freedom of maneuver of those at the very center of the system. "As techniques of government, the totalitarian devices appear simple and ingeniously effective. They assure not only an absolute power monopoly, but unparalleled certainty that all commands

17

will always be carried out; the multiplicity of the transmission belts, the confusion of the hierarchy, secure the dictator's complete independence of all his inferiors and make possible the swift and surprising changes in policy for which totalitarianism has become famous."[12]

There are thus at least two distinctive characteristics of the totalitarian role structure: (1) the predominance of the coercive roles, and (2) the functional instability of the power roles—bureaucracy, party, army, and secret police. The predominance of the coercive role structure is reflected in its penetration of all of the other role structures. Thus all forms of organization and communication become saturated with a coercive flavor. This predominance of coercion is reflected in the celebrated definition of the state as "bodies of armed men" in Lenin's *State and Revolution*. It is also reflected in the doctrine of the "potential enemy of the state," a conception under which almost any behavior may be arbitrarily defined as disloyal behavior. This eliminates the predictability of the impact of coercion and renders it an omnipresent force, however limited its application may be in a quantitative sense.

The functional instability among the power roles has as its main purpose the prevention of any stable delegation of power, and the consequent diffusion of power and creation of other power centers. This pattern was apparently quite marked in the development of the Nazi regime and has been observable in the uneasy balance established in the Soviet Union between party, bureaucracy, army, and secret police. In the nature of the case there must be a stabler delegation of power among the economic allocative roles, but even these roles are penetrated by the coercive role structure and manipulated within limits. A third class of roles is illustrated by the electoral process and the representative system, as well as the practice of "self-criticism" in the party. While there is a set of norms under which these activities are supposed to influence power and policy making, they are rather to be understood as mobilizing devices, as devices intended to create a facade of consent.

THE CONTINENTAL EUROPEAN
POLITICAL SYSTEMS

We refer here primarily to France, Germany, and Italy. The Scandinavian and Low Countries stand somewhere in between the Continental pattern and the Anglo-American. What is most marked about the Continental European systems if the fragmentation of political culture; but this fragmentation is rather different from that of the non-Western systems. For in the non-Western systems we are dealing with mixed political cultures involving the most striking contrasts. The Western political culture arising out of a very different development pattern is introduced bodily, so to speak, from the outside. In the Continental

European systems we are dealing with a pattern of political culture characterized by an uneven pattern of development. There are significant survivals, "outcroppings," of older cultures and their political manifestations. But all of the cultural variations have common roots and share a common heritage.

In view of this developmental pattern it may be appropriate to speak of the Continental European systems as having political subcultures. There is indeed in all the examples of this type of system a surviving pre-industrial subculture (e.g., the Catholic *Ancien Régime* areas in France, Southern Italy, and the Islands, and parts of Bavaria). The historical background of all three of these systems is characterized by a failure on the part of the middle classes in the nineteenth century to carry through a thorough-going secularization of the political culture. Thus another political subculture in these political systems constitutes remnants of the older middle classes who are still primarily concerned with the secularization of the political system itself. A third group of political subcultures is associated with the modernized and industrialized parts of these societies. But because they emerged in an only partially secularized political culture, their potentialities for "political market" behavior were thwarted. As major political subcultures there are thus these three: (1) the pre-industrial, primarily Catholic components, (2) the older middle-class components, and (3) the industrial components proper. But the political culture is more complex than this. Since in the last century the political issues have involved the very survival of these subcultures, and the basic form of the political system itself, the political actors have not come to politics with specific bargainable differences but rather with conflicting and mutually exclusive designs for the political culture and political system. This has involved a further fragmentation at the level of ideology and political organizations. Thus the pre-industrial, primarily Catholic element has both an adaptive, semisecular wing and an antisecular wing. The middle classes are divided into conservative wings in uneasy alliance with clerical pre-republican elements, and left-wings in uneasy friendship with socialists. Finally, the industrial workers are divided according to the degree of their alienation from the political system as a whole. The organized political manifestations of this fragmented political culture take the form of "movements" or sects, rather than of political parties. This means that political affiliation is more of an act of faith than of agency.

Perhaps the most pronounced characteristic of the political role structure in these areas is what one might call a general alienation from the political market. The political culture pattern is not adapted to the political system. For while these countries have adopted parliaments and popular elections, they are not appropriately oriented to these institutions. The political actors come to the market not to exchange, compromise, and adapt, but to preach, exhort, convert, and transform the political system into something other than a bargaining agency. What bargaining and exhanging does occur tends to take the form of under-the-counter   19 transactions. Thus demoralization (*"transformism"*) is an almost inescapable consequence of this combination of political culture and system. In contrast, the normatively consistent, morally confident actor in this type of political system is the *militant* who remains within the confines of his political subculture, continually reaffirms his special norms, and scolds his parliamentarians.

This suggests another essential characteristic of this type of role structure, which places it in contrast to the Anglo-American. There is not an individuation of the political roles, but rather the roles are embedded in the subcultures and tend to constitute separate subsystems of roles. Thus the Catholic subculture has the Church itself, the Catholic schools, propaganda organizations such as Catholic Action, Catholic trade unions, or worker organizations, a Catholic party or parties, and a Catholic press. The Communist subculture—the subculture of the political "alienates"— similarly has a complete and separate system of roles. The socialist and "liberal" subcultures tend in the same direction but are less fully organized and less exclusive. Thus one would have to say that the center of gravity in these political systems is not in the formal-legal role structure but in the political subcultures. Thus "immobilism" would appear to be a normal property of this kind of political system, and it is not so much an "immobilism" of formal-legal institutions as a consequence of the condition of the political culture. Needless to say, this portrayal of the Continental European political system has been exaggerated for purposes of contrast and comparison.

Two other general aspects of the role structure of these countries call for comment. First, there is a higher degree of substitutability of roles than in the Anglo-American political systems and a lesser degree than in the non-Western systems. Thus parties may manipulate pressure groups in the sense of making their decisions for them (the Communist case); interest groups such as the Church and Catholic Action may manipulate parties and trade unions; and interest groups may operate directly in the legislative process, although this last pattern occurs in the Anglo-American system as well. The "immobilism" of the formally political organs often leads to a predominance of the bureaucracy in policy making.

A second general characteristic, which is a consequence of the immobilism of the political system as a whole, is the ever-present threat of what is often called the "Caesaristic" breakthrough. As in the non-Western area, although the situations and causes are different, these systems tend always to be threatened by, and sometimes to be swept away by, movements of charismatic nationalism which break through the boundaries of the political subcultures and overcome immobilism through coercive action and organization. In other words, these systems have a totalitarian potentiality in them. The fragmented political culture may be transformed into a synthetically homogeneous one and the stalemated role structure mobilized by the introduction of the coercive pattern already described.

In conclusion perhaps the point might be made that conceptual and terminological growth in the sciences is as inevitable as the growth of language itself. But just as all the slang and neologisms of the moment do not find a permanent place in the language, so also all of the conceptual jargon which the restless minds of scholars invent—sometimes to facilitate communication with their colleagues and sometimes to confound them— will not find its permanent place in the vocabulary of the disciplines. The ultimate criterion of admission or rejection is the facilitation of understanding, and this, fortunately enough, is not in the hands of the restless and inventive scholar, but in the hands of the future scholarly generations who will try them out for "fit." If I may be permitted to conclude with a minor note of blasphemy, it may be said of new concepts as it was said of the salvation of souls . . . "there shall be weeping and gnashing of teeth, for many are called but few are chosen."

NOTES

1. See in particular Max Weber, *The Theory of Social and Economic Organization*, trans. A. M. Henderson and Talcott Parsons (New York: Oxford University Press, 1947), pp. 87 ff.

2. See David Easton, *The Political System: An Inquiry into the State of Political Science* (New York: Alfred A. Knopf, 1953), pp. 90 ff.

3. Talcott Parsons and Edward A. Shils, eds., *Toward a General Theory of Action* (Cambridge, Mass.: Harvard University Press, 1951), p. 23.

4. From Max Weber, *Essays in Sociology*, trans. H. H. Gerth and C. Wright Mills (New York: Oxford University Press, 1946), p. 78.

5. Parsons and Shils, *Toward a General Theory*, pp. 58 ff.

6. Franz Neumann, *Behemoth: The Structure and Practice of National Socialism* (New York: Oxford University Press, 1942), pp. 459 ff.

7. Hannah Arendt, *The Origins of Totalitarianism* (New York: Harcourt Brace Jovanovich, 1951), p. 388.

8. Merle Fainsod, *How Russia is Ruled* (Cambridge, Mass.: Harvard University Press, 1953), pp. 354 ff.

9. Carl J. Friedrich, ed., *Totalitarianism* (Cambridge, Mass.: Harvard University Press, 1954), pp. 47 ff.

10. Alex Inkeles in *ibid.*, pp. 88 ff.

11. Barrington Moore, Jr., *Terror And Progress USSR: Some Sources of Change and Stability in the Soviet Dictatorship* (Cambridge, Mass.: Harvard University Press, 1954), pp. 154 ff.

12. Arendt, *Totalitarianism*, p. 389.

THE NON-WESTERN
POLITICAL PROCESS

Lucian W. Pye

The purpose of this article is to outline some of the dominant and distinctive characteristics of the non-Western political process. In recent years, both the student of comparative politics and the field worker in the newly emergent and economically underdeveloped countries have found it helpful to think in terms of a general category of non-Western politics.[1]

There are, of course, great differences among the non-Western societies. Indeed, in the past, comparative analysis was impeded by the appreciation of the rich diversity in the cultural traditions and the historical circumstances of the Western impact; students and researchers found it necessary to concentrate on particular cultures, and as a consequence attention was generally directed to the unique features of each society. Recently, however, attempts to set forth some of the characteristics common to the political life of countries experiencing profound social change have stimulated fruitful discussions among specialists on the different non-Western regions as well as among general students of comparative politics.

For this discussion to continue, it is necessary for specialists on the different areas to advance, in the form of rather bold and unqualified statements, generalized models of the political process common in non-Western societies.[2] Then, by examining the ways in which particular non-Western countries differ from the generalized models, it becomes possible to engage in significant comparative analysis.

1. *In non-Western societies the political sphere is not sharply differentiated from the spheres of social and personal relations.* Among the most powerful influences of the traditional order in any society in transition are those forces which impede the development of the distinct sphere of

From Lucian W. Pye, "The Non-Western Political Process," *Journal of Politics* 20 (August 1958): 468-86. Reprinted by permission of the author and the publisher.

politics. In most non-Western societies, just as in traditional societies, the pattern of political relationship is largely determined by the pattern of social and personal relations. Power, prestige, and influence are based largely on social status. The political struggle tends to revolve around issues of prestige, influence, and even of personalities, and not primarily around questions of alternative courses of policy action.

The elite who dominate the national politics of most non-Western countries generally represent a remarkably homogeneous group in terms of educational experience and social background. Indeed, the path by which individuals are recruited into their political roles, where not dependent upon ascriptive considerations, is essentially an acculturation process. It is those who have become urbanized, have received the appropriate forms of education, and have demonstrated skill in establishing the necessary personal relations who are admitted to the ranks of the elite. Thus, there is in most non-Western societies a distinctive elite culture in which the criteria of performance are based largely on nonpolitical considerations. To be politically effective in national politics, one must effectively pass through such a process of acculturation.

At the village level it is even more difficult to distinguish a distinct political sphere. The social status of the individual and his personal ties largely determine his political behavior and the range of his influence. The lack of a clear political sphere in such communities places severe limits on the effectiveness of those who come from the outside to perform a political role, be it that of an administrative agent of the national government or of a representative of a national party. Indeed, the success of such agents generally depends more on the manner in which they relate themselves to the social structure of the community than on the substance of their political views.

The fundamental framework of non-Western politics is a communal one, and all political behavior is strongly colored by considerations of communal identification. In the more conspicuous cases the larger communal groupings follow ethnic or religious lines. But behind these divisions there lie the smaller but often more tightly knit social groupings that range from the powerful community of Westernized leaders to the social structure of each individual village.

This essentially communal framework of politics makes it extremely difficult for ideas to command influence in themselves. The response to any advocate of a particular point of view tends to be attuned more to his social position than to the content of his views. Under these conditions it is inappropriate to conceive of an open market place where political ideas can freely compete on their own merits for support. Political discussion tends rather to assume the form of either intracommunal debate or one group justifying its position toward another.

The communal framework also sharply limits freedom in altering political allegiances. Any change in political identification generally requires a change in one's social and personal relationships; conversely, any change in social relations tends to result in a change in political identification. The fortunate village youth who receives a modern education tends to move to the city, establish himself in a new subsociety, and become associated with a political group that may in no way reflect the political views of his original community. Even among the national politicians in the city, shifts in political ties are generally accompanied by changes in social and personal associations.

2. *Political parties in non-Western societies tend to take on a world view and represent a way of life.* The lack of a clearly differentiated political sphere means that political associations or groups cannot be clearly oriented to a distinct political arena but tend to be oriented to some aspect of the communal framework of politics. In reflecting the communal base of politics, political parties tend to represent total ways of life. Attempts to organize parties in terms of particular political principles or limited policy objectives generally result either in failure or in the adoption of a broad ethic which soon obscures the initial objective. Usually political parties represent some subsociety or simply the personality of a particularly influential individual.

Even secular parties devoted to achieving national sovereignty have tended to develop their own unique world views. Indeed, successful parties tend to become social movements. The indigenous basis for political parties is usually regional, ethnic, or religious groupings, all of which stress considerations not usually emphasized in Western secular politics. When a party is merely the personal projection of an individual leader it is usually not just his explicitly political views but all facets of his personality which are significant in determining the character of the movement.

* * *

3. *The political process in non-Western societies is characterized by a prevalence of cliques.* The lack of a distinct political sphere and the tendency for political parties to have a world view together provide a framework within which the most structured units of decision making tend to be personal cliques. Although general considerations of social status determine the broad outlines of power and influence, the particular pattern of political relationships at any time is largely determined by decisions made at the personal level. This is the case because the social structure in non-Western societies is characterized by functionally diffuse relationships; individuals and groups do not have sharply defined and highly specific functions and thus do not represent specific interests that distinguish them from other groupings. There is no clearly structured setting that can provide a focus for the more refined pattern of day-to-day political activities. Hence, in arriving at their expectations about the probable behavior of others, those involved in the political process must rely heavily upon judgments about personality and the particular relations of the various actors to each other. The pattern of personal associations provides one of the firmest guides for understanding and action within the political process. Personal cliques are likely to become the key units of

24

decision making in the political process of most non-Western societies.

* * *

4. *The character of political loyalty in non-Western societies gives to the leadership of political groups a high degree of freedom in determining matters of strategy and tactics.* The communal framework of politics and the tendency for political parties to have world views means that political loyalty is governed more by a sense of identification with the concrete group than by identification with the professed policy goals of the group. The expectation is that the leaders will seek to maximize all the interests of all the members of the group and not just seek to advance particular policies or values.

So long as the leaders appear to be working in the interest of the group as a whole, they usually do not have to be concerned that the loyalties of the members will be tested by current decisions. Under such conditions, it is possible for leadership to become firmly institutionalized within the group without the particular leaders having to make any strong commitments to a specific set of principles or to a given political strategy.

Problems relating to the loyalty of the membership can generally be handled more effectively by decisions about intragroup relations than by decisions about the goals or external policies of the group. So long as harmonious relations exist within the group, it is generally possible for the leaders to make drastic changes in strategy. Indeed, it is not uncommon for the membership to feel that matters relating to external policy should be left solely to the leadership, and it may not disturb them that such decisions reflect mainly the idiosyncrasies of their leaders.

5. *Opposition parties and aspiring elites tend to appear as revolutionary movements in non-Western politics.* Since the current leadership in non-Western countries generally conceives of itself as seeking to effect changes in all aspects of life, and since all the political associations tend to have world views, any prospective change in national leadership is likely to seem to have revolutionary implications. The fact that the ruling party in most non-Western countries identifies itself with an effort to bring about total change in the society makes it difficult to limit the sphere of political controversy. Issues are not likely to remain as isolated and specific questions but tend to become associated with fundamental questions about the destiny of the society.

In addition, the broad and diffuse interests of the ruling elites make it easy for them to maintain that they represent the interest of the entire nation. Those seeking power are thus often placed in the position of appearing to be, at best, obstructionists of progress and, at worst, enemies of the country. Competition is not between parties that represent different functional specific interests or between groups that claim greater administrative skills; rather, the struggle takes on some of the qualities of a conflict between differing ways of life.

This situation is important in explaining the failure of responsible opposition parties to develop in most non-Western countries. For example, 25 the Congress Party in India has been able to identify itself with the destiny of the entire country to such a degree that the opposition parties find it difficult to avoid appearing either as enemies of India's progress or as groups seeking precisely the same objectives as Congress. Since the frustration of opposition groups encourages them to turn to extremist measures, they may in fact come to be revolutionary movements.

6. *The non-Western political process is characterized by a lack of integration among the participants, and this situation is a function of the lack of a unified communications system in the society.* In most non-Western societies there is not a single general political process that is the focus of most political activities throughout the population; rather, there are several distinct and nearly unrelated political processes. The most conspicuous division is that between the dominant national politics of the more urban elements and the more traditional village level of politics. The conflicts that are central to the one may hardly appear in the other.

Those who participate, for example, in the political life of the village are not an integral part of the national politics, since they can act without regard to developments at the central level. Possibly even more significant is the fact that at the village level all the various village groups have their separate and autonomous political processes.

This situation is a reflection of, and is reinforced by, the communication system common to non-Western societies, where the media of mass communication generally reach only to elements of the urban population and to those who participate in the national political process. The vast majority of the people participate only in the traditional word-of-mouth communication system. Even when the media of mass communications do reach the village, through readers of newspapers or owners of radios, there is almost no "feedback" from the village level. The radio talks *to* the villagers but does not talk *with* them. The views of the vast majority of the population are not reflected in the mass media. Indeed, it is often the case that the Westerner has less difficulty than the majority of the indigenous population in understanding the intellectual and moral standards reflected in the media of mass communication, not only because these media are controlled by the more Westernized elements but also because the media may be consciously seeking to relate themselves more to the standards of the international systems of communication than to the local scene.

The lack of a unified communication system and the fact that the participants are not integrated into a common political process limit the types of political issues that can arise in non-Western societies. For example, although these are essentially agrarian societies in which industrial development is just beginning to take place, there has not yet appeared (in their politics) one of the issues basic to the history of Western politics: the clash between industry and agriculture, between town and countryside. Questions of agriculture usually arise in politics when the urbanized leaders advance plans for increasing production and developing village life. The values and concepts of the rural element are not effectively represented in the national political process largely because its fragmented character and the lack of a unified communications system leave the rural elements without a basis for mobilizing their combined strength and effectively advancing their demands on the government. It is possible that in time the rural masses, discovering that they have much in common, will find ways to mobilize their interests and so exert their full potential influence on the nation's political life. Such a development would drastically alter the national political character. In the meantime, however, the fragmented political process of the non-Western societies means that fundamentally agrarian countries will continue to have a form of national politics that is more urbanized than that commonly found in the industrial West. In many cases one city alone dominates the politics of an entire country.

7. *The non-Western political process is characterized by a high rate of recruitment of new elements to political roles.*[3] The spread of popular politics in traditional societies has meant a constant increase in the number of participants and the types of organizations involved in the political process. This development has been stimulated by the extraordinary rise in the urban population, which has greatly increased the number of people who have some understanding about, and feeling for, politics at the national level. A basic feature of the acculturation process which creates the subsociety of the elite is the development of attitudes common to urban life. It is generally out of the rapid urban growth that there emerge the aspiring elites who demand to be heard. In almost all non-Western societies, there is a distinct strata of urban dwellers who are excluded from direct participation in national politics but whose existence affects the behavior of the current elite.

The more gradual reaching out of the mass media to the countryside has stimulated a broadening awareness that, although participation in the nation's political life is formally open to all, the rural elements actually have little access to the means of influence. In some places political parties, in seeking to reach the less urbanized elements, have opened up new channels for communicating with the powerful at the nation's center which may or may not be more effective than the old channels of the civil administration. In any case, the existence of multiple channels of contact with the national government tends to increase the number of people anxious to participate in national decision making.

8. *The non-Western political process is characterized by sharp differences in the political orientation of the generations.* The process of social change in most non-Western societies results in a lack of continuity in the circumstances under which people are recruited to politics. Those who took part in the revolutionary movement against a colonial ruler are not necessarily regarded as indispensable leaders by the new generations; but their revolutionary role is still put forward as sufficient reason for their continued elite status. As a result, in some countries, as in Indonesia and Burma, groups that were not involved in the revolution feel that they are

27

now being arbitrarily excluded from the inner circle of national politics. For these people, the current elite is claiming its status on the basis of ascriptive rather than achievement considerations.

This problem in non-Western societies is further complicated by demographic factors, for such societies are composed of rapidly growing populations that have a high birth rate. In Singapore, Malaya, and Burma, over half the population is under voting age, and the median age in most non-Western countries is in the low twenties. There is thus a constant pressure from the younger generation, whose demands for political influence conflict with the claims of current leaders who conceive of themselves as being still young and with many more years of active life ahead. In most of the newly independent countries, the initial tendency was for cabinet ministers and high officials to be in their thirties and forties, a condition which has colored the career expectations of the youth of succeeding generations, who now face frustration if they cannot achieve comparable status at the same age.

This telescoping of the generations has sharpened the clash of views so that intellectually there is an abnormal gap in political orientations, creating a potential for extreme reversal in policy, should the aspiring elites gain power. Ideas and symbols which are deeply felt by the current leaders, including those relating to the West, may have little meaning for a generation which has not experienced colonial rule.

9. *In non-Western societies there is little consensus as to the legitimate ends and means of political action.* The fundamental fact that non-Western societies are engrossed in a process of discontinuous social change precludes the possibility of a widely shared agreement as to the appropriate ends and means of political activities. In all the important non-Western countries, there are people who have assimilated Western culture to the point that their attitudes and concepts about politics differ little from those common in the West. At the other extreme there is the village peasant who has been little touched by Western influences. Living in different worlds, these individuals can hardly be expected to display a common approach toward political action.

The national leadership, recruited from people who have generally become highly urbanized, is in a position to set the standards for what may appear to be a widely shared consensus about politics. However, more often than not, this apparent national agreement is a reflection only of the distinct qualities of the elite subsociety. The mass of the population cannot fully appreciate the values and concepts which underlie the judgments of the elite and which guide its behavior.

The lack of a distinct political sphere increases the difficulties in achieving agreement about the legitimate scope and forms of political activities. The setting is not one in which political issues are relatively isolated and thus easily communicated and discussed. Instead, a knowledge of national politics requires an intimate acquaintance with the total social life of the elite. The fact that loyalty to the particular group rather than support of general principles is the key to most political behavior strengthens the tendency toward a distinct and individual rather than a shared orientation towards politics.

The situation is further complicated by the fact that, since most of the groupings within the political process represent total ways of life, few are concerned with limited and specific interests. The functionally diffuse character of most groups means that each tends to have its own approaches to political action in terms of both ends and means. Under these circumstances, the relationship of means to ends tends to be more organic than rational and functional. Indeed, in the gross behavior of the groups it is difficult to distinguish their primary goals from their operational measures. Consequently, the political actors in non-Western societies tend to demonstrate quite conspicuously the often-forgotten fact that people generally show greater imagination and ingenuity in discovering goals to match their means than in expanding their capabilities in order to reach distant goals.

Given the character of the groups, it is difficult to distinguish within the general political discourse of the society a distinction between discussions of desired objectives and analyses of appropriate means of political action.

10. *In non-Western societies the intensity and breadth of political discussion has little relationship to political decision making.* Western observers are impressed with what they feel is a paradoxical situation in most non-Western countries: the masses seem to be apathetic toward political action and yet, considering the crude systems of communications, they are remarkably well informed about political events. Peasants and villagers often engage in lengthy discussions on matters related to the political world that lies outside their immediate lives, but they rarely seem prepared to translate the information they receive into action that might influence the course of national politics.

The villagers are often responding in the traditional manner to national politics. In most traditional societies, an important function of the elite was to provide entertainment and material for discussion for the common people; but discussions in villages and teashops could center on the activities of an official without creating the expectation that discussion should lead to action. Thus the contemporary world of elite politics provides a drama for the common people, just as in many traditional cultures the popular forms of literature and drama stressed court life and the world of officialdom.

A second explanation for this pattern of behavior is that one of the important factors in determining social status and prestige within the village or local community is often a command of information about the wider world; knowledge of developments in the sphere of national and even international politics has a value in itself. But skill in discussing political matters again does not raise any expectations of actual participation in the world of politics.

29

Finally, many of the common people in non-Western societies find it desirable to keep informed about political developments in order to be able to adapt their lives to any major changes. Since their lives have often been drastically disrupted by political events, they have come to believe it prudent to seek advance warning of any developments which might again affect their lives; but it has not necessarily encouraged them to believe that their actions might influence such developments.

11. *In the non-Western political process there is a high degree of substitutability of roles.*[4] It seems that in non-Western societies most politically relevant roles are not clearly differentiated but have a functionally diffuse rather than a functionally specific character. For example, the civil bureaucracy is not usually limited to the role of a politically neutral instrument of public administration but may assume some of the functions of a political party or act as an interest group. Sometimes armies act as governments. Even within bureaucracies and governments, individuals may be formally called upon to perform several roles.

A shortage of competent personnel encourages such behavior either because one group may feel that the other is not performing its role in an effective manner or because the few skilled administrators are forced to take on concurrent assignments. However, the more fundamental reason for this phenomenon is that in societies just emerging from traditional status, it is not generally expected that any particular group or organization will limit itself to performing a clearly specified function. Under these conditions there usually are not sharply defined divisions of labor in any sphere of life. All groups tend to have considerable freedom in trying to maximize their general influence.

12. *In the non-Western political process there are relatively few explicitly organized interest groups with functionally specific roles.* Although there are often large numbers of informal asscciations in non-Western countries, such groups tend to adopt diffuse orientations that cover all phases of life in much the same manner as the political parties and cliques. It is the rare association that represents a limited and functionally specific interest. Organizations which in name and formal structure are modeled after Western interest groups, such as trade unions and chambers of commerce, generally do not have a clearly defined focus.

In many cases groups, such as trade unions and peasant associations that in form would appear to represent a specific interest, are in fact agents of the government or of a dominant party or movement. Their function is primarily to mobilize the support of a segment of the population for the purposes of the dominant group, and not primarily to represent the interests of their constituency.

In situations where the associations are autonomous, the tendency is for them to act as protective associations and not as pressure groups. That is, their activities are concentrated on protecting their members from the consequences of governmental decisions and the political power of others.

They do not seek to apply pressure openly on the government in order to influence positively the formation of public policy.

This role of the protective association is generally a well developed one in traditional societies and in countries under colonial rule. Under such authoritarian circumstances, since informal associations could have little hope of affecting the formal law-making process, they tended to focus on the law-enforcing process. Success in obtaining preferential treatment for their membership did not require that they mobilize general popular support. On the contrary, activities directed to broadly articulating their views were generally self-defeating. They were likely to be more successful if they worked quietly and informally to establish preferential relations with the policy-enforcing agents of the government. Under such conditions each association generally preferred to operate separately in order to gain special favors. The strategy of uniting in coalitions and alliances to present the appearance of making a popular demand on the government, as is common in an open democratic political process composed of pressure groups, would only weaken the position of all the informal associations in a traditional society, for it would represent a direct challenge to the existing governmental elite.

This approach to political activity common in traditional societies still lingers on in many non-Western societies. Informal associations tend to protect all the interests of their members in relations with the government. At the same time, many interests in the society are not explicitly organized. Although the process of social change is creating the basis for new interests, the formation of explicit interest groups rarely moves at the same pace. Often the new groups turn to the more traditional informal associations and only very gradually change their character. In other cases interest groups that fundamentally represent the newly developing aspects of the society perform according to the standards of the traditional groups.

From this brief discussion we may note that when interest groups act as protective associations, focusing on the law-enforcing process and seeking special treatment for their members, they are likely to avoid articulating publicly their goals and are likely to base their requests for special favors on particularistic rather than universalistic considerations. In appealing to policy-enforcement agents, prudence dictates the desirability of framing a request as an isolated demand; for any suggestion that a request constitutes a widespread demand, consistent with the general interest of the public good, would threaten the preserve of the lawmakers, who were presumed to be unapproachable in most traditional societies.

We may sum up these observations by formulating a general hypothesis that would read: "Whenever the formally constituted lawmakers are more distant from and more inaccessible to the general public than the law-enforcing agencies, the political process of the society will be characterized by a high degree of latency, and interests will be represented by informally organized groups seeking diffuse but particularistically

31

defined goals which will not be broadly articulated nor claimed to be in the general interest." The corollary of this hypothesis would, of course, read: "Whenever the formally constituted lawmakers are less distant from and more accessible to the general public than the law-enforcing agencies, the political process of the society will be open and manifest, and interests will be represented by explicitly organized groups seeking specific but universalistically defined goals which will be broadly articulated and claimed to be in the general interest."

13. *In the non-Western political process the national leadership must appeal to an undifferentiated public.* The lack of explicitly organized interest groups and the fact that not all participants are continuously represented in the political process deprive the national leadership of any readily available means for calculating the relative distribution of attitudes and values throughout the society. The national politician cannot easily determine the relative power of those in favor of a particular measure and those opposed; he cannot readily estimate the amount of effort needed to gain the support of the doubtful elements.

It is usually only within the circle of the elite or within the administrative structure that the national leaders can distinguish specific points of view and the relative backing that each commands. In turning to the population as a whole, the leaders find that they have few guides as to how the public may be divided over particular issues. Thus, in seeking popular support, the politician cannot direct his appeal to the interests of particular groups. Unable to identify or intelligently discriminate among the various interests latent in the public, the political leader is inclined to resort to broad generalized statements rather than to adopt specific positions on concrete issues. This situation also means that, whether the question is one of national or of merely local import, the leadership must appear to be striving to mobilize the entire population.

The inability to speak to a differentiated public encourages a strong propensity toward skillful and highly emotional forms of political articulation on the part of non-Western leaders. Forced to reach for the broadest possible appeals, the political leader tends at times to concentrate heavily on nationalistic sentiments and to present himself as a representative of the nation as a whole rather than of particular interests within the society. This is one of the reasons why some leaders of non-Western countries are often seen paradoxically both as extreme nationalists and as men out of touch with the masses.

14. *The unstructured character of the non-Western political process encourages leaders to adopt more clearly defined positions on international issues than on domestic issues.* Confronted with an undifferentiated public, leaders of non-Western countries often find the international political process more clearly structured than the domestic political scene. Consequently, they can make more refined calculations as to the advantages in taking a definite position in world politics. This situation not only encourages the leaders of some non-Western countries to seek a role

in world politics that is out of proportion to their nation's power, but it also allows such leaders to concentrate more on international than on domestic affairs. It should also be noted that in adopting a supranational role, the current leaders of non-Western countries can heighten the impression that their domestic opposition is an enemy of the national interest.

15. *In non-Western societies the affective or expressive aspect of politics tends to override the problem-solving or public-policy aspect of politics.* Traditional societies have generally developed to a very high order the affective and expressive aspects of politics. Pomp and ceremony are usually basic features of traditional politics, and those who are members of the ruling elite in such societies are generally expected to lead more interesting and exciting lives than those not involved in politics. In contrast, traditional societies have not usually emphasized politics as a means for solving social problems. Questions of policy in such societies are largely limited to providing certain minimum social and economic functions and maintaining the way of life of the elite.

Although in transitional societies there is generally a greater awareness of the potentialities of politics as a means of rationally solving social problems, the expressive aspects of politics usually continue to occupy a central place in determining the character of political behavior. The peculiar Western assumption that issues of public policy are the most important aspect of politics, and practically the only legitimate concern of those with power, is not always applicable to non-Western politics. Indeed, in most non-Western societies the general assumption is not that those with power are committed to searching out and solving problems, but rather that they are the fortunate participants in the central drama of life. Politics is supposed to be exciting and emotionally satisfying.

In part the stress on the affective or expressive aspect of politics is related to the fact that, in most non-Western countries, questions of personal loyalties and identification are recognized as providing the basic issues of politics and the bond between leader and follower is generally an emotional one. In fact, in many non-Western societies, it is considered highly improper and even immoral for people to make loyalty contingent upon their leaders' ability to solve problems of public policy.

In the many non-Western societies in which the problem of national integration is of central importance, the national leaders often feel they must emphasize the symbols and sentiments of national unity since substantive problems of policy may divide the people. It should be noted that the governmental power base of many non-Western leaders encourages them to employ symbols and slogans customarily associated with administrative policy in their efforts to strengthen national unity. The Western observer may assume that statements employing such symbols represent policy intentions when in fact their function is to create national loyalty and to condition the public to think more in policy terms.

16. *Charismatic leaders tend to prevail in non-Western politics.*[5] Max

33

Weber, in highlighting the characteristics of charismatic authority, specifically related the emergence of charismatic personalities to situations in which the hold of tradition has been weakened. By implication, he suggested that societies experiencing cultural change provide an ideal setting for such leaders since a society in which there is confusion over values is more susceptible to a leader who conveys a sense of mission and appears to be God-sent.

The problem of political communication further reinforces the position of the charismatic leader. Since the population does not share the leadership's modes of reason or standards of judgment, it is diffcult to communicate subtle points of view. Communication of emotions is not confronted with such barriers, especially if it is related to considerations of human character and personality. All groups within the population can feel confident of their abilities to judge the worth of a man for what he is, even though they cannot understand his mode of reasoning.

So long as a society has difficulties in communication, the charismatic leader possesses great advantage over his opponents, even though they may have greater ability in rational planning. However, the very lack of precision in the image that a charismatic leader casts, especially in relation to operational policy, does make it possible for opposition to develop as long as it does not directly challenge the leader's charisma.

* * *

Charisma is likely to wear thin. A critical question in most non-Western societies that now have charismatic leaders is whether such leadership will in the meantime become institutionalized in the form of rational-legal practices. This was the pattern in Turkey under Kemal Ataturk. Or will the passing of the charismatic leader be followed by confusion and chaos? The critical factor seems to be whether or not the leader encourages the development of functionally specific groups within the society that can genuinely represent particular interests.

17. *The non-Western political process operates largely without benefit of political "brokers."* In most non-Western societies there seems to be no institutionalized role for carrying out the tasks of, first, clarifying and delimiting the distribution of demands and interests within the population, and, next, engaging in the bargaining operation necessary to accommodate and maximize the satisfaction of those demands and interests in a fashion consistent with the requirements of public policy and administration. In other words, there are no political "brokers."

* * *

In most non-Western societies, the role of the political "broker" has been partially filled by those who perform a "mediator's" role, which consists largely of transmitting the views of the elite to the masses. Such "mediators" are people sufficiently acculturated to the elite society to understand its views but who still have contacts with the more traditional masses. In performing their role, they engage essentially in a public relations operation for the elite, and only to a marginal degree do they

34

communicate to the elite the views of the public. They do not find it essential to identify and articulate the values of their public. Generally, since their influence depends upon their relations with the national leadership, they have not sought to develop an autonomous basis of power or to identify themselves with particular segments of the population as must the political "broker." As a consequence, they have not acted in a fashion that would stimulate the emergence of functionally specific interest groups.

NOTES

1. For two excellent discussions of the implications for comparative politics of the current interest in non-Western political systems, see: Sigmund Neumann, "Comparative Politics: A Half-Century Appraisal," *Journal of Politics* 19 (August 1957): 269-90; and Dankwart A. Rustow, "New Horizons for Comparative Politics," *World Politics* 9 (July 1957): 530-49.

2. The picture of the non-Western political process contained in the following pages was strongly influenced by: George McT. Kahin, Guy J. Pauker, and Lucian W. Pye, "Comparative Politics in Non-Western Countries," *American Political Science Review* 49 (December 1955): 1022-41; Gabriel A. Almond, "Comparative Political Systems," *Journal of Politics* 18 (August 1956): 391-409; Rustow, "New Horizons," and also his *Politics and Westernization in the Near East* (Princeton: Center of International Studies, 1956).

3. Kahin, Pauker, and Pye, "Comparative Politics," p. 1024.

4. See Almond, "Political Systems," p. 30.

5. Kahin, Pauker, and Pye, "Comparative Politics," p. 1025.

APPROACHES TO THE STUDY
OF POLITICAL DEVELOPMENT

Robert A. Packenham

Interest in the politics of the developing areas has increased steadily since World War II, and scholars have now produced a sizable collection of single-country monographs, several regional studies, and at least one attempt at a global synthesis.[1] This literature has tended to stress various conditions as the primary correlates or determinants of political development. This research note offers a taxonomy of five approaches to the study of political development. The taxonomy draws upon both traditional and contemporary sources, and studies of both "developing" and "developed" areas, to derive a framework for ordering the literature on political development produced in the past two decades. The five approaches are (1) "legal-formal," (2) "economic," (3) "administrative," (4) "social system," and (5) "political culture."

Of course, not all writings on political development have been or could be included.[2] To add another caveat, this taxonomy is presented as *a* way rather than *the* way to think about political development studies, but it is a way that has been useful.[3] Some authors are mentioned who wrote about "developed" rather than "developing" countries; we hope they do not mind being placed in this framework. Finally, the taxonomy deals only with the conditions of political development. What is meant by "political development" itself varies from writer to writer and therefore has not been employed as a criterion.

THE LEGAL-FORMAL APPROACH

Some writers have suggested that political development is primarily a

From Robert A. Packenham, "Approaches to the Study of Political Development," *World Politics* 17, no. 1, pp. 108-20. Copyright © 1964 by the Princeton University Press. Reprinted by permission of the publisher.

function of a *legal-formal constitution that prescribes such features as equal protection under the law, the rule of law, regular elections by secret ballot, federalism, and/or the separation of powers.*

This notion was clearly implied, if not stated explicitly, in much of the work in formal political science in Europe and the United States during roughly the last 100 years.[4] Illustrations of this approach are the works of Theodore Woolsey, Woodrow Wilson, John W. Burgess and, until recently, most comparative government textbooks in the United States.[5] Historical, descriptive (as distinguished from theoretical), and legal-formal studies continued to be the dominant preoccupation of American political scientists at least until 1950.[6]

The legal-formal approach has been less apparent in writings about the developing areas than about the United States and Western Europe. The literature on politics in Latin America has perhaps embodied it to a greater extent than work on other developing areas, although this may be changing.[7] In general, one of the most notable characteristics of studies of the politics of the developing areas is how far the pendulum has swung away from legal-formal to economic, administrative, sociological, and psychological factors as explanatory variables.

THE ECONOMIC APPROACH

A very common view is that political development is primarily a function of a *level of economic development sufficient to serve the material needs of the people and to enhance a reasonable harmony between economic aspirations and satisfactions.*

One immediately thinks of the works of Europeans, particularly Karl Marx, as classic cases of the economic approach to politics. But intellectual history in the United States also has been receptive to this idea. There is a long tradition in American social thought regarding the importance of economic factors— notably, property—for political liberty and the conduct of political affairs.[8] More broadly, there is also a tradition, recently being rediscovered, of looking at the relations of the economy, as the independent variable, to the polity, as the dependent variable.[9]

Coming on the heels of this tradition, and himself a part of it, Charles A. Beard presented the economic approach to politics more forcefully than any other prominent American scholar. He also gave it the aura of science.[10] On the research front, this meant that Beard's thesis absorbed much of the interest in the "new science of politics" that was developing as a reaction to the legal-formalism of the time.[11] On the teaching side, Beard's influence on instruction in American history has been pervasive.[12] For decades American elementary and secondary school pupils have been socialized to Beard's doctrine, even though the first systematic effort to test the thesis advanced by Beard in his *Economic Interpretation of the*

37

Constitution was not published until 40 years after the book's appearance in 1913.[13]

Against this historical background, it is not surprising that Americans writing about political development should be very much interested in its economic roots. It is in such a context that the famous "proposal" by Millikan and Rostow,[14] which appears to be based upon the economic approach, was seen and, frequently, criticized. The criticism often made was that the authors posited a too-close relationship between economic and political development.[15] This alleged shortcoming was frequently attributed in part to the traditional receptivity of Americans to the economic approach.

It is true that the relationship between economic and political development is not one to one. However, this fact should not be allowed to obscure the very important statistical correlation that seems rather well established between level of economic development and political democracy, when the latter is defined in terms of political competitiveness. Using slightly different but roughly comparable indices of economic development and political democracy, Lipset, Coleman, Hagen, and Cutright all found such a correlation.[16] The implication of this finding for the policy maker would seem to be that political democracy *usually* requires economic development. It is countries like India, which (happily) insists on remaining democratic in spite of its relatively low level of economic development, that keep the correlation less than one to one and that make necessary the qualification "usually." But India is an exception. There are also exceptions of the opposite sort. The same data that demonstrate the correlation also show that relatively high levels of economic development are in the deviant cases associated with a lack of political competitiveness and even with political autocracy.[17]

If one's index of political development shifts from political competitiveness to level of political contentment, the relation to economic development seems more complex. On the one hand, one study examines the hypothesis that there is a direct relationship between "political vulnerability," a complex notion measured in terms of three economic indices, and political discontent, measured in terms of Communist voting. A "rudimentary" test in the Indian national elections of 1951-1952 "tended to support the hypothesis," although further testing was strongly urged.[18] On the other hand, there are studies that report a negative correlation. Brinton found, in his study of revolutions, that they occurred in the United States, England, France, and Russia when the economies were on the upturn.[19] Tocqueville supports this view of the French Revolution, concluding that "The French found their situations more intolerable the better it became."[20] Davison reports a positive correlation between income and Communist voting in Sweden's 1952 elections.[21]

In a middle position are studies suggesting that there may be a correlation between economic development and political contentment, even in modernizing societies, but that the correlation is about as strong with social and psychological as with economic factors.[22] Lipset and Davies have tried to reconcile these various views. They suggest that the relationship between economic development and political contentment is best understood in dynamic terms.[23] Davies, for example, writes: "Revolutions are most likely to occur when a prolonged period of objective economic and social development is followed by a short period of sharp reversal. . . . The actual state of socio-economic development is less significant than the expectation that past progress, now blocked, can and must continue in the future."[24] As Davies himself points out, it would be useful to know more about what constitute "long" and "short" periods.[25]

THE ADMINISTRATIVE APPROACH

Under this heading are grouped those writers who have tended to argue that political development is primarily a function of the *administrative capacity to maintain law and order efficiently and effectively and to perform governmental output functions rationally and neutrally.* This approach stresses the output side of the Easton input-output model.[26]

Historically, the case for political development in terms of advanced administration has been put most brilliantly by Max Weber. "Weber saw bureaucratization as an institutional form inherent in all democracies."[27] It was characterized by neutrality, rationality, and achievement rather than by ascriptive criteria as the basis for selection and promotion.

Another historical source of the administrative approach to political development is the writings of the English colonial administrators about their experiences in the nineteenth and early twentieth centuries. From their point of view, the first priority for the political development of the then colonial, now developing, peoples was better administration. Thus they stressed this aspect of political development in their writings.[28]

More recently, as their relations with the developing countries have increased, Americans have observed problems similar to those of the English colonial officers of that earlier day. As a result some writers have, like the English, stressed the need for efficient government and a capacity for carrying on public services and maintaining law, order, and stability as the hallmarks of political development. The stimulus to this set of writings seems primarily to have been the authors' views of the needs of U.S. foreign policy.[29]

Another recent manifestation of the administrative approach may be found in the work of organization and communications theorists. Organization theorists think of political development as the creation of "more effective, more adaptive, more complex, and more rationalized organization."[30] A communications theorist advances the hypothesis that stability, in the context of social mobilization, depends upon increasing income rates *and* an increasing capability of the government to bear its

39

communications "load."[31] Such theories merge the administrative with the social system approach (see below). The stimulus to this set of writings seems primarily to have been interest in the theory of socio-political change rather than the needs of U.S. foreign policy.

A major strength of the administrative approach seems to be that it emphasizes the very real need for governments to maintain law and order and to get things done on a relatively rational and efficient, yet humane, basis. To the extent that these theories indicate *how* such performance can be achieved, they are even more useful. By raising and providing preliminary answers to the question of how the "irrational" can be a means to the "rational" in administration, organization theory has an especially important contribution to make to the understanding of political development.

A danger in the administrative approach may be that, in stressing the need for achievement, it sometimes gives inadequate attention to the problem of democratic political development.[32] In this connection a promising avenue of research is, again, organization theory. Early students of organizations, like Frederick W. Taylor and his successors in the scientific management movement, argued that efficiency is related to "having clearly defined roles, or offices, based on universalistic norms, functionally specific relationships, and rigid adherence to achievement considerations."[33] Organization theorists today are finding that informal, particularistic, functionally diffuse forms of relationships can and do contribute, or can be made to contribute, to organizational effectiveness. In this lies the promise as well of the kind of pluralism of activities and attitudes that seems necessary for democratic political development.

THE SOCIAL SYSTEM APPROACH

Still another approach is the idea that political development is primarily a function of a *social system that facilitates popular participation in governmental and political processes at all levels and the bridging of regional, religious, caste, linguistic, tribal, or other cleavages.*

There are at least four ways in which this approach has been expressed. One is in terms of social correlates of democracy. These include relatively high "scores" on such sociological variables as an open class system, literacy and/or education, high participation in voluntary organizations, urbanization, and communications systems. These social correlates of democracy, like the economic correlates, seem pretty well established.[34]

A second way is to see the development of nationhood in terms of a dynamic "communications grid" or network of "social communication." The outstanding exponent and major initiator of this approach as a theoretical construct is Karl W. Deutsch.[35] Several studies have used

Deutsch's framework as guides to study national and even supranational political communities.[36]

A third group of expressions of the social system approach may be gathered together under the broad rubric of the "group" approach to politics. This approach has a tradition at least as old as Tocqueville and as recent as David Truman. To generalize about so diverse a group is always a mistake in part, but we may gain some understanding if we try to formulate the central theme of these many writers. It might be put this way: A complex infrastructure of groups provides the differential centers of decision making, the shared power base, and the overall social vitality that are required for democracy. The case for this is put not only on moral grounds ("group participation in politics is a good thing because each group ought to have its say"), but also on existential grounds ("group participation is functional because it is necessary for the vitality of the system and because there are serious cognitive limits on men's capacity for central planning").[37] In the literature on the politics of the developing areas, two recent manifestations of this approach are Robert E. Scott's *Mexican Government in Transition*[38] and Myron Weiner's *The Politics of Scarcity: Public Pressure and Political Response in India.*[39]

A fourth expression of the social system approach is structure-function analysis, especially as put forth by Gabriel A. Almond.[40] Almond defines a political system in terms of universal political functions. These are used as a basis for identifying important political structures. Ideally this scheme provides a basis for truly comparative analysis and, to the extent that the structures and functions can be propositionally related to one another, the basis for general theory.

Now it is possible, drawing from each of these four elements of the social system approach, to construct a very rough model of the social foundations for political development. The legal-formal approach conceived of the conditions of the developed political system primarily in terms of constitutional forms; the economic approach, in terms of economic output and, sometimes, distribution; and the administrative approach, in terms of administrative capacity. This approach suggests a society where there is a relatively large number of *groups,*[41] *organizations,* or *institutions.* People *associate* themselves voluntarily with these groups. They form new associations from time to time. People belong to several groups at one time; in each group the memberships are different; hence there are *cross-cutting memberships* and *multiple loyalties.* In addition to these horizontal links, there are *vertical links*—namely, links between groups at different levels. Groups in such a linkage relationship may be said to perform the *aggregation* function. They are a point of *access* for the *articulated demands* of the "lower"-level groups in the linkage chain. The *class structure* is neither *polarized* nor *rigid,* which further facilitates access. Through these mechanisms, in the developed political system, all *major* groups have *reasonable* access to political decisions.

41

THE POLITICAL CULTURE APPROACH[42]

Here are found writings which see political development as primarily a function of the political culture—that is, *the set of attitudinal and personality characteristics that enables the members of the political system both to accept the privileges and to bear the responsibilities of a democratic political process.*

Political culture is, obviously, largely a psychological concept. The psychological mechanisms at work occur on at least two levels: (1) the level of attitudes or sets of expectations about political roles held by members of the polity, and (2) the level of personality.

The concept of political culture at the level of attitudes has been mostly a postwar development.[43] It received its name in a classic formulation in 1956.[44] Other works using it include Leites's and Wylie's studies on France; Banfield's on southern Italy; Lerner's on the Middle (Near) East; Binder's on Iran; Apter's on Africa; Almond's and Verba's on the United States, United Kingdom, Germany, Italy, and Mexico; and Lipset's on the United States as a "new nation."[45]

These studies are notable for spotlighting a hitherto neglected dimension of political development. The psychological characteristics named as requisites or inhibitors of political development go under varied headings: for example, unwillingness to accept political responsibility (Leites and Wylie), "amoral familism" (Banfield), empathy (Lerner), and a mixed "civic culture" (Almond and Verba). While these groupings are differently named partly because they measure different phenomena, they also tap a common root—namely, psychological predispositions here called "political culture."

At the personality level of the political culture, less work has been done on the developing areas than on the United States.[46] One outstanding work is Lucian W. Pye's study of the Burmese political system.[47] The thesis of this book is that political development, which is defined in terms of nation building, is fundamentally a problem of personal identity, trust, and psychic well-being. That is, the politically developed society is one in which participants' personalities are sufficiently secure and well-integrated to enable them to bear psychologically the privileges and responsibilities of independence and self-government. This is an extraordinary thesis, if one considers it in the light of traditional explanations of political development. For rather than, say, constitutional forms or administrative capacity or even economic development, Pye is arguing that the priority problem in political development is "identity" and psychic health. Though not all observers may go so far as Pye, his thesis is extremely provocative. The notion that the new nations of Asia and Africa face an identity crisis upon independence will strike a responsive chord among many students of those areas. Nor will the phenomenon be wholly foreign to Latin Americanists, even though most of the Latin countries have been formally independent for more than a century.[48]

There is considerable geographic distribution among these studies. Latin America seems least well represented. For example, in the literature cited, only the book by Almond and Verba draws upon research in a Latin American country (Mexico is one of the five countries surveyed). Yet, judging from the frequent references to *personalismo, caudillismo, machismo, jeitos*, and so on in many of these countries, who would deny that political culture is an important variable there, too?

It would be possible to add still other approaches. For example, a sixth might be the "geographical" approach—that is, the body of writing arguing that political development is primarily a function of land and other geographic factors. Among its foremost exponents would be Achille Loria,[49] Frederick Jackson Turner,[50] Karl A. Wittfogel[51] and, more broadly, the geopolitical school of international relations theorists.[52] And a seventh approach might deal with "stages of modernization": those theories which see political development as part of a total modernization process involving legal-formal, economic, social, psychological, and administrative aspects to a roughly equal extent. This process occurs by stages over time. Rather than emphasizing one or another dimension of the conditions of development (e.g., economic conditions), these theories stress various points of development, such as the "take-off" stage.[53]

Instead of elaborating these approaches further, however, we conclude with the hope that this taxonomy may help to identify and order the literature on political development and that, by so doing, it may illuminate some important dimensions of the conditions of political development—not only for scholars, but also for the policy makers whose Herculean task it is to understand and to deal effectively with political change in the developing nations.

NOTES

1. Gabriel A. Almond and James S. Coleman, eds., *The Politics of the Developing Areas* (Princeton 1960).

2. Three books not discussed elsewhere but directly relevant are Lucian W. Pye, ed., *Communications and Political Development* (Princeton 1963); Joseph LaPalombara, ed., *Bureaucracy and Political Development* (Princeton 1963); and Robert E. Ward and Dankwart A. Rustow, eds., *The Political Modernization of Japan and Turkey* (Princeton 1964). These are the first of a projected series of seven "Studies in Political Development" sponsored by the Committee on Comparative Politics of the Social Science Research Council. The other volumes also will be published by Princeton University Press and will deal with "Education and Political Development," "Political Parties and Political Development," "Comparative Political Culture," and "A Theory of Political Modernization."

43

3. Some of the studies grouped as examples of one approach have characteristics that legitimately suggest they might be placed under another heading. For example, we would call Professor Deutsch's social mobilization approach primarily a social system one, although his hypothesis clearly contains elements of the political culture and administrative approaches as well. The social system and political culture approaches are particularly closely related. Those works which build on Max Weber and Talcott Parsons—such as Seymour Martin Lipset's *The First New Nation: The United States in Historical and Comparative Perspective* (New York 1963) and David Apter's two books on African political systems, *The Gold Coast in Transition* (Princeton 1955) and *The Political Kingdom in Uganda: A Study in Bureaucratic Nationalism* (Princeton, 1961)—are included in the political culture approach, even though the relationship of values to social system is intimate. Many theories overlap somewhat, but each tends to emphasize one approach more than the others. In spite of the problem of overlapping, this taxonomy seems reasonable and useful.

4. Harry Eckstein, "A Perspective on Comparative Politics, Past and Present," unpublished manuscript, n.d. (c. 1961), pp. 27-44; UNESCO, *Contemporary Political Science*, Publication No. 426 (Paris, 1950); and Austin Ranney, *The Governing of Men* (New York, 1956), chap. 24, especially pp. 576-84.

5. See Theodore D. Woolsey, *Political Science, or, The State: Theoretically and Practically Considered*, 2 vols. (New York, 1878); Woodrow Wilson, *The State: Elements of Historical and Practical Politics: A Sketch of Institutional History and Administration* (Boston, 1892); and John W. Burgess, *Political Science and Comparative Constitutional Law*, 2 vols. (Boston and London, 1891). See also Eckstein, "A Perspective on Comparative Politics," pp. 39-45, and Bernard Crick, *The American Science of Politics* (Berkeley, 1959).

   Examples of comparative government textbooks on Europe are Gwendolen M. Carter, John H. Herz, and John C. Ranney, *Major Foreign Powers* (New York, 1957), and R. Taylor Cole and others, *European Political Systems* (New York, 1953). Examples of Latin American texts that devote large proportions of their discussions to constitutions which exist for the most part on paper (as the authors themselves sometimes point out) are Austin F. Macdonald, *Latin American Politics and Government* (New York, 1949, 1954), and Miguel Jorrin, *Governments of Latin America* (New York, 1953). Recently some texts have incorporated other approaches more or less systematically. See especially Almond and Coleman, eds., *Developing Areas*, and Samuel H. Beer and Adam B. Ulam, eds., *Patterns of Government: The Major Political Systems of Europe* (New York, 1962). 1962).

6. Claude E. Hawley and Lewis A. Dexter, "Recent Political Science Research in American Universities," *American Political Science Review* 46 (June 1952): 470-85. See also Gabriel A. Almond, *The American People and Foreign Policy* (New York, 1960), pp. 154-57.

44   7. Merle Kling, "Area Studies and Comparative Politics—The Latin

American Experience" (Paper prepared for delivery at the 1963 Annual Meeting of the American Political Science Association, New York City, September 4-7, 1963).

8. David Fellman has traced this strain from its origins in seventeenth-century England through the end of the Jacksonian era, which he takes to be about 1850. "The Economic Interpretation in Early American Political Theory" (Ph.D. diss., Yale University, 1934).

9. This tradition has been interpreted as a "common theme" in "liberalism, classical economics, Marxism, conservatism and Saint Simonism—[as well as] much of modern sociology." Reinhard Bendix, *Max Weber: An Intellectual Portrait* (Garden City, N.Y., 1962), pp. 487-88. See also Sheldon S. Wolin, *Politics and Vision* (Boston, 1960), chaps. 9 and 10.

10. See Charles Beard, *An Economic Interpretation of the Constitution* (New York, 1935), chap. 1, "Historical Interpretation in the United States."

11. See Morton White, *Social Thought in America: The Revolt Against Formalism* (New York, 1949), pp. 74, 109, 125-27; Lee Benson, *Turner and Beard: American Historical Writing Reconsidered* (Glencoe, Ill., 1960); and Robert E. Osgood, *Ideals and Self-Interest in America's Foreign Relations: The Great Transformation of the Twentieth Century* (Chicago, 1953, 1955), pp. 371-76.

12. See Maurice Blinkoff, "The Influence of Charles A. Beard upon American Historiography," *University of Buffalo Studies* 12 (May 1936): 4-84.

13. Both Benson and Robert E. Brown, *Charles A. Beard and the Constitution* (Princeton, 1956), make this point. Brown's book in 1956 and Forrest McDonald, *We, the People: The Economic Origins of the Constitution* (Chicago, 1958), appear to have been the first systematic tests of Beard's thesis.

14. Max F. Millikan and W. W. Rostow, *A Proposal: Key to an Effective Foreign Policy* (New York, 1957).

15. It should be noted that the authors state flatly that they reject the "crude materialist thesis that progress consists exclusively in 'extra food in the stomach' ..." (*ibid.*, p. 21). There are parts of the book (especially pp. 21-42) which indicate adherence to the social system and political culture approaches (see below) to political development. However, the proposal itself, which is guided by a "banking concept," is not very clearly tied to these approaches and does seem to reflect the economic approach to a greater extent; see especially chaps. 6 and 7.

16. Seymour Martin Lipset, *Political Man: The Social Bases of Politics* (Garden City, N.Y., 1960), chap. 2; James S. Coleman, "The Political Systems of the Developing Areas," in Almond and Coleman, *Developing Areas*, pp. 538-44; Everett E. Hagen, "A Framework for Analyzing Economic and Political Change," in Robert E. Asher et al., *Development of the Emerging Countries: An Agenda for Research*

45

(Washington, 1962), pp. 1-8; and Phillips Cutright, "National Political Development: Measurement and Analysis," *American Sociological Review* 28 (April 1963): 253-64.

Lyle W. Shannon has found positive correlations between level of economic development and political independence, i.e., formal self-government. However, his work does not deal with political development after independence. See his "Is Level of Economic Development Related to Capacity for Self-Government?" *American Journal of Economics and Sociology* 17 (July 1958): 367-82; "Socio-economic Development and Political Status," *Social Problems* 7 (Fall 1959): 157-69; and "Socio-economic Development and Demographic Variables as Predictors of Political Change," *Sociological Quarterly* 3 (January 1962): 27-63.

17. In Coleman's data, for example, Cuba, Venezuela, and the United Arab Republic rank high in economic development but low in political competitiveness; Hagen's three exceptions are Cuba, the U.A.R., and Iraq. Other obvious examples are Nazi Germany, the U.S.S.R., and de Gaulle's France.

18. Charles Wolf, Jr., *Foreign Aid: Theory and Practice in Southern Asia* (Princeton, 1960), p. 408.

19. Crane Brinton, *The Anatomy of Revolution* (New York, 1959), pp. 264-79.

20. Alexis de Tocqueville, *On the State of Society in France Before the Revolution of 1789* (London, 1888), p. 152, quoted in Wolf, *Foreign Aid*, p. 304n.

21. W. Phillips Davison, "A Review of Sven Rydenfelt's Communism in Sweden," p-570, RAND Corporation (1954), pp. 27-29, cited in ibid.

22. William Buchanan and Hadley Cantril, *How Nations See Each Other* (Urbana, 1953), pp. 30-37; Hagen, "A Framework," pp. 36-38; and James C. Davies, "Toward a Theory of Revolution," *American Sociological Review* 27 (February 1962): 5-19.

23. Davies, pp. 5-6, and Lipset, *Political Man*, pp. 63-64.

24. Davies, "Toward a Theory" pp. 5-6.

25. Ibid., p. 19.

26. David Easton, "An Approach to the Analysis of Political Systems," *World Politics* 9 (April 1957): 383-400.

27. Lipset, *Political Man*, p. 29.

28. Research on these works would be useful. One might start with the writings of John Stuart Mill—for example, the final chapters of *Representative Government*.

29. Examples are: Foreign Policy Research Institute of the University of Pennsylvania, "A Study of United States Military Assistance Programs in Underdeveloped Areas," Annex C, Volume II, *Supplement to the Composite Report of the President's Committee to Study the Military Assistance Program* (Washington, 1959), esp. pp. 77-80; John H. Badgley, "Burma's Political Crisis," *Pacific Affairs* 31 (December 1958): 350-51; Zbigniew Brzezinski, "The Politics of Under-

development," *World Politics* 9 (October 1956): 55-75; Guy Pauker, "Southeast Asia as a Problem Area in the Next Decade," *World Politics* 11 (April 1959): 342-45; and Howard Wriggins, "Foreign Assistance and Political Development," in Asher et al., *Development of the Emerging Countries*, pp. 181-214.

30. Lucian W. Pye, *Politics, Personality and Nation Building: Burma's Search for Identity* (New Haven and London 1962), p. 38. See also Philip Selznick, *Leadership and Administration* (Evanston, 1957); Herbert A. Simon, *Administrative Behavior: A Study of Decision-Making Processes in Administrative Organization* (New York, 1947); James A. March and Herbert A. Simon, *Organizations* (New York, 1958); and the valuable discussion in Wolin, *Politics and Vision*, chap. 10.

31. Karl W. Deutsch, "Toward an Inventory of Basic Trends and Patterns in Comparative and International Politics," *American Political Science Review* 54 (March 1960): 38-39.

32. For a statement of this view, see Fred W. Riggs, "Bureaucrats and Political Development: A Paradoxical View," in LaPalombara, *Bureaucracy*, pp. 120-67.

33. The quotation is from Pye, *Politics, Personality and Nation Building*, p. 39. Taylor's book is *The Principles of Scientific Management* (New York, 1911).

34. For example, see Lipset, *Political Man*, chap. 2; and Cutright, "National Political Development"; Hagen, "A Framework"; and Buchanan and Cantril, *How Nations See Each Other*.

35. His most comprehensive statement is *Nationalism and Social Communication* (New York, 1953). See also "The Growth of Nations," *World Politics* 5 (January, 1953): 168-96.

36. James S. Coleman, *Nigeria: Background to Nationalism* (Berkeley and Los Angeles, 1960); Rupert Emerson, *From Empire to Nation: The Rise to Self-Assertion of Asian and African Peoples* (Cambridge, Mass., 1960); Selig Harrison, *India: The Most Dangerous Decades* (Princeton, 1960); and Karl Deutsch et al., *Political Community and the North Atlantic Area* (Princeton, 1957).

37. On the latter point, see Robert A. Dahl and Charles E. Lindblom, *Politics, Economics and Welfare* (New York, 1953), pp. 78-88; and two articles by Lindblom, "The Science of Muddling Through," *Public Administration Review* 19 (Spring 1959): 79-88, and "Policy Analysis," *American Economic Review* 47 (June 1958): 298-312.

38. Urbana, 1959.

39. Chicago, 1962. See also William Kornhauser, *The Politics of Mass Society* (New York, 1959); this study, however, draws its data from the U.S. and Western Europe.

40. See "Introduction: A Functional Approach to Comparative Politics," in Almond and Coleman, *Developing Areas*, pp. 3-64.

41. Groups in a conscious, rather than a categoric, sense are what is meant here.

42. There is a rich literature on "national character" and politics, much of which might be subsumed under this approach. For some central propositions and bibliographical references, see Nathan Leites, "Psycho-Cultural Hypotheses About Political Acts," *World Politics* 1 (October 1948): 102-19; Alex Inkeles and Daniel Levinson, "National Character: The Study of Modal Personality and Sociocultural Systems," in Gardner Lindzey, ed., *Handbook of Social Psychology* (Reading, Mass., 1954), II, pp. 977-1020; and Gabriel A. Almond and Sidney Verba, *The Civic Culture: Political Attitudes and Democracy in Five Nations* (Princeton 1963), pp. 12-36, especially 13n.

43. One can, of course, trace its lineage back about as far as one chooses. The whole idea owes perhaps more to Max Weber than to any other single modern social scientist. In the United States, no discussion of the historical background to the notion of political culture should omit the work of Graham Wallas, Walter Lippmann, Charles E. Merriam, and Harold D. Lasswell. Talcott Parsons has been extremely influential in transmitting and revising the insights of Max Weber. Nevertheless, the concept of political culture as a major determinant of political change and development does not seem to have become prominent until the 1950s.

44. Gabriel A. Almond, "Comparative Political Systems," *Journal of Politics* 18 (August 1956): 391-409.

45. Nathan Leites, *On the Game of Politics in France* (Stanford, 1959); Laurence William Wylie, *Village in the Vaucleuse* (Cambridge, Mass., 1958); Edward C. Banfield, *The Moral Basis of a Backward Society* (Glencoe, 1958); Daniel Lerner, *The Passing of Traditional Society: Modernizing the Middle East* (Glencoe, 1958); Leonard Binder, *Iran: Political Development in a Changing Society* (Berkeley and Los Angeles, 1962); Apter, *The Gold Coast in Transition* and *The Political Kingdom in Uganda*; Almond and Verba, *The Civic Culture*; Lipset, *The First New Nation*. See also Harry Eckstein, *A Theory of Stable Democracy* (Princeton, 1961).

46. In the U.S. arena, Harold D. Lasswell was a pioneer; see *Psychopathology and Politics* (Chicago, 1930)·and *Power and Personality* (New York, 1948). Other important works are T. W. Adorno and others, *The Authoritarian Personality* (New York, 1950); M. Brewster Smith, Jerome S. Bruner, and Robert W. White, *Opinions and Personality* (New York, 1956); and Robert E. Lane, *Political Ideology: Why the American Common Man Believes What He Does* (New York and London, 1962). In the field of political biography, see Alexander and Juliette George, *Woodrow Wilson and Colonel House: A Personality Study* (New York, 1956); Erik Erikson, *Young Man Luther: A Study in Psychoanalysis and History* (New York, 1958); Alex Gottfried, *Boss Cermak of Chicago* (Seattle, 1962); and Arnold A. Rogow, *James Forrestal: A Study of Personality, Politics, and Policy* (New York, 1963).

47. *Politics, Personality and Nation Building*. Others may be noted. Gabriel A. Almond's *The Appeals of Communism* (Princeton, 1954) is relevant, although it is based upon material drawn from ex-Party

members in the United States, United Kingdom, Italy, and France. It stimulated and served as a guide for an earlier volume by Lucian W. Pye, *Guerrilla Communism in Malaya: Its Social and Political Meaning* (Princeton, 1956), which also leans heavily on personality to explain political development.

Two other volumes, both by non-political scientists interested principally in economic development but also in broader social change, are especially noteworthy. These are Everett E. Hagen, *On the Theory of Social Change: How Economic Growth Begins* (Homewood, Ill., 1962), and David C. McClelland, *The Achieving Society* (Princeton, 1961). It is at least quite interesting that scholars with backgrounds and disciplines as different as Pye (a political scientist), Hagen (an economist), and McClelland (a psychologist) should all turn to personality to try to account for political, social, and economic change.

We know of few psychological biographies of political leaders in developing countries, although this field has rich research possibilities. To get an idea of this richness, see the revealing essay by Susanne Hoeber Rudolph, "The New Courage: An Essay on Gandhi's Psychology," *World Politics* 16 (October 1963): 98-117.

48. "The difference between the twenties and the sixties in Brazil is that today the Brazilians have discovered themselves. They have taken a good look and they like what they see. They no longer wish to be Europeans, and their intellectuals no longer escape to Paris to find something to write about. They no longer describe themselves, or are so described by their own intellectuals, as a mongrel race, inferior because it consists of a mixed people. On the contrary, they find their creative freedom, their pride in the present, their confidence in the future precisely in this fact—that they are a mixed, a universal people. The social democracy of Brazil, and the pride Brazilians have discovered in being what they are, has released a font of creative enthusiasm." Frank Tannenbaum, in the Introduction to Gilberto Freyre, *The Mansions and the Shanties: The Making of Modern Brazil* (New York, 1963), p. xi.

49. See Benson, *Turner and Beard*, pp. 1-92 and *passim*. According to Benson, Loria's "fundamental proposition was that the relationship of man to the amount of 'free land' available for cultivation holds the key to human history," including the nature of the political system. Ibid., pp. 4 and 6-9.

50. "American democracy was born of no theorist's dream; it was not carried in the *Sarah Constant* to Virginia, nor in the *Mayflower* to Plymouth. It came out of the American forest, and it gained new strength each time it touched a new frontier. Not the constitution, but free land and an abundance of natural resources open to a fit people, made the democratic type of society in America for three centuries while it occupied its empire." *The Frontier in American History* (New York, 1920), p. 293, quoted in Fellman, "Economic Interpretation," p. 294. For a reinterpretation of the Turner thesis, see David M. Potter, *People of Plenty* (Chicago, 1954).

51. See *Oriental Despotism* (New Haven, 1957) for his thesis of the tyrannical "hydraulic society."

52. For example, see Sir Halford John Mackinder, *Britain and the British Seas* (New York, 1902), and "The Geographic Pivot of History," *Geographic Journal* 23 (April 1904); 421-37; Alfred Thayer Mahan, *The Influence of Sea Power upon History, 1660-1783* (New York, 1957); and Nicholas John Spykman, *The Geography of the Peace* (New York, 1944).

53. See especially Max F. Millikan and Donald M. Blackmer, eds., *The Emerging Nations: Their Growth and United States Policy* (Boston, 1961). For earlier statements of this approach in more narrowly economic form, see Millikan and Rostow, *Effective Foreign Policy*, chap. 5, and W. W. Rostow, *The Stages of Economic Growth: A Non-Communist Manifesto* (Cambridge, Eng., 1960).

SUGGESTIONS FOR FURTHER READING
PART ONE: APPROACHES TO THE STUDY OF COMPARATIVE POLITICAL SYSTEMS

Almond, Gabriel A. "A Developmental Approach to Political Systems." *World Politics* 17 (January 1965): 183-214.

Almond, Gabriel A. "Introduction: A Functional Approach to Comparative Politics." In *The Politics of Developing Areas,* edited by Gabriel A. Almond and James S. Coleman, pp. 3-64. Princeton: Princeton University Press, 1960.

Almond, Gabriel A., and Coleman, James S., eds. *The Politics of the Developing Areas.* Princeton: Princeton University Press, 1960.

Almond, Gabriel A., and Powell, G. Bingham, Jr. *Comparative Politics: A Developmental Approach.* Boston: Little, Brown and Co., 1966.

Anderson, Charles W.; von der Mehden, Fred R.; and Young, Crawford. *Issues of Political Development.* Englewood Cliffs, N.J.: Prentice-Hall, 1967.

Hah, Chong-Do, and Schneider, Jeanne. "A Critique of Current Studies on Political Development and Modernization." *Social Research* 35 (Spring 1968): 130-58.

Pye, Lucian W. "The Non-Western Political Process." *The Journal of Politics* 20, no. 3 (August 1958): 468-86.

Shils, Edward. "On the Comparative Study of the New States." In *Old Societies and New States,* edited by Clifford Geertz, pp. 1-26. New York: Free Press, 1963.

PART TWO
the
meaning
of political
development

S. N. Eisenstadt defines political development or modernization as the capacity of modern society "to adapt itself to
continuous changing demands, to absorb them in terms of
policy-making, and to assure its own continuity in face of
continuous new demands and new forms of political organization."[1] This, however, does not imply that any modern society
is always fully able to cope with new problems which are
continuously created within it. "The ability to deal with continuous change of political demands," writes Eisenstadt, "is the
crucial test of such sustained political growth, of political
development, or modernization."[2]

Moreover, modernization involves the development of institutional structures capable of absorbing change. The main structural aspects of modernization have been identified as the
development of a high degree of differentiation or specialization; the development of specialized or diversified types of
social organizations; and the development of wide nontraditional "national" or supernational group identification.[3]
Political development also means change in social relations—
from status to contract basis—and a change from traditional and
undifferentiated institutions to new politically differentiated
institutions of viability.   53

Karl Deutsch defines political modernization in terms of participation or mobilization. He suggests that modernization is dependent upon mass participation in the form of increased political decentralization. Widespread political participation is regarded as the key to political development. Political involvement is maximized with higher levels of education, exposure to mass media, and industrialization. These preconditions of political participation may intensify demands (inputs) on rule-making bodies, stimulate participation, broaden the elite, and center public attention on public needs at the national level.[4]

Emphasis on political participation as the key to political development is common among observers. Daniel Lerner observes that participation, industrialization, urbanization, and literacy characterize modern society, while low participation, lack of division of labor, weak bonds of interdependence, and localism and provincialism characterize traditional society. The latter conditions reflect the absence of shared symbols such as national "ideology" which enable members of the polity to achieve a "consensus" by articulating and adjusting their opinions. On the other hand, modern polities are participatory in that they function by consensus, which suggests that persons making decisions on public matters must often concur with other members of the political system in order to maintain "a stable common governance."[5]

Modernization is a dynamic process which transforms the political system in order to meet the changing demands for a more versatile participation of politically activated social groups in the political decision-making processes. Political development or modernization is an unceasing process which any political system has to undergo in order to meet the challenges of technology, industrialization, and urbanization.

David E. Apter defines modernization as follows:

> The dynamic aspect of modernization for the study of politics can be expressed in the general proposition that modernization is a process of increasing complexity in human affairs within which the polity must act. This is why it creates severe political problems. Politics becomes, in large measure, the business of coping with role differentiation while integrating organizational structures. Political actions that arise from such increasing complexity, however, are not pure responses by political leaders outside a political context. The question is, what is the political context? In the sense in which the phrase is used here, it refers to the particular arrangements by which

government exercises authority. As these structures change, so will political responses, and as political responses change, so will structures.[6]

Some scholars view political development as a movement from one stage to another, a process of growth over a period of time. For example, economists may observe and measure development in terms of gross national product (GNP), per capita income, investments, and output. For other social scientists, political development means democracy, political parties, urbanization, interest groups, a high level of literacy, representative government, industrialization, technological innovations, economic planning, and a role in the international arena. Political development also means the continuous emergence of new situations and problems in a series of stages each of which reflects distinctive characteristics and needs. In brief, political development signifies the capacity of the political system to sustain continuous change.

In the first article of this section, Karl von Vorys discusses social disorganization and weak national ties in traditional societies. He states that "The combination of frail national ties and disrupted small-scale societies generates anomic pressures which no political system can long endure." Only government can take the initiative by asserting control over the rate and course of socio-economic change. Governments in many newly independent states, however, suffer from serious limitations on their capacity to coerce at the time when their capacity to persuade is minimal. Governments in newly rising states do not possess the capacity to direct the course and rate of social and economic change. Von Vorys concludes that "they will yet have to develop this capacity through steady and balanced increments in their capacities of coercion and persuasion."

In his article "Patterns (Structures) of Modernization and Political Development," Marion J. Levy, Jr. examines the distinction between relatively modernized and relatively nonmodernized societies. The more modern societies have a greater ratio of inanimate to animate sources of power and, to a greater extent, human efforts are multiplied by the use of tools. The foci of differences by the relatively modernized and relatively nonmodernized societies include: specialization of organizations, interdependency, relationship emphases, patterns of centralization, media of exchange, and markets. Moreover, differences exist in bureaucracies, family considerations, and

55

town-village interdependencies. Levy states that "change in a consistent direction, family strains, problems of control, reactions, mobs, and problems of knowledge are seen as the differences it makes."

Levy moves to the examination of many of the advantages and disadvantages of the late comers (newly independent states). Finally, he states that alterations in town-village imbalances, creative uses of the armed forces, the use of politics as recreation, and the trickle effect may be viewed as possible avenues of control.

S. N. Eisenstadt discusses the general characteristics of political modernization which include the development of highly differentiated political structures in terms of specific political roles and institutions, unification and centralization of the political system, and the continuous spread of political power to wider groups in society. Furthermore, political modernization is characterized by the weakening of traditional elites and traditional legitimation of the rulers. Political modernization is also characterized by popular participation in the political processes.

The political process in modern political systems is characterized by the continuous interaction between institutional and noninstitutional interests. Eisenstadt examines how interests are aggregated and articulated in modern political systems and states that forms of articulation of interests have existed in various ways, even in premodern systems, but with differences. He discusses these differences in some detail.

At different stages in the development of modern political systems, different problems and different political organizations have developed. The major problem of political modernization is the ability of any system to adapt itself to changing demands and forms of political organization. Eisenstadt analyzes the patterns of absorption of political change in constitutional (multiparty) political systems, totalitarian regimes, and semiautocratic systems.

The various new states, namely the post-colonial ones, tend to evince in the initial stages of their development some common characteristics or problems with relation to change. The emphasis on change, progress, and economic development is part of their basic political and ideological orientation. However, their capacity to absorb changes is very limited when measured against their high aspirations for change. The leaders of the new states are faced with many problems, the solutions of which may influence the extent of institutionalization of viable political systems.

Eisenstadt attempts to explain the extent to which various modernizing elites and social groups may evince different attitudes to change and propensities or recourse to develop different organizational structures. The stability and continuity of modern or modernizing political systems is greatly influenced by broader social conditions, especially the interrelationship between the modernizing elites and the broader strata of the population.

NOTES

1. S. N. Eisenstadt, "Theories of Social and Political Evolution and Development," in *The Social Science: Problems and Orientations* (The Hague: Mouton, 1968), p. 184.

2. Eisenstadt, "Evolution and Development," p. 184.

3. Eisenstadt, "Evolution and Development," pp. 184-85.

4. Samuel P. Huntington, "Political Development and Political Decay," *World Politics* 17 (April 1965): 388.

5. Daniel Lerner, *The Passing of Traditional Society: Modernizing the Middle East* (New York: Free Press, 1958), p. 50.

6. David E. Apter, *The Politics of Modernization* (Chicago: University of Chicago Press, 1965), pp. 3-4.

TOWARD A CONCEPT
OF POLITICAL DEVELOPMENT

Karl von Vorys

It is becoming uncomfortably apparent that there are few newly independent countries about which it could be said with some confidence that their political systems will survive this decade. Revolutions occur with distressing regularity; demonstrations and riots seem endemic. Politics rarely means contests *within* the framework of the political system. Invariably it is the contest *about* the political system. We may commence an effort toward an operational concept of political development with the proposition that a political system which can provide for the functional requirement of long-term persistence from its own resources is not only in the interest of these new states, but is essential to the maintenance of international order as well. We may proceed by indicating the essential political features of a successful process toward this goal.

SOCIAL DISORGANIZATION

The political system in newly independent states is in constant peril as it is not sustained by a social system on a corresponding—national—scale which serves as the focus of orientation. For centuries, perhaps millennia, a vast number of traditional societies—tribes and kinship groups—operated at a small-scale equilibrium in most of Asia and Africa. Each was socially definitive. It made and enforced rules. It ascribed and rewarded roles. Each was also economically nearly self-sufficient. It produced its own food and traded its modest surplus for other necessities with local artisans. Except

From Karl von Vorys, "Toward a Concept of Political Development," *Annals of the American Academy of Political and Social Science* 358 (March 1965): 15-19. Reprinted by permission of the author and The American Academy of Political and Social Science.

in times of cataclysm it provided at least subsistence to all members. This is not to say that the traditional small-scale societies were free from stresses and strains. They were not. Their long-term persistence was assured, however, by the absence of alternatives. There were few outside contacts, and even in these, whether the subject was marriage or property, the critical test remained family identification. Ostracism was a most potent punishment.

The traditional small-scale societies are no longer in equilibrium. They are no longer socially definitive. Increasingly, urbanization offers alternatives while traditional rules appear inappropriate, and their implementation seems ineffective. Increasingly, the confidence of the hierarchy is sapped by men of inferior ascriptive standing who through competitive accomplishments earn substantial increments in rewards. Increasingly, the authority of the hierarchy is undermined by a younger generation with more education than its elders and by women with a vote equal to that of their husbands. Nor are the traditional small-scale societies economically self-sufficient any longer. The last decades saw a population explosion in Asia and parts of Africa. Abruptly the size of the kinship groups to be sustained by the small agricultural holdings has expanded rapidly while the holdings themselves have shrunk by subdivision and fragmentation. Simultaneously the introduction of industry has offered a formidable competition gradually invading rural markets, reducing and in some instances eliminating altogether the income of artisans.

The disruption of the traditional small-scale societies, however, has not been accompanied by potent forces pressing toward reintegration on the national scale. In view of the genesis of most newly independent states, this is surely not surprising. They emerged, after all, from artificial political entities contrived to preserve mercantile privileges and to serve colonial administrative conveniences. Their borders often enclose a collection of most diverse ethnic and cultural groups while separating arbitrarily segments of the same tribal group. Nor did the independence movement yield sufficient impetus for a national focus of orientation. In those territories where the struggle was short, perhaps perfunctory, the mobilization of the predominantly rural masses was neither necessary nor accomplished. Even where independence was gained only after prolonged agitation and strife, mass support was rarely attracted by a common drive *for* national unity. More often it reflected a common resentment *against* the centralizing pressures of colonial rule and the hope that with the withdrawal of the foreign power the strain upon the traditional small-scale societies would be at least reduced, if not eliminated.

The combination of frail national ties and disrupted small-scale societies generates anomic pressures which no political system can long endure. Some may hope that the very condition of disequilibrium will be sufficient stimulus for re-equilibration or that some "invisible hand" will provide adequate impetus for social and economic integration on the national scale. Reliance upon automatic mechanisms, however, is a very risky undertaking, particularly since their existence is far from satisfactorily demonstrated. The goal of a political system with long-term persistence is better served by a more secular initiative capable of reasserting control over the rate and course of social and economic change.

GOVERNMENT INITIATIVE

There is a distinct paucity of sources for such initiative. Only the government seems to have the potential to play this role adequately. It is, after all, the most comprehensive—if not the only—organizational structure on the national scale. It also contains the preponderant share of managerial resources. Above all, it has already staked out an exclusive claim to the performance of this task. Still, at this point even the government lacks the necessary control to provide effective initiative. To be sure, supported by international recognition of sovereignty and international definition of equality, governments determine foreign policy and regulate the movement of persons and goods across international borders. Many even possess the capacity to prevent territorial secession. When it comes to efforts requiring compliance by the masses—and social and economic reintegration does involve compliance by the masses—then performance is not at all impressive. Tax collection is sparse; evasions are massive. Subscriptions for public bonds by individuals are negligible. Price controls are ineffective. Public exhortations for family planning are unavailing. Most important, central law enforcement is rather tenuous. In the countryside order is still primarily assured through the authority and sanctions of the traditional hierarchies. In the towns and cities, strikes, mass demonstrations, and riots remain unchecked, and most agitators escape punishment. In consequence, if it is to serve as an effective source of initiative, the government must first develop its capacity to control.

CAPACITY TO CONTROL

Government control is a function of both coercion and persuasion. At different times and in different political systems there is a substantial variation in the mix. The critical problem in newly independent states is that the government suffers from serious limitations upon its capacity to coerce at the time when its capacity to persuade is minimal. Let us be more specific.

A basic restraint upon governmental capacity to coerce is the peculiar double standard in the popular attitude to force. Private violence as a means to settle individual and intergroup disputes or to support political demands against the government is routine and appears quite proper. In contrast the legitimacy of public force is far from generally accepted. Invariably, it evokes intense resentment not only from those who are its targets, but also from the population at large. For a husband to kill his wife and her lover if found together or for a family to continue a blood feud is considered in the finest tradition. For the government to punish such murders is unacceptable. Students, labor unions, and political groups may strike, demonstrate, damage property, even assault policemen as a matter of course. When the authorities respond with tear gas and arrests, they are roundly condemned.

This double standard may have its roots in the hostility of the small-scale societies to any and all external sources of sanction. It has undoubtedly been reinforced by the resentment generated against the colonial government during the struggle for independence. In any case, this double standard is largely responsible for a condition where even a moderate use of public force in support of such minimal governmental functions as collection of taxes, administration of justice, and maintenance of law and order produces a response of violence by individuals and groups.

The outbreak of violence places the government in a most difficult predicament. An attempt at repression would certainly trigger further violence, and that in turn would present a need for intensified repression. To sustain for long an escalation of coercion, however, is beyond the capacity of the government. Communications are minimal. Policies can be disseminated only slowly and inaccurately. Deviations are reported only rarely and unreliably. Transportation is rudimentary. Most villages are not accessible by road or railroad. Some are hardly accessible at all. Coercive personnel are modest in number; their reliability is open to doubt. The police force is now staffed by native sons, heirs to centuries of tradition, raised in small-scale societies. Invariably they feel more identified with the people upon whom they exercise power than with the government whose power they exercise. The constables are poorly trained and ill-paid. Not unnaturally, their turnover rate is high, and corruption is rampant. Aware of these restraints the government is reluctant to compel compliance with its policies or to enforce its laws. It is inclined to acquiesce in disorders short of anarchy. Aware of these restraints, political-action groups are inclined to ignore government initiative and are prone to support their demands with violence in the streets.

If the people are not disposed to submit to compulsion, neither are they prepared to comply voluntarily. Their experience with government has been a thoroughly bad one. In the past it meant foreign and/or arbitrary rule. It meant tax levies and military recruitment. All too often it meant personal abuse. The government's more recent record is scarcely more conducive to generation of public confidence There were hopes that the withdrawal of the colonial rulers would relieve the pressure upon the traditional small-scale societies. Instead the drive toward centralization intensified and was frequently accompanied by vigorous campaigns of

61

cultural assimilation. There were expectations that independence would bring a more egalitarian distribution of income and an improvement in the standard of living. Instead, in spite of much publicized efforts of government planning and public sector investments, wealth continued to accumulate in the hands of a few, while the real income of the masses increased very slowly, if at all. Especially, there were visions of self-determination and popular participation in political decision making. Instead, civil rights were invaded, political parties were dissolved, and elections were postponed or manipulated. Gradually, if not abruptly, hegemony accrued to a civilian and/or military bureaucracy whose skills are administrative and whose sensitivity to public opinion is not pronounced.

COERCION AND PERSUASION

It is conceivable that the government may improve the efficacy of its control by maximizing only its capacity to persuade. It is conceivable, though not very likely. The short histories of newly independent states are replete with constitutions which were cavalierly abandoned, representative assemblies which were promptly isolated from their constituents, and political parties which degenerated into tools of sectional and private interests. The fact is that the government can offer few incentives to entice voluntary compliance. It may dispose of some jobs which become available in the expanding bureaucracy, a few others in public corporations and expropriated foreign business firms. Massive efforts of capital formation and a steady influx of foreign aid may raise per capita incomes by modest percentages. However, it takes coercion—more coercion than the government can now muster—to increase domestic saving significantly and thus propel the economy into self-sustained growth. It takes coercion—more coercion than the government can now muster—to assure some semblance of an equitable distribution of income. It takes coercion—more coercion than the government can now muster—to offer the villager effective protection from roving gangs or hostile tribes.

Another alternative is concentrating upon the capacity to coerce. Since independence a motley group of dictators, lifetime presidents, and even great "redeemers" have seized the governments of various newly independent states. Few, if any, have chosen the path of expanding control by relying primarily upon instruments of compulsion. Presumably this remarkable fact is not due to their extraordinary commitment to democratic ideals. More plausibly, it reflects a sober assessment that such would be an unfruitful course. The government could presumably recruit a large enough army and even equip it with foreign weapons. Such armies may indeed be effective in guarding the borders or thwarting secession. In times of internal crises they could even succeed in restoring public order.

Their performance is less likely to be impressive when the challenges are not concentrated or when resistance is widespread and passive. It may become negligible when instead of *responding* to challenge the army is called upon to implement policy. The government could also, no doubt, improve the equipment and increase the size of the police forces. It requires persuasion, however—more persuasion than the government can now muster—to assure that these forces will in fact be prepared to use their coercive power. It requires persuasion—more persuasion than the government can now muster—to avoid a public response of violence to attempts at coercion. Finally it requires persuasion—more persuasion than the government can now muster—to sustain wide-scale effectiveness of coercion by public cooperation in providing information about prohibited behavior and public assistance in the apprehension of criminals and agitators. There remains, then, the final alternative: expansion of governmental control through a gradual and balanced development of both capacities. To gauge the proper rate and the correct combination is at the very core of the process.

POLITICAL DEVELOPMENT

We are, then, dealing with a special kind of process, one which is more specific than political change and one which is distinct from modernization. It is a process which has its origins in the disequilibrium of mounting anomic pressures, not in the equilibrium of traditional societies. It is a process whose goal is a political system which can provide for the functional requirements of long-term persistence, a system which will probably meet the tests of modernity, but which does not have to do so. It is a process which includes social and economic changes, but whose focus is the development of the governmental capacity to direct the course and the rate of social and economic change. It is a process which will rest largely upon social and economic accomplishments, but whose progress is measured by increments in the government's capacities to coerce and persuade. Above all, it is a political process which, in fact, will accomplish its political goal. It is a process which may well be described as political development.

PATTERNS (STRUCTURES)
OF MODERNIZATION
AND POLITICAL DEVELOPMENT

Marion J. Levy, Jr.

In discussing the problems of "modernization" for the developing nations—whatever term or euphemism we use—we deal with a peculiar problem in social history. We are confronted—whether for good or for bad—with a universal social solvent. The patterns of the relatively modernized societies, once developed, have shown a universal tendency to penetrate any social context whose participants have come in contact with them. From many points of view it makes little difference whether these patterns penetrate at least partially by the will and preference of relatively nonmodernized peoples or whether they have the patterns thrust upon them. The patterns always penetrate; once the penetration has begun, the previous indigenous patterns always change; and they always change in the direction of some of the patterns of the relatively modernized society. The changes, once begun, are by no means necessarily successful from the point of view of either outsiders or insiders, but lack of success and dissatisfaction with them hardly impede the disruption of the previous patterns—rather the opposite.

INTRODUCTION

Throughout this paper I shall use a distinction between relatively modernized and relatively nonmodernized societies as locations along a continuum. Regardless of where the dividing point lies, certain examples of societies or nations are sufficiently far on one side or the other of such

From Marion J. Levy, Jr., "Patterns (Structures) of Modernization and Political Development," *Annals of the American Academy of Political and Social Science* 358 (March 1965): 30-40. Reprinted by permission of the author and The American Academy of Political and Social Science.

a point as to make discussions reasonably clear. The United States is a relatively modernized society; the societies of Tokugawa, Japan, traditional China, modern China, and India are relatively nonmodernized. I consider any society the more modernized the greater the ratio of inanimate to animate sources of power and the greater the extent to which human efforts are multiplied by the use of tools. I consider any society relatively modernized if comparatively small changes increasing the ratio of animate to inanimate sources of power would have very far-reaching implications for the general social structure. In this sense there are no societies totally lacking in all elements of modernization, and that is the reason I have used quotation marks around the word modernization when it first appeared above.

I assume that on the most general levels of consideration all societies must be identical and that all variations at less abstract levels constitute overlays on these common elements. All relatively modernized societies have developed out of relatively nonmodernized ones, some with only minor importations from abroad. All relatively nonmodernized societies have more in common as regards social structure than any one of them has with any case of a relatively modernized society and vice-versa.

I have chosen modernization as a focus because the problem of political development at issue here is a special facet of this more general category. In the discussion of modernization I have tried to focus attention on problems of maximum relevance to questions of coordination and control.

All statements here should be considered to be hypotheses about the facts. I do not present any such hypotheses without believing them to be tenable, but my beliefs are not to be confused with proof.

FOCI OF DIFFERENCES BETWEEN RELATIVELY MODERNIZED AND RELATIVELY NONMODERNIZED SOCIETIES

Specialization of Organizations

There is a type of specialization—not unknown in relatively nonmodernized contexts, but carried very much further in relatively modernized contexts—that is independent of the kind of products produced or operations performed in terms of the organization. It is a specialized orientation to a single aspect of behavior. Organizations that are predominantly economically oriented (for example, business firms or factories), predominantly politically oriented (for example, governments and political parties), predominantly educationally oriented (for example, schools), predominantly religiously oriented, predominantly recreationally oriented, and the like are enormously elaborated in relatively modernized contexts. Relatively nonspecialized organizations such as family units are not eliminated or unimportant in such contexts. Nevertheless, one of the

65

critical differences is that, when such specialized organizations exist in relatively nonmodernized contexts, only a relatively small proportion of the general population operate often or much in terms of them. The vast majority of the members of any relatively modernized society operate continuously in terms of such organizations, in addition to the operations they continue to carry out in other contexts. This is, of course, what is dubbed the "compartmentalization" of life in highly modernized contexts. This change has far-reaching implications for people accustomed to carrying out the vast majority of their activities in relatively nonspecialized contexts. It is a new context for many, and it changes the implications of behavior in terms of the relatively nonspecialized contexts in which they continue to act. The increase of such contexts at one and the same time undermines previous family stability and increases the relevance of the family as the "castle of the me" for modern man.

Interdependency

A close correlate of the increased specialization of organizations is the high level of interdependency characteristic of relatively modernized society. In no society are there organizations whose members are capable of complete self-sufficiency, but the levels of self-sufficiency attained in terms of organizations such as the family, the village, and the like is frequently high. The level of self-sufficiency of the members of all organizations up to and including nations continues to decline with increases in modernization.

Relationship Emphases

Relatively modernized, by contrast with relatively nonmodernized, contexts are featured by great emphases both ideally and actually on what have come in the trade to be known as the patterns of rationality, universalism, and functional specificity as opposed to emphases on tradition, particularism, and functional diffuseness. Explicit emphases in many contexts on using knowledge that is presumably scientifically justified (rationality), of selecting people and judging them on the basis of what they can do that is relevant as opposed to who they are (universalism), and on precisely defined and delimited relationships (functional specificity) are requisites for a relatively modernized society. The most common form of the fallacy of misplaced dichotomy is to imply or assert that in relatively modernized contexts there are not, or are only negligible, emphases on tradition, particularism, and functional diffuseness. The family is always relevant for these societies and is always predominantly traditional, particularistic, and functionally diffuse. In relatively nonmodernized contexts there are often some actual emphases on rationality, universalism, and functional specificity, and sometimes there are ideal patterns of this sort as well—for example, the examination patterns of the Chinese bureaucracy. Nevertheless, both ideally and actually, the vast majority of the members of all of the relatively nonmodernized societies operate in nearly all their organizational contexts on predominantly traditional, particularistic, and functionally diffuse bases. What is done because it is predominantly traditional is not necessarily irrational, and indeed frequently coincides with rationality given the means at the disposal of the people concerned. The same cannot be said of the other two aspects, although here, given the contexts in which they are emphasized, they may not make the kind of differences usually supposed. For example, predominantly particularistic criteria for employment do not necessarily under these circumstances lower the level of efficiency of the personnel engaged in a given job.

Patterns of Centralization

All relatively nonmodernized societies stable over relatively long periods of time are examples of quite specific combinations of centralization and decentralization. Moreover, however much the patterns of centralization may have been emphasized, these systems as a whole were never overwhelmingly centralized, if stable. It is only with the patterns of relatively modernized societies that the logistics of overwhelming central-ization become either feasible or economic—regardless of ethical considera-tions. In all of the relatively modernized contexts the levels of centraliza-tion continually rise over long periods of time. We tend to think of all centralization as heading toward governmental organizations. Increasingly this is the case with relatively modernized societies, but it is by no means exclusively the case. Most observers would probably agree that the centralization of the government of the Soviet Union has been carried to considerably greater lengths than that of the United States, but in some senses the much greater development of communication facilities consti-tutes greater over-all centralization of United States society.

For late-comers to the process, the requirements of coordination and control are always strategic, and they are always strategic at a point in time at which the probability is overwhelming that the previously existing patterns of coordination and control will be radically undercut. So far only the Meiji Japanese have shown "virtuosity" in avoiding these effects.

Generalized Media of Exchange and Markets

All relatively modernized contexts require much greater emphases on monetary devices and markets. Media of exchange—monies—vary enor-mously in their levels of generalization, that is, in the number of things that can be exchanged or evaluated in terms of money. For example,

67

characteristically in feudal contexts land is not subject to free and easy purchase and sale.

The whole subject of money is a matter about which academics are exceedingly skittish, and even nonacademics seem to feel that a preoccupation with money is one of the crassest forms of materialism. None of us hesitates to affirm the opinion that travel is broadening, but so is the use of money. Few things so affect a people's horizons of the possible as the increased use of money. Above all it spreads comparisons. Whether one likes it or not, if a Rembrandt painting has sold for $2.5 million and the latest edition of *Fanny Hill* sells for $2.50—regardless of ideology—a relation of the one as 10^6 more costly than the other has been established. Correspondingly to tell a peasant who has never even considered the possibility of getting an education for his son that an education costs a given amount—even if that amount is one that he does not think he has any prospect of achieving—tells him that, if he can make certain accumulations, he can achieve an education for his son. It is not entirely correct that money cannot buy an education. By contrast with any relatively nonmodernized context the level of generalization of the media of exchange and the use of money in general always increase. They will continue to do so until or unless a completely managed and centralized organization for allocation of goods and services under government auspices is achieved. Such centralization, however, in turn implies other problems—especially the problem of adequate knowledge.

Markets are by no means unknown in relatively nonmodernized contexts, but they always multiply in relatively modernized contexts. There are, by definition, always some degrees of freedom associated with a market. These degrees of freedom, if broad enough and if the number of participants in the market is great enough, spread out and hence minimize the problem of error, and always pose problems of control. In the absence of adequate knowledge for efficient rationality about direct allocation of goods and services, a market minimizes the problem of errors by diffusing them among a relatively large and less powerful set. Of course, this cannot be done without leaving to members of the market the possibility of using their allocations in ways that may not be deemed desirable. It is one of the ironies of modern ideological disputes that "capitalism" and the associated presence of high degrees of freedom in the markets concerned is supposed quite broadly to increase the implications of allocations of goods and services for the allocations of power and responsibility. Actually such patterns are perhaps the most efficient device found by man to minimize such implications. Societies which may be described as feudal, fascist, and socialist are always ones in terms of which allocations of power and responsibility and allocations of goods and services are more directly and immediately interdependent than capitalistic societies.

Fit in General Structure

The implication of a given pattern may vary enormously depending on how that pattern fits into the general social structure. The many common emphases of Japanese and Chinese family patterns were enormously modified by virtue of the fact that the Chinese was expected to give his loyalty first and last to his family whereas the Tokugawa Japanese was, ideally, prepared to sacrifice his family interests for those of his overlord. Correspondingly, during modernization the retention of previously existing patterns does not mean that they have the same implications as before, nor does it mean that a given pattern may be taken over directly and used efficiently. The ancient ideal patterns of social mobility in China, initially at least, had negative implications for modernization whereas the closed class patterns of Japan had positive implications. The inherited positions of the Tokugawa bureaucracy were, via a civil service by adoption, less vulnerable to corruption than those of the Chinese bureaucracy.

Bureaucracy

This whole question is so frequently commented upon that it need not detain the argument here. The bureaucracies in relatively modernized contexts must be on a different basis than those in relatively nonmodernized contexts. In relatively modernized contexts members of bureaucracies are not only faced by the necessity of high levels of ingenuity and skill in devising both patterns of government and physical plant. They are also faced by the twin problems of rapid obsolescence and far-reaching implications of relatively minor failures in maintenance.

A critical question for members of all relatively modernized societies is how to recruit, maintain, and insulate such organizations from other contexts. For late-comers to the process this poses a special problem. Not only are the previous nonbureaucratic contexts still very much present, but the bureaucrats themselves constitute one of the great sources of dissidence. Bureaucrats in general are easily frustrated, and in the process of modernization the new bureaucrats are first made both ideally and actually elite, and then are likely to be radically frustrated.

Family Considerations

From a theoretical point of view the family is an interesting organization. It is the one organization that we feel sure.has existed in all known societies. Furthermore, the overwhelming majority of members of all known societies, including the most modernized, have roles in some family or other throughout their life histories. All nonfamily organizations

69

can be divided into two categories. The first is those relative to which, ideally speaking, family considerations are supposed to make a difference. Most of the relatively nonmodernized societies are ones whose members regard nepotism as a virtue rather than as a vice. Under these circumstances it is better than an even-money bet that, both ideally and actually, what happens to one in terms of one's family will affect the way in which one behaves in nonfamily contexts. The other type of nonfamily organization is that in terms of which family considerations are not supposed to affect how one behaves. The proliferation of such organizations in relatively modernized contexts is enormous. Most of the specialized organizations referred to are of this sort, and all of the bureaucracies, ideally, are. In the context of these organizations what happens to one in terms of one's family supposedly does not affect one's behavior; actually, it is exceedingly likely to. Finally, in the context of all known societies much basic learning—for example, walking, talking, eating, sleeping, bodily control, adjustments to patterns of authority, allocations of goods and services, and responses to affection—is acquired in family contexts. Even in the most highly modernized contexts where the "functions of the family" are alleged to be withering away, this holds. Thus, family organizations are not likely to be negligible matters for understanding any social setting.

Moreover, in all relatively nonmodernized contexts the vast majority of all behavior of all individuals is actually likely to be family-oriented even if it is not ideally so. The average member of such societies rarely operates outside a family context. The average member of all relatively nonmodernized societies acquires the vast majority of all of the learning that he acquires throughout his life cycle—not just his basic learning—in a family context. The various bases of precedence in the family context ordinarily reinforce one another. The family head is ordinarily the representative of the oldest generation, is in fact the oldest individual, and a male. Furthermore, insofar as individuals are controlled, the vast majority of individuals in relatively nonmodernized contexts are controlled on a family basis. The major form of decentralization of control is to the family head in such contexts. This is one of the reasons why the general problems of social control for all the late-comers to this process are so closely related to questions of family disintegration. The fact that, with the introduction of the new patterns, the individual may for the first time have learned something of importance to his performance of adult roles from someone other than an older member of his own family may undermine the ordinary reinforcement of respect for the control of the older members. Previous lack of defiance may have been more a function of lack of conceived alternatives than of a lack of dissatisfaction with the forms of control as they existed. This as much as anything else is relevant to the explosive disintegration of so many social patterns under the impact of modernization.

Town-Village Interdependencies

The vast majority of all of the members of all of the relatively nonmodernized societies are rural rather than urban. They are villagers rather than townspeople. They are also overwhelmingly preoccupied with sedentary forms of agriculture. If the societies are of considerable scale in terms of numbers of members and territorial limits, they are without exception—never mind how they came to be—accustomed to some level of what they regard as essentially a one-way flow of goods and services from rural to urban contexts. The main forms of such flows are, of course, rent, taxes (or feudal dues), interest, and profits. The rurals take this as a way of life. They do not ordinarily defy or resist unless there is some increase beyond customary limits. They do not regard themselves as recipients of a continuous flow of goods and services from urban contexts. Above all, they are not accustomed to the urban contexts as a source of goods or devices or ideas that systematically increase productivity per acre. This latter expectation is one of the most revolutionary features of relatively modernized societies and has reached its most extraordinary development in the case of modern United States society. Our great comparative advantage in problems of modernization is surely our agrarian "know how" (which in a curious sense we do not understand). It is relatively speaking much easier to reproduce our factories than our productivity per acre.

THE DIFFERENCE IT MAKES

Change

Once contact is made with members of a relatively modernized society, change in that direction begins—even if the change from the point of view of all concerned is a dismal failure.

Families and Strains

Family contexts always are a focus of strain. And the new possibilities of learning and alternative forms of employment furnish explosive outlets for those strains.

Problems of Control

The problems of control are maximized just as most of the bases for control are undercut—especially the bases of family control. In some sense all of the late-comers, as they modernize, are in for political instability.

71

Furthermore, initial successes in control are not necessarily harbingers of success. There is hardly a case in which there is not sufficient control initially to get some more or less spectacular increases in productivity in the form of a factory here or an improved communications facility there started. The real trick is to coordinate such increases in productivity and such changes once a large number of them have come into existence. So far, many more late-comers have tried than have succeeded. This is what makes Japan so spectacular.

Individualism by Default

There is likely to be individualism by default in all cases of modernization rather than stable forms of individualism by ideal. People are more likely to be radically cut loose as far as their horizons of what they can do or attempt is concerned than to pick up the kind of patterns of individualism that we tend to think of. The context in terms of which they have ordinarily made their decisions—most usually the family context—is either no longer available to them or no longer relevant. Individualism by default always increases the possibilities of ruthless behavior and, especially if concentrated among virtuosi of individualism by default, considerably complicates problems of control.

ADVANTAGES AND DISADVANTAGES OF LATE-COMERS

Advantages: Late-comers to the process have certain obvious advantages. For one thing they are not traveling in *terra incognita.* Unlike the indigenous developers of these patterns they have conceptions, right or wrong, about where they are going. Second, there exists the possibility of borrowing initial expertise in planning, capital accumulation, skills, patterns of organization, and the like. Third, there is the possibility of skipping some of the early stages associated with the process elsewhere. Fourth, the leaders among late-comers—because the problem is not *terra incognita*—may be able to solidify their leadership by holding out prospects elsewhere achieved. Fifth, late-comers are always in the position to take over some of the fruits of the process elsewhere without the cost of invention or previous obsolescence. Not only are the late-comers likely to ask for assistance, but regardless of motivation those who have previously achieved in these respects are likely to offer or insist on assistance.

Disadvantages: The disadvantages of late-comers are in general of three sorts. There are problems of scale, problems of conversion, and problems of disappointment. Late-comers, in order to get into the process at all, must do some things from the very outset on a fairly large scale.

Characteristically these are things which the indigenous developers were able to carry out over long periods of time in relatively small steps. Most spectacular among these are the development of modern communication and educational facilities. Universal literacy, for example, is something that "needs" achieving for these people as soon as possible. The larger the problems of scale, the greater the implications of any failures in coordination and control.

The second disadvantage of late-comers has to do with the problem of conversion of resources, materials, skills, and the like from one employment to another. For those who modernized gradually over long periods of time the materials and skills at hand were converted into new ones. In Great Britain the carpenters, the blacksmiths, and the wrights of one period, working with the materials at hand, created the materials and skills for the next stage. For the late-comers the problem is different. No amount of ingenuity and skill permits one to use the carpenters, blacksmiths, and wrights at hand plus the materials available to make a modern milling machine. Some of the conversions to be made are always of this order. Short of everything needed in this fashion being an outright gift from abroad—and that poses problems of a different sort—as a minimum there is the problem of reorientation of pre-existing forms of productivity so as to accumulate foreign exchange or its equivalent.

The third disadvantage of late-comers is that of disappointment. These people get involved in the process with a view to what it will do for them. They and their leaders have expectations which did not exist for the indigenous developers, but in the process someone always gets hurt. Things do not always turn out according to either expectations or hopes. In some cases there is the illusion of falling farther and farther behind even though in relative terms one is gaining. Late-comers are exceedingly likely to experience the frustration of running harder and harder only to seem to be less likely to catch up.

Fundamentalist Reactions

In this process someone always gets hurt. Someone is always disappointed. In the midst of the disintegration of the old someone always sees villainy *as* the introduction of the new. The cry that things were better in the good old days always occurs to someone, always appeals to someone, and someone always acts on it. Attempts to turn the clock back are no less radical in their implications than attempts to push the clock forward beyond one's means. The main difference lies in the fact that the former are unintentionally radical and the latter are often unthinkingly radical.

Mobs

One of the earliest importations now is always radical improvement in   73 the means of communication—and with that the probability of mass appeals—and with that the possibility of the use of mobs. The temptation to use mobs is something that should be indulged in by those out of power seeking to gain it but never attempted by those in power. For those in power the use of mobs means instability. One can endow the members of a mob with power but one cannot hold them effectively responsible. The former is more likely to be seen as the short-cut means to the ends of some of the leaders involved.

The Problem of Adequate Knowledge

The more highly centralized a given system becomes, the more strategic is adequate knowledge to the levels of explicit planning necessary. For late-comers to the process, with their special disadvantages and their special problems of coordination and control, adequate knowledge is a critical problem. Usually neither they nor we know much about their own societies. Certainly far less is known explicitly than is necessary to take fully into account the bases from which change takes place. Furthermore, given the state of the social sciences, with certain notable exceptions in particular areas of the field of economics, the prospects are not favorable that we will soon come into possession of the knowledge we need. The state of theory in most of these fields is a scandal, and we need more analysis of a high order of these problems than seems in immediate prospect. In the world in which we live today radicalism has little to do with the ideology of left and right. Increasingly radicals take the form of conservative radicals who would unwittingly cut the levels of centralization below the minimum requisite for the kinds of contexts in which they live, and the liberal radicals who would increase the level of centralization beyond the limits of adequate knowledge for operating in terms of centralized patterns. In the absence of improvements in the social sciences well beyond sophisticated techniques of gathering and assessing data, members of both highly modernized and relatively nonmodernized societies alike are in far greater danger from ignorance than from population explosions or entropy.

POSSIBLE AVENUES OF CONTROL

Alterations of Town-Village Imbalances

As indicated above, these societies are overwhelmingly likely to be predominantly agrarian. For most people in the past the terms modernization and industrialization have been considered almost synonymous. Only recently have the revolutionary implications of highly modernized agrarian productivity been recognized for what they are. At almost every turn in all of the relatively nonmodernized cases, when one speaks of capital formation, of controlling people—whatever one speaks of—one speaks of handling farmers. It is no longer possible to satisfy farmers in these areas by the strategy of allocating titles of land to them. For the remainder of this century the major strategy of modernization for late-comers will have to be increasingly an attempt to improve productivity per acre systematically and continuously first, and to increase productivity in industry in the ordinary sense in urban settings no more rapidly than is necessary to support such increases in productivity per acre in the rural areas. One of the major obstacles to this at present is that to the late-comers themselves it is the factories, the automobiles, the computers that symbolize modernization, and not the somewhat more subtle continuous increase in productivity per acre.

Creative Use of Armed Forces

We tend to consider armed forces as essentially negative in impact and available primarily for external use. For most people in the world the relevance of armed forces for the maintenance of internal order will, short of a holocaust, be more important than their uses in external forays. The late-comers are going to maintain armed forces—the more modern the better as far as they are concerned. We have not generally considered the armed forces for what they are. Under relatively nonmodernized conditions the armed forces are more likely to be a focus of preoccupation with rationality, universalism, functional specificity, and the like than anything else. Furthermore, in the modernization situation armed forces offer certain advantages. First, the things that the leaders will want the members of their armed forces to be good at are usually directly convertible to nonmilitary contexts. Driving a military truck is not in principle different from driving a civilian truck. Second, problems of control of the members of armed forces are usually minimal. Mass mutinies are relatively rare in history and do not occur save in the context of general social disintegration. The real problem of handling members of armed forces is the problem of containing palace revolutions engineered by cliques. Third, armed forces are likely to be set up on the basis of universal conscription and that affords those in control the possibility of the selection of the ablest people both physically and mentally for the impact of the training to be given. Fourth, for reasons having to do with the focusing of attention, elimination of interference, and the like, the inculcation of new patterns in an armed force context is almost always carried out in "camps." These involve, potentially at least, high levels of isolation from the population at large, and creative thought in the matter could probably increase those rates. This means that the armed forces probably offer a more promising context for the maximization of new elements of modernization with a minimization of problems of uncontrolled feedback

75

than any other single social device. The feedback will not be eliminated, but it is more amenable to control than most. One is aided in this by the inevitable emphasis on discipline characteristic of armed force contexts.

Politics as Recreation

One of the most important changes in American institutional life has been a switch from politics as recreation to recreation as politics. There was a time in this country when alternative forms of specialized recreation were relatively undeveloped. Furthermore, this was the period in which something approaching mass participation in the specialized political contexts of life was a new and heady experience. During the last century politics was a major form of entertainment for large audiences. That was the day of the two- to three-hour political speech. That was the day of people who came with their entire families in their wagons with lunches, picnicking to hear the politicians of their day. Except for occasional flurries today, such as debates between presidential candidates, party conventions when televised for the first time, and the like, politics is no longer a major form of recreation. Recreation becomes a special form of politics when each party has its own Hollywood folk, and when an increasing number of people with leisure at their command find political participation as amateurs at the grassroot level more fascinating than bridge. With the introduction of mass communication media there is likely to be among all of the late-comers a considerable period of politics as recreation. Ideology may be terribly important, but one can hardly witness or look at films of the demonstrations of the 1960s in Japan, of the freedom chanters in Africa, or elsewhere, without being struck by the recreational aspects of these occasions. If this is at all correct, it holds the prospect of substituting other forms of recreation for politics as recreation. The counterploy for youth intrigued and active in one political camp may well be nonideologically oriented driving schools or the furtherance of dating patterns rather than alternative ideological themes in an alternative political context. Mass participation in anything except *labor corvées* has been rare throughout social history, let alone mass participation in the specialized political contexts of life. It is exceedingly likely to be heady stuff. It is not frivolous to think of the recreational implications of participation in politics.

The Trickle Effect

The trickle effect is an increasing possibility as income distribution becomes more unimodal and as the standard of living continues to improve. One of the implications of the trickle effect was first suggested by Professor Lloyd Fallers.[1] Relatively modernized contexts are likely to emphasize social mobility to a higher degree than their participants achieve it. If new and relatively costly consumer goods are continuously generated, if they are first used by people in higher income brackets, if there is enough of a continuity in income distribution for them to trickle down to lower and lower income brackets as they catch on, their cost can be reduced by larger markets so that they will trickle down even faster. They will first have acquired an aura of upper-class usage and prestige. If there is a continuous flow of such goods trickling down through income levels, Fallers maintained that one would get from this an illusion of social mobility even in the absence of actual social mobility. He reasoned that this would operate much in the same way that a man sitting stationary in a train on one side of the platform has the illusion of moving in the opposite direction when a train on the opposite side of the platform pulls out. It may be possible to use the trickle effect as a method of control, as an offset to some of the problems of frustration previously mentioned. If this is true, it is vital that one have an increasingly distributed per capita income, not just an increasing earned per capita income. It is also implicit in the trickle effect that very early attempts at equalization of income or attempts, however nugatory, to block the association of higher income with higher prestige are great mistakes. Such attempts cannot be successful, but they can be made.

CONCLUSION

There is more to this than theorizing. Neither we nor they have a real alternative to trying to carry out modernization. We are not going to be able to modernize primarily in terms of the traditional patterns of the societies concerned or to preserve those patterns to any considerable extent. As time goes on they and we will come increasingly to resemble one another—not necessarily because they come to be more like what we are now, but because the patterns of modernization are such that the more highly modernized societies become, the more they resemble one another. We and the Japanese, for example, may be more like one another in the year 1990 than either of us will be like what we are today. In addition to the problems of adequate knowledge for late-comers and for the members of relatively modernized societies already stressed we face—all of us— increasingly another special problem, and this is truly new under the sun. We face the problem of socialization for an unknown future. The rate of social change in both relatively modernized and modernizing contexts is itself revolutionary. Prior to our day the vast majority of all individuals in world history lived out their lives in the expectation that their lots would be roughly modeled on the lots of their parents and that their children's lots would be modeled on theirs. Both as an ideal and as an actuality we expect the lives of our children as adults to be removed from ours. But

77

how does one educate children for an unknown future? We had better learn how.

NOTES

1. See Lloyd Fallers, "A Note on the Trickle Effect," *Public Opinion Quarterly* 18, no. 3: 314-21.

POLITICAL MODERNIZATION: SOME COMPARATIVE NOTES

S. N. Eisenstadt

Throughout the world we witness today the continuous spread of modern forms of political organization and process. This process is, in a way, much more ubiquitous and general than that of economic growth and development to which so much attention has been paid, and it does also serve a basic prerequisite or condition of economic development. Moreover, in many of the so-called new countries the goal of economic development is more of a political goal than a fact of economic life, and much of the fate of economic development is nowadays in the hands of the politicians.

The political forms and processes which develop in these New States may sometimes seem to be entirely new—different from those which were connected with the establishment of modern political frameworks in Europe, the United States, the Dominions or Latin America. And yet the very fact that we designate them as modern shows that there may exist affinity and similarity in the very forms and in some of the elements of the political process.

It is the purpose of this paper to explore some of these affinities as well as the major differences between the various types of modern political regimes.[1]

Historically, political modernization can be equated with those types of political systems which have developed in Western Europe from the seventeenth century, and have then spread to other European countries, to the American and in the nineteenth and twentieth centuries to Asian and African continents.

Typologically, political modernization is characterized by the develop-

From S. N. Eisenstadt, "Political Modernization: Some Comparative Notes," *International Journal of Comparative Sociology* 5 (March 1964): 3-24. Reprinted by permission of the publisher.

ment of a series of features within a political system. Some—but not all—of these features have existed also in premodern political systems, often serving as precursors to modernization and as important conditions of initial modernization.

The most general traits of political modernization are, on the one hand, continuous development of a high extent of differentiation, unification and centralization of the political system, and on the other hand, continuous development of a high extent of "free-floating" (i.e. noncommitted to any ascriptive groups) political power and resources.

These general traits are manifest in several more concrete characteristics:

The first such characteristic of political modernization is the development of a highly differentiated political structure in terms of specific political roles and institutions, of the centralization of the polity and of development of specific political goals and orientations.

Second, political modernization is characterized by growing extension of the scope of the central legal, administrative and political activities and their permeation into all spheres and regions of the society.

Third, it is characterized by the continuous spread of potential political power to wider groups in the society—ultimately to all adult citizens.

Further, it is characterized by the weakening of traditional elites and of traditional legitimation of the rulers, and by the establishment of some sort of ideological and usually also institutional accountability of the rulers to the ruled who are the holders of the potential political power.

All these characteristics are, of course, connected with the continuous growth of great fluidity of political support, with the lack of ascriptive commitment of political support, with the lack of ascriptive commitment of political allegiance to any given ruler or group. This necessitates that the rulers, in order to maintain themselves effectively in power and receive support for the specific goals which they propagate and for the policies they want to implement, have to search continuously the political support of the ruled, or at least of large or vocal parts thereof; and have to mobilize continuously full political support.

The culmination of this process, as it has gradually developed in the outright modern systems, is the participation of the ruled in the selection of the rulers, in the setting up of the major political goals, and to a smaller extent, also in the formulation of policies. The formal expression of this is the system of elections, as it has evolved, in different ways, in most modern political systems.

Unlike the rulers of traditional regimes the rulers of the totalitarian regimes cannot take the political passivity and/or traditional identification of their subjects for granted and are even afraid of such passivity—just because such passivity may become in these systems a potential focus for the crystallization of the potential political power of the citizens. The difference between modern democratic or semidemocratic and totalitarian political systems lies not in the fact of the spread of such power—which is common to all of them—but in the ways in which the rulers react to this power.

The preceding analysis does not imply that no charismatic and traditional (feudal) relations exist between rulers and ruled in a modern political system. But traditional legitimation cannot be predominant in any modern political system where the rule or ideology of "accountancy" of the rulers to the ruled be the predominant ones. These may be either charismatic, or legal—rational or "social" in the sense of devotion to secular social values (a category which may be akin to Weber's *"Wertrational"* but which he did not use in his classification of types of legitimation).[2]

The political process in modern, as in all other types of political systems, is characterized by the continuous interaction between the political institutions, the rulers on the one hand, and other spheres and groups of the society on the other hand. The major social groups put before the rulers various types of demands for policy decisions. At the same time, these groups make various types of resources available to the rulers' political institutions. These resources are made available through the activities of various political elites which compete for them and organize them within the frameworks of the major political institutions.

As in all other political systems so in the modern ones, the rulers have to deal both with "objective" problems such as international relations and alliances, budget taxes, mobilization of economic resources, on the one hand, and with mobilization of political support on the other hand. But the connection between these two is in modern political systems much more close than in other types of political systems, because the growing participation of wider strata of population in the political process makes these groups much more sensitive and interested in—although not necessarily always better able to understand—these "objective" problems.

Similarly, the articulation of political demands and activities in modern political systems is much more closely related to the provision of resources to the political elite than in other types of political systems. Some effective political organization of the ruled is here almost a basic prerequisite of the continuous provision of resources to the polity. Because of this the availability—at different levels—of elites which are able to mobilize resources and political support and at the same time to articulate political demands is of crucial importance for the working of these systems.

At different stages of the development of modernization there developed different patterns of articulation and aggregation of political demands and of mobilization of political support; but some general institutional devices, which have developed in most modern political systems, can be discerned.[3]

Among the specific types of organizations through which political demands are articulated are interest groups, social movements, "public opinion" and political parties. The first three may to some extent be seen as components of the last i.e., of parties which are the most articulate forms of modern political organization, and which perform also crucial functions of *aggregation* of political demands; but this is true only in part as the various interest groups, social movements and various forms of public opinion have also autonomous existence and orientations of their own.

The interest group or the pressure group is usually oriented to gaining concrete, specific interests—be they economic, religious, cultural or political—and is interested in the wider broader political machinery of the party or of the State, only or mainly, in so far as it can directly promote this interest (or at least assure its optimal promotion in a given situation). There are, of course, many diverse types of such interest groups—economic, professional, religious, ethnic or tribal—and their specific interests may vary greatly from situation to situation.

The second type of organization through which political orientations and demands are articulated and aggregated in modern political systems are social movements. A social movement usually aims at the development of some new total society or polity. It attempts to infuse certain values or goals into a given institutional structure or to transform such a structure according to these aims and values. These aims are usually inclusive and diffuse. A social movement usually has a strong "future" orientation and tends to depict the future as greatly different from the present and to fight for the realization of this change. It very often contains some apocalyptical, semi-Messianic elements, and it tends usually to make demands of total obedience or loyalty on its members and to make extreme distinctions between friends and foes.

The third element through which political demands are articulated in modern political systems is what can be called "general, diffuse, intelligent interest in public issues." By this is meant people or groups who have a rather more flexible attitude to both specific interests and to "total" ideas and claims, who are not firmly attached to any given interest group, movement or organization, and who are interested mainly in the "sober" evaluation of a political programme in values and concrete possibilities.

Each of these forms of articulation of interests has existed in various forms also in premodern systems, but with differences. One such difference was that with the partial exception of petitions or entreaties by interest groups or cliques, the representation of the political activities and orientations of such groups was not usually firmly legitimized within the central political institutions, while social or social-religious movements were largely apolitical or "nonlegitimate" from the point of view of the existing political institutions.

The second such difference was that these groups were mostly concerned with petitioning the rulers for various concrete benefits, and not with the determination of major political goals or the selection of rulers.

The third was rooted in the fact that it is only in the modern political systems that these different interest groups and movements tend to become integrated, even if only to some extent, into the framework of common continuous political activity and organization, such as political parties, or other organizations which perform similar functions of continuous mobilization of support and interpretation of different political demands. Such integration is attained by the parties (or other party-line organizations), through the development of specific party organs, leadership and programs, and through the aggregation within the party, of various concrete interests under some more general rules or aims which may be of some appeal to a wider public, and through the translation, as it were, of the inclusive, diffuse aims of the social movements into more realistic terms of concrete political goals, issues and dilemmas.[4]

Different parties may evince, of course, different degrees of predominance of each of these elements. But whatever such relative predominance, the integration of each of these elements into the parties is never complete, and interest groups social movements and different organs of public opinion, tend to develop autonomous orientations, which in many situations tend to "burst" the frameworks imposed on them by the parties. They tend to maintain their autonomous orientations through the presentation of their own demands directly to the central political institutions—be they the executive, legislature or bureaucracy—without the mediation of any given party, through attempts to mobilize support and resources for themselves directly, and not through a party, as well as through attempts to aggregate within their own frameworks different political demands. This tendency is, of course, facilitated by the parallel tendency of the major central political institutions to perform themselves directly the major functions of political aggregations.

The various characteristics of modern political systems tended, of course, to develop gradually in various modern regimes. These characteristics developed in the wider framework of social, economic and cultural modernization. The combined impact of these conditions and of the basic characteristics of modern political systems gave rise to continuous generation of new types of political demands and organizations, which the central political institutions have had to absorb.

At different stages of the development of modern political systems, there have developed different problems which became important, and different types of organizational frameworks through which such problems were dealt with. Thus at certain stages of modernization, the problem of suffrage and of the definition of the new political community, of attainment of its independence, assumed most central importance. In other spheres or at other stages, there were mainly problems of religious toleration or of so-called secularization of culture that were most prominent. While still in other stages or in other phases of modernization

83

the economic and social problems as well as problems of organization were most pertinent. The development of each of these problems was usually connected with the entrance of different new groups and strata into the political arena.

The nature of their major problems as well as of the various groups which become involved in them at any given stage has greatly influenced, as we shall see, the ways in which political demands and concentrations became articulated and organized, and the degrees to which they could be subsumed under broader policy orientations.

But perhaps the most important aspect of this question to bear in mind is that within any modern political system new problems and forms of political organization tend to develop continuously and new groups are continuously drawn into the central political orbit.

Hence, the central problem of political modernization is the ability of any system to adapt itself to these changing demands, to absorb them in terms of policy making and to assure its own continuity in the face of continuous new demands and new forms of political organization.

Modern political systems are then faced not only, as any other political system, with the problem of how to maintain in general some balance between political demands and policies, but also with the problem of how to maintain such a balance through the absorption of demands and patterns of political organization which are, potentially at least, continuously changing.

In other words, political modernization creates in its wake problems of sustained political growth as its central problem. The ability to deal with continuous changes in political demands is the crucial test of such sustained political growth of political development and is the crucial focus of modern political systems or of political modernization.

It is true that such a modern system may retard further political modernization—but this does not mean that it is necessarily a nonmodern system. There is a basic difference between, let us say, pre-1950s Nepal and Franco's Spain or even Salazar's Portugal. This difference lies in the fact that the last try to suppress or manipulate political demands which are to some extent rooted in the basic social characteristics of the system, but to which it does deny free political expression—i.e., expression in terms of articulate demands made on the central political authorities for formulation of policies and for participation in the ultimate decision making. In a "traditional" system, on the other hand, the problem does not exist in this sense because various groups and strata do not evince, on the whole, such orientations.

Although the propensity to generate changes and also to some extent to absorb them is built into the institutional structure of modern political systems, the capacity to deal with such changes effectively varies greatly between different modern regimes.

The history of modern political systems is, of course, full of cases of unsuccessful adaptation, or of lack of adaptation of existing political structures to new types of political demands and organization. In such cases the capacity for continuous political growth and for continuous sustenance of such growth may be blocked or impaired.

Such impairment of political growth or development may become manifest either in the nonability of the various groups to formulate their demands in an articulated way, in the nonprovision of resources by various groups to the political elites and institutions, or by the development of too intensive demands which the existing institutions cannot absorb.

The "external" manifestations of such a blocking are usually some type of political "eruptions," i.e., of more or less violent outbreaks of political activities and development of symbols which are oriented against the existing system and its symbols.

The more "primitive" types of such eruptions—various mob activities and outbursts—develop when there are no elites available which are able to organize and articulate the potential political demands of different groups.

The more articulated types of such eruptions are usually very closely related to, or manifest in the development of some types of organized political activity which are, however, not in accord with the frameworks and premises of the existing parties and political institutions, and whose leaders do not find a way to integrate their demands within the framework of these parties and institutions, or in the lack of integration of interest groups into any wider common framework, or the noninstitutionalism of social movements within the framework of parties and policy making.

Insofar as such eruptions are not merely transitory their structural outcomes may cause the disintegration of a given political system, or the successful suppression, by the rulers, of the new political demands and organization to a level (sometimes the former level, sometimes a somewhat new level) with which they and the political institutions are capable of dealing.

In principle any modern political system can deal with the problem of absorbing change in several different ways:

One such way is to attempt to minimize the development of any changes which would generate new political demands and patterns of development.

The second is to control and manipulate such changes and their political expressions within relatively strict limits imposed by the rulers.

The third is to absorb (obviously with certain—but relatively feasible and changing—limits) such new demands and organizations.

Obviously, in any concrete regime there always exists some mixture of these different attitudes to political change, but the nature of this mixture varies between different regimes and different regimes vary as to the relative predominance of each of them.

Within "constitutional" and democratic systems[5] (many of which have developed from more "traditional" centralized oligarchic regimes), the capacity to absorb changing political demands and organizations usually is not a *fully conscious* political goal but it has been rather attained—insofar as it is attained—through the pliability, flexibility of the political institutions and through the sensitivity of the major political and social elites to the continuously changing demands and forms of political organization. Although obviously the rulers and those who compete for the ruling positions initiate political reforms and changes and articulate the major policies, the initial crucial impetus to such changes usually comes in these regimes from within the fold of various social, professional or cultural groups, from different interest groups, social movements, from the more diffuse general public opinion, and from the political elites which appeal to such groups, compete for their support and attempt to integrate them in the framework of political parties. The varied impetuses become articulated as political demands through the active participation and articulation of the various competing elites into various, often innovating, policies and into new institutional frameworks.

In this way, political innovations tend in these regimes to be initiated and articulated by political leadership (be it the leadership of a party or of a more independent group) and by different parties which absorb the impulses for change from within social groups and strata, and which mobilize wider support for various goals and policies.

The major areas of political decision making and of institutionalization of political changes and innovations are usually centered, at least formally, in the legislature, in the executive *acting with the legislature* and also in the bureaucracy. It is in these more central organs in which the major policies are, if not decided on, at least fully and publicly articulated, presented and discussed.

The importance both of mass parties and bureaucracies as arenas of decision making has been growing continuously with growing differentiation of the social structure, with continuous modernization and with the growth of complex social and economic problems on the one hand, and with growing political mobilization of the wider masses on the other hand; and many crucial political decisions and functions have become concentrated within them in all modern regimes—constitutional or totalitarian.

But in the constitutional regimes neither the parties nor the bureaucracy have become the *only* areas of political discussion, innovation, and decision making. Executive and legislative organs continued to maintain some of their—at least symbolic—positions of control, as the main frameworks of independent public opinion and leadership, and as the main areas in which political innovation became institutionalized.

The innovating ability of the democratic elites and the possibility of institutionalizing various innovations were to no small degree dependent on the ability of the parties and their leadership to integrate various diverging interest groups, and to institutionalize the more intensive demands and orientations of social movements and hence also on the continuous existence and political ability of some independent leadership and public opinion.

The various eruptions to which these regimes were prone tended mostly to develop insofar as the parties were not able to assure, within their frameworks, such aggregation of interest groups and social movements.

The nature and organizational contents of the eruptions which tend to develop in the constitutional regimes differ greatly according to the level of differentiation of the social structure, and of the extension of political participation of the broader social groups within it.

Thus in the early stages of modernization, when these regimes were ruled by relatively small oligarchies, and when political participation and suffrage were limited, most of the eruptions took on the form of relatively unorganized, highly activistic, movements and outlines oriented either at the attainment of immediate needs or to the obtainment of political rights and inclusion in the body politic.

With growing extension of social differentiation and political participation, there tended to develop more organized eruptions which became mostly organized in various social movements or violent interest groups.[6]

This tendency within these regimes to the development of more organized eruptions is rooted in the fact that by their very nature such regimes encourage certain levels of articulation and aggregation of political demands and of mobilization and organization of political support. The eruptions that tend to develop within these regimes derive their strength more from the lack of absorption of such demands by the existing political institution than from the nonavailability of any type of leadership to organize and articulate such demands, although in some instances—especially, but not only, in the initial stages of modernization—cases of lack of any adequate leadership, of erosion of the active political leadership, may also develop.

The eruptions which developed in these regimes may have been absorbed by them—as was the case in England, the United States, Scandinavia, Holland, Switzerland to some extent, in Belgium and Uruguay—while others may give rise to disruptions of the system and its change into other types of systems—as was the case in Italy, Germany, and to some extent in France before the Fourth Republic, and in many Latin American countries.

The patterns of absorption of political change within totalitarian regimes[7] are, of course, different from those of the constitutional (multi-party) ones. In the totalitarian regimes, political, social and economic change are consciously and deliberately fostered and directed by the political elite which, at the same time, attempts to minimize the autonomous political expression of various social groups and their *political* reaction to the changes initiated by the elite. The expression of political demands of these various groups is carefully molded by the rulers within organizations over which they attempt to maintain almost complete control and any attempts to break through this control is looked upon by them as a very grave political aberration.

The various social changes here are formulated as political goals of the regime and their political contents and expression are set and controlled by the political elite.

Thus these regimes are characterized both by direction, manipulation and control of change by the ruling elite, and by the minimization of the actual *political* expressions of the reactions of various groups to such changes.

The major media of political modernization, innovation and decision making are here the party and the party leadership, and to some extent the bureaucracy, while the legislature performs purely ritual functions and the executive (as distinct from the party leadership), although important in several aspects, plays mainly only a secondary, routine, role. Although the relations between the party and the bureaucracy are, in these regimes, often delicate and precarious, yet it is through the juxtaposition of these two that the major impetus to change, as well as the control and manipulation of its expressions are organized and institutionalized. The party leadership and the party tend usually to serve as the major centers of innovation and of active manipulation and mobilization of political support, while the bureaucracy tends more to deal with the "routine" administration of the new conditions generated by the changes initiated by the political leadership and the party.

The continuity of such fostered change and the regime's ability to control it are closely connected with the close interweaving of various interest groups and of (very often nonexistent or suppressed) social movements in the monolithic party framework. The almost total integration of interest groups and of the nuclei of social movements or public opinion in the party or their control by the bureaucracy is of crucial importance for the ability of the elite to manipulate and control the political expression of change. Any attempt on behalf of such groups to more autonomous public debate or presentation of their demands is usually envisaged as a very serious potential threat to the regime, as potential breeding ground for eruption and hence gives rise to many repressive measures.

The continuity of these regimes is greatly dependent on the maintenance of a balance between the repressive measures aimed at the minimization of such autonomous political expression and the flexibility and ability of the ruling elite to aggregate changing demands and orientations into the framework of the party and the bureaucracy, without at the same time allowing them more autonomous forms of expression.

The eruptions that tend to develop in these regimes are much less organized than those that develop in the constitutional regimes. They take here the form of mob activities and outbreaks, of "subversive" clique activities of different interest groups or of some outbursts of "free" public opinion or of underground nuclei or remnants of social movements. These regimes may also be threatened by the potentially "secessional" or usurpational tendencies of their apparatus—be they the army, the secret police, some parts of the bureaucracy or even regional sectors of the party. But by their very nature these regimes do not engender the development of the more organized and articulated forms of eruption and political activities. As until now we did not have any examples of internal systematic changes of totalitarian regimes except under the impact of defeat in war, it is impossible to designate either the exact range of the absorptive capacity or the types of regimes which may succeed them.

Seemingly similar, but in many crucial aspects, different[8] attitudes to change can be found in those regimes like Turkey or Mexico in which new, modern or modernizing regimes were established through a revolutionary group or congeries of groups which evolved into a full fledged party with relatively strong monolithic tendencies, and which attempted to direct social and political changes into certain well-defined channels. But their goals of social, economic, or political change were usually less far-reaching and disruptive of previous conditions than those of the totalitarian regimes, while politically the internal structure of the parties was also to some extent (especially in Mexico) less monolithic than in totalitarian regimes.

The party and to some extent the executive served here as the main foci of political decision making and of political innovation. Parties were the main foci of political and often social innovation, of the formulation of various policies which aimed at cliques and of mobilization of support for new policies. At the same time, however, these parties did not aim or succeed in effecting a close and monolithic integration of various groups, movements and independent public opinion and in the total negation of their autonomous political expression. Usually they allowed—whether willingly or unwillingly—some such expression. Hence there developed within them some recourse to the legislative and to the executive as media of political discourse, innovation and decision making, and to the bureaucracy as an important, and to some extent, autonomous instrument of implementation and execution of such policies.

In later stages of development these characteristics enabled an increase in the importance of bureaucracy and even of the legislature as media of political decision making and innovation.

A different constellation of attitudes to change and structural arrange- ments can be seen among semi-autocratic or autocratic (civil or military) dictatorships which have developed in different countries and especially in Eastern Europe during the interwar period, in some Middle Eastern countries, and to some extent in Latin America.[9] In many ways they were akin to the more traditional autocracies, although here there was also official emphasis on some change—on what might be called technical modernization, especially modernization in military and technical fields. But the whole outlook and orientation of the ruling elite was here usually very conservative, with a much stronger emphasis on the maintenance of the prevailing social structure, even if connected with some changes in the composition of the bureaucracy and some subelite groups.

Hence here we find that executives and "conservative" bureaucracies were much more predominant in the political process and in political decision making than parties and the parties that did develop were used (with different degrees of success) by the executive and bureaucracy and the military mainly as instruments of mobilization of some limited political support from different social groups, as additional arenas of political patronage and of control of such groups, but rarely as agents of social-political change and innovation.

Hence it was the executive and conservative bureaucracy that usually constitute in these regimes the main arenas of decision making and political innovation.

The capacity of these regimes to absorb political changes has been usually small. Much of the efforts of the rulers were directed towards keeping a relatively low level of political demands and articulation, and to the maintenance of the relative preponderance of interest groups (as against social movements, free public opinion and parties) as the main organs of political articulation, and to the aggregation within the bureaucracy of many of the demands of the various interest groups.

The eruptions that tend to develop in these regimes may take on a great variety of forms ranging from mob outbreaks up to the more organized forms of social movements, parties and public opinion.

Insofar as these eruptions were not absorbed with the preexisting system or suppressed by the elite, they gave rise to changes of the regimes.

Some such changes may have given rise to a type of regime not greatly different from the preceding one, while others may have given rise to other types of regimes—mainly to some variants of the one party regime or in very exceptional cases, to constitutional ones.

At the end of the scale of modern regimes from the point of view of attitudes to change we find the semi-autocratic regimes such as the more traditional regimes of the nineteenth century or, in the twentieth century, the Franco and Salazar regimes.[10] These regimes attempt to minimize the development of social and political changes—even to the extent of the impediment of the full development of the major characteristics of modern political system, i.e., in terms of extension of suffrage, spread of political power, etc.

They are characterized by the predominance of the executive and the bureaucracy and by the small importance of both legislative bodies and parties as arenas of political process, innovation and decision making. In these regimes the bureaucracy and executive tend to deal directly with various interest groups and tend to look askance on attempts to integrate such interest groups into any wider, active party political frameworks; they attempt to suppress any social movements and more independent expressions of public opinion, and employ towards them various repressive measures, so as to minimize the possibilities of their developing into active and highly articulated political elements and organizations.

These measures of control are often effected not through the mobilization of support by a monopolistic party, but mainly through attempts not to raise the level of political demands, and to minimize the possibility of the development of free expression and articulation of such demands. However, they can but rarely entirely succeed in these endeavors. Because of their need for some free resources and political support, they usually have to countenance some sort of political organizations and some—even if limited—forms of public opinion. Hence, the eruptions which tend to develop may take the form not only of mob outbreaks, but also of more organized and articulated forms of political activity and of expression of public opinion.

The concrete forms of such eruptions depend here greatly on the level of differentiation of the social structure as well as on the extent to which the existing political institutions allow some political organization and expression. The absorptive capacity of these regimes has, on the whole, been a rather limited one—although many of them have successfully maintained themselves for long periods of time. Under the impact of the more violent eruptions they have become often transformed into other types of regimes—whether constitutional, totalitarian or some other types which will be shortly discussed.

The various New States, especially the post-colonial ones, hold a rather special position from the point of view of their attitudes towards change and the ability to absorb it.[11]

Truly enough within the New States there tend to develop a great variety of regimes—comprising according to Shils' classification, the traditional oligarchy, various types of modernizing oligarchies (civil or military), totalitarian regimes and tutelary democracies—resembling in many ways some of the types of regimes described above.

But whatever the differences between them, most of the New States—especially those which have developed from former colonial states—tend to evince, especially in the initial stages of their development, some common characteristics or problems with relation to change.

Among most of them (with the partial exception of those ruled by traditional oligarchies) the emphasis on change, progress, and economic development is one of the main tenets of their political and ideological orientations. But at the same time, their institutional capacity to absorb changes may be disproportionately small to their aspirations for change, although it necessarily greatly differs among the different New States according to varied conditions—some of which will be discussed later.

This strong emphasis on change is usually connected in most of these states with the relatively great importance—especially in initial phases—of parties as centers of political innovation, and as the main organs, together with the executive, of political decision making, through which attempts are made to institutionalize the manifold changes to which they aspire.

But the ability of these regimes to implement these various changes is often limited and very often they are barely able to maintain their own continuity and stability. This relatively small extent of institutional ability to absorb change develops insofar as basic political symbols and administrative and political frameworks are weak, and various autonomous interest groups are weak and underdeveloped.[1][2]

This discrepancy between the strong emphasis on change and the relative weakness of the institutional frameworks which have to absorb them can be seen in the nature of the eruptions which tend to develop in these regimes.

These eruptions are characterized by a combination of what may be called very primitive outbreaks and outbursts on the one hand, with the much more organized and articulated eruptions in the form of organized social and political movements, on the other hand. The exact nature, scope and persistence of these eruptions, as well as the regime's ability to absorb them, varies greatly between these various New States and naturally may greatly influence their stability and continuity.

Here of central importance is the fact that the rulers of these countries are faced—more than rulers of other types of regimes hitherto discussed—with the simultaneous development of several different problems, the solution of which may greatly influence the extent of institutionalization of stable modern political systems. The rulers of these regimes are faced first, with the problem of creation and spread of a general identification with the new polity, with the maintenance of general, continuous interest in different complex political issues and problems and with mobilization of support for its own program; second, with maintaining themselves in power and third, with finding adequate ways and means of solving various outstanding social, economic and political problems which are or appear of foremost importance to them.

Insofar as the development of these various aspects of political orientations reinforce one another, the prospects for the development of a realistic and critical attitude towards political issues and of the possibility of getting political support in terms of realistic programs are relatively great. But insofar as these different political orientations contradict one another—and such a possibility can be seen as to some extent inherent in some of the basic conditions of these states—various unrealistic and "destructive" attitudes towards political life may easily develop and the different types of eruptions which were analyzed above can easily develop.

This special constellation of conditions in the New States, the lack or weakness of long-standing political frameworks, the relatively high level of political demands, the possible cleavages within the elites in their pursuit of popular support may easily create conditions under which the elites may be unable to assure the initial institutionalization of political frameworks capable of absorption of change and may give way to regimes with a lower level of such ability.

The crucial stage for all these regimes comes when various new political forces—i.e., forces not fully represented by the original nationalist elite—be they regional, trade-union, new rural leaders—emerge, often through the policies of development of the nationalist elites, and create, through their demands, potential splits within the elite and strains on the working of the central institutions. In some cases, as for instance, in Pakistan or Indonesia,[13] these developments have precipitated a downfall of the initial regime; in others, like India, Ceylon, Nigeria, Guinea and Tunisia, they are still attempting to absorb these new groups and demands within the initial frameworks.[14]

The preceding analysis, preliminary as it has been, has indicated some of the major problems in the comparative analysis of political modernization. First it has shown that the process of political modernization can take on, within the framework of the basic common characteristics outlined above, a great variety of institutional and structural forms. Second, this analysis has also shown that various modern or modernizing political regimes do not only differ in various structural-institutional arrangements, but evince also great differences in their attitudes to change and in their ability to absorb continuous change within their institutional frameworks. We have then to see whether it is possible to explain, first, this variety of structural forms of political modernization, and second, whether there exist any relations between some aspects of this structural variety on the one hand, and the attitudes to change and the constitutional ability to absorb change on the other hand.

From this point of view, it might be useful to analyze the process of modernization and of the establishment of modern political frameworks as a social process, and especially as a continuous process of interaction between what has been called "modernizing" elites and wider groups and strata of the population.

Perhaps the most important concept here is that of the modernizing elite—a concept which recognizes the fact that it is some more active group or groups which provides at least the initial push to modernization in different institutional spheres.[15]

This approach does basically assume—although the full implications of this assumption have not been made explicit—that the process of modernization is, like many other types of creation of new institutional structures, borne or developed by "charismatic" groups or personalities—even if the nature of its characteristics differ greatly from those of older, "classical" religious types of charisma, and that what may be called the institutionalization of modernization is not unlike the various processes of routinization of charisma which were analyzed by Weber.

93

In order to be able to understand the process of modernization, the institutionalization of modern frameworks, it is important to analyze the relations between the innovating groups and the broader institutional setting, and especially their relations to the pre-existing institutional structure and the social orientations of those elites which held the power positions within it, on the one hand, and to the broader groups and strata of the society—those groups and strata which have to provide the basic resources, be they manpower, labor resources, social or political support for implementation of more differentiated, modern goals—on the other hand.

Accordingly it might be worth while to attempt to explain the structural differences attendant on processes of modernization in different societies by the differences in the orientations and goals of the major modernizing elites on the one hand, and in the modernizing tendencies and orientations of the broader social strata on the other. In other words, we may attempt to see to what extent various modernizing elites and social groups may evince different attitudes to change and propensities to develop or have recourse to different organizational structures.

Thus it seems that ruling traditional autocratic or oligarchic elites which are interested to minimize change or to limit it mostly to technical spheres tend to use mostly the executive branch of the government and a relatively conservative bureaucracy and to limit, insofar as possible, the development of free organs public opinion and leadership, or legislative organs or of widespread parties.

Insofar as they are interested in promoting controlled change, but at the same time to minimize the political participation and mobilization of wider groups, they will attempt to develop and use continuously expanding and modernized bureaucracies, but to limit the development of parties and autonomous legislative bodies.[16]

Nonautocratic elites—whether oligarchic or recruited from wider groups and strata and having a more flexible attitude to change, i.e., being committed to the implementation of various differentiated goals, such as economic advancement, cultural activities, extension of the suffrage etc. have usually tended to have recourse to a greater variety of structural forms, to various organs of public opinion, to legislative groups and "cliques." With growing differentiation of the social structure they tend to expand their activities to bureaucracies and parties alike without however abandoning the other organs.

Revolutionary elites stemming usually from social movements and aiming at institutionalizing total change tend to develop, above all, mass parties and to use also to some extent bureaucracies.

A tentative parallel analysis may be attempted with regard to the nature of articulation of political demands among different types of groups and strata.

The most important conditions influencing the nature of such articulation seem to be "closure" or traditionality of these groups on the one hand, and their placement within the social structure, the extent of their internal cohesion and of their interrelations with other strata on the other hand.

The more traditional and "closed" such groups are the less they are usually articulated politically and whatever political activities they undertake are in usually the form of intermittent interest or petitioning groups with direct relations to the executive or bureaucracy.

Insofar as social groups become internally more modernized and flexible they tend to develop more articulate, specialized, interests and organizations and also to evince certain propensities to participate in wider political frameworks and to develop some orientations to the central political institutions.

Insofar as their internal cohesion is small and they are alienated from other strata and elites, then their ability to participate in wider frameworks tends to be relatively small and is usually limited only to intermittent participation in extremist social movements.

Insofar as their internal cohesion and attachment to other groups is relatively high, they might show a greater ability or propensity to participation and integration in such wider frameworks.

Both social movements and more diffuse public leadership tend to develop especially among various secondary elite groups and intellectuals who are caught in processes of change and differentiation and to some extent dislocated through these processes. The extent of their propensity to become integrated into some existing or emerging wider frameworks or parties is also greatly dependent on the extent to which the groups from which they are recruited are cohesive and not alienated from one another.

The preceding analysis does also indicate some of the conditions of stability and continuity of modern or modernizing political systems.

It clearly indicates that such stability or continuity does not depend on any one structural form and is not confined to any such form. It depends rather on the extent of compatibility between the types of structural organizations used and developed by the elites and the levels and types of political articulation of the broader groups and strata of the society.

The stability or continuity of different modern political regimes can be maintained on different levels of institutional ability to absorb change, ranging from the most minimal extent of such ability up to most flexible and differentiated modern systems, and on each such level it is connected with a different constellation of structural forms within the central political institutions, of ways of aggregation of political interests and orientations and of articulation of political activities and demands.

On the other hand, the tendencies to instability, to outbreak of eruptions and transformations of modern regimes is usually manifest in the lack of compatibility between the types of structural organizations used by the rulers and the levels of political articulation of broader groups and strata. Such lack of compatibility may also develop on different levels of institutional ability to absorb change and take on different structural forms.

The focus of such compatibility is the articulation and formulation of political demands on the one hand, and the ability of the elites and political frameworks to absorb such demands in terms of policies on the other hand. It is within this context that aggregation of diverse political interests and orientations in political parties or other organizations, and the ability of different elites to subsume such various interests in terms of effective policies becomes crucially important.

But whatever these structural forms that tend to develop in modern regimes their stability is greatly influenced both by some "structural" aspects of the central political institutions and by broader social conditions—especially by some aspects of the interrelation between the modernizing elites on the one hand and the broader groups of the society on the other hand.

The most important structural aspect of central institutions which influences the stability of modern or modernizing regimes is the development of some ability of institutionalizing the various impetus to political change which tend always to develop with continuing modernization.

The preceding analysis indicates, first, that while impetus to political change and innovation can be located in all the different types of political organizations and institutions, there are some forms of political organizations which seem to be especially prone to become the force of such innovations and of the institutionalization of political change. One such arena of political innovation is the political party, especially a party which develops from a social movement, and within which different interest groups are integrated through the activities of a central political leadership and elites. The leaders of such parties are committed to some goals of change and they have to attempt to mobilize broad support and to integrate different interest groups and broader public opinion so as to assure the maximization of such support.

A second important locus of impending impetus to change and political innovations may come from what has been called independent leadership and public opinion, ranging from relatively organized political leadership and social, political, professional and cultural elites to different types of more diffuse "public opinion."

While such leadership may be found in any and every form of political organization, it tends to direct some at least of its activities and innovating impulses to parties and to representative-legislative frameworks.

However, the possibility of the institutionalization of changes and of the absorption of such changes and innovations is greatly dependent on the degree to which the innovating groups and organizations become closely related to the executive and bureaucracy, and are able to develop such frameworks and work within them.

It is the bureaucracy and the executive that provide some of the indispensable frameworks for the provision of administrative services to the various groups and strata in the population, for the regulation of political processes and for the maintenance of continuity of political frameworks.

Moreover, as the executive usually serves also as the symbol of political community, it plays therefore a very important part in the assurance of the continuity of the political system.

Hence, the possibility of some continuous institutionalization of political innovation of absorption of changing political demands and organizations, which constitutes, as we have seen, the crucial test of political modernization, is greatly dependent on the extent to which these frameworks are continuously functioning and some continuous and viable modus vivendi between them and the more "innovating" organizations and agencies can be established.

The establishment of such modus vivendi greatly depends on the one hand on the aggregation of different types of interest groups, social movements in the wider framework of different parties or other groups which perform such functions. On the other hand, the establishment of such modus vivendi between the different political institutions greatly facilitates the ability of the political elites to effect some integration of interests and social movements within the framework of political parties or party-line organizations.

The nature of such aggregation and subsumption of varied interests and demands under some general policy principles varies greatly between different types of regimes and at different stages of their development, but some such integration of diverse political interests, activities and organization within the frameworks of "party-political" activities constitutes a basic prerequisite of the stability or continuity of any modern political system.

Each of these regimes has developed, as we have seen, some mechanisms through which it attempted to deal with change according to its own basic attitudes and to maintain, in this way, it own continuity. The exact nature of these mechanisms varied, as we have indicated, between the different regimes as did also their relative success in absorbing changes according to their premises and in maintaining their own continuity.

Contrariwise, the lack of ability of elites—and of institutional frameworks—to integrate and aggregate the political demands of various groups would often spell the possibility of outbreaks of eruptions and of ultimate breakdown of a regime.

But the stability and continuity of modern or modernizing political systems is also greatly influenced by broader social conditions and especially by some of the interrelations between the modernizing elites and the broader strata of the population. It is beyond the scope of this paper to go in detail into this problem, which anyhow would necessitate

97

much new research, but some preliminary indications might not be out of place.

The continuity and stability of modern regimes is greatly dependent first, on the general level of development of "internal" modernization of the different strata which take part in the process of modernization and of their internal cohesion. Second, it is dependent on the extent of compatibility or affinity between the modernizing elites and the major social strata.

The extent of such compatibility and affinity between the modernizing elites and the major groups and strata as well as the structure, propensity of modernization, and cohesion of the major strata, greatly influence the patterns of organization of political activities and demands as well as the concomitant eruptions that tend to develop throughout the process of modernization.

Insofar as there exists some such affinity, even if it is a rather passive one, between the modernizing elite and the major groups and strata, then the process of political modernization tends to develop relatively smoothly with but little eruptions.

Under such conditions the ability of the major elites to aggregate various interest groups into some wider types of political organization and to institutionalize the different types of political demands and political organization is relatively high.

The stronger and more cohesive internally are the major strata, and the more they are able to participate in the process of modernization in various institutional spheres, the greater is, on the one hand, the extent of resources which they are able to put at the disposal of various modern institutions and organizations, and on the other hand also their ability to articulate realistic political demands and to influence the formulation of major political goals and policies by the elites.

Insofar as the elites are more set on modernization then the broader groups and strata but there still exists some affinity between them, then the range of change which the regime is capable of absorbing will usually be smaller but it may still be able to develop relatively smoothly.

The smaller such affinity and the more set are the elites on a definite course of modernization, the more would they have to take recourse to coercive measures.

Insofar as both the elites and the broader groups evince only a limited interest in modernization the stability of the regimes can be maintained on a relatively low level of absorption of change.

Insofar as there exists or develops an extreme lack of affinity between the modernizing elites and the modernizing tendencies of broader groups and strata, the institutional settings are not able to foster some such affinity and the elites would not be able to aggregate the political demands of the broader groups.

In such cases, the various groups and strata tend, on the one hand, to develop discrete interest groups which cannot be easily integrated into any order, while on the other hand tend also to develop various extreme social movements which do not evince a strong tendency to institutionalization of their demands within the existing political framework.

Under these latter conditions attempts may be made by some such extreme elites to "smash" the existing interest group and/or to integrate the newly emerging strata into a monolithic framework.

In general, such conditions may easily give rise to a great variety of eruptions—either eruptions which become, as it were, thresholds for new types of regimes or which may easily create a condition of continuous semi-institutionalized instability and stagnation.

The preceding analysis has necessarily been preliminary and tentative but it might perhaps indicate some possibilities of comparative-research in the field of modernization.

NOTES

1. Some of these considerations have been presented by the author in a fuller way in "Bureaucracy and Political Development," in *Bureaucracy and Political Development*, ed. J. La Polambara (Princeton: Princeton University Press, 1963) and will be also dealt with in greater detail in a forthcoming publication by the author.

2. For a fuller exposition of the differences between premodern and modern political systems, see S. N. Eisenstadt, *The Political Systems of Empires* (New York: Free Press of Glencoe, 1963), esp. chap. 13.

3. On some of these concepts, see G. Almond, "Introduction: A Functional Approach to Comparative Politics," in *The Politics of Developing Areas*, ed. G. Almond and J. S. Coleman (Princeton: Princeton University Press, 1960), pp. 3-64. See also Eisenstadt, *The Political Systems of Empires*, and "Patterns of Political Leadership and Support" (Papers of the International Conference on Representation, Government and National Progress, Ibadan, Nigeria, 1959).

4. See Eisenstadt, *The Political Systems of Empires*.

5. See: C. J. Friedrich, *Constitutional Government and Democracy* (Boston, 1950); H. Finer, *The Theory and Practice of Modern Government* (New York, 1949); S. Neumann, ed. *Modern Political Parties* (Chicago: University of Chicago Press, 1956); S. M. Lipset, *Political Man* (New York, 1960); S. H. Beer and A. B. Ulam, eds., *Patterns of Government: The Major Political Systems of Europe* (New York, 1969).

6. See: M. Kaplan, ed., *The Revolution in World Politics* (New York: J. Wiley, 1962), esp. pts. 1 and 2.

7. The literature on the USSR is of course immense but some of the points most important from the point of view of our analysis can be found in: M. Fainsod, *How Russia is Ruled*, (Cambridge, Mass.: Harvard University Press, 1955) Z. K. Brzezinski, *Ideology and Power in Soviet Politics* (New York: Praeger Publishers, 1962); J. A.

Armstrong, *The Politics of Totalitarianism: The Communist Party of the Soviet Union from 1934 to the Present* (New York: Random House, 1961).

8. See: H. Cline, *Mexico—Revolution to Evolution* (London: Oxford University Press, 1962); R. Scott, *Mexican Government in Transition* (Urbana: University of Illinois Press, 1959); K. Karpat, *Turkey's Politics: the Transition to a Multy-Party System* (Princeton: Princeton University Press, 1959).

9. See: E. Lieuwen, *Venezuela* (London: Oxford University Press, 1960); K. H. Silvert, *The Conflict Society—Reaction and Revolution in Latin America* (New Orleans: Hauser Press, 1961); J. Johnson, *Political Change in Latin America, the Emergence of the Middle Sectors* (Stanford: Stanford University Press, 1958); and see also A. Curtis Wilgus, ed., *The Caribbean—Its Political Problem* (Gainesville: University of Florida Press, 1962); D. Thomson, *Europe Since Napoleon* (New York: Alfred A. Knopf), chap. 27; H. Seton-Watson, *Eastern Europe between the Wars (1918-1941)* (London, 1945).

10. See: Thomson, *Europe Since Napoleon*, chaps. 8 and 27; E. J. Hughes, *Report from Spain* (New York, 1947); E. Allison Peers, *Spain in Eclipse 1937 to 43* (London, 1943); M. Derrick, *The Portugal of Salazar* (New York, 1939).

11. See: S. N. Eisenstadt, *Essays on the Sociological Aspects of Political and Economic Development* (The Hague, 1961); J. N. Kautsky, ed., *Political Change in Underdeveloped Countries, Nationalism and Communism* (New York: John Wiley and Sons, 1962); and E. Shils, *Political Development in New States* (The Hague: Mouton, 1962).

12. See: S. N. Eisenstadt, *Problems of Emerging Bureaucracies in Developing Areas and New States,* North American Conference on the Social Implications of Industrialization and Technological Change (Chicago, 1966, forthcoming).

13. For some very pertinent analysis of the development in Indonesia, see H. Feith, *The Decline of Institutional Democracy in Indonesia* (Ithaca: Cornell University Press, 1962); on Pakistan, Khalid bin Sayeed, "Collapse of Parliamentary Democracy in Pakistan" *Middle East Journal* 13, no. 4 (Autumn 1959): 389-407.

14. Myron Weiner, *The Politics of Scarcity. Public Pressure and Political Response in India* (Chicago: University of Chicago Press, 1962); G. Carter, ed., *African One-Party States* (Ithaca: Cornell University Press, 1962).

15. See on this concept C. Kerr, et al., *Industrialism and Industrial Men* (Cambridge, Mass.: Harvard University Press, 1960); D. McClelland, *The Achieving Society* (Princeton: Van Nostrand Reinhold Co., 1960): E. Hagen, *On the Theory of Social Change* (Homewood Ill: Dorsey Press, 1962), especially chap. 10; and C. Geertz, "Social Change and Economic Modernization in Two Indonesian Towns," in E. Hagen, *Social Change*, pp. 385-421.

16. The early Japanese experience is very instructive from this point of

view. See H. Norman, *Japan's Emergence as a Modern State* (New York: Institute of Public Relations, 1940), and R. N. Bellah, "Values and Social Change in Modern Japan" in Asian Cultural Studies, no. 3, *Studies on Modernization of Japan*, Intern. It may be compared with the German imperial experience under Bismarck.

SUGGESTIONS FOR FURTHER READING
PART TWO: THE MEANING OF POLITICAL DEVELOPMENT

Almond, Gabriel A. *Political Development: Essays in Heuristic Theory.* Boston: Little, Brown and Co., 1970.

Apter, David E. *The Politics of Modernization.* Chicago: University of Chicago Press, 1965.

Badgley, John. *Asian Development: Problems and Prognosis.* New York: Free Press, 1971.

Black C. E. *The Dynamics of Modernization: A Study in Comparative History.* New York: Harper & Row, 1966.

Eisenstadt, S. N. *Modernization: Protest and Change.* Englewood Cliffs, N. J.: Prentice-Hall, 1966.

Eisenstadt, S. N. *The Political Systems of Empires.* New York: Free Press of Glencoe, 1963.

Harts, Louis. *The Founding of New Societies: Studies in the History of the United States, Latin America, South Africa, Canada, and Australia.* New York: Harcourt Brace Jovanovich, 1964.

Horowitz, Irving Louis. *Three Worlds of Development: The Theory and Practice of International Stratification.* New York: Oxford University Press, 1966.

Organski, A. F. K. *The Stages of Political Development.* New York: Alfred A. Knopf, 1965.

Pennock, J. Roland, ed. *Self-Government in Modernizing Nations.* Englewood Cliffs, N. J.: Prentice-Hall, 1964.

Pye, Lucian W. *Aspects of Political Development.* Boston: Little, Brown and Co., 1966.

Pye, Lucian W., and Verba, Sidney, eds. *Political Culture and Political Development.* Princeton: Princeton University Press, 1965.

Weiner, Myron, ed. *Modernization: The Dynamics of Growth.* New York: Basic Books, 1966.

Welch, Claude E., Jr., ed. *Political Modernization: A Reader in Comparative Political Change.* 2d ed. Belmont, Calif.: Wadsworth Publishing Co., 1971.

PART THREE
dilemmas
of traditional
and transitional
societies

Traditional societies are characterized by their hierarchical social structure and tend to be custom-bound, ascriptive, and predominantly rural and agricultural. The extended family (father, mother, children, brothers and sisters, grandparents, uncles, and other relatives) serves as the center of activity in traditional societies. The family is the primary agent of socialization and social control. It shapes the attitudes and behavior of the individual and determines his status in life. Status in traditional societies is ascribed rather than determined by achievement. The family also serves as an economic and political unit.

Transitional societies, on the other hand, are those which have one foot in modern society and the other in traditional society. In fact, a large segment of the population in transitional societies remains custom-bound with parochial loyalties while only a small segment, the educated few, is modern in its attitudes and outlook and its loyalties are national rather than parochial. We should note, however, that the modernizing elites in traditional and transitional societies are not fully integrated into a new set of values and way of life patterned on modern lines. Social norms and customs remain deeply rooted in society and regulate most aspects of daily life.

103

Traditional and transitional societies face many dilemmas in their quest for modernity. There is the inevitable breakdown or disintegration of traditional norms and customs which pervade every level of society and every aspect of daily life. Also, there are the complex problems of disparities between the elites and the masses, the urban and the rural, the educated few and the illiterate many, the very rich and the very poor, and the skilled few and the unskilled many. Such disparities create instability, frustration, and alienation of the masses from the power elites and vice versa. Modernization also creates special problems. The unskilled, illiterate, and tradition-bound rural people find it difficult to accept urban values and ways of life even while dissatisfied with rural life.

The movement of traditional and transitional societies toward modernity does not imply the disappearance of traditional norms, customs, and social divisions. Particularism is a universal phenomenon. Although cultural values are weakened by social change they continue to influence political loyalties. Also, we should bear in mind that traditional and transitional societies differ in their response to modernization. The speed and ease of adaptation to modernity depends upon the nature of their traditional values, social classes, elites, political systems, and ideology, to mention only a few. The stresses and strains of transition can be eased by the use of tradition, as was the case in Japan. S.N. Eisenstadt writes:

> The history of modern societies is, of course, full of cases of unsuccessful adaptation, or lack of adaptation, of existing structures to new types of problems and organizations and of inability on the part of the major institutions to incorporate, even in a partial way, the various changes and movements of protest that are inherent in the process of modernization. In such cases the capacity for continuous growth and sustenance of such growth may be blocked or impaired. The external manifestation of such blocking is usually some type of eruption—i.e., more or less violent outbreaks of social and political activity and the development of symbols that are oriented against the existing system and its symbols.[1]

The selections that follow examine the role of tradition and the processes of change associated with the breakdown of traditional societies. In the initial article, "The Role of Traditionalism in the Political Modernization of Ghana and Uganda," David E. Apter examines the question of why some traditional systems can innovate more easily than others. He states that the answer lies in part in the type of traditionalism in a society and its receptivity to change. Innovation has been "traditionalized" in Uganda.

Apter discusses how innovation was incorporated in the East African kingdom of Buganda. In Buganda he writes, "All novelty came to be regarded as a device for strengthening tradition." In the Ashanti Confederacy of West Africa, however, the forces of modernism and traditionalism clashed. Ghana has been unable to make use of traditionalism in support of innovation. Since the government lacks the support of the traditional sector of society, the burdens of modernization on Ghana have become more intense and the state relatively autocratic. Apter concludes by summarizing the salient points of contrast between the two systems.

In the next article, "Political Modernization and Political Culture in Japan," Robert E. Ward states that Japan's experience with the political modernization process seems to suggest that authoritarian forms of political organization can be very effective in the early stages of the modernization process. Authoritarian forms of political organization may not hinder the gradual emergence of more democratic forms of political organization. He further suggests that the gradual transition from authoritarian to democratic forms of political organization may be essential to the emergence of politics which are both more modern and durably democratic.

Samuel P. Huntington maintains that rapid increase in mobilization and participation undermines political institutions. "Rapid modernization," Huntington writes, "produces not political development, but political decay." Political development should be viewed as the institutionalization of political organizations and procedures. The institutionalization of any particular organization or procedure can be measured by its adaptability, complexity, autonomy, and coherence. Huntington discusses the meaning of adaptability and states that it is a function of environmental challenge and age.

Huntington turns his attention to the discussion of complexity and simplicity of organizations. Complex organizations are more highly institutionalized. Complexity involves both multiplication of organizational subunits, hierarchically and functionally, and differentiation of separate types of organizational subunits. Simple traditional political systems are overwhelmed and destroyed by the modernization process.

The third measure of institutionalization is the extent to

105

which political organizations exist independently of other social groups and methods of behavior. Finally, the more unified and coherent an organization is, the more highly institutionalized it is; the greater the disunity of the organization, the less its institutionalization.

Huntington examines the processes of mobilization and institutionalization. He states that rapid mobilization and political participation are directly responsible for the decay of political instituions, discontinuity, and the rise of mass movements. Rapid socio-economic change calls into question existing values and behavior patterns. It often leads to corruption. Huntington concludes that the political party is the only modern organization which can effectively be a source of authority and legitimacy and which can be institutionalized.

NOTE

1. S.N. Eisenstadt, "Modernization and Conditions of Sustained Growth," *World Politics* 16 (July 1964): 578.

THE ROLE OF
TRADITIONALISM IN THE
POLITICAL MODERNIZATION
OF GHANA AND UGANDA

David E. Apter

Social analysts have long been preoccupied with those features of traditional culture and belief which affect the direction of change and the receptivity of a society to innovation. In spite of the very considerable literature concerned with acculturation, there have been few efforts to examine different types of traditional systems with respect to the problems they pose for political modernization. We attempt this form of analysis here. The plan is to examine two countries, Ghana and Uganda, which are engaged in the effort to build a national society. Each is experimenting with constitutional forms and each has had to deal with the problem of traditionalism. Indeed, the central problem of those concerned with building national, as distinct from local, political institutions has been to create overarching political parties, voluntary associations, and governmental forms that bridge older parochialisms. Moreover, just as tradition is a source of parochial strengths and social pride, so its characteristics vary widely. There are some who argue that any understanding of modernity in Africa must be based on an examination of the variants of the traditional systems.

In this article, we shall compare recent political events in Ghana and Uganda, and try to show how they have been shaped by the nature of traditionalism. By this means we can illustrate the implications of two different kinds of traditionalism and the problems they pose for modern nation-builders.

TRADITIONALISM

The importance of traditional factors in change was not the discovery of Max Weber, as some have thought. Such antecedent greats as Marx and Coulanges sought to link to the problem of modernization those stable symbols, artifacts, and values transmitted by the people of a society through generations. Marx was particularly concerned with its economic aspects; Coulanges with its religious aspects. Since that time, the study of tradition has been either directly or indirectly brought into the most contemporary concerns. Most recently, Lerner has observed the behavioral consequences and durability of tradition by exploring degrees of participation in mass media of communication. Fallers has dealt with it in terms of bureaucracy. My own concern has focused on the functional implications of traditional political forms for modern ones.[1]

Nor is interest in tradition a peculiarity of social scientists. Politicians, no less than academics, recognize that traditional factors which under some circumstances seem to create immobilities in social structure, and abort or minimize innovation, at other times can open the door to an entirely different range of behaviors. Administrators who in Mali Federation (formerly Senegal and French Sudan) for years sought with only small success to establish effective local units of government, possessing cultural and solidary features satisfying to the population, now find the very same measures enthusiastically taken up by African leaders and interpreted as peculiar to the genius of Africans. Under the ideology of *negritude*, the meaning attached to community development, cooperation, and communalism has been transformed into a living and continuous feature of the African past. By this means, innovation has been "traditionalized" and made comfortable. Change is not strange or foreign, requiring new roles or learning. Traditionalism puts novelty on trial rather than the people that novelty is supposed to serve. The lesson of Mali is that contemporary administrators and political leaders in Africa who can learn to enlist traditionalism in the service of innovation will indeed be contributing to successful political modernization.

Traditionalism, as distinct from tradition, we can define as validations of current behavior stemming from immemorial prescriptive norms. It is not that traditionalist systems do not change, but rather that innovation—i.e., extra-systemic action—has to be mediated within the social system and charged to antecedent values. Modernism, in contrast, presupposes a much remoter relationship between antecedent values and new goals. Modern systems, with their complex and highly differentiated social structures, value change itself.

These distinctions between modernism and traditionalism, valid as they are, leave unanswered the question why some traditional systems can innovate more easily than others. Answers have been sought in the structural features of traditional societies, while traditionalism has remained a more or less undifferentiated concept.

The discussion here accordingly distinguishes between two types of traditionalism. The first can be called *instrumental;* the second, *consummatory.*[2] Each kind exhibits certain structural tendencies. The combination of value type and structural tendency determines the problems that confront political leaders as they seek to build modern nations. We shall examine these combinations in Ghana and Uganda.

As we are using the term, instrumental systems are those which can innovate easily by spreading the blanket of tradition upon change itself. In such systems, those who are called upon to arbitrate in matters of custom, and to interpret in some official capacity, are easily persuaded to find traditional counterparts in contemporary events. Such systems can innovate without appearing to alter their social institutions fundamentally. Rather, innovation is made to serve immemoriality. The characteristic structural expression of instrumental traditionalism is a military type of system with hierarchical authority stemming from a single king or command figure.[3] Appointive ranks in the system tend to underwrite the king as the central source of authority. A heavy reliance on performance is a characteristic of office and the chief who fails to serve his king loyally and well is subject to removal or death. Religion is decidedly secondary in such a system, whose primary value is service to the king or state. Examples of such systems are Morocco, Ethiopia, and Buganda.[4]

The traditionalism of consummatory systems is much more complex. They were first described by Fustel de Coulanges when, deploring the simplistic interpretations of Greece and Rome as prototypes for modern societies, he wrote that examining the institutions of those two systems without a knowledge of their religious notions left them "obscure, whimsical, and inexplicable." He went on to say:

> A comparison of beliefs and laws shows that a primitive religion constituted the Greek and Roman family, established marriage and paternal authority, fixed the order of relationship, and consecrated the right of property, and the right of inheritance. This same religion, after having enlarged and extended the family, formed a still larger association, the city, and reigned in that as it had reigned in the family. From it came all the institutions, as well as all the private laws, of the ancients. It was from this that the city received all its principles, its rules, its usages and its magistracies.[5]

Thus society, the state, authority, and the like are all part of an elaborately sustained, high-solidarity system in which religion as a cognitive guide is pervasive. Such systems have been hostile to innovation. Change has produced fundamental social upheavals such as migration to towns. Broken are the warmth and intimacy of custom. Not only were ancient Greece and Rome examples of such systems, but so was Ashanti.[6]

Our general hypothesis is that the instrumental-hierarchical type of system can innovate with ease until the kingship principle is challenged, at which point the entire system joins together to resist change. In other words, such systems are highly resistant to political rather than other forms of modernization, and in particular cannot easily supplant the hierarchical principle of authority with a representative one.

Consummatory values are more significantly rooted where the structural expression of authority is pyramidal rather than hierarchical. Pyramidal structure means that patterns of subordinacy and superordinacy are limited to such activities as war or court appeals. For most purposes a chief or political leader is responsible to his social group rather than to a senior chief or official. The chiefs at each level of the pyramid thus have similar powers and are relatively autonomous of one another. Such a structural form relies heavily on semisegmental kinship relationships. The autonomy of the chief or political leader is thus a reflection of the autonomy of the kinship unit itself.

The consummatory-pyramidal systems are highly resistant to all forms of innovation, and the consequences of change are external political groupings that form as new solidary associations cutting across the older ones. In other words, new social structures with a political focus emerge, with the object of tearing down the older ones. Let us examine these processes in Ghana and Uganda.

TWO TRADITIONAL SYSTEMS

Buganda, one of the most important kingdom states in the lake area of Eastern Africa, was regarded very favorably by Europeans who first came upon the country in the latter half of the nineteenth century. First Arabs, and then British and French missionaries, were welcomed by the king, or *Kabaka*, of Buganda. Kabaka Mutesa I encouraged competitive performances by the three religious groups—Muslim, Catholic and Protestant. Although he died a pagan, he was intensely interested in Christianity.

To the Baganda, adoption of Christianity came to denote a superior technological and educational status. The older religious system, associated with the institution of clanship which was itself giving way to a hierarchical chieftaincy system, disappeared without producing much internal strain. Christianity easily passed muster as an aid to the Baganda in maintaining their society. The only point of concern was the fact that missionaries, in gaining adherents, tended to usurp the functions of chiefs. Since the latter remained responsible to the Kabaka, while the missionaries were not, a disturbing element was introduced into the political system.

Competition among religions, however, resulted in religious wars. These were eventually resolved by allocating fixed numbers of chieftaincies to Catholics, Protestants, and Muslims. The religious factions became tantamount to political parties within Buganda.

The missionaries themselves commented on how quickly the Baganda took to education and became ardent religionists as well.[7] After British intervention and the establishment of the Protectorate over Uganda, regular Catholic and Protestant school systems were established. The chiefs were the best educated group in the population. Catholic chiefs were products of Kisubi, the Catholic school, and Protestant chiefs were products of King's College, Budo. Both were modeled after British public schools.

Moreover, freehold land tenure was introduced and 8,000 square miles were distributed among 1,000 chiefs and notables, who thereby became a kind of squirearchy. The recipients of the land were mainly Catholics and Protestants.

Whatever the innovated structure, whether civil service chieftaincy, a parliament and council of ministers, modern education, or freehold tenure, it strengthened the system. The instrumental quality of hierarchical kingship was never defeated. The innovations that were most easily accepted were those that strengthened the Buganda government and also facilitated the individual's efficiency within it.

As a result, the organization of political life, which had been the crucial social structure in Buganda, was regarded as continuing from the past, with each innovation simply perfecting and strengthening an established system. All novelty came to be regarded as a device for strengthening tradition. As we shall indicate below, the main form of nationalism which emerged was that of a modernizing autocracy in which the government of the Kabaka and the Kabaka himself represented effective nationalism.

In Ashanti, on the other hand, responses to innovation were relatively complicated. Chieftaincy, despite its tiers of relatively autonomous powers with respect to various units of government, was nevertheless hemmed in with restrictions. Chieftaincy faced inward to the people to whom, by lineage and totem, the chief or headman was related. Instead of the individual atomism of Buganda, which was held together by regard for the Kabaka and the external force of hierarchical authority, the Ashanti chief was linked with an elaborate system of religiously sanctioned self-restraints on behavior. When land alienation began to occur in undue measure, for example, chieftaincy was affected and the stable confines of the social system were undermined. When Christianity was introduced, it helped to weaken the traditions of chieftaincy and removed the control that the dead ancestors exercised over the living. The result was excesses by chiefs, who turned to British authorities for their support. When education was introduced, chiefs had to be ordered to send their children to school. While they could not disobey the orders of district officers, they often sent the children of their slave lineages rather than the children of royal blood. The succeeding generations of chiefs were thus by no means the best educated. The support required for the authority of the chiefs violated customary restraints on behavior. The excesses of the chiefs soon came to be regarded as perversions of traditional society, from which younger and more educated elements began to disaffiliate. Christianity helped ease the process of disaffiliation and there developed, along with an increase in urbanization and the growth of villages, the phenomenon of the

111

urban village Christian and the rural village pagan. Most important, a series of wars between the British and the Ashanti was a token of the inability of Ashanti to absorb those innovating effects of a system of colonial rule which was basically common to both Buganda and Ashanti. In the end the *Asantehene*, or king of Ashanti, had to be exiled. Indeed, from 1901 to 1935, the Ashanti Confederacy did not exist as such.[8]

Within the context of the term "traditional," both Ashanti and Buganda were traditional systems. Both required validations of current behavior by appeal to immemoriality. Both had myths of origin involving a powerful figure associated with the formation of the society, and with whom the king had claims to ancestry. In the case of the Ashanti, the powers of origin descended to the Golden Stool rather than to a person. In Buganda, descent was reckoned through the line of kings, or Kabakas. That the preservation of power and continuity should reside in an object in the case of Ashanti—as distinct from a person, as in Buganda—is not without significance. For, in Ashanti, those in power serve the present by serving the past. It is a symbol of ancestral concern which is the visible repository of authority. In Buganda the king was, as both Roscoe and Fallers have called him, despotic.[9] While there was—and still is—pomp and ceremony around the king he was not regarded as a descendant of living ancestors. He was rather the punishing, aggressive, and virile representative of a dynamic people expanding their military hegemony in the Lake Victoria region. Hence the essentially religious and theocratic nature of the Ashanti state, and the more secular and military character of Buganda.

There were other important differences between these societies. In Ashanti, the system of political organization had its prototype in the extended family, which included up to a hundred members, possessing strong solidary affiliations. Families lived together in villages and it was unusual for an Ashanti to live alone or with only his immediate family.

In addition, the Ashanti had an elaborate lineage system whereby recruitment to office and the allocation of rights and duties were organized. The core political unit was the village. The largest unit was the division, over which there was a paramount chief. Kumasi, which established a compact with the other Ashanti divisions in a historical episode veiled in mystery and magic, became the center of a Confederacy. An elaborate balance of checks and controls on authority extended from the village level to the division, including restrictions on the exercise of power by the Asantehene, or king of the Ashanti Confederacy.

The system in Buganda was much simpler in one respect, and much more complex in others. Unlike the chief in Ashanti, who was a religious figure, a lineage figure and, moreover, elected to office, the chief in Buganda was appointed by the king, or Kabaka, and was responsible to him. The chief was subject to summary dismissal at the pleasure of the Kabaka. Much closer to the Ashanti pattern was an earlier, pre-Kabaka, clan system which continued to play a part in subsequent periods. The king was both *Sabataka* (head of all the clans) and Kabaka.

112

Every Muganda is a member of a clan. Clans are hereditary. The elders of clans had responsibilities over the family, the social conduct of individuals, and inheritance. Chiefs, who were appointed, reflected the powers of the Kabaka. Clan elders, who were elected from eligible lineages, reflected religious and immemorial powers. These two principles of authority were in constant conflict. Increasingly, performance in serving the Kabaka and thereby the state became the basis of chieftaincy. Performance and service became readily identifiable since Buganda, as a military system, was in process of expanding at the expense of her neighbors.

The acceptance of hierarchical authority thus was associated with successful national aggrandizement and the pure authority of the Kabaka was not mitigated by any other countervailing principle. Tension within the system was produced by conflicts between clanship and chieftaincy. But the Kabaka represented the central authority in both systems—i.e., Sabataka or head of all the clans, and Kabaka or head of all the chiefs.

Two effects were immediately observable from the twin systems of organization in Buganda united by a system of autocratic and hierarchical kingship. Clans were scattered throughout the country. In any area an individual on the move could find a clansman and receive certain benefits from him. This not only facilitated mobility but also ensured considerable uniformity of custom and behavior throughout the system.

The chiefs, who were territorial governors for the king, were also military leaders. Their followers were loyal to the chief because the chief reflected the Kabaka's authority. This military-administrative system of organization included a massive network of military roads converging, radially, upon the center or capital. Yet the capital itself was often moved, so that there was no "center" and hinterland."

The result was a "suburban" pattern of life in which clanship counterposed chieftaincy in daily life, but each man's eyes centered upon the king. In time of war, which was often, the military administrative system required almost no modification. The necessary mobilizations took place under the chiefs. Food continued to be produced, and family life managed to go on quite well. In contrast, Ashanti had to shift to a quite different military formation in time of war, and then returned to their peacetime pyramidal organization when war was over.[10]

What were some of the controversial issues which the Kiganda system was unable to absorb? The most characteristic one was an inability to adjust to any permanent limitation on the power of the Kabaka. Whether a Muganda were chief or peasant, educated or not, he maintained the same unabashed veneration for the office of the Kabaka. Or, to put the matter another way, the principle of national aggrandizement was never lost, and the Kabaka was its symbol. Each of the major conflicts which aroused the Baganda and posed serious problems for the Protectorate government centered around possible dangers to the autonomy of Buganda or diminutions of the authority of the Kabaka.

113

In contrast to Ashanti, then, the Baganda have instrumental values. Ends are relatively well defined and essentially patriotic.

Both Baganda and Ashanti developed their own forms of tribal parochialism. The former were adept in retaining considerable political autonomy, and the Uganda Agreement of 1900, which stipulated the relations between Baganda and British, became a legal bulwark of ethnic nationalism and political parochialism. In Ashanti, where no such constitutional relationship existed, internal conflict was widely manifested throughout the entire area, creating instabilities which eventually led to mass nationalism. In more contemporary terms, in Buganda nationalist politicians have so far been able to make little headway and are regarded by the Buganda government as malcontents and ne'er-do-wells. One finds there an absorbing situation, in which the British authorities are anxious to see nationalist political parties develop on an all-Uganda pattern as the solution to building a modern state.[11] In Ghana, the party nationalists have become tantamount to the state itself, regarding chiefs dimly, to say the least. Not only have they taken active steps to break the chief's power, but the Asantehene, the paramount chief of Ashanti, has been their particular target. In the last encounter between the Asantehene and the party government, it was the former who had to admit defeat. The quasi-religious character of traditional society has been replaced by the quasi-religious character of modern nationalism in Ghana. We can analyze these developments more closely.

CONTRASTING EFFORTS AT POLITICAL MODERNIZATION

Uganda and Ghana are in the process of modernization. Practically, this has meant establishing parliamentary institutions by means of which the whole country is governed. Ghana achieved the level of political development in 1950 which Uganda now hopes to achieve. In other respects as well, Ghana has developed more rapidly. National income per head in Ghana is double that of Uganda. More effective internal transport and trade facilities are found in Ghana and Africans participate actively in all aspects of technical and commercial life. In Uganda, Asians and Europeans still monopolize the more important sectors of the economy and are the predominant racial groups in the civil service. In contrast, Africanization of the civil service in Ghana is virtually complete, with only a few senior positions and technical services still performed by Europeans, and these mostly on contract.

Ghana is economically well off for an African country.[12] Since 1951, 80 percent of its internal savings has been based upon a single cash crop, cocoa. Other sources of income are gold, bauxite, manganese, industrial diamonds, and timber. It has advanced economically under a series of development plans, the first of which was primarily concerned with expanding basic transportation facilities. Railways were extended, a deep-water port built at Takoradi. The principle of a reserve fund for economic contingencies was established early. The first ten-year development plan was launched at the end of World War I and, except during the period of the world depression, Ghana has been development conscious. Both under the later stages of colonialism and under her present nationalistic government, she has been a social-welfare state.

What was the effect of innovation? Traditional chieftaincy and social organization increasingly became a focus for internal resentments. Bitter conflict over land developed. The pattern of self-restraints on behavior was upset. Land alienation in the form of concessions was common. Considerable friction developed between chiefs who took their seats not only in traditional councils, but on the legislative council and other conciliar bodies set up by the government, and the urban, educated elites which emerged with the spread of modern commerce. Each emerging group thought itself destined to inherit political power. The result was cultural withdrawal which prepared the ground for mass nationalism in Ghana after the Second World War. The chiefs, failing to consider the sources of mass nationalism, regarded it as simply an event in a long and stable cultural tradition which would only help to restore chieftaincy to its proper role.

The Western-educated elites regarded the nationalists as usurpers of their roles. The British viewed them as dangerous malcontents, subversive of public peace and good order. Such rejection gave fervor to the nationalists of the Convention People's Party (CPP), who by adherence to the party gave a new coherence to Ghana as a national society. They brought about a closer integration of the different peoples making up the territory, and they made economic and political institutions African rather than foreign by using them in the interests of self-government. Politics had already become polarized between traditional and secular authorities during the colonial period. Now the fundamental issues of traditionalism and modernity became wrapped up in more complex conflicts over democracy itself.

The major achievement of the CPP in Ghana was the organization and maintenance of an effective mass political organization. This resulted in centers of communication in the towns and villages, requiring members who could coordinate the activities of others. By building the CPP into a social group, a fraternity of the disadvantaged was encouraged to mold society in its favor by means of national political institutions and political freedom. A widely diverse membership was provided with a feeling of confidence in the future. Self-government was the goal. New opportunities were to be achieved thereby. A vision of a new society which was as vague as it was powerful was the moral claim of the CPP.

Yet in creating a mass political organization devoted to achieving independence, the CPP incorporated elements which had no long-run

115

natural inclinations toward one another. More particularly, traditional groupings formed centers of opposition to Dr. Nkrumah both inside and outside the party. The main source of opposition was Ashanti. The Asantehene and his council helped plan the organization of an opposition, the National Liberation Movement (NLM), which itself renewed an old alliance between intellectuals and traditional authorities.[13]

With demands for a federal system of government, the situation rapidly grew dangerous. One Cabinet minister, a leading CPP figure from Ashanti, was ambushed outside his house and his sister killed. Government leaders did not dare to go to Ashanti for almost two years. Moreover, the appearance of successful traditionalism in Ashanti encouraged other opposition groups to form. In Accra, in Nkrumah's own constituency, there was formed an Accra people's movement which was essentially parochial and anti-Nkrumah. Everywhere traditionalism and the natural organization of the ethnic and tribal group seemed the only possible alternative to party rule by the Convention People's Party.

The conflicts over traditionalism and the future of democracy were sharpest during the period just prior to independence. In the general election of 1956, the candidates of seven parties and 45 independents ran for office. In spite of the fact that the NLM was able to put only 39 candidates in the field, and the CPP was well enough organized to contest all 104 seats, the latter received only 398,141 votes and the combined opposition received 299,116. This opposition vote was extremely high, considering the fact that a vote for the CPP was considered a vote for independence. Approximately 50 percent of the electorate voted. In the post-independence period, the opposition was smashed. A series of acts rushed through Parliament were designed to break the power of traditional authorities. So successful were these efforts that, when elections to the Kumasi Municipal Council were held in February 1958, the CPP won 17 out of 24 seats—a remarkable achievement.

In attacking traditionalism, movements of the CPP type take on the characteristic of inviolability. They have a tendency to brand splinter groups and the opposition as playing into the hands of the "feudal" elements in society. The idea of party fealty is stressed more than any other.

The pattern which can be clearly seen in this conflict between traditionalism and modernism is thus the continuous affiliation to and disaffiliation from powerful social groupings that each make total claims on the allegiance and support of its members. The clear loser in such a situation is the opposition. In crucial respects, therefore, countries like Ghana find that in attacking tradition and supporting modernity they become one-party systems. It is not that there is no opposition, but that organized party opposition finds itself in difficult circumstances. Traditionalism, which serves the opposition as an effective rallying ground for popular support, is branded as subversive.[14] Indeed, at the Accra African Peoples' Conference in December 1958, tribalism and religious separatism

116

were defined as evil practices by Africa's leading nationalists. It was resolved that "those African traditional institutions whether political, social, or economic which have clearly shown their reactionary character and their sordid support for colonialism be condemned."[15]

What, then, has political modernization meant in Ghana? Attacking tradition has resulted in the development of an "organization weapon" type of party which, constantly on the attack, probes for weaknesses in the system. It seeks to jostle the public into functionally useful roles for the pursuit of modernization. To prevent the loss of power, and to modernize as rapidly as possible, are the basic goals of those who have inherited the mantle of British power. Modernization has come to require a host of attitudes of mind and social organizations antithetical to traditional ways of doing things. Political modernization therefore attacks head-on traditional ways of believing and acting.

In these respects, the Ghana government has been unable to make use of traditionalism to support innovation. The past has become a dead weight on the present government, which by the use of inducements, and by occasional kicks and blows as well, seeks to drive people toward a new way of life. Because of the government's loss of support in the traditional sectors of society, the burdens of modernization on Ghana have become more intense. Unlike Senegal, where the blending of traditionalism and modernity has eased the transition to new political and economic forms, in Ghana traditionalism has not provided a genuine source of pride and inspiration. Unlike the French African concept of *negritude*, the slogan "African personality" has remained largely devoid of content.[16] Ghana, in assuming the heavy burdens of modernization without the supports of traditionalism, has become a relatively autocratic system.

Uganda shows a completely different political pattern. Unlike Ghana, which is a maritime nation, Uganda is situated inland on the shores of Lake Victoria.[17] It is roughly the same size as Ghana, with an area of 80,000 square miles and a population of approximately 6 millions.[18]

By virtue of its superior institutions and successful collaboration with the British, Buganda was made a privileged area. The Uganda Agreement of 1900 formally recognized these privileges, and elsewhere in the country the Kiganda pattern of territorial organization was established—a three-tiered system of local government, each with a chief and a council (*Lukiko*) and ranging in scope from the parish to the county. The British retained an appointive chieftaincy system, but one which followed the practice of a regular civil service, with chiefs being promoted, transferred and retired. Theirs was the task of maintaining peace and good order, collecting taxes, and otherwise taking care of the areas under their jurisdiction. Buganda, as a province, formed the model for the other ethnic groups to follow in the districts. In more recent times the parliament of Buganda, the Great Lukoko, has been the model for the district councils, which have become the object of considerable tribal parochialism in the districts outside of Buganda.

117

The three races, African, Asian, and European, live in uneasy proximity. Asians are involved in petty commerce, and increasingly in larger commercial enterprises in urban centers such as Kampala, while Europeans generally remain in charge of major commercial operations. Few Europeans were successful in farming in Uganda, where a situation comparable to that of the white settlers in Kenya never developed. Asians and Europeans have always tended to collaborate in representing the commercial interests of the country.[19] Asians were represented on the Legislative Council along with Europeans from the very onset, after World War I. No Africans were represented on the Legislative Council, nor was it regarded as desirable that they should be, until after the Second World War. It was widely held that Buganda's own Lukiko served as her political outlet, and the same situation was thought to prevail in the districts. It was regarded as essential to the interests of Africans that the principle of trusteeship, the mainstay of administration during the interwar period, should be maintained through the Governor and his staff.[20]

Until the present day, nationalism in Uganda was largely expressed through the Buganda government "establishment." There is now stirring the kind of "modern" nationalism which is increasingly inclined to limit the powers of the Kabaka and make of Uganda a united, self-governing nation. But modernism as an ideology is confined to a very few. Indeed, it has been largely pre-empted by the Buganda government. Let us examine the process by which this occurred.

Although the Baganda did not suffer national defeats as did the Ashanti, religious wars in the latter part of the nineteenth century resulted in the deposition and restoration of the Kabaka by Europeans on two occasions. The Baganda have never gotten over that. Given the special position of the Kabaka in the structure of Kiganda society, cavalier treatment of them on the part of the Europeans deeply wounded and aggrieved the Baganda. Even during the period of their closest collaboration with the British (roughly from 1900 to 1926), such grievances were nursed. A singular touchiness has thus characterized relations between the British and the Baganda. Unlike the more typical case in the districts, changes in political organization have, if they originated with the Protectorate government, been stoutly resisted. The Kabaka as a symbol of modern nationalism has been continuously strengthened and now has more power than at any time since British control.

When the Agreement of 1900 was signed, the Lukiko, or African parliament, dominated by the chiefs, was empowered to distribute land on a freehold basis to the most important people in Buganda. The three chief ministers received the largest estates (with the exception of the Kabaka himself), while others were given land according to their chieftaincy rank, or their general status.[21] Few pagans received any land.

Since chieftaincies had been divided up according to religion, both Protestants and Catholics of wealth came to have a considerable stake in the modified system. By fixing the proportions of chieftaincy along religious lines, family wealth and position were distributed in the same manner. Both Protestants and Catholics had some wealthy families in possession of land, and in important positions in the community. The Muslims suffered most of all the religious groups, while paganism quickly disappeared.

Those in the clan system who had been traditionally entitled to certain burial estates or clan lands, and who lost those lands during the parceling-out of freehold, became the first political force in Buganda. The clan system thus formed the "natural" opposition to a government of chiefs. This resulted in considerable internal dissension. Gradually the *bataka*, or clan groups, came to represent the *bakopi*, or peasantry. Land holding had become almost synonymous with prestige and social position.[22] Indeed, it appeared for a time that the system would become based on dynastic land-holding families, and the principle of easy access to political office and performance would be eliminated. Yet other innovations helped to prevent this. For example, the expanded educational system, which was enthusiastically supported by the Baganda, did not limit facilities to the children of chiefs, but included peasant children as well. Education was regarded as a major basis for entry into the political hierarchy (which remained the only major social organization throughout Buganda).

The instrumental values of the Baganda, colliding with a threatening monopoly of political roles by families of the senior chiefs who had received land, or by important Protestant and Catholic leaders, prevailed over both elites without altering the autocratic principle of hierarchical kingship. This allowed progressive modification of the Lukiko and greater opportunities to the public as a whole. Unlike the consummatory system of Ashanti, where individuals had virtually to withdraw from the traditional system in order to seek new careers and opportunities in a different kind of society, the Kiganda system was modified in practice, while posing few contradictions in principle.

Although the Buganda government was often in conflict with the peasantry, such conflicts appeared in the guise of government and its loyal opposition. The British, through a Resident, built up the influence of the chiefs and the ministers of the Buganda government. They regarded them as modern because of the ease and alacrity with which they learned to collect taxes, adapted themselves to methods of bookkeeping, and were able to control the public.

Thus the autocratic principle has prevailed in Buganda until the present. Innovations, it is widely believed, have come not from an alien source, but through the Buganda government itself. With the country's leaders able to maintain social discipline, because to act irresponsibly is to act against the Kabaka, a sense of awe and formality in social relations has helped retain public support. To keep the public "on the alert" and politically conscious, skirmishes against the intervention of the Residency are constantly fought.

119

As a result, the Baganda have regarded themselves as exceedingly blessed in a state of political autonomy. The Buganda government has been the most successful nationalist "party" in the country. Success in the economic field as well, particularly with the cotton and coffee crops, brought the Baganda considerable wealth as compared with the rest of Uganda. To add to their complacency, they had, by such visible indicators as tin roofs on their houses, number of bicycles, number of laborers from elsewhere working for them, and number of educated people, the highest standard of living in the Protectorate. They were able to absorb new forms of income, and to accept the standards of education, knowledge, skill, and training as requirements for a job such as chieftaincy, while retaining the essential character of their political system.

The freehold system, the chieftaincy system, the method of recruitment, the standards of selection, the acceptance of cash crops, all helped to make Buganda extremely modern in many ways. *But the prerequisite to accepting any modern feature on the political level was that some real or mythical traditional counterpart had to be found for it.* Hence, if the Lukiko was now a regular council with minutes, committees, and a budget, it was nevertheless regarded as an age-old institution. If chiefs were now almost invariably large landowners or related to the original holders of freehold, in custom those responsible for the control over "heads," i.e., over families and soldiers, were found to be the equivalent.

In 1955 several important measures were passed. In the districts, the District Councils Ordinance gave the councils both executive and legislative powers, enabling them to make bylaws on a wide range of subjects.[23] In Buganda, after the deportation of the Kabaka for refusing to cooperate with the Protectorate government (part of his effort to retain autonomy for Buganda), a new agreement was signed which enhanced the powers of the Lukiko, made the Kabaka in effect a constitutional monarch, and gave the Baganda three new ministries—Health, Education, and Natural Resources—in addition to the three they already had (Prime Minister, Chief Justice, and Treasurer).[24] These reforms in effect gave to Buganda and to the district governments substantive warrants of authority and responsibility to attend to most of the economic and social schemes which are regarded as necessary to modernization. In Buganda the autocratic nature of the system has now come under attack—but the attack is still exceedingly mild. Elsewhere, in the districts, the effort to achieve local autonomy is regarded as the essence of political modernity.

What the system in Buganda cannot resolve are challenges to the principle of autocratic or hierarchical kingship. Resisting the first direct elections to be held in Buganda in 1958, the Baganda saw themselves threatened by devolution of authority to an African national government. Opposed to the nationalism of political parties, they regard representative government on an all-Uganda basis as tantamount to the destruction of their own society. In a pamphlet justifying the position of Buganda, the *Katikiro*, or Prime Minister, recently pointed out that the "peaceful growth of Western democracy in Buganda has been possible because the Baganda's customs and traditions are adaptable to new ideas which do not seek to uproot their fundamental political conceptions. . . ." Yet the pamphlet also warns that "The Baganda cannot exist as a people unless the Kabaka is the Head of the political structure in his Kingdom. Therefore, any constitution which envisages placing any other ruler or any foreign monarch in the position of the Kabaka of Buganda has no other intention but to cause the Baganda to cease to be a nation." More importantly, he concludes: "From time immemorial the Baganda have known no other ruler above their Kabaka in his Kingdom, and still they do not recognize any other person whose authority does not derive from the Kabaka and is exercised on his behalf."[25]

As a result of this position, it is the Protectorate government and British officials who are trying to build a modern national state in Uganda. How well they have succeeded is indicated by the fact that in the first direct elections in 1958, Buganda refused to participate, as did several other districts.[26]

Still more recently, a constitutional committee has recommended the establishment of responsible government at the center, with a legislature possessing 72 elected seats.[27] The Buganda government voiced its bitter opposition, but non-Baganda see in it the possibility of a political society not dominated by Buganda. With the Baganda anxious to secede from Uganda entirely if that is necessary to maintain the position of the Kabaka and the Buganda kingdom, there is bitter conflict between the Buganda government, on the one hand, and party politicians allied to British authorities, on the other.

There is now emerging among many Baganda an awareness that the absorptive capacity of the traditional system and its instrumental values has been reached. This is taken by the traditionalists to indicate a need for secession if the system is to be preserved. Younger groups are anxious to build a larger national society, a united Uganda. These are regarded as traitors by the traditionalists. However, the traditionalists are not antimodern. Quite the contrary, as we have seen, they have built up a modern if miniature state in Buganda and now that very modernity is used as a justification for autonomy.

The result is that political parties remain largely ineffective both in Buganda and in Uganda as a whole. Recently, in an effort to gain popular support, several parties included anti-Asian riots aimed at reducing the economic and commercial power of Indians. But in spite of such efforts, political parties remain weak and the Buganda government continues to be the main source of parochial nationalism. Political party leaders hope that when responsible government develops at the center and the financial resources of the country are allocated on the basis of popular government, the strength of the Buganda government will be diminished. The struggle to obtain parliamentary institutions is less concerned with Britain or the colonial administration than was the case in Ghana. Rather, it is directed

against the Buganda government because of its unwillingness to subordinate hierarchical authority to the principle of representative government.
Thus the ethnic nationalism of Buganda remains the most important
political obstacle to self-government and has crippled political party
growth, rendering the political heart of the country virtually lifeless.[28]

As has been pointed out above, however, non-Baganda groups are
developing a new political party that has been launched by recently
elected African representatives of the Legislative Council. They seek to
make the Legislative Council the crucial political organ in Uganda, and are
reluctant to be tied to the tail of Kiganda parochialism. Thus the
possibility presents itself that the central conciliar institutions of Uganda
will now tend to favor the rest of the country. Grants in aid, development
plans, and educational schemes can now become the target of competitive
nationalism, fought out in the context of competing parochialisms. In that
event, neither the traditional institutions nor their insularity will long be
maintained.

Moreover, direct elections to the Buganda Lukiko will bring party
politics strongly into the Buganda sphere.[29] It is possible that competitive
nationalism can be transformed into federal government at the center.
Federal government is a compromise system brought about by conflict
among the constituent states, and conflict is necessary for its vitality. What
is possible in the Uganda situation is political modernization in a federal
system, in which the several traditional states will be allowed to modernize
their institutions on their own terms. In the demand for federalism all
groups see some hope for their survival. Federalism itself has come to
mean political modernism.

CONCLUSION

In both Ghana and Uganda tribal or ethnic parochialism has persisted
with widely varying results. Kiganda parochialism has itself been a form of
modernism. Civil service chieftaincy and bureaucratic norms have bol-
stered the kingdom. Indeed, the Buganda government is widely regarded as
the most progressive force in the country. Hence, for the Baganda, to be
modern is to be parochial.

In Ashanti, modernism clashed directly with traditionalism. The
religious aspect of the traditional political and social structure was an
important part of a network of suitable restraints on behavior. When these
were disrupted by innovations in commercial enterprise and colonialism,
traditional authority was quickly undermined. Yet because traditional
authority was so much a part of daily life and custom, those who broke
with tradition found themselves in drastic need of new and powerful social
affiliations, for to break with tradition was to break with family, lineage,
and ancestral fidelity.

In contrast to Ashanti, Buganda remains the most powerful solidary association possible. Social satisfactions are still achieved within Buganda and its government for all those who belong to the kingdom. In Ashanti the formation of a new political party was itself a process of forming new and powerful symbolic attachments. The Ashanti members of the CPP became fiercely devoted to the organization. The messianic role of the leader was based on the development of a new morality to supplant the old. Hence the deep cleavages in society which remained after self-government had been obtained posed the problem of nation-building after independence rather than before it.

We can summarize some of the more salient points of contrast between the two systems as follows:

1. *Absorption of innovation.* Ashanti, with its consummatory-pyramidal system, was unable to control the effects of innovation. Ashanti tended to shrink from contact with the modern world. Early missionaries were imprisoned. The Ashanti wars were efforts to expel the British, as a foreign body, from the body politic. The effects of contact loosened the hold of traditionalism, although it remained a powerful force.

Buganda was able to control innovation. The European presence was absorbed and rendered useful. By careful planning and the use of modernizing agencies, the Buganda government increased its autonomy and control as time went on, rather than suffering partial decay.

2. *Internal divisions and discontinuities.* What had hitherto been reinforcing social institutions of the consummatory system of Ashanti rapidly broke down into competing power groups and sources of internal antagonism and weakness. Thus the development of conflicts between youth and age, royals and non-royals, slaves and non-slaves, were all examples of conflict over the continuing strength of particularistic criteria which could be reconciled only so long as older religious and institutional checks were sustained. Such social controls were highly internalized, with authority variously distributed. As soon as the continuity of past and present was disrupted, the various groupings rapidly came to compete.

In Buganda the internal conflict continued, as in the period prior to contact, between clanship and chieftaincy—all, however, under the umbrella of the king as both Sabataka, head of all the clans, and Kabaka, or king. The advantages of appointive chieftaincy had long been apparent in the military undertakings of the kingdom and a secular tendency inherent in the system was simply reinforced by contact with the British. The system was able to modify itself to restrain the old conflicts sufficiently so that the principle of hierarchic kingship did not require substantial alteration. Allegiance did not become confused.

3. *Competition for affiliations.* Internal conflict in Ashanti produced widespread attitudes of guilt. Cleavages divided the extended and nuclear families. Social breaks which meant modifying one's religious practices and sundering ties with the past (and one's ancestors) led to migration of individuals to urban areas which supported very different patterns of social

123

life. These created more fundamental differences in outlook between urban and rural groups who, within one generation, had grown apart but were still not socially distant. The Ashanti were able to retain affiliations among those who represented orthodoxy. However, breaking such affiliations could not be resolved by the simple acceptance of heterodoxy. Rather a new orthodoxy had to be posed against the old. Thus the new affiliations of the political party assumed the proportions of a militant church movement.

In Buganda, there was relatively easy adaptation of internal cleavage to serve the larger purposes of the state. As a result, no Baganda repudiated their chiefs or the Kabaka. The Buganda government was itself a source of modernism, and no incompatibility between modernism and traditionalism resulted in the enforced disaffiliation of discontented groups. No discontented urban groups emerged, anxiety-ridden and seeking drastic change.

4. Legitimacy conflicts. Just as innovation could not be controlled in Ashanti, so the secular authority of the colonial government was posed against the traditional authority of the chiefs. Immemorial prescriptive rights clashed with concepts of efficiency and performance as a basis of authority. In Buganda, the autocratic principle prevailed and two oligarchies, British and Baganda, worked alongside one another. They were in constant competition, but they did not challenge each other's legitimacy. Both were oriented to efficiency and performance.

In Ashanti almost any outside activity, by being resisted, posed an ultimate legitimacy problem. So closely interrelated were the elements of social life and belief that they conformed nicely to Durkheim's concept of a fragile and mechanical society. Ultimately all threats were threats against legitimacy. Hence not only was colonialism viewed as a threat to traditional legitimacy, but nationalism was even more so. The conflict between lineage and ancestral sanction (immemoriality) for current acts and secular forces was introduced by colonialism, and helped to produce the nationalism which then had to break the power of traditionalism and its residual hold upon the public. Thus modern nationalism in Ghana is essentially an effort to create a wider legitimacy which introduces some of the same instrumental characteristics which Buganda possessed traditionally. *The result is a growth of an autocratic principle of leadership in Ghana*—the organizational weapon serving as its own justification.

In contrast, in Buganda, the conflict over legitimacy never emerged in sharp form in the colonial-Buganda government relationship. Indeed, even when the Kabaka was exiled, early in the relationship, or more recently when the present Kabaka was deported, the principle of the Kabakaship was not questioned by the Protectorate government authorities.

However, now that the problem of building wider affiliations has been tackled effectively by the Protectorate government, political parties are challenging the principle of hierarchical authority. *They are seeking to supplant hierarchical authority with representative authority as* a means of building a modern nation. They do not, however, need to create attitudes of universalism and performance as the basis of political recruitment since these are already widespread and traditional.

Where the consummatory-pyramidal system prevailed, there developed fierce competition between traditional and secular leaders to monopolize allegiance. This was expressed by the latter in efforts to build overarching and autocratic institutions which by autocratic means fostered egalitarianism in political recruitment and the exercise of authority. The problem was to prevent social atomism while mobilizing those resources of the society which could capitalize on change itself. This put exceedingly heavy burdens on political nationalists, whose need for organizational control and support became all important.

In the instrumental-hierarchical system prevailing in Buganda, change has aided parochialism and modernism of a local sort, making political modernism of the national state more difficult to achieve. Where consummatory values prevail in the traditional sector, the political leaders lose the advantages of traditionalism. Their need is to find new ways and means of employing it to ease the burdens of political development. Where instrumental values prevail, the local and national forms of modernism need to be brought into some kind of useful identity, so that instrumental traditionalism can reinforce political modernization at the national level.

Ghana shows the effects of a single-party unitary government and its difficulties in modernization. Can a modernizing nation be created through a federal system of government in which the parts will reinforce the whole? In this respect, Uganda represents a potential alternative to the Ghana pattern. Out of regard for instrumental traditionalism, Uganda may find a political compromise proximate to the needs of the public, achieving modernity with both prudence and freedom.

Modernism and traditionalism have become key political issues. Buganda has retained both her tribalism and her separatism, penalizing the political advance of the country as a whole. Ashanti, the last stronghold of tribalism in Ghana, has been defeated by modernism in the form of nationalism. Buganda and Ashanti, Uganda and Ghana, both facing similar problems in different ways, shed some light on the politics of modernization in contemporary Africa.

NOTES

1. See D. Lerner *et al.*, *The Passing of Traditional Society* (Glencoe, Ill., 1958); L. A. Fallers, *Bantu Bureaucracy* (Cambridge: 1956); and D. E. Apter, *The Gold Coast in Transition* (Princeton, N. J., 1955).

2. As we are using the terms, "instrumental" systems are those characterized by a large sector of intermediate ends separate from and independent of ultimate ends; "consummatory" systems are those characterized by a close relationship between intermediate and ultimate ends. The terms are derived from Parsons' categories of "cognitive-instrumental meanings" and "expressive-integrative meanings." See T. Parsons *et al.*, *Working Papers in the Theory of Action* (Glencoe, Ill., 1953), p. 105.

   In our sense, the difference between instrumental and consummatory values can be illustrated by the following example. Consider two traditional systems, one consummatory and the other instrumental in value type. Both are short-hoe cultures and an effort is made to introduce new agricultural techniques, particularly the use of tractors. In the consummatory system, changing from the short hand-hoe system will so corrupt the ritual of hoe-making, the division of men's and women's work, the religious practices associated with both, and the relationship between agricultural rituals and the authority of chiefs that it would be impossible to consider a tractor only in terms of increasing agricultural productivity. In the instrumental system, by contrast, the tractor would simply be viewed in terms of its ability to expand agricultural output and would not affect the ultimate ends of the system. In the first instance, such an innovation represents a threat to the system. In the second instance, it is far likelier to strengthen the system by increasing farm income.

3. For a discussion of hierarchical authority, see A. Southall, *Alur Society* (Cambridge, 1956), esp. chap. 6. See also D. E. Apter, *The Political Kingdom in Uganda: A Study of Bureaucratic Nationalism* (Princeton, N. J., forthcoming).

4. The reader should note that the name Uganda refers to the entire country, the Uganda Protectorate, which includes many different tribes; Buganda is a tribe within Uganda; the Baganda are the people (plural) of Buganda; a Muganda is a single member of the Buganda tribe; and Kiganda is the adjective form.

5. Fustel de Coulanges, *The Ancient City* (New York: Doubleday Anchor Books, n.d.), p. 13.

6. Such systems can innovate, however. Indeed, the philosophy prevailing in Senegal today is similar to that described by Coulanges, but the religious system is pervaded by humanistic socialism. Hence to build upon traditional solidarities, the emphasis on family, corporatism in institutions, personalism, and the like go hand in hand with joint participation in communal economic efforts. By this means, work is ennobled and given new meaning in traditional terms. See, for example, the expression of this point of view in *L'Economie africaine*,

126

M. Mamadou Dia, (Paris, 1957), and "Economie et culture devant les élites africaines," Présence africaine 14-15 (June-September 1957): 58-72.

7. See R. P. Ashe, *Chronicles of Uganda* (London, 1894); and A. R. Tucker, *Eighteen Years in Uganda and East Africa* (London, 1908), *passim.*

8. J. N. Matson, *Warrington's Notes on Ashanti Custom*, 2d ed. (Cape Coast: Prospect Printing Press, 1941).

9. See, in particular, John Roscoe, *The Baganda* (London, 1911), p. 232.

10. Ashanti had a complex hierarchy of chiefs. At the pinnacle of the hierarchy was the *omanhene*, or divisional chief. Independent in his sphere of authority, he was nevertheless hedged about with restrictions. His was a religious role symbolizing lineage relationships to ancestors, and only members of a founder's or royal lineage were eligible to be elected to chieftaincy. The same held true for village chiefs and headmen. During war a division chief and others would take a position in the army and a more hierarchical system of authority would come to prevail. See E. Meyerowitz, *The Sacred State of the Akan* (London, 1951), especially chap. 10.

11. See *Report of the Constitutional Committee, 1959* (Wild Report), Entebbe, Government Printer, 1959, pp. 33-35.

12. A population of approximately 5 million in an area of over 90,000 square miles is divided into several main tribal groups. The northern peoples are chiefly grouped in Muslim kingdoms. The central group is the seat of the once-powerful Ashanti Confederacy. The southern groups—Fante, Ga, Ewe, and others—have had the longest contact with Western commerce and education. There are old families inhabiting the former "factories" of early traders who intermarried with the local people and established their own family dynasties. See J. Boyon, *Le Ghana* (Paris, 1958), pp. 7-10.

13. In 1957 the NLM joined with other tribal parties like the *Ga Shifimo Kpee* to become the United Party. The former leader of the party, Dr. K. A. Busia, is currently in Holland, Ghana's first real political exile.

14. At the same time, the parliamentary opposition in Ghana has been effective on occasions. There are times when the CPP backbench threatens to bolt party whips and vote with the opposition. Such a threat has been a useful means of modifying the position of the government on several issues, not the least of which was modification of the Emergency Powers Bill, while the constitutional changes of early 1957 were incorporated under pressure from the opposition. Bitterly contested decisions which often resulted in suspensions of parliamentary sessions have been those involving basic liberties. Three such measures were the Ghana Nationality and Citizenship Bill, the Emergency Powers Bill, and the Deportation Bill. For an excellent study of Ghana's parliament, see D. G. Austin, "The Ghana Parliament's First Year," *Parliamentary Affairs* 11, no. 3 (Summer 1958): 350-60.

15. All-African Peoples' Conference, Resolution on Tribalism, Religious Separatism, and Traditional Institutions, *Conference Resolutions*, vol. I, no. 4, issued by the Conference Secretariat, Accra, 1958.

16. It is interesting to note that while the term "African personality" is widely attributed to Nkrumah, it is in Nigeria that an effort is being made to give it a content. Examples of such efforts are the journals Black Orpheus and Odú, which, as cultural and literary journals, seek to give a philosophic and cultural significance to the term.

17. Blessed with an exceedingly good climate and well-distributed rainfall, most of Uganda is fertile agricultural country. To supplement her two main crops, cotton and coffee, she needs more diverse export commodities, and copper and other raw materials are being successfully exploited on an increasing scale.

18. See *Colonial Report*, (Entebbe, Government Printer, 1959). Buganda represents approximately 20 percent of the population of Uganda.

19. The Indian Association and the Uganda Chamber of Commerce were instruments of that cooperation.

20. For a discussion of this period, see K. Ingham, *The Making of Modern Uganda* (London, 1958), *passim*.

21. Uganda Agreement of 1900, para. 15. See *Laws of the Uganda Protectorate, Native Agreements and Buganda Native Laws*, London, 1936, pp. 1380-81.

22. Important in preventing such dissension from assuming proportions of "class conflict" was the fact that peasants could, and did, buy freehold land. Moreover, no landless peasantry was created. Everyone could get a leasehold property at a nominal and fixed rental. This deterred migration to towns, and no urban-rural cleavage developed. Buganda remains a rural "suburbia." See A. W. Southall and P. C. W. Gutkind, *Townsmen in the Making*, East African Studies No. 9 (Kampala: East African Institution of Social Research, 1956), *passim*.

23. See *District Councils Ordinance, 1955* (Entebbe, Government Printer, 1955).

24. See *Buganda Agreement of 1955* (Entebbe, Government Printer, 1955).

25. M. Kintu, *Buganda's Position*, Information Department, Kabaka's Government (Kampala: Uganda Printing and Publishing Co., 1960), pp. 1-2.

26. See C. P. S. Allen, *A Report on the First Direct Elections to the Legislative Council of the Uganda Protectorate* (Entebbe: Government Printer, 1959), Appendix J.

27. See the Wild Report, *Report of the Constitutional Committee*, which anxiously notes the need for political parties in order to create effective central government.

28. It must be pointed out, however, that in Uganda, unlike colonial Ghana, everyone knows that self-government is forthcoming. Lack of such certainty helped to develop an effective nationalist movement in Ghana, where to remain outside the party was tantamount to being

procolonialist. In Uganda, all groups know that the country will eventually get self-government, and there is far more effort on the part of each of them to retain and expand their influence and power. Foreknowledge of self-government, in that sense, has helped to diminish the urgency of nationalism.

29. Already in the new Lukiko, elected in 1959 (without direct election methods), five political parties are represented, a predominantly Catholic party supplying 80 percent of all party representatives. The Buganda government has accepted the principle of direct elections but has steadfastly refused to implement it.

POLITICAL MODERNIZATION AND POLITICAL CULTURE IN JAPAN

Robert E. Ward

* * *

The course of political modernization in Japan raises some interesting questions with respect to the form and organization of authority in modernizing societies. . . . States which have achieved modernity may have democratic, totalitarian, or some intermediate type of political organization. The form of government does not seem to be a defining factor in mature cases of political modernization. The experience of Japan, however, makes one wonder if the same judgment applies with respect to forms of political organization in all earlier stages of the political modernization process. Is the process neutral in this respect throughout, or can one identify stages which demand authoritarian forms of government and which are antipathetic on grounds of developmental efficiency and potentiality to the introduction of democratic institutions on more than a very restricted basis? The question is of great importance from the standpoint of those who would prefer to see "backward" political systems develop along lines which are both modern and democratic. These are compatible but not necessary consequences of the developmental process. This poses the problem of how one can maximize the probability that developing politics will become both modern and democratic.

The experience of Japan alone certainly cannot provide definitive answers to either of the above questions. But neither is it irrelevant, and in circumstances where it represents the sole mature non-Western exemplar of the modernization process in all of Asia, it should be examined with unusual care and attention. The Japanese experience seems to suggest: (1) that authoritarian forms of political organization can be extraordinarily effective in the early stages of the modernization process; (2) that they

From Robert E. Ward, "Political Modernization and Political Culture in Japan, "*World Politics* 15, no. 4, pp. 588-96. Copyright © 1963 by the Princeton University Press. Reprinted by permission of the publisher.

need not debar the gradual emergence of more democratic forms of political organization; and (3) that some such process of gradual transition from authoritarian to democratic forms may be essential to the emergence of politics that are both modern and durably democratic. It should be emphasized again that these are no more than highly tentative hypotheses based upon the experience of Japan, but they do possess at least this much historical sanction and support. Let us then consider in a general way selected aspects of Japan's experience with the political modernization process which relate to the above three propositions.

First, authoritarian forms of political organization can be extraordinarily effective in the early stages of the modernization process. It is implied—though not demonstrable on the basis of the Japanese experience —that democratic forms are significantly less effective and that their early introduction may in fact result in conditions that will seriously inhibit the prospects of long-term democratic development.

This contention rests primarily on observations with respect to the relationship between the political modernization process and the process of social modernization in a general or total sense. The former is not autonomous, not a goal in itself. It is instrumentally related to the larger process and goal and should serve and expedite its purposes. This larger process of modernization entails for the society concerned, especially in the critical early or "take-off" stages, a series of shocks and strains of major proportions. It equally creates emancipations and new opportunities for some, but for major segments of the population this is apt to be a lengthy period of adjustment to new economic, social, and political situations and demands. Large-scale material and psychological stresses are invariably involved. One of the routine consequences of such a situation— at least in the non-Western world of the late nineteenth and the twentieth centuries—seems to be a greatly expanded role for government. A certain and perhaps very important amount of the modernization process may still take place under private auspices, but in recent times the needs and expectations which set the standards of modernization have been so urgent and expensive that national governments have had to assume a leading and dominant role. Only power organized at this level seemed capable of massing the resources and taking and enforcing the wide-ranging and difficult decisions involved.

This primacy of government in the modernizing process is more or less taken for granted throughout the underdeveloped world today. The situation was doubtless historically different in the case of the modernization of certain Western European societies and their offshoots, but in present-day underdeveloped societies there simply are no plausible and politically viable alternatives to the primacy of government as an agent of modernization. This was also true in the Japanese case at the time of the Restoration.

The overriding problems and goals of the 1870s and 1880s in Japan were well expressed by the popular political slogan of the day—*fukoku*   131 *kyōhei* (a strong and wealthy nation). This captures the essence of the complex of forces and aspirations which underlay the Restoration movement and motivated its leaders in the difficult days that followed the initial successes of 1868. The greatest and most urgent needs were for national unity and the creation of armed strength sufficient to guarantee the national security against both real and fancied dangers of foreign imperialist aggression and economic exploitation. Instrumental thereto, of course, was the creation of a strong and stable government to lead the nation along suitable paths. Fortunately for Japan, her leaders were wise enough to define these goals in broad and constructive terms. Military strength meant to them far more than a large army and navy well-equipped with Western armaments; it also meant the industrial plant to sustain and expand such a military establishment and appropriate training for the men who must staff it. National wealth came to mean a radical diversification of the predominantly agrarian economy, urbanization, systematic mass and higher education, planned industrialization, new commercial and financial institutions, and a variety of other commitments which were perceived as essential to survival and effective competitive status in a Western-dominated world. Not all of these commitments were either generally perceived or welcomed at the outset by the leadership group, but in their search for national unity, strength, and security they found themselves embarked upon a species of "modernization spiral" similar in some respects to the "inflationary spiral" of the economists. The most intelligent and able of them adapted to the general course set by the imperatives which these goals entailed; the others were eliminated from leadership circles.

The realization of national goals of this sort did not come easily to a society such as Japan's, even given the forms of covert preparation for modernization which had characterized the later Tokugawa Period. The really critical years between 1868 and 1890 must sometimes have seemed an unending series of crises. Civil war, the threat of international war and the fact of foreign economic exploitation, a series of economic crises, inflation and deflation, the recurrent threat of samurai conspiracies against the government, the embitterment of the peasantry at the failure of the government to improve their lot, the dearth of desperately needed technical knowledge and personnel, and all of the widespread fears and tensions which attend a time of new beginnings—these were merely some of the problems which constantly confronted the new political leadership. Yet, by 1890, policies capable of dealing with all of these problems had been developed and the country was firmly embarked on the path to modernization. The foreign threats had been faced and Japan's international position was secure; the menace of civil war had been permanently liquidated; the structural vestiges of feudalism had been eliminated and the country effectively unified; the position and authority of the government had been confirmed and regularized by constitutional arrangements; the economy had been stabilized and a promising start made upon its diversification and industrialization; a system of mass compulsory education had been inaugurated and mass media of communication established; in every critical category the strength of Japan showed remarkable and promising improvements.

Under such circumstances it may be that some measure of democratic participation could successfully have been introduced into the political system. There were those who advocated such changes. The *Jiyūminken Undō* (Freedom and Popular Rights Movement), for example, called for the establishment of a national parliament, a limited suffrage, and some dispersion of political authority. Had this been attempted during these years, the results need not have been fatal to the modernization of Japan. But under conditions of more or less constant political or economic crisis, widespread popular disaffection and lack of understanding of the necessity for the sacrifices entailed by many government programs, the unpredictable qualities and perils of the country's foreign relations, and what we have learned in general of the limitations of fledgling democratic institutions in largely unprepared contexts, it is difficult to envisage the feasibility or practicality of any very significant democratic innovations at this time.

These years from 1868 to 1890, or some similar period, would seem to be a time in Japan's modernization when an authoritarian form of political organization offered distinct advantages where rapidity of response, flexibility, planning, and effective action were concerned. This is said with full appreciation of the fumbling and shortcomings of authoritarian leadership groups and irresponsible bureaucracies—including the Japanese of this period—in all of these departments. It thus assumes the availability of some at least minimally competent and unified political leadership. If this is not available—and there are obviously cases where it is not—political modernization is not a practicable proposition for the countries concerned.

In the Japanese case, however, it seems on balance highly improbable that (1) the addition of any significant or effective democratic institutions to the decision-making apparatus at such a stage of national development could have had other than deleterious effects upon the speed and decisiveness with which urgent problems were handled; and that (2) this stage of the modernization process, beset as it inevitably was by so many and such desperate problems, would have been an appropriate time to launch so delicate an experiment as democratization.

Our second hypothesis was that the dominance of authoritarian forms of political organization in the initial stages of the political modernization process need not debar the gradual emergence of democratic forms of organization. This is not intended to imply any quality of inevitability in such a development, although in a secular sense some such tendency may exist.

In the Japanese case, no significant measures of democratization were introduced into the political system until the enactment of the Meiji

Constitution in 1890, 22 years after the Restoration. Even then it is very doubtful if any of the authors of this document thought of their handiwork as an act of democratic innovation. It is certain that their so-called "liberal" opposition did not. Rather does it seem that the Meiji leadership group conceived of this constitution primarily as a means of regularizing the structure and operations of political authority—the absence of any rationalized or stable structure and the continual innovation and experimentation of the intervening years must have been very trying—and of further unifying and solidifying both the country and their own authority. As a consequence of this and a variety of later developments, there has been a tendency to undervalue both the degree of political change which the Meiji Constitution brought to Japan and the measure of democratic development which took place under it.

It is helpful to look at the Meiji Constitution and its attendant basic laws both in terms of the general political standards and practices of 1890 and in terms of its actual operations as well as its legal and political theory. If this is done, one will note that it makes public, explicit, and authoritative a particular theory of sovereignty and the state, and derives from this a functionally differentiated and rationally organized governmental structure; it establishes the legal status of citizens and specifies their political and civil rights and duties; it distinguishes legislative, executive, and judicial functions and, although establishing a dominant and protected position for the executive, does provide for their separate institutionalization; it specifies legal equality before the law and creates means for the assertion of popular against official rights; it establishes a restricted but expansible franchise and, in terms of this, a popularly elected house in the national legislature; it provides for some measure of decentralization in government, and renders inevitable the introduction of a much greater measure of pluralism into both the Japanese oligarchy and the political system in general.

Against the background of Tokugawa and Restoration political practices, these are notable and democratic innovations. They did not, of course, put an end to the period of authoritarian political rule in Japan. But they certainly launched a process of democratization which has continued to play a major, although usually not dominant, part in Japanese politics ever since. In this sense the history of the democratization of Japan, viewed in the light of present circumstances, is a product of erosive and catalytic agents. Much of the story is told, until 1932 at least, in terms of the erosion of the authoritarian political forms and practices characteristic of the preconstitutional period. This process never reached the point of establishing what the contemporary West would regard as an authentically democratic political system, but, by the 1920s, the degree of pluralism, responsibility, and popular participation characterizing Japanese politics would certainly have surprised, and probably appalled, the great leaders of the Restoration Period. Between the 1920s and the 1960s there intervened, of course, the resurgence of military and ultranationalist rule, the war, and the Allied Occupation of Japan. This last acted as a catalytic agent on the submerged but still vital forms of Japanese democracy and gave them institutional and legal advantages, authority, and prestige beyond what they could have hoped for on the basis of their own political position and strength. The consequence has been a great and apparently sudden florescence of Western-style democracy in Japan. In fact, however, the roots of this development lie deep in the political experience of post-1890 Japan.

There are two things about this gradual emergence of democratic politics from the authoritarian system of pre-1890 Japan which might have more general validity and interest. The first is that even the concession of a very carefully restricted and seemingly impotent governmental role to a popularly elected body can, over a period of time, have consequences well nigh fatal to sustained authoritarian rule. It would be hard to be optimistic about the influence or authority of the Japanese House of Representatives in terms of the provisions of the Meiji Constitution or the relevant basic laws. These faithfully reflect and implement the desire of the founders to make of the House an appealing but powerless sop to the demands of the opposition and public opinion. But the lessons to be learned from the subsequent history of the lower house are: (1) that it provides a means of institutionalizing and enlarging the role of political parties; (2) that, in modernizing circumstances, even vested powers of obstructing the smooth and effective flow of governmental decisions and actions can be critical—positive powers of initiation and control are not necessary; and (3) that in circumstances where a popularly chosen body can thus blackmail an authoritarian leadership, there is a fair possibility of forcing the latter into piecemeal but cumulative accommodations which are democratic in tendency.

The second generalization suggested by the history of democratic development in Japan relates to the conditions necessary to support an effectively authoritarian system of government. Japanese experience suggests the existence of a close relationship between effective authoritarian rule and the unity and solidarity of the oligarchy involved. The limits involved cannot be described with much precision, but authoritarian government in Japan began to disintegrate as the heretofore fairly solidary oligarchy began to split into competing cliques and factions. The probability of such rifts seems to be very high in modernizing societies. The development of role specialization and professionalization even at high levels is an essential part of the process of modernization, and this makes it hard for an oligarchy to maintain the degree of unity and cohesion feasible in revolutionary or in simpler times. Pluralism in this sense seems to be built into the process. And as an oligarchy breaks down into competing factions in this fashion, the terms of political competition in that society undergo an important change. Extra-oligarchic groups such as emergent political parties acquire new room for maneuver and new political leverages, and the ex-oligarchic cliques themselves acquire new

135

incentives for broadening the basis of their support. Out of these altered political circumstances are apt to come new political alliances involving elements of the former oligarchy with elements of more popularly based bodies—in particular, with political parties. The total process is dilutive from the standpoint of authoritarian government and supportive of the gradual emergence of greater degrees of pluralism and democracy.

It is not intended to depict either of the foregoing generalizations on the basis of Japanese experience as controlling or inevitable. But they did occur within a fairly authoritarian context in Japan's case and there seem to be some reasons for regarding them as of more general validity. The conclusion would seem to be that an initial or early stage of authoritarian government on the path to modernization (1) does not commit a polity to long-term adherence to authoritarian forms; (2) does not necessarily make an authoritarian course of development probable; and (3) may even contain built-in elements calculated with time and development to break down and liberalize such authoritarian forms.

Our third hypothesis is even more tentatively stated and adds up to a feeling that some such process of gradual transition from authoritarian to democratic forms may be essential to the emergence of a political system which is both modern and durably democratic. In this connection Japan's experience suggests several notions of possible interest.

First, our commonly employed systems of periodization may involve serious distortions where the history of political modernization is concerned. Thus, in Japan's case, while the feudal-modern or Tokugawa-Restoration frameworks have a plausible amount of relevance to the emergence of a modern Japanese political system, they also serve to obscure important aspects of the process. They are calculated, as is the prewar-postwar framework, to produce an overemphasis on the significance of certain dramatic and allegedly "revolutionary" events in a country's history—in this case, the Restoration or the 1945 defeat plus the Occupation. This is conducive to a dichotomous view of the political development process which seriously overstates the enduring importance of alleged discontinuities in a national history at the expense of the less dramatic but fundamentally more important continuities.

Second, if the history of the development of democracy in Japan is weighted for this distorting effect of the commonly employed categories and system of periodization, the differences in preparation, timing, and depth of democratic experience which are often held to distinguish a democratic political system in Japan from its Western analogues would perhaps seem appreciably less valid and important than is usually assumed. The two patterns of development probably have more in common than is generally recognized.

Third, if the foregoing assumptions are valid, one is tempted to conclude that all practicing and at least ostensibly solid and durable democracies today are the products of lengthy and multifaceted evolutionary processes. In the Japanese case, if one looks only to the direct antecedents, 73 years intervene between the Meiji Constitution and the present. But far longer periods of preparation are involved if one looks to the less direct consequences of the introduction of mass literacy or a rationalized bureaucratic structure. In this sense it is questionable whether history provides any very encouraging examples of short-cuts to the achievement of a democratic political system.

Finally, such a train of argument suggests the importance of the relationship existing between a "modern" political system and a "democratic" political system. One hesitates to claim that all or a specific proportion of the attributes of a modern polity must be achieved before a society becomes capable of durably democratic performance or achievement, but Japan's experience at least suggests an important correlation between the two. It is hard to specify the proportions involved, but, in a rough and approximate way, one might say that perhaps only modern societies with modern political cultures . . . are practical candidates for democratization.

POLITICAL DEVELOPMENT
AND POLITICAL DECAY

Samuel P. Huntington

"Among the laws that rule human societies," de Tocqueville said, "there is one which seems to be more precise and clear than all others. If men are to remain civilized or to become so, the art of associating together must grow and improve in the same ratio in which the equality of conditions is increased."[1] In much of the world today, equality of political participation is growing much more rapidly than is the "art of associating together." The rates of mobilization and participation are high; the rates of organization and institutionalization are low. De Tocqueville's precondition for civilized society is in danger, if it is not already undermined. In these societies, the conflict between mobilization and institutionalization is the crux of politics. Yet in the fast-growing literature on the politics of the developing areas, political institutionalization usually receives scant treatment. Writers on political development emphasize the processes of modernization and the closely related phenomena of social mobilization and increasing political participation. A balanced view of the politics of contemporary Asia, Africa, and Latin America requires more attention to the "art of associating together" and the growth of political institutions. For this purpose, it is useful to distinguish political development from modernization and to identify political development with the institutionalization of political organizations and procedures. Rapid increases in mobilization and participation, the principal political aspects of modernization, undermine political institutions. Rapid

From Samuel P. Huntington, "Political Development and Political Decay," *World Politics* 17, no. 3, pp. 386-430. Copyright © 1965 by the Princeton University Press. Reprinted by permission of the publisher.

modernization, in brief, produces not political development, but political decay.

* * *

POLITICAL DEVELOPMENT AS INSTITUTIONALIZATION

There is thus much to be gained (as well as something to be lost) by conceiving of political development as a process independent of, although obviously affected by, the process of modernization. In view of the crucial importance of the relationship between mobilization and participation, on the one hand, and the growth of political organizations, on the other, it is useful for many purposes to define political development as the institutionalization of political organizations and procedures. This concept liberates development from modernization. It can be applied to the analysis of political systems of any sort, not just modern ones. It can be defined in reasonably precise ways which are at least theoretically capable of measurement. As a concept, it does not suggest that movement is likely to be in only one direction: institutions, we know, decay and dissolve as well as grow and mature. Most significantly, it focuses attention on the reciprocal interaction between the on-going social processes of modernization, on the one hand, and the strength, stability, or weakness of political structures, traditional, transitional, or modern, on the other.[2]

The strength of political organizations and procedures varies with their *scope of support* and their *level of institutionalization*. Scope refers simply to the extent to which the political organizations and procedures encompass activity in the society. If only a small upper-class group belongs to political organizations and behaves in terms of a set of procedures, the scope is limited. If, on the other hand, a large segment of the population is politically organized and follows the political procedures, the scope is broad. Institutions are stable, valued, recurring patterns of behavior. Organizations and procedures vary in their degree of institutionalization. Harvard University and the newly opened suburban high school are both organizations, but Harvard is much more of an institution than is the high school. The seniority system in Congress and President Johnson's select press conferences are both procedures, but seniority is much more institutionalized than are Mr. Johnson's methods of dealing with the press. Institutionalization is the process by which organizations and procedures acquire value and stability. The level of institutionalization of any political system can be defined by the adaptability, complexity, autonomy, and coherence of its organizations and procedures. So also, the level of institutionalization of any particular organization or procedure can be measured by its adaptability, complexity, autonomy, and coherence. If these criteria can be identified and measured, political systems can be compared in terms of their levels of institutionalization. Furthermore, it will be possible to measure increases and decreases in the institutionalization of particular organizations and procedures within a political system.

139

Adaptability-Rigidity

The more adaptable an organization or procedure is, the more highly institutionalized it is; the less adaptable and more rigid it is, the lower its level of institutionalization. Adaptability is an acquired organizational characteristic. It is, in a rough sense, a function of environmental challenge and age. The more challenges which have arisen in its environment and the greater its age, the more adaptable it is. Rigidity is more characteristic of young organizations than of old ones. Old organizations and procedures, however, are not necessarily adaptable if they have existed in a static environment. In addition, if over a period of time an organization has developed a set of responses for dealing effectively with one type of problem, and if it is then confronted with an entirely different type of problem requiring a different response, the organization may well be a victim of its past successes and be unable to adjust to the new challenge. In general, however, the first hurdle is the biggest one. Success in adapting to one environmental challenge paves the way for successful adaptation to subsequent environmental challenges. If, for instance, the probability of successful adjustment to the first challenge is 50 percent, the probability of successful adjustment to the second challenge might be 75 percent, to the third challenge 87½ percent, to the fourth 93¾ percent, and so on. Some changes in environment, moreover, such as changes in personnel, are inevitable for all organizations. Other changes in environment may be produced by the organization itself; if, for instance, it successfully completes the task which it was originally created to accomplish. So long as it is recognized that environments can differ in the challenges which they pose to organizations, the adaptability of an organization can in a rough sense be measured by its age. Its age, in turn, can be measured in three ways.

One is simply chronological: the longer an organization or procedure has been in existence, the higher the level of institutionalization. The older an organization is, the more likely it is to continue to exist through any specified future time period. The probability that an organization which is 100 years old will survive one additional year, it might be hypothesized, is perhaps 100 times greater than the probability that an organization one year old will survive one additional year. Political institutions are thus not created overnight. Political development, in this sense, is slow, particularly when compared with the seemingly much more rapid pace of economic development. In some instances, particular types of experience may substitute for time: fierce conflict or other serious challenges may transform organizations into institutions much more rapidly than normal circumstances. But such intensive experiences are rare, and even with such experiences time is still required. "A major paty," Ashoka Mehta has observed, in commenting on why communism is helpless in India, "cannot be created in a day. In China a great party was forged by the revolution. Other major parties can be or are born of revolutions in other countries.

But it is simply impossible, through normal channels, to forge a great party, to reach and galvanize millions of men in half a million villages."[3]

A second measure of adaptability is generational age. So long as an organization still has its first set of leaders, so long as procedure is still performed by those who first performed it, its adaptability is still in doubt. The more often the organization has surmounted the problem of peaceful succession and replaced one set of leaders with another, the more highly institutionalized it is. In considerable measure, of course, generational age is a function of chronological age. But political parties and governments may continue for decades under the leadership of one generation. The founders of organizations—whether parties, governments, or business corporations—are often young. Hence the gap between chronological age and generational age is apt to be greater in the early history of an organization than later in its career. This gap produces tensions between the first leaders of the organization and the next generation immediately behind them, which can look forward to a lifetime in the shadow of the first generation. In the middle of the 1960s the Chinese Communist Party was 45 years old, but in large part it was still led by its first generation of leaders. An organization may also change leadership without changing generations of leadership. One generation differs from another in terms of its formative experiences. Simple replacement of one set of leaders by another, i.e., surmounting a succession crisis, counts for something in terms of institutional adaptability, but it is not as significant as a shift in leadership generations, i.e., the replacement of one set of leaders by another set with significantly different organizational experiences. The shift from Lenin to Stalin was an intra-generation succession; the shift from Stalin to Khrushchev was an inter-generation succession.

Thirdly, organizational adaptability can be measured in functional terms. An organization's functions, of course, can be defined in an almost infinite number of ways. (This is a major appeal and a major limitation of the functional approach to organizations.) Usually an organization is created to perform one particular function. When that function is no longer needed, the organization faces a major crisis. It either finds a new function or reconciles itself to a lingering death. An organization which has adapted itself to changes in its environment and has survived one or more changes in its principal functions is more highly institutionalized than one which has not. Not functional specificity but functional adaptability is the true measure of a highly developed organization. Institutionalization makes the organization more than simply an instrument to achieve certain purposes.[4] Instead its leaders and members come to value it for its own sake, and it develops a life of its own quite apart from the specific functions it may perform at any given time. The organization triumphs over its function.

Organizations and individuals thus differ significantly in their cumulative capacity to adapt to changes. Individuals usually grow up through childhood and adolescence without deep commitments to highly specific functions. The process of commitment begins in late adolescence. As the individual becomes more and more committed to the performance of certain functions, he finds it increasingly difficult to change those functions and to unlearn the responses which he has acquired to meet environmental changes. His personality has been formed; he has become "set in his ways." Organizations, on the other hand, are usually created to perform very specific functions. When the organization confronts a changing environment, it must, if it is to survive, weaken its commitment to its original functions. As the organization matures, it becomes "unset" in its ways.

* * *

Complexity-Simplicity

The more complicated an organization is, the more highly institutionalized it is. Complexity may involve both multiplication of organizational subunits, hierarchically and functionally, and differentiation of separate types of organizational subunits. The greater the number and variety of subunits, the greater the ability of the organization to secure and maintain the loyalties of its members. In addition, an organization which has many purposes is better able to adjust itself to the loss of any one purpose than an organization which has only one purpose. The diversified corporation is obviously less vulnerable than that which produces one product for one market. The differentiation of subunits within an organization may or may not be along functional lines. If it is functional in character, the subunits themselves are less highly institutionalized than the whole of which they are a part. Changes in the functions of the whole, however, are fairly easily reflected by changes in the power and roles of its subunits. If the subunits are multifunctional, they have greater institutional strength, but they may also, for that very reason, contribute less flexibility to the organization as a whole. Hence, a political system with parties of "social integration," in Neumann's terms, has less institutional flexibility than one with parties of "individual representation."[5]

Relatively primitive and simple traditional political systems are usually overwhelmed and destroyed in the modernization process. More complex traditional systems are more likely to adapt to these new demands. Japan, for instance, was able to adjust its traditional political institutions to the modern world because of their relative complexity. For two and a half centuries before 1868, the emperor had reigned and the Tokugawa shogun had ruled. The stability of the political order, however, did not depend solely on the stability of the shogunate. When the authority of the shogunate decayed, another traditional institution, the emperor, was available to become the instrument of the modernizing samurai. The collapse of the shogun involved not the overthrow of the political order but the "restoration" of the emperor. The simplest political system is that which depends on one individual. It is also, of course, the least stable. Tyrannies, Aristotle pointed out, are virtually all "quite short-lived."[6] A political system with several different political institutions, on the other hand, is much more likely to adapt. The needs of one age may be met by one set of instituions; the needs of the next by a different set. The system possesses within itself the means of its own renewal and adaptation. In the American system, for instance, President, Senate, House of Representatives, Supreme Court, and state governments have played different roles at different times in history. As new problems arise, the initiative in dealing with them may be taken first by one institution, then by another. In contrast, the French system of the Third and Fourth Republics centered authority in the National Assembly and the national bureaucracy. If, as was frequently the case, the Assembly was too divided to act and the bureaucracy lacked the authority to act, the system was unable to adapt to environmental changes and to deal with new policy problems. When in the 1950s the Assembly was unable to handle the dissolution of the French Empire, there was no other institution, such as an independent executive, to step into the breach. As a result, an extraconstitutional force, the military, intervened in politics, and in due course a new institution, the de Gaulle Presidency, was created which was able to handle the problem. "A state without the means of some change," Burke observed of an earlier French crisis, "is without the means of its conservation."[7]

* * *

Autonomy-Subordination

A third measure of institutionalization is the extent to which political organizations and procedures exist independently of other social groupings and methods of behavior. How well is the political sphere differentiated from other spheres? In a highly devloped political system, political organizations have an integrity which they lack in less developed systems. In some measure, they are insulated from the impact of nonpolitical groups and procedures. In less developed political systems, they are highly vulnerable to outside influences.

At its most concrete level, autonomy involves the relations between social forces, on the one hand, and political organizations, on the other. Social forces include the groupings of men for social and economic activities: families, clans, work groups, churches, ethnic and linguistic groupings. Political institutionalization, in the sense of autonomy, means the development of political organizations and procedures which are not simply expressions of the interests of particular social groups. A political organization which is the instrument of a social group—family, clan, 143 class—lacks autonomy and institutionalization. If the state, in the traditional Marxist claim, is really the "executive committee of the bourgeoisie," then it is not much of an institution. A judiciary is independent to the extent that it adheres to distinctly judicial norms and to the extent that its perspectives and behavior are independent of those of other political institutions and social groupings. As with the judiciary, the autonomy of political institutions is measured by the extent to which they have their own interests and values distinguishable from those of other social forces. As with the judiciary, the autonomy of political institutions is likely to be the result of competition among social forces. A political party, for instance, which expresses the interests of only one group in society—whether labor, business, or farmers—is less autonomous than one which articulates and aggregates the interests of several social groups. The latter type of party has a clearly defined existence apart from particular social forces. So also with legislatures, executives, and bureaucracies. Political procedures, like political organizations, also have varying degrees of autonomy. A highly developed political system has procedures to minimize, if not to eliminate, the role of violence in the system and to restrict to explicitly defined channels the influence of wealth in the system. To the extent that political officials can be toppled by a few soldiers or influenced by a few dollars, the organizations and procedures lack autonomy. Political organizations and procedures which lack autonomy are, in common parlance, said to be corrupt.

Political organizations and procedures which are vulnerable to nonpolitical influences from within the society are also usually vulnerable to influences from outside the society. They are easily penetrated by agents, groups, and ideas from other political systems. Thus, a *coup d'état* in one political system may easily "trigger" a *coup d'état* by similar groups in other less-developed political systems.[8] In some instances, apparently, a regime can be overthrown by smuggling into the country a few agents and a handful of weapons. In other instances, a regime may be overthrown by the exchange of a few words and a few thousand dollars between a foreign ambassador and some disaffected colonels. The Soviet and American governments presumably spend substantial sums attempting to bribe high officials of less well-insulated political systems which they would not think of wasting in attempting to influence high officials in each other's political system.

In every society affected by social change, new groups arise to participate in politics. Where the political system lacks autonomy, these groups gain entry into politics without becoming identified with the established political organizations or acquiescing in the established political procedures. The political organizations and procedures are unable to stand up against the impact of a new social force. Conversely, in a developed political system, the autonomy of the system is protected by mechanisms which restrict and moderate the impact of new groups. These mechanisms either slow down the entry of new groups into politics or, through a process of political socialization, impel changes in the attitudes and behavior of the most politically active members of the new group. In a highly institutionalized political system, the most important positions of leadership can normally be achieved only by those who have served an apprenticeship in less important positions. The complexity of a political system contributes to its autonomy by providing a variety of organizations and positions in which individuals are prepared for the highest offices. In a sense, the top positions of leadership are the inner core of the political system; the less powerful positions, the peripheral organizations, and the semipolitical organizations are the filters through which individuals desiring access to the core must pass. Thus the political system assimilates new social forces and new personnel without sacrificing its institutional integrity. In a political system which lacks such defenses, new men, new viewpoints, new social groups may replace each other at the core of the system with bewildering rapidity.

Coherence-Disunity

The more unified and coherent an organization is, the more highly institutionalized it is; the greater the disunity of the organization, the less its institutionalization. Some measure of consensus, of course, is a prerequisite for any social group. An effective organization requires, at a minimum, substantial consensus on the functional boundaries of the group and on the procedures for resolving disputes on issues which come up within those boundaries. The consensus must extend to those active in the system. Nonparticipants or those only sporadically and marginally participant in the system do not have to share the consensus and usually, in fact, do not share it to the same extent as the participants.[9] In theory, an organization can be autonomous without being coherent and coherent without being autonomous. In actuality, however, the two are often closely linked together. Autonomy becomes a means to coherence, enabling the organization to develop an esprit and style which become distinctive marks of its behavior. Autonomy also prevents the intrusion of disruptive external forces, although, of course, it does not protect against disruption from internal sources. Rapid or substantial expansions in the membership of an organization or in the participants in a system tend to weaken coherence. The Ottoman Ruling Institution, for instance, retained its vitality and coherence as long as admission was restricted and recruits were "put through an elaborate education, with selection and specialization at every stage." The Institution perished when "everybody pressed in to share its privileges. . . . Numbers were increased; discipline and efficiency declined."[10]

Unity, esprit, morale, and discipline are needed in governments as well as in regiments. Numbers, weapons, and strategy all count in war, but major deficiencies in any one of those may still be counterbalanced by superior coherence and discipline. So also in politics. The problems of creating coherent political organizations are more difficult but not fundamentally different from those involved in the creation of coherent military organizations. "The sustaining sentiment of a military force," David Rapoport has argued, "has much in common with that which cements any group of men engaged in politics—the willingness of most individuals to bridle private or personal impulses for the sake of general social objectives. Comrades must trust each other's ability to resist the innumerable temptations that threaten the group's solidarity; otherwise, in trying social situations the desire to fend for oneself becomes overwhelming."[11] The capacities for coordination and discipline are crucial to both war and politics, and historically societies which have been skilled at organizing the one have also been adept at organizing the other. "The relationship of efficient social organization in the arts of peace and in the arts of group conflict," one anthropologist has observed,

> is almost absolute, whether one is speaking of civilization or sub-civilization. Successful war depends upon team work and consensus, both of which require command and discipline. Command and discipline, furthermore, can eventually be no more than symbols of something deeper and more real than they themselves.[12]

Societies, such as Sparta, Rome, and Britain, which have been admired by their contemporaries for the authority and justice of their laws have also been admired for the coherence and discipline of their armies. Discipline and development go hand in hand.

* * *

Experience tells us that levels of institutionalization differ. Measuring that difference may be difficult, but it is not impossible. Only by measuring institutionalization will we be able to buttress or disprove hypotheses about the relation between social, economic, and demographic changes, on the one hand, and variations in political structure, on the other.

MOBILIZATION VS. INSTITUTIONALIZATION: PUBLIC INTERESTS, DEGENERATION, AND THE CORRUPT POLITY

Mobilization and Institutionalization

Social mobilization and political participation are rapidly increasing in Asia, Africa, and Latin America. These processes, in turn, are directly responsible for the deterioration of political institutions in these areas. As Kornhauser has conclusively demonstrated for the Western world, rapid industrialization and urbanization create discontinuities which give rise to mass society. "The *rapid* influx of large numbers of people into *newly* developing urban areas invites mass movements."[13] In areas and industries with very rapid industrial growth, the creation and institutionalization of unions lag, and mass movements are likely among the workers. As unions are organized, they are highly vulnerable to outside influences in their early stages. "The rapid influx of large numbers of people into a new organization (as well as a new area) provides opportunities for mass-oriented elites to penetrate the organization. This is particularly true during the formative periods of organizations, for at such times external constraints must carry the burden of social control until the new participants have come to internalize the values of the organization."[14]

So also in politics. Rapid economic growth breeds political instability.[15] Political mobilization, moreover, does not necessarily require the building of factories or even movement to the cities. It may result simply from increases in communications, which can stimulate major increases in aspirations that may be only partially, if at all, satisfied. The result is a "revolution of rising frustrations."[16] Increases in literacy and education may bring more political instability. By Asian standards, Burma, Ceylon, and the Republic of Korea are all highly literate, but no one of them is a model of political stability. Nor does literacy necessarily stimulate democracy: with roughly 75 percent literacy, Cuba was the fifth most literate country in Latin America (ranking behind Argentina, Uruguay, Chile, and Costa Rica), but the first to go Communist; so also Kerala, with one of the highest literacy rates in India, was the first Indian state to elect a Communist government.[17] Literacy, as Daniel Lerner has suggested, "may be dysfunctional—indeed a serious impediment—to modernization in the societies now seeking (all too rapidly) to transform their institutions."[18]

Increased communication may thus generate demands for more "modernity" than can be delivered. It may also stimulate a reaction against modernity and activate traditional forces. Since the political arena is normally dominated by the more modern groups, it can bring into the arena new, antimodern groups and break whatever consensus exists among the leading political participants. It may also mobilize minority ethnic groups who had been indifferent to politics but who now acquire a self-consciousness and divide the political system along ethnic lines. Nationalism, it has often been assumed, makes for national integration. But in actuality, nationalism and other forms of ethnic consciousness often stimulate political disintegration, tearing apart the body politic.

Sharp increases in voting and other forms of political participation can also have deleterious effects on political institutions. In Latin America since the 1930s, increases in voting and increases in political instability have gone hand in hand.

> Age requirements were lowered, property and literacy requirements were reduced or discarded, and the unscrubbed, unschooled millions on the farms were enfranchised in the name of democracy. They were

147

swept into the political life of the republics so rapidly that existing parties could not absorb many of them, and they learned little about working within the existing political system.[19]

The personal identity crises of the elites, caught between traditional and modern cultures, may create additional problems: "In transitional countries the political process often has to bear to an inordinate degree the stresses and strains of people responding to personal needs and seeking solutions to intensely personal problems."[20] Rapid social and economic change calls into question existing values and behavior patterns. It thus often breeds personal corruption. In some circumstances this corruption may play a positive role in the modernizing process, enabling dynamic new groups to get things done which would have been blocked by the existing value system and social structure. At the same time, however, corruption undermines the autonomy and coherence of political institutions. It is hardly accidental that in the 1870s and 1880s a high rate of American economic development coincided with a low point in American governmental integrity.[21]

Institutional decay has become a common phenomenon of the modernizing countries. Coups d'état and military interventions in politics are one index of low levels of political institutionalization: they occur where political institutions lack autonomy and coherence.

***

The differences which may exist in mobilization and institutionalization suggest four ideal-types of politics (see Table 1). Modern, developed, civic polities (the United States, the Soviet Union) have high levels of both mobilization and institutionalization. Primitive polities (such as Banfield's backward society) have low levels of both. Contained polities are highly institutionalized but have low levels of mobilization and participation. The dominat political institutions of contained polities may be either traditional (e.g., monarchies) or modern (e.g., political parties). If they are the former, such polities may well confront great difficulties in adjusting to rising levels of social mobilization. The traditional institutions may wither or collapse, and the result would be a corrupt polity with a high rate of participation but a low level of institutionalization. In the corrupt society, politics is, in Macaulay's phrase, "all sail and no anchor."[22] This type of polity characterizes much, if not most, of the modernizing world. Many of the more advanced Latin American countries, for instance, have achieved comparatively high indices of literacy, per capita national income, and urbanization. But their politics remains notably underdeveloped. Distrust and hatred have produced a continuing low level of political institutionalization. "There is no good faith in America, either among men or among nations," Bolivar once lamented. "Treaties are paper, constitutions books, elections battles, liberty anarchy, and life a torment. The only thing one can do in America is emigrate."[23] Over a century later, the same complaint was heard: "We are not, or do not represent a respectable nation . . . not because we are poor, but because we are disorganized," argued an Ecuadorian newspaper. "With a politics of ambush and of permanent mistrust, one for the other, we . . . cannot properly organize a republic . . . and without organization we cannot merit or attain respect from other nations."[24] So long as a country like Argentina retains a politics of coup and counter-coup and a feeble state surrounded by massive social forces, it cannot be considered politically developed, no matter how urbane and prosperous and educated are its citizens.

TABLE 1. TYPES OF POLITICAL SYSTEMS

Social Mobilization	Political Institutionalization	
	High	Low
High	Civic	Corrupt
Low	Contained	Primitive

In reverse fashion, a country may be politically highly developed, with modern political institutions, while still very backward in terms of modernization. India, for instance, is typically held to be the epitome of the underdeveloped society. Judged by the usual criteria of modernization, it was at the bottom of the ladder during the 1950s: per capita GNP of $72, 80 percent illiterate, over 80 percent of the population in rural areas, 70 percent of the work force in agriculture, a dozen major languages, deep caste and religious differences. Yet in terms of political institutionaliz-ation, India was far from backward. Indeed, it ranked high not only in comparison with other modernizing countries in Asia, Africa, and Latin America, but also in comparison with many much more modern European countries. A well-developed political system has strong and distinct institutions to perform both the "input" and the "output" functions of politics. India entered independence with not only two organizations, but two highly developed—adaptable, complex, autonomous, and coherent—institutions ready to assume primary responsibility for these functions. The Congress Party, founded in 1885, was one of the oldest and best-organized political parties in the world; the Indian Civil Service, dating from the early nineteenth century, has been appropriately hailed as "one of the greatest administrative systems of all time."[25] The stable, effective, and democratic government of India during the first 15 years of independence rested far more on this institutional inheritance than it did on the charisma of Nehru. In addition, the relatively slow pace of modernization and social mobilization in India did not create demands and strains which the Party and the bureaucracy were unable to handle. So long as these two organizations maintain their institutional strength, it is ridiculous to think of India as politically underdeveloped, no matter how low her per capita income or how high her illiteracy rate.

Almost no other country which became independent after World War II

149

was institutionally as well prepared as India for self-government. In countries like Pakistan and the Sudan, institutional evolution was unbalanced; the civil and military bureaucracies were more highly developed than the political parties, and the military had strong incentives to move into the institutional vacuum on the input side of the political system and to attempt to perform interest aggregation functions. This pattern, of course, has also been common in Latin America. In countries like Guatemala, El Salvador, Peru, and Argentina, John J. Johnson has pointed out, the military is "the country's best organized institution and is thus in a better position to give objective expression to the national will" than are parties or interest groups.[26] In a very different category is a country like North Vietnam, which fought its way into independence with a highly disciplined political organization but which was distinctly weak on the administrative side. The Latin American parallel here would be Mexico, where, as Johnson puts it, "not the armed forces but the PRI is the best organized institution, and the party rather than the armed forces has been the unifying force at the national level." In yet a fourth category are those unfortunate states, such as the Congo, which were born with neither political nor administrative institutions. Many of these new states deficient at independence in one or both types of institutions have also been confronted by high rates of social mobilization and rapidly increasing demands on the political system.

* * *

STRATEGIES OF
INSTITUTIONAL DEVELOPMENT

If decay of political institutions is a widespread phenomenon in the "developing" countries and if a major cause of this decay is the high rate of social mobilization, it behooves us, as social scientists, to call a spade a spade and to incorporate these tendencies into any general model of political change which we employ to understand the politics of these areas. If effective political institutions are necessary for stable and eventually democratic government and if they are also a precondition of sustained economic growth, it behooves us, as policy analysts, to suggest strategies of institutional development. In doing this, we should recognize two general considerations affecting probabilities of success in institution-building.

First, the psychological and cultural characteristics of peoples differ markedly and with them their abilities at developing political institutions. Where age-old patterns of thought and behavior have to be changed, quite obviously the creation of political institutions is a far more difficult task than otherwise. "The Tokugawa Japanese could not, as did the Chinese, put family above government," one expert has observed. "The samurai was expected to be loyal to his official superior first, his family second. In mores generally the primacy of the organization over the person was constantly reiterated."[27] This difference in Japanese and Chinese attitudes toward authority undoubtedly accounts in part for their differences in modernization and development. The Japanese peacefully and smoothly created new political institutions and amalgamated them with old ones. The weakness of traditional Chinese political institutions, on the other hand, led to 40 years of revolution and civil war before modern political institutions could be developed and extended throughout Chinese society.

Second, the potentialities for institution-building differ markedly from society to society, but in all societies political organizations can be built. Institutions result from the slow interaction of conscious effort and existing culture. Organizations, however, are the product of conscious, purposeful effort. The forms of this effort may vary from a Meiji Restoration to a Communist Revolution. But in each case a distinct group of identifiable people set about adapting old organizations or building new ones. "Nation-building" has recently become a popular subject, and doubts have been raised about whether nations can be "built."[28] These doubts have a fairly solid basis. Nations are one type of social force, and historically they have emerged over long periods of time. Organization-building, however, differs from nation-building. Political organizations require time for development, but they do not require as much time as national communities. Indeed, most of those who speak of nation-building in such places as tropical Africa see organization-building as the first step in this process. Political parties have to be welded out of tribal groups; the parties create governments; and the governments may, eventually, bring into existence nations. Many of the doubts which people have about the possibilities of nation-building do not apply to organization-building.

Given our hypotheses about the relation of social mobilization to institutionalization, there are two obvious methods of furthering institutional development. First, anything which slows social mobilization presumably creates conditions more favorable to the preservation and strengthening of institutions. Secondly, strategies can be developed and applied directly to the problem of institution-building.

Slowing Mobilization

Social mobilization can be moderated in many ways. Three methods are: to increase the complexity of social structure; to limit or reduce communications in society; and to minimize competition among segments of the political elite.[29]

In general, the more highly stratified a society is and the more complicated its social structure, the more gradual is the process of political mobilization. The divisions between class and class, occupation and occupation, rural and urban, constitute a series of breakwaters which divide the society and permit the political mobilization of one group at a time. On the other hand, a highly homogeneous society, or a society which has only a single horizontal line of division between an oligarchy that has everything and a peasantry that has nothing, or a society which is divided not horizontally but vertically into ethnic and communal groups, has more difficulty moderating the process of mobilization. Thus, mobilization should be slower in India than in the new African states where horizontal divisions are weak and tribal divisions strong, or in those Latin American countries where the middle strata are weak and a small oligarchy confronts a peasant mass. A society with many horizontal divisions gains through the slower entry of social groups into politics. It may, however, also lose something in that political organizations, when they do develop, may form along class and stratum lines and thus lack the autonomy of more broadly based political organizations. Political parties in countries like Chile and Sweden have been largely the spokesmen for distinct classes; caste associations seem destined to play a significant role in Indian politics. The disruptive effects of political organizations identified with social strata may be reduced if other political institutions exist which appeal to loyalties across class or caste lines. In Sweden, loyalty to the monarchy and the Riksdag mitigates the effects of class-based parties, and in India the caste associations must, in general, seek their goals within the much more extensive framework of the Congress Party. In most societies, the social structure must be largely accepted as given. Where it is subject to governmental manipulation and influence, mobilization will be slowed by government policies which enhance the complexity of social stratification.

The communications network of a society is undoubtedly much more subject to governmental influence. Rapid gains in some of the most desired areas of modernization—such as mass media exposure, literacy, and education—may have to be purchased at the price of severe losses in political stability. This is not to argue that political institutionalization as a value should take precedence over all others: if this were the case, modernization would never be good. It is simply to argue that governments must balance the values won through rapid increases in communications against the values jeopardized by losses in political stability. Thus, governmental policies may be wisely directed to reducing the number of university graduates, particularly those with skills which are not in demand in the society. Students and unemployed university graduates have been a concern common to the nationalistic military regime in South Korea, the socialist military regime in Burma, and the traditional military regime in Thailand. The efforts by General Ne Win in Burma to cut back the number of univeristy graduates may well be imitated by other governments facing similar challenges. Much has been made of the problems caused by the extension of the suffrage to large numbers of illiterates. But limited political participation by illiterates may well, as in India, be less dangerous to political institutions than participation by literates. The latter typically have higher aspirations and make more demands on government. Political participation by illiterates, moreover, is more likely to remain limited, whereas participation by literates is much more likely to snowball with potentially disastrous effects on political stability. A governing elite may also affect the intensity of communications and the rate of political mobilization by its policies on economic development. Large, isolated factories, as Kornhauser has shown, are more likely to give rise to extremist movements than smaller plants more closely integrated into the surrounding community.[30] Self-interest in political survival may lead governing elites to decrease the priority of rapid economic change.

The uncontrolled mobilization of people into politics is also slowed by minimizing the competition among political elites. Hence mobilization is likely to have less disturbing effects on political institutions in one-party systems than in two-party or multiparty systems. In many new states and modernizing countries, a vast gap exists between the modernized elite and the tradition-oriented mass. If the elite divides against itself, its factions appeal to the masses for support. This produces rapid mobilization of the masses into politics at the same time that it destroys whatever consensus previously existed among the politically active on the need for modernization. Mobilization frequently means the mobilization of tradition; modern politics become the vehicle of traditional purposes. In Burma during the first part of this century, the "general pattern was one in which the modernizers first fell out among themselves whenever they were confronted with demanding choices of policy, and then tended to seek support from among the more traditional elements, which in time gained the ascendency."[31] In Turkey a rough balance between the mobilization of people into politics and the development of political institutions existed so long as the Republican People's Party retained a political monopoly. The conscious decision to permit an opposition party, however, broadened the scope of political competition beyond the urban, Westernized elite. The Democratic Party mobilized the peasants into politics, strengthened the forces of traditionalism, and broke the previous consensus. This led the party leaders to attempt to maintain themselves in power through semilegal means and to induce the army to join them in suppressing the Republican opposition. The army, however, was committed to modernization and seized power in a *coup d'état*, dissolving the Democratic Party and executing many of its top leaders. In due course, the military withdrew from direct conduct of the government, and democratic elections led to a multiparty system in which no party has a clear majority. Thus from a relatively stable one-party system, Turkey passed through a brief two-party era to military rule and a multiparty system: the familiar syndrome of states where mobilization has outrun institutionalization. In the process, not only were political institutions weakened, but the traditional-minded were brought into politics in such a way as to create obstacles to the achievement of many modernizing goals.

153

Creating Institutions

"Dans la naissance des sociétés ce sont les chefs des républiques qui font l'institution; et c'est ensuite l'institution qui forme les chefs des républiques," said Montesquieu.[32] But in the contemporary world, political leaders prefer modernization to institution-building, and no matter who leads modernization, the process itself generates conflicting demands and inducements which obstruct the growth of political institutions. Where modernization is undertaken by traditional leaders working through traditional political institutions, the efforts of the traditional leaders to reform can unleash and stimulate social forces which threaten the traditional political institutions. Traditional leaders can modernize and reform their realms, but, where substantial social elements oppose reform, they have yet to demonstrate they can put through reforms without undermining the institutions through which they are working. The problem is: how can the traditional political institutions be adapted to accommodate the social forces unleashed by modernization? Historically, except for Japan, traditional political institutions have been adapted to the modern world only where a high degree of political centralization was not required for modernization and where traditional (i.e., feudal) representative institutions retained their vitality (as in Great Britain and Sweden). If modernization requires the centralization of power in a "reform monarch" or "revolutionary emperor," it means the weakening or destruction of whatever traditional representative institutions may exist and thus complicates still further the assimilation of those social forces created by modernization. The concentration of power also makes the traditional regime (like the eighteenth-century French monarchy) more vulnerable to forcible overthrow. *The vulnerability of a traditional regime to revolution varies directly with the capability of the regime for modernization.* For traditional rulers, the imperatives of modernization conflict with the imperatives of institution-building.

If the traditional political institutions are weak, or if they have been displaced and suppressed during periods of colonial rule, adaptation is impossible. In societies which have undergone colonial rule, incubation can serve as a substitute for adaptation. Unfortunately, the opportunity for incubation was missed in most colonial societies, with a few prominent exceptions such as India and the Philippines. Incubation requires a colonial administration which is willing to permit and *to contend with* a nationalist movement for many years, thus furnishing the time, the struggle, and the slowly increasing responsibility which are the ingredients of institution-building. In general, however, colonial powers tend to postpone incubation for as long as possible and then, when they see independence as inevitable, to bring it about as quickly as possible. Consequently, most of the states which became independent in the 1950s and 1960s had little opportunity to incubate political institutions while still under colonial tutelage.

Where traditional political institutions are weak, or collapse, or are overthrown, authority frequently comes to rest with charismatic leaders who attempt to bridge the gap between tradition and modernity by a highly personal appeal. To the extent that these leaders are able to concentrate power in themselves, it might be supposed that they would be in a position to push institutional development and to perform the role of "Great Legislator" or "Founding Father." The reform of corrupt states or the creation of new ones, Machiavelli argued, must be the work of one man alone. A conflict exists, however, between the interests of the individual and the interests of institutionalization. Institutionalization of power means the limitation of power which might otherwise be wielded personally and arbitrarily. The would-be institution-builder needs personal power to create institutions but he cannot create institutions without relinquishing personal power. Resolving this dilemma is not easy. It can be done only by leaders who combine rare political skill and rare devotion to purpose. It was done by Mustafa Kemal who, for almost two decades, managed to maintain his own personal power, to push through major modernizing reforms, and to create a political institution to carry on the government after his death. Atatürk has been a conscious model for many contemporary modernizing leaders, but few, if any, seem likely to duplicate his achievement.

The military junta or military dictatorship is another type of regime common in modernizing countries. It too confronts a distinct set of problems in the conflict between its own impulses to modernization and the needs of institution-building. The military officers who seize power in a modernizing country frequently do so in reaction to the "chaos," "stalemate," "corruption," and "reactionary" character of the civilian regimes which preceded them. The officers are usually passionately devoted to measures of social reform, particularly those which benefit the peasantry (whose interests have frequently been overlooked by the anterior civilian regime). A rationalistic approach to societal problems often makes the officers modernizers par excellence. At the same time, however, they are frequently indifferent or hostile to the needs of political institution-building. The military typically assert that they have taken over the government only temporarily until conditions can be "cleaned up" and authority restored to a purified civilian regime. The officers thus confront an organizational dilemma. They can eliminate or exclude from politics individual civilian politicians, but they are ill-prepared to make fundamental changes in political processes and institutions. If they turn back power to the civilians, the same conditions to which they originally objected tend to reappear (Burma). If they attempt to restore civilian government and to continue in power as a civilian political group (Turkey, South Korea), they open themselves to these same corrupting influences and may pave the way for a second military takeover by a younger generation of colonels who purge the civilianized generals, just as the generals had earlier purged the civilians. Finally, if the military leaders retain power indefinitely, they need to create authoritative political

155

organizations which legitimize and institutionalize their power. Concern with their own personal authority and unfamiliarity with the needs of political institution-building create problems in the fulfillment of this task. It is still too early to say for certain what sort of authoritative political institutions, if any, will be produced by regimes led by military officers such as Nasser and Ayub Khan.

The Primacy of Party

Charismatic leaders and military chiefs have thus had little success in building modern political institutions. The reason lies in the nature of modern politics. In the absence of traditional political institutions, the only modern organization which can become a source of authority and which can be effectively institutionalized is the political party. *The importance of the political party in providing legitimacy and stability in a modernizing political system varies inversely with the institutional inheritance of the system from traditional society.* Traditional systems do not have political parties. Unlike bureaucracy, the party is a distinctly modern form of political organization. Where traditional political institutions (such as monarchies and feudal parliaments) are carried over into the modern era, parties play secondary, supplementary roles in the political system. The other institutions are the primary source of continuity and legitimacy. Parties typically originate within the legislatures and then gradually extend themselves into society. They adapt themselves to the existing framework of the political system and typically reflect in their own operations the organizational and procedural principles embodied in that system. They broaden participation in the traditional institutions, thus adapting those institutions to the requirements of the modern polity. They help make the traditional institutions legitimate in terms of popular sovereignty, but they are not themselves a source of legitimacy. Their own legitimacy derives from the contributions they make to the political system.

Where traditional political institutions collapse or are weak or nonexistent, the role of the party is entirely different from what it is in those polities with institutional continuity. In such situations, strong party organization is the only long-run alternative to the instability of a corrupt or praetorian or mass society. The party is not just a supplementary organization; it is instead the source of legitimacy and authority. In the absence of traditional sources of legitimacy, legitimacy is sought in ideology, charisma, popular sovereignty. To be lasting, each of these principles of legitimacy must be embodied in a party. Instead of the party reflecting the state, the state becomes the creation of the party and the instrument of the party. The actions of government are legitimate to the extent that they reflect the will of the party. The party is the source of legitimacy because it is the institutional embodiment of national sovereignity, the popular will, or the dictatorship of the proletariat.

Where traditional political institutions are weak or nonexistent, the prerequisite of stability is at least one highly institutionalized political party. States with one such party are markedly more stable than states which lack such a party. States with no parties or many weak parties are the least stable. Where traditional political institutions are smashed by revolution, post-revolutionary order depends on the emergence of one strong party: witness the otherwise very different histories of the Chinese, Mexican, Russian, and Turkish revolutions. Where new states emerge from colonialism with one strong party, the problem is to maintain the strength of that party. In many African countries the nationalist party was the single important modern organization to exist before independence. The party

> was generally well organized. The conditions of the political struggle and the dedication of the top elite to the party as the prime instrument of political change led the elite to give the major portion of their energies and resources to building a solid, responsive organization capable of disciplined action in response to directives from the top and able to ferret out and exploit feelings of dissatisfaction among the masses for political ends.[33]

weakened by the many competing demands on organizational resources. A marked dispersion of resources means a decline in the overall level of political institutionalization. "Talents that once were available for the crucial work of party organization," one observer has warned, "may now be preoccupied with running a ministry or government bureau. . . . Unless new sources of loyal organizational and administrative talents can be found immediately, the party's organization—and, therefore, the major link between the regime and the masses—is likely to be weakened."[34]

The need for concentration applies not only to the allocation of resources among types of organizations but also to the scope of organization. In many modernizing countries, the political leaders attempt too much too fast; they try to build mass organizations when they should concentrate on elite organizations. Organizations do not have to be large to be effective and to play a crucial role in the political process: the Bolshevik Party in 1917 is one example; the Indian Civil Service (which numbered only 1,157 men at independence) is another. Overextension of one's resources in organization-building is as dangerous as overextension of one's troops in a military campaign. (The strategic hamlet program in South Vietnam is an example of both.) Concentration is a key principle of politics as well as strategy.

* * *

American social scientists have devoted much attention to the competitiveness of political systems, devising various ways of measuring that competitiveness and classifying systems according to their degree of competitiveness.[35] The more parties which exist within a system,

157

presumably the more competitive it is. Yet the proliferation of parties usually means the dispersion of organization and leadership talents and the existence of a large number of weak parties. If sufficient resources are available to support more than one well-organized party, this is all to the good. But most modernizing countries will be well off if they can create just one strong party organization. *In modernizing systems, party institutionalization usually varies inversely with party competitiveness.* Modernizing states with multiparty systems are much more unstable and prone to military intervention than modernizing states with one party, with one dominant party, or with two parties. The most unstable systems and those most prone to military intervention are the multiparty systems and the no-party systems. The weak institutionalization of parties in the multiparty system makes that system extremely fragile. The step from many parties to no parties and from no parties to many parties is an easy one. In their institutional weakness, the no-party system and the multiparty system closely resemble each other.

* * *

TABLE 2. DISTRIBUTION OF COUPS AND COUP ATTEMPTS
IN MODERNIZING COUNTRIES SINCE INDEPENDENCE

Type of Political System	Number of Countries	Countries with Coups	
		Number	Percent
Communist	3	0	0
One-party	18	2	11
One-party dominant	12	3	25
Two-party	11	5	45
Multiparty	22	15	68
No effective parties	17	14	83

SOURCE: Figures are somewhat revised and adapted from the similar table in Fred R. von der Mehden, *Politics of the Developing Nations* (Englewood Cliffs, N.J., 1964), p. 65.

NOTES

1. Alexis de Tocqueville, *Democracy in America,* ed. Phillips Bradley (New York, 1955), pp. 11, 118.

2. The concept of institutionalization has, of course, been used by other writers concerned with political development—most notably, S. N. Eisenstadt. His definition, however, differs significantly from my approach here. See, in particular, his "Initial Institutional Patterns of Political Modernization," *Civilisations* 12, no. 4 (1962): 461-72, and 13, no. 1 (1963): 15-26; "Institutionalization and Change," *American Sociological Review* 29 (April 1964): 235-47; "Social Change.

Differentiation and Evolution," *ibid.* 29 (June 1964): 375-86.

3. Ashoka Mehta, in *World Technology and Human Destiny*, ed. Raymond Aron (Ann Arbor, 1963), p. 133.

4. See the very useful discussion in Philip Selznick's small classic, *Leadership in Administration* (New York, 1957), pp. 5ff.

5. Sigmund Neumann, "Toward a Comparative Study of Political Parties," in *Modern Political Parties*, ed. Sigmund Neumann (Chicago, 1956), pp. 403-5.

6. *Politics*, trans. Ernest Barker (London, 1946), p. 254.

7. Edmund Burke, *Reflections on the Revolution in France* (Chicago, 1955), p. 37.

8. See Samuel P. Huntington, "Patterns of Violence in World Politics," in *Changing Patterns of Military Politics*, ed. Samuel P. Huntington (New York, 1962), pp. 44-47.

9. See, e.g., Herbert McCloskey, "Consensus and Ideology in American Politics," *American Political Science Review* 18 (June 1964): 361ff.; Samuel Stouffer, *Communism, Conformity, and Civil Liberties* (New York, 1955), *passim.*

10. Arnold J. Toynbee, *A Study of History*, Abridgement of Vols. I-VI, ed. D. C. Somervell (New York, 1947), pp. 176-77.

11. David C. Rapoport, "A Comparative Theory of Military and Political Types," in *Changing Patterns of Military Politics*, ed. Huntington, p. 79.

12. Harry Holbert Turney-High, *Primitive War* (Columbia, S.C., 1949), pp. 235-36.

13. William Kornhauser, *The Politics of Mass Society* (Glencoe, 1959), p. 145.

14. *Ibid.*, p. 146.

15. See Mancur Olson, Jr., "Rapid Growth as a Destabilizing Force," *Journal of Economic History* 27 (December 1963): 529-52; and Bert F. Hoselitz and Myron Weiner, "Economic Development and Political Stability in India," *Dissent* 8 (Spring 1961): 172-79.

16. See Daniel Lerner, "Toward a Communication Theory of Modernization," in *Communications and Political Development*, ed. Lucian W. Pye (Princeton, 1963), pp. 330ff.

17. Cf. Karl W. Deutsch, "Social Mobilization and Political Development," *American Political Science Review* 55 (September 1961): 496.

18. Daniel Lerner, "The Transformation of Institutions," mimeographed, p. 19.

19. John J. Johnson, *The Military and Society in Latin America* (Stanford, 1964), pp. 98-99.

20. Lucian W. Pye, *Politics, Personality and Nation Building* (New Haven, 1962), pp. 4-5.

21. See, in general, Ronald E. Wraith and Edgar Simpkins, *Corruption in Developing Countries* (London, 1963).

159

22. Thomas B. Macaulay, letter to Henry S. Randall, Courtlandt Village, New York, 23 May 1857, printed in "What Did Macaulay Say About America?" *Bulletin of the New York Public Library* 29 (July 1925): 477-79.

23. Simon Bolivar, quoted in *Expectant Peoples: Nationalism and Development*, ed. K. H. Silvert (New York, 1963), p. 347.

24. *El Dia*, Quito, November 27, 1943, quoted in *The Making of the Good Neighbor Policy*, Bryce Wood (New York, 1961), p. 318.

25. Ralph Braibanti, "Public Bureaucracy and Judiciary in Pakistan," in *Bureaucracy and Political Development* ed. Joseph LaPalombara (Princeton, 1963), p. 373.

26. Johnson, *Military and Society*, p. 143.

27. John Whitney Hall, "The Nature of Traditional Society: Japan," in *Political Modernization in Japan and Turkey*, ed. Robert E. Ward and Dankwart A. Rustow (Princeton, 1964), p. 19.

28. See Karl W. Deutsch and William J. Foltz, eds., *Nation-Building* (New York, 1963), *passim*, but especially the contributions of Joseph R Strayer and Carl J. Friedrich.

29. These are not, of course, the only ways of slowing mobilization. Myron Weiner, for instance, has suggested that one practical method is "localization": channeling political interests and activity away from the great issues of national politics to the more immediate and concrete problems of the village and community. This is certainly one motive behind both community development programs and "basic democracies."

30. Kornhauser, *Politics of Mass Society*, pp. 150-58.

31. Pye, *Politics, Personality and Nation Building*, p. 114.

32. Charles de Secondat, Baron Montesquieu, *Considérations sur les causes de la grandeur des romains et de leur décadence*, in *Oeuvres*, 1 (Paris, 1828), pp. 119-20.

33. William J. Foltz, "Building the Newest Nations: Short-Run Strategies and Long-Run Problems," in *Nation-Building*, ed. Deutsch and Foltz, p. 121.

34. *Ibid.*, pp. 123-24.

35. See James S. Coleman, in *Politics of the Developing Areas*, ed. Almond and Coleman, Conclusion; Phillips Cutright, "National Political Development: Its Measurement and Social Correlates," in *Politics and Social Life*, ed. Nelson W. Polsby, Robert A. Dentler, and Paul A. Smith (Boston, 1963), pp. 569-82; Fred R. von der Mehden, *Politics of the Developing Nations*, (Englewood Cliffs, N. J., 1964), pp. 54-64.

SUGGESTIONS FOR FURTHER READING
PART THREE: DILEMMAS OF TRADITIONAL
AND TRANSITIONAL SOCIETIES

Apter, David E. *Ghana in Transition.* New York: Atheneum Publishers, 1963.

Apter, David E. *The Gold Coast in Transition.* Princeton: Princeton University Press, 1955.

Apter, David E. *The Politics of Modernization.* Chicago: University of Chicago Press, 1965.

Barringer, Herbert R.; Blanksten, George I.; and Mack, Raymond W., eds. *Social Change in Developing Areas.* Cambridge, Mass.: Schenkman Publishing Co., 1965.

Binder, Leonard. *Iran: Political Development in a Changing Society.* Berkeley: University of California Press, 1962.

Geertz, Clifford, ed. *Old Societies and New States: The Quest for Modernity in Asia and Africa.* New York: Free Press, 1963.

Hagen, Everett. *On the Theory of Social Change.* Homewood, Ill.: Dorsey Press, 1962.

Halpern, Manfred. *The Politics of Social Change in the Middle East and North Africa.* Princeton: Princeton University Press, 1963.

Huntington, Samuel P. *Political Order in Changing Societies.* New Haven: Yale University Press, 1968.

Johnson, John J. *Political Change in Latin America: The Emergence of the Middle Sectors.* Stanford: Stanford University Press, 1958.

Lerner, Daniel. *The Passing of Traditional Society: Modernizing the Middle East.* New York: Free Press of Glencoe, 1958.

Levy, Marion J., Jr. *Modernization and the Structure of Societies.* Princeton: Princeton University Press, 1966.

Marris, Peter. *Family and Social Change in an African City.* London: Routledge & Kegan Paul, 1961.

McCord, William. *The Springtime of Freedom: The Evolution of Developing Societies.* New York: Oxford University Press, 1965.

Micaud, D. *Tunisia: The Politics of Modernization.* New York: Praeger Publishers, 1964.

Pye, Lucian W. *Aspects of Political Development.* Boston: Little, Brown and Co., 1966.

Pye, Lucian W., and Verba, Sidney, eds. *Political Culture and Political Development.* Princeton: Princeton University Press, 1965.

Rustow, Dankwart A., and Ward, Robert E., eds. *Political Modernization in Japan and Turkey.* Princeton: Princeton University Press, 1964.

Shils, Edward. *Political Development in the New States.* The Hague: Mouton, 1962.

Sinai, I. R. *The Challenge of Modernization.* London: Chatto and Windus, 1964.

161

PART FOUR
nation-building:
modernization
and
political
integration

Building a nation is a difficult and complex task. The difficulty stems from the conflict of loyalties between tribalism and nationalism. In traditional and transitional societies, particularly in rural areas, the individual is loyal to his family and tribe, and region and ethnic community, and his concept and attachment to the nation-state is very weak if it exists at all.

Political development presupposes a minimum level of national awareness and unity of beliefs and symbols. Moreover, it presupposes political participation, shared political ideologies, a general consensus, a linkage between the rulers and the ruled and the city and the country, and as Myron Weiner points out in the initial article in this chapter, the integration of citizens into a common political process.

Many Asian and African states have sought to achieve national unity or political integration by creating a one-party political system. Sidney Verba aptly states: "The development of a clear and unambiguous sense of identity is more than a facilitating factor in the creation of a nation; it may be in some sense the major constituting factor of a new nation."[1] Verba

163

defines national identity as "the beliefs of individuals and the extent to which they consider themselves members of their nation-state . . . the identification with the nation may be and often is one of the basic beliefs that serve to define an individual for himself."[2]

National integration means the creation of a sense of oneness between diverse linguistic, ethnic, and religious communities. It also means bridging the gap between rulers and ruled and city and country. The modernizing elites of many African and Asian countries face many difficult problems in unifying their societies which have often been called mosaic societies. First, the ruling elites are attempting to create a unified modern state modeled after the Western state system. In their impatience they become oblivious of the fact that unity in Western states was achieved gradually over three centuries. Second, by pressing upon their many minority groups they are more likely to provoke resistance to national integration.

In the first article, "Political Integration and Political Development," Myron Weiner analyzes the problems of integration which all nations confront in the course of their political development. The concept of "integration" may refer to establishing a national territorial unit and a national identity, establishing a central national authority over subordinate political units, linking the government with the governed, achieving a value consensus which is essential to social order, or creating the capacity of people in a society to organize for some common purpose. Weiner examines various paths which might be taken to deal with these problems. Political leaders have major strategy options and policy choices available to them which may facilitate the resolution of integration problems.

W. Howard Wriggins' analysis of Ceylon seems to reaffirm the thesis that modernization may increase tension. According to Wriggins the conflict between separate ethnic, linguistic, and religious groups impedes national unity and creates a "plural" or "mosaic" society. Equally important is the horizontal stratification which sharply divides socio-economic classes from one another. Awareness of mutual differences has increased rather than diminished since independence. Furthermore, awareness of economic competition has increased as the population has grown. Ceylonese politicians have attempted to exploit the language issue which has helped to incite riots. Wriggins concludes that a sense of Ceylonese nationhood is not yet clear.

Consolidation of ethnic communities into one nation has yet to be accomplished. A strong sense of Ceylonese identity has yet to transcend communal loyalties or the split between the Tamil and Sinhalese communities.

Political instability occurs when institutions fail to meet the demands placed upon them. Political instability in Latin America results from three interacting factors: (1) entrepreneurial deficiencies; (2) high degrees of role substitutability among politically relevant performance entities; and (3) urbanization and overpopulation. Kenneth F. Johnson discusses in some detail each of these interacting factors and concludes that popular frustration and alienation are manifested in popular support for radical and action-oriented movements which voice mistrust of government and hatred for the dominant classes. This situation prompts the armies and bureaucracies to seize power and consequently political instability moves across the continuum from latent to overt.

NOTES

1. Sidney Verba, "Comparative Political Culture," in *Political Culture and Political Development,* ed. Lucian W. Pye and Sidney Verba (Princeton: Princeton University Press, 1965), p. 530.

2. *Ibid.*, p. 529.

POLITICAL INTEGRATION
AND POLITICAL DEVELOPMENT

Myron Weiner

It is often said of the developing nations that they are "unintegrated" and that their central problem, often more pressing than that of economic development, is the achievement of "integration." The term "integration" is now widely used to cover an extraordinarily large range of political phenomena. It is the purpose of this article to analyze the various uses of this term, to show how they are related, then to suggest some of the alternative strategies pursued by governments to cope with each of these "integration" problems.

DEFINITIONS

1. Integration may refer to the process of bringing together culturally and socially discrete groups into a single territorial unit and the establishment of a national identity. When used in this sense "integration" generally presumes the existence of an ethnically plural society in which each group is characterized by its own language or other self-conscious cultural qualities, but the problem may also exist in a political system which is made up of once distinct independent political units with which people identified. National integration thus refers specifically to the problem of creating a sense of territorial nationality which overshadows— or eliminates—subordinate parochial loyalties.[1]

2. Integration is often used in the related sense to refer to the problem of establishing national central authority over subordinate political units

From Myron Weiner, "Political Integration and Political Development," *Annals of the American Academy of Political and Social Science* 358 (March 1965): 53-64. Reprinted by permission of the author and The American Academy of Political and Social Science.

or regions which may or may not coincide with distinct cultural or social groups. While the term "national integration" is concerned with the subjective feelings which individuals belonging to different social groups or historically distinct political units have toward the nation, "territorial integration" refers to the objective control which central authority has over the entire territory under its claimed jurisdiction.[2]

3. The term "integration" is often used to refer to the problem of linking government with the governed. Implied in this usage is the familiar notion of a "gap" between the elite and the mass, characterized by marked differences in aspirations and values.[3] The "gap" may be widest in a society with a passive population and modernizing elite, but a relatively stable if frustrating relationship may exist. More often the masses are beginning to become organized and concerned with exercising influence, while the elite responds with attempts to coerce, persuade, or control the masses. It is under these conditions of conflict and often internal war that we customarily speak of "disintegration."

4. Integration is sometimes used to refer to the minimum value consensus necessary to maintain a social order. These may be end values concerning justice and equity, the desirability of economic development as a goal, the sharing of a common history, heroes, and symbols, and, in general, an agreement as to what constitutes desirable and undesirable social ends. Or the values may center on means, that is, on the instrumentalities and procedures for the achievement of goals and for resolving conflicts. Here the concern is with legal norms, with the legitimacy of the constitutional framework and the procedures by which it should operate—in short, on desirable and undesirable conduct.

5. Finally, we may speak of "integrative behavior," referring to the capacity of people in a society to organize for some common purposes. At the most elementary level all societies have the capacity to create some kind of kinship organization—a device whereby societies propagate themselves and care for and socialize their young. As other needs and desires arise within a society we may ask whether the capacity grows to create new organizations to carry out new purposes. In some societies the capacity to organize is limited to a small elite and is only associated with those who have authority.[4] Only the state, therefore, has a capacity to expand for the carrying out of new functions. In still other societies organizational capacities are more evenly spread throughout the population, and individuals without coercive authority have the readiness to organize with others. Societies differ, therefore, in the extent to which organizational proclivities are pervasive or not, and whether organizations are simply expressive in character—that is, confined to kinship and status—or purposive.

The term "integration" thus covers a vast range of human relationships and attitudes—the integration of diverse and discrete cultural loyalties and the development of a sense of nationality; the integration of political units into a common territorial framework with a government which can   167 exercise authority; the integration of the rulers and the ruled; the integration of the citizen into a common political process; and, finally, the integration of individuals into organizations for purposive activities. As diverse as these definitions are, they are united by a common thread. These are all attempts to define what it is *which holds a society and a political system together.* Scholars of the developing areas have groped for some such notions of integration, for they recognize that in one or more of these senses the political systems they are studying do not appear to hold together *at a level commensurate with what their political leadership needs to carry out their goals.* If each scholar has in his mind a different notion of "integration," it is often because he is generalizing from one or more specific societies with which he is familiar and which is facing some kind of "integration" problem. Since there are many ways in which systems may fall apart, there are as many ways of defining "integration."

To avoid further confusion we shall use a qualifying adjective hereafter when we speak of one kind of integration problem. We shall thus speak of national integration territorial integration, value integration, elite-mass integration, and integrative behavior and use the term integration alone when we are referring to the generalized problem of holding a system together.

FORMS AND STRATEGIES

Transitional or developing political systems are generally less integrated than either traditional or modern systems. This is because these systems cannot readily perform the functions which the national leadership—or in some instances, the populace too—expects them to perform. In other words, as the functions of a system expand—or the political leadership aspires to expand the functions of the system—a new level of integration is required. When we speak of political development, therefore, we are concerned first with the expanding functions of the political system, secondly with the new level of integration thereby required to carry out these functions, and, finally, with the capacity of the political system to cope with these new problems of integration. It is necessary, therefore, that we now take a more concrete look at the kinds of expanding functions which occur in the course of political development, the specific integrative problems which these pose, and the public policy choices available to governmental elites for coping with each of these integrative problems.

National Integration

It is useful to ask why it is that new nations with pluralistic social orders require more national integration than did the colonial regimes which preceded them. The obvious answer is that colonial governments were not concerned with national loyalties but with creating classes who would be loyal to them as a colonial power. Colonial governments, therefore, paid little or no attention to the teaching of a "national" language or culture, but stressed instead the teaching of the colonial language and culture. We are all familiar with the fact that educated Vietnamese, Indonesians, Nigerians, Indians, and Algerians were educated in French, English, and Dutch rather than in their own languages and traditions. Although the colonialist viewed the development of national loyalties as a threat to his political authority, the new leadership views it as essential to its own maintenance. Moreover, since the colonial rulers permitted only limited participation, the parochial sentiments of local people rarely entered into the making of any significant decisions of essential interest to policy makers. Once the new nations permit a greater measure of public participation, then the integration requirements of the system are higher. Moreover, the new elite in the new nations have higher standards of national integration than those of their former colonial rulers and this, too, creates new integration problems.

So long, for example, as export-import duties were imposed by a colonial ruler whose primary concern was with the impact of commercial policies upon their trade and commerce, then no questions of national integration were involved. Once these areas of policy are in the hands of a national regime, then issues immediately arise as to which sections of the country—and therefore which communities—are to be affected adversely or in a beneficial fashion by trade policies. Once educational policy is determined by national rather than colonial needs, the issues of language policy, location of educational facilities, the levels of educational investment, and the question of who bears the costs of education all affect the relations of culturally discrete groups. Finally, once the state takes on new investment responsibilities—whether for roads and post offices or for steel mills and power dams—questions of equity are posed by the regions, tribes, and linguistic groups which make up plural societies. Even if the assent of constituent groups is not necessary for the making of such decisions—that is, if an authoritarian framework is maintained—at least acquiescence is called for.

How nations have handled the problems of national integration is a matter of historical record. Clifford Geertz[5] has pointed out that public policy in the first instance is effected by patterns of social organization in plural societies. These patterns include (1) countries in which a single group is dominant in numbers and authority and there are one or more minority groups; (2) countries in which a single group is dominant in authority but not numbers; (3) countries in which no single group by itself commands a majority nor is a single group politically dominant; and (4) countries of any combination in which one or more minorities cut across international boundaries. Examples of the first group are prewar Poland (68 percent Polish), comtemporary Ceylon (70 percent Sinhalese), and

169

Indonesia (53 percent Javanese). The dominant minority case is best exemplified by South Africa (21 percent "white"). The best examples of complete pluralism with no majorities are India, Nigeria, and Malaya and, in Europe, Yugoslavia and Czechoslovakia. And finally, among the minorities which cross international boundaries, the most troublesome politically have been the Kurds, the Macedonians, the Basques, the Armenians, and the Pathans. In contemporary Africa, there are dozens of tribes which are cut by international boundaries, and in Southeast Asia there are substantial Chinese and Indian minorities.

In general there are two public policy strategies for the achievement of national integration: (1) the elimination of the distinctive cultural traits of minority communities into some kind of "national" culture, usually that of the dominant cultural group—a policy generally referred to as assimilationist: "Americanization," "Burmanization," "detribalization"; (2) the establishment of national loyalties without eliminating subordinate cultures—the policy of "unity in diversity," politically characterized by "ethnic arithmetic." In practice, of course, political systems rarely follow either policy in an unqualified manner but pursue policies on a spectrum somewhere in between, often simultaneously pursuing elements from both strategies.

The history of ethnic minorities in national states is full of tragedy. If today the future of the Watusi in East Africa, the Hindus in East Pakistan, the Turks in Cyprus and the Greeks in Turkey, and Indians in Burma and Ceylon is uncertain, let us recall the fate of minorities in the heterogeneous areas of East Europe. Poland in 1921 had minorities totalling 32 percent of the population. Since then 2.5 million Polish Jews have been killed or left the country and over 9 million Germans have been repatriated. Border shifts and population exchanges have also removed Ruthenian, white Russian, and Lithuanian minorities, so that today only 2 percent of the population of Poland belongs to ethnic minorities. Similarly, the Turkish minority in Bulgaria was considerably reduced at the end of the Second World War when 250,000 Turks were forced to emigrate to Turkey in 1950, and 3 million Germans and 200,000 Hungarians have been repatriated from Czechoslovakia since the war. Killings, the transfers of populations, and territorial changes have made most Eastern European countries more homogeneous today than they were at the beginning of the Second World War. Yugoslavia and Czechoslovakia are the only remaining East European countries which lack a single numerically dominant ethnic group.[6]

It is sad to recount an unpleasant historical fact—that few countries have successfully separated political loyalties from cultural loyalties. The dominant social groups have looked with suspicion upon the loyalty of those who are culturally different—generally, though not always (but here, too, we have self-fulfilling prophecies at work) with good reason. Where killings, population transfers, or territorial changes have not occurred, the typical pattern has been to absorb the ethnic minority into the dominant culture or to create a new amalgam culture. Where cultural and racial differences continue in Europe or the United States, they are generally accompanied by political tensions. No wonder that so many leaders of the new nations look upon assimilation and homogenization as desirable and that strong political movements press for population transfers in Cyprus, India, and Pakistan, and are likely to grow in importance in sub-Sahara Africa. It remains to be seen whether the ideal of unity and diversity, that is, *political* unity and *cultural* diversity, can be the foundation for modern states. Perhaps the most promising prospects are those in which no single ethnic group dominates—Nigeria, India, and Malaysia. The factors at work in prewar Eastern Europe seem tragically in the process of being duplicated in many of the developing nations: the drive by minorities for ethnic determination, the unsuccessful effort by newly established states to establish their own economic and political viability, the inability of states to establish integration without obliterating cultures—and often peoples—through assimilation, population transfers or genocide, and, finally, the efforts of larger more powerful states to establish control or absorb unintegrated, fragile political systems.

Territorial Integration

The associations of states with fixed territories is a relatively modern phenomenon. The fluctuating "boundaries" of historic empires, and the fuzziness at the peripheries where kinship ties and tributary arrangements marked the end of a state are no longer acceptable arrangements in a world where sovereignty is characterized by an exclusive control over territory. In time the control over territory may be accompanied by a feeling of common nationality—our "national integration," but there must first of all be territorial integration. For most new states—and historic ones as well—the establishment of a territory precedes the establishment of subjective loyalties. A Congo nation cannot be achieved, obviously, without there being a Congo state, and the first order of business in the Congo has been the establishment by the central government of its authority over constituent territorial units. Some scholars have distinguished between the state and the nation, the former referring to the existence of central authority with the capacity to control a given territory and the latter to the extent of subjective loyalty on the part of the population within that territory to the state. There are, of course, instances where the "nation" in this sense precedes the "state"—as in the case of Israel and, according to some, Pakistan—but more typically the "state" precedes the "nation." "Nation-building," to use the increasingly popular phrase, thus presumes the prior existence of a state in control of a specified—and, in most instances, internationally recognized—territory. Territorial integration is thus related to the problem of *state-building* as distinct from *nation-building*.

171

Colonial rulers did not always establish central authority over the entire territory under their *de jure* control. The filling of the gap between *de jure* and *de facto* control has, in most instances, been left to the new regimes which took power after independence. Thus, the areas under *indirect* control by colonial authorities have been placed under the *direct* control of the new governments—in India, Pakistan, Malaya and in many areas of Africa. This process has been accomplished with relatively little bloodshed and international disturbance—although the dispute over Kashmir is an important exception—largely because the colonial regimes denied these quasi-independent pockets of authority the right to create their own armies.

The more serious problem of territorial integration has been the efforts of the new regimes to take control over border areas which were, in effect, unadministered by the colonial governments. Since both sides of a boundary were often governed by the same colonial power—as in French West Africa—or by a weak independent power—as in the Indian-Tibetan and Indian-Chinese borders—the colonial government often made no effort to establish *de facto* authority. Moreover, some of these areas are often occupied by recalcitrant tribes who forcefully resisted efforts toward their incorporation in a larger nation-state.

Some of the new governments have wisely not sought to demonstrate that they can exercise control over all subordinate authorities—wisely, because their capacity to do so is often exceedingly limited. But no modern government can tolerate for long a situation in which its laws are not obeyed in portions of its territory. As the new regimes begin to expand their functions, their need to exercise control grows. As an internal market is established, there is a need for a uniform legal code enforceable in courts of law; as state expenditures grow, no area can be exempt from the tax collectors; with the growth in transportation and communication there is a need for postal officers and personnel for the regulation in the public interest of communication and transport facilities. Finally, there is pride, for no government claiming international recognition will willingly admit that it cannot exercise authority in areas under its recognized jurisdiction, for to do so is to invite the strong to penetrate into the territory of the weak.

Value Integration

The integration of values—whatever else it encompasses—at a minimum means that there are acceptable procedures for the resolution of conflict. All societies—including traditional societies—have conflicts, and all societies have procedures for their resolution. But as societies begin to modernize, conflicts multiply rapidly, and the procedures for the settlement of conflict are not always satisfactory. There are societies where the right of traditional authority to resolve conflict remained intact during the early phases of modernization—Japan comes readily to mind—and who were thereby able to avoid large-scale violence. But these are the exceptions. Why does the system require a new level of value integration?

First of all, the scale and volume of conflict increases in societies experiencing modernization. The status of social groups is frequently changed, even reversed, as education opens new occupational opportunities, as the suffrage increases the political importance of numbers, and as industrial expansion provides new opportunities for employment and wealth. A caste or tribe, once low in status and wealth, may now rise or at least see the opportunity for mobility. And social groups once high in power, status, and wealth may now feel threatened. Traditional rivalries are aggravated, and new conflicts are created as social relationships change.

The modernization process also creates new occupational roles and these new roles often conflict with the old. The new local government officer may be opposed by the tribal and caste leader. The textile manufacturer may be opposed by producers of hand-loomed cloth. The doctor may be opposed by a traditional healer. To these, one could add an enormous list of conflicts associated with modernization: the conflicts between management and labor characteristic of the early stages of industrial development, the hostility of landlords to government land-reform legislation, the hostility of regions, tribes, and religious groups with one another as they find it necessary to compete—often for the first time—in a common political system where public policies have important consequences for their social and economic positions. Finally, we should note the importance of ideological conflicts so often found in developing societies as individuals try to find an intellectually and emotionally satisfying framework for recreating order out of a world of change and conflict.

There are two modal strategies for integrating values in a developing society. One stresses the importance of consensus and is concerned with maximizing uniformity. This view of consensus, in its extreme, emphasizes as a goal the avoidance of both conflict and competition through either coercion or exhortation. A second view of the way integrative values may be maximized emphasizes the interplay of individual and group interests. Public policy is thus not the consequence of a "right" policy upon which all agree, but the best policy possible in a situation in which there are differences of interests and sentiments.

Since most developing societies lack integrative values, political leaders in new nations are often self-conscious of their strategies. In practice, of course, neither of these two strategies is pursued in a "pure" fashion, for a leadership which believes in consensus without conflict may be willing to permit the interplay of some competitive interests while, on the other hand, regimes committed to open competition often set limits as to which viewpoints can be publicly expressed.

173

Though movements often develop aimed at the elimination of conflict—Communists, for example, see class harmony as the culmination of a period of struggle—such movements in practice simply add another element of conflict. The problem has been one of finding acceptable procedures and institutions for the management of conflict. It is striking to note the growth of dispute-settling institutions in modern societies. When these bodies are successful, it is often possible to prevent conflicts from entering a country's political life. Here we have in mind the social work agencies, churches and other religious bodies, lawyers and the courts, labor-management conciliation bodies and employee councils, and inter-racial and interreligious bodies. The psychiatrist, the lawyer, the social worker, and the labor mediator all perform integrating roles in the modern society. In the absence of these or equivalent roles and institutions in rapidly changing societies in which conflict is growing, it is no wonder that conflicts move quickly from the factory, the university, and the village into political life.

A modern political system has no single mechanism, no single procedure, no single institution for the resolution of conflict; indeed, it is precisely the multiplicity of individuals, institutions, and procedures for dispute settlement that characterizes the modern political system—both democratic and totalitarian. In contrast, developing societies with an increasing range of internal conflict, typically lack such individuals, institutions, and procedures. It is as if mankind's capacity to generate conflict is greater than his capacity to find methods for resolving conflict; the lag is clearly greatest in societies in which fundamental economic and social relationships are rapidly changing.

Elite-Mass Integration

The mere existence of differences in goals and values between the governing elite and the governed mass hardly constitutes disintegration so long as those who are governed accept the right of the governors to govern. British political culture stresses the obligations of citizens toward their government; the American political culture stresses the importance of political participation. In both, a high degree of elite-mass integration exists. At the other extreme are societies faced with the problem of internal war, and in between are many countries whose governments are so cut off from the masses whom they govern that they can neither mobilize the masses nor be influenced by them. The integration of elite and mass, between governors and the governed, occurs not when differences among the two disappear, but when a pattern of authority and consent is established. In no society is consent so great that authority can be dispensed with, and in no society is government so powerful and so internally cohesive that it can survive for long only through the exercise of cohesive authority. We need to stress here that both totalitarian and democratic regimes are capable of establishing elite-mass integration and that the establishment of a new pattern of relations between government and populace is particularly important during the early phase of development when political participation on a large scale is beginning to take place.

It is commonplace to speak of the "gap" between governors and the governed in the new nations, implying that some fundamental cultural and attitudinal gaps exist between the "elite" and the "mass," the former being secular-minded, English- or French-speaking, and Western-educated, if not Western-oriented, while the latter remain oriented toward traditional values, are fundamentally religious, and are vernacular-speaking.[7] In more concrete political terms, the government may be concerned with increasing savings and investment and, in general, the postponement of immediate economic gratification in order to maximize long-range growth, while the public may be more concerned with immediate gains in income and, more fundamentally, equitable distribution or social justice irrespective of its developmental consequences. Often the governmental elite itself may be split with one section concerned with satisfying public demands in order to win popular support while the other is more concerned with maximizing growth rates, eliminating parochial sentiments, establishing a secular society, or achieving international recognition. The elite-mass gap also implies that communications are inadequate, that is, that the elite is oriented toward persuading the mass to change their orientation, but the feedback of political demands is not heard or, if heard, not responded to.

Perhaps too much is made of the attitudinal "gap" between governors and governed; what is more important perhaps is the attitude of government toward its citizens. Nationalist leaders out of power are typically populist. They generally identify with the mass and see in the "simple peasant" and the "working class" qualities which will make a good society possible. But once the nationalist leadership takes power and satisfies its desire for social status it tends to view the mass as an impediment to its goals of establishing a "modern," "unified," and "powerful" state. From being the champion of the masses the elite often becomes their detractor.

In all political systems, those of developing as well as developed societies, there are differences in outlook between those who govern and those who are governed. In a developed system, however, those who govern are accessible to influence by those who are governed—even in a totalitarian system—and those who are governed are readily available for mobilization by the government. In modern societies governments are so engaged in effecting the economy, social welfare, and defense that there must be a closer interaction between government and the governed.[8] Governments must mobilize individuals to save, invest, pay taxes, serve in the army, obey laws. Modern governments must also know what the public will tolerate and must be able to anticipate, before policies are pursued, what the public reaction to a given policy might be. Moreover, the modern

175

government is increasingly armed with sophisticated tools of economic analysis and public opinion surveys to increase its capacity to predict both the economic and political consequences of its actions. In contrast, the elites of new nations are constantly talking to the masses; it is not that they do not hear the masses, but what they hear is often so inappropriate to what they wish to do. To ban opposition parties, muzzle the press, and restrict freedom of speech and assembly does indeed close two-way channels of communication, but often this is precisely what is intended.

But whatever their fear of the masses, governmental elites in new nations cannot do without them. While the elite may be unsympathetic to mass efforts to exercise influence, the elite does want to mobilize the masses for its goals. In some developing societies an organizational revolution is already under way as men join together for increasingly complex tasks to create political parties, newspapers, corporations, trade unions, and caste and tribal associations. Governmental elites are confronted with a choice during the early stages of this development. Should they seek to make these new organizations instruments of the authoritative structures or should these organizations be permitted to become autonomous bodies, either politically neutral or concerned with influencing government? When the state is strong and the organizational structures of society weak—a condition often found in the early phases of postcolonial societies with a strong bureaucratic legacy—then government leadership clearly has such an option.[9] It is at this point that the classic issue of the relationship of liberty and authority arises, and the elite may choose to move in one direction rather than the other.

The choices made are often shaped by dramatic domestic or international crises of the moment. But they are also affected by the society's tradition of elite-mass relations. The traditional aloofness, for example, of the mandarin bureaucracy toward the Vietnamese populace and the traditional disdain of the Buddhist and Catholic Vietnamese toward the *montagnards* or "pagan" hill peoples have probably been more important factors affecting elite-mass relations in contemporary Vietnam than any strategic or ideological considerations on the part of the Vietnamese government. Similarly, the behavior of many African leaders can often be understood better by exploring the customary patterns of authority in traditional tribal society than by reference to any compulsions inherent in the development process.

In the analysis of elite-masses relations much attention is rightly given to the development of "infra-structures"—that is, political parties, newspapers, universities, and the like—which can provide a two-way communication channel between government and populace.[10] Much attention is also given to the development of a "middle strata" of individuals who can serve as links—newspapermen, lobbyists, party bosses, and precinct workers. While in the long run these developments are of great importance, in the short run so much depends upon the attitude of the governmental elites, whether the elites fundamentally feel—and behave—as if they were alienated from and even antagonistic to the masses as they are, or whether the elites perceive the values of the masses as essentially being congruent to their own aims.

Integrative Behavior

The readiness of individuals to work together in an organized fashion for common purposes and to behave in a fashion conducive to the achievement of these common purposes is an essential behavioral pattern of complex modern societies. Modern societies have all encountered organizational revolutions—in some respects as essential and as revolutionary as the technological revolution which has made the modern world. To send a missile into outer space, to produce millions of automobiles a year, to conduct research and development, to manage complex mass media all require new organizational skills. During the last few decades we have begun to understand the nature of managerial skills and the complexity of organizations—how they carry out their many purposes, how they adapt themselves to a changing environment, and how they change that environment. We know less about why some societies are more successful than others in creating men and women capable of establishing, maintaining, and adapting complex organizations for the achievement of common purposes.

The consequences of an organizational lag as an impediment to development are, however, quite apparent. The inability of many political leaders to maintain internal party and government unity in many new nations has resulted in the collapse of parliamentary government and the establishment of military dictatorships. The much vaunted organizational skill of the military has also often failed in many new nations. In Ceylon a planned military coup collapsed when several of the conspirators spoke of their plans so openly that even a disorganized civilian government had time to take action, and in many Latin-American countries, and now in Vietnam, the military has proven to be as incapable of maintaining cohesive authority as their civilian predecessors.

The capacity—or lack of capacity—to organize with one's fellow men may be a general quality of societies. A society with a high organizational capacity appears to be organizationally competent at creating industrial organizations, bureaucracies, political parties, universities, and the like. Germany, Japan, the United States, the Soviet Union, Great Britain come quickly to mind. In contrast, one is struck by a generalized incompetence in many new nations where organizational breakdowns seem to be greater bottlenecks to economic growth than breakdowns in machinery. In some new countries technological innovations—such as industrial plants, railways, telegraph and postal systems—have expanded more rapidly than the human capacities to make the technologies work, with the result that mail is lost, the transport system does not function with any regularity,

177

industrial managers cannot implement their decisions, and government administrative regulations impede rather than facilitate the management of public sector plants. Though some scholars have argued that the skill to create complex institutions will accompany or follow technological innovation, there is good reason to think that organizational skills are a prerequisite for much political and economic development. In fact, the pattern of interpersonal relations appears to be more conducive to organization-building in some traditional societies than in others. Just as the presence of entrepreneurial talents in the traditional society is a key element in whether or not economic growth occurs, so may the presence of organizational talents be an important element in whether there emerges a leadership with the capacity to run a political party, an interest association, or a government.[11]

Surprisingly little is known about the conditions for the development of effectual political organizations. If the modernization process does produce political organizations, why is it that in some societies these organizations are effectual and in others they are not? By effectual, we mean the capacity of an organization to establish sufficient internal cohesion and external support to play some significant role in the decision-making or decision-implementing process. The multiplication of ineffectual political organizations tends to result either in a highly fragmented unintegrated political process in which government is unable to make or implement public policy, or in a political system in which the authoritative structures make all decisions completely independently of the political process outside of government. In the latter case we may have a dual political process, one inside of government which is meaningful and one outside of government which, in policy terms, is meaningless.

Some scholars have suggested that political organization is a consequence of increased occupational differentiation which in turn results from economic growth and technological change—an assumption, incidentally, of much foreign economic assistance. The difficulty with viewing political change as a consequence of social changes which in turn are the consequence of economic development is that, however logical this sequence may appear to be, in the history of change no such sequence can be uniformly found. Indeed, political organization often precedes large-scale economic change and may be an important factor in whether or not there is large-scale economic change.

In recent years greater attention has been given to the psychocultural components of political organization. Attention is given to the existence of trust and distrust and the capacity of individuals to relate personal ambition with some notion of the public good and of moral behavior. For explanations, psychologists focus on the process of primary socialization.

While psychologists focus on the working of the mind, sociologists and social anthropologists have been concerned with the working of society, and focus on the rules that effect the relationship among men—why they are kept and why they are broken. Sociologists have given attention to the complex of rules that organize social relationships, the patterns of superordination and subordination as among and between groups and individuals, how these change, and what effects they have on political and social relationships. While psychologists give attention to the primary process of socialization, sociologists and social anthropologists are concerned with the way in which the individual, during his entire life, comes to learn the rules and, under certain circumstances, to break them. It is from these two complementary views of man that we may expect the more systematic study of politically integrative and disintegrative behavior.

CONCLUSION

We have tried to suggest in this essay that there are many different kinds of integration problems faced by developing nations, for there are innumerable ways in which societies and political systems fall apart. A high rate of social and economic change creates new demands and new tasks for government which are often malintegrative. The desire of the governing elite or the governed masses, for whatever reasons, to increase the functions of government are often causes of integration problems. Since modern states as well as modernizing states are often taking on new functions, it would be quite inappropriate to view integration as some terminal state. Moreover, the problems of integration in the developing areas are particularly acute because so many fundamentally new tasks or major enlargements of old tasks are now being taken on. Once the state actively becomes concerned with the mobilization and allocation of resources, new patterns of integration between elite and mass are called for. Once the state takes on the responsibilities of public education and invokes sentiments of "national" solidarity, then the integration of social groups to one another becomes an issue. And once men endeavor to create corporations, newspapers, political parties, and professional associations because they perceive their individual interests served by common actions, a new set of values is called for which provides for the integration of new structures into the political process. The challenges of integration thus arise out of the new tasks which men create for themselves.

NOTES

1. This is perhaps the most common use of the term. For a precise view of the many attempts to define "nationality," see Rupert Emerson, *From Empire to Empire* (Boston: Beacon Press, 1960), especially Part 2: "The Anatomy of the Nation." K. H. Silvert, the editor of a collection of studies of nationalism prepared by the American Universities Field Staff, *Expectant Peoples: Nationalism and Development* (New York: Random House, 1963), suggests as a working definition of nationalism the acceptance of the state as the impersonal and ultimate arbiter of human affairs (p. 19). See also Karl W. Deutsch, *Nationalism and Social Communication* (New York: John Wiley and Sons, 1953) and Karl W. Deutsch and William J. Foltz, eds., *Nation-Building* (New York: Atherton Press, 1963).

2. For a discussion of some of the problems of territorial control in Africa see James S. Coleman, "Problems of Political Integration in Emergent Africa," *Western Political Quarterly* (March 1955): 844-57.

3. For an explanation of this use of the term integration in the literature see Leonard Binder, "National Integration and Political Development," *American Political Science Review* (September 1964): 622-31. Elite-mass integration is also one of the usages in James S. Coleman and Carl G. Rosberg, eds., *Political Parties and National Integration in Africa* (Berkeley: University of California, 1964). They use integration in two senses: "(1) political integration, which refers to the progressive bridging of the elite-mass gap on the vertical plane in the course of developing an integrated political process and a participant political community, and (2) territorial integration, which refers to the progressive reduction of cultural and regional tensions and discontinuities on the horizontal plane in the process of creating a homogeneous territorial political community" (p. 9). These two definitions correspond with our first and third definitions.

4. For an analysis of the attitudes which inhibit organized activity see Edward Banfield, *The Moral Basis of a Backward Society* (Glencoe, Ill.: Free Press, 1958). Though Banfield's study is confined to a single village in Italy, he raises the general problem of analyzing the capacities of a people to organize for common purposes.

5. See Clifford Geertz, "The Integrative Revolution: Primordial Sentiments and Civil Politics in the New States," in *Old Societies and New Nations*, ed. Clifford Geertz (New York: Free Press, 1963).

6. These figures are taken from Lewis M. Alexander, *World Political Patterns* (Chicago: Rand McNally), pp. 277-325.

7. For a critique of "gap" theories of political development, see Ann Ruth Willner, "The Underdeveloped Study of Political Development," *World Politics* (April 1964): 468-82.

8. Karl Deutsch has pointed out that governments of industrial societies, whether totalitarian or democratic, spend a larger proportion of their GNP than do governments in underdeveloped economies, irrespective of their ideologies.

9. This theme is amplified by Fred W. Riggs, "Bureaucrats and Political Development: A Paradoxical View," in *Bureaucracy and Political Development*, ed. Joseph LaPalombara (Princeton: Princeton University Press, 1963).

10. For a discussion of the role of infra-structures in political development, see Edward Shils, *Political Development in the New States* (The Hague: Mouton, 1962).

11. For an attempt to relate traditional patterns of social and political relations to modern party-building, see Myron Weiner, "Traditional Role Performance and the Development of Modern Political Parties: The Indian Case," *Journal of Politics* (November 1964). The problems of party-building in a new nation are treated in my *Party-Building in a New Nation: The Indian National Congress* (Chicago: University of Chicago Press, 1967).

181

IMPEDIMENTS TO UNITY IN NEW NATIONS: THE CASE OF CEYLON

W. Howard Wriggins

In their search for nationhood since World War II, many peoples of Asia and Africa have discovered that independence from western rule is only the first and perhaps the easiest step. Once the foreigner has gone, the larger problem looms of creating a viable political society. Divisions and competitive strivings held in check when outsiders controlled affairs are suddenly released. Ethnic, religious and regional differences, that seemed less important so long as colonial administrators ruled, boil up after independence and more often than not come to dominate the loyalties and inspire the ambitions that move men in politics. To their dismay, responsible leaders find themselves heading not the homogeneous, modern nation state they dreamed of before independence, but a congeries of separate groups. The simple, unifying purpose of the independence struggle fades away, leaving a host of contradictions and cleavages.

Indonesia is wracked by repeated resistance to Jakarta. Burma has been beset by periodic insurrection, supported in part by regional and ethnic hostility to Rangoon. The nightmare of India's Nehru is the growth of regional and linguistic differences. Imminent disintegration of the ex-Belgian Congo dramatizes the extreme case.

Are the difficulties impeding national consolidation mainly the fruit of irresponsible political leadership, as ex-colonial administrators are tempted to allege? Are ill-considered linguistic and educational reforms to blame, reforms that wiser statesmanship could have avoided? What other social and political developments sharpen antagonisms and impede the building of a viable nation state? Would more rapid economic development solve

From W. Howard Wriggins, "Impediments to Unity in New Nations: The Case of Ceylon," *American Political Science Review* 55 (June 1961): 313-20. Reprinted by permission of the author and the American Political Science Association.

the problems of marked diversity, as the proponents of take-off aid programs often assert?

THE PRICE OF THE UNION

No doubt repeated appeals to regional, ethnic or traditional differences stunt the growth of a sense of common nationhood. Yet political leaders usually have substantial reasons for stressing their attachment to such divisions in the body politic. Unlike the colonial administrator who preceded him, the elected politician must elicit support; he cannot impose allegiance. So long as the bulk of citizens are moved by appeals to local or traditional ties, there is no surer way of winning political backing than by demonstrating attachment to parochial loyalties. It remains an essential part of political campaigning in Scotland or Wales, as it does in Louisiana or in Maine. In Great Britain and the United States, to be sure, tacit understandings by now set bounds beyond which regional or certain other special interests cannot profitably be pressed at the expense of an overriding national interest. In new countries, the pressures for asserting regional, ethnic or traditional values are many times greater, tacit understandings of the proper limits as not yet agreed upon, and people are little aware of a public interest that must take priority if the national community is to solve its problems effectively and survive.

In India, as Selig Harrison reminds us, many members of the Congress Party—and even the Communist Party—draw their strength mainly from regional or traditional interests so insistent that an overarching identity with policies of concern to all of India in many instances is not possible. In Indonesia, many politicians and administrators feel impelled to insist upon regional interest, reenforced by traditional attachments and religious differences. Not even Sukarno can count any more upon a freely given nationwide support; he has had to reach adjustment with the army to help him hold the nation's multiplicity together. In Pakistan, differences between Urdu-speaking, Moghul-influenced West Pakistan and Bengali-speaking, Hindu-influenced East Pakistan are profound. Any political man from East Pakistan who does not speak out for his region's peculiar interests is likely to lose indispensable political support at home. However understandable these political imperatives may be, it often appears that spokesmen for parochial interests press their claims excessively, disregarding the likely disruptive consequences to the whole of what they seek to achieve for the part.

In nearly all the countries of South and Southeast Asia, linguistic legislation and educational reform have had high priority. Yet governments and legislators on the side of the largest language group have persistently and seriously underestimated the strength of linguistic loyalties among minorities. In India, for example, legislation provides that Hindi shall

183

replace English as the official language, at a pace defined by an official time-table. At the same time, the efforts to promote Hindi have sharpened minority anxieties about the larger ambitions of the Hindi-speaking segments of the population, and consolidated their loyalties to their own languages. In Malaya, Chinese are antagonized by Malay efforts to strengthen the position of Malay. In Ceylon, Tamils have bitterly opposed efforts of the Sinhalese majority to raise the status of Sinhalese. Each such measure may promote national consolidation in the long run, but it usually favors immediately one group more than another, and changes the terms on which groups compete for opportunity, wealth and power. Those who promote the reforms find it hard to imagine why the minorities should feel so bitter, a lack of empathy that impedes taking steps to assuage minority anxieties, or otherwise to ease what may be an unavoidable transition.

Educational reforms adopted on grounds of excellent principles—the right to universal education, for example, or the right to have children taught in the language of their parents—may have disruptive side effects which can be foreseen but are not taken seriously. A rapidly expanded school system without appropriate changes in the curriculum produces large numbers of educated citizens who are ambitious for status but for whom there are no proper jobs. Teaching children only in the vernaculars segregates them into ethnic groups from the outset and weakens communication between communities. A leadership which transcends the traditional differences such as developed, with all its inequities, under the British and to a more limited extent, under the French colonial systems is no longer produced. Neither by-product is examined with care, and sufficient countermeasures are not taken, with the result that communal awareness is heightened and competition for all-too-scarce opportunities is sharpened.

Economic development providing new opportunities and greater hope for the future would be likely to mitigate this competition in the long run, but in the politically crucial short run it does not eliminate the attachment to old divisions. At the outset, development is likely to favor those most adaptable and ready to seize new opportunities, who are often ethnic and linguistic minorities such as the Marwaris in India or aliens, like the Chinese, in Indonesia. If this process is allowed to run its course, divisions and antagonisms are aggravated. If it is interrupted by political intervention in favor of the majority, resentments among these minorities are heightened. Improved means of communication may at first arouse more perception of group differences and sharpen conflicting ambitions.

Modernization may provoke its own reaction, as traditionalist groups organize to oppose innovation and to weaken the power of those who are responsible for it. Thus, in the short run, at least, modernization may increase group tensions. However much urbanization and industrialization may eventually free men from their traditional loyalties and make a new basis for integration possible, the transition is more likely to be immediately disruptive than to ease group relations.

The struggle for independence provokes the turning back to prewestern cultural roots. But as the early history of each country is explored, it is discovered that the ancestors of those presently engaged in common opposition to the European fought one another in bloody wars or gradual incursions upon one another's territory. When independence is finally achieved, these historical struggles take on a new urgency as groups compete for opportunity and status in the new country.

Hence, the task of national consolidation, however urgent it may be, poses very difficult problems. A close look at Ceylon's experience with relations between its majority and minority populations will illustrate these observations. The country's small size permits clearer analysis of interacting social, political, and economic factors than is possible in massive India or less organized Burma or Indonesia. Of all the new Asian countries, Ceylon seemed to have the best chance of making a successful transition to modern statehood. It began its independence most auspiciously with seasoned leadership drawn from nearly all important ethnic groups. The population was 60 percent literate at independence. It had longer experience with nationwide elections on the basis of a universal franchise to represent single-member, territorial constituencies than any other country. Per capita GNP was higher than in any other country in the area apart from Japan. Its recent experience of relative harmony among classes and racial groups was such that there had been no insurrection, no partition, no sharp class struggle. Yet in 1956 and 1958, unprecedented riots left deep antagonisms that will be hard to soften in the future; the hitherto orderly processes of representative government were interrupted by emergency governor's rule, and the Prime Minister was assassinated.

A detailed examination of this deterioration where high hopes were entertained may shed some light on what other countries have in store. For despite their many differences, virtually all the former colonial countries on the edge of Asia share certain fundamental characteristics that complicate their search for national consolidation. First, there are fissures in the indigenous social order, often regionally defined, that separate ethnic, linguistic and religious groups from one another. In most there are also important minorities who have come to the country within the past century, brought by European enterprisers or drawn by economic opportunities during the colonial period. Indian Tamils in Ceylon, Bengalis in Burma, Chinese in Thailand, Vietnam and Indonesia are the legacy that must be dealt with. Both of these impediments to national unity are usually identified as "communal" differences, creating a "plural" or "mosaic" society. Second, the horizontal stratifications are no less important, dividing socio-economic classes sharply from one another. By education, language and culture, the leading elements are in many respects alien to the masses they must lead. The nearest analogues to this stratification in the contemporary West are perhaps to be found in Latin America, Spain or southern Italy.

IMPEDIMENTS TO UNITY IN CEYLON

The Social Structure

The social structure of Asian countries provides an underlying element of disunity; the plural society in Ceylon is simpler than most others in the area. The majority Sinhalese community comprises nearly 70 percent of the total population. There are two Tamil-speaking minorities: approximately 12 percent of the population have lived on the island for many centuries; another 10 percent are relative newcomers who arrived during the colonial period to man the tea and rubber estates and develop wholesale businesses. A Muslim minority of some 5 percent and a Burgher community descended from mixed European and Ceylonese marriages form the balance.

The Sinhalese are largely Buddhists and speak Sinhalese, an Aryan language related to Bengali; the Tamils are Hindus who speak the Dravidian language Tamil. The Muslims, descendants of Arab traders, speak Sinhalese or Tamil and perhaps English as well, depending upon where they live. The Burghers claim English as their mother-tongue, though many speak Sinhalese too. Perhaps 8 percent of the population are Christians, divided between Sinhalese and Tamils, though nearly all the Burghers are Christians. There are also caste groupings, less strict than in India, which need not detain us. These are the gross contours of the plural society in Ceylon.

Members of the Sinhalese and Tamil communities speak different languages, lead different lives, and follow differing family customs. Although many individuals in both communities are fully accepted within the other, the two groups hold unflattering views of each other. Their attitudes show clearly differentiated and mutually critical stereotypes. Sinhalese and Tamils consider themselves to be markedly different. Each sees in the other traits it does not admire. Group distrust lies not far beneath the surface. Each community tends to form a network of mutual confidence and assistance when a member is faced with harm from those outside his own community. Some, though by no means all, trade unions, the Christian churches, larger business enterprises and the public service have provided opportunities for mingling and common activity. The army, though drawing on all communities, remains small and professionalized, playing only a minor role in national integration. The communities are therefore brought together by few institutions.

Other divisions in the society complicate the fundamental Sinhalese-Tamil difference. In many ways as profound is the fissure that separates the mass of the population from the English-speaking, western educated elite who represent roughly 8 percent of the total. An exact appraisal of this social distance is difficult, since the man who appears most at home in the western offices or salons of the capital may quickly shed his western

186

ways when he returns to the family village. There are, of course, gradations in the degree of westernization, from the Oxford graduate raised in an English-speaking Ceylonese family, at one extreme, to the graduate of grammar school who has learned his English after primary school, on the other. Yet the division between the trousered men who command English and the rest is a visible, striking reality, and one profoundly felt by the millions who are not part of that elite. It is significant because the distribution of wealth, opportunity and power no longer depends alone upon family ties and family relations to the land, as in the traditional society. This is still important. But today, and for several generations already, real influence on the national state and often wealth have depended in addition upon the acquired skills of English education and western social ways.

Regardless of whether they were Sinhalese, Tamils, or Burghers in origin, the English-educated formed a stratum that lay across the ethnic and linguistic differences. These Tamils and Sinhalese had many close friendships that ignored communal lines. The English-educated articulated the desire for independence. Their vision usually encompassed all communities living in some degree of mutual acceptance in a gradually modernizing, unifying Ceylonese nationhood. As elsewhere in Asia, they inherited political power when the colonial rulers withdrew, in 1948.

But they were not politically homogeneous. Indeed, they competed among themselves for the opportunities of office. They were divided on political-ideological as well as religious grounds, and visions were accentuated as their leading position in the society became less sure.

Growing Awareness of Differences

Awareness of mutual differences has increased rather than diminished since independence. First, a cultural revival came to Ceylon only after independence, expressing the need to assert a cultural idiom distinct from western ways. As Sinhalese and Tamils each explored their own pasts, they recalled battles won from the other; they gained a sense of inferiority or superiority toward each other. In their search, they found no common Ceylonese tradition, only separate Sinhalese and Tamil pasts. The statewide alien rule no longer formed a common opponent uniting the different groups.

Second, an expanded educational system carried schooling to ever higher grades in the vernacular languages. More and more young people graduated from upper levels of the school system, reared entirely within one or the other vernacular culture without the unifying experience of English education.

Third, mutual understanding between the ethnic communities seemed to diminish. The vernacular press, for example, gained importance as literacy increased and as the wider masses became more actively concerned with public issues. This enhanced the distance between the Sinhalese and Tamils, since each vernacular paper tended to stress those aspects of public issues and cultural traditions which editors believed would appeal to their differentiated audiences. The press thus tended to provide contrasting and often contradictory interpretations of public problems to the different ethnic communities, hardening differences and sharpening distrust.

Fourth, with independence the Sinhalese majority expected that the Tamil and other minorities would assimilate to the Sinhalese way of life. But a sense of cultural superiority among the Tamils led them to resist the majority's effort to realize this expectation. Tamils feel a part of the capacious Indian tradition; they believe they have a culture rich in art, literature and religious insight. Becoming part of the Sinhalese cultural world is taken to mean abandoning this great tradition. Conversely, a sense of Sinhalese cultural inferiority has made many in the majority community unusually sensitive. There are only 8 million Sinhalese in all the world. In Ceylon itself reside 2 million Tamil-speaking people; across in India there are some 28 million more. The Sinhalese are often fearful of being overwhelmed by their Tamil neighbors; the Ceylon Tamils fear being swamped by the island's majority Sinhalese. Ironically, both groups are beset with something akin to minority feelings, each oversensitive to the other's criticisms and fearful of the other's ambitions.

These differences set the stage for invidious communal comparisons. Moreover, modernization has not gone so far that an individual's professional or financial achievement is seen as his personal accomplishment. On the contrary, an individual's achievement still reflects more upon the position of his communal group. When communal differences become projected into politics, every act of members of one community is looked at for its political significance—to see, that is, whether it enhances or diminishes the relative political influence of his own community. Past political contests between communities are disinterred and over-elaborate political strategies and tactics are attributed to moves made by members of the other community that often had no political intention behind them.

Fifth, a growing awareness among the masses concerning the privileged position of the westernized elite and a clearer cultural consciousness led to an increasing resentment against that elite. Articulate leaders of the independence movement from among the westernized talked of welfare, of democracy and of majority rule. But positions of control in the society were still filled by men of high birth or those fortunate enough to have been able to learn English. In a period of growing cultural self-awareness, this was not the democracy that had been preached by the leadership for many decades. The country still seemed to be ruled by an oligarchy of men alienated from indigenous traditions and cultures.

Moreover, their efforts to modernize their country, though cautious, provoked anxiety and resentment in important groups in the countryside who were among the intermediaries between the urban politicians and the rural masses. Practitioners of traditional *ayurvedic* medicine resented the resources invested in modern, western-type medical services; Buddhist monks, keepers of the Sinhalese tradition, opposed the growing emphasis on materialistic values; vernacular teachers protested against their second-class professional status by comparison with the higher pay and respect accorded to English-speaking teachers; local officials opposed the growing influence and size of the capital's bureaucracy.

Economic Competition

Awareness of economic competition increased as the population grew. The expanding school system turned out more liberal arts graduates who aspired to enter the coveted public service than the service could absorb. After an initial expansion to replace colonial officials and provide new economic and social service functions, public service hiring fell off just as more graduates began to enter the job market.

The students who could not find work form an articulate group, with time on their hands and an acute sense of grievance. They possess the skills necessary for political activity. Had there been other job opportunities, their frustrated ambitions for public service careers would not have mattered so desperately. But economic development that produced white collar jobs was disappointingly slow. The jobs they sought were not to be found in the government or elsewhere, and their liberal arts education had not fitted them for much else.

This increased the potentiality for tension between communities in part because the communal structure of Ceylon is relatively simple and readily lends itself to statistical comparisons. It was possible to argue, for example, that although the Sinhalese represented some 70 percent of the population, they held only 60-65 percent of the public service jobs, while the Ceylon Tamils, representing only 12 percent of the population, held some 20 percent of the jobs. In a time of growing unemployment in lower jobs as well, a politician could prove his devotion to the majority community by pointing the finger at the Tamils who had "usurped" more than their fair share of the best jobs.

Clearing and irrigating jungle land to be settled by peasants from the overcrowded Sinhalese and Tamil areas became a bitter apple of discord between the two communities. The land had lain under the rule of malaria, empty and desolate, until DDT made its reconquest possible. Tamils consider these new lands to be areas they have traditionally inhabited. The Sinhalese see much historical evidence to prove that Buddhist civilization once flourished before the jungle and malaria made their conquest. Both argue that settlement of peasants from the other community represents encroachment. And since political representation goes according to territorial constituencies, a significant change in the population structure of such areas would alter the balance of communal representation in the House of Representatives. Hence, even land development has sharpened group conflict.

189

Political Imperatives

The background of political leaders and the electoral imperatives provided other potentialities for social tension.

The principal political figures have come from the westernized elite. Broadly speaking, national electoral politics has been a struggle for office between men of this socio-economic class. Each has sought those relationships and issues that would carry influence and "project his image" across the social and linguistic gulf that separated him from the mass of voters. A convenient way of identifying himself with the voters was to demonstrate that he was more closely attached to the cultural and religious values of his constituents than his opponent, who could usually be charged with being too much like the former colonial rulers in style of life and language.

After independence, Ceylon was ruled by a coalition of moderately conservative men from the English-educated, land-owning, professional families in both Sinhalese and Tamil communities. Their support in the countryside was reenforced by the semifeudal fact that the rural masses tended to vote the way the rural notable, landowner or employer wished. But as new men from lesser origins entered the westernized elite, as cultural revival accented indigenous virtues often flouted by the more modern, westernized man, as democratic ideology penetrated the country-side, the westernized could not assume that their ruling position would continue. Their right to control affairs was bound to be tested. More direct appeals to mass sentiments often seemed the way to ensure continued political success.

Until 1956 the opposition parties were splintered, as in India, and the majority party could not be effectively challenged on the floor of the House of Representatives or at the hustings. The urban population was relatively small and underrepresented in a House designed to give greater representation to backward rural areas. Only if the opposition could undercut the government party in the countryside could it hope to displace the men who had ruled since independence.

In rural areas, between the notables and landowners who dominated national politics and the peasant and town masses, is a rural middle class of men who are prominent in their towns and villages. Buddhist monks, elected village officials, teachers skilled in the vernacular languages, practitioners of traditional *ayurvedic* medicine are such men. Opposition agitation in 1956 drew them into political activity that contributed decisively to the opposition's electoral victory that year. This agitation precipitated the elements of potential disunity into communal discord and violent conflict. The particular issue of import to them all concerned the matter of language.

190

LANGUAGE AND POLITICS

The "Language Question"

It is difficult in the United States, where one language predominates, to appreciate the intensity of emotions that the "language question" can arouse. In a plural society, language distinguishes one man from his neighbor, gives him access to his own cultural tradition, is the canonical representation of his religion and the instrument for communicating about it. English had been the colonial ruler's language. Language differences had much to do with the distribution of opportunity, wealth and political power. Widespread resentment against the airs and privileges of the English-educated, the power and aloofness of the English-speaking public service, the cultural snobbishness of the westernized city man, made the demotion of English virtually inevitable.

As independence neared, two vexed questions of government policy toward the country's languages had to be answered. In what language should the children be taught and what should be the country's official language (or languages) of government?

After sharp and protracted debates, it was decided that Sinhalese and Tamil children should learn in their own language, while English would be taught as a second language. The policy solution was obvious enough, but the debates on the matter added to communal sensitivities. Each year they were renewed as the Opposition accused the government of not pressing ahead rapidly enough with the necessary language changeover in the higher grades of the schools. As a by-product of this decision—and significant for the long run—there would no longer be produced an islandwide elite from all communities who had passed together through the same educational experience.

Electoral Politics

Intense feelings were provoked over the issue of the language or languages to be designated as official languages of state. Seeking to undercut the ruling coalition, the political opposition found the language question an unusually effective means for mobilizing the rural middle class in the majority community—the teachers, native physicians, the *bhikkhus* and local elected officials. Each one, for different reasons, experienced some sense of threat from westernizing, modernizing changes or some resentment against the westernized elite. Each rallied behind traditional communal symbols. They all believed that if Sinhalese were made the sole official language, their cultural and religious tradition would receive greater attention and their opportunities and status would be commensurately improved.

191

All who opposed making Sinhalese the sole official language were held to be standing in the way of legitimate—and national—aspirations. The Tamils opposed such a change and were therefore considered opponents. In the excitement of platform polemics, which were remarkably colorful and keyed to traditional allusions and indigenous fancy, many politicians made no distinction between Tamil invaders of 1,000 years ago and contemporary Ceylon Tamils. Ancient antagonisms were thus revived and combined with contemporary competition for scarce opportunity and uncertain status.

Many among the western-educated Sinhalese were generally opposed to the changes. But their will and power were sapped by two circumstances. In the first place, they feared that speaking out on behalf of moderation and a gradual transition to Sinhalese as the official language would turn the wrath of ardent Sinhalese against them, leading to the accusation that they were allies of the Tamils in a cause which they felt was all but lost already. Secondly, many experienced a growing sense of guilt that they had allowed themselves to become so alienated from their own tradition. In the name of their community's tradition, which they now sensed they had neglected, they were prepared to acquiesce in the changes even though these would seriously undermine their hitherto privileged position and risk bringing on dramatic communal difficulties.

As the Tamils saw it, to make Sinhalese the sole official language put Tamil in an inferior position and would no doubt give the Sinhalese-speaking people a competitive advantage as entrants to the public service, to teaching, university and other desirable careers. Pride in their culture was hurt; even their status as accepted inhabitants of Ceylon seemed brought in doubt.

In the 1956 election, the Sinhalese opposition, skillfully led by Bandaranaike, was successful in displacing the formerly ruling United National Party by a landslide vote. The ruling party had been vulnerable on other counts as well, but it was primarily linguistic politics that brought it down.

Electoral By-products

As a by-product of the campaign, communal antagonisms were at a new high for the country. The successful Prime Minister—like his defeated opponents—had assumed that communal antagonism could be turned up for tactical purposes and then turned down when the political need was gone. But new pressure groups organized among extremist Sinhalese and a vigorous minority of the clergy were not prepared to allow the new Prime Minister to moderate these antagonisms until their full aspirations were met. The Tamils, frightened by the upsurge of anti-Tamil sentiment, became more rigid.

Riots in 1956 followed close on the heels of the election and the debate in the House of Representatives over a language bill designed to give Sinhalese sole official standing. In the face of dramatic activities by the newly organized pressure groups, all provisions designed to safeguard Tamil interests were removed from the bill before it was submitted to debate. Starting in Colombo, vicious riots spread rapidly and over 100 were killed.

If bold political leadership, putting extremists on both sides in their place, might have cut through the fear and tension of communal intransigence, none appeared.

In 1958 more serious riots occurred. The police had become demoralized as a result of politically inspired transfers and because of restraining orders pressed upon the Prime Minister by his Marxist cabinet colleagues with political trade union interests to promote. The police were unable to restore order as rioting, looting, and burning spread. Several hundreds were killed—some say as many as 2,000. In the end, 10,000 Tamils and 2,000 Sinhalese sought refuge in army-managed refugee camps. When the army was finally called out, order was quickly restored. But a deeper gulf of fear now separated the minority Ceylon Tamil community from the majority Sinhalese.

As a tragic climax to these events, the Prime Minister was assassinated on his own verandah in September 1959 by a monk, a student of *ayurvedic* medicine. The case is under adjudication and there may be obscure political or even economic foundations for what at first appeared to be an act of a religious and cultural enthusiast who found the Prime Minister unable to carry out the promises he had made in the heat of political campaigning.

CONCLUSIONS

Apart from the tragedy of the hundreds killed during the riots and the assassination of the Prime Minister himself, the two rounds of communal riots left the country divided as it had not been for centuries. What conclusions can be drawn from these unhappy events?

1. The social structure of the plural society remains a stubborn social and political fact. Modernizing currents have not yet undermined the primary loyalty of the mass voters to traditional linguistic communities. A sense of Ceylonese nationhood is not yet clear.

2. Efforts to assert cultural independence from the West lead to explorations of the country's tradition. But this reaffirms diverse traditions and a past of local conflict which enlivens communal awareness and antagonisms. These differences increase after independence is achieved when the common opponent, the western ruler, no longer provides a focus for unifying antagonism.

3. Important rural middle class figures feel sufficiently threatened by

193

modern, secular influences to be particularly susceptible to traditional appeals that have, as their by-products, profound communal implications. These men are potential intermediaries between the westernized political leaders and opposition and the rural voters. They can therefore play an important role in politics when they are drawn into political activity, and they are by no means always carriers of modernization to the rural masses.

4. The earlier equation between education and opportunity has been disrupted and ever-higher levels of education are conducted in the vernaculars. Economic diversification and growth have not kept pace with expanding educational opportunities, resulting in a middle-class unemployment. This contributes particularly and directly to communal competition. Since the newly educated middle classes are largely trained in the vernacular languages, they identify only with their own parochial community. They do not comprehend a wider loyalty to the country as a whole, and they see their job futures in terms of their language community only.

5. Unavoidable decisions have to be made regarding the language or languages to replace English in the schools and in the government. These are bound to cause communal discord unless handled with great finesse.

6. Where a ruling elite is at a notable linguistic and cultural distance from the masses in a representative political system, those who seek to replace elected representatives may easily evoke communal and ethnic enthusiasms as a means of enlisting mass political support.

7. As one side effect of such electoral politics, communal anxieties may be greatly increased and new pressure groups develop to further press communal and religious claims. This stiffens the inflexibility of minority leaders and leaves a new government relatively little room for maneuver as it seeks an adjustment of contradictory claims.

8. A new government that is indecisive in domestic affairs and allows the vigor of the police to deteriorate unwittingly encourages extremists in both camps. Outbreaks of mob violence create further anxiety and antagonism for the future.

9. Rapid economic growth providing new opportunities to the most frustrated probably would mitigate such conflicts. In itself, however, it would not be sufficient to prevent them, and in the short run, at least, it may provide additional grounds for group antagonism.

In sum, those forces which divide, which separate one group from another grow in strength after independence—in school, in political activity and sometimes in economic life. Cultural revival enlivens the recollection of historic divisions and group conflicts; steps toward modernization arouse resistance from traditionalists who, feeling threatened, fall back on vernacular cultural values as protection. Rapidly expanding the liberal arts school system in the vernaculars at a time when the colonial administrator's *lingua franca* must be replaced produces educated unemployed, stops the creation of a nationwide elite, and provokes minority anxieties about their own future opportunities.

Simultaneously, a westernized elite at a cultural distance from the masses and not having solved important public problems is an easy target of criticism and scorn for those who would use ethnic enthusiasm as a means of replacing the leaders who gained power at independence. As a result of such political developments, new pressure groups form around divisive, parochial purposes while new leadership may only encourage extremists if it is indecisive.

In the Ceylon setting, the westernized elite no longer can be as self-assured as it used to be. Consolidation of ethnic communities into one nation is farther away today than it was ten years ago. The task of mending the social fabric will tax the skill and statesmanship of the new government of Mrs. Sirimavo Bandaranaike, widow of the former Prime Minister, whose electoral coalition won handsomely in June 1960. In other new countries, too, national consolidation remains one of the crucial problems of the future, demanding quite as much courage and foresight as the more familiar problems of economic development.

CAUSAL FACTORS IN LATIN AMERICAN POLITICAL INSTABILITY

Kenneth F. Johnson

* * *

THE INSTABILITY SYSTEM

Political instability occurs when the governing instituions of organized society are ineffective in gratifying popular wants and expectations. In that sense, governments are "maximizers," to use David Apter's term, sending out streams of satisfactions.[1] Failure of governments to gratify popular wants leads to political alienation in varying degrees of intensity. Alienation, in turn, is not a fixed quality but varies according to a number of causal factors. Political alienation may be defined as a deeply felt resentment toward social and governing institutions which is so intense as to be manifested in happenings which contribute to political instability. Political instability, accordingly, is defined as a state of conflict between governments and (competing) power groups which is characterized by overt acts of violence, by support for extreme political radicalism, or by apathy in the face of movements which are committed to extreme, radical, or violent dislocations of the status quo.[2] Thus, political alienation is seen as a widely shared attitude-potential and instability is viewed as those phenomena proceeding therefrom.

* * *

From Kenneth F. Johnson, "Causal Factors in Latin American Political Instability," *Western Political Quarterly* 27 (September 1964): 435-41. Reprinted by permission of the author and The University of Utah, copyright holder.

Causal factors in Latin American political instability may be viewed as actors in a circular or self-reinforcing system. Their cumulative effect is a barrier to the drives of Latin American nations toward economic development and political stability. As a result of low socioeconomic development, maldistribution of wealth reaches critical levels; frustration of mobility expectations is widespread and produces popular elite alienation, disaffection, and outright aggression toward the state.

Political instability in Latin America results from the circular interaction of three general categories of factors: (1) entrepreneurial deficiencies (includes passive and flight capital, social values and cultural influences, religious institutions, illiteracy); (2) high degrees of role substitutability among politically relevant performance entities; and (3) accelerated urbanization and overpopulation.

Entrepreneurial Deficiencies

As a human dynamic, entrepreneurship is defined as "the function of perceiving and effectuating new combinations of factors of production in order to take advantage of existing or anticipated market situations."[3] The commercial entrepreneur deals in ideas, supported by capital from credit or familial sources, in such a way as to realize a marginal profit. Governmental entrepreneurship relates largely to leadership expertise at problem solving through public policy and administration. Both entrepreneurial forms require available active capital for effective functioning. The relative absence of entrepreneurship accounts for much of Latin America's backwardness and contributes to political instability.

Chronic to all underdeveloped countries is illiteracy, a tremendous entrepreneurial deficiency, which has been abundantly treated in the literature on Latin American political change and, requiring no further elaboration here, will be passed over in preference for other factors.

Social attitudes and values act to inhibit entrepreneurial growth in Latin America. Throughout the area, there is a general lack of individual preparedness to take big financial risks in order to capture lucrative gains. Although many Latin Americans are willing to invest in stocks, bonds, mutual funds, and securities, the majority of investors prefer something safer such as land or independently issued credit at high rates of interest. One frequently hears stories of private money caches both great and small. According to informal reports, one would expect fairly impressive sums to appear if all of these passive investors were to declare their resources.

Because a genuinely competitive and collaborative spirit is lacking, Latin Americans are suspicious of impersonal institutions which control and allocate capital. Investors prefer to keep their funds out of banks and government-sponsored lending institutions where they might otherwise be available for entrepreneurial use as development capital. Reluctance to mobilize capital for entrepreneurship accompanies failure to achieve volume marketing conditions through increased unit output. According to

197

testimony and empirical observation in Colombia and Mexico, there seems to be an ingrained notion that it is better to sell a few items at a high price than to improve one's total income through promotion of volume sales at a reduced price.[4]

Another entrepreneurial deficiency lies in the problem of excessive centralization of decision making where allocation of credit for commercial development is concerned. In Mexico, for instance, major credit decisions are regularly made at the "home office" level which normally means the capital city.[5] Moreover, thousands of decisions of relatively small consequence also require central validation. Interviews in both Mexico and Colombia revealed the belief among businessmen that provincial locations are definitely less favored than central ones where credit dispensation is concerned. In Mexico, for instance, major credit decisions are regularly made at the associated with parasitic development of certain cities at the expense of regional economies.[6]

Still a further barrier to effective entrepreneurship is found in Latin American religious institutions. Drawing on the works of Tawney and Weber, the general proposition may be made that the Roman Catholic ethic, being preoccupied with achieving and preserving grace in the sight of God, discourages the vigorous competitive spirit needed for accomplishment within an entrepreneurial value hierarchy.[7] Besides Roman Catholicism, anthropologists have noted in certain Indian societies value systems which discourage capital formation for other than ceremonial purposes. Eric Wolf found that the Maya Indians of Mexico and Guatemala accumulate capital for annual religious displays which wipe out family savings.[8] Specifically Wolf says of the Maya, "he is not a capitalist nor free of restrictions; his economic goal is not capital accumulation but subsistence and participation in the religio-political system of his community."[9]

Ultimately, in the deep recesses of Latin American culture, one comes to the inescapable conclusion that collusion rather than collaboration is the dominant characteristic of human enterprise. As John A. Crow writes of the Mexicans, "Mexican society, composed as it is of many . . . personal islands, is lacking in social cohesion, solidarity, collective enterprise, collaboration, and human charity.[10] The absence of a truly collaborative spirit is an enormous enterpreneurial deficiency which Latin America cannot easily overcome.

Entrepreneurial deficiencies constitute a market imperfection which allows capital to flow into passive rather than active forms. The process is circular and affects the public and private sectors of the economy jointly. Exploitive tributary taxation and corrupt fiscal allocation by governments discourage private investment and capital formation. Public fiscal dishonesty inspires nonpayment of taxes and wastes much of whatever funds are collected. Accumulated capital is hoarded or invested in ritual and prestige items or in usurious investments with proceeds concealed from taxation or exported abroad. Public treasuries are thus impoverished and public services remain at low levels. Controlling value systems sustain corrupt public officials and inhibit adoption of policies aimed at socioeconomic betterment. Low entrepreneurial growth means that Latin American economies cannot absorb rapid population increase without hardship. Frustration of mobility expectations is therefore widespread and dictates to political alienation and instability.

Role Substitutability Among Politically Relevant Performance Entities

Gabriel Almond's definition of a pre-industrial political system emphasized the relative ease with which performance entities could usurp each other's natural role. This condition has been endemic to Latin America and is a major causal factor in political instability. George Blanksten notes that in some Latin American countries the army performs a number of unspecialized and undifferentiated functions ranging from administering public education to conducting elections.[11] With increasing functional differentiation in the private economy, Blanksten sees the possibility of a trend toward "more specialized functions of political institutions . . . and basic alterations in the commitments of governing elites."[12] Whereas in Colombia, Peru, and Ecuador the Church is landowner, public educator, and political practitioner as well as a religious institution, "with the march of the developmental process it is likely that the last of these functions will tend to become the exclusive, specialized and differentiated role of the Church."[13]

The prevailing lack of role specialization and interdependence among performance entities in Latin America is a continuing invitation to armies and government bureaucracies to usurp each other in a power grab. Likewise, the failure of Latin American universities to become specialized seats of learning has relegated student groups to extreme and radical political roles. The same may be said for trade unions which, in countries such as Bolivia, Venezuela, and Argentina, constitute veritable "parties" in themselves and are frequently embroiled in extreme acts which contribute to political instability.

The apparent ease with which performance entities have usurped each other in Latin America may be partly explained in terms of the relative absence of social pluralism within that political culture. Involving as it does a multiplicity of overlapping group memberships, social pluralism has a decidedly moderating effect upon political behavior. One's performance in a given membership context is certain to have implications for other memberships as well. Social pluralism is one of the hallmarks of Latin America's incipient middle class which has been viewed by Charles Wagley as moderately conservative.[14] According to John J. Johnson, the Latin American middle sectors are "harmonizers" which avoid the dangers inherent in strictly negative and absolute postulates.[15]

199

Because of the relative lack of social pluralism in Latin America, performance entities become psychologically compartmentalized and politically semi-autonomous. Vocational roles tend to circumscribe social attitudes and political attachments. Armies, bureaucracies, legislatures, are found each with its own highly subjective *élan vital*, an aggressive expansionist force marked by the all-consuming lust for control and easily infused with a moral purpose to justify intrusion upon other roles. For many Latin Americans, a career in the army or government bureaucracy is life's only road to socioeconomic mobility.

* * *

Urbanization and Overpopulation

During the past several decades, urbanization in Latin America has taken on proportions of acute social change.[16] Rural-to-urban migratory patterns complicate efforts to promote urban economic growth and to stimulate new agrarian entrepreneurship. Displaced peasants seek welfare and opportunity in great cities. Frustration of their expectations produces alienation and, thus, urbanization exacerbates existing symptoms of political instability.

The following causes of Latin America's accelerated urbanization may be listed at this point: (1) urban industrialization and the promise of a better life lures unemployed groups from the country; (2) exploitation of rural workers by *latifundistas* forces exodus as does material impoverishment of *minifundistas*;[17] (3) terror and violence perpetuated by bandit groups especially in Colombia, Venezuela, and Peru make rural life unbearable,[18] (4) certain legal structures promote social and economic development of a capital or central city at the expense of the rest of the country as in the case of Haiti;[19] (5) many peasants are motivated to leave their farms because of exploitation by the bureaucracy of an agrarian reform program as in the case of Mexico;[20] and (6) in at least one country, Colombia, there is specific evidence that service in the military brings many young peasants into the city who are unwilling to return to an agrarian life upon completion of their duty.[21] These motivational factors for rural-to-urban migration have meaning for the majority of Latin American nations. Urbanization has brought increased demands upon governments and socioeconomic systems for accommodation of the expanding work force. Because of the entrepreneurial deficiencies discussed earlier, popular expectations for achievement and mobility are frustrated which leads to political alienation and instability.

A concomitant of urbanization has been overpopulation in both urban and rural areas. Though government programs of disease control have sharply reduced infant mortality throughout Latin America, urbanization has not produced a significant decline in over-all fertility rates.[22] While rural populations have continued to grow, rural food production has not always kept pace with urban needs. This keeps food prices high and militates against the already depressed and alienated social sectors. Migrants to the cities find that large families are no longer the asset they were in the country as family incomes are dissipated by nonproducing members who continue to consume. With children under 15 years making up approximately 40 percent of Latin America's total population, the need to provide for these dependents heavily burdens the head of a household. He is at a major disadvantage in seeking to improve his level of living through accumulation of capital for investment or for family emergency.[23]

As Latin American overpopulation continues, pressure mounts upon the already inadequate rural land forcing more and more persons into the great cities where entrepreneurial deficiencies make it doubtful that their wants will be gratified. Growing popular frustration and alienation are manifest in popular support for aggressive radical movements which voice mistrust of government and hatred for the dominant classes.[24] At this point, opportunities for usurpation of governing roles may be seized upon by armies, bureaucracies, or other power groupings and political instability moves across the continuum from latent to overt.

* * *

NOTES

1. David E. Apter, "A Comparative Method for the Study of Politics," *American Journal of Sociology* 64 (1958): 225.

2. Apathy on the part of politically relevant populations is considered a reinforcement factor in the sense of tacit endorsement through inaction.

3. Charles Wolf and Sidney Sufrin, *Capital Formation and Foreign Investment in Underdeveloped Areas* (Syracuse: Syracuse University Press, 1968), p. 21—derived from Joseph Schumpeter, "Economic Theory and Entrepreneurial History," in *Change and the Entrepreneur* (Cambridge: Harvard University Press, 1949), pp. 23-24.

4. In Bogotá, for instance, the author learned that there are hundreds of dwellings remaining vacant much of the year because proprietors favor a high and prestigeful rental price even though a lower one might bring more tenants and an improved total income for the landlord.

5. Paul Lamartine Yates, *El desarrollo regional de México* (México: Banco de Mexico: segunda edición, 1962), p. 205.

6. Gunnar Myrdal, *Economic Theory and Under-Developed Regions* (London: Duckworth, 1957). Myrdal contends that, because of the unhampered play of market forces, development exhibits excessive centralizing tendencies (backwash effects) favoring certain cities at the expense of a more equitable regional development. He views the latter as desirable and labels this phenomenon "spread effects" (p. 55).

Along this same line, the extreme political and economic centralizing tendencies of certain areas have been viewed by Alfred P. Thorne as conducive to oligopoly and monopolistic competition; cf. "Monopolio, oligopolio y el desarrollo económico de las áreas subdesarrolladas en América y el Caribe," *Revista de Ciencias Sociales* 4, (1960): 125-42; see also Ragnar Nurkse, *Problems of Capital Formation in Underdeveloped Countries* (New York: Oxford University Press, 1953).

7. R. H. Tawney, *Religion and the Rise of Capitalism* (New York: Harcourt Brace Jovanovich, 1926). Tawney speaks of barriers to entrepreneurship in the sense of ideology rather than specifically in terms of capital formation. In contrasting Roman Catholic and Calvinist-Puritan views toward commercial enterprise he says that Puritanism "indeed, in short, that money-making if not free from spiritual dangers ... could be, and ought to be, carried on for the greater glory of God." (p. 199).

8. Eric R. Wolf, *Sons of the Shaking Earth* (Chicago: University of Chicago Press, 1959), p. 216.

9. *Ibid.*, p. 224.

10. John A. Crow, *Mexico Today* (New York: Harper Row, 1957), p. 320. Dishonesty in public management is facilitated by multilinear relationships within the extended family or *compadrazgo* and also through the *camaradería (cuello)* complex. "Cuello, a favorite expression among the Ladinos, indicates that a legal matter may be accelerated, or a job for which one is not totally qualified might be secured through the personal influence of an acquaintance who is in power or knows a third party who can be influenced. The *cuello* complex depends upon the strength of friendship established and is often measured in terms of the number of favors dispensed to each other." Cf. Ruben E. Reina, "Two Patterns of Friendship in a Guatemalan Community," *American Anthropologist* 61 (February 1959): 44-50. On the cultural problem of self-affirmation and extreme individualism, see Francisco Miró Quesada, "The Impact of Metaphysics on Latin-American Ideology," *Journal of the History of Ideas* 24 (1963): 539-52.

11. George I. Blanksten, "The Aspiration for Economic Development," *Annals* 334 (March 1961): 17.

12. *Ibid.*, p. 19.

13. *Ibid.*, p. 17.

14. Charles Wagley, "The Brazilian Revolution: Social Changes Since 1930," in *Social Change in Latin America Today*, ed. Lymon Bryson (New York: Harper & Row, 1960), pp. 221-22.

15. John J. Johnson, "The Political Role of the Latin American Middle Sectors," *Annals* 334 (March 1961): 25.

16. This contention is based on the author's "Urbanization and Political Change in Latin America" (Ph.D. diss., Ann Arbor, University Microfilms, 1963).

17. See Robert Carlyle Beyer, "Land Distribution and Tenure in Colombia," *Journal of Inter-American Studies* 3 (April 1961): 281-91, *passim.*

18. See Roberto Pineda Giraldo, *El impacto de la violencia en el Tolima: El caso de El Líbano* (Bogotá: Universidad Nacional de Colombia, 1960).

19. Achille Aristide treats this problem in *Problemes Haitiens* (Port-au-Prince: Imprimierie de L'Etat, 1958).

20. See Rodrigo García Treviño, *Precios Mordidas* (México: Editorial America, 1953).

21. Kenneth F. Johnson and Fernando Gallo C., "Encuesta para un grupo de infantes de marina" (Cartagena: Facultad de Economia de la Universidad de Cartagena, 1962, unpublished sample survey).

22. Pertinent here are a series of studies done by Harold L. Geisert and Carr B. Lavell which were published by George Washington University Press in 1959 and 1960: cf. Geisert, *Population Problems in Mexico and Central America,* and *The Caribbean: Population and Resources;* and Lavell, *Population Growth and Development of South America.* On the topic of birth control, see J. Stycos, Curt Back, Reuben Hill, "Contraception and Catholicism in Puerto Rico," *Milbank Memorial Fund Quarterly* 34 (April 1956): 150-59.

23. Geisert, *Population Problems.*

24. This theme is prominent in Oscar Lewis' study of the slums in Mexico City: *The Children of Sanchez; Autobiography of a Mexican Family* (New York: Random House, 1961), p. xxvii.

SUGGESTIONS FOR FURTHER READING
PART FOUR: NATION-BUILDING: MODERNIZATION
AND POLITICAL INTEGRATION

Ake, Claude. *A Theory of Political Integration.* Homewood, Ill.: Dorsey Press, 1967.

Ashford, Douglas E. *National Development and Local Reform: Political Participation in Morocco, Tunisia, and Pakistan.* Princeton: Princeton University Press, 1967.

Bendix, Reinhard. *Nation-Building and Citizenship.* New York: John Wiley & Sons, 1964.

Coleman, James S., and Rosberg, Carl G., Jr., eds. *Political Parties and National Integration in Tropical Africa.* Berkeley and Los Angeles: University of California Press, 1966.

Deutsch, Karl W. *Nationalism and Social Communication: An Inquiry into the Foundations of Nationality.* 2d ed. Cambridge, Mass.: M.I.T. Press, 1966.

Deutsch, Karl W., and Foltz, William J., eds. *Nation-Building.* New York: Atherton Press, 1966.

203

Johnson, Willard R. *The Cameroon Federation: Political Integration in a Fragmentary Society.* Princeton: Princeton University Press, 1970.

Pye, Lucian W., ed. *Communications and Political Development.* Princeton: Princeton University Press, 1963.

Pye, Lucian W. *Politics, Personality and Nation-Building: Burma's Quest for Identity.* New Haven: Yale University Press, 1962.

PART FIVE
economic development and social change

Developing states in Asia, Africa, and Latin America differ in their approach to development and their ability to achieve a state of self-sustained growth. They also differ in their susceptibility and resistance to the process of social and cultural change brought about by technology, industrialization, and urbanization. They vary in their gross national product, per capita income, economic performance, educational expenditures, defense expenditures, population, national identity or integration, illiteracy rate, morale of certain classes, performance of civil servants, and type of leadership.

Economic development in the developing states of Asia, the Middle East, Africa, and Latin America is not bound by any particular ideology or value system. This does not mean, however, that economic and social progress will not affect ideological and value systems of society. To be sure, development involves basic changes in national behavior and often poses a threat to national unity. Development is not a guarantee to political stability. In fact, change is essentially disruptive.

Economic development is apt to create a gap between the rising expectations and real achievements. Put in another way, there is little relationship between plans and proposals on the

207

one hand and resources on the other. Many of the best conceived plans will generally contain certain features that cannot work out satisfactorily. When development plans are drawn, many people tend to expect immediate results or even miracles. Consequently, the gap between the "revolution of rising expectations" and achievement leads to the "revolution of rising frustrations" and growing dissatisfaction. Economic development is neither easy nor an automatic process. Tradition-bound, agricultural societies cannot hope to become industrialized until the preconditions for the take-off are established over a relatively long period of time. These preconditions include the breakdown of traditionalism and the existing feudal or semifeudal relationships; the development of new ways of doing things; the expansion of educational facilities; the encouragement of savings which must be channeled into investment; the expansion of the market and financial institutions; and the reorganization of the social and economic structure. This reorganization means that power, wealth, and privilege are apt to undergo radical shifts or even cause the elimination of the previously dominant vested interests. Restrictions of social mobility and equal opportunity created by caste system or class must be broken and distribution of rewards must be made on prescriptive (merit) rather than ascriptive basis. There must be administrative and land reforms and reorganization of the tax structure. People must be prepared to accept new forms of organizations and new centers of social and political power.

Economic development is not a process which breeds social contentment. Technical, economic, and ecological changes affect the social and cultural fabric of society. As society becomes more industrialized and urbanized and moves from subsistence farming toward the commercial production of agricultural goods, family relations, working relations, and community relations change. Rapid economic development may be a destabilizing process in many ways. It disrupts traditional social groups such as the family, caste, or class and consequently creates circumstances conducive to revolutionary protest. Second, it increases geographic mobility which undermines traditional family ties and in particular, encourages rapid migration from rural areas to cities which produces alienation and political extremism. Third, it requires a general restriction on consumption and thus creates popular discontent. Finally, it increases regional and ethnic conflict over the distribution of consumption and investment. Among the factors that inhibit economic progress and modernization, the following are paramount:

1. capital shortage
2. low per capita income
3. low saving level
4. lack of technological skill
5. poor utilization of national and human resources
6. low productivity
7. high birth rate and declining mortality rates
8. high illiteracy rate
9. agrarian economy
10. inadequate communication and transportation systems
11. scarcity of natural resources
12. limited social mobility
13. unfavorable political conditions
14. weak and arbitrary tax system
15. corruption in public administration
16. absence of a strong middle class
17. tradition-bound society
18. lack of land reforms
19. lack of organized marketing
20. suspicion of and discrimination against foreign exports and capital.

Developing states find themselves in a vicious circle of poverty. Illiteracy, lack of technological knowledge, tradition-oriented social institutions and values, etc., produce underdevelopment of resources, in turn leading to low income and low output. Low income contributes to low consumption demand and a low level of savings devoted to capital formation and investment. While low capital formation may be adequate for such projects as schools, roads, and housing, it is inadequate for purposes of eradicating those traditional orientations of the masses that bolster existing institutional imperfections.[1]

Underdevelopment cannot be mitigated by concentration upon one or two factors such as socio-ecological environment (caste system, rural-urban dichotomy, traditional values and attitudes, etc.), population explosion, capital formation, or technological knowledge. The problem facing developing nations is multicausal, encompassing all such factors, each interacting with the others. These interlocking problems are the hard political realities which characterize, in various degrees, most of the developing countries in the twentieth century.[2]

In the following three articles Hagen, Spengler, and Rose explore in detail the process of economic development and social change in developing societies. Everett E. Hagen states that the requirements for the transition to economic growth are: (1) fairly widespread creativity—problem-solving ability, and a tendency to use it and (2) attitudes toward manual-technical labor and the physical world. He points out that a theory of economic growth must give attention to the forces which change those two aspects of personality. The presence of low level creativity helps explain the absence of innovation in the social and political fields. In psychological terms the central characteristics of creativity include high need for achievement, high need for autonomy, and high need for order.

Hagen raises the questions of how did social change ever occur and how did technological progress and economic development ever begin? His answer is formulated in the concept of harsh "withdrawal of status respect." Hagen finds that the innovative and creative individual is the one who has been alienated from traditional values and belongs to a rejected group. As Hagen puts it, "The fact that the disparaging group . . . was traditional, is one of the reasons why the disparaged group rejected traditional values and turned to innovation."

J. J. Spengler focuses his discussion on the political conditions and political consequences of economic development in developing nations. He discusses the indicators of under-development and the determinants of economic growth. Growth-favoring factors are intercorrelated and tend to cluster even as do growth-retarding factors. Spengler identifies the specific positive or negative roles or functions of government which directly or indirectly affect economic growth. Moreover, he lists what he regards as the minimal political conditions for economic development. These minimal requirements include (1) minimal public services; (2) growth-supporting and growth-stimulating arrangements; (3) personnel; and (4) political instruments. Spengler proceeds to show that as economic development moves ahead, growth-affecting political conditions and requirements change. In general, he states, "economic development tends eventually to be accompanied by both political and economic decentralization."

The article by Arnold Rose uses sociological concepts to explain economic development or the lack of it in India. Rose seeks to interpret economic behavior in a context of social institutions and cultural values. In other words, he examines the culture and social system of India for characteristics that would seem to promote economic inefficiency or efficiency. For example, he examines the impact of the joint family, caste systems, and the Hindu religious values on the economy and offers several suggestions for increasing the economic efficiency of India. He states that agricultural policy, bureaucracy, and the status-conception of government officials have hampered economic activity in India. There are also the problems of population explosion and superstitions which hinder economic development. Rose concludes his article by discussing the factors facilitating economic development.

NOTES

1. A. J. Kondonassis, "Concepts of Economic Development with Special Reference to Underdeveloped Countries," in *The Emergent Nations*, ed. Oliver Benson (Norman, Okla.: Graduate International Studies Program, University of Oklahoma, 1963), pp. 81-82.
2. Gilbert Abcarian and George S. Masannat, *Contemporary Political Systems* (New York: Charles Scribner's Sons, 1970), p. 294.

HOW
ECONOMIC GROWTH BEGINS:
A THEORY
OF SOCIAL CHANGE

Everett E. Hagen

This paper proposes a theory of how a "traditional" society becomes one in which continuing technical progress (hence continuing rise in per capita production and income) is occurring. I shall define a traditional state of society in the following section. The hypotheses which I present to explain the change from this state to one of continuing technological progress may be relevant also to the analysis of other types of social change.

The theory does not suggest some one key factor as causing social change independently of other forces. Rather, it presents a general model of society, and deals with interrelationships among elements of the physical environment, social structure, personality, and culture. This does not imply a thesis that almost anything may cause something, so that one must remain eclectic and confused. Rather, certain factors seem of especial importance in initiating change, but their influence can be understood only by tracing interrelationships through the society. It is implied that general system analysis is a fruitful path to advance in societal theory. Since presented in brief compass, the model is necessarily presented rather starkly here.[1]

The purely economic theories of barriers which explain the absence of growth seem inadequate. The assumption that the income of entire populations is too low to make saving easy; that markets in low-income countries are too small to induce investment; that costly lumps of expenditure for transport facilities, power plants, etc., which low-income countries cannot provide, are a requisite to growth—these and related

From Everett E. Hagen, "How Economic Growth Begins: A Theory of Social Change," *Journal of Social Issues* 14 (January 1963): 20-34.

theories are internally consistent but seem without great relevance to reality. Empirical study of low-income societies demonstrates that the supposed conditions and requirements do not in fact exist or are not of great importance. Neither are the differences among nations with respect to growth explained by differences in the degree of contact with the West. Contact with the technical knowledge of the West is a requisite for growth, but forces quite independent of the degree of contact determine whether a nation uses that knowledge. The most spectacular example of this fact is that among the four great Asian nations, Indonesia and India had the most contact with the West during the period 1600-1900, China had an intermediate amount, and Japan the least. Moreover, Indonesia and India experienced the most Western investment, China an intermediate amount, and Japan none whatever until her economic growth was already well under way. Yet among the four countries Japan began to develop first, and has developed rapidly; Indonesia is the laggard,; and if China solves her agricultural problem her growth will probably be faster than that of India.

These facts suggest some hypotheses which a theory of growth should not emphasize. Certain other facts give more positive indications of the elements with which a plausible theory must deal.

Economic growth has everywhere occurred interwoven with political and social change. Lipset and Coleman have demonstrated the correlation between economic change and the transition from authoritarian to "competitive" politics in Asia, Africa, and Latin America, and the same relationship is found in every country elsewhere that has entered upon economic growth.[2] The timing is such that it is clear that the economic growth does not occur first and cause the political-social change. Rather, the two are mutually dependent. Whatever the forces for change may be, they impinge on every aspect of human behavior. A theory of the transition to economic growth which does not simultaneously explain political change, or explains it merely as a consequence of the economic change, is thus suspect.

One last consideration will serve to lead up to the exposition of the model. It is this: the concept is rather widely held in the West that the present low-income societies can advance technically simply by imitating the technical methods already developed in the West. That concept is ethnocentric and incorrect. Mere imitation is impossible. A productive enterprise or process in the West depends for its efficiency on its position in a technical complex of facilities for supplies, services, transportation, and communication, and on a complex of economic, legal, and other social institutions. The management methods which work well within the plant and in its relationships to other units, depend on a complex of attitudes toward interpersonal relationships which are not closely paralleled by attitudes elsewhere. When the process is lifted out of its complex, to adapt it so that it will function in an underdeveloped economy requires technical and especially social and cultural creativity of a high order.

213

Requirements for the transition to economic growth, then, are (1) fairly widespread creativity—problem-solving ability, and a tendency to use it—and (2) attitudes toward manual-technical labor and the physical world such that the creative energies are channeled into innovation in the technology of production rather than in the technology of art, war, philosophy, politics, or other fields. I believe that exploration of these facets of the process of economic growth is a useful approach to a theory of social change.

What is in point is not widespread genius but a high degree of creativity in a few individuals and a moderately high level in a larger number. I shall suggest reasons to believe that the traditional state of a society is associated with a rather low level of creativity among the members of the society. Further, the persons in traditional society who are in position to innovate are the elite—perhaps the lower elite, but certainly not the peasants and urban menials. It is well known that being concerned with tools, machinery, and in general physical processes seems demeaning to the elite and is repugnant to them. It seems to me that a theory of economic growth must give considerable attention to the forces which change those two aspects of personality.

THE STABILITY OF
TRADITIONAL SOCIETY

When I refer to a traditional society I have in mind a traditional agricultural society, for while there have also been traditional hunting and fishing societies and traditional pastoral societies,[3] they can hardly accumulate many artifacts and hence continuing technical progress is hardly possible in them. A traditional agricultural society is of course one in which things are done in traditional ways, but two other characteristics which have been typical of the world's traditional societies and turn out to be essential qualities of the type are also worthy of note here.

First, the social structure is hierarchical and authoritarian in all of its aspects—economic, political, religious. The existence of an authoritarian hierarchy does not refer merely to a large mass who were submissive and to a small class who rule. Rather, every individual in a traditional hierarchy except perhaps for one or a few at the very apex is submissive to authoritarian decisions above him, and in turn exercises authority on persons below him. And this is true even of the lowliest peasant, who as he grows older and becomes a husband, a father, and an elder in his village, becomes increasingly an authority in some aspects of his social relations.

Secondly, one's status in the society is, with little qualification, inherited. One does not earn it; one is born to it. The families of the politically dominating groups, who usually also are economically powerful landed groups, provide the officers of the armed forces and the professional classes as well as the political leaders. Lesser elites also perpetuate their status, though with somewhat greater mobility.

214 These characteristics of the society as well as its techniques of

production are traditional and change very slowly. While the model of a completely unchanging traditional society is a construct, an ideal type, it is sufficiently relevant to reality to be useful. From the beginning of agriculture in the world until say 1600 the traditional state of society persisted everywhere except that occasionally, here and there, was a bursting out of the traditional mode for a few hundred years, then a lapse back into it, sometimes at the original technical level, sometimes at a higher one. The present-day transition to economic growth is such a bursting out. We must ask, Why has the traditional state of society been so persistent? and then, Why have the bursts of change occurred? Or at least, Why have the modern bursts of change occurred?

One condition sometimes suggested as an answer to the first question is that the instruments of power were in the hands of the elite. The traditional authoritarian hierarchical state persisted, it is suggested, because the elite kept the simple folk in subjection by force. This explanation seems inadequate. It is possible for a small group to keep an unwilling 97 percent of a society in subjection by force for a decade or two, or perhaps for a generation or two, though if the subjection persists even this long one must ask whether it really was entirely unpleasing. But that the masses were kept in subjection primarily by force for many centuries seems improbable. The authoritarian hierarchical traditional social structure must have persisted because submitting to authority above one, as well as exercising authority, was satisfying, and secondly because the conditions of life recreated personalities, generation after generation, in which it continued to be so.

Creative and Uncreative Personality

To suggest probable reasons why authoritarian social structure was satisfying, let me digress to discuss certain aspects of personality.

Many elite individuals in traditional societies are prevented from using their energies effectively in economic development by their repugnance to being concerned with the grubby material aspects of life. The repugnance includes being concerned with the details of running a business effectively, as well as performing manual-technical labor—"getting their hands dirty." Often the repugnance is largely unconscious; the individuals concerned often deny it, because it does not occur to them that any middle- or upper-class person anywhere would have any more favorable attitude toward engaging in such activity than they have. Why does this attitude exist?

It is deep rooted. I would explain it as follows. Every person in any society who holds or gains privileged position in life must justify it to himself, in order to be comfortable. If he has gained it by his abilities, justification is easy. The person who gains it by the accident of birth is forced to feel that it is due him because he is essentially superior to the simple folk. Typically, the elite individual in traditional societies feels that his innate superiority consists in being more refined than the simple folk.

215

One evidence of his greater refinement is that he does not like the grubby attention to the material details of life which is one of their distinguishing characteristics. However this attitude may have developed historically, once it exists the elite child acquires it from infancy on by perceiving the words, the attitudes, the tone of voice of his elders. By the time he is six or eight years old, it is deeply bred into his personality.

This attitude alone would not contribute to the lack of innovation in social and political fields. Presence of a low level of creativity, however, would help to explain absence of innovation in these fields as well as in techniques of production.

The explanation of a low level of creativity and justification for the assertion that it exists are more complex.

One component of creativity is intelligence, and intelligence is in part due to biological characteristics. However, although individuals differ greatly in inherited intellectual capacity, the best evidence suggests no reason to assume any appreciable average difference in this respect between the individuals of traditional societies and those of other societies. There are varying degrees of innate intelligence in both. Persons in traditional societies are not less creative because they are less intelligent.

A more relevant component is certain attitudes. In formal psychological terms, I would suggest as characteristics central to creativity high need (for) achievement, high need autonomy, high need order (though this needs further definition), and a sense of the phenomena about one as forming a system which is conceptually comprehensible, rather than merely being arbitrary external bundles.

A person who has high need achievement feels a sense of increased pleasure (or quite possibly a lessening of chronic anxiety, which is the same thing) when he faces a problem or notes a new and irregular phenomenon in a field of interest to him; by the pleasure he anticipates in using his capacities he is drawn to use his energies to understand and master the situation. A person with high need autonomy takes for granted that when he has explored a situation in an area of interest to him, his evaluation of it is satisfactory. He does not think he "knows it all"; he seeks ideas; but when he has thus gained a perspective he assumes that his discriminations and evaluations are good; he feels no anxiety about whether the judgments of other persons differ from his. He does not rebel against the conventional view for the sake of rebelling, but neither does he accept it because it is generally accepted. In Rogers' phrase, the "locus of evaluative judgment is within him."[4]

A person with high need autonomy and also high need order, in the sense in which I use that phrase here, tolerates disorder without discomfort, because sensing that the world is an orderly place, he knows that within the disorder there is complex and satisfying order, and he is willing to tolerate the disorder, and in fact even enjoys it somewhat, until the greater order shall suggest itself to him. Such a person is alert to phenomena which contradict his previous assumptions about the scheme of things, for he assumes that he will be able to perceive the order implicit in them and thus gain an enlarged understanding of the world. In Poincaré's terms, he has a "capacity to be surprised"; in Rogers', "openness to experience."[5]

These characteristics are not fully independent of each other. In technical jargon, they may not be orthogonal. This categorization of personality therefore does not quite go to the roots of things. But it will do for my present purpose.

This personality complex may be contrasted with one which for the moment I shall term merely uncreative. It includes low need achievement and need autonomy, high need dependence, high need submission-dominance, and a sense of the world as consisting of arbitrary forces.

If an individual does not trust his own capacity to analyze problems, then when he faces a problem, anxiety rises in him. He anticipates failure, and avoids problems. He will find comfort in the consensus of a group (not on a majority decision opposed by a minority, for this involves a clash of judgment and the necessity of choosing between the two judgments). He will find it comfortable to rely on authority for guidance—the authority of older men or of the appropriate person in the hierarchy of authority and status which is always found in a traditional society. He will enjoy having a position of authority himself; one reason for this is that if he must make a decision, he can give it the sanction of his authority; persons below him, if they in turn find it comfortable to rely on authority, will not question his decision, and he does not need to feel anxiety lest analysis of it would prove it to have been wrong. It is right because a person with the proper authority made it.

A person with such needs will avoid noting phenomena that do not meet his preconceptions, for their existence presents a problem. In any event, since he senses the world as consisting mainly of arbitrary forces, an unexpected phenomenon provides no clue to him. It is simply a possible source of failure or danger.

I shall suggest below that the experiences in infancy and childhood which give a person this perception of the world inculcate rage and need aggression in him, but also fear of his own need aggression, and therefore anxiety in any situation within his group in which power relationships are not clearly defined and conflict leading to aggressiveness might occur. Hence he likes a clearly defined structure of hierarchical authority, in which it is obviously proper for him to submit to someone above him or give orders to persons below him, without clash of judgment. In addition, his need aggression also causes him to feel pleasure in dominating those below him—his children, his juniors, his social inferiors.

Thus there are dual reasons why the authoritarian hierarchy is satisying. It is appropriate to give this personality type not merely the negative label "uncreative" but also the positive one "authoritarian."[6]

While it is evident that these two personality types exist, to this point it is purely an assumption that authoritarian personality is typical in traditional societies. One reason for thinking that this is true is that this hypothesis explains many things about traditional societies which otherwise are puzzling. It explains, for example, why many persons in traditional societies not only follow traditional methods, but seem to cling almost compulsively to them, even though to an outsider trial of a new method seems so clearly to their advantage. It explains why the method of decision of local problems in so many traditional societies is by consensus of the village elders, through a long process of finding a least-common-denominator solution on which all can agree, rather than by majority vote. It explains, too, why authoritarian social and political systems have persisted in such societies for such long periods.

That a hypothesis explains a number of phenomena which are otherwise puzzling is strong reason for accepting it. However, there is also more direct reason for believing that authoritarian personality is unusually prevalent in traditional societies. This reason lies in the existence of some evidence that childhood environment and childhood training in traditional societies are of the kind which tend to produce such personality.

Perhaps the factor which is most important in determining whether childhood environment will be such as to cause the formation of creative personality or such as to cause the formation of authoritarian personality is the opinions of the parents concerning the nature of infants and children. Suppose that the parents take for granted that infants are oganisms which, while delicate and in need of protection for a time, have great potentials; organisms which as they unfold will develop capacity for understanding and managing life. A mother who regards this as an axiomatic fact of life will if she is sensible take precautions to keep her child's explorations of the world around him from causing harm or alarm to him, but she will let him explore his world and will watch with interest and pleasure as his muscular capacities develop, his range of activity expands, and he accomplishes in endless succession the hundreds of new achievements which occur during infancy and childhood.

His repeated use of his new physiological capacities, as they unfold, is from his viewpoint problem solving—intensely interesting problem solving. Assume that it is successful because his mother has taken safeguards so that he will not fall out of his crib, cut himself, break the glassware, fall down stairs, etc., and because his mother offers advice and restraint when necessary. Assume, however, that his venturings do not meet repeated restraint, because his mother trusts his developing capacities and does not check his every step. Then he will repeatedly feel joy at his own successful problem solving and pleasure in his mother's pleasure. There will be deeply built into him the pattern that initiative is rewarded, that his judgment is adequate, that solving problems is fun.

If his mother wants him to be self-reliant, presses him to do things as soon as his capacities have developed, usually refuses to let him lapse into babyhood after he has gained capacities, and shows displeasure when he does not do things for himself, then the stimulus of her displeasure when

218

he does not show initiative will be combined with that of her pleasure when he does so. I have mentioned only his mother. During the first year or more of his life, her attitude is the most important one in his life; after that the attitude of his father (and so that of his siblings) toward his behavior will also be important.

Suppose, alternatively, that the child's parents have as a part of their personalities the judgment that children are fragile organisms without much innate potential capacity to understand or manage the world. Then during the first two years or so of life the mother is apt to treat the child over-solicitously, and to shield him somewhat anxiously from harm. In doing so, unintentionally she also keeps the child from using his unfolding initiative. The use of initiative come to alarm him, because it alarms her. Then, after these first few years of life, when the parents think the child is old enough to be trained, parents with the view that children are without much potential inner capacity train the child by a continual stream of commands and instructions concerning what is good to do and not good to do, the proper relationships to them and to others, and in general how he should live. Exercise of initiative on his part frequently brings alarm and displeasure and hence causes him anxiety. He can avoid anxiety only by passively obeying the instructions of these powerful persons so important in his life. The instructions will often seem arbitrary to him and the repeated frustration of his initiative will create anger in him. He will repress it, but this does not mean that it disappears.

The practices and attitudes of older siblings and playmates who have been brought up under the same influences will provide models which in various ways will reinforce the same lesson.

The impact of these parental attitudes on the child may be reinforced by certain related attitudes of the parents. The existence of any child restricts the freedom of his parents, and interferes with their relations to each other. Moreover, the child exerts a will independent of theirs, and they are not always sure that they can control him. If the parents, especially the mother, are relaxed confident people, they will not be disturbed by these problems. Suppose, however, that they are somewhat anxious persons who feel that they themselves do not understand the world (as they are apt to feel if their own childhood was like that which I have just described). Then their child may repeatedly make them anxious, and unconsciously they may hate him for causing them anxiety and also interfering with their freedom. The child is sure to sense their hostility; it will both make him more afraid to venture and increase his pleasure in venting his frustrations by controlling someone below him later in life.

Exposure to the one or the other of these parental attitudes will have an impact on the child through infancy and childhood, but for brevity I shall mention specifically only the most conspicuous manifestation, that during the "period of infantile genitality," which usually occupies about the fourth and fifth years of life. At this age a boy knows that he is a male, like his father, and that he will become big, like his father, and he begins

219

to wonder whether he can successfully rival his father. Specifically, he becomes a rival of his father for his mother's attentions. If his father and mother are perceptive and understanding persons, they will accept him into their fellowship and let him gain an adequate degree of the feminine attention he needs. However, without anxiety or arbitrariness, they will teach him that he can postpone his demands when the circumstances require it, and need not feel anxiety at the postponement. He will learn, as before, that one's initiative must be judicious, and he will also reinforce powerfully the earlier lesson that the exercise of his initiative is safe and brings pleasure.

If the father is weak and the mother is not arbitrary and somewhat rejecting, the son may gain his mother's attentions not because his parents understand his needs and meet them but because his father gives up at the boy's aggressive persistence. In this case too the son will learn that initiative is successful, though he will learn it with overtones of anxiety.

Suppose, however, that the parents doubt their own ability to manage problems, and, having no faith in the capacities of children, regard the boy's initiative as a danger rather than a valuable attribute. Then they will be disturbed by the boy's emerging rivalry with his father during the period of infantile sexuality, will resent the boy's encroachment, and will "put the boy in his place." The experience will reinforce the anxiety and alarm that the boy felt earlier at the exercise of initiative. It will also reinforce the anger that the boy felt earlier at his parents' arbitrary restrictions, and since he cannot vent his anger at his parents, there is apt to build up in him an unformed desire to exercise arbitrary authority himself, and lord it over someone under him, later in life—just as the college freshman humiliated by hazing at the hands of sophomores often waits his turn to vent his humiliation on the new freshmen the next year.

The impact of the one or other type of parental personality on girls during this period is not quite parallel to that on boys, because of the different sexual role which girls have already learned. The differences will not be discussed here.

In these ways, creative or authoritarian personality is formed. There are many other aspects to the process, and many other aspects of authoritarian and creative personalities, which cannot be discussed here.[7] This brief discussion will, I hope, give the general flavor of both the personality types and the process which forms them.

I think that the reader may already have realized that the parental attitudes which tend to create authoritarian personality in the children are themselves components of authoritarian personality in the parents. That is, persons in whom authoritarian personality was created by the circumstances of their childhoods are apt to have such a view of life that they will in turn create an environment which will cause authoritarian personalities to appear in their children. The type, like most other personality types, tends to be self-perpetuating.

220   It is of great importance, then, that the scattered evidence which is

available suggests that precisely the sort of childhood environment and training sketched above as conducive to the emergence of authoritarian personality is the sort prevalent in traditional societies. Fairly intensive sketches of childhood environment in Burma by Hazel Histon[8] and in Java by Hildred Geertz,[9] and more fragmentary sketches relating to many Latin societies, indicate that in all of these cases childhood environment is precisely of this type. These sketches refer primarily to the simple folk, but there is some empirical evidence to suggest that they are true of personality and childhood environment among the elite as well.

And there is even more convincing evidence that various of the conspicuous characteristics of authoritarian personality are present in many traditional societies in Latin America and Asia. Though our knowledge concerning African countries is more limited, they are probably present in those countries as well. Hence it seems likely that a low level of creativity is also characteristic of such societies.

Presumably this personality type developed initially because the every day phenomena of the physical world were bewildering to unscientific man. Convinced of his inability to fathom the world, man began to protect his children jealously when they were infants and then train them minutely in the way in which they should behave to be safe. And so authoritarian personality appeared and perpetuated itself. Repugnance to concerning oneself with the humble material matters of life and with manual-technical labor also appeared among the elite, in the way sketched earlier in this essay, and tended to perpetuate itself.

SOCIAL CHANGE

How, then, did social change ever occur? and technological progress and economic development ever begin?

Study of a number of countries in which there has occurred a transition from a traditional state to continuing economic development suggests that an important factor initiating change was some historical shift which caused some group or groups of the lesser elite, who previously had had a respected and valued place in the social hierarchy, to feel that they no longer were respected and valued. This derogation in some societies consisted of explicit indication of contempt for the functions or position of the lesser elite, in others of behavior by a new higher elite which seemed immoral, unmanly, or irreligious to the groups below them, and thus indicated contempt for the moral standards of the lesser elite.

I shall omit the example of England, which is complex and difficult to mention briefly, and shall refer briefly to highlights of three other examples. In the 1650s the Tsar of Russia and Patriarch of Moscow, to attain diplomatic ends by adopting Greek practices, ordered certain changes in the ritual of the Orthodox church which the faithful felt to be heretical and to endanger their souls. There followed conflict and

221

persecution, in waves of varying severity, even down to 1900. The Old Believers, who were the victims of this withdrawal of respect for their status in the society, were prominent in economic development in Russia in the nineteenth century. Concerning the twentieth I have no information.

In Japan the feudal group known as the Tokugawa, who gained national power in 1600, imposed a peace which deprived the samurai of their traditional function; imposed rigid distinctions among social classes which had the effect of relegating the so-called wealthy peasants, descendants of the lesser elite, to the rank of peasant; and to some extent demeaned other feudal groups, the so-called outer clans. It was the lesser samurai and wealthy peasants, apparently especially of the outer clans, who were the innovators in Japan's industrial revolution.

In Colombia, in the 1530s the Spanish settled on a high plateau around Bogota and in the valleys around Cali and Medellin. Through historical developments I shall not sketch, during the next two centuries the settlers of the other two areas came to look down on those in Antioquia, the valley around Medellin. The social friction continues to the present; and the Antioqueños have been the leaders in economic innovation out of all proportion to their numbers in the population.

I shall call such events "withdrawal of status respect" from the group no longer accorded its old place. It is important to note that the situation is one in which a group of the elite once had full status respect and later lost it. What are the results? Let me speculate concerning them.

I suggest that among the adults of the first generation so affected, the reaction is anger and anxiety. Their children, however, seeing that their parents' role in life causes anxiety, do not find it a fully satisfying model. Alternative roles are in general not open to them, and so they respond by repressing somewhat within themselves their parents' values—by ceasing to have *any* role values with the same clarity and intensity their parents did. The process, I suggest, is cumulative in successive generations, and in the second or third or fourth generation there appears pronounced "normlessness," shiftlessness, anomie, or, in Merton's term, retreatism. It can be observed, for example, in Negroes of the southern United States, American Indians on any reservation, first and second generation immigrants, and colonial subjects.[10] Historical records suggest that it also characterized the Antioqueños, the samurai, and the Old Believers.

There is reason to suspect that retreatism affects men more than women because of the differences between the normal social roles of the sexes. After several generations, then, there will appear men who are retreatist and weak, but women who are less so. The women will probably feel some pity for their children's lot in life, and will cherish them tenderly. But, reacting to the ineffectiveness of their husbands, the women will have an intense desire that their sons shall be more effective, and will respond with delight to each achievement in infancy and boyhood. During the period of infantile sexuality, the boy will win in the rivalry with his father, both because his initiative pleases his mother and because his father is weak.

Obviously not all home environments in some generation of a group of the lesser elite from whom status respect has been withdrawn will be like this, but it is plausible to believe that some such environment will appear occasionally, or even fairly often. Some combinations and intensities of such maternal attitudes, combined with weakness in the father, provide an almost ideal environment for the formation of an anxious driving type of creativity.

Where a considerable degree of creativity is inculcated, but the anxiety is great, a variant type of individual may appear, one who gives himself security by being traditional and authoritarian in most aspects of his behavior, and then dares to be bold and creative in some other aspect. Henry Ford was such a person, as was J. Pierpont Morgan. And this type has been important in economic development in Japan, the Soviet Union, and Germany.

Thus, I suggest, there gradually emerges a group of individuals, creative, alienated from traditional values, driven by a gnawing burning drive to prove themselves (to themselves, as well as to their fellows), seeking for an area in which to do so, preferably an area in which they can gain power, and preferably also one in which in some symbolic way they can vent their rage at the elites who have caused their troubles. Moreover, their (perhaps unconscious) rage at the group disparaging them will cause them to turn against some of the values of the group disparaging them. The fact that the disparaging group, in the cases cited above, was traditional, is one of the reasons why the disparaged group rejected traditional values and turned to innovation.

What they turn to will be determined in part by the models they find during their childhood somewhere in their history or their folklore or the tales their elders tell them of the life around them, and in part by the objective opportunities of the world around them. In the modern world, to few socially rebellious groups of traditional societies will any other road to power, recognition, and proof to oneself of one's ability seem as inviting as economic prowess, and creative individuals in most such groups will become economic innovators. In the cases of England, Japan, and Colombia, which I have examined in some detail, such groups have provided a disproportionate share of the leaders in the transition to economic growth.

A word is in point concerning the complexity of the situation in colonial societies. Here there has been rather harsh withdrawal of status respect, but by invading groups from the West who became colonial conquerors. These groups have not traditional but "modern" values toward manual-technical work. The tendency of disparaged groups to reject the values of the disparaging group may cause them to reject engaging their energies in the occupations of the conquerors. Thus even though they desire to gain symbols of economic power, an additional

223

emotional block is put in the way of the indigenous elite becoming effective industrialists. This fact may explain some of the ambivalence and erratic behavior sometimes manifested.

The theory of some of whose central points have been sketched so briefly above proceeds in broad sweeps, and of course is subject to a corresponding margin of error. It seems plausible to me because it is internally consistent and because it explains many aspects of social, political, and economic behavior in low-income countries for which no other very logical explanation seems available.

If it is correct it does not follow that economic growth will succeed only where certain rather special historical conditions have existed. For the forces of modern history have caused social tensions among the social classes of low-income societies themselves, by virtue of which some degree of withdrawal of status respect has existed among the indigenous social classes of almost all of them, and what values various groups are alienated from or drawn to is confused and uncertain. However, innovational personality is clearly appearing, in varying degree. The drive for security, self-reassurance, and power will surely lead many innovational individuals to technological innovation, though frequently within social forms differing from those of the West.

NOTES

1. The model is presented at greater length in E. E. Hagen, *On The Theory of Social Change* (Homewood, Ill.: Dorsey Press, 1962). This paper is in essence an abstract of various chapters of that book.

2. S. Lipset, "Some Social Requisites of Democracy: Economic Development and Political Legitimacy," *American Political Science Review* 53 (March 1959); G. A. Almond, J. S. Coleman et al., *The Politics of the Developing Areas* (Princeton: Princeton University Press, 1960). Adapting their method slightly, I used it in "A Framework for Analyzing Economic and Political Change," in *Development of the Emerging Countries: An Agenda for Research,* R. Asher et al. (Washington, D.C.: The Brookings Institution, 1962).

3. Industrial societies will probably also become traditional in time, which is to say that technical progress will come to an end, at least for a time.

4. H. H. Anderson, ed., *Creativity and Its Cultivation* (New York: Harper & Row, 1959), p. 76.

5. Poincaré's phrase is quoted by Erich Fromm in *ibid.*, p. 48; Rogers' is at *ibid.*, p. 75.

6. It is not congruent in all respects with the one portrayed by Adorno and associates in *The Authoritarian Personality.*

7. For example, models are important in personality formation, and it is of interest to ask where the son of a weak father obtains models of

successful behavior. There are several possibilities. This and other complexities must be passed over here.

8. H. Histon, "Family Patterns and Paranoidal Personality Structure in Boston and Burma" (Ph.D. diss., Radcliffe College, April 1959).

9. H. Geertz, *The Javanese Family* (New York: Free Press of Glencoe, 1955) and "The Vocabulary of Emotion: A Study of Javanese Socialization Processes," *Psychiatry* 22 (August 1959): 225-37.

10. In groups who are not of the lower elite, but instead are of the "simple folk," the later reaction may be not creative innovation but violent social revolt. For lack of space, that branch of the theory cannot be expounded here.

ECONOMIC DEVELOPMENT: POLITICAL PRECONDITIONS AND POLITICAL CONSEQUENCES

J. J. Spengler

"For good or ill, life under the conditions imposed by the modern industrial system . . . is in the long run incompatible with the prepossessions of mediaevalism."
Thorstein Veblen, in "The Opportunity of Japan"

This paper has to do with the political preconditions and the political consequences of economic development. It relates principally to the underdeveloped world, a term which embraces Asia (with the exception of Soviet Asia, Japan and Israel), almost all of Africa, much of Latin America and portions of Southern and Eastern Europe. Around 1950, according to Shannon, 147 of the world's 195 political entities, embracing about 54 percent of the world's landed area, were classifiable as underdeveloped. Within areas variously described as underdeveloped live between 60 and 75 percent of the world's population.[1]

After passing in review some of the characteristics of the under-developed world and touching upon the determinants of economic development, I shall examine, in order . . . the specific roles or functions of government affecting economic development, the minimum political preconditions of economic development and the changes that take place in some of these preconditions as economic development proceeds.

CONCOMITANTS OR INDICATORS OF UNDERDEVELOPMENT

Of the concomitants or indicators of economic development, the cultural and the political are most significant for the present discussion,

From Joseph J. Spengler, "Economic Development: Political Precondi-tions and Political Consequences," *Journal of Politics* 22 (August 1960): 387-416. Reprinted by permission of the author and the publisher.

though the economic, the technological and the demographic are most important from the immediately economic point of view. Here it is necessary only to note that, in the underdeveloped world, per capita income, capital equipment and capital formation are very low; inferior technologies predominate; enterprise is lacking; accessible natural resources are badly exploited; natality and (usually) natural increase are relatively high, in part because so much of the population is rural and agricultural; and the age composition of the population is unfavorable to productivity and the education of youth.[2]

Economic backwardness is associated with various cultural circumstances unfavorable to economic growth. Society is tradition-bound, stable and disposed to preserve stability. The family often is of the extended sort. Land may be communally owned and operated. Educational attainment, together with literacy, is low. Much economic activity may remain unmonetized and free of the regulative influence of markets. The "middle class" is unimportant, and the socio-legal system in effect usually unduly restricts enterprise. The values stressed may not encourage economic development, and incentives favorable to work and enterprise may be weak. And so on. Of course, as a country progresses economically, its cultural environment becomes more favorable to economic progress, within limits. It is usually assumed, however, that the rapidity with which a nation's cultural environment becomes favorable to economic development may be increased through appropriate governmental action, particularly when there are at hand successful working models. It is also taken for granted that persistent economic growth is most likely to get under way *after* suitable institutional arrangements have been established in respect of law, family, education, motivation, reward systems, and the like.

Developed countries resemble each other more closely in economic than in political respects, since the prerequisites to economic development are more specific and exacting than those essential to political development and self-government. Underdeveloped countries resemble one another in some but not in all respects, in part because a given political condition may be favorable to economic development under some circumstances, but not under others. For example, while sometimes absolutist regimes have effectively promoted economic development (*e.g.*, in the Soviet Union), at other times they have retarded it by establishing sanctions against deviant persons who might initiate development.[3] Similarly, parliamentary regimes have sometimes fostered and sometimes retarded economic growth. Self-government, though typically a concomitant of economic development, has not always brought it about. The pseudo-biblical precept engraved on Premier K. Nkrumah's statue in Accra ("Seek ye first the political kingdom and all other things shall be added unto you") has yet to acquire the status of a political axiom. For while only nine negligibly populated non-self-governing political units out of a total of 106 units so describable were economically developed around

227

1950, but 39 of the 89 self-governing political entities were so classifiable. Moreover, the 50 self-governing underdeveloped entities included 55 percent of the world's population, whereas the 97 non-self-governing underdeveloped units included only 8 percent.[4] Of the political characteristics common to all underdeveloped countries, the most important is a dearth of administrative personnel possessed of technical competence and other requisite attributes.

* * *

DETERMINANTS OF ECONOMIC DEVELOPMENT

The determinants of economic development have been variously classified. One may, with Lewis, group them under three principal heads: (1) wide-ranging efforts to economize in the sense of minimizing input per unit of output, or of maximizing output per unit of input; (2) "the increase of knowledge and its application," particularly to production; (3) "increasing the amount of capital or other resources per head."[5] But such a grouping, even though it allows adequate weight to the role of the entrepreneur, tends to understate the roles of cultural, political and other noneconomic factors. It may also overlook social-structural and related obstacles to the formation and the effective investment of capital. There is merit, therefore, in lists of determinants such as the one Rostow has proposed. He suggests that growth depends upon certain propensities which reflect a society's underlying value system and summarize its response to its environment: (1) the propensity to develop fundamental physical and social science; (2) "the propensity to apply science to economic ends"; (3) "the propensity to accept innovations"; (4) "the propensity to seek material advance"; (5) "the propensity to consume, by which saving also is conditioned; (6) "the propensity to have children." The propensities are related, on the one hand, to the more immediate economic causes of economic growth, and, on the other, to determinants or circumstances underlying the propensities in question.[6]

Typological studies suggest that growth-favoring factors, being intercorrelated, tend to cluster even as do growth-retarding factors. Facilitation of a society's economic development therefore initially entails the introduction and the strengthening of enough favorable factors. In proportion as these variables are loosely instead of tightly interconnected, initial growth-favoring changes must be large if they are to be propagated through the system of interrelated variables and bring about new, intervariable equilibria that remain sufficiently unstable to make for continuing growth.

* * *

SPECIFIC ROLES OR FUNCTIONS
OF GOVERNMENT

The state, of course, may contribute, positively or negatively, to economic development by pursuing courses which indirectly or directly affect economic growth. It may contribute indirectly through actions suited to strengthen the private sector, and directly by carrying on appropriate activities in the public sector. An economy is not always reducible, of course, to terms of a private sector and a public sector. The two sectors may overlap and become intermixed, inasmuch as many of the choices available lie on a continuum running from one extreme to the other.[7]

The negative actions of government include failure to maintain law and order; corruption in public administration, together with plundering of commercial and other enterprising classes; exploitation of submerged classes, together with denial to them of access to superior occupations; abuse or exclusion of foreigners possessing requisite skills, enterprise, capital, new tastes, *etc.*; nonmaintenance of essential public services; failure to provide critical assistance and stimuli to economic sectors in which development may be triggered off; unduly restrictive regulation of economic activities; diversion of an excessive fraction of the community's surplus above consumption into unproductive forms of public capital; imposition of taxes which are arbitrary, uncertain and of a sort to blunt incentive; waste of resources in war; premature development of effective trade unions, together with "welfare-state" legislation; denial of adequate returns on private investments in public utilities, *etc.*; and diversion of resources from economic to uneconomic activities.

Economic activity can be carried on in the private sector, with some prospect of eventuating in continuing economic development only if certain functions are satisfactorily performed by the government. These include: (1) the maintenance of law and order and security against aggression; (2) sufficient support of education and public health; (3) adequate support of basic research, of the introduction of scientific findings from abroad and of the diffusion of applied scientific knowledge through agricultural extension and similar services; (4) provision, insofar as economically indicated and possible, of certain basic forms of overhead capital. Just as, through (2) and (3), the state may foster the development of a more effective labor force, so through (1) it may augment the capacity of the society to withstand the tensions that accompany economic development.

Satisfying the money requirements of economic development presupposes performance of at least two sets of functions: (5) control of the issue and supply of paper money and bank credit, through an effective central banking system and in a manner capable of preventing marked inflation; (6) making provision, insofar as practicable and necessary, for action on the part of the central banking system and cognate agencies to prevent undue deflation. It does not seem advisable for an underdeveloped country to pursue monetary policies designed to maintain full employment. Its situation, together with the nature of its unemployment (much of it in agriculture and of long standing), differs from that encountered in developed countries; moreover, factor immobility is too great and bottlenecks are too many to permit such policies to work. (7) Provision needs to be made for the establishment, under public or public-private auspices, of financial institutions suited to assemble small savings (*e.g.*, savings banks), to supply short-term and intermediate credit, to channel long-term capital from its sources to securities markets and to facilitate the inflow of foreign capital. (8) The government may contribute notably to the formation of attitudes favorable to economic development. (9) It may influence the uses to which resources are put (*e.g.*, through conservation policies, zoning regulations, *etc.*), the manner in which industry is dispersed in space (so as to prevent excessive concentration, depressed areas, *etc.*), the degree of specialization (*e.g.*, to prevent monoculture, *etc.*). (10) Should the government undertake to influence income distribution, it must proceed warily lest capital formation, the acquisition of skill, the suitable distribution of the labor force, *etc.*, be checked. (11) The system of taxes employed should be so constituted as to diminish private capital formation and economic incentive very little. (12) To meet the many needs of a developing economy, a well-tested, stable, appropriately-oriented, and explicit legal and administrative structure is required, together with effective administrative and judicial personnel. Among the needs that must be met are: provision for the establishment and operation of required types of business organization (*e.g.*, partnership, private corporation, cooperative, public and quasi-public corporations, trade union) and for the associated forms of decision-making power; rules facilitating the holding and the conveyance of property; guarantees of mobility and of freedom of entry on the part of labor and other factors of production into employments for which they are technically qualified; suitable definitions and regulations relating to contractual content, sanctions, limitations, *etc.*; rules insofar as required to avert retardation of growth by quasi-monopolistic and related arrangements; and so on. (13) A government may facilitate economic development by institutionalizing public as well as private initiative, since both are likely to be required, and by drawing on the relevant experience of countries which have achieved high levels of development.

More positive action may be undertaken by a government. It may undertake reform of the system of land tenure. It may attempt to step up capital formation and investment through facilitation of foreign loans, higher taxation and limited inflation, or through the use of unemployed and underemployed manpower to construct economic overhead capital (*e.g.*, highways, railways). The success of such measures turns largely on whether resources are diverted from consumption or from the formation of private capital (which, frequently, is put to more productive use than public capital), and on whether increases in money-income restore to nonsavers (*e.g.*, wage-earners) what inflation and increased taxes have taken away from them. The state may draw up a plan to put resources to particular uses and attempt to implement it by giving to entrepreneurs acting in conformity therewith greater access to resources in short supply (*e.g.*, capital, foreign exchange, skilled labor). It may attempt to affect the course of development directly, by setting up a development corporation to which it channels public revenue, by utilizing public revenue to finance the construction of economic and social overhead capital, by establishing specific agencies to perform entrepreneurial functions, and so on.

MINIMAL POLITICAL CONDITIONS FOR ECONOMIC DEVELOPMENT

While it is not possible always to distinguish sharply between political and economic factors, it is possible to identify a number of essentially political conditions,[8] most of which are prerequisite to economic development in the present-day underdeveloped world. The kind of society envisaged is noncommunist (in the contemporary empirical sense); it may be democratic in the American or British sense, or "dictatorial" in the Latin-American sense. The minimal requirements may be grouped under four main heads: minimal public services; growth-supporting and growth-stimulating arrangements; personnel; and political instruments.

Minimal Public Services

If the state does not make provision for certain minimal services, not much economic activity can be carried on, and little impetus can be given to economic growth. It is, of course, a matter of judgment how large at the minimum the supply of any of these services must be. Here it is noted only that this minimum must be met and that as it is increased economic growth tends (within limits) to be stimulated, though not necessarily in proportion to the increase in services. Having already discussed these services, I shall merely list what the state needs to do:
1. Maintain law, order and security.
2. Support education and public health.
3. Provide for the issue and suitably controlled supply of paper money and bank credit.
4. Provide for the creation of banks to assemble savings, to supply short-term and intermediate credit and to afford access to domestic and foreign long-term capital.
5. Provide as much of a legal and administrative structure as is required to permit various types of business organization to function, to maintain

private and public property and to prevent excessive monopolization of important activities.

6. Treat foreign personnel and capital so that as much is attracted as is warranted by the desire to get economic development under way.

Growth-Supporting and Growth-Stimulating Arrangements

Only the last-mentioned of the services just enumerated actually gives impetus to economic development. Impetus is supplied by entrepreneurs, private or public, but it can be provided only if they have access to capital, to land and natural resources, and to technology that reduces input requirements and creates new goods. Accordingly, the state must pursue positive policies calculated to give support to entrepreneurs while minimizing the impact of policies that are unwelcome to enterprise.

1. Tax revenue needs to be raised through taxes that diminish very little both incentive to economic activity and propensity to form capital.

2. Governmental expenditure should, insofar as possible, assume forms essential or relatively conducive to economic growth.

3. Inasmuch as effective highly centralized planning under government auspices is quite out of the question in most, if not all, underdeveloped countries, reliance must be placed largely upon decentralized, private economic decision making which provides entrepreneurs and others with ample incentive to uncover and test potential opportunities. Hence the state must support a climate of opinion in which entrepreneurial decisions can be made freely and effectively.

4. The state must support basic research, together with the adaptation and diffusion of applied technological knowledge.

5. The state must facilitate the provision of economic and social overhead capital where need for it is indicated, even though the prospective current return on such capital is insufficient to attract private investment.

6. It is desirable, on a number of grounds, among them national prestige, that something like a five-year plan be kept in effect, and that there be established a development corporation, perhaps to help administer such plan and perform various other functions now normally carried on by such corporations. It is desirable that such a plan be subject to revision from year to year as the relative importance of different objects of investment changes. Such a plan, together with changes in it, needs to be made in consultation with the private sector; for, since much of the investment undertaken should serve to increase the productivity of private facilities, or to assist newly-developing private enterprise, it should be directed into channels where it gives greatest stimulus to long-run growth. Given such a plan, public capital expenditures are more likely to be made in light of their comparative capacity to stimulate economic growth, and if

a public development corporation has been established, better direction tends to be given to expenditures included under 4 and 5. The existence of such a plan may even facilitate foreign borrowing. It is always essential, however, whether such a plan be in existence or not, that attention be directed to estimating whether public or private investment expenditure would be the more productive. It is essential also to recognize that the effectiveness with which a development corporation can function turns on its position in the governmental hierarchy and, therefore, varies as this position changes.

7. It is possible, given the arrangements described under 6, that the ever present tendency to inflation can be better kept under control. For then budgetary practice can be more nearly arranged to keep governmental income and outgo in balance, unless imbalance in the private sector indicates some need for an offsetting imbalance in the public sector.

8. It has already been noted that the effectiveness of governmental economic policy is much less subject to critical assessment and rectification than is private economic policy. Furthermore, in many underdeveloped countries there do not exist competent private agencies (e.g., universities, research bureaus) which are both free and able to evaluate governmental economic policies. Hence, governmental expenditure tends to be less conducive to development than it might be. It is essential, therefore, that such competent and free critical agencies be developed and that they have access to the information requisite for periodical assessments of governmental economic policies.[9]

Personnel

Under this head we consider personnel in the employ of agencies of the state. In any economy with both a public and a private sector, between which personnel are free to migrate, it is not possible to specify the number of employees in the public sector, or their quality, since migration may modify both number and quality. From the standpoint of a country's development, of course, migration of relatively skilled personnel from one sector to the other necessarily weakens the capacity of the personnel-losing sector to contribute to economic development. Respecting governmental personnel, at least two conditions may be laid down as essential to economic development.

1. *Quantity and quality of governmental personnel.* The available information indicates that, as yet, in all of the underdeveloped countries, the supply of suitable personnel available to fill governmental posts, particularly those having to do with economic development, is insufficient for getting economic growth under way. Furthermore, much of this personnel is short of technical knowledge, probity and other qualities essential to effective performance. The defects noted—in quantity and

233

quality—are similar to those characteristics of personnel in the private sector. It is generally true that personnel improve in quality at about the same rate in both the public and the private sector, and it is probable that the degree of shortage of qualified personnel is no more pronounced in the public than in the private sector.[10] The shortage of qualified governmental personnel is particularly serious in many underdeveloped countries in which the government is being counted upon to perform much of the innovating and pioneering role largely performed by the private entrepreneur in the West.[11]

The stock of qualified personnel at the disposal of a government thus sets an upper limit to the developmental functions that it can undertake. While a government may draw personnel from the private sector in order to raise this limit, it does not follow that development will thereby be made greater. The outcome depends upon where the personnel in question could make the greater contribution to economic development, in the private or in the public sector. It is essential, therefore, that the stock of qualified personnel be increased in both the private and the public sector, through investment in appropriate education, and so on.

2. *Disposition of governmental personnel.* Because of the shortage of qualified personnel that can perform functions which the state may need but not undertake, it is particularly important that use of governmental personnel be carefully economized. Governmental personnel should be employed only in undertakings in which the input of personnel per unit of output is relatively low, with high priority being given to the performance of the "minimal public services" discussed above. Such personnel should not be engaged in the performance of tasks which nongovernmental personnel can do quite (if not more) effectively, in part because *technically qualified* personnel tend to be more scarce in the public than in the private sector. For, under civil service regulations, the attributes specified as being requisite in those who would perform given sets of tasks tend to be greater than is required in reality or in the private sector. For example, one may need to possess, if he would perform a set of tasks S efficiently only attributes $abcd$; and yet he may be required by civil service regulations to possess, at a minimum, attributes $abcdef$ to qualify for the occupational post to which responsibility for the performance of S is assigned. In this instance, attributes ef are nonessential; moreover, in the private sector, they tend to be treated as nonessential, with the result that in this sector under *ceteris paribus* conditions the potential supply of performers of S is relatively greater than in the public sector. It is largely because civil service rules so frequently are inimical to the economical use of manpower, skilled and otherwise, that efforts have been made, though not with much success, to exempt public corporations and companies from the incidence of these rules.[12] Economical use of a nation's more skilled manpower virtually requires, therefore, that the bulk of the business of transforming inputs into outputs, be these indicated by the market or by agencies of the state, be confined to the private sector.[13]

Political Instruments

Under this head are considered the roles of two instruments, here labeled "political," namely, party structure and welfare state.

1. *Party structure.* As has been indicated, the economic and social costs of economic development are bound to be heavy; there is scope for much controversy regarding priorities; and there are many individuals whose situation will be affected adversely, at least for some time, by economic development. The resulting burden will vary with country, of course, being much greater in heavily populated, low-income countries (*e.g.*, in Asia) than in those where population pressure is less marked and the capacity to increase per capita income is greater (*e.g.*, in much of Latin America and parts of Africa). In many of these countries (especially in those situated in Asia), economic development is much more likely to be realized, given one dominant political party (*e.g.*, the Congress Party in India), or a pair of parties,[14] each strongly committed to economic development, than given a multiplicity of parties (as in pre-1940 France).[15] Only a well-entrenched party, or a pair of parties strongly committed to economic development, is likely to be able to keep the ideology of development effectively alive, to impose the necessary costs of development on the population, and yet to remain in office long enough to get economic growth effectively under way.[16] A dictatorship might find itself in a somewhat similar position, given that it sought to promote economic growth and had fairly widespread support.[17]

2. *Welfare state.* This term is used to denote a state which diverts a considerable fraction of the national income to the support of so-called welfare objectives (various forms of social security, highly subsidized housing) and which sanctions legislation (*e.g.*, minimum-wage legislation) and institutions (*e.g.*, a strong trade-union movement) which exercise heavy upward pressure on real wage rates. While it may be granted that some provision for state-administered social-welfare objectives is essential (particularly since the security-providing extended family and clan and village organizations will probably be undergoing dissolution), and while it may be admitted that some increase in real wages is necessary (to sustain faith in the gradual advent of a better economic world), it is not compatible with capital formation and economic development for these two objectives to be given strong support. Nor need they be, inasmuch as a rising per capita income is compatible with an increasing rate of capital formation so long as both output per head and the marginal propensity to save are rising. It may be concluded, therefore, that, for the present and for some years to come, no more than a quite limited welfare-state is compatible with a high rate of economic growth in presently under-developed lands. For this reason a multiparty system is not compatible with economic growth; it is too likely to give in to ever present demands for "liberal" welfare-state provisions.

ECONOMIC DEVELOPMENT AND
CHANGING POLITICAL CONDITIONS

As economic development proceeds, growth-affecting political conditions and requirements change. Per capita expenditure for education and health tends to increase significantly. Institutional provisions respecting "money" become more complex. There is greater emphasis upon preventing deflation; monetary policy is increasingly directed to narrowing economic fluctuations and fostering fuller employment; less attention is given to cushioning fluctuations in the prices of primary goods. Moreover, as an economy progresses, its banking system becomes more differentiated, and its ratio of paper to physical assets rises. The legal structure also becomes more complex and differentiated as does the public and the private organizational structure for which legal institutions must design appropriate rules.[18] Foreign economic relations tend to become subject to greater regulation, much of it restrictive, especially after external trade has begun to lag behind national income.

As an economy advances, it may tolerate larger amounts of growth-checking taxation and public expenditure, since the economic system itself becomes more autonomous and more able and willing to supply growth capital. While emphasis upon governmental intervention and centralized economic planning may for a time increase as an economy progresses, it eventually tends to decline insofar as the need for economic and social overhead capital and for state aid to newly developing industries falls off. This outcome is quite likely. Such increase in emphasis upon the public sector may, for a time, make conditions worse in the private sector, though this is not a necessary outcome. Development corporations are not likely to be continued after an economy has become autonomous and characterized by self-sustaining growth. Budgetary policy becomes of greater importance as the economy progresses, particularly if, as some believe, the advent of "affluence" makes greater freedom increasingly necessary, together with the supply of "cultural" and "collective" goods and services, the production and/or distribution of which are not considered well suited to private enterprise. Economic progress is attended also by a great increase in the competence of private criticism of governmental economic policies, though not necessarily in its effectiveness.

While highly skilled personnel are always in short supply, governmental personnel tend to improve in quantity and quality as an economy improves, thereby permitting the government to undertake more of those economic tasks of which it is empirically capable, given adequacy of personnel. Rising income is associated with the increase of skilled personnel, income and personnel interacting through time to augment each other.

In general, as has been implied, economic development tends eventually to be accompanied by both political and economic decentralization. It is accompanied by decentralization of both legal norm-making power and use-determining, economic decision-making power, with both forms becoming more widely distributed in space and among households and/or corporate groups. The disposition of economic power in space and among groups and individuals tends to be rather closely associated with that of political power. Political decentralization entails the distribution of norm-making power among a plurality of groups or organs, together with the subjection of centralized norm-making to restraints imposed by dispersed, norm-affecting groups whose initially heterogeneous aspirations enter into such consensus as comes to underlie norms held valid for all members of a society.[19] Economic decentralization requires that the mechanisms employed to discover what final goods and services should be produced reflect an ever widening range of consumer preferences, be these mechanisms "free markets" in which price and effective economic demand rule, or political devices designed to register such noneconomic indicators as votes. Such decentralization results because, as an economy becomes more consumer-oriented, centralized determination of what is to be produced becomes increasingly difficult.

Among the concomitants of decentralization are the decline of one-party rule and the rise of the welfare state. An effective one-party system, though often favorable to economic growth, appears to be incompatible with a complex economy in which consumer goods, together with a high level of education, have come to play a paramount role. Similarly, the welfare state, though initially incompatible with the effective development of economically retarded lands, eventually becomes a part of the set of arrangements whereby, in high-income economies, collective goods and services are supplied and expenditure is kept abreast of "full-employment" output in pacific times.

NOTES

1. See L. W. Shannon, *Underdeveloped Areas* (New York, 1957), pp. 6-12, 478-79. *See also* P. T. Bauer and B. S. Yamey, *The Economics of Underdeveloped Countries* (London, 1957), chap. 1; N. S. Buchanan and H. S. Ellis, *Approaches To Economic Development* (New York, 1955), chap. 1; G. M. Meier and R. R. Baldwin, *Economic Development* (New York, 1957), chap. 1 and pp. 478-79; Eugene Staley, *The Future of Underdeveloped Countries* (New York, 1954), chap. 1.

2. *E.g.*, see Harvey Leibenstein, *Economic Backwardness and Economic Growth* (New York, 1957), chaps. 4-5; Benjamin Higgins, *Economic Development* (New York, 1959), Part I.

3. See B. F. Hoselitz, "Noneconomic Factors in Economic Growth," *American Economic Review*, 47 (May 1957), p. 39; also Talcott Parsons, *Structure and Process in Modern Societies* (Glencoe, 1960),

pp. 101-2, 106. In the eighteenth and early nineteenth centuries, states often indirectly fostered economic growth by allowing freedom of action to private individuals whose enterprise gave rise to economic development.

4. Shannon, op. cit., p. 27, also pp. 468*ff.*; idem, "Is Level of Development Related to Capacity for Self-Government?" *American Journal of Economics and Sociology*, 17 (July 1958), 367-81, and "A Re-examination of the Concept 'Capacity for Self-Government'," *Journal of Negro Education*, 26 (Spring 1957), 135-44. See also W. S. and E. S. Woytinsky, *World Commerce and Governments* (New York 1955), pp. 563-67, 582-83, 586.

5. William Arthur Lewis, *The Theory of Economic Growth* (London, 1955), p. 11.

6. See W. W. Rostow, *The Process of Economic Growth* (New York, 1952), chaps. 1-3. For yet another list of factors which directly or indirectly affect economic development, *see* J. J. Spengler, "Economic Factors in the Development of Densely Populated Areas," *Proceedings of the American Philosophical Society* 95 (1951): 21-24.

7. In this section, I draw heavily upon Lewis, op. cit., chap. 7. See also Parsons, *Structure and Process* . . ., chaps. 3-4; R. A. Dahl and C. E. Lindblom, *Politics, Economics and Welfare*, pp. 6-8; and, on the limitations to which governmental development efforts are subject, Bauer and Yamey, op. cit., and Buchanan and Ellis, op. cit.

8. For analysis of political science research on such conditions, see Ralph Braibanti, "The Relevance of Political Science to the Analysis of Underdeveloped Areas," in Braibanti and J. J. Spengler (eds.), *Tradition, Values and Socio-Economic Development* (Durham, 1960).

9. On this problem, see Shils, "The Intellectuals, Public Opinion, and Economic Development," *Economic Development and Cultural Change*, VI (1951): 56-62.

10. We may turn to several sources for indications of shortages of governmental personnel sufficiently qualified to fill the posts to which they are assigned. Each year, in its Annual Report, the Consultative Committee on the Colombo Plan discusses the shortage of technical personnel and the role of technical assistance under the plan in somewhat alleviating this shortage. Similarly, in the reports of Missions of the International Bank for Reconstruction and Development, the development-retarding effects of shortages of technical personnel, together with qualitative defects in the technical attainments of such personnel, are noted. See also J. J. Spengler, "Public Bureaucracy, Resource Structure, and Economic Development: A Note," *Kyklos* 11 (Fasc. 4, 1958), 459-86; F. W. Riggs, "Public Administration: A Neglected Factor in Economic Development," *Annals of the American Academy of Political and Social Science* 305 (May 1956), 70-80; P. Franck, "Economic Planners in Afghanistan," *Economic Development and Cultural Change* 1 (February 1953), 323-40.

11. On how this shortage retards development, see *e.g.*, H. W. Singer,

238

"Obstacles to Economic Development," *Social Research* 20 (Spring 1953), 19-31; also Shils, op. cit., pp. 55-56.

12. *E.g.*, see A. H. Hanson, *Public Enterprise and Economic Development* (London, 1959), pp. 459-64.

13. See *ibid.*, chap. 15, also chaps. 5, 11-14; also Spengler, "Public Bureaucracy..." loc. cit. The discussion above relates to mixed economies. Weaknesses inherent in bureaucratic undertakings in mixed economies are present also in centralized economies, but their output-depressing effects may be swamped by very high rates of capital formation. *E.g.*, see Janos Kornai, *Overcentralization in Economic Administration* (London, 1959); also M. Polanyi, *The Logic of Liberty* (London, 1951), chaps. 8-10.

14. Normally, in a two-party country with attitudes distributed rather regularly along a continuum, the platforms of the two parties will tend to be quite similar (given allowance for ambiguities), since each will take a position calculated to appeal to a majority of the voters, and each will arrive at much the same estimate regarding the content of this position (again making allowance for certain differences in "party" appeal). This is the kind of situation found in the United States. If attitudes are not distributed fairly evenly along a continuum, or if there are more than two parties, the party (or parties) temporarily in power will not have a sufficiently strong and persisting mandate from the voters to carry out a development program. This line of argument is based upon H. Hotelling's "Stability in Competition," *Economic Journal* 39 (March 1929): 41-57, esp. part ii.

15. The above argument must make allowance for a country's stage of development and for its social structure at or near the time its growth is getting effectively under way. In nineteenth-century Germany and Japan, the social structure, together with cognate conditions, was favorable. Capital formation could continue at high levels and labor remained content with the share going to it. This seems to have been true also in Britain and France in that the trade-union movement was not strong at the time economic development was getting under way. In general, the underlying population did not resist bearing the costs of development, any more than did the post-1945 German population; hence the presence of two or more parties did not prove inimical to development. A similar situation is not so likely to be found in present-day underdeveloped countries. *E.g.*, see Karl de Schweinitz, "Industrialization, Labor Controls, and Democracy," *Economic Development and Cultural Change* 7 (July 1959): 385-404, and comments on this article by Robert Freedman, together with de Schweinitz's reply, in *ibid.* 8 (January 1960), 192-98. Of course, union pressure may operate, in a quite imperfectly competitive society, to compel entrepreneurs to improve methods of production, *etc.* See A. Sturmthal, "Unions and Economic Development," *ibid.*, pp. 204-5.

16. As was noted earlier, even when there is not initially a single party,

the processes associated with carrying out a development program tend to channel power into the hands of a single party. See Z. Brzezinski, "The Politics of Underdevelopment," *World Politics* 9 (October 1956): 62-64. The fact that economic development in the West was accomplished under predominantly private entrepreneurial leadership, democratic auspices, and the political leadership of two or more parties has little influence today in underdeveloped countries (see *ibid.*, pp. 58-59; E. A. Shils, "The Intellectuals . . . : 55-56. Furthermore, the examples of Russia and China are at hand, and the Communist Party is now representing itself as the political instrument through which industrialization is to be achieved. See J. H. Kautsky, "What Neo-Maoism Shows," *New Leader* 40 (16 December 1957). Presumably, in countries where durable political parties have been lacking, development is likely to be retarded. If this be true, and if D. A. Rustow is correct in remarking the absence of durable political parties from a number of underdeveloped countries (see *ibid.*, pp. 58-59; Shils, "The Intellectuals," pp. 55-56). Further-terrent to growth. See D.A. Rustow, "New Horizons for Comparative Politics," *World Politics* 9 (July 1957): 541-42.

17. The above analysis suggests that, if there are but two parties, a parliamentary system may be better suited to foster economic growth than a federal system of the sort found in the United States. Under the latter, power is more widely dispersed, with the result that, except in times of crisis, it is very difficult to focus attention, effort and resources upon as costly an undertaking as economic development.

18. *E.g.*, see E. V. Rostow's account of the newly acquired rules of public law, in *Planning for Freedom* (New Haven, 1959).

19. See Hans Kelsen, "Centralization and Decentralization," in Harvard Tercentenary Conference, *Authority and the Individual* (Cambridge, 1937), pp. 210-39, esp. 212-13, 216-17, 223, 227-29; also 231-32 on struggles for local autonomy, and 233-34 on federalism as a form of decentralization.

SOCIOLOGICAL FACTORS AFFECTING ECONOMIC DEVELOPMENT IN INDIA

Arnold M. Rose

THE SOCIOLOGICAL APPROACH
TO ECONOMIC DEVELOPMENT

Experts in agriculture, industry, government, finance, public works, engineering, medicine, and public health become frustrated when they try to apply their knowledge and skills to technologically underdeveloped societies. Despite the vast amount of technical and material aid given to the underdeveloped societies since 1946, there has been a growing gap in per capita income between the rich and the poor nations. Some of the poor nations have even slipped in an absolute as well as a relative sense, India has slipped absolutely in agriculture, and it has regressed relatively on several other economic indices. In an effort to explain and correct this regression, economists have talked about a new economic theory,[1] psychologists have offered a new theory of motivation,[2] and anthropologists and sociologists have made on-the-spot studies of the failures.[3]

One difficulty of the new psychological theories is that they fail to take into account specific institutions and cultural values. McClelland, for example, has done research on the relation between a psychological need for achievement and economic development, but he adopts an ethnocentric definition of need for achievement in terms of material advancement. In India, the role model and high status individual has traditionally been the Brahman (priest-scholar) or even the *sadhu* (religious beggar): Status striving or achievement in India—as Srinvas[4] points out in

From Arnold M. Rose, "Sociological Factors Affecting Economic Development in India," *Studies in Comparative International Dvelopment.* Copyright © Volume 3, Number 9, (1967-1968) *Studies in Comparative International Development*, Rutgers University, New Brunswick, N. J. Reprinted by permission of the publisher.

his concept of "sanskritization"—means copying the vegetarianism and anti-manual-labor practices of the Brahman, which work *against* economic development. The Indian may not lack a need for achievement, but he seeks to achieve, from a developmental point of view, the wrong things.

One difficulty of many anthropological-sociological studies is that they have rarely taken a macroscopic view of economic development. In an effort to keep close to the known facts, they have taken segmentalized and small-scale soundings. The present study seeks to broaden this sociological perspective, by taking a macroscopic view of economic development in India. The general approach will be to interpret economic behavior in a context of social institutions and cultural values. Both theoretical and institutional economics developed in the context of Western civilization, and some of the conditions prevailing in underdeveloped societies were beyond the imagination of Western economists. Even when these economists visit an underdeveloped society with a culture and social system very different from anything they have known, they have great difficulty in recognizing its economic problems. For example, in India the demand for nearly *all* goods and services is far less elastic than economic demand for "necessities" in the West. This inelasticity of demand creates certain rigidities and inefficiencies in the production system, which preclude many of the reforms economists would suggest if they were advising a Western nation. It is difficult for them to imagine that choice in terms of shifting production among goods and services with greater or lesser elasticity of demand is practically meaningless in the Indian context. In this study, I will examine the culture and social system of India (from the standpoint of a sociologist or anthropologist) for characteristics that would seem to promote economic inefficiency or efficiency (from the standpoint of an economist). I will offer suggestions for increasing the economic efficiency of India that seem to be compatible with India's institutions and value structure, rather than compatible with the advice that would normally be offered by a Western-oriented economist. I do not claim to be original in many of these observations or suggestions, but I hope to be more comprehensive and to take a wider perspective than has hitherto appeared in published writings.

THE EFFECTS OF THE JOINT FAMILY AND CASTE SYSTEMS

Two of India's unique institutions are its joint family and caste systems. These are linked, for a caste in India is like a huge extended family. It ranges in size from several thousand people to many millions, all related consanguineously. While tradition has the castes categorized into five great *varnas*, with the Brahmans on top and the Untouchables at the bottom, the operating caste is the *jati*. It is differentiated not only according to occupation and status, but also according to region. The *jati* is endogamous, and this is what gives a family-like character to the caste. The *joint family* is a three-generation group of close relatives, which traditionally lived together in a compound under the direction of the senior male and shared economic benefits and obligations. Only half of India's people still live in joint families,[5] but there remains a strong sense of mutual obligation among family members even when they no longer live together.

Perhaps the most detrimental influence of the joint-family system on the economy is that it encourages dependency and submissiveness. Indian men and women are not supposed to make major decisions for themselves unless they are heads of families. Many a 40-year-old Indian man will go to his father or elder brother (or, when away from home, to his employer or professor) with a request for decision making that would be permitted a 10-year-old child in the West. Adult Indians occasionally exploit their economic claims on the joint family to avoid work, but this is atypical; the basic problem is lack of suitable jobs. The joint family provides nurturance for the migrating laborer, who might otherwise become anomic in the city, and thus it does serve as a valuable stabilizing influence on personality. But it does not encourage toughness in the face of adversity—what the British used to calll "fiber." In instances such as India's willingness to become dependent on food from the United States rather than take drastic action to become self-sufficient in food production, the softness of the Indian personality is an overwhelming force working against economic development.

Mutual obligations are much weaker, in the caste than in the joint family, but they still exist. Members of a caste identify with one another in a way that Indians do not typically identify with any other institution, even the home village. It is often said that the caste system is breaking down in India, but this is true mainly in that the grosser discriminations against the lower castes are diminishing and some castes are broadening their occupational activities. The hierarchy of castes is breaking down, but castism—loyalty to caste and thinking of oneself in terms of one's caste—is becoming strengthened.[6] Only among the highly educated and Western-oriented Indians in the largest cities is loyalty to the caste diminishing. For most Indians, caste loyalty is becoming stronger as the caste spirit enters into modern institutions of government and industry, and as caste associations develop to provide social welfare benefits, school scholarships, and pressure-group influences on government.[7]

The joint family and the caste provide certain economic benefits to their members. The joint family partly substitutes for a social security system, by caring for the elderly and the unemployed. It takes care of a villager's wife and children when he goes off to work in the city. It permits some pooling of savings for investment and of land for more efficient agriculture. Caste members try to help their brethren find jobs; they raise funds to send youngsters to school or college; they provide orientation for the dislocated villager when he first arrives in the city; and they may even provide the migrant with temporary housing at little or no cost. Skilled workers teach members of their caste the formal and informal techniques of their trade.

Some of these benefits to individuals aid the economy as a whole, but the net effect of caste on the economy is negative. The caste as a traditional occupational group hinders occupational mobility: Economic needs and demands may go unfilled in a community if there are insufficient workers to engage in the specific economic activity "belonging" to their caste. For example, even if a shortage develops in land-produced foods, fish still cannot be caught except by fishermen, and the fisherman caste cannot be readily expanded to take advantage of a sudden increase in demand. There are unemployed men in villages with shortages of carpenters and stone masons, but the unemployed will not take these jobs because the work is beneath their caste or because it "belongs" to the carpenters' and stone masons' castes. The latter, in turn, will not teach persons outside their caste the minimal skills of their hereditary occupations. Caste is occupationally restrictive in the same way that the European guilds of the Middle Ages were or the modern "closed unions" are. As modern technology opens up a new occupation, there is a greater lag than would be found in the West in getting workers into this occupation, because one or a few castes claim it as their monopoly, and they are inevitably slower in providing sufficient workers for it than if the occupation were thrown open to all comers. However, caste is more restrictive of labor mobility for the traditional occupations than for the newer ones: Morris found that caste did not create much hindrance in setting up factories in Jamshedpur and Bombay.[8]

Selection of workers for an occupation is not on the basis of aptitude or interest, but on the basis of family background. "Once the worker in industry has obtained a job, he seeks to cling to it. He attempts to give it a hereditary character, preserving it for his son if possible."[9] This lowers economic efficiency and produces a large number of occupational misfits.

The caste system creates nepotism on a vast scale. The obligation to help one's caste member find a job or gain promotion extends to nearly every industry and government office in India.[10] This leads to the placement of unqualified people, and it demoralizes the qualified who see their chances for economic advancement reduced or even eliminated because their caste fellows are not in the key positions.[11]

Big industries and government offices are run like family enterprises. Only caste members are fully trusted by the key leaders. Risk capital is not always available to promising entrepreneurs because they are not trusted by those of other castes. Even administrators who pass on government loans regularly violate the rules to aid their own caste brothers. Wealth is hoarded by certain rich castes or caste-equivalent groups, such as the Marwaris, rather than invested.

244   The requirement that each economic task be performed by a given

caste, and only by that caste, results in frequent underemployment.[12] The smallest village must have its own barber, its own sweeper and scavenger, and its own carpenter, even when there is not enough work to keep them busy. Often the local agriculturalists will use their own resources to keep a member of each service caste around. Oscar Lewis found that 33 percent of the able-bodied males in the small agricultural village he studied were not engaged in farming at all.[13] Many a rich Indian family will have its own Brahman (priest), its own Dhobi (washerman), its own Chamar (sweeper and scavenger), and other servants for whom there are not enough tasks to keep them employed more than a dozen hours a week. In a village of Northern India, Opler found that there were 18 castes that operated on the hereditary employer-customer relationship system among castes (called the *jajmaniparjussia* system), although the custom is declining.[14]

The provision of many social welfare and other benefits by caste and regional groups has reduced the pressure that might otherwise be exerted on the government to provide these benefits on an impartial and universal basis. Weak castes—which are often the lower castes and the smaller ones—are not able to do much for their members. Thus the society is built on discrimination that is often economic in character. Socialism is one of modern India's professed ideals, but few governments in the world provide so few social services and allow such uncontrolled exploitation of workers by private enterprise—enterprise often organized and sustained by government loans.

India is not yet a nation in a sociological or psychological sense. It is still a collection of mutually suspicious and mutually hostile extended families. This aspect of the social structure prevents cooperation between groups even when selfish interest would rationally dictate cooperation. The ties of family and caste still inhibit the cooperative effort that is implicit in the institutions of the market, the corporation, the trade union, and even the government. As nineteenth-century social evolutionist Sir Henry Maine put it, India has not yet shifted from "status" to "contract" as its dominant means of ordering interpersonal relationships.

Indians tend to use the term "community" where I use "caste," because the latter term has historically been applied only to Hindu groups. But caste extends well beyond the Hindus in India, since the minority Muslims, Christians, Buddhists, and even Jews[15] have internal caste-like divisions. Sometimes groups that are in origin mixtures of several castes, but come from a common region, will be treated as a single caste. This is true of the Marwaris, originally of Rajasthan, of the Sindis (refugees from Sind, West Pakistan), and sometimes of the refugees from East Pakistan. The Indians apply their concept of "community"—which includes all the defining characteristics of caste—to everyone. Rules of status relationship, endogamous marriage, occupational limitation—the central criteria of caste—are applied to small religious groups like the Parsis, or to foreigners like Europeans and Americans. In the same logical and anthropological

245

sense of "caste" (rather than the narrower legal or religious sense), it is almost impossible for an Indian to conceive of an individual independent of his caste: A stranger is immediately identified as to caste just as he is to his sex or age group. A man usually reveals his caste in his name, his speech, his manner, his bearing, and his occupation.[16] Caste in India is changing in its structure and functions, but it pervades Indian life today as much as it ever did.

THE EFFECTS OF HINDU
RELIGIOUS VALUES

Associated with caste are certain Hindu values that have considerable significance for economic life. There is a hierarchy of nearly everything in India—not only castes, but animals and plants, age and sex groups, machines and books. New and unfamiliar techniques and procedures are quickly assigned a place in a hierarchy. The outsider or innovator can readily learn to manipulate this valuation system.[17]

High caste Indians will not perform the tasks of low caste Indians even when there is great need because of the belief in "pollution."[18] Nightsoil, fish, and bones are not used as fertilizers by many peasants, because these fertilizers are regarded as polluting. Caste Hindus often require their Untouchable employees to carry such fertilizers to the fields, but even then, the caste Hindus will not work the soil until the fertilizer has "disappeared." Higher caste Indians will not engage in manual labor even under duress because it is polluting for their caste to do so. The Untouchables are still not allowed access to community resources such as wells in some villages, because their presence is regarded as polluting to upper-caste Hindus. This is now against the law, but there is a lag in enforcement.

Not only are certain tasks polluting because they are low on the hierarchy, but so are certain foods. Status aspirations often take the form of the lower castes' aping the Brahmans by refusing to eat meat, fish, fowl, and eggs. This seems to be true for about half the population of India. When prosperity comes to a middle or low caste family, it will begin engaging in conspicuous nonconsumption of these polluted foods. There are also nonreligious food restrictions. In certain parts of India, the only "edible" grain is rice, in other parts, it is wheat or millet. Most Indians restrict their diet so markedly that they are undernourished even when they have the income to purchase well-balanced meals. The higher castes require that their food be prepared and served only by cooks of the same high caste. This sets restrictions on travel and requires duplication of services. Where a town can only economically support one hotel, it must have two—one for Brahmans and the other for all other castes.

The basic Hindu values of *dharma* (duty; predetermined role) and *karma* (destiny; fate) inhibit economic development because they discourage this-worldly activity and innovation, and because they fatalistically consider change to be part of the uncontrollable order of the universe.[19] Just as Calvinism encouraged hard work, capital savings and investment, avoidance of waste, etc., the Hindu values encourage disdain of economic productivity, earning solely for the needs of the day, and avoidance of accumulating wealth. Some anthropologists have pointed out that these Hindu values are part of the "great tradition," which is scarcely known to the average Indian peasant; he follows the animist-like cult of the "little tradition" and seeks to maximize his economic profits just as a European peasant would. But even in the "little tradition" there is the belief that if a peasant is poor, God must have wanted him to be so. Also, there is the popular belief that nature should be adjusted to rather than conquered. The distinction between "great tradition" and "little tradition" is found in all societies, and it may be especially strong in India: The Brahmans theoretically are the carriers of the "great tradition," and the lower castes are enjoined against practicing it (although some do so in the Indian equivalent of status-striving). There may be some Hindu values of the "great tradition" that encourage savings and hard work, and this makes it difficult to conclude that traditional values inhibit modernization.[20] Pending detailed studies of just exactly what values the Indian peasant and worker actually hold, speculation as to the effect of these values on economic development is probably useless. Yet it must be recognized that religious values do exert strong control in Indian society: Religion permeates the economic and political institutions to an extent not found in Western societies, and even the intellectuals and the top political and business leaders are not secularized.[21]

The Indian economist-journalist, Kasum Nair, reported after interviewing peasants in several parts of India that they have no aspirations to raise their incomes markedly.[22] This attitude probably exists among European peasants and workers too. Most people in tradition-bound and highly stratified societies aspire to only a little more than they already have. But that "little more" can be enough to encourage initial economic expansion. And even in India, there are certain caste-like groups such as the Marwaris, regional groups outside their home states like the Gujeratis, the ruling families of pre-Independence times, and the businessmen of present-day Bombay and Bangalore who seem to have unlimited desire for wealth and power.

Modern India's values have been greatly influenced by Mohandas K. Gandhi, and some have asserted that the Gandhian values have worked against modernization. Kennedy asserts:[23]

> Gandhi's emphasis on the peasant in his village as the soul of India and the key to its future, his strictures on industrialism, his disdain for material things, his lack of interest and participation in the complex institutional machinery of modern community life, includ-

247

ing politics and government, and his conspicuous personal success in bypassing such machinery have all had great appeal for the transcendentally minded. His example sustains their moral, nonempirical approach to the political and economic problems of society, their disinclination for studying these problems or assuming responsibilities in the humdrum affairs of community or nation, and their distaste for politics and suspicion of politicians.

Defenders of Gandhi claim that he favored village hand-production techniques only as a short-run expedient to reduce underemployment, and not as a substitute for mechanized production when capital became available.[24] Neither government leaders nor the masses have shown real resistance to mechanized production, even though they have not been efficient in achieving it. Gandhi did favor rapid change in some respects, such as removing the restrictions on Untouchables. He sought to put pressures on government, and to use extra-governmental associations of people to inaugurate social changes. Thus, it is difficult to agree that Gandhi helped keep India immobile.

HOW INDIA DEALS WITH THREE ASPECTS OF DEVELOPMENT

It is difficult to ascertain whether Indian *values* keep India economically backward, but it is certain that many Indian *institutions*—even besides caste and the joint family—inhibit economic development. The basic problem of economic development, is that of increasing productivity by shifting a plow-and-bullock agricultural economy to a rationalized machine-and-office economy.[25] This problem has several facets: accumulating large amounts of capital for investment; training managers, technicians, and workers; and moving workers out of traditional village occupations into "modern" occupations.

Capital Accumulation

For India, capital accumulation offers little fundamental difficulty. The old local rulers exploited the country and accumulated vast stores of gold and jewels, which could be used today in direct payments or as foreign exchange. The ancient merchant castes also did very well in accumulating wealth, but only some of them are willing to lend this money—at exorbitant interest rates.[26] Most Indians put their savings into gold and jewels, rather than depositing them in banks. When they need cash, they pawn the gold and jewels. There are some rational reasons for this: There is always the threat of devaluation of currency, and in 1949 and 1966 devaluation actually occurred. During the interval between those years, there was a black market in currency. Land ownership has been speculative because of various efforts at land reform. Hence, there are few alternatives for the saver except to hoard his wealth in gold and jewels. Not until 1962 did the government of India begin to place some restrictions on the private hoarding of gold, and only in 1965 did it begin to "borrow" from the gold-and-jewel accumulations of the wealthy.

A great number of foreigners—particularly Americans, Germans, and British—are willing to invest in Indian enterprises. But they are prevented or discouraged from doing so by the government of India, which requires their conformity to dysfunctional bureaucratic rules, which sets narrow limits to the profits that they can remove from the country, which requires participation in ill-designed "plans," and which—most difficult of all—requires bribes, and tariff payments, to bring capital equipment into the country. This stems from a natural fear of "economic imperialism," in a people who remember how, three centuries ago, the Europeans started with trade and ended up ruling the country.

Education For The Modern Economy

India is making progress in getting trained technicians and professionals—she is permitting the U.S.A., Great Britain, and other countries to train thousands of her youth at practically no cost to herself. The majority of these Ph.D.'s, M.S.'s, and engineers eventually return to India. Their salaries are low, but they get rewards in high prestige and sense of achievement in their own pioneering economy. Some of the high-level skills, especially that of business management, remain in very short supply. India is not giving adequate higher education to her youth in many fields. There are over 40 universities in the country, and over a thousand colleges and technical schools, but in many the curricula and pedagogy are so poor that they have an inhibitory rather than stimulating effect on the economy.[27] Except for the new agricultural and engineering colleges, the Indian universities are mistraining youth for the jobs that exist now or will soon exist if the economy becomes more efficient. Too many students go into the humanities or into law and then find there are no jobs for them.[28] The inadequate training of many professors, their low pay and low status compared with civil servants and businessmen, their heavy teaching loads, their traditional reliance on the lecture method to the virtual exclusion of other methods, and their disdain of the students do not make for effective teaching. And the humanistically trained graduates are not equipped to teach courses in technical and business education, for which there is great need.

Elementary and secondary education are also deficient in India. Only about 25 percent of adult Indians have enough education to make them literate in any language, and only about 50 percent of the children get *any* schooling.[29]

249

Labor Mobility And The Effect Of
Linguistic And Religious Differences

A growing manufacturing establishment is attracting rural peasants to jobs in the industrial cities—particularly to Bangalore, Bombay, Ahmedabad, Kanpur, Durgapur, Jamshedpur, and Calcutta. The need for educated, English-speaking clerical workers and small merchants is drawing qualified persons from Kerala, Madras, and Gujerat states, as well as refugees from Pakistan, to the same cities, plus Delhi. There are several influences that inhibit the integration of these people into a permanent work force. The joint family—unlike the Western nuclear family—seldom migrates as a unit. It provides a "nest" for the migrating worker's wife and children in the home village, where the worker visits his family once or twice a year. Often he will do this for ten, twenty, or more years, never thinking of himself as a permanent part of the industrial labor force. The high sex ratio of the industrial cities reveals the extent of this practice (1961 data): Bombay, 176 men per 100 women; Calcutta, 166 men per 100 women; Kanpur, 143 men per 100 women; and Ahmedabad, 131 men per 100 women. The ratio is even higher among the working classes and migrants.[30]

There is also much attachment to caste and village. The Untouchable *Camars* of Uttar Pradesh, while brutally depressed and exploited in their village, feel a strong loyalty to it. "Although there is much temporary geographic mobility of *Camars* from the village to the city, over the last three generations only one family of *Camars* from Madhopur is known to have settled permanently in a city."[31] The city worker will sometimes be able to save up enough wealth to return home permanently, thus depriving the industrial centers of his acquired skills and experience. If he is given a higher wage as an incentive for efficient work, he will use the money to return home sooner, or he will stay longer on his annual or semi-annual visit. Japan built hotels with house mothers to supervise them, in order to attract respectable country girls to work in the factories. These girls soon married boys who also migrated from rural areas, and new city families were thus established. But the strong emphasis in India on parent-arranged marriages might prevent similar success with such a program.

The diversity of languages of India creates a handicap for the migrating workers, especially since many come from the South Indian states where the languages are very different from those of the great cities of the North. The language barrier makes it difficult for plant foremen and other supervisors to give orders and explain work assignments to their subordinates. It also makes it difficult for migrants to adjust to city life when even the shop signs and the cinema offerings remain a mystery to them. The workers typically live in an ethnic enclave where they associate in off-hours only with persons of their own regional and language group.

Industrialization and urbanization are thus not creating the "melting pot" that ultimately aided economic development in the United States.

The Indian government has declared Hindi to be the national language, but it has done little to provide adult education facilities in which the people can learn Hindi. The South Indian worker in a northern city is likely to find English a more useful language than Hindi, since it allows him to communicate also with foreigners and with South Indians from states other than his own. This continued use of English as a second language clashes with government promotion of Hindi.

Religious differences (particularly between Hindus and Muslims) create similar barriers in many parts of North India, particularly in the Punjab and in West Bengal, where they have been exacerbated by friction with Pakistan and the presence of Hindu refugees from Pakistan. Violent riots and other forms of civil disorder are common. Strong prejudice and discrimination set restrictions on the efficient use of manpower. India has little national integration or national loyalty, despite its cultural unity based on Hinduism.[32]

THE ROLE OF GOVERNMENT
IN ECONOMIC DEVELOPMENT

Government has facilitated economic development in India in many ways. It has maintained a more stable civil order than exists in most underdeveloped countries. There has been no serious threat of revolution since independence from Britain took place in 1947, although there was much violence attending the partition of the Indian subcontinent between India and Pakistan. Civil liberties and civil rights are fairly well maintained in India, and despite their many deficiencies, the police protect the citizenry about as well as they do in the West.[33] The government has also been a major source of capital investment for industry, both by direct entrepreneurship and outright ownership of certain industrial establishments, and by providing capital loans for private investors and entrepreneurs. Progressive taxation has turned some savings into capital and has reduced extreme wealth at the top. Government five-year plans have provided some guidance for production into fairly predictable markets. Public works—especially roads, railroads, post facilities—could be greatly improved, but they are adequate to keep the productive and distributive systems functioning. Despite the many criticisms, India's government has served its people and its economy better than most governments in Asia, Africa, and Latin America.

But there are also significant ways in which the federal and state governments of India have hampered economic development. Foremost has been the failure to improve agriculture. While in the manufacturing sector, the growth rate has stayed close to 8 percent per year since 1960, food-grain production has been more or less static.[34] Wheat output has been particularly poor; it fell by nearly 20 percent from 1961 to 1964.[35]

251

As one prominent economist has noted, "The bulk of the increase in [agricultural] production in the last decade has come from extension of area and only a small proportion from increase in yields."[36] The government has invested very little in irrigation systems, fertilizer plants, and agricultural equipment, but some action was under way by 1966—largely because of pressure from the United States, which has been compensating for India's huge food deficiency. Some needed improvements in agriculture do not require much capital; they merely require organization of the available underemployed rural manpower. But the government is not providing this leadership. Among the rural activities that could be organized with little capital investment are the construction of tanks (ponds), wells, and irrigation channels such as the Pakistanis are building; the construction and maintenance of rural roads; and the improvement of land through reforestation or clearance. The maintenance of the rural status quo seems to come from the urban and international orientation of educated government officials,[37] and from the alliance between the politically dominant Congress party and the traditional, conservative landowners. India passed legislation for land reform in the early 1950s, but it has not been implemented. Landowners are scarecely taxed, even though few of them contribute much capital or labor to agricultural production. Approximately 45 percent of India's national income is derived from agriculture, but land taxation takes less than 1 percent of the gross value of agricultural output.[38]

> About 10 percent of the agricultural population of India constitutes a privileged minority. They own more than half the total cultivated area, and their per capita income is significantly higher than even the major segments of organized industry and commerce, yet they are among the least taxed groups in the country . . . . Their tax burden is merely 5 percent of their income.[39]

The Indian government also maintains a system of agricultural zones, and food may be transported between zones only with severe governmental limitations. This system, inaugurated by the British, is maintained by the political leaders of the relatively food-rich states. The system keeps food plentiful and prices low in certain states, while people in other parts of the country starve. From the standpoint of the national economy, the zonal system provides little incentive for the relatively efficient food producers in the food-rich states to produce more. It would depress their prices. This zone system is one of the most amazing examples since eighteenth-century Europe of a government's depressing economic productivity by restricting markets.

Another depressing government influence is the corruption of the lower bureaucracy. Moral obligations run almost exclusively along family and caste lines,[40] and government officials are no different from anyone else in this respect. They often expect a personal payment for each service provided, unless the service is for a family member or fellow caste member. Petty corruption by lower officials, often considered a way of compensating for their low salaries, adds extra cost to accomplishing any kind of business. Especially serious for the society is the corruption found among top officials. Their operations usually involve large amounts of money—enough to wreck otherwise good government programs or promising economic activities.[41] These officials are brazen enough to demand bribes from foreign investors and even from foreign embassies.

The status-conception of the government official is another political factor hampering economic activity in India. Like most educated persons in India, he regards anything that will get his hands dirty as demeaning. Many community development agents in rural India, who correspond roughly to agricultural extension agents in the United States, simply refuse to do their jobs beyond giving an occasional lecture to the peasants.[42] The author has visited several villages in India where he was told that the community development agent refused to step out of his car or jeep: He called the villagers to his car, where he gave them a lecture.

The Indian bureaucracy is especially well developed, since there is great pressure on the government to provide jobs for educated persons, since a "socialistic" society has a great number of functions for government officials to administer, and since bureaucracy is thought of as a way of checking against violation of statutes.[43] Civil servants want to show that they are earning their low salaries and high status, so they create a web of red tape designed to confound everyone (except their relatives). Prime Minister Nehru himself was appalled by the amount of red tape, but offered no specific solutions:[44]

> I have looked into the Civil Service Rules. I was astonished how, in spite of impediments these rules put, the government has func-tioned. I cannot conceive how these rules can be wholly applicable to India today. The whole background and environment of independence requires a new approach to our problems. Unfortu-nately, we are all bound hand and foot with something which has no place today. We have to get rid of it.

The red tape is associated with much officiousness—civil servants are very conscious of their high status in a highly status-conscious society. Insofar as these bureaucratic rules and their officious administration are applied to economic activity, they limit it.

Large-scale corruption among powerful top officials, especially in a socialist society where government is expected to take large-scale initiative in creating industry, allows the very rapid accumulation of wealth by certain entrepreneurs. These entrepreneurs are often relatives of the top officials. The unprincipled and rampant capitalism—albeit state capitalism—of modern India is reminiscent of the "robber baron" days of American and British capitalism. The result is economic monopoly, which restricts the economic development of competitors and damages the economy as a whole. It remains to be seen whether "socialist" India, which displays one of the most unrestrained and self-seeking forms of capitalism in the contemporary world,[45] will move in the American

253

direction of controlling monopoly. Since the Indian tradition is not to re-invest excess income, but to hoard it, this uncontrolled capitalism is further damaging to the economy. And as Kennedy has pointed out, the Indian government official has a "moralistic reluctance to admit or encourage the materialistic and competitive nature of the Indian peasant."[46] Officials are often moralistic where their own, or their caste's, interests are not involved.

In sum, the government restrains economic development by aiding both the traditional landlords in the rural areas and the modern "robber barons" who control much of the industry in the cities. The great bulk of the population is exploited, without contributing much to capital investment in agriculture or to industry in the private sector. Of course, the government has also stimulated the economy in several ways—by maintaining public order, by constructing a reasonably good transportation system, and by investing directly in industry and in public works such as dams and their connected irrigation systems. The government has tried to restrain the more vicious discriminations against the Untouchables, to provide some protection for the most helpless, and to set some limits on economic exploitation. But its laws in these matters are often poorly enforced, since there is a widespread attitude among Indians that once a law is passed, that takes care of the problem.

OTHER PROBLEMS OF AGRICULTURE

In considering the failure of growth in agriculture, the backward land tenure system deserves emphasis. Twenty-two percent of the rural households do not own any land at all, and another 25 percent hold less than one acre.[47] A United Nations *Report* on land reform[48] makes this comment:

It is evident that the tenancy system ... is a powerful obstacle to economic development, in three ways. ... The tenant has little incentive to increase his output, since a large share in such increase will accrue to the landlord, who has incurred no part of its cost. ... The high share of the produce taken by the landowner may leave the peasant with a bare subsistence minimum, with no margin for investment; in a bad year, he gets more heavily in debt; in a good year, he can reduce his indebtedness ... it means that wealth is held in the form of land, and that the accumulation of capital does not lead to productive investment. In Asia, the landowner is also a money-lender and in this capacity depends more on interest on loans to small cultivators than on increased income from the improvement of land.

The debt-bondage referred to in this *Report* creates what amounts to peonage. Not only do the majority of the Indian peasants own little or no land, but land holdings tend to be fragmented as a result of the dowry and inheritance systems.

After the failure of the government's land reform laws in the early 1950s, the religious leader Vinoba Bhave sought to accomplish the same purpose by voluntary gifts of land (*bhoodan*) to be redistributed to the poorest peasants. Later he added to his program the complete redistribution of a village's land into a modified cooperative (*gramdan*), which was designed to consolidate holdings as well as to equalize them. The results have been spotty. In some places there was a genuine altruism in giving up productive land, and the *bhoodan* officials worked closely with the peasants; in other places the land donated was worthless, or the *bhoodan* or *gramdan* officials simply acted like old-fashioned feudal landlords—exploitative and dictatorial.[49] The total area covered by Bhave's movement was a relatively small part of rural India.

It is unlikely that the agricultural technology that has proved so successful in the United States can serve India. Fertilizer may have to be different where the peasant has no funds for investment in commercial fertilizers, and where there are two or three crops a year instead of one. An entirely different concept has to be applied to agricultural machinery in a land where labor is very cheap and capital is practically nonexistent (or lent at usurious rates), where draft animals are too weak to lift heavy equipment and gasoline is not available to run motors, where land holdings are tiny and broken up, and where social values may condemn drastic disturbance of the soil. Techniques of controlling plant disease and insects have to be revised where the diseases and insects are different from those that plague Western agriculture. New types of crops have to be experimented with where wind, terrain, water supply, and market demand are markedly different from what they have been in the West. Substitutes must be found for crop-rotation and fallow-year techniques where demand is extremely inelastic and poverty is so great that it will not tolerate temporary cutbacks in production. Since agricultural extension experts consider it beneath their dignity to give personal instruction to the peasant on his own land, the best means of communicating to peasants would seem to be by demonstration-lectures at a central school, aided by radio reiteration of techniques and day-to-day advice about when to seed and when to plow. New assembly and marketing institutions have to be devised where individual production is very small and the number of crop producers very large. New distribution schemes have to be formulated where transportation is inadequate and politics regularly interferes with the market (regularly causing hoarding and black-marketing of crops, for example).

Food wastage is endemic in India. Wild and semidomesticated animals roam the villages and cities at will, stealing food produced by man. Cows consume far more food than they return in work or food. Rats exist in incredible numbers all over India. Indians, who have generally shown little compunction about killing each other (as long as it is not in a situation

255

known as "war"), are religiously and ethically enjoined against killing these animals. Some modern-minded Indians have advocated fitting cows with birth control devices. The cattle are permitted to go anywhere, and they trample almost as much food as they eat.

As food becomes increasingly scarce, the rats get an increasing share of it. Shortages are accompanied by private hoarding and government storage, and both practices accommodate the rats. Food storage in a society without good mechanical and transportation facilities also means spoilage through moisture: Much of the stored grain sprouts, molds, or rots before it can be eaten. India lacks most food-preserving processes found in the West. The wood shortage means that practically no food is smoked (dried cow dung is the common household fuel, and it is useful for slow cooking, but it cannot be used for smoking or canning). The lack of refrigeration means that food cannot be frozen. Unsanitary practices, as well as the lack of fuel, make canning and preserving unfeasible. India has much milk, but apparently little of it is canned, powdered, or even made into cheese. Some fruits are preserved by being dried in the sun, but the lack of protection means a heavy percentage of loss to wild animals and insects.

Perhaps just as bad as the material conditions affecting food are the psychocultural ones. Indians eat very little by Western standards, and many of them believe they can get along on far less in an emergency. Probably most Indians are not aware that they face starvation. Because it is bad politics, government officials do not inform them of the nationwide desperation. Macroscopic statistics on food shortages mean little even to educated Indians, since they think in local or family terms only rather than in nationwide terms. This may be a psychological defense against the terrible reality of India's food shortage, but one gets the impression that the cultural roots of the attitude are far deeper than that: The sense of social responsibility seldom extends beyond the family, the village, or the caste. For whatever reason, Indians seem apathetic about the food shortage, except when the government reduces the precious rice ration. Then they riot in a usually temporarily successful effort to force the government to raise it again. Scattered and gradual starvation is endemic in India, and it remains to be seen how much this can increase before it results in serious efforts to take individual or organized action concerning food shortages. The United States ships about 20 percent of its total agricultural product to India. If this supply were curtailed, many Indians would starve immediately.

THE URBAN ECONOMY

India's manufacturing is far more rational and modern than its food production and distribution. Industrial output has been increasing at the laudable rate of 8 percent per year and some industries are quite efficient within the context of a cheap and overly exploited labor supply. Indian steel production—much of it under the direction of the remarkable Tata family (who are Parsis, a small religious minority)—is said to be more efficient than that of the United States or many other Western countries. But there are serious lacks in industry. Entrepreneurs often "milk" their firms rather than reinvesting and expanding. There is a serious shortage of trained managers and supervisors. With little guidance, laborers work hard but inefficiently. Even the Ford Foundation schools of management— expensively and excellently staffed—do not produce many trained managers.

India has a vast reservoir of skilled craftsmen that are far from fully employed. The government has made many successful efforts to develop the so-called "cottage industries" or handicrafts. Madras cloth, for example, has even achieved a noteworthy market abroad. But the total effort is so far small compared with the possibilities. Many beautiful and useful Indian craft products could find large markets abroad if there were a systematic effort to develop these markets, but Indian businessmen and commerce officials seem to know little about business practices in the West. They also need to learn that, for the West, marketable products require good materials as well as good workmanship. The skills themselves might be rechanneled into producing items with a wider market. The artistry of ivory or wood carving might be rechanneled into watch-making or the production of transistor radios (which ought to find a considerable market even within India). The human material of India is most promising, but it needs to be organized and directed. India needs more big-thinking and modern-minded entrepreneurs like the Tata family. Their shortage suggests again the inadequacies of the system of higher education.

THE DEMOGRAPHIC FACTOR

The failure of food output to increase since 1960 is especially serious in view of India's rapid population growth. The rate of increase is presently about 2.5 percent per year. The problem is that the application of an improved medical and public health technology has sharply reduced the death rate, while the birth rate has remained relatively constant. Between 1901 and 1964, the average length of life in India doubled—from about 24 years to about 48 years. (The average life span in the United States today is about 72 years, and it is somewhat higher in ten other Western countries.) In this period 1901-1964, India's crude death rate fell from 42.6 per 1,000 per year to 19.0. The birth rate has started to fall too, as modern techniques of birth control are adopted by the educated and upper class people of the cities, although increased possibility of living through the child-bearing ages has buoyed it up.

The "family planning" movement has scarcely diffused to the villages,   257 where about 80 percent of the Indian population lives.[50] Some of the failure can be attributed to the fact that earlier methods of birth control were ill-adapted for use by impoverished, ignorant peasants. This is now being overcome by the low-cost "coil," which can easily be inserted into or withdrawn from the vagina, and which can be left constantly in place and remain effective for at least a year. American philanthropic foundations, and recently the U.S. government itself, are trying to provide more such materials. The current Minister of Health, who is himself a highly qualified demographer, promises to do a better job of distributing birth control information. Training village women to communicate the need and to instruct others in the techniques seems to be promising, but it will take some time to get this program into large-scale operation.

SUPERSTITION

Another factor in the culture and social structure of India that hinders its economic development is superstituion. Superstition and the reliance on magic are found in all societies. What differentiates India from the West is that, in India, the *educated* man believes in magic. The reliance on amulets among physicians, on astrologers among cabinet officers, and on the distribution of tea leaves at the bottom of a cup among university professors is quite common in India. Astrology is governed by complicated mathematics, and authentic astrologers must study several years before practicing their art. Thus it has a "scientific" quality, and its practitioners take on the character of professionals.[51]

Magical practices are found at all social levels in India, and the consequences of reliance on them by the higher decision makers are significant in inhibiting economic development. Cabinet ministers and businessmen postpone their actions until dates that astrologers calculate are propitious. They choose locations for investment in these magical terms. Even scientists working for the Ford Foundation have been known to postpone a trip because a last-minute horoscope proved unfavorable. The wife of the late prime minister, Lal Bahadur Shastri, would not move to a larger house from their small one because her astrologer said that its address was lucky, so all the business of state had to be conducted from this small inadequate base. Shastri's temporary successor, Gulzarilal Nanda, was entrapped by scandal because he tried to prevent legal action against his astrologer's son, who was accused of improper financial operations.[52]

Perhaps related to superstition is the uneconomical Indian custom of spending large sums for religious celebrations. Poor and rich families alike will spend half their savings on a marriage or birth celebration. This diverts capital from producers' goods to consumers' goods.

258

FACTORS FACILITATING
ECONOMIC DEVELOPMENT

I have attempted to summarize the factors arising from India's culture and social structure that inhibit its economic development. Advice as to future economic development can be valuable only if it is based on hard-headed understanding of these factors. Just as the agricultural expert must devise new technologies for India's particular social and geographic circumstances, so must the economist devise new development plans that will include variables from India's culture and social structure. Failure to do so thus far has kept Western economic aid from being very productive.[53]

Some Indian institutions are readily divisible, so that an effort to eliminate the parts that impede economic development need not reduce the effectiveness of the parts that facilitate long-term economic goals. The central government, for example, despite its inhibitory features, provides two great assets for development: a strong tradition of maintaining order within a framework of democracy, and a set of social ideals guiding its top officials.[54] This is partly the heritage of British rule, although the Hindu value of *ahimsa*, or nonviolence, reinforced by Gandhi and his followers has aided the tradition of order. Even the students who engage in riots do not seem to seek revolution or violence for its own sake, but rather correction of specific defects. Another government asset is the orientation toward action. Whatever their religious heritage of fatalism and their familistic tendency to avoid coming to grips with difficult problems ("leave it to father"), Indian government officials maintain the socially healthy myth that every problem can ultimately be solved. This does not seem to be very effective in the short run, but it keeps them open to possible solutions in the long run.

The Indian people favor charismatic leaders. Their acceptance of leadership by Gandhi or Nehru seems to have been more genuine than other peoples' acceptance of leadership by, say, Sukarno or Nasser or Nkrumah. Indian leaders like Vinoba Bhave and Jayaprakash Narayan today have the charismatic power to motivate large sections of the population to "better" behavior. Acceptance of charisma is not necessarily a positive force for economic development, but so far in the history of independent India, it has had that effect. Indians seek "saintly" leaders, and can be motivated by them toward progressive action, if the leaders are themselves progressive.

Another facilitating institution, surprisingly strong and extensive in India, is the voluntary association (*samaj*). The Indian people have a tradition of associating themselves into formal groups to accomplish some limited purpose. In the upper classes, it is often a social-welfare organization that seeks to mitigate the extremes of poverty among some group or in some area, or a social-reform movement that seeks to reduce

259

the evils of prostitution or drunkenness. In the middle and lower classes, the tendency to join voluntary associations is weaker, but it does exist. Many caste associations have social-welfare functions, and there are popular cross-caste associations with recreational or educational functions. Likely the net effect of these voluntary associations—as in other nations like Sweden, Britain, and the United States—will be progressive. This seems to be true even of the religious revival associations, such as the Brahmo Samaj, the Arya Samaj, and the Ramakrishna Mission.

Much has been made of the fatalistic orientation to life encouraged by the Hindu religion and its negative implications for economic development. I agree with this, but there are also two characteristics of the Hindu religion that *aid* India's acceptance of social change. First is the absence of an organized priesthood. There are holy man (*sadhus*) and village Brahmans, who are mostly conservatives, but they do not have the power to organize massive resistance to social change in the way that the Muslim Ulemas, the Roman Catholic upper clergy, and the Buddhist priesthood do in some other countries. Hinduism is a way of life rather than an organized religion, and while its capacity to penetrate all other aspects of Indian culture tends to slow down social change, it can scarcely mount an organized power play against economic development.

Hinduism is also an open religion. It accepts new movements by incorporating them into its value system and structure. It has been tolerant of reform movements within its own body, from Buddhism beginning in the sixth century B.C., through Sikhism in the fifteenth century, to the modern religious movements. It has even been tolerant of foreign religious influences, such as the successive waves of Christian missions. (Only the aggressive Muslim faith has evoked organized hostility from Hindu leaders and masses.) This Hindu tradition of tolerance seems to bode well for economic development. The Indians, except for a small group in the Jan Sangh political movement, have never mounted a crusade against Western influence, such as has occurred in other parts of Asia. Indian openness to Western influence may not yet have resulted in the transmission of much besides the forms of democratic government, but it suggests that India can accept more from the West without destructive social disorganization or ideological upheavals.

Another Indian tradition, long held in abeyance under Muslim influence but now reasserting itself, is the positive evaluation of women. While menstruating women were regarded as polluting in the Hindu "great tradition," they were not regarded as innately inferior to men and treated as beasts of burden. Under Muslim influence, most Indian women lived in *purdah* for centuries (and still do in many villages), but now they are taking their places as equals of men. They are bound to be an economic (and intellectual and political) resource, rather than a social waste as they have been in the Muslim world. Whereas Pakistan's Fatima Jinnah is an exception to Muslim social values, and tolerated in politics solely because she is the sister of Mohammed Ali Jinnah, Indira Gandhi and Viyalakshmi

Pandit, although aided in their political careers by their close relationship to Nehru, are no exception to Hindu social values. Indian women play a leading role in intellectual activities, in the arts, and in voluntary associations, and they are now beginning to assume positions of economic leadership.

Indians have a strong tradition of craftsmanship. The ideals of skilled workmanship have yet to be applied to India's modern economic problems, but the country's promising airplane, steel, and textile industries may herald world-competitive enterprises once Indian businessmen learn what is really needed to be competitive. The Indians may prove to be like the Japanese: The Japanese produced shoddy goods before World War II, but once they learned to use high-quality materials, their traditions of hard work and skill thrust them into positions of leading competition on the world market. It might be worth while to send some young Indian businessmen to American schools of business for a year or two, or have them learn "on the job" within American industry. The results might be as favorable as they have been in training Indian scientists and statisticians in the United States. But such an experiment might also fail because so much of what the Indians would learn about business in the United States would be inapplicable to India. American business education to India, in the management schools at Calcutta and Ahmedabad, has so far produced only very limited results.

India has much wealth, but this wealth is hoarded or lent out at usurious rates. A carefully planned effort to use this wealth in capital development, by government "borrowing" and use in foreign trade for imports of selected machinery, could provide the needed "take-off into sustained growth."[55] Of course, it could also be allowed to dribble away or disappear into the new hoardings of corrupt politicians. But if some incorruptible, economics-trained, top-level government official were put in charge if the hoarded gold and jewels of India, he would have a major resource to drag his country out of economic stagnation.

CONCLUSION

It is not simply one tradition, institution, value, or national characteristic trait that keeps India economically backward. It is the cumulative and interrelated effect of all of the inhibiting factors considered in this study, although caste, or "community," comes closer than any of the other influences to being a keystone in the blockage. It will not do—as some Indian and Western scholars are now doing—to point to similar specific institutions or values in economically developed societies, and to say that these did not prevent those societies from developing. It is true that white Americans have held down the Negroes just as caste Hindus have held down the Untouchables. And it is true that the French hoard gold just as the Indians do. But the fact that other countries have uneconomic practices is beside the point for India. India has an unusual *number* of these uneconomic practices, and it can *least afford* them. India is not making enough economic progress to satisfy its growing population and its aspirations. It is not even approaching a "take-off into the sustained growth." If the United States needs a revolution in its race relations, and is now getting it, India needs a revolution in many of its institutions and other cultural practices—and India may *not* be getting it.

NOTES

1. Gunnar Myrdal, *Economic Theory and Under-Developed Regions* (London: Gerald Duckworth and Co., 1957). See also Myrdal's forthcoming study of South Asian economies. Economist Everett Hagen has used psychological theory to explain economic development or the lack of it. See, *On the Theory of Social Change* (Homewood, Ill.: Dorsey Press, 1962). Economist Bert Hoselitz has used anthropological and sociological concepts to interpret economic underdevelopment. Harvey Leibenstein has kept closer to orthodox economic analysis in his *Economic Backwardness and Economic Growth* (New York: John Wiley & Sons, 1957). Indian economist N. V. Sovani has turned to sociology for aid in understanding why India has not made greater economic progress: "Non-economic Aspects of India's Economic Development," in *Administration and Economic Development in India*, ed. Ralph Braibanti and Joseph H. Spengler (Durham, N.C.: Duke University Press, 1963), pp. 260-80.

2. David C. McClelland, *The Achieving Society* (Princeton: Van Nostrand Reinhold, 1961).

3. See, for example, the village studies of India by A. R. Beale, B. S. Cohn, S. C. Dube, Oscar Lewis, G. R. Madan, McKim Marriott, Morris Opler, E. K. Gough, D. G. Mandelbaum, Milton Singer, M. N. Srinvas, and G. P. Steed. For summaries of village studies, see: *India's Villages* (Calcutta: West Bengal Government Press, 1955); McKim Marriott, ed., *Village India*, in *American Anthropologist* 57: 3: part 2 (June 1955): xix, 269.

4. M. N. Srinvas, *Religion and Society Among the Coorgs of South India* (Oxford: Clarendon Press, 1952), pp. 30-31, 212-27.

5. See, for example, Ramkrishna Mukherjee, *The Sociologist and Social Change in India Today* (New Delhi: Prentice-Hall of India, 1965).

6. Robert O. Tilman, "The Influence of Caste on Indian Economic Development," in *India's Economic Development*, ed. Braibanti and Spengler, pp. 202-23, esp. p. 219. Tilman believes the caste system is having progressively less effect on economic development because some castes are moving into nontraditional occupations. In my view, this trend is outweighed by the other trends in caste discussed in this paper.

7. F. G. Bailey, *Caste and the Economic Frontier* (London: Oxford University Press, 1958); Ramkrishna Mukherjee, "Caste and Economic Structure in West Bengal in Present Times," in *Sociology, Social Research, and Social Problems in India*, ed. R. N. Saksena (Bombay: Asia Publishing House, 1961); M. N. Srinvas, *Caste in Modern India and Other Essays* (Bombay: Asia Publishing House, 1962), pp. 15-41.

8. Morris David Morris, "The Labor Market in India," in *Labor Commitment and Social Change in Developing Areas*, ed. Wilbert E. Moore and Arnold S. Feldman (New York: Social Service Research Council, 1960).

9. *Ibid.*, p. 189.

10. The only large-scale exception is the Tata enterprises. It is said in India that the only reason for this is that there aren't enough Parsis to fill all the top jobs in this huge industrial empire.

11. Ethnic and family nepotism takes place in the West also, but not nearly to the same extent as in India, where it is sanctioned by caste and joint-family ideals.

12. The economic aspects of underemployment in underdeveloped countries are considered in Leibenstein, *Economic Backwardness*, pp. 58-76, and in N. H. Majumdar, "Some Aspects of Under-Employment," *Indian Economic Journal* 5 (July 1957): 1-18.

13. Oscar Lewis "Urbanization Without Breakdown," *Scientific Monthly* 75 (1952): 31-41.

14. Morris E. Opler, *Village Life in Northern India* (Chicago: Delphian Society, 1950), pp. 293-96.

15. It is estimated from the 1961 census that 84.0 percent of Indians are Hindu, 10.2 percent Muslims, 2.4 percent Christians, 1.8 percent Sikhs, 0.8 percent Buddhists, and 0.8 percent of other smaller religious groups.

16. There has been some reduction in the correlation of names with caste in recent years. In South India, some Hindus have been dropping their caste names. When there are religious conversions—from Islam to Christianity, or from Hinduism to Islam—the families who convert are no longer likely to change their name, even though they have changed their "community."
    Voting in India is largely along caste lines. Even the large Communist parties of Kerala and Andhra Pradesh are made up of caste coalitions, and ideological Communists (rare outside Calcutta) will often vote along caste lines for non-Communist candidates. See Lloyd I. and Susanne H. Rudolph, "The Political Role of India's Caste Associations," *Pacific Affairs* 33 (March 1960): 5-22.

17. If a top-caste stranger, like an American, identifies an innovation as high in its respective hierarchy, it will be given more acceptance than if it is introduced with little attention to its status. Sometimes it is of economic value to introduce something as low in its hierarchy: When recently-introduced deer in a certain community were beginning to destroy crops and the villagers refused to molest the deer because they

associated them with cows (the highest animal), a Westerner was successful in redefining the deer as akin to horses (a much lower species), and they were readily brought under control.

18. Victor S. D'Souza, "Implications of Occupational Prestige for Employment Policy in India," *Artha Vijnana* 1 (September 1959): 233-47.

19. Much of the Western speculation about the inhibiting role of Hindu values on economic development has stemmed from Max Weber's *Religion of India: The Sociology of Hinduism* American edition (Glencoe, Ill.: The Free Press, 1958) published in Germany during the First World War. For more recent speculation, see "India's Cultural Values and Economic Development: A Discussion," *Economic Development and Cultural Change* 7 (October 1958): 1-13, and other writings cited there. *Also see* Sovani, "Economic Development," pp. 264-71.

20. Milton Singer, "Changing Craft Traditions in India," in *Labor Commitment*, ed. Moore and Feldman, pp. 273-75.

21. Edward Shils, *The Intellectual between Tradition and Modernity—The Indian Situation* (Comparative Studies in Society and History—Supp. I, 1964).

22. Kusum Nair, *Blossoms in the Dust* (New York: Praeger Publishers, 1963).

23. Van Dusen Kennedy, "India: Tendermindedness vs. Tough Problems," *Industrial Relations* 5 (October 1965): 11.

24. M. L. Dantwala, "The Case for Village and Small-Scale Industries," *Indian Economic Journal* 3 (January 1956): 269-77.

25. *See* Leibenstein, *Economic Backwardness*, especially chapter 9.

26. As recently as December 1965, after 17 years of desperate need for foreign exchange and investment funds, the government of India was hesitant to tax or confiscate the 1.1 billion in gold bullion alone (not counting the jewels and other valuables) of the now-deceased Nizam of Hyderabad. Instead, the former princely rulers are still given up to $2 million a year each, as tax-free income, in compensation for their loss of ruling powers. According to Kamaraj Nadar, former prime minister of Madras state, the gold in the pawn shops of Madras city alone was worth Rs 120,000,000, or about $24,000,000, when (in 1964) the government limited private ownership of gold.

27. Margaret Cormack, *She Who Rides a Peacock* (Bombay and London: Asia Publishing House, 1961), esp. chapters 9 and 12. Kennedy ("India: Tendermindedness vs. Tough Problems," pp. 17-18): "The ills which keep Indian higher education from playing its proper role are many. . . . They include rapid expansion in the face of inadequate physical facilities, particularly libraries and laboratories; too many poor and mediocre faculty members; a system of promotion and departmental government that fails to attract and reward the ablest young men; undue political interference and control; a crippling instruction problem resulting from the fact that the average standard

of competence in English . . . is declining among entering students and that increasing resort is being had to regional languages for which there is a dearth of textbooks and supporting academic literature; a curricular and degree-earning system which, being geared to prescribed syllabi and standard external examinations, encourages rote learning and minimum study at the expense of creative teaching and intellectual inquiry. The results are distressing—low academic standards, high failure rates, low morale among teachers and students, and recurring indiscipline among students."

28. A. G. Deshmukh and A. R. Kamat, "Wastage in College Education— Arts Students," *Artha Vijnana* 2 (March 1960): 28-44; "Science Students," *ibid.* 2 (June 1960): 122-40; "Stagnation in College Education," *ibid.* 2 (September 1960): 173-88.

29. Cormack, *She Who Rides a Peacock*, pp. 33 ff.

30. Bella Dutt Gupta, *Contemporary Social Problems in India* (Calcutta: Vidyodaya Library, 1964), p. 14.

31. Bernard J. Cohn, "The Changing Status of a Depressed Caste," in *Village India*, ed. Marriott, pp. 64, 67.

32. Sovani, "Economic Development," pp. 268-69.

33. Rioting, including violent student deomonstrations, creates special problems for the police. See Philip G. Altbach, "The Transformation of the Indian Student Movement," *Asian Survey* 6:8 (August 1966): 448-60.

34. K. N. Raj, *Indian Economic Growth: Performance and Prospects* (New Delhi: Allied Publishers, 1965), pp. 2-6.

35. Ibid., and A. K. Sen, "PL 480 and India," *Now* 2 (12 November 1965): 11.

36. Raj, *Indian Economic Growth*, p. 11.

37. Richard D. Lambert, "The Social and Psychological Determinants of Savings and Investments in Developing Societies," in *Development and Society*, ed. David E. Novack and Robert Lekachman (New York: St. Martin's Press, 1964), pp. 270 ff.

38. Myron Weiner, *Politics of Scarcity* (Chicago: University of Chicago Press, 1962), p. 151.

39. Ashok Mitra, "Tax Burden for Indian Agriculture," in *India's Economic Development*, ed. Braibanti and Spengler, p. 303.

40. See Kingsley Davis, "Social and Demographic Aspects of Economic Development in India," in *Economic Growth: Brazil, India, and Japan*, ed. S. Kuznets, W. E. Moore, and J. J. Spengler (Durham, N.C.: Duke University Press, 1955), pp. 306-8.

41. Ronald Wraith and Edgar Simpkins, *Corruption in Developing Countries* (London: George Allen and Unwin, 1963), p. 203.

42. The weakness of the bureaucracy in relation to rural community development is discussed by Hugh Tinker, "The Village in the Framework of Development," in *India's Economic Development*, ed. Braibanti and Spengler, especially pp. 131-33.

43. The Indian civil service was created by the British, whose primary concern was that the government of India maintain law and order. Thus the British, relatively unbureaucratic themselves, founded a tremendous bureaucracy in India. They managed to keep it quite honest while they were in authority. Sovani ("Economic Development," p. 269) maintains, with considerable evidence, that British bureaucracy killed what initiative there existed in village institutions, such as the *panchayat*. If government's purpose now is to stimulate the economy, it must reorient itself away from the primary emphasis on restrictive maintenance of order. *See* Joseph LaPalombara, *Bureaucracy and Political Development* (Princeton: Princeton University Press, 1963).

44. Quoted from M. B. Desai, *Report on the Administrative Survey of the Surat District* (Bombay, 1958), p. 81. Despite his brave words, Nehru's fatalism reveals itself in this quotation.

45. D. R. Gadgil, "Social Change and Liberal Democracy in New States," *Artha Vijnana* 1:3 (September 1959): 183-86.

46. Kennedy, "India: Tendermindedness vs. Tough Problems," p. 15.

47. Mitra, "Tax Burden for Indian Agriculture," p. 298.

48. Novack and Lekachman, eds., *Development and Society*, p. 115.

49. Partha Mukherjee (Ph.D. diss., Patna University, 1966).

50. M. V. Raman, "Knowledge and Practice of Contraception in India: A Survey of Some Recent Studies," *Artha Vijnana* 5 (June 1963): 81-96.

51. There are certain uses of mathematics in the social sciences in the United States that are not dissimilar to those of astrologers in India, so perhaps we should not differentiate too sharply between East and West.

52. *New York Times*, 28 February 1966, p. 3.

53. Julius F. Hilliard, "A Perspective on International Development," unpublished paper (Ford Foundation, November 1965).

54. The strengths of the Indian bureaucracy are discussed by Ralph Braibanti in his chapter in *India's Economic Development*, ed. Braibanti and Spengler, pp. 3-68.

55. W. W. Rostow, "The Take-Off into Sustained Growth," *Economic Journal* 66 (March 1956): 25-48.

SUGGESTIONS FOR FURTHER READING
PART FIVE: ECONOMIC DEVELOPMENT AND SOCIAL CHANGE

Brown, Lester R. *Seeds of Change: The Green Revolution and Development in the 1970's*. New York: Praeger Publishers, 1970.

Eisenstadt, S. N. *Essays on Sociological Aspects of Political and Economic Development*. The Hague: Mouton, 1961.

Heilbroner, Robert L. *The Great Ascent: The Struggle for Economic Development in Our Time.* New York: Harper & Row, 1963.

Holt, Robert T., and Turner, John E. *The Political Basis of Economic Development: An Exploration in Comparative Political Analysis.* Princeton: Van Nostrand Reinhold, 1966.

Hunter, Guy. *Modernizing Peasant Societies: A Comparative Study in Asia and Africa.* New York: Oxford University Press, 1969.

Johnson, Harry G. *Economic Policies Toward Less Developed Countries.* Washington, D. C.: The Brookings Institution, 1967.

Kunkel, John H. *Society and Economic Growth: A Behavioral Perspective of Social Change.* New York: Oxford University Press, 1970.

Leibenstein, Harvey. *Economic Backwardness and Economic Growth: Studies in the Theory of Economic Development.* New York: John Wiley & Sons, 1957.

Millikan, Max F., and Hapgood, David. *No Easy Harvest: The Dilemma of Agriculture in Underdeveloped Countries.* Boston: Little, Brown and Co., 1967.

Myrdal, Gunnar. *Economic Theory and Underdeveloped Regions.* New York: Harper & Row, 1957.

Novack, David E., and Lekachman, Robert, eds. *Development and Society: the Dynamics of Economic Change.* New York: St. Martin's Press, 1964.

Pearson, Lester B. *Partners in Development: Report of the Commission on International Development.* New York: Praeger Publishers, 1969.

Rostow, W. W. *Politics and the Stages of Growth.* Cambridge, Mass.: Cambridge University Press, 1971.

Rostow, W. W. *The Progress of Economic Growth.* 2d ed. New York: W. W. Norton & Co., 1962.

Ward, Barbara. *The Rich Nations and the Poor Nations.* New York: W. W. Norton & Co., 1962.

PART SIX
ideologies
and political
development

Many African, Middle Eastern, and Asian leaders assert in
varying degrees that their underdevelopment was brought about
by Western imperialism or neocolonialism. Some of the Afro-
Asian leaders subscribe in varying degrees to Marxist-Leninist
interpretation of imperialism as the highest stage of capitalism
and place the blame for their underdevelopment on the West
rather than upon themselves. Nationalist leaders found it easier
to place the responsibility for their underdevelopment on
outside powers and the Marxist-Leninist ideology provided a
simple explanation to many of the Afro-Asian peoples. Although such a simple explanation ignores the many and complex factors involved in the development process, as we have
discussed in our previous chapters, it provides a rationale for
political action and mobilization of the masses.

Ideology is used by political elites to unify their people
regardless of social cleavages which may have existed in the
past. The unified society is then mobilized behind a developmental plan and organized to carry out developmental tasks.
Political elites exert their leadership by appealing to nationalism
or "Arab Socialism," "African Socialism," "Islamic Socialism,"
"Destourian Socialism," or other types of "ism." These leaders
may draw a picture of a new society in terms of nationalism or
socialism. The use of ideology in modernizing society was
succinctly described by David E. Apter:

> What gives an ideology its real force and conviction during its period of maximum effectiveness is its contribution to establishing identity and solidarity. If an ideology can reduce anxiety and increase self-confidence, if it can displace fear to a foreign or outside group, and if it can give individuals a sense of their own worth and significance, then an ideology will be powerful on an individual level. In other words, it must satisfy an identity function.[1]

Apter further states:

> For the political leader, if an ideology can be sufficiently generalized and if it can be made the basis of shared feelings and a universal language of understanding in the sense of communicating a common condition under which many labor, it will be useful in building solidarity. The powerful ideologies, then, are those that at crucial moments during the cycle of perception give individuals a sense of identity and solidarity with their fellows—all in a political context.[2]

Many political leaders in developing states use socialist ideology in order to undermine the prevailing hierarchies of power and prestige which are associated with traditionalism. Many African, Middle Eastern, Asian, and Latin American political leaders use socialism in a non-Marxist sense. They repudiate or are silent on the question of class conflict which is one of the major tenets of Marxism-Leninism. Their concept of the role of property is vague. Government is accepted as the major source of development.

Some political elites in developing states have sought the support of the masses for their development programs by carefully appealing to the people on the basis of traditional ethos of the community and the use of religious symbols. Egypt during Nasser's rule is a case in point. Muslim attachment to Islamic heritage made it all the more imperative for the rulers to accommodate themselves and their policies to public religious sentiment. Professor P. J. Vatikiotis has stated:

> The military rulers of the U.A.R. (Egypt) have been faced with the difficult task of devising a secular formula for national identification and orientation, to replace the traditional one of Islam. Although considered to belong to the most modern secularly orientated national institution in Egypt, the officers in power today continue to use Islam and the traditional ethos of the Egyptian community as instruments to legitimate their authority and to command the allegiance of all classes in a still undifferentiated public. At the same time, their use of traditional symbols has permitted the army rulers to attain a certain degree of political consensus among the masses without, however conceding to them any great measure of participation in the political process and the making of policy.[3]

The political leadership in Egypt is trying to rebuild a nation on the following pillars: democratic, cooperative socialism; freedom from capitalistic monopoly; abolition of feudalism; a strong national army; social justice for all citizens; and a sound democracy where all members of the political body take an active part in the political processes of the government. In pursuing their socialist plans for rebuilding their nation Egypt's leaders supported their actions by Islamic proclivities which call for equality between citizens, and the end of monopoly and exploitation. The essence of the Islamic message has always been centered around the assertion of human dignity and worth. Egyptian socialism is thus justified on religious rather than Marxist grounds. The incompatibility of religion, however, and twentieth-century Egyptian socialism arises only when religious doctrines are subjected to reactionary interpretation. Thus, the late President Nasser has asserted:

> Every religion contains a message of, a call to, progress. Reaction, however, ever ready to monopolize the good things of the earth, has in the past harnessed religion to the service of its own greed, wilfully distorting the essential truths to check the course of progress.

> The essence of all religions is the assertion of man's right to dignity and freedom. The very doctrine of reward and punishment is based on the concept of equality of opportunity for every man before God; each individual begins his religious and moral life with a *tabula rasa*, a clean sheet, later to be inscribed with the acts performed of his own free will.

> For the will to be free, the person must be free. True religion cannot tolerate a restrictive system of class distinction, by virtue of which the majority inherit the terrestial punishment of poverty, ignorance and disease, while a small minority monopolize the reward of all prosperity.[4]

In the preceding pages we sketched briefly how ideology can be used as a vehicle by political elites in order to unify and solidify their people in their quest for modernization. Political elites use nationalism, different kinds of socialism, traditional ethos of the community, and religious symbols in order to move their societies from traditionalism to modernity.

In the following three articles we will examine systematically the role of nationalism, religion, and socialism in the political development in Afro-Asian states. The first article by Rupert Emerson introduces the reader to "the most important single force behind the revolutionary drive of the rising peoples of

271

Asia and Africa"—nationalism. The ordinary poverty-stricken peoples in Africa and Asia are willing to endure temporary economic privation in order to gain national salvation. Nationalism, Emerson explains, has characteristically been the property of the constantly expanding minority elites many of whom received their education in Western institutions. The educated elites in the emergent nations are generally oriented toward the West and modernization in spite of their passionate attacks on alleged Western imperialism. Although the educated nationalist elites in the Afro-Asian countries hope to establish democratic institutions and viable political systems, nationalism as a dynamic force can turn in undemocratic or antidemocratic directions. Thus, Emerson concludes that nationalism by itself can provide very few answers to the multitude of questions facing the newly independent Afro-Asian peoples.

Gordon P. Means examines the changing role of Islam in Malaysia and evaluates its impact upon the modernization of the political system. There has been no conflict between Islamic religion and the beliefs and practices of the recipient society partly because Islam has no religious hierarchy standing apart from society. Means discusses the role of religion in precolonial Malay society and states that religion has played an important role in providing social integration and cohesion in the primary group relations of life within the Malay village. During this period Islam has adapted to most existing Malay institutions, beliefs, and practices and it can hardly be said that it promoted the modernization of social structures, beliefs, values, and attitudes of Malay society.

The colonial period witnessed greatly improved communications which brought about changes in the character of Muslim religious elites and thus created tensions between the folk religions of the Malay village and certain religious elites. This tension created strong impulse for change and reform. However, the Islamic reform movement was dogmatic and fundamentalist in character. Means turns his attention to the discussion of Islamic law and administration under British colonial rule. Colonial authorities attempted to avoid any policies that might disrupt Islam as a "cultural gyroscope" for Malay society.

The role of Islam in the postwar era and the role of government in religious affairs are examined. Means concludes that Islam has been a significant force in the political modernization to the extent it promoted popular participation in the political system. Also, it has helped the Malays to overcome their parochial loyalties. On the other hand, there are certain features of Islam that tend to impede other aspects of modernization, particularly economic development. John N. Hazard points out that Keita pressed hard to establish a Soviet model in Mali by moving directly into socialism. He discusses Keita's economic and land policies and the major reasons for their failure and the fall of Keita. Hazard states that Lenin's system of economic administration has economic merit, as evidenced by its use in varying forms in many countries, but it functions with difficulty in developing societies. For its success it requires diffused managerial skill, knowledge of complex cost accounting methods and administrative efficiency. Mali lacked these essential requirements. Moreover, Keita was inept in handling public relations and lacked the experience to operate Lenin's system. Hazard concludes that although Keita was ousted from power, "Mali remains too important as a focal point in Africa for operations and for proof of the viability of the Marxian socialist system for the U.S.S.R. and China to leave it alone, unless all hope has to be abandoned."

NOTES

1. David E. Apter, *The Politics of Modernization* (Chicago: University of Chicago Press, 1965), p. 328.

2. *Ibid.*

3. P. J. Vatikiotis, *The Egyptian Army in Politics: Pattern For New Nations* (Bloomington: Indiana University Press, 1961), pp. 190-91.

4. *Arab Observer*, no. 169, 16 September 1963, p. 19. *See* my article "Nasser's Search For New Order," *The Muslim World* 56, no. 2 (1966): 87-95, for a more detailed discussion.

NATIONALISM
AND POLITICAL
DEVELOPMENT

Rupert Emerson

If it were necessary to select the most important single force behind the revolutionary drive of the rising peoples of Asia and Africa, the choice would inevitably go to nationalism. For none of its potential rivals can an effective case be made. Indeed, almost all of them contribute in one fashion or another to the mounting nationalist demand. Arnold Toynbee, profuse with capitals, may denounce Nationalism as a "disastrous corruption," "a perversion of Industrialism and Democracy," or "the monstrous outcome of the impact of our modern Western Democracy upon the Parochial State"; but to the peoples newly asserting their claim to equal status in the world, nationalism is the essence of what they seek.

In the debates in the United Nations on the Covenants on Human Rights the right of self-determination has frequently been considered the foundation on which all other rights rest; self-determination denied, no other right can be secure. It is in this light that peoples around the globe have viewed nationalism, assuming that the remaining goods they seek will flow from its attainment. The usual version of this goal is an acknowledged equality expressed in sovereign independence; more rarely, an adequate substitute may be found in free association with another country as is the case between Puerto Rico and the United States, or between British Togoland and Ghana, or perhaps within the French Community.

The prime rival to nationalism as a driving force is presumed to be the desire for an improved standard of living. From time to time it is asserted that the ordinary poverty-stricken Asian and African is really interested only in seeing an end put to his poverty. This is a highly dubious proposition. The evidence indicates that he regards at least temporary

From Rupert Emerson, "Nationalism and Political Development," *Journal of Politics* 22 (February 1960): 3-28. Reprinted by permission of the author and the publisher.

economic privation as an appropriate price to pay for national salvation. It has also been contended that his real demand is for a transition to modernity, as manifested in economic and social development. In some part the pressure for economic development derives from the same root as the desire for an improved standard of living. However, it also has nationalist implications in its drive for equality.

However strong the urge toward better living conditions and economic development, it tends always to take second place to the political claims of nationalism. The individual who protects his economic position by refusing to undertake the sacrifices which patriotism demands reads himself out of the community of right-minded, nation-fearing men. As one of the standard phrases of nationalism has it: we would rather be governed like hell by ourselves than well by someone else. Furthermore, the issue between nationalism and material advancement here posed is seen as a quite unreal one since the nationalist creed normally embraces the belief that material improvement will surely follow in the wake of national self-realization. Both well-being and economic development are considered unattainable in the shadow of imperialism. Only when the national destiny is safely entrusted to national and not alien hands is it possible to move confidently ahead on the path which leads to wealth, strength, and modernity. Nationalism opens the way to a new economic era, and the latter in turn lends new power to the nation.

Communism might be put forward as a contemporary threat to nationalism and undoubtedly, in certain cases, individuals and groups have given to the Party a priority which they deny to the nation. More frequently, however, and particularly in the revolt against imperialist domination, Communism is seen as an alternative means of reaching national goals. Although objective reality may contradict them, Asian and African Communists are far more likely to view their Party membership as a positive expression of their nationalism than as a negation of it. Official Communist dogma itself puts self-determination in the forefront of its doctrines (even though the small print always carefully reduces it to an instrument to be used for Party purposes) and distinguishes between the rightful patriotism of the unfree peoples and the proper devotion to proletarian internationalism of those whose national identity is old-established. It has often been contended that the success of the Communists in Asian countries hinges upon their ability to identify themselves with the local nationalist cause.

The priority of nationalism has been vigorously affirmed by both Jawaharlal Nehru and Kwame Nkrumah. In his opening address to the IPR conference at Lucknow in 1950, the Indian Prime Minister described nationalism as a war-cry which warms the heart of almost every Asian: "Any other force, any other activity that may seek to function, must define itself in terms of this nationalism. . . . No argument in any country of Asia is going to have weight if it goes counter to the nationalist spirit of the country, Communism or no Communism." Supporting much the same

275

theme, Ghana's Prime Minister cited the motto of the Convention People's Party, which was his own creation. "We prefer self-government with danger to servitude in tranquillity" and followed it up with what he called the party's policy, "Seek ye first the political kingdom and all things shall be added unto you."[1] It is to the attainment of the political kingdom of the nation that the guiding spirits of the new states and their followers have looked, confident that the nation came first and that the rest would follow after.

It is a great deal easier to assert the priority given nationalism than to lay out with any measure of precision its content. Rarely does nationalism represent a coherent and positive body of doctrine and belief, reaching significantly beyond insistence on the establishment of an independent state. Freedom from partition or alien intrusion is normally a far better defined matter than are the uses to which freedom would be put. In the speech cited above, Nehru commented on the fact that a large element in nationalism is negative. "Nationalism is essentially an anti-feeling," he has written elsewhere, "and it feeds and fattens on hatred and anger against other national groups, and especially against the foreign rulers of a subject country."[2]

The negative or 'anti'-character of nationalism in a colonial setting is simple enough to explain, but it is by no means unique to colonialism. Everywhere the national "we" has been to a considerable degree defined by contrast to the alien and opposing "they," and in most instances no operationally significant statement of what the nation stands for can be expected. Indeed, this may be held to be a standard feature of all nationalism until one arrives at what Carlton Hayes called integral nationalism or what might today be called totalitarian nationalism. I take it to be characteristic of liberal nationalism that its particular content remains very largely unspecified, allowing for a multitude of sins as well as virtues. The Fourth of July oration of the past, praising America's blue skies and broad horizons, its heroes and its great achievements, reached an approximately acceptable level of specificity. It roused a glow of pride in being an American and yet did not rule out any significant number of Americans who were heretical on one or another point mentioned by the speaker. Tom Paine, George Washington, Alexander Hamilton, Thomas Jefferson, and Andrew Jackson must all fit within the American heritage; New England, the South, the Middle West and the Far West must find an equal place. If any of them are to be ruled out by authorized fiat we have come to the proto-Fascist phase when some body arrogates to itself the right to determine among Americans what is to be accepted as American. France must embrace the *ancien régime*, the Revolution, Napoleon, and the twists and turnings of the last century and a half. To demand that each nation have a single positive content and program for nationalism is to ask that it select from a diverse history certain strands which alone will constitute its legitimate national heritage. Not far down this road lies the *Gleichschaltung* of the Nazis.

The new states are however, peculiarly divided within themselves by the gaps which separate different elements in the population. Not only do they have as diverse and internally contradictory a history as do other peoples, but they are also afflicted by an unusual degree of distance between the bulk of the population and the newly arisen leadership. The most notable gap is the one which divides the active, Western-educated urban group from the inert, uneducated, tradition-bound mass mainly composed of the peasantry. It is the first group from which the heirs of empire have been drawn to constitute the new elite, putting its stamp on the states which it has been largely responsible for bringing into being. Here are the makings of a fundamental dilemma. It is arguable that any nation's claim to a distinctive place in the sun must be derived from the past which has shaped it in this peculiar national fashion, yet the entire leadership of the new states tends to be made up of those most removed from the traditional society of their ancestors. Nationalism has characteristically been the property of the constantly expanding but still relatively slight minority most influenced by the West.

The social structure in Asian and African nations, then, is that a newly fashioned elite, oriented toward the West and modernization despite its passionate repudiation of Western imperial control, has taken a predominant lead in societies the bulk of whose members are still close to their ancestral past. In such a circumstance the definition of the national purpose must evidently be a hazardous process. We do not as yet have any accurate evidence or body of precedent by means of which to determine what course the new states are likely to take. We do not know whether the gaps which are now so apparent will be filled with greater or less speed, and whether the mass will tend to move in the Westernizing and modernizing direction of its currently ruling elite (which seems most probable) or the elite move toward re-absorption into the mass and the older patterns of life (which is highly unlikely as a general phenomenon). Against the current trend toward an optimistic view of the prospects for development must be set the general failure of almost all non-Western countries save Japan to swing into the modern stream during the last century. Furthermore, the record shows that many Latin American countries not only relapsed into lethargy but also made little headway in achieving the national integration of different elements of their population. It may be that a similar decline into stagnation on the part of Africa and Asia is precluded by the speed at which the world now moves and the new modes of production, transport and communication which work to break down old barriers and isolationisms. The precedents of the past have perhaps become irrelevant in the face of such developments as the deep penetration of virtually every society by Western forces and ideas, the inescapable pressure of outside events, and the presence of Communism, ready to exploit every difficulty or failure. Both what has already happened and the widespread expectations for a different kind of future render a return to the old ways impossible. The clear probability is that the West has loosed forces the forward sweep of which can only temporarily be diverted or checked, though no reliable estimate can be made either of the speed of change or of the form it will take. The nationalist movements have themselves been the spearhead of the demand for change.

The existence of great gaps in the society of the new states raises a further question. How real is the solidarity of a nation when it is so profoundly divided within itself? It is evident that no single and all-embracing answer can be given to such a question since the backgrounds and present situations of the different countries vary so greatly. What can be said of Egypt has no necessary bearing for Ghana or the Philippines, and India's prospects may be quite unrelated to those of its neighbors, Pakistan, Burma, Ceylon, and Afghanistan. Precisely the 'anti'-character of nationalist movements in colonial or quasi-colonial countries is likely to lend a deceptive sense of national unity. The fact that a people can stage a consolidated anti-imperial movement conveys no assurance that it will be able to maintain political coherence once the imperial enemy has vanished. It is, of course, true that the mere carrying on of an extended and concerted struggle is in itself a significant factor in the creation of national sentiment, but a more basic identity is necessary if the national unity is to endure. The sense of belonging together through the experience of a common history and of facing a common destiny is not something which can be created overnight.

How great importance should be attached to the gap between the Western-oriented elite and the mass is not a matter on which a precise estimate can now be given. When a nationalist movement has gotten into full swing, the people at large are likely to follow the lead of the active nationalist elite though they may have given little prior evidence of political interest. One commentator has remarked that there is no difference between African peoples which is as great as their collective difference from the Europeans who have ruled them. When India was aflame with nationalism in the 1930s, Gandhi and his lieutenants were able to win the support of many whose knowledge of what the struggle involved must have been slight. Similarly, when the euphemistically labelled police actions of the Dutch were carrying colonial warfare to the Indonesians, an unexpectedly broad segment of the population gave its backing to the nationalist forces. And yet the gap remains. The mass has so far demonstrated only meagre interest in taking an active part in day-to-day political life. The leaders, for their part, have often shown an inclination to see themselves as an elite, properly entrusted with the destinies of their untutored countrymen. "Guided democracy," which Sukarno considers suitable to the present state of development in Indonesia, also describes the elite conception of government in many other countries. Nor have the mass of the people up to this point been inclined to challenge the elitist claim of their new leaders, although the military have presented a decisive challenge in several countries. Where democratic institutions survive for an extended time and the people come to feel that political power is actually in their hands, the present relationship between mass and elite may take on a quite different cast.

* * *

The nation establishes the demographic and geographic frontiers of the state. For the survival of the state nationalism furnishes another vital element in that it supplies the emotional cement which holds the members of the state together when disagreements threaten to pull them apart. What the social contract sought to provide by engaging men in formal obligations to each other came to be provided in the contemporary world by the social-historical fact of being born, brought up, and educated within the close-knit and emotion-laden confines of the nation. In the theory of the national era the state exists in order to realize the purposes of the nation, and, short of external attack, it can maintain its unity as long as the "We" of the nation takes priority over all the divergent pulls which might distract and disrupt.

Does nationalism have a clear tendency to produce one or another type of political institution? The answer to this question must be a slightly hesitant "No"; slightly hesitant because nationalism has in it democratic elements which cannot be ignored even where it has turned in ruthlessly authoritarian directions.

In fact, to assign to nationalism any particular political coloration is presumably impossible since it has been associated with almost every conceivable regime and attitude. Even though an impressive case can be made for the proposition that every true nationalism rests on democratic underpinnings of sorts, there are many ardent and unmistakable nationalisms in which democracy as a specific type of political system is either nonexistent or is no more than a facade of outward conformity with current political fashions. Where the general constellation of forces has been such as to promote democracy, as most notably in Western Europe and the countries which it has settled overseas, nationalism has maintained a predominantly democratic outlook; where the foundations of democracy have been weak, as in most of the rest of the world, nationalism has betrayed the democratic promise which the nineteenth-century liberal saw in it and has become an instrument of the established ruling groups or of totalitarianism. It is, of course, always the champion of self-government in the sense of national as opposed to alien rule, but it is only accidentally self-government in the sense of rule by the many as opposed to rule by the few. Reduced to its bare bones, nationalism is no more than the assertion that this particular community is arrayed against the rest of mankind. This sense of separate identity can by itself give no clue as to how the community may choose to manage its own affairs.

At a time when nationalism in the West has often drifted in reactionary or militarist directions and when the most dangerous and abhorrent elements in it have so recently been arrogantly paraded by the Fascists and

279

Nazis, it may appear paradoxical, or even outrageous folly to suggest the existence of an essential bond between nationalism and democracy; yet both in idea and in actual historical development there has been such a bond. Hans Kohn has put the matter in the extreme form of saying that "nationalism is inconceivable without the ideas of popular sovereignty preceding—without a complete revision of the position of ruler and ruled, of classes and castes."[3] On the face of the historical record no statement as uncompromisingly sweeping as this can be sustained . . . and yet it has more than a germ of fundamental truth.

Once full-fledged nationalism has appeared, a transformation of deep and lasting importance in the relations of people, rulers, and state tends to occur. Even in the Fascist variants the role which the people play is sharply distinguished from their role in the earlier type of dictatorship or monarchy, as witness the efforts of Fuehrer and Duce to carry the masses with them, to give at least the appearance of popular consultation through plebiscitary techniques, and to spread the tentacles of the Party down into every cranny of the society. This, certainly, is not democracy in any acceptable sense, and yet it is equally certainly a perverse offshoot from democratic roots. The Leader and the Party put themselves forward as emanations of the popular will, as a truer distillation of the national *volonté générale* than the people themselves can produce.

To reduce the question to its most basic terms, the argument linking democracy and nationalism would run something as follows. Nationalism is peculiarly a product of or a response to the distinctive forces which have gone into the shaping of the modern world. Those forces are inherently and inevitably "democratic" in the sense that they mobilize submerged elements and classes of society into new social roles, eat away at traditional attachments and relationships, and work toward the building of a new great society into which, in principle, all men are actively drawn. Obviously what is involved here is by no means necessarily a democratic constitutional structure nor even an immediate approximation of a society striving toward egalitarianism, although both of these are likely to be present at least as active aspirations. Far more, it is the general conception, derived from the changing social scene, that the people, the mass of ordinary humans, are of consequence, that they are achieving a sense both of their own worth and of their right and ability to do something about it, and that the leaders must speak in their name. The national era comes to be an era of mass communications and mass production, inescapably headed toward mass politics.

The heart of the argument is the proposition that the rise of nationalism is normally associated with deep-running social ferment and change which disrupt the old order of society and bring about a rise in social consequence and awareness of ever-widening segments and classes of the people at large. On this basis nationalism is seen as one of the major and typical manifestations of what Karl Mannheim has spoken of as "the fundamental democratization of society," the stirring "into action of those classes who formerly played a passive part in political life."[4] As the peoples themselves—or, at least, a significant new element among them—begin to come of age and to a new consciousness of themselves, they demand a new place in a society in process of transformation. One of the characteristic forms which this demand has taken is insistence upon the centrality of the national community and upon the latter's right to make the state the sovereign organ of its identity and will. The people, after all, compose the nation, and it is not beyond the bounds of reason to suggest the revolutionary importance of the fact that the social-political community which has come to occupy the center of the contemporary stage—taking over the state in its own name and establishing a new criterion of legitimacy—should, therefore, be defined in terms of the people. In the new dispensation the state could no longer be seen as made up of the ruler and those who happened to be his subjects, but became in principle the emanation and instrument of the nation. The forward thrust of the bourgeoisie in Europe and later of the masses, had its close overseas parallel in the awakening rebellion of colonial people, in roughly similar circumstances and under similar leadership.

The rise of democracy as a political phenomenon has coincided too closely with the emergence of nations as conscious entities to be explained in terms of random chance. The lines of interconnection between the two are many. The most evident is the one which has already been briefly discussed: the fact that nationalism is one of the major manifestations of the modern social ferment which overturns traditional relationships and gives new consequence to formerly submerged elements of society.

A second line of interconnection is the immense prestige which democracy has achieved—even among those who have no serious intent of practicing it. Democracy is taken as an ultimate good to which all peoples must aspire, but which only the advanced peoples can hope to master. The imperial centers—Britain, France, the Low Countries, the United States—which have so largely set the tone for the world as it has evolved in the last century and more, have established the pattern of democratic supremacy, and have, at least until recently, made no effort to conceal their belief that the "lesser breeds of man" could not be trusted to manage a democratic system. The imperial powers themselves, properly democratic at home, must impose a benevolently autocratic rule on the peoples whose tutelage they had undertaken. For the nationalists struggling to win their equality with the imperial masters here was a challenge: democracy was the political system whose realization would serve as a symbol that the bonds of inferiority had been broken.

Nor was the striving for democratic institutions only a matter of prestige. Assuming the nationalist leaders to be in almost every instance the product of Western education at home or abroad, the political philosophy and political history with which they were imbued pointed to democracy as the form of government which represented man's highest achievement and as the form which modern man naturally adopted. If

281

they lived and studied abroad, they were likely to come in contact with democratic institutions, and in dependent countries the imperial author-ities grudgingly introduced installments of democracy at which their wards were allowed to try their hand under close supervision. Political education in both a formal and a practical sense had the concepts and institutions of democracy in large part at its center, and other approaches to democracy were made in the new era through the upcoming political parties, trade unions, cooperative organizations, and other such bodies, all of which represented popular adaptation to the new Western forces coming in under the aegis of imperialism.

Furthermore, a swing in the democratic direction was a matter of vital political necessity for the nationalists. Their legitimacy in the eyes of their imperial opponents, and, no doubt, in their own as well, rested in very considerable part on their ability to demonstrate that they had the mass of their people behind them. If it could be established that they spoke for a nation with the blessing of its people, their moral claim to take over approached the irrefutable. To this moral aspect of their struggle must be added the hard political fact that if they were to represent enough of a political force to have a serious impact on the imperial power whose position they contested, they must be able to enlist the masses in battle behind them. Particularly in the colonial areas the effective strength of the nationalists rested upon their ability to have a larger hold on the loyalty of the people than could be exercised by the colonial officials. As the grandest sample of all, when the Indian National Congress under Gandhi's guidance became a mass organization in the 1920s and 1930s the British authorities could no longer maintain the claim that the people at large really preferred alien rule nor could they count on having their orders generally obeyed. Prisons and bayonets still served to keep the system temporarily in operation, but they were an unacceptable substitute for consent.

In these and other fashions nationalism works to promote democracy, but it also contains ingredients which can with the greatest of ease turn in undemocratic or antidemocratic directions. Wherever nationalism is the main driving force, there is the temptation to give priority to the attainment of national unity, strength, and independence. In such circumstances the liberalism of democratic nationalism may yield to the demand for unity put forward in the name of the nation itself. The problem is always present of giving specific content to the national will and singling out those who formulate it. Rousseau's *volonté générale*, itself only precariously identified with the concrete wills of actual human beings, is sublimated by Hegel into a *Volksgeist* which manifests itself in a realm above that of ordinary mortals but must be brought down to earth. The national will speaks with irresistible authority, yet whose voice speaks for it? The national soul may reside in the simple peasant, villager, or worker, but his ignorance and lack of experience of the great world render him, it may be contended, unable to give it true expression. In his stead the elite or the charismatic leader takes over as the emanation of the national will. The nation is sovereign, but the exercise of that sovereignty, so the argument all too fluently runs, should, for the good for the nation itself, be entrusted to those who can use it rightly. By this time the national democracy is well on the way toward transformation into nationalist autocracy; and it was down this road that the Germans were stampeded into the disaster of Nazism.

If the nation is one entity with a single sacred destiny, how can it be allowed to dissipate its energies in internal disaffection and conflict, particularly when it is threatened by external danger and is embarked on basic internal reconstruction? In the actual situation of the new states the attraction of power and the estimate of national need combine to enhance the already strong elitist tendency of Western-oriented leaders who are amply aware of the illiteracy, backwardness, and inexperience of the bulk of their countrymen. And where the civilian elites do not themselves step in to furnish the "guided democracy," the military are likely to be standing by to impose their version of order and of the national will on peoples whose ability to manage the democratic constitutions they have decreed for themselves is minimal. Latin America and the Middle East furnish unhappy models which are already having their imitators elsewhere, often with explicit insistence that the democratic order is being overturned only in order to lay solider foundations for a return to democracy. At the next remove the Communists will gladly furnish their own improved rendering of democracy.

No great confidence can be placed in the general populace as the defender of threatened democratic institutions. Poverty-ridden peoples in a climate of rising expectations are not likely to make their first concern the preservation of political forms and liberties whose meaning is obscure to them and whose promise appears of less significance than other prospects that are held out to them. If democracy fails to produce results with adequate speed and if authoritarian methods seem to hold the remedy, the masses cannot be counted on to rise to the defense of unfamiliar political machineries. In general they lack not only the democratic tradition but also the more basic tradition of standing up to do battle for their rights against the remote and superior authorities who have through the ages pushed them around. Nothing in their experience has brought home to them the belief that they are the possessors of human rights and fundamental freedoms which they are entitled to and able to defend. The present array of democratic institutions has been imposed on them from above almost as much as any of the previous systems; certainly the constitutions have not been adopted in response to a demand from below. All too often it is probable that the people would feel more at home with a government which, in traditional style, tells them what to do.

Whatever their composition, the ruling authorities in this democratic or post-democratic age will seek popular consent or approval to establish the legitimacy of their title to power, but this can be handled through the familiar plebiscitary techniques without disturbing the people by placing alternatives before them.

In the West nationalism is now often denounced as being a divisive and anachronistic force—bad enough at any time and intolerable in the atomic era. From this the moral is drawn, most frequently in France, that the Asian and African peoples should resign themselves to recognition that the world has arrived at a time of interdependence which renders a demand for sovereignty absurd. Of the grievousness of nationalism's faults there can be no doubt. They can exact a high price, yet what is bought at that price is also of great value, particularly, perhaps, for those who are just entering into the modern national phase. The divisiveness of nationalism has a different bearing for the people of the new states than for those who are old established and even outgrowing their nationhood, and the element of anachronism is to be measured not only by the calendar but by the life span of the particular nationalisms as well.

Even for the Western peoples whose reaping of the fruits of nationalism is of relatively old standing the undermining of the nation by insistence on its shortcomings could create a worse rather than a better situation unless preferable forms of community, acceptable to the people, were ready at hand. The brotherhood of man finds much of its present working expression within the nation, even though its other face is hostility to those outside. Whatever changes in the structure of the global society may lie just around the corner, they are still sufficiently concealed to make it impossible to see the form and nature of the nation's successors. We have, unhappily, no necessary reason to assume that if the nation were to lose its hold the next stage would mark any appreciable advance toward a more desirable world. France presented no pretty picture in the years just before World War II when the idea of the nation had lost its force for both the right and the left, and many in the center as well.

In the newly rising countries nationalism has functions to perform which it has largely exhausted in the West. While in the West the nation has come to represent the actual outer boundaries of communal allegiance for most men or has set limits which are already found too confining, in Asia and Africa it constitutes a great potential widening of the social and political horizons of most of the people. Far from forcing men to live within restricted quarters, it opens new doors and windows. Where men's lives have traditionally been bounded by family, tribe, or caste, by village, market town, or petty state, the emergence of nationalism creates pressures which force men into larger communities, as nationalism is itself a response to similar pressures. That lesser communities can put up strong resistance to full absorption into the nation, or what claims to be the nation, is demonstrated on a small scale by the existence in all countries of isolated pockets of people who have not effectively been drawn into the broader national society. On a larger scale there are any number of evidences of growing pains such as the demands of linguistic communities in India, the revolts in different parts of Indonesia, and Nigeria's troubles with its tribes and regions. In some instances, as in Pakistan's split from India, even the assertion that there is a single nation embracing the peoples concerned may be successfully denied. For many individuals and groups considerable time will surely elapse before their social-political consciousness expands to the new national limits, but the forces of the modern world are on the whole conspiring to make man's age-old parochialism impossible.

For the leaders and organizers of national movements it is obviously a matter of the first importance to wean as many people as possible away from their more local attachments and bring them to active awareness of their national ties. In addition to ethical and religious considerations Gandhi was moved by a simple political calculation in pleading the case for the untouchables: if the latter remained outside the national fold, the Indian nation could bring that much less pressure to bear on the British in its struggle for independence. In taking the national cause to the masses, men like Gandhi, Sukarno, Nasser, and Nkrumah have not only immeasurably strengthened their political position but have also taken a creative part in shaping the nations they represent. All the agitation and propaganda associated with nationalist parties and upheavals dramatize the issues and serve to make the nation a living reality for people who have had no consciousness of its existence. To the extent that the new concept is grasped, the peasant isolated in his village becomes a citizen of a nation which takes its place in the world's councils. The nation is itself still far removed from meeting the needs of an age of jet planes, radio, and intercontinental ballistic missiles, but it is at least an advance in social magnitude over what preceded it.

To the national unity which it brings to the new states nationalism adds another vital ingredient for survival: a revolutionary zeal and a sense of devotion to the nation and the state which is to be its instrument. In the new states and in those which are in process of formation the nation is not something which can be taken casually for granted but an exciting new achievement, worthy of love and sacrifices. Independence has been won as the result of campaigns whose emotional momentum in some part carries over and may be utilized in dealing with the problems of the difficult years ahead. Particularly in colonial areas but also to some extent in any country still living under some variant of the *ancien régime*, the nation and nationalism open the possibility of tapping sources of popular energy and participation which no alien or old-style autocratic ruler could hope to tap. To carry on warfare, to put through major reforms, or to require present sacrifices for future benefits enlists a new dimension of popular support if it can be called for by national leaders as a part of the nation's due.

How long the zeal and devotion will last and how usefully they can be channeled into dealing with the post-independence tasks are questions the answers to which the heirs to imperial power must anxiously seek. Certainly there can be no simple transference. At the extreme the

285

youngster who has carried on years of guerrilla warfare against the Dutch in Indonesia or against the French in Indochina or Algeria is unlikely to be the most suitable candidate for a desk job in the Ministry of Reconstruction and not even perhaps for the routines of a peacetime army. More broadly, the demonstrated ability of the nationalist leadership to perform the political function of rallying the people against imperial domination can give no guarantee of ability to perform another and quite different job. A strong case can be made for the proposition that the sacrifices and basic social changes which development calls for can only be got across to the people by the political leader and not by the expert or bureaucrat, but the nationalist revolutionary who has been victorious in one setting may fumble badly in another. The dramatic and heroic temper of nationalist battle is far from being a wholly suitable mood in which to tackle the problems of managing a stable and progressive polity and a modernized and expanding economy.

Nationalism by itself gives the answer to virtually none of the particular problems arising from the ubiquitous demand for development and, indeed, to very few of the multitude of questions which confront peoples coming to independence.[5] Its most vital contribution is in the realms of the intangibles of the spirit: the restoration of self-respect, the building up of morale, and the stimulation of social solidarity. It does not, however, determine the choice between alternative and often conflicting values, each legitimately put forward as embraced within the national destiny; it does not provide all the good things associated with independence; and it does not establish the institutions necessary for further advance. One must look elsewhere than to nationalism to decide even such over-all questions as whether a free enterprise system or Communism, liberal democracy or centralized authoritarianism, is most fitting and the vast majority of lesser decisions must also be taken primarily on other than nationalist grounds. In almost every instance, to hold up the concept of the national interest as the determinant of decision and action is to produce an empty symbol whose content is in dispute between different factions within the nation. Even in the realm of foreign affairs where nationalism most evidently comes into play, it is likely to give no conclusive answer to questions concerning entry into this alliance or that, neutralism or commitment. The danger is also real that nationalism may serve as an actual impediment to advance, as, for instance, in curtailing access to alien goods, skill, and capital, and it can always be paraded as a screen to hide domestic failures or abuses.

The dimensions of the task which lie ahead of the new states are staggering. They cannot rest content with taking their new-found sovereignty and enjoying it, as they might have at some earlier point in history. Both national pride and the imperatives of survival now demand that they move speedily into the modern world, rivalling the achievements of peoples who have long preceded them on the road. Despite illiteracy, inexperience, and tragic shortages of trained manpower, the latest model

286

of the welfare state plus modernized armed forces is to be produced by governments equipped with all the trappings of parliamentary democracy. Economic systems are to be transformed and the remnants of backwardness wiped from the slate. The new national community is to take its place in the organized society of nations, be represented at a multitude of international conferences and meetings, and furnish an appropriate quota of personnel for international secretariats.

In moving toward goals such as these, nationalism can be of immense assistance if it is wisely and skillfully used by those responsible for the guidance of the new states. If it is used merely to inflame and obscure, its contribution can be disastrous.

NOTES

1. The citation from Nehru is to be found in William L. Holland, ed., *Asian Nationalism and the West* (New York, 1953), pp. 353-54: Nkrumah's statement appears in his autobiography, *Ghana* (New York, 1957), pp. 162-63. In his opening speech at the Pan-African Conference in Accra on 8 December 1958, Prime Minister Nkrumah repeated this conviction: "My first advice to you who are struggling to be free is to aim for the attainment of the Political Kingdom—that is to say, the complete independence and self-determination of your territories. When you have achieved the Political Kingdom all else will follow. Only with the acquisition of political power—real power through the attainment of sovereign independence—will you be in a position to reshape your lives and destiny; only then will you be able to resolve the vexatious problems which harrass our Continent."

2. Jawaharlal Nehru, *Toward Freedom* (New York, 1941), p. 74.

3. Hans Kohn, *The Idea of Nationalism* (New York, 1941), p. 3.

4. Karl Mannheim, *Man and Society in an Age of Reconstruction* (London, 1940), p. 44.

5. I have elaborated somewhat on this theme in "The Progress of Nationalism" in *Nationalism and Progress in Free Asia*, ed. Philip W. Thayer (Baltimore, 1956), pp. 71-82.

287

THE ROLE OF ISLAM
IN THE POLITICAL
DEVELOPMENT OF MALAYSIA

Gordon P. Means

The concept of political development has been almost as widely accepted among social scientists who study the non-Western world as economic development has been accepted among contemporary economists. In both instances, there is the assumption that we can examine a specific country and, by empirical analysis of certain critical indicators, determine with some degree of precision how "modern" that society is. Presumably, such analysis can also aid in identifying factors that either inhibit or accelerate "progress" as defined by the characteristics that are said, by typological definition, to be "modern." While there is no unanimity on the typological characteristics of a "modern political system," we can find fairly widespread agreement about certain characteristics of a modern social and political order.

The typology of a modern political system is usually described as one that has a high degree of occupational and skill specialization, functionally specific nonascriptive structures, a prevalence of voluntary associations, a secular national political authority seeking to exercise rational controls over man and his environment to achieve secular-instrumental values, and a basis in universalistic achievement norms. Despite slight differences in various typologies of a modern society, there is near universal agreement that its political structures must be secular and pursue secular utilitarian values. While these typologies may be colored by the experience of the advanced industrial states of the West where the principles of the separation of church and state have been for the most part widely accepted, it is also implicit in the notion that modernization means maximizing rational and scientific knowledge to meet man's present physical and material needs on this earth. [1]

From Gordon P. Means, "The Role of Islam in the Political Development of Malaysia," *Comparative Politics* 1 (January 1969): 264-84. Reprinted by permission of the author and the publisher.

If this is to be the yardstick of modernization, we may ask a related question: What is the role of religion in the process of modernization? Is it one of the major obstacles that must be abolished or pushed aside in the process of modernization?

Because of the attributes ascribed to a modern political system, it is easy to arrive at the conclusion that religion, tied as it so often is to tradition, is an impediment to political development. Variations on this theme have been stated rather explicitly by Werner Levi, David Apter, W. F. Wertheim, and others, not to mention Karl Marx and a large number of his apostles.[2] Yet it is by no means clear that religion is necessarily an impediment to political development and modernization. Max Weber and R. H. Tawney both examined the positive contributions of Protestantism to the economic and political development of the West.[3] Their findings have prompted others to examine the question of whether the role of religion is an inevitable impediment to progress or whether there are forces within the great religions of Asia and Africa which, like Protestantism, can liberate new energies and create new norms and attitudes that break tradition and promote economic and political development.

In the Epilogue to a book he edited, Robert N. Bellah states the thesis that religion can perform the function of "a cybernetic control mechanism" both for a society and for the personality of those who constitute it. He gives the following explanation:

Perhaps the central function of a religion is to act as a cultural gyroscope, to provide a stable set of definitions of the world and, correlatively, of the self, so that both the transience and the crises of life can be faced with some equanimity by the society or person in question. It is this stability, continuity, and coherence provided by the commitment to a set of religious symbols (or perhaps better to what they symbolize) that give religion such a prominent place in defining the identity of a group or person.[4]

He goes on to suggest that the role of religion becomes more important in periods of great social crisis, since religion can make change more tolerable by reference to what does not change.

The proposition stated by Professor Bellah presumes that a particular religion must possess an adaptive capacity for change as well as stability if it is to perform the requisite functions ascribed to it by him. A religion must therefore be able to be accommodative to those social and political changes most conducive to modernization. In short, Bellah's thesis suggests that religion can assist in the process of social transformation by inhibiting social disintegration, provided that it develops a reformist, "modernist" strain, somewhat similar to the Protestant Reformation of Christendom. In the following paragraph he explains what kind of transformation must take place to facilitate the process of modernization.

It must be able to rephrase its religious symbol system to give meaning to cultural creativity in worldly pursuits. It must be able to channel motivation disciplined through religious obligation into

289

worldly occupations. It must contribute to the development of a solidary and integrated national community, which it seeks neither to dominate nor to divide, although this necessity certainly does not imply sanctioning the nation as a religious ultimate. It must give positive meaning to the long-term process of social development and be able to value it highly as a social goal, again without necessarily taking social progress itself as a religious absolute. It must contribute to the ideal of a responsible and disciplined personality. As part of the new balance between religious and secular in modern society, it must be able to accept its own role as a private voluntary association and recognize that this role is not incompatible with its role as bearer of the society's ultimate values. This list of requisites is of course an ideal typical construction. ... If modernization is to be successfully accomplished, either traditional religion must be able to make this transition, at least in large part, or it must be able to withdraw from major spheres of life and allow secular ideologies to complete the transition.[5]

In this article I propose to examine the changing role of Islam in Malaysia and to evaluate its impact upon the modernization of the political system.

ISLAM IN TRADITIONAL MALAY SOCIETY

Fragmentary historical evidence indicates that Persian or Arab Muslims established some contacts with the Malay Archipelago as early as the seventh century. Whether Muslim communities of converts or settlers were established during the first few centuries of contact is subject to much speculation and dispute. We do know, however, that mass conversions to Islam did not take place until the thirteenth century. At that time Sufi mystics from India were zealously engaged in an extensive campaign of proselyting.[6] Intensified contacts between India and the island empires of Southeast Asia provided them with new opportunities for their missionary endeavors.

Before the great wave of Muslim conversions took place, the people of the area either were animists or combined animism with an admixture of Hinduism and Buddhism. The conversion to Islam of a large proportion of the coastal populations of peninsular and insular Southeast Asia took place without disrupting the existing societies. The new religion did not displace existing political and social elites or challenge too many existing social values and practices. Usually when the Ruler embraced the new religion, his subjects, by force of example and royal sanction, were quite willing to be counted as Muslims.

The variety of Islam that took root in Southeast Asis facilitated the process of adaptation between Islam and the recipient culture. Most of the

290

great Muslim missionaries to Southeast Asia were Sufi mystics of the Sunni sect. Sufism's transcendentalist view of God, its emphasis upon mystical personal communion with God, and its view that God manifests his power in all things, animate and inanimate, gave to Islam its amazing ability to tolerate and adapt to the beliefs and practices of the pre-Muslim society. These eclectic qualities of Islam are noted by Professor Gibb:

> ... There is in the mental makeup of nearly all the Muslim peoples a strong infusion of what we may call the 'raw material of pantheism.' I mean the heritage of primitive animism, the belief in spirits, in *jinns*, in *afrits*. . . . And though some of these animistic beliefs and practices were definitely rejected by Islam and remained outside it, yet a certain number of them gained admission and eased the way for the worship of saints and 'marabouts'; the belief in a hierarchy of living *walis*, who exercise divinely conferred powers in this world; and other such elements, which were taken up into Sufi thought.[7]

The syncretic combination of the Sufi Muslim tradition with the animist-Hindu-Buddhist elements in Malay culture was achieved with very little tension or conflict, in part because Islam has no religious hierarchy standing apart from society. Instead, Islam acknowledges that the Ruler must be the ultimate authority on Muslim affairs. Leadership of religious institutions was thus exercised by the raja class and local elites, who undoubtedly sought to interpret Islam so as to make it easily compatible with their role in society and with the existing beliefs, customs, and practices of the Malays. In essential aspects, Muslim law was adopted, but not at the expense of displacing *adat* customary law. The Muslim system of worship and Muslim religious practices were followed, but the worship of a host of local spirits, ghosts, saints (*walis*), and holy places (*keramat*)[8] also continued, in a slightly altered form. Each village had an imam to perform Muslim rites, but also continued to employ other functionaries (a *bomoh* and a *pawang*) who practiced magical-religious mysteries and spells to control the spirits that brought health and fortune, or illness and calamity, to the villagers.[9]

THE ROLE OF RELIGION IN PRECOLONIAL MALAY SOCIETY

It is exceedingly difficult to define the role of religion in traditional Malay society, since nearly all aspects of life assumed a religious significance. The problem of analysis is complicated by the fact that social institutions performed multiple and overlapping functions. Religion thus contributed to the performance of numerous functions in society, while performing few functions exclusively. Without attempting an exhaustive analysis, we can make a few observations, primarily as a point of reference for noting significant changes that took place during the colonial era and after.[10]

In the traditional Malay political system, religion helped to symbolize the unity of the state. This function was performed in a rather minimal way, since religion did not define the parameters of the political system. Malays exhibited strong parochial identity with their state, symbolized more by their sultan than by their religion. Nonetheless, the Islamic concept of *dar al-Islam* (the place of Islam) and *dar al-harb* (the place of war, i.e., the abode of infidels) helped to define those who were legitimately excluded from the political system. To be a Malay meant being a Muslim, but to be the subject of a particular state also meant giving professions of fealty and obeisance (*menghadap*) to the Malay-Muslim ruler. In Malay the process of conversion to Islam was called *masok Melayu*, which literally means "to enter the Malay community." The ceremony marking the entrance to adulthood of the Malay youth was called *masok jawi* (to become a Malay-Muslim).[11] (Both terms are still in use.) Thus, Islam was acknowledged to be a precondition of political and social participation in Malay society, but not the only requirement for the privileges of participation.[12]

In the Malay political system, religion played some role in legitimizing authority. Yet despite its highly legalistic character, Islam did not provide an effective set of "rules of the game" for political contests. It was thus not particularly effective in stabilizing the political system against civil strife and the collapse of royal authority. The most important bases of legitimizing a claim to power were not essentially religious, since all rival claimants to a throne would be Muslim and could put forth about the same claims of religious legitimacy. Royal title, superior lineage, the support of major chiefs, control of the capital and its royal palace, and the strength of supporting military forces were more important in claiming legitimacy. Religious sanctification became more important after rivals had been disposed of. Then the proper ceremonies and religious forms assisted in legitimizing the incumbent's authority against the machinations of ambitious rivals.

It is significant to note that most of the ceremonies and concepts associated with the institution of the Ruler[13] reveal many more Hindu beliefs and practices than Muslim.[14] Hindu concepts of divine kingship were only reinforced by the Muslim view that the Ruler has an obligation to God to protect the faith and be "God's shadow" on earth.[15] If a Ruler could produce (or manufacture) a genealogy (*salasilah*) tracing his lineage to some famous Muslim monarch, his claim to office was strengthened. However, apart from this and from the Muslim justification of rule by sultans, the use of Muslim prayers in some rituals at the court, and the Ruler's observance of Muslim practices for his personal life, Islam was not a pillar of royal authority. No public rituals of a distinctively Islamic character were employed to legitimize the crown. No Muslim judges (*kathis*) were employed at the royal courts and no central Muslim institutions were maintained at the capital to act as a center for religious activities or observances within the state.[16] While Islamic jurisprudence influenced legal codes in some states, these laws appear to have been largely ignored in administration and in the settlement of disputes.[17] Even though the Ruler was depicted as God's shadow on earth and was acknowledged to be the highest authority on matters both religious and secular, Muslim institutions were not actively supported by royal power and revenues. Islam was a state religion largely in symbolic form.

In precolonial Malaya, religious institutions were primarily local in character. Each kampong (village) maintained either a mosque (*masjid*) or a prayer house (*surau*),[18] depending upon its size and wealth. The village elders selected, usually from among their own number, a mosque committee to supervise the maintenance of the mosque or prayer house and to oversee the religious life of the community. Someone from the village who was believed to be devout and knew something about Muslim practices and the Koran would be appointed to be imam. The imam was responsible for leading the group prayers and for giving guidance on matters of religion (and perhaps also on Malay magic). He would have an assistant (*bilal*), who made the call to prayers, and would sometimes also have some lesser functionaries.

Village life centered on the mosque or prayer house. Apart from their use for regular prayers, these structures also served as both social and political meeting places for village affairs. Affiliated with the mosque would be some organized system of religious instruction for the children. If the imam could read Arabic, he might act as a religious teacher in a village *pondok* ("hut") school or give instruction in his home. Otherwise, someone from outside the kampong would have to be recruited if a Muslim religious school were to be maintained for the children of the village. All these religious institutions were maintained by the villagers' donations of services or goods and by the traditional Islamic *zakat* and *fitrah* taxes, which are obligatory for all Muslims.

Before the advent of British rule, each kampong was largely self-sufficient in meeting its religious needs. Residents of the kampong or its immediate environs held the key religious and magical-religious offices. Travel within the state was difficult, while travel to Arabia was practically nonexistent except for Arab and Indian merchant-traders. Consequently, the capitals and port cities would count among their number only a few Arab, Indian, and Malay hajis, who had made the pilgrimage to Mecca. In all likelihood, these few would be the ones who monopolized the key religious offices of those cities. But, in the countryside, a Muslim folk-religion existed without external supports and without the recruitment of expatriate religious elites with specialized religious knowledge from Islamic centers abroad. Thus, the beliefs and values of the religious functionaries in the village were not significantly different from those of the other inhabitants. Under these circumstances, religious tensions within a village were minimal. Likewise, the formal rituals of Islam, which were

293

practiced everywhere, cloaked a substantial cultural diversity and variety of local religious practices within a state and between Malay states.[19]

Space does not permit a description of the traditional religious beliefs and practices of the Malays.[20] We can, however, consider the more important functions of religion in the social and political system of the Malay village.

Religion played a central role in providing social integration and social cohesion in the primary group relations of life within the Malay village. Social solidarity was promoted by the common prayers, rituals, rites and festivals.[21] The cycles of life—planting, harvesting, marriage, birth, puberty, death—were all cloaked in religious mystery. Special rites and ceremonies were celebrated to mark each of these events. Most peasant Malays were quite conscientious in performing daily prayers and worshiped regularly at the local mosque, prayer house, and shrines. They also observed the fasting month of Ramadan and the major Islamic holy days. Most of the rites and ceremonies were public in nature, thus strengthening social integration and a sense of identity with the community. The same is true of the quasi-religious *kenduri* communal feasts,[22] which each adult male villager gave for his friends and village notables at the time of rites of passage, on religious holidays, and when he was seeking to influence the inhabitants of the spirit world. These feasts were important agents of social integration helping to alleviate conflicts within the kampong.

The roles of village functionaries and the local social-status and ranking system were partly defined by the religious beliefs and attitudes of the village. All community functionaries were legitimized in their office by religious rituals and by reference to religious sources of authority. Sometimes the religious leader of the community (usually the imam) would even outrank the village headman (*penghulu*) in status and deference. Similarly, those individuals who proved themselves to be particularly devout in their religious obligations and offered more than the usual number of *kenduries*, or performed the optional but meritorious duties (*sunnat*) recommended in the Koran were treated with great respect and given positions of status and power in the village. Frequently, the pious and devout were assumed to have thereby gained extraordinary powers over the supernatural world, and villagers would then seek their advice and help in time of need. Besides gaining status, the pious would also obtain certain free services from their fellow villagers and be frequent guests at *kenduries*.[23]

In summary, Islam, in its syncretic Malay form, became a vital social force, particularly at the village level. It performed a number of socially significant functions, frequently in conjunction with other institutions. While Islam infused new and rich cultural elements into Malay society, it appeared to make that society somewhat more resistant to external cultural influences by giving its adherents the complacency and ethnocentrism that come from a feeling of cultural and religious superiority. Before the impact of the West, Islam was a vital and expanding force in peninsular and insular Southeast Asia. Yet Islam did not make a substantial transformation of the recipient society. Instead, Islam adapted to that society in harmony with most existing institutions, beliefs, and practices. During this period, Islam can hardly be described as a religion that promoted in a discernible way the modernization of social structures, values, and attitudes of Malay society.

THE COLONIAL IMPACT ON
THE ROLE OF RELIGION

Western impact on Malay society did not come to all states at the same time, nor was it of uniform intensity. Except for Malacca and the islands of Penang and Singapore, the Malay States were independent of foreign control until the last quarter of the nineteenth century.[24] While the presence of Western traders and trading posts from the beginning of the sixteenth century on made some impact on Malay society, the most significant changes came only after the extension of a colonial administration over the Malay States. Except in Malacca, this extension took place only after 1874, and for some states it was delayed until after the turn of the century. Despite the differential impact of the West on various Malay States, in the long run the consequences were much the same. Therefore, the details of local variations need not concern us in this article.

The colonial era witnessed greatly improved communications (and consequently increased internal contacts within traditional society) and greatly intensified exchanges with foreign cultures. While the most obvious initial changes in Malay society did not involve religion, the cumulative effect of improved communications gradually brought about significant changes in Malay religious institutions, beliefs, and practices. Improved contacts among Malays made some of them more aware of the parochial character of their religious beliefs and practices, despite their common profession of Islamic orthodoxy. For the more enlightened, the contradictions between Islam and the Malay folk religion became all too apparent.[25] Furthermore, improved communications with the Middle East and India facilitated a gradual transformation of religious elites in Malay society. Through the years the number who travelled to Mecca as haj pilgrims increased substantially.[26] While contacts with Arabia were usually temporary and rather superficial, the haj did involve fairly intensive religious indoctrination and brought the pilgrim into contacts with Muslims from other lands. Upon his return, the new haji was likely to expose certain "non-Muslim" practices in Malay society, partly to demonstrate his new piety and strengthen his claim to higher status and prestige in Malay society.[27] Improved communications also made possible an infusion of Arabs and Indian Muslims (known locally as Jawi

295

Peranakan) into elite positions in Malay society. Arabs could capitalize on the common belief of Muslims that practically all Arabs are direct descendents of Muhammad, and both Arabs and Indian Muslims who came to Southeast Asia were often better informed on orthodox Muslim practices than were indigenous Malay leaders.[28] All these factors gradually brought about changes in the character of Muslim religious elites and thus created tensions between the folk religion of the Malay kampong and the demands of orthodox Islam.[29].

The infusion of new religious ideas and some expatriate religious elites into Malay society created divisions between the society and the elites, as well as among the elites themselves. An open factional split developed between Kaum Muda (Young Faction) and Kaum Tua (Old Faction) shortly after the turn of the century.[30] The Kaum Muda elites were "modernist-reformist" and the bearers of the religious and political ideas emanating from the "Manar circle" and al-Azhar University in Cairo. The leaders of this movement tended to be urban-based Arabs, Jawi Peranakan, or Indonesians, and frequently were the products of Arabic education in *madrasah* schools[31] or had obtained an Islamic education abroad, usually in Egypt or India. Initially, few of the Kaum Muda were of peninsular Malay origin. They operated primarily from Singapore and Penang where they had no worry about Islamic religious censorship, which could be enforced against them in the Malay States. By the 1930s the Kaum Muda movement had become actively politicized, and it began to challenge the leadership of the traditional elites in Malay society. While it never became a mass movement, it did help to generate nationalist and anticolonial sentiments based on pan-Islamic doctrines. It also promoted the ancillary concept of the union of all Muslims in Southeast Asia into a single state of Indonesia Raya (Greater Indonesia).

The resistance, represented by Kaum Tua, came primarily from the traditional rural *ulama* (Muslim "scholars") who were usually the products of the village Muslim *pondok* schools. Their opposition to the new doctrines was shared by many of the traditional Malay political elites who formed part of the Malay royal court circle in each state. In time, the religious and political ideas of Kaum Muda began to win converts among educated Malay elites, at the Malay courts, and even among some religious leaders in the kampongs of Malaya. This religious cleavage in Malay society created a dynamic tension between certain religious elites and the folk society of the peasant Malays, thus creating a strong impulse for change and reform.[32] However, the "modernism" of the Islamic reform movement was fundamentalist and dogmatic in character. Its ideology contained the seeds of nationalism stressing the political mobilization of the Malay community, based upon a reaffirmation of Islamic faith and rediscovery of its great tradition. In certain respects the fundamentalist modernism of this movement was similar in its thrust to the Protestant Reformation in Christendom.

ISLAMIC LAW AND ADMINISTRATION
UNDER COLONIAL RULE

The extension of British colonial administration to the Malay States involved a restructuring of Islamic religious institutions. The treaties the British made with the Malay Rulers stated that the Ruler agreed to "receive and provide a suitable residence for a British Officer ... whose advice must be asked and acted upon on all questions other than those touching Malay Religion and Custom."[33] Deprived of substantial power in other areas, the role of the Ruler as the protector of "Malay Religion and Custom" became that much more important. Because of the difficulty of defining Malay Custom, British rule did involve some impingement upon that sphere, but the British were very careful to follow a policy of passive protection of Islam and noninterference in Islamic affairs. As Islamic rituals at the Malay courts became more important, the Rulers and their State Councils also began to assume greater responsibility for religious affairs. After 1884. various states began to create for the first time a centralized administrative structure and legal system for Muslim affairs.[34]

Islamic religious courts were established in each state to enforce both Muslim and *adat* law. A *kathi* was appointed for each district to administer Muslim affairs, to try cases within his jurisdiction, and to supervise the operation of mosques in his district. At the *mukim* level (a subdistrict within the jurisdiction of a mosque) the *kathi* would be assisted by a *naib-kathi* who, unlike the *kathi*, did not receive a government salary, but retained fees and fines for his services. At the top of the judicial system was the chief *kathi* for each Malay State. Although Muslim affairs were legally the responsibility of the Ruler, through the years a confusing variety of committees and offices were created by various Rulers to assist them or relieve them of these duties. Such institutions as a Council of Theologians (*Majlis Ugama*), a Shari'ah Committee (to interpret Muslim law), and a Kathis Committee were to be found in many of the Malay States. Some states established a Department of Religious Affairs under the supervision of a Council of Religion and Malay Customs (*Majlis Ugama Islam dan Adat Melayu*) to administer religious affairs.[35]

Although Islam enjoyed state support in the Malay States and was recognized as the official state religion, it remained in a backwash for most of the colonial period. Muslim courts had few powers and very narrow jurisdiction.[36] In comparison with the administration of other state programs, Muslim administration was haphazard and lethargic. Yet, the British were careful to pay public deference to Islam in matters of ceremony and public holidays and in meager and ritualistic financial support for Islamic institutions. Likewise, by both administrative decree and law, restrictions were placed on proselyting of Muslims by non-Muslim missionaries.[37] Despite the preferential treatment of Islam, the religion did not acquire any new vigor or dynamism, particularly since those who were charged with responsibility for the administration and leadership of religious affairs were either the traditional political elites of Malay society or the rural conservative religious elites who were the products of the village *pondok* schools or the Malay vernacular primary schools.

Apart from the restrictions on proselyting among Muslims, the colonial administration followed a policy of upholding the religious freedoms of non-Muslims. Members of any faith could establish places of worship, could engage in missionary work among the non-Malays, and could establish schools, medical services, and other institutions. The authorities were careful to show impartiality to the other religions found in the country—Hinduism, Sikhism, Confucianism, Taoism, Buddhism, and Christianity. Yet in practice, Christian churches had some advantages under colonial rule. British administrators may not have been faithful churchgoers, but were more likely to cooperate with and be sensitive to the wishes of European and American missionaries than of other religious groups. Church-operated schools that complied with educational standards set by the government became eligible for grants-in-aid that greatly assisted the expansion of Christian mission schools.[38]

Because the Straits Settlements were not "Malay States" but Crown Colonies directly under the British flag, Islam was not the official religion in Penang, Malacca, and Singapore. Therefore the policies protecting Islam did not apply there. Instead, the Church of England was the established church and received a small annual grant in addition to donations of public land for church buildings. Yet even in the Straits Settlements, British administrators discouraged (but did not prohibit) Christian missions from working among Malays because of possible Malay reaction to such endeavors.

In their early contacts with the Malays, the British discovered that Islam was a powerful factor in Malay society and that cooperation with the Malays was impossible if Islam appeared to be threatened. Therefore colonial religious policy sought to placate the Malays and assure them that their traditional way of life was not being destroyed under colonial rule. Likewise, the preservation and protection of Islam provided the Malays with psychological assurance that the country continued to be theirs despite the influx of vast numbers of Chinese and Indian immigrants.[39] In every respect, the religious policies of the colonial administration were designed to harmonize with the government's general policy toward the Malays. The British sought to gain the support of the Malay royalty and traditional elites in ruling the country, while protecting the Malay peasant from alien exploitation and allowing him to preserve his traditional way of life with minimal adjustments to the modern world. Colonial religious policies were admirably suited to assist in the pursuit of these goals. The colonial authorities correctly assessed the role of Islam in the prewar years as being a stabilizing and conservative force. They thus attempted to avoid any policies that might disrupt Islam as a "cultural gyroscope" for Malay society.

ISLAM IN THE POSTWAR ERA

Toward the end of the interwar period, the role of Islam in Malay life had begun to change, primarily as a result of the ferment caused by the "modernist" Kaum Muda movement. By this time, Islam could no longer be considered a single, fairly uniform, religious and ideological value system. While the main thrust of Islamic values had been traditional and conservative, this new movement reflected a dynamism within Malay society. Kaum Muda began exposing Malays to new values, attitudes, perceptions, and a vision of a future society that were neither conservative nor supportive of traditional Malay social practices. Instead, these new ideas challenged traditional Malay society and the authority of traditional elites by espousing political and social reforms, popular democracy, and pan-Islamic nationalism.

However, it was significant that this new wine was being served in the old bottles of Islamic orthodoxy. In this way the symbolic unity of Islam was not being assaulted, and those who accepted these new elements of religious and political faith could do so with the conviction and the psychological assurance that they were not converts to alien beliefs, attitudes, and values, but rather were rediscovering their cultural and religious heritage in its ancient and unadulterated form. For this reason, within Malay society, politics and religion were very closely linked, particularly in the early stages of development of Malay nationalism.

Because most Malays view Islam as the core of their culture and of their society, they exhibit extremely strong affective attachments to their religion. For a century or more Islam has probably had a latent capacity as a catalyst for political mobilization of the Malays. Yet during the early stages of the development of Malay nationalism, this power of religion was largely untapped by emergent nationalist elites, perhaps because their religious views were rather out of harmony with the Islamic folk religion of the peasant Malays. For example, in the postwar period the Malay Nationalist party was the first important Malay party to be founded. It tended to represent urban Malays with fairly radical views. While some of its leaders had been affiliated with the Kaum Muda movement, little attention was given by the MNP to religious issues. Instead the party stressed its opposition to colonialism and to the role of the Malay Rulers.[40] Likewise, when the United Malays National Organization (UMNO) was founded in 1946 by Dato Onn, its appeal was not based primarily upon religion. This party gained mass support among the Malays almost overnight by mobilizing them to resist the postwar constitutional arrangements that the British were planning for Malaya. Since these proposals sought eventually to give the immigrant communities equal access to political power, Dato Onn capitalized on the fear of political and economic domination by the immigrant communities to arouse the Malays to political action. Thus, religion was not a critical factor in the politics of

299

the country until after the Malays had already become fairly effectively mobilized.

In this observer's view, Malay politicians became far more sensitized to the religious aspects of politics after 1950. That was the year in which crowds of Muslims rioted in Singapore to protest the Maria Hertog case.[41] To most Muslims the decision in this case appeared to violate fundamental tenets of their faith, and it was interpreted by many Muslims as a direct attack by an infidel court upon Islam. More important, however, the intense feelings aroused by this case provided an object lesson to Malay politicians that religion might be utilized to tap the "primordial sentiments" of the bulk of Malay society.[42] As various politicians discovered the power of religion as a device to gain the support of Malay voters, Malay politics became more openly involved with religious questions.

An example of the shift from an essentially secular political idiom to a religious idiom is provided by the career of Dr. Burhanuddin bin Mohamed Noor.[43] During the 1930s he was a leading member of Kesatuan Melayu Muda, a radical Malay nationalist organization closely tied to the Indonesian nationalist movement and noted for its opposition to the Malay Rulers. After the war Dr. Burhanuddin became president of the Malay Nationalist party, which followed in the KMM tradition. We have already noted that the MNP, in pursuit of radical Malay nationalist goals, was essentially secular in its orientation. When the Malayan Communist party began its insurrection in 1948, the MNP disbanded because it wished to support neither side in that contest. Dr. Burhanuddin temporarily faded from public view, but when the Maria Hertog case came to public attention in 1950, he became a political activist in mobilizing Malay protest demonstrations. For a short period he attempted to bring all Malay parties into a united front, but he failed to gain a mass following.[44] Finally, following the first federal elections of 1955, Dr. Burhanuddin joined the Pan-Malayan Islamic party and very quickly became its president.[45] Thereafter, his political appeals were unabashedly religious. The protection and promotion of Islam against infidel influences became a powerful theme used to mobilize mass Malay support and to give religious legitimacy to the more extreme communal demands of the party. Under Dr. Burhanuddin's leadership the PMIP became the second largest Malay party and the most formidable opposition party in the country. By fusing radical Malay nationalism with an intense religious appeal, Dr. Burhanuddin was able to gain mass support among Malays and was able to overcome some of the conservative bias of most Malay peasants. His emphasis upon Malay Islamic identity made it possible for him to bridge the differences between modernist and conservative-traditional Islamic factions and thereby to encourage both to give their support to the PMIP.

In subsequent elections the PMIP presented a substantial challenge to the ruling Alliance coalition, particularly in areas where rural Malays predominated. For example, in the 1959 elections, the PMIP won 41 out of 53 state Legislative Council seats in the two predominantly Malay states of Trengganu and Kelantan; it won 13 of the 16 parliamentary seats for those states.[46] The exploitation of religious sentiments for political objectives by the PMIP stimulated other Malay parties to follow suit. Party Negara was a Malay-oriented party that had been founded by Dato Onn after his rather disastrous attempt to create a "noncommunal" political party in 1952. During the 1955 elections Party Negara was no match for UMNO, and it suffered total defeat. Later, however, it began to play much more on the religious sentiments of the Malays and had some success in Trengganu in the 1959 elections.

The intensification of religious appeals for the Malay vote stimulated the ruling Alliance Government to give more attention to religious issues. The Malay party in that coalition, UMNO, tried to recruit Malay religious leaders into its ranks to give the party religious legitimacy. By 1959 UMNO had organized an Ulama Section to represent Muslim religious leaders and to give added emphasis to the pledges put in the UMNO constitution to safeguard and promote Islam in Malaya.[47] The intensity of UMNO's religious appeal was muted primarily because of its participation in the multi-communal Alliance coalition with the Malayan Chinese Association and the Malayan Indian Congress. However, despite these restraints, the Alliance gradually became more sensitive to Malay demands for public policies to promote and protect Islam. Thus, a shift away from secular politics was a characteristic of the whole political system in the years following Malayan independence.

THE CHANGING ROLE OF GOVERNMENT IN RELIGIOUS AFFAIRS

Because religion was considered to be a matter of state concern under the colonial regime, the state governments have always been more sensitive than the federal government to religious issues. Consequently, demands by Malays for strengthening Islam were made first at the state level. By 1950 most of the Malay states had established a Department of Religious Affairs to improve Muslim administration and provide new services for the Muslim community. Increasing funds were made available for mosque construction. State governments assumed greater responsibility for the enforcement of Muslim criminal and moral codes. In many areas, what had been considered to be a religious obligation was made a matter of law, enforced and punished in the courts. Thus, for example, Muslim alms taxes, which had been treated as voluntary, were made a matter of legal obligation with penalties for nonpayment of those taxes by Muslims. Similarly, other laws penalized Western dating practices (under the *khalwat* law), violation of Muslim moral codes, failure to perform religious obligations such as fasting requirements or, for males, attendance at Friday

301

prayers at the mosque. In addition, state governments assumed greater responsibility for defining and interpreting orthodox Muslim doctrines and for protecting the Muslim community from those who were thereby defined as heretics. For example, anyone who taught or propagated religious doctrines among Muslims without the permission of the state religious authorities or anyone who circulated publications defined as heretical was liable to rather severe punishment. These laws not only prohibited non-Muslim missionary activity and proselyting among Muslims, but also prohibited unrecognized Muslim sects from propagating their doctrines.[48]

Federal involvement in religious affairs was practically nonexistent before Malaya gained her independence. The constitution that went into effect at the time of Malaya's independence in 1957 made Islam the official religion for the entire federation, including Penang and Malacca, which had been Crown Colonies and thus had no Muslim ruler. The Paramount Ruler (Yang di-Pertuan Agong) assumed responsibilities for Islam in those two states (and later also for Singapore during the period it was in the federation). The Ruler's Council composed of all the Malay Rulers began to consider religious affairs from a federal perspective, and the Keeper of the Ruler's Seal exercised some authority for the coordination of Muslim affairs at the federal level. Likewise, after 1957, increasing sums of federal money were allocated to the states for mosque construction. Muslim administration, and Muslim welfare.

Perhaps more than for any other reason, federal involvement in religious affairs came about because the constitution sanctions a system of special rights tied to religion. Malays are given legal privileges in four general areas. Preferential quota systems favoring Malays operate (1) for admission to the public service, (2) for award of government scholarships, and (3) for allocation of permits and licenses for certain trades and businesses. Further, (4) large areas of land have been set aside as "Malay Reservations" where only Malays may own land. Since the constitution defines a Malay as one who professes the Muslim religion, habitually speaks the Malay language, and conforms to Malay custom, these special rights are given with a religious qualification.[49] Thus, a Malay who abandoned his religion would also lose his claim to special privileges.[50] If for no other reason, this system of Malay special privileges has thrust religious questions into the center of political controversy, making a secular approach to politics almost impossible.

Once committed to making religion a federal as well as a state matter, the federal government instituted a number of policies designed to promote Islam. All schools, even government-aided Christian mission schools, are required to provide compulsory Islamic religious instruction for Muslims if more than 15 Muslims attend a school. Non-Muslims may receive instruction in their faith, but not during school hours or by teachers paid in full or in part from government funds, even though they volunteer their services. Islamic religious education is paid for by the government, while non-Islamic religious education is subject to restrictive regulations.[51] Likewise, the Board of Film Censors refuses to allow any films or scenes that they feel might be contrary to Islam or might offend Muslims. Movies with Biblical or Christian religious themes have been proscribed. Similar discrimination applies to religious broadcasting, with Muslim services being broadcast regularly throughout the year and non-Muslim religious services permitted only on a few major religious holidays.

The federal government has taken some measures designed to restrict non-Muslim missionary activity and to promote the conversion of non-Muslims to Islam. Foreign missionaries are restricted to a ten-year residence limitation in the country. Non-Muslims may not propagate their religion among Muslims in Malaya, and while that restriction is not applicable to Sabah and Sarawak, the federal authorities have issued warnings against such endeavors in those two states. The federal government has also adopted policies designed to persuade or coerce Malaya's animist jungle aborigines to accept Islam and become "integrated" into the Malay community.[52] Most of the 60,000 to 80,000 Malayan aborigines have resisted attempts to convert them to Islam. The Malays have been their traditional oppressors, and conversion to Islam is interpreted by them to be a form of subjugation to Malay authority. Furthermore, Islamic dietary laws prohibit the consumption of their available meat, such as pork, reptiles, monkeys, and carnivorous animals. Although foreign Christian missions have been prohibited from working among these people since 1940, about two thousand aborigines have adopted Christianity, in part because it provides one bulwark against the pressure for integration into the Malay-Muslim community.

When Malaysia came into being, a problem arose concerning the status of Islam in the new states joining the wider union. Briefly, the solution worked out was to allow Islam to remain the official religion for the entire federation, but to permit the states entering the federation to avoid becoming involved in administration of Islamic law. Malaya's system of special privileges and support for Islam was substantially curtailed in the new states of Sabah and Sarawak. In the Borneo states, financial aid to Muslim institutions requires the consent of the governor of the state, and federal funds given to Islam in Malaya are to be matched proportionately by funds for general social-welfare purposes in Sabah and Sarawak. Likewise, in these two states, any law restricting the propagation of religious doctrine among Muslims requires the consent of a two-thirds majority of the State Assembly.[53]

Although largely exempted from the Malayan pattern of mosque-state relations, the Borneo states have been under increasing pressure from the federal government to follow the lead of Western Malaysia, on the argument that nation-building is facilitated by uniform policies. However, since Muslims constitute only 28.9 percent of the combined population of Sarawak and Sabah, these states have developed strong resistance to

303

federal pressures to abandon more secular policies in favor of those supportive of Islam. The religious issue has been deliberately suppressed in public debate because it is such a potentially explosive issue. Even so it has been an important factor contributing to a series of crises between the federal government and the political leaders of Sarawak and Sabah.[54]

THE EFFECTS OF RELIGIOUS POLICIES
UPON MODERNIZATION

From this very brief summary of the role of Islam in Malaysia, we can identify some of the effects of religion upon the processes of modernization. It is clear that Islam has been a significant force in the political mobilization of the Malays, even though the first mass mobilization was begun without too much emphasis upon their religious identity. To the extent that religion has prompted popular participation in the political system, it has contributed to political modernization. Likewise, religion has helped the Malays to overcome their parochial loyalties and has probably contributed to their increasing desire to create a dynamic community of Muslims who have both economic and political power appropriate to their numbers.

Yet these contributions of religion to the process of modernization must be weighed against the features of Islam that impede certain other aspects of modernization. Unlike the Protestant ethic, as analyzed by Max Weber, Islam does not appear to create among its believers "worldly asceticism," the "compulsion to save," or the "release of acquisitive activity" in the form of economic competition and hard work.[55] Among Muslims, a good share of their savings is invested for noneconomic purposes, such as for the haj, for religious festivals, or for *kenduries.* Although the government has attempted to inculcate values conducive to economic development and a pragmatic-instrumentalist approach to both political and economic problems, the value system inherent in Islam has not been substantially altered. Furthermore, government policies are more likely to support the traditional Islamic value system than to challenge it. The government's promotion and subsidizing of the haj, its investment of fairly large sums of money for support of Islam,[56] and its acceptance of a shorter working day and lower standards of productivity for Muslims during the fasting month are only a few examples of government encouragement of traditional religious priorities. Paradoxically, although the government is dedicated to modernizing the country, its religious policies have inhibited doctrinal diversification and have tended to dampen some of the most dynamic and modernist trends within Islam in Malaysia.

All too frequently, the traditional religions of Asia have been assumed to present an almost insurmountable obstacle to political and economic development because of their value systems and the perceptions of the world they perpetuate. In saying that Islam does not contribute much to an achievement ethic, we must avoid the pitfall of concluding that it prevents the development of new ideas and attitudes associated with modernization. Many other factors are making their impact upon the Muslim community, such as urbanization, modern industrial and economic structures, education, mass communications, and increasing contacts with other peoples and cultures. Some cross-cultural empirical studies in other developing countries suggest that religious attitudes and values may be only a slight impediment, if any at all, when these other agents of social change are present.[57]

In Malaysia, the Muslim community is subject to many pressures for change in both attitudes and behavior patterns. Malaysia's economic growth, its modern communications system, and its educational system are all making an impact upon the Malays, even though they were partially insulated from these developments for many years. Consequently, an increasing number of Malays are becoming westernized, modernized, and increasingly secular in outlook. Yet because of state enforcement of religious obligations and the virtual impossibility for a Malay to renounce his religion without severe legal and social penalties, these modernizing Malay elites are forced to mask their secular attitudes and values by means of ritualistic identification with Islam. Malays who no longer hold to traditional religious norms are as yet unwilling to challenge those norms openly. Hypocrisy and compartmentalization of religion from everyday life provide ways of accommodating the conflicting demands of religion and modernization. Eventually Islam will be challenged by those members of the Muslim community who are already secular, pragmatic, and rationalist in their outlook, attitudes, and behavior. How soon such a challenge will develop is hard to determine. However, the institutional and legal support given to Islam by the state undoubtedly tends to delay that confrontation and increases the incidence of ritualized hypocrisy among the most educated and modern elements of Malay society.

In evaluating the role of religion in the political development of Malaysia, we must not restrict ourselves to the Muslim community, particularly since Muslims constitute only about 47 percent of the total population of Malaysia. There is little question that governmental support of Islam has the enthusiastic approval of most Muslims and these policies contribute to the fairly stable political support the present government enjoys. However, these policies are resented by a large proportion of Malaysia's non-Muslim population. The use of religion to mobilize the Malays and give them a sense of community identity transcending parochial loyalties has been offset by the increasing alienation of non-Muslims from the political system. In many ways the government emphasizes the basic Malay character of the country, and its policies toward Islam are symbolically important as evidence of its pro-Malay orientation. It is little wonder, then, that non-Muslim ethnic and cultural minorities express continued anxiety and nagging doubt about their place in the nation and find it difficult to develop strong loyalties to Malaysia.

While Non-Muslims enjoy a fairly high degree of religious liberty, apart from the restrictions on their proselyting among Muslims, they resent having their taxes go for the support of Islam, and they resent even more the preferential treatment given to Malays. Paradoxically, most restrictions on religious liberty apply to Muslims, but since Muslims also enjoy the benfits associated with their religious identity, they almost never voice demands for religious liberty as it is understood in the West. The concept of the separation of religion from state affairs is alien to Islamic tradition and would be opposed by most Muslims in Malaysia today. Under these circumstances, it is inconceivable that Malaysia will become a secular state and abandon its system of privileges and preferential treatment given to Islam and to Malays. Since religious divisions are nearly coterminous with ethnic-cultural divisions, present policies create obstacles to national integration by exacerbating the already serious communal cleavage in the political system between Malays and non-Malays.

With this brief survey of the role of religion in Malaysia, it should be apparent that it is extremely difficult to determine with precision or clarity whether religion has impeded or promoted political and economic development. The ledger is a mixture of red- and black-ink entries that are difficult to add and subtract to make a total. Islam has certainly been a stimulant to important social and political changes with the Malay community. Yet, if we refer to the commonly applied typology of modernization, we see that in protecting Islam, the government is not exclusively dedicated to pursuing secular-instrumental values and makes major exceptions to universalistic achievement norms. Religion is probably an important "cultural gyroscope," as suggested by Robert Bellah. However, Islam is not accepting a role as a "private voluntary association," and government support of Islam is tending to make Islam more doctrinaire and thus somewhat more resistant to pressures for the reformation of traditional beliefs and practices to harmonize with a modernized society. But most important, Islam does not facilitate the "development of a solidary and integrated national community, which it seeks neither to dominate nor to divide. . . . "[58]

NOTES

1. See Karl W. Deutsch, *The Nerves of Government* (New York, 1963), pp. 248-54.

   At present the modern state is not expected to provide in a positive way for man's spiritual needs, although there is increasing concern about the psychological well-being of men subject to the stress of modern life. Whether this will result in a reevaluation of the relationship between the modern secular state and religion is difficult to determine. Nonetheless, it appears that if such developments occur, they will be based on instrumental-secular values.

   Works on political modernization and political development are too numerous to mention. However, the works of the following authors can be considered as a starting point: David Apter, Leonard Binder, S. N. Eisenstadt, Daniel Lerner, Marion J. Levy, Jr., John D. Montgomery, Lucian W. Pye, Fred W. Riggs, Edward Shils, I. R. Sinai, William J. Siffin, and Myron Weiner.

2. David Apter, *The Politics of Modernization* (Chicago, 1965), passim; Werner Levi, "Religion and Political Development: A Theoretical Analysis," a paper presented to the Annual Meeting, American Political Science Association, September 1966; W. F. Wertheim, "Religious Reform Movements in South and Southeast Asia," *Archives de sociologie des religions* 12 (1961), 53-66.

3. See Max Weber, *The Protestant Ethic and the Spirit of Capitalism* (London, 1930); and R. H. Tawney, *Religion and the Rise of Capitalism* (New York, 1926).

4. Robert N. Bellah, *Religion and Progress in Modern Asia* (New York, 1965), p. 173.

5. *Ibid.* pp. 202-3.

6. S. Q. Fatimi, *Islam Comes to Malaysia* (Singapore, 1963), pp. 37-70; Christopher H. Wake, "Malacca's Early Kings and the Reception of Islam," in Colin Jack-Hinton, ed., *Papers on Early South-east Asian History* (Singapore, 1964), pp. 104-28.

7. H. A. R. Gibb, *Modern Trends in Islam* (Chicago, 1947), pp. 22-23.

8. For an account of modern *keramat* worship practices see Mohammad Zain bin Mahamood, "A Study of Keramat Worship," academic exercise, Department of Malay Studies, University of Malaya, Singapore, 1959. Also note, Syed Naguib al-Attas, *Some Aspects of Sufism as Understood and Practiced Among the Malays* (Singapore, 1963); and A. G. S. Danaraj, *Mysticism in Malaya* (Singapore, 1964).

9. In general, a *bomoh* is a Malay witch doctor whose aid is sought to control spirits that affect the health and welfare of individuals, while a *pawang* generally specializes in spirits affecting nature, such as the weather, fertility and growth of crops, and natural disasters. For an account of Malay magical practices see Walter William Skeat, *Malay Magic* (London, 1900; reprinted, 1965): R. J. Wilkinson, *Malay Beliefs* (London, 1906), reprinted in *Journal of the Malayan Branch, Royal Asiatic Society*, 30, Part 4 (November 1957).

10. For an evaluation of the role of religion in traditional and primitive societies, see Paul Radin, *Primitive Religion* (New York, 1937), pp. 3-39; and Sir Edward Burnett Tylor, *Religion and Primitive Culture* (New York, 1958), pp. 444-47 et passim.

11. More modern surviving practices of this ceremony are described by Thomas M. Fraser, Jr. *Rusembilan: A Malay Fishing Village in Southern Thailand* (Ithaca, 1960), pp. 201-4.

12. At the village level, participation in political life depended on established residence as well as having proper ascriptive and status credentials. See J. M. Gullick, *Indigenous Political Systems of Western Malaya* (London, 1958), pp. 22-43.

13. The Hindu title for the Ruler is raja, while the Muslim title is sultan. Malays continued to employ both titles even after conversion to Islam.

14. See Sir Richard Winstedt, *The Malays, A Cultural History*, 3d ed. (London, 1953), pp. 63-90. Similarly, one of the most important powers associated with kingship was that of *daulat*, a supernatural power believed to be acquired by the ruler at his coronation ceremonies. This concept appears to be essentially animist in origin and is related to the view that the monarch is also a magician who acquires control of supernatural power derived from the spirit world.

15. L. Richmond Wheeler, *The Modern Malay* (London, 1928), pp. 100-102.

16. J. M. Gullick, *Indigenous Political Systems*, p. 139.

17. *Ibid.*, p. 114. For an example of legal codes with Islamic content, see J. Rigby, *The Ninety-nine Laws of Perak* (Kuala Lumpur, 1908).

18. A *masjid* is of permanent construction and is appropriate for formal Friday worship, while a *surau* is a more simple structure and cannot be used for Friday prayers or certain other formal ceremonies.

19. J.M. Gullick, *Indigenous Political Systems*, pp. 136-37.

20. Malay accounts of precolonial religious practices cannot be relied upon for accuracy. Moreover, those that have survived concentrate on the court ceremonies rather than on religious practices of the rural villages. However, traditional religious practices can be reconstructed from more recent accounts of rural Malay life since beliefs and practices in the rural areas have been slow in changing. See for example: Fraser, *Rusembilan;* Skeat, *Malay Magic;* Wilkinson, *Malay Beliefs;* Winstedt, *The Malays*, pp. 18-44; and R. O. Winstedt, *Shaman Saiva and Sufi* (London, 1925).

21. For some observations on the "integrating energy inherent in religious rites," see Joachim Wach, *Sociology of Religion* (Chicago, 1944), p. 42.

22. *Kenduri* feasts were viewed as "acts of merit" designed both to serve the community and to propitiate the good and evil spirits that controlled the fate of the individual and his community. Among non-Islamic peoples of Southeast Asia similar practices exist, such as the *ruai* festivals of the Ibans or the *mithun* sacrificial "feasts of merit" practiced by Nagas and other tribal peoples of Burma and Northeast India. In Java these feasts are known as *selamatan*. For an excellent description of these last feasts and an analysis of their religious significance and their role in Javanese society, see Clifford Geertz, *The Religion of Java* (New York, 1960), pp. 11-118.

23. For an account of more modern manifestations of the religious basis of status, see S. Husin Ali, *Social Stratification in Kampong Bangan* (Singapore, 1964), pp. 58-79; Mohammad Daud bin Hashim, "Religious Institutions Amongst the Malays of Signapore," academic exercise, Department of Social Studies, University of Malaya, 1958; and M. G. Swift, *Malay Peasant Society in Jelebu* (London, 1965), pp. 143-66.

24. The first European expedition reached Malayan waters in 1509. The Portuguese captured Malacca two years later, finally losing it to the Dutch in 1641. During the Napoleonic Wars the Dutch surrendered it to the English, who had acquired Penang Island by treaty in 1785 and later secured control of Singapore Island in a similar manner in 1819. Only after the Larut Wars ended in 1874 did the British embark upon a policy of bringing the Malay States under British protection by imposing treaties upon the Malay Rulers which provided for British Advisors or British Residents to administer these states according to British principles of law and order, but in the name of the Malay Rulers. British control and the colonial administrative apparatus were quite quickly established in Selangor, Negri Sembilan, Perak, and Pahang, but came more slowly in Johore, Kedah, Perlis, Kelantan, and Trengganu. See N. J. Ryan, *The Making of Modern Malaya*, 2d ed. (Kuala Lumpur, 1965); J. Kennedy, *A History of Malaya* (London, 1962); and C. Northcote Parkinson, *British Intervention in Malaya, 1867-1877* (Singapore, 1960).

25. The conflict between Islam and the *adat* customary law was particularly acute in Negri Sembilan (where the Minangkabaus from Sumatra had settled) because of the contradiction between Islam and their matrilineal *adat* laws. For an account of the institutions and practices of Negri Sembilan, see Winstedt, *The Malays*, pp. 187-90; P. E. de J. de Jong, *Minangkabau and Negri Sembilan: Socio-political Study in Indonesia* (The Hague, 1952); and G. A. de C. de Moubray, *Matriarchy in the Malay Peninsula and Neighbouring Countries* (London, 1931).

26. Contact with Mecca was much easier after the opening of the Suez Canal in 1869. By 1957 the volume of pilgrims from Malaya reached the figure of 4,273. See *Muslim World*, XLVIII, no. 1 (1958), 77.

27. For an account of the institution of the haj and the economic and social consequences of such pilgrimages, see Mohammad Soffian bin Abdul Rahim, "The Institution of the Haj Among the Malays of Singapore," academic exercise, Department of Social Studies, University of Singapore, 1962; H. A. R. Gibb and J. H. Kramers, eds. *Shorter Encyclopaedia of Islam* (London, 1961), pp. 121-25.

28. For an analysis of the place of Arabs and Indian Muslims in Malay society, see William R. Roff, *The Origins of Malay Nationalism* (New Haven, 1967), pp. 39-55 et passim.

29. In many respects Malay society exhibited the same religious tensions that affected Islamic societies elsewhere in the world. Beginning in the eighteenth century, Islam had been split between Sufi transcendentalists and the strict monists who formulated in uncompromising terms the "otherness of God" and wished to purge Islam of Sufism with its pantheistic tendencies. The puritanical Hanbalite Wahhabi movement (following the teachings of Muhammad Ibn Abd al-Wahhab) was one expression of this Islamic reform movement. Jamal ad-Din al-Afghani and Shaikh Muhammad Abduh carried this reform movement much further, attempting both to purify Islam and to borrow from the West certain ideas and practices that would

strengthen Islam so that is culture and religious traditions could be defended more effectively against Christian missions and against the impact of Western colonial rule. The leaders of this reform movement came to be known as the "Manar group," after its journal, *al-Manar*, while the University of al-Azhar in Cairo became the center for spreading the "modernist" ideas of these disciples of Muhammad Abduh. See Gibb, *Modern Trends*, pp. 25-62.

30. Roff, *Origins*, pp. 56-90. See also the earlier version of this chapter by Roff, "Kaum Muda—Kaum Tua: Innovation and Reaction Among the Malays, 1900-1941," in K. G. Tregonning, ed. *Papers on Malayan History* (Singapore, 1962), pp. 162-92.

31. Madrasah schools were established, usually in urban areas, to teach Koranic studies and Arabic. Most of them became centers for dissemination of *al-Manar* religious, social, and political doctrines. They maintained higher standards and were far more politicized than the village *pondok* schools.

32. A similar but more serious cleavage had developed within Indonesian society between the *abangan* and the *santri*. These religious and cultural differences are analyzed in some detail in Geertz, *Religion of Java*, pp. 11-226. The Islamic revivalist movement flourished in parts of Sumatra and created severe conflicts, particularly among the Minangkabaus. The orthodox Padri movement, which began about 1799, spawned a number of wars and later gave religious zeal to the Achinese in their extended conflicts with the Dutch during the nineteenth century. These religious movements in Sumatra may have influenced Islamic revivalism in Malaya. See Marion Fredricks, "Social Aspects of Malay Society," academic exercise, Department of History, University of Malaya, Singapore, 1961, pp. 29-38.

33. The text of the first such treaty, The Pangkor Engagement, is reproduced in Parkinson, *British Intervention*, Appendix A, pp. 323-25.

34. Roff, *Origins*, pp. 67-74. See also Ahmad Ibrahim, *Islamic Law in Malaya* (Singapore, 1965). The latter book gives a thorough account of substantive Muslim law in Malaya, but it provides practically no account of the bureaucratic and judicial structures created to administer these laws.

By 1890 English officers filled practically all judicial positions in the Malay States. Therefore, a separate system of religious courts manned by Malay *kathis* became necessary if English officers were not to interpret and enforce Muslim laws. See Eileen Tan Siew Lean, "Administration of Justice in the Malay States, 1874-1896," academic exercise, Department of History, University of Malaya, Singapore, 1959, pp. 49-51, 72-73.

35. For a good account of the administrative arrangements in Perak, see Mohamed Khalil bin Hussein, "The Department of Religious Affairs, Perak," academic exercise, Malay Studies Department, University of Malaya, Singapore, 1958.

36. The Muslim courts' jurisdiction applied only to Muslims, and their

primary responsibility was to register Muslim marriages and divorces and to distribute property after death or divorce. In civil cases these courts were limited to disputes of less than M$125, and in criminal cases the maximum penalty was M$10 fine. *See* Mohamed Khalil bin Hussein, pp. 12-15.

37. For example see *The Laws of the State of Kedah, IV* (Kedah, 1934), "Supervision of Alien Missionaries, Enactment No. 119." Where no statutes existed, the prerogative powers of the Malay Rulers "to safeguard the Muslim Religion" were available to prevent non-Muslim missionaries from working among the Malays. Similar but less stringent restrictions were also applied to missionary work among Malaya's animist aborigines because the Malays considered them to be dependent peoples destined eventually to become Muslims. The Malay term for these aboriginal peoples is *Sakai*, which means "slave."

38. The Methodists have been the most active in the educational field in Malaya, followed by the Catholics, Anglicans, and Presbyterians. In the Federation of Malaya and Singapore together, the Methodist schools had an enrollment of 17,472 in 1940 and by 1963 the figure had risen to 69,357 See Ho Seng Ong, *Methodist Schools in Malaysia* (Petaling Jaya, 1964), p. 27; Federation of Malaya, *Annual Report on Education, 1957* (Kuala Lumpur, n.d.).

39. When the state governments began to establish vernacular schools for the Malays, attendance was disappointingly poor because some Malays feared that their children might lose their religious faith. After Islamic studies became the main subject of the Malay government schools, attendance soared. See Roff, *Origins*, pp. 25-26.

40. For accounts of the political stands taken by the MNP see *Straits Times*, October 21, 1946, p. 1; March 10, 1948, p. 4; and March 23, 1948, p. 6. Also see Mohammad Yunus Hamidi, *Sejarah Pergerakan Politik Melayu Semenanjong* (Kuala Lumpur, n.d. [1961], pp. 65-68 The more radical Malay party, affiliated with MNP, Angkatan Pemuda Insaf (API), in its first manifesto made no mention of any religious issue. See *Malaya Tribune*, December 25, 1946, p. 1.

41. Born of Dutch parents, Maria Hertog was left as a small child in the care of an Indonesian servant when the Japanese invaded Southeast Asia. After the war the parents could not at first find their daughter, but finally traced her to the east coast of Malaya where she was living as a Malay with her foster mother. Maria did not want to return to her parents, but a court order was secured to obtain custody over her. Although she was only 13 years old at the time, her foster mother arranged her marriage to a Malay, since under Muslim law this action made her legally the responsibility of her husband. The conflict between Muslim law and common law was carried through a number of appeals with religious fanatics among the Malays interpreting the case as being one of Christianity versus Islam. Maria eventually was given into the custody of her parents, but the decision triggered serious anti-European riots, resulting in 18 people killed and 180 injured. *See* Lionel Leach, Chairman, *Report of the Singapore Riots Inquiry Commission, 1951* (Singapore, 1951).

311

42. Clifford Geertz coined this phrase and uses it to refer to the subnational community loyalties that bound premodern societies together and that persist in present-day transitional societies. See Geertz, ed. "The Integrative Revolution," *Old Societies and New States* (New York, 1963), pp. 105-57.

43. Information on Dr. Burhanuddin was obtained from a parliamentary survey conducted by the author, from newspaper accounts, and from J. Victor Morais, ed. *The Who's Who in Malaysia*, 1963 (Kuala Lumpur, n.d.), p. 41. Born in Perak in 1911, Dr. Burhanuddin studied in Malaya, the Dutch East Indies, and later in India, where he obtained a degree in homeopathic medicine. During the 1930's he became a journalist and edited a Malay magazine published in Singapore. From 1937 to 1940 he taught in an Arabic *madrasah* school in Singapore.

44. Dr. Burhanuddin campaigned on behalf of Barisan Kebangsaan Melayu (Malay Nationalist Front) which had as its objective the union of all Malay nationalist parties into a single organization for common political action. Dato Onn of UMNO was also a member, but he tended to ignore the BKM, thus leaving it powerless and ineffective.

45. The PMIP was founded in 1948 at a conference of Muslim religious leaders. Although organizationally weak, it had shown surprising strength in the 1955 election and was able to elect the lone opposition member to the Federal Legislative Council, thus preventing a clean sweep by the UMNO-MCA-MIC Alliance.

46. *Report on the Parliamentary and State Elections, 1959* (Kuala Lumpur, 1960).

47. Daniel E. Moore, "The United Malays National Organization and the 1959 Malayan Elections," unpub. diss., University of California, Berkeley, 1960, pp. 59-60.

48. For a more extended description of Muslim offenses, see Gordon P. Means, "State and Religion in Malaya and Malaysia," in M. M. Thomas and M. Abel, eds. *Religion, State and Ideologies in East Asia* (Bangalore, 1965), pp. 106-26; and Ahmad Ibrahim, *Islamic Law*, esp. pp. 315-66. Among the more important state statutes governing Muslim administration and defining Muslim offenses are the following: Johore: *Council of Religion Enactment, 1949*, No. 2 of 1949; Selangor: *Administration of Muslim Law Enactment, 1952*, No. 3 of 1952; Trengganu: *The Administration of Islamic Law Enactment, 1955 (1375)*, No. 4 of 1955; Pahang: *Administration of the Law of the Religion of Islam Enactment, 1956*, No. 5 of 1956; Negri Sembilan: *Council of Muslim Religion Enactment, 1957*, No. 1 of 1957; Malacca: *Administration of Muslim Law Enactment, 1959*, No. 1 of 1959; Penang: *Administration of Muslim Law Enactment, 1959*, No. 3 of 1959; Kedah: *Administration of Muslim Law Enforcement, 1962*, No. 9 of 1962.

49. *Constitution of the Federation of Malaya* (1957), Art. 160 (2).

50. By existing Muslim laws there is no procedure for a Muslim to renounce or change his religion, in part because Koranic law treated

apostasy as a serious crime. However, it is possible for a Muslim to be freed from the legal obligations of Islam and removed from the jurisdiction of the Muslim courts by means of petition to the Ruler. As far as can be determined, four or five Malays have sought to renounce their religion in recent years, but their petitions were not approved, since such action would appear to give the Ruler's sanction to apostasy. Nonetheless, unofficially they have been treated as exempt from prosecution in Muslim courts.

51. See Federation of Malaya, *The Report of the Education Review Committee, 1960*, pp. 47-48, 50, 70; Federation of Malaya, Ministry of Education, *Circular 93* (June 1960); Federation of Malaya, *Education Act, 1961*, No. 43 of 1961, p. 235 et passim.

52. The statement of policy designed to be a guideline for the Department of Aborigines is contained in Federation of Malaya, Ministry of Interior, *Blue Book, 1961*.

53. Malaysia, *The Federal Constitution, Together With Sections 73 to 96 of the Malaysia Act* (Kuala Lumpur, 1964), Art. 161D, p. 108. Also note: Mohamed Suffian, "Religious Freedom and the Position of Islam in Malaysia," *World Muslim League Magazine* 3, No. 2 (1966), 40-43.

54. For a more detailed account of these tensions and crises, see Gordon P. Means, "Eastern Malaysia: The Politics of Federalism," *Asian Survey*, VIII (April 1968), 289-308.

55. Weber, *Protestant Ethic*, pp. 155-183.

56. In 1957 the states of Malaya spent an estimated sum of M$7,784,021 for Muslim affairs, not including the funds spent by the federal government or the over M$3 million collected from *zakat and fitrah* taxes. The states spent 4.6 percent of their expenditures for support of Islam in 1957. The total sum had increased about 200 percent by 1963 and has continued to rise since then. In 1960 the federal government estimated that its support for Muslim religious instruction would be M$5.4 million in 1961 and rise to M$13.6 million by 1982. These figures do not include other costs of supporting Islam, such as the construction of the M$10 million National Mosque and the hundreds of other mosques that have been constructed. Some estimates of Muslim expenditures are made by M. Suffian Hashim, "The Relationship Between Islam and the State in Malaya," *Intisari*, I, no. 1 (n.d. [1962]), 21.

57. See Amar Kumar Singh, "Hindu Culture and Economic Development in India," *Conspectus*, 3 (First Quarter, 1967), 9-32; Alex Inkeles, "The Modernization of Man," in Myron Weiner, ed. *Modernization: The Dynamics of Growth* (New York, 1966), pp. 133-50.

58. Bellah, *Religion and Progress*, cited in fn. 5.

MARXIAN SOCIALISM IN AFRICA: THE CASE OF MALI

John N. Hazard

The ouster and arrest of Modibo Keita in Bamako on November 19, 1968, marked the end of an era, not only for Mali but for West Africa. The most doctrinaire of Black Africa's Marxist inspired leaders had fallen after nearly a decade of trying to introduce orthodox Marxism-Leninism into his tribally constituted society.

No other African president had taken such a firm position. In 1958 Sékou Touré of Guinea had declared complete independence from what he believed to be "neo-colonial" controls exerted by French capital, but even he had not declared himself a Marxist in Keita's terms. Touré professed a "noncapitalist way," but he denied that he had created forces that could lead only to communism.[1] For him the inevitability preached by the Marxian historical materialists was unreal. He was emphatic in denying that he was a prisoner of doctrine, saying always that his people had retained their power to choose what would come after achieving abundance.

Another of Keita's neighbors, Léopold Sédar Senghor of Senegal, had departed even further from the doctrinaire views of his former partner in the short-lived Federation of Mali. Senghor accepted only the "young" Marx who, in his view, typified the humanism essential to an African society. Senghor rejected Stalin's development of the dictatorship of the proletariat as a "soulless monster."[2] His admiration was for Soviet economic progress. He indicated his readiness to utilize Soviet experience as a model, but he wanted to create a doctrinal "mutation." His future lay in what he called "African socialism," epitomized by his catchword "negritude."[3] He wanted to create something new, a product of socialist

From John N. Hazard, "Marxian Socialism in Africa: The Case of Mali," *Comparative Politics* 2 (October 1969): 1-15. Reprinted by permission of the author and the publisher.

institutions functioning within a society permeated with the traditional humanistic values of Black Africa.

Keita expressed his admiration of the Soviet model in 1962 on the occasion of a visit to the Kremlin, but he entered an African reservation: "Our socialism will not be for us the manifestation of a tendency to copy servilely what others have done."[4] He planned to adapt the Marxian pattern to his society. His position was no defiance of orthodoxy, for Lenin had preached the need for just such an approach—although in practice he had tended to dictate, and Stalin carried dictation to the extreme. The Mongolian communists of the 1920s provided the Soviet leaders with the first chance to experiment with the applicability of the Soviet model outside the Union of Soviet Socialist Republics. They adapted the Soviet system to a nomadic life for which it was hardly intended; but they met with such success, in Stalin's view, that he concluded he had found a form of universal applicability. Only when Tito resisted in Yugoslavia was he given cause to reconsider and, even then, his reaction was to isolate and attempt to unseat Tito. Not until the Polish and Hungarian riots of 1956 were the doctrinaire specialists in the Kremlin forced to agree that there might be various "roads to socialism."

Keita rose to power in post-1956 circumstances when Marxists outside the U.S.S.R. could adapt Soviet patterns to local conditions without limitation on every detail, but he sought to preserve more of the "core" concepts than his neighbors, Touré and Senghor. To him, Senghor had become a traitor to Marxism by revising his doctrine to create something new. Keita's position was dramatized by his formula "socialism in Africa"[5] in contrast to Senghor's "African socialism." To a doctrinaire Marxist there is a real difference implied in these phrases, although to nonbelievers the contrast seems little more than semantic.

Equipped with his doctrinaire formula, Keita pressed hard to establish a political, economic, and social pattern along the lines of the U.S.S.R. He felt the need of doing so in order to express his determination to skip Russia's feudal and capitalist stages of development and even the period of Soviet history when the neo-capitalism of the New Economic Policy was given rein (1921-1928). His policy of vaulting directly into socialism was designed to avoid creating an African capitalist class from which he anticipated no good. He put himself in sharp contrast to Jomo Kenyatta of Kenya. The latter spoke out against creating in Africa the antagonistic class divisions of nineteenth-century Europe, but he anticipated Africanizing capital. This was to be done in part by providing the means for Africans to purchase stock in British companies and by granting loans to Africans to establish their own firms.[6] Keita wanted none of this, for he put his entire faith in state industry, supplemented in a very limited way by foreign concessions to be conducted under strict state control. The latter was to be established through joint ownership of stock and the appointment of Malian state officials as key corporate officials.

Although Keita's investment policy was to encourage foreign capitalists

315

to invest on promise of preservation of the right to withdraw profits, his 1962 investment code was restrictive.[7] The foreigners' activity was limited to production, and they were to be required to conform to the developmental provisions of the state economic plan. To avoid possible sabotage from foreign bankers, he permitted only one French bank to remain in operation in Bamako, and he cut his ties with the French franc. His explanation was orthodox: "History teaches us that political power always and necessarily is accompanied by the royal power to coin money; that monetary power is inseparable from national sovereignty."[8]

Keita's independence proved untenable, and by 1964 he began moving toward economic rapprochement with the franc. Not until 1967, however, when his economy had collapsed, was he willing to swallow his words and reestablish his link with the franc. This move frightened the Malian left. To placate his left wing and to protect his political system from the hostile influences which he expected to creep through the opened economic door, he suspended sessions of his National Assembly and even abolished the political bureau of his monopolistic political party, "l'Union Soudanaise— R.D.A." He began to rule with the aid of a narrowly constituted group which he called the Committee for the Defense of the Revolution. It was these protective measures that finally led to his undoing, but Keita seems not to have anticipated that, in closing one door to revolution, he had opened another. Perhaps it was because his preventive measures seemed logical from the Marxist viewpoint. He saw political power based on economic power as do all Marxists and, consequently, his first step was to insure protection from the economically powerful.

Keita's opponents in a Military Liberation Committee spoke out immediately after his ouster.[9] They decried his land use plan, inviting the villagers to abolish the communally tilled field, to return all land to private farming, and to sell their produce on the open market.[10] They had reason to expect this proposal to be popular, for during his presidency Keita had moved increasingly in the direction of the Soviet collective farm[11] and had created state corporations to monopolize the purchase of basic crops. Beyond that he had moved cautiously, for he had not applied Lenin's policy of land nationalization. Perhaps his caution stemmed from his fear of the continuing strength of the traditionalist elements of the villages. His approach was to leave customary land rights as they were, except when the state needed land for industry or transport. Then the Minister of Rural Economy issued a decree of acquisition and registration in the name of the state, but only after publication of notice and a hearing to determine customary claims.[12] Those who had acquired "title" under provisions of French colonial law were not disturbed unless specific state needs required acquisition of their plots. Even then the owners were not to be unduly antagonized, for officials were ordered to proceed with a unilateral determination of value only after having made every effort to reach a friendly accord.

316   The land policy for the surface did not apply to valuable subsoil rights,

an area in which the tribesmen had no political force. These were monopolized by the state, for Keita wanted no African land owner or tribal user to become a strong capitalist on discovery of subsoil resources. Only public authorities were permitted to exploit precious metals and gems, although such authorities might be publicly licensed prospectors' cooperatives as well as state enterprises.[13]

In spite of the precautions taken to avoid tribal hostility, Keita turned his land policy into the Achilles heel of his Marxian socialist program. His successors accused him of fostering "collective farms," but this was an oversimplification. He had never gone to the extreme of Soviet agricultural policy. He was only in the early stages in which he took advantage of tribal custom to further Lenin's concept of collectivization of use. He ordered expansion of traditional "common fields" of each village. This was to be accomplished not only by plowing virgin lands, but also by transforming plots tilled by individual families. The expansion was to continue by degrees until the "common fields" became the major asset of the village. A state department called the "Action Rurale" was to help in the process by aiding villagers to form cooperatives and to draft laws on cooperatives.[14] Similar cooperatives were to be encouraged among fishermen, for Keita believed cooperatives to be what they were for Lenin, namely "transmission belts to socialism."

Private trade in crops was restricted by a requirement that basic non-grain crops be sold only to state enterprises at fixed prices, while cereals were to be commercialized only through the newly created village cooperatives. All agriculture was subjected to a program of state agricultural planning established by an Institute for Rural Economy.

Keita was demonstrating his faith in a Marxian socialist road to socialism comparable to the one developed in Rumania, where land was not "nationalized" by the communists but absorbed from private owners by peasant cooperatives. The cooperatives pooled the privately owned plots of members and tilled them collectively. Keita failed where the Rumanians succeeded, probably for lack of local leadership. His strength was in the *comités* of his monopoly party; but their unpopularity is seen in the fact that they were quickly disbanded at the time of the coup against him. The party form had evidently failed to take firm root in the village social structure in spite of Keita's efforts to emulate the instruments of the communist parties of Eastern Europe.

Europeans with long experience in Mali had predicted leadership failure. They did not believe that the villagers could be brought to such respect for discipline that the village could be ruled with an iron hand and held together in that manner in the face of opposition. Keita himself was probably to blame for the power crisis, for he had introduced a notable variation from Lenin's pattern of elite leadership. Although he insisted that his political party face no opposition, he thought it unnecessary, until he approached his downfall, to create a party composed solely of the elite. Unlike Lenin, Keita had made no effort to reserve membership for militants. He had opened the party doors to all who knocked.[15] He had exhorted party members to study Marxism-Leninism and to develop discipline, but he had established no screening procedures to see that only those who met an exacting test could gain admission. He seemed to believe, until it was too late, that he had ample time to establish respect for discipline in the oncoming generation and to ignore the mature citizen until the last moment. He concentrated his political education on youth, to create in them a firm understanding of what they had to do and why. Keita's supporting forces were not, therefore, already in existence but were projected for the future; many were still at universities in the communist world, learning the art of government and administration. Still others were learning Russian from Soviet Komsomols in Mali's lycées, and a few were studying Marxism-Leninism from Soviet professors in Mali's National School of Administration.

Keita had reason to believe that his youth plan would work. Indeed, foreign authors reported increasingly during later years that the militant youth returning from communist schools were advancing swiftly up the political and technical ladders and would soon be strong enough to turn the state in the direction of a complete duplication of the Leninist pattern.[16] But those who remained at home proved to be the weak spot, for they were not so strongly imbued with Leninist doctrine. A visitor to the National School of Administration in the autumn of 1966 found that the Soviet professors who taught the key political subjects were not making a strong impression. Their lectures in halting French were declared unintelligible. The copiously supplied Soviet texts in French translation remained in the library, unsoiled by use. Indeed, some students reported that there was little interest in "theory" and that their major purpose in studying was merely to become traditional professionals by learning the techniques of law and administration from the able French technicians who provided the bulk of the teaching staff.

The conflict in approach between the communist-educated youth and most of those trained at home may have created a second major cause of Keita's fall. His failure was more than inability to excite his villagers to make the sacrifices he deemed essential for their salvation. It was also his inability to create with adequate speed a broadly based, dedicated, and disciplined leadership throughout his whole political apparatus. Those who were not converted remained politically strong, and they seemed to have sensed the threat to their future in the rising group of foreign-trained Marxist doctrinaires. Some of these traditionalists were in the Army; and from this position they controlled immediately exercisable power. Calling upon the dissident villagers to revolt against threatened "collectivization" and upon the noncommitted urbanites to revolt against restraints on private enterprise which had greatly reduced the goods for sale, they garnered enough popular support to oust a man in whom large segments of the population had lost confidence.

Appreciation of Keita's weakness was not limited to the grassroots, where communal customs were being trampled under foot, but it appeared also at higher administrative levels. Those who understood finance saw the mounting deficits of the state enterprises charged with operating the national economy, although they could do nothing to remedy this until French experts returned in February 1967. Keita had followed Lenin's model, created to help the state-owned economy of the early 1920s to compete with the private enterprise still permitted to exist. Thus, he operated the economy not through state bureaus of the ministry functioning under budgetary allocations from the treasury, but under public corporations made responsible for the conservation of their capital and asked to pay their way.[17]

Lenin's system of economic administration undoubtedly has economic merit, as evidenced by its use in varying forms in many lands, but it functions with difficulty in the developing societies. For its success it requires widely diffused managerial skills, knowledge of complex cost accounting methods, and, most important, the determination on the part of administrators to avoid waste and corruption. All of these qualities are in limited supply in the developing countries. A private enterprise economy also suffers from the shortage, but being smaller and more immediately responsive to the open market, its shortcomings become evident sooner than when they are lost in a large bureaucracy. In addition, the market mechanism punishes the incompetent and the corrupt faster than a prosecutor can find erring or absconding bureaucrats in the state machine.

Eastern Europeans are well aware of their problems in this area. Their attempt to create a "market-socialism" by establishing some features of the open market, by fixing prices on rational grounds, and by charging interest on capital are well-known. Keita had little experience in this field and few skilled persons. In consequence, his state enterprises operated with great waste and consequent high cost. Losses were heavy, and even the French experts who returned to Mali when the Malian and French francs were again linked in 1967 had difficulty in rectifying the situation. The currency continued to fall until made convertible in March 1968.

While economic decay played a major part in Keita's fall,[18] it seems to have been paired with inept handling of public relations. One of the slogans of the Army lieutenants who led the coup against Keita was "restore the elections." Marxist leaders in Eastern Europe never overlook elections, even though, to western eyes, they offer little but positive expression of choice. Lenin fostered the "soviets" as popularly elected councils of deputies chosen by factory workers and peasants. He had no choice in 1917, for his Bolsheviks were but a minority, and he needed a coalition of leftist parties to rule. Still, even after political power was safely in the hands of the Communist party and wholly monopolized, Stalin continued the "soviet" system which provided popularly elected assemblies at every level of government: village, city, county, province, republic, and federation.

319

The "soviets" have served a useful purpose, even though they would not satisfy westerners. They permit citizens to participate in an election act; to express grievances to deputies in their consultation rooms; to hear reports on what was done; to present statements of what ought to be done; and to participate from the galleries in watching the proceedings. The "soviets" have helped to satisfy the mass's desire for participation and, thus, to reduce the burden of governing them, even though the intellectuals find them small comfort.

Keita overlooked this opportunity. His oversight may have resulted from lack of an experience that would have fitted him to operate Lenin's system. The French colonial system had given almost no opportunity to practice popular representation. Villages were in the hands of their chiefs who functioned under customary powers. High levels were directed by colonial officials. Only the largest cities were organized as "communes" through which the urban elite could share, in a limited way, in policy making. Keita had begun to change this pattern to introduce Lenin's scheme, but he moved slowly, and finally reversed the process in the face of economic crisis.

At the village level, Keita created a council, elected by universal suffrage and including women as well as men.[19] But its powers were limited, for it could not elect the "village chief." Its function was to nominate a candidate, who was then appointed by the central government. The village council existed primarily as conciliator, to resolve disputes over land and property matters, and to maintain public order. The political authority in the village was the village *comité*, whose duties were stated to be "first of all the role of mobilization in the bosom of the masses, which it is charged to educate." Here was the arm of Keita's party, controlled from above under the Leninist principle of "democratic centralism," through which the center has the major role within the hierarchical party structure.

The municipalities had popularly elected Municipal Councils which chose the Mayor and his deputies from their membership; but, in the main, these were conceived as primarily consultative.[20] The Minister of the Interior had to consent to decisions on nine critical matters, and municipal borrowing and expenditures of size had to be approved by the Council of Ministers.

Under Keita's system, at intermediate levels of government the Malians did not participate at all.[21] A chief governed the *arrondissement* at the level next above the village, being named by, and directly subordinate to, the next superior, the *commandant* of the *cercle*. The latter's importance was enhanced by the requirement that he be a political figure of proven responsibility. His link with the party was assured by dual authority: administration of the *cercle* and political education of the party's *comités* within his *cercle*. To assure his loyalty he was named by the governor of the *région*. The governors were, of course, named by the government and instructed to work closely with the party body of the *région*.

While there were plans under Keita to expand the regional financial council into a Regional Assembly elected by universal suffrage in the same manner as the Provincial Soviet in the U.S.S.R., this never occurred. Keita's only high level popularly elected body was, therefore, the National Assembly; but even this was insulated from popular control. Its members were chosen on a single list prepared by the monopoly party and named to represent the country at large.[22] No deputy had association with a specific, comprehensibly-small locality, so he could not become a spokesman for his electors as deputies from small election districts in the U.S.S.R. appear to be.

It was this National Assembly in which Keita lost confidence at the time of rejoining the franc bloc in 1967, presumably because he felt it impossible to rely on a disciplined party to prevent his colleagues from succumbing to what were expected to be the blandishments of French capitalists returning with the franc. By suspending the National Assembly and substituting a more circumscribed "Legislative Delegation," Keita lost the confidence of his people, some of whom had come to look upon the National Assembly, with all its limitations, as a symbol of their sovereignty.

Finally, there was the exacerbation of grievances created by the people's militia. In emulation of U.S.S.R. models, Keita had created a youth corps of lads from 15 to 20 years of age, commissioned to preserve public order in public places. Perhaps because they had not been indoctrinated and trained as well as their Soviet counterparts, they ran wild. They became marauders, beating people who displeased them, taunting elderly women and even raping younger ones. They came to be hated by many of the citizens in the cities, and especially in the capital city. This hatred rubbed off on Keita and his regime and became a powerful factor in support of the army's call for a return to law and order in the streets.

While there are some elements that can be identified as playing a part in Keita's fall, it is equally important for the evaluation of influences on power in West Africa to identify some elements that played no part. The most important is tribalism. Although Keita was a Bambara, and his successor a Malinki, this was not proof that Keita's fall was due to his tribal origin. West Africans from neighboring states declare that this was not a factor.[23] Further, there was no charge of corruption against Keita. He was always accepted as the soul of honesty. Proof of his personal qualities was given by the Army's offer to him that he remain as president under the new regime. Only when he refused to abandon his Marxian socialism was he imprisoned. ... But at the time of his fall, no one either within the country or abroad was presenting them as reason to oust him.

Another factor which played no part in Keita's downfall was religion. Keita had abandoned the anti-religious policies of his Marxist models. He had even moved to include within his program the Islamic faith of the vast majority of his people. He specifically rejected atheism, saying in 1962,

321

"There is no religion more socialist than the Moslem religion because it teaches among its principles that the rich must give to the poor, must divide their goods in order to relieve the suffering of others."[24] While departing from Marxism on this score, he sought to explain his departure in terms that would have been understandable to Russians. He defended his position on the ground that religion in Mali had never made itself the agent of the colonial system; nor had it, even in the remote past, been an instrument of the feudal system. Furthermore, Islam had not caused resignation on the part of the people. All of these are points that the Bolsheviks had made in their attacks on the Orthodox Church.

Having accepted religion as a continuing factor in Mali's social life, Keita set about to limit its excesses. Primarily this took the form of an attack upon polygamy, but a restrained attack. Unlike Sékou Touré in Guinea, who thought the year 1968 opportune for the abolition of polygamy, Keita decreed no abolition. His 1962 Family Code[25] provided simply that monogamy was to be enforced only if the parties to a marriage included a commitment to monogamy in the marriage contract. If the contract were amended with the consent of the first wife, a second might be married in keeping with Islamic law. Short of that, a second marriage subjected the husband to state prosecution and the exaction of criminal penalties.

The new code followed models commonly accepted elsewhere in the modern world by recognizing only secular marriages, but it went one step further. It imposed a fine on those who participated in a religious marriage before civil registration. Its primary target was the arranged marriage, since consent was made a requisite for validity. It met custom halfway, however, for it provided under a betrothal agreement that, if a marriage had been arranged and gifts exchanged, the fiancé had the right to prevent the marriage of his fiancée to another man until his expenses had been repaid. Judges were authorized to fix the damages.

A further limitation was put upon the custom of giving large gifts on the occasion of a marriage. Under the new code, a prospective husband's gift to the bride's father or head of family on the occasion of marriage might not exceed 20,000 francs ($90) for an unmarried girl or 10,000 francs ($45) for a previously married woman. In the event of divorce, the aggrieved party could demand return of the gifts. Those who exceeded the limitations might be prosecuted under the Criminal Code.

Keita had also moved cautiously to avoid upsetting his people's sense of "justice." He introduced no Moscow-type criminal or civil law and initiated no unfamiliar judicial procedures. His code[26] established no "state economic crimes" with high penalties, including death, as did the U.S.S.R. pattern. The only two provisions suggestive of the approach of Soviet jurists were a prohibition of vagabondage on the ground that "Labor is the duty of every Malian," and a 1964 amendment establishing a mild form of "economic crime."[27] This latter, which was defined as fraud, contraband, and other voluntary and premeditated infractions committed

322

against the economic, financial, and banking institutions, carried the relatively light penalties of confiscation of property and disqualification for ten years from civil rights and from employment in state agencies. Even imprisonment was not permitted for the offense.

In civil and commercial law the French rules were kept in force with little change. The major communist influence here, as in other Marxist-oriented economies, was withdrawal of productive property from the operation of the civil and commercial codes to create a public sector. Other amendments were designed to protect debtors, but in a fashion no more surprising than in capitalist states: rent freezes and rent fixing.

Judicial procedure underwent some change under Keita because the customary law courts were combined with the state courts, but otherwise the well-known practices still prevailed.[28] Judges were not elected as in the U.S.S.R., nor were there two lay assessors on every bench. The French system of a single professional judge appointed as a civil servant prevailed. Prosecutors were completely within the French tradition of the *Parquet* and so was the bar. Keita's only change was to infuse politics into the judiciary by telling them that they were not members of a separate branch of government but completely responsible to the party as was any other civil servant. When some objected, he insisted that they participate in party meetings and show political interest. It may be that this attitude helped to estrange the judiciary who had undergone French training, but, if so, they can easily revert to French attitudes in the post-Keita period, since no structural change will be required.

For the villagers the loss of the customary courts was softened by a provision to have customary law experts upon the bench when the professional judge had to decide issues involving customary law. This meant that the traditional wise men of the tribal community sat in their flowing robes alongside the French-style professional judge, so that the courtroom was not entirely a court of the outsider. Further, no one had to go to court to settle a dispute, for mediation was urged as a desirable procedure in dispute resolution, and this could be conducted by village elders.

What Malians will demand now that Keita is gone is still problematical. Quite possibly they will wish to continue to call their society "socialist" as do their neighbors, for the concept is popular in Africa regardless of content. They will probably look at Senghor's Senegal, which many know well as the country at the other end of their only railroad to the sea and as their previous partner in federation. They may even look further afield at the Ivory Coast, which has experienced swift development under a program of private enterprise.

If Senegal becomes the model,[29] Mali, under the Army, will still have a national economic plan, although by no means as detailed as the plan under which Keita operated. Foreign investors will be invited to enter the country, and their investments will be guaranteed insofar as they will be authorized to withdraw profits. Private trade will be permitted to flourish.

Perhaps the Lebanese will even find it advantageous to return as taxes are reduced on their activities as merchants. Exports and imports will still be controlled when they relate to key items of the economy. Basic industries will remain under state ownership. The Malian trade unions were adamant on this point when Army leaders sought their cooperation in ousting Keita. For socialist thought has penetrated so deeply into the trade unionists' mentality that they cannot accept a return to private ownership of major industries. They will not tolerate the emergence of a class of rich Africans with unlimited power to exploit industrial workers. This means that French capital will be invited to return, but investors will be treated as concessionnaires, subject perhaps to eventual ouster if the Malian economy becomes strong enough to permit the state to buy them out.

It is possible that lesser industry may be stimulated through seeking to establish a Malian private sector by granting loans to enterprising individuals. Such a program would run into strong theoretical opposition and practical difficulties, however. There are still influential Malians who fear capitalism in uncontrolled form. Also there are few with the skills necessary to organize and operate industry at any level above that of the artisan.

Cooperatives will be encouraged, but as marketing units rather than producing units. No collectivization of agriculture on the Soviet model, or even on that of the first stages of European-type cooperatives, can presently be foreseen.

Whatever the program, the new Malian leaders can expect to feel pressures from citizens who have been trained in Marxian socialist countries and who possess intelligence and skills. There will also be pressures from abroad, for Mali's economy is heavily dependent upon Eastern European technical experts and on the credits granted to pay the latters' wages. The U.S.S.R. has large outstanding loans for the repayment of which the Soviet government could become very demanding. The new leadership must both satisfy the demand for political reform and prove that the economic life of the country can be stabilized. This will be a difficult task in a country that lacks natural resources, unless some new ones can be found. Soviet experts were engaged in exploration for minerals at the time of Keita's fall. Unless they, or western experts, are successful in finding presently unknown resources, Mali's economic future looks bleak.

Will the communists of Eastern Europe and Asia leave the new Malian regime free to develop as it wishes? This seems unlikely, for Mali has long been the brightest star in Africa for communists of the U.S.S.R. and China. When slogans were published annually on Soviet holidays, the greetings to Mali were placed immediately after the group of greetings to peoples within the inner group of fourteen members of the Marxian socialist commonwealth. Hope ran high that Mali would adhere to the group, although no such adherence was proclaimed.

Soviet strategists are realists. Perhaps they realize that Keita could not be kept in power in the face of a determined attack upon him. This explanation for Soviet reluctance to include Mali within the commonwealth, as Cuba was included, was given two years ago by a Pole in a conversation with the author. In explanation of Keita's continuing position outside the commonwealth, he reported that, to a Marxist, there can be no event to suggest a break in the inevitable progress of states from capitalism to socialism. Historical materialism cannot be thwarted. The events of Keita's ouster give credence to such an explanation, for it happened quickly and the Soviet forces, including even the many technicians within Mali, could do nothing. Indeed, the latter accepted the coup and immediately returned to their jobs. But they remain in the wings and may move back to center stage if the West fails to provide the massive aid needed.

Mali remains too important as a focal point in Africa for operations and for proof of the viability of the Marxian socialist system for the U.S.S.R. and China to leave it alone, unless all hope has to be abandoned. The Marxist East has done better in Mali than elsewhere in training large numbers of Malians, and this group cannot be expected to remain silent once the first flush of excitement abates. Social revolution takes time, and Marxists do not permit themselves to become discouraged by what they believe to be no more than temporary setbacks in the progress of the dialectic of history.

NOTES

1. Sékou Touré, *L'Afrique et la Révolution* (Conakry, n.d.), p. 168. Touré's works appear in a series, some volumes of which bear numbers, although each has a different title. This volume is numbered 13 in the series.

2. Léopold Sédar Senghor, *On African Socialism*, translated and with an introduction by Mercer Cook (New York, 1964), p. 33.

3. Léopold Sédar Senghor, *Liberté 1: Négritude et Humanisme* (Paris, 1964), pp. 8-9.

4. Speech at Kremlin Palace, 22 May 1962, reprinted in Modibo Keita, *Discours et Interventions* (Bamako-Moscow, 1965), p. 43.

5. *2e Seminaire de l'Union Soudanaise—R.D.A. Bamako, les 5-6-7 Septembre 1962* (Bamako, n.d.), p. 73.

6. "Statement by the President," in *African Socialism and its Application to Planning in Kenya* (Nairobi, n.d.), p. i.

7. Law No. 62-5 AN, 5 January 1962 [1962] *Journal Officiel de la République du Mali* [cited hereinafter as *JORM*], no. 110, p. 112.

8. Speech to the National Assembly, 30 June 1962, in Keita, *Discours*, p. 141.

9. See Lloyd Garrison, "President of Mali Is Ousted by Army," *New York Times*, 20 November 1968, p. 1. Also see Alfred Friendly, Jr.

"Leaders of Coup in Mali Request Economic Aid," *ibid.*, 23 November 1968, p. 5.

10. See "New Mali Leaders Consolidating Rule," *ibid.*, 22 November 1968, p. 8.

11. Modibo Keita, "Speech on Sixth Anniversary," 22 September 1966, in *L'Essor* (Bamako), 26 September 1966, p. 4.

12. Law of 12 May 1959, discussed in Blanc, "Chronique fonciére: Quelques lois Guinéennes et Maliennes récentes," *Receuil Penant* 72 (1962): 297.

13. Law No. 20 PG, 25 February 1964 [1964] *JORM*, no. 166, p. 236.

14. Law No. 61-66 AN, 18 May 1961 [1961] *JORM*, no. 90, p. xxii.

15. Speech of Political Secretary, *VIᵉ Congrés de l'Union Soudainaise—R.D.A.—Bamako, les 10-11-12 Septembre 1962* (Bamako, 1963), p. 107.

16. F. Schatten, *Communism in Africa* (London, 1966), p. 166.

17. Model statute of 16 January 1963, discussed in Seydou Madane Sy, *Recherches sur l'exercice des pouvoirs en Afrique Noire—Côte d'Ivoire, Guinée, Mali* (Paris, 1965), p. 49. For adaptation of the model to a specific corporation, see Law no. 63-65 AN, 26 December 1963 [1964] *JORM*, no. 162, p. 112.

18. For a post-Keita analysis by an African economist, depicting Mali's economic decay, see J. Vangsi, "La lecon d'un échec," *Jeune Afrique*, no. 421 (27 January-2 February 1969), p. 26.

19. These were created within the République Soudanaise on 28 March 1959, and continued when Mali was established under Law no. 63-32 AN, 31 May 1963 [1963] *JORM*, no. 147, p. 382.

20. Law No. 66-9 AN, 31 March 1966 [1966] *JORM*, no. 218, p. VII.

21. For territorial structure of the Republic, see Mali Constitution, Art. 41. Law No. 60-1, 22 September 1960 [1960] *JORM*, no. 65, p. III.

22. Ordinance No. 65 bis (Electoral Law), 24 November 1960 [1960] *JORM*, no. 73 at p. I.

23. Information gained from West African friends of the author, who shall remain nameless.

24. Keita, *Discours*, p. 108.

25. Law No. 62-17 AN, 3 February 1962 [1962] *JORM*, no. 111, p. I. Also published in République du Mali, Ministére de la Justice, *La Justice en République du Mali* (Bamako-Moscow, 1965), p. 362.

26. Law No. 99 AN, 3 August 1961 [1961] *JORM*, no. 98, p. 1. Also published in *La Justice en République du Mali*, p. 51.

27. Law No. 63-92 AN, 1 February 1964 [1964] *JORM*, no. 162, p. 91.

28. Law on the Judicial System, No. 61-55 AN, 15 May 1961 [1961] *JORM*, no. 90, p. II. Also published in *La Justice en République du Mali*, p. 6.

29. For the author's conception of Senghor's model, see John N. Hazard, "Negritude, Socialism and the Law," *Columbia Law Review* 65 (1965): 788.

SUGGESTIONS FOR FURTHER READING
PART SIX: IDEOLOGIES AND POLITICAL DEVELOPMENT

Binder, Leonard. *The Ideological Revolution in the Middle East.* New York: John Wiley & Sons, 1964.

Brockway, A. Fenner. *African Socialism.* London: Bodley Head, 1963.

Coleman, James. *Nigeria: Background to Nationalism.* Berkeley and Los Angeles: University of California Press, 1958.

Cottam, Richard W. *Nationalism in Iran.* Pittsburgh: University of Pittsburgh Press, 1964.

Emerson, Rupert. *From Empire to Nation: The Rise of Self-Assertion of Asian and African People.* Cambridge, Mass.: Harvard University Press, 1960.

Gordon, David C. *Self-Determination and History in the Third World.* Princeton: Princeton University Press, 1971.

Hughes, A. J. *East Africa: The Search for Unity.* Baltimore: Penguin Books, 1963.

Kautsky, John H. *Communism and the Politics of Development: Persistent Myths and Changing Behavior.* New York: John Wiley & Sons, 1968.

Kautsky, John, ed. *Political Change in Underdeveloped Countries: Nationalism and Communism.* New York: John Wiley & Sons, 1962.

Lasswell, Harold D., and Lerner, David, eds. *World Revolutionary Elites: Studies in Coercive Ideological Movements.* Cambridge, Mass.: M.I.T. Press, 1965.

Nkrumah, Kwame. *Africa Must Unite.* New York: Praeger Publishers, 1963.

Nuseibeh, Hazem Zaki. *The Ideas of Arab Nationalism.* Ithaca: Cornell University Press, 1956.

Nye, Joseph S. *Pan-Africanism and East African Integration.* Cambridge, Mass.: Harvard University Press, 1965.

Senghor, Leopold. *African Socialism.* New York: American Society of African Culture, 1959.

Senghor, Leopold. *On African Socialism.* New York: Praeger Publishers, 1964.

Sigmund, Paul E., ed. *The Ideologies of the Developing Nations.* rev. ed. New York: Praeger Publishers, 1967.

Silvert, K. H., ed. *Expectant Peoples: Nationalism and Development.* New York: Random House, 1963.

Smith, Donald Eugene. *Religion and Political Development.* Boston: Little, Brown and Co., 1970.

Ward, Barbara. *Nationalism and Ideology.* New York: W. W. Norton & Co., 1966.

Welch, Claude E., Jr. *Dream of Unity: Pan-Africanism and Political Unification in West Africa.* Ithaca: Cornell University Press, 1966.

PART SEVEN
the elites, parties, military, and bureaucracy and political development

Since the end of the Second World War the politics of the emergent nations have been directed by new and relatively young persons. These new leaders or elites include civilians—college professors, lawyers, doctors, engineers, students, high school teachers, civil servants or bureaucrats—and the military. The new political elites are nationalistic and revolutionary in their policies. Many of the elites in developing nations are Western educated. They are interested in action and results and often use nationalism to achieve their goals as we have discussed in the previous chapter. They tend to emphasize competence, performance, and ability rather than ascriptive rights (family, wealth, and status) as the sole criteria for public service. Their ascension to power has drastically altered socio-economic systems by challenging the political supremacy of the landed aristocracy. Political elites in developing states are those who wield political power in the political system and are able to manipulate the developmental process.

Throughout the developing nations of Asia, Africa, the Middle East, and Latin America, political and often socio-economic leadership in society is in the hands of the young and educated men who recognize the value and importance of science and technology. Naturally, they are oriented toward the scientific-technological culture which often leads to conflict with old norms and traditions of the past. Generally, the new elites in developing states are the urban-educated group who espouse modern values, the military officers who are entering the middle class, the bureaucrats who are achievement-oriented, and those of the traditional elites who come to recognize and accept reforms, political innovation, and social change as essential aspects of the modernization process.

Modernizing elites in a large number of the developing nations are antagonistic to the dominant values of the society and are more likely to reject traditional elements and accept what is modern and advanced. The more traditional the society, the more conflict there will be between the modernizing elites and those groups that insist on preserving the status quo. Modernizing elites must stimulate change, not only of technological nature, but also in social mores. They must create social and political institutions that will mobilize the nation and create political, economic, and social integration. In the first three articles we will examine the role of leadership and development in Tunisia, the patterns of elite succession in the process of development, and finally, the revolutionary and managerial types of elites in modernizing regimes.

In his article, "Leadership and Development," Charles A. Micaud examines developmental programs in Tunisia, the new structural reforms, and the capacity of the political system to adapt itself to rapid social change. Also, he raises the question of political leadership and its role in the process of development. He examines Destourian socialism under the leadership of Habib Bourguiba. Destourian socialism is used as a vehicle to maintain political and social cohesion. Micaud points out the basic features of Bourguiba's assumptions which aim at transforming man and society. Destourian socialism is pragmatic in its search for efficiency and adaptability to new conditions. It proposes the theory of "social function of property" and gives emphasis to cooperatives.

Micaud also examines Bourguiba's strategy for change, the role of Ben Salah, former minister of Plan and Nation Economy, the role of the party in implanting new structures, and the problems of organization and regional and local leadership. He concludes that the gap between elites and masses is yet to be bridged and raises the question of whether the political culture imparted by the one-party rule and the unitary ideology can be adequate once people develop new needs through education and place new demands upon the political system. Moreover, he raises the question of what will happen to the regime that depended upon the rule of one man. Micaud entertains a number of illusions about the Tunisian experiment in social engineering, including the important role played by the Destour party.

In the next article John H. Kautsky examines the diversification and proliferation of elite grouping in terms of major group conflicts and the various patterns of political change that may take shape in the course of economic development. He discusses how economic development from without affects the major social grouping in traditional society as well as the new ones created by that impact. Moreover, he analyzes the reaction of both old and new groups to modernization from without in the form of anticolonial movement.

Kautsky then traces some of the patterns of political change that have been and may yet be evolving in many parts of the world that have been subjected to the impact of economic change from without. He states that the modernizing efforts of aristocratic regimes will eventually lead to their overthrow. A similar fate probably awaits rulers of traditional societies. Kautsky reviews at length the role of the military and moves on to a discussion of conflicts in regimes that fall somewhere between those of modernizing aristocrats and of modernizers. Also, he analyses the various elements of conflict between modernizers after they come to power. Coups of one group of modernizers against another become more frequent.

Although revolutionary modernizers have come to power, we cannot assume that managerial modernizers will emerge in great numbers or must necessarily come to power at all. Also, we cannot assume that all underdeveloped societies will become highly industrialized. However, it is not unreasonable to predict an indefinite period of widespread discontent and governmental instability for societies that cannot move on to effective industrialization.

In his second article, "Revolutionary and Managerial Elites in Modernizing Regimes," Kautsky suggests that as industrialization proceeds, the managerial elites replace revolutionary ones.

However, sufficient evidence is not yet available to test this hypothesis, although the general thesis finds support in the experience of few countries that have made substantial progress toward industrialization. Kautsky discusses in detail the major differences between revolutionary modernizers and managerial elites with respect to (1) their background, experience, and training, (2) their attitudes, and (3) their policies.

Kautsky concludes that we cannot distinguish sharply between revolutionary and managerial elites on the basis of available evidence at this juncture. He writes, "we cannot test, much less validate, the hypothesis that industrialization and the replacement of revolutionary by managerial modernizers accompany each other if we cannot clearly distinguish between the two types of modernizers."

The impact of political parties on political development is examined by David E. Apter and Aristide R. Zolberg. Parties can act as vehicles by which modernizing elites achieve societal transformation and create national unity and solidarity and democratic systems. David E. Apter indicates that opposition in new nations needs a more limited and specialized role in order to gain general acceptance and protect its position. It must be responsible. However, the outlook for opposition in new nations is bleak. Fear that opposition will lead to factionalism, separatism, and corruption is widespread in new states. Apter discusses the single dominant party and the multiparty systems in new nations. Also, he discusses the functions of an opposition in presenting interests and providing information, criticism, and alternatives to government policies.

Apter discusses how an opposition can aid the government in three important spheres of a democratic system, namely, preservation of political values, helping to control the acts of the executive by conciliar control and advice, and finally, giving coherence and meaning to the representative system. An opposition must be able to strike a balance between being an enemy and a contender for the government. An opposition in new nations must be responsible in order to help in the struggle for unity, freedom, social justice, and racial equality.

In his study of the Ivory Coast, Aristide R. Zolberg points out that although the Parté Démocratique de Cote d'Ivoire (PDCI) has contributed to national integration, it also has created certain structures that are obstacles to national integration. He deals with the problem of particularism and the possible rise of dissident groups which might accentuate centrifugal tendencies and lead to the use of coercive measures by the government. He concludes that the contributions of the PDCI to the development of a new society in the Ivory Coast cannot be assessed at this juncture. In the long run, however, it is likely that the integrative functions of the PDCI will overshadow the negative consequences of its activities.

In many emergent nations the military remains the principal force capable of establishing a viable political system. It controls the instruments of power and has a cohesive organization. More than any other group it reflects the national interest and possesses the capacity to unify a disunited and often apathetic political community. In recent years there have been many cases of military intervention in domestic politics aimed at restoring order by destroying corrupt civilian regimes. Such intervention has taken place in Egypt, Syria, Lebanon, Iraq, Sudan, Yemen, Pakistan, Turkey, Burma, Indonesia, Thailand, Vietnam, Korea, Ghana, and the Congo, among many others.

In what sense does the military function as a unifying force in the emergent nations? It helps to foster a sense of national identity and thereby minimizes the considerable differences among subcultural, tribal, and ethnic groups. Its capacity for creating a sense of identification is based on its organizational unity and environment. Its members are socialized to an awareness of belonging to a corporate body with unified military functions. The military gives its members the organizational, material, and psychological resources to cope with problems they may face. Men with diverse ethnic and social backgrounds are given a common experience and come to think of themselves as Burmese, Indonesians, Ghanians, or Nigerians.[1]

There are two aspects to the military as an instrument for developing national identity and socialization. The first relates to the consequences of military service, and the second to the symbolic values the military provides for the people as a whole. In states where religious and ethnic hostilities are present or where there is an established military tradition, the military assumes immediate importance. In certain states of Sub-Sahara Africa, however, the role of the military as a socializing force is limited by its newness and size.[2]

Military elites play a key role in the transition from traditional to Western orientations. The soldier is required to move away from localized, particularistic relationships into the more modern, impersonal, and universalistic relations of an industrialized society.[3] The young recruit is compelled to recognize and identify himself with the larger political order. He learns to assume some definite relationship to the national political community. In this sense the military acts as a politicizing agency. The recruit is likely to comprehend that events in the political community do not just happen by fate or chance but rather are determined by human decisions. He may come to recognize that much of life can be changed and that human wishes and decisions have enormous consequences.[4]

The technological orientation of the military colors its conception of national progress. If the intellectual class possesses technological knowledge and experience, the military tends to view it as an ally. If, however, the technocrats are too few, as in the Middle East, Africa, and Asia, young officers are apt to look upon themselves as the only hope for modernizing society.

In the three articles by Bill, Needler, and Hopkins we will examine the role of the military in the Middle East and Latin America and the relationship between civilian government and military organizations in developing countries. James A. Bill analyzes the role of the military in the social-political changes taking place in the Middle East. He discusses the two schools of thought concerning the role of the military. The military may act to preserve traditional values or to introduce new ones. Also, he examines four general categories into which the military coup may fall. Moreover, Bill discusses the significance of military-civilian group interaction under two general categories: (1) military-civilian group interaction in the immediate seizure of power, and (2) military-civilian group interaction in the maintenance of power. Bill states that in terms of a successful program of modernization, military-civilian relations after the seizure of power are more crucial than relations at the time of actual seizure of power.

Bill turns his attention to the discussion of the internal cleavage and conflict in Middle Eastern officer corps which take place prior to and during the seizure of power by young officers. Intramilitary conflict, we should bear in mind, varies in intensity and direction from one state to another. Intramilitary struggles leave their impact upon the society in which they occur. Military coups in Turkey and Egypt have brought about change in traditional social and political patterns. The military elite seeking to modernize its society must first stabilize its own position and consolidate its powers although this may necessitate a certain amount of authoritarianism. The major problem facing modernizing military elites is how to mobilize and gain the support of their societies behind their efforts. Modernizing elites must understand, however, that authoritarianism may well act as an obstacle to modernization.

While Bill's article examines the modernizing role of the military in the Middle East, Martin C. Needler's article considers the role of the military in Latin America. Needler raises three important empirical questions: (1) Have coups d'etat become more or less frequent? (2) What changes have been taking place in the functions of the coup in relation to changes occurring in the larger society? and (3) What are the effects of changes in the Latin American military on the form, structure, and timing of the coup d'etat, and what political significance do these effects have? He examines each of these questions in detail and concludes that military intervention occurs when economic conditions are deteriorating. Also, military coups d'etat have tended to take place more often in the period immediately prior to a presidential election and/or inauguration and these coups are accompanied by violence. Moreover, there is a tendency for conflict to develop between "hard-line" and "soft-line" groups which indicates readiness to restore constitutional procedures.

Keith Hopkins examines the relations between civilian government and military organizations in developing countries. He discusses the images the military have of themselves, the images of the military held by different groups within society, and the image as contrasted with reality. Hopkins examines at length the cohesiveness of the military and states that it is not dependent upon social origin but rather upon professionalism and career experiences combined with the pervasiveness of military life which inculcate a sense of identity in the military officer.

He examines S. E. Finer's typology of civil-military relations and the social structure and its impact upon military relations with civilian governments. The military may intervene in politics because of inadequacies of professional politicians, or it may be invited or blackmailed to intervene; or still it may act on its own initiative to preserve traditional social and political patterns or to speed modernization and improve its own posi-

335

tion. The military intervenes when there is a power vacuum. Intervention is made easier because of the relative weakness of the masses and the restricted sphere of governmental activity.

Finally, he discusses the syndrome of military government and concludes that new nations spend large sums of money on the military, because the military carries out many useful programs and contributes to national unity and development. However, the record is not impressive. "Military involvement in politics is symptomatic of the centripetality of conflict; the more the dissensus, the more alternative sources of power become involved in the dispute."

The bureaucrats are the final group of "modernizing elites" to be considered. S. C. Dube states that "Bureaucracy forms an important element of the modernizing elite in many of the economically less developed countries which have attained national independence during the last two decades." Economic planning requires highly specialized knowledge and manipulative skills and the implementation of these plans calls for administrative insights. Integration of local, regional, and national planning demands knowledge and skills which the bureaucracy possesses.

Bureaucracies in new nations were the first to make the transition from traditionalism to modernity. Bureaucracies in their respective countries, Dube writes,

> were among the pioneers who sought to break away from traditionally affective and emotional-based communal society and to set in motion the forces that were to contribute towards the emergence of a different type of society—a society characterized by affective neutrality and based on rational ends-means calculations for individual goals.

Dube discusses the features of these bureaucracies as they emerged and crystallized during the colonial phase and their problems in the context of (1) the culture of politics, (2) the emerging ethos, and (3) the expanding sphere of State activities and the new institutional arrangements. Dube notes that in the new order the sovereignty of politics largely replaces the supremacy of administration. In this culture of politics there is the tendency to merge the political roles with personal and social roles. Administration becomes largely personal. In many of the newly independent states "the bureaucracy was trained well enough to accept political direction, and only in a few

exceptional cases did it try to gain the upper hand." Adjustment in this political culture, however, was difficult. Moreover,
the emerging ethos presented bureaucracy with many problems.
It should be noted that bureaucracy, by and large, has "resisted
innovation in its structural arrangements." New approaches are
discussed and to some degree accepted, but only in rare cases
are they given a fair trial.

Robert N. Kearney and Richard L. Harris discuss the impact
of the social, cultural, and political environment on the contemporary bureaucracy in Ceylon. They examine the prestige of the
public service, the social stratification and the bureaucratic
structures, the influence of the educational system, the impact
of ethnic and religious communities, and the caste and family
influence on the functioning of bureaucracy. Finally, they
analyze the political environment and its impact on bureaucracy. They conclude that political interference appears to have
damaged bureaucratic morale and effectiveness, although the
extent of the effect is difficult to measure. Family and communal loyalties combined with the influence of caste have
probably helped in reducing the impartiality of the bureaucracy. Moreover, adaptation and adjustment to changing circumstances following independence have been the major
sources of stress in the contemporary bureaucracy. The bureaucracy has been very vulnerable to political pressures and growing nationalist currents. Kearney and Harris state that the
exclusiveness of the bureaucracy made the process of adjustment to the political trends arising after independence difficult.

NOTES

1. Morris Janowitz, *The Military in the Political Development of New
   Nations* (Chicago: University of Chicago Press, 1964), pp. 80-81.
2. Janowitz, *New Nations*, pp. 81-82.
3. Lucian W. Pye, "Armies in the Process of Political Modernization, " in
   The Role of the Military in Underdeveloped Countries, ed. John J.
   Johnson (Princeton: Princeton University Press, 1962), p. 89.
4. Pye, "Process of Political Modernization," p. 83.

LEADERSHIP
AND DEVELOPMENT:
THE CASE OF TUNISIA

Charles A. Micaud

With the introduction of "Planning" in 1961, Tunisia quickened the pace of its development and embarked on a radical transformation of economic and social structures through the rapid expansion of the cooperative sector in agriculture and trade. From 1964 on, the year of the nationalization of colon lands and of the launching of the second four-year Plan, the reform moved at increasing tempo. Hundreds of agricultural production cooperatives were created in the Northwest and in the South and Center. These transformed the conditions of life of almost a quarter of the population, while tens of thousands of shopkeepers and merchants, a highly vocal and influential group, were regrouped willy-nilly into new commercial units and consumer cooperatives. In early 1969, agricultural production cooperatives were being rapidly introduced in the densely populated Sahel and in the rich olive tree forest around Sfax, despite the risks of infuriating peasants who have a strong sense of individual ownership.

There are few governments of developing nations that would have dared embark on a revolutionary program of such magnitude and speed that it challenges the capacity of the political system to absorb tensions and maintain social cohesion. Despite signs of displeasure and some mute opposition to the scope and speed of the reforms, even within the party,[1] the Tunisian political system has weathered the storm. Good crops in 1969, coming after several years of drought, ought to ease tensions and facilitate the consolidation of the new structures, one of the main targets of the new four-year Plan.

The structural reforms test the solidity and adaptability of the political

From Charles A. Micaud, "Leadership and Development," *Comparative Politics* 1 (July 1969): 468-84. Reprinted by permission of the author and the publisher.

system and its power to combine political stability and rapid social change. It raises the problem of political leadership and its role in the process of development. Through what methods and under what sets of conditions can leadership succeed in combining the radical restructuring of society with maintenance of a broad political consensus? How can bold experimentation insert itself within the old unitary ideology and step-by-step strategy characteristic of "Bourguibism"?

Political science has somewhat neglected the problem of political leadership and its impact on development. Perhaps this is because it is a variable that does not lend itself well to empirical and comparative analysis; or perhaps because there are only a few leaders who seem inventive or forceful enough to handle competently problems that have baffled the theoreticians of development. Their roles as initiators of development policies are considered of lesser relevance than the impact of economic, social, and cultural forces in which the leader appears as little more than a marginal actor doomed to fail if he attempts to manipulate forces necessarily above his control. The narrowness of his margin of freedom is taken for granted, all the more so since few statesmen stay in power long enough or seem consistent enough in their modernization efforts to have much impact.

The leader of a liberation movement is understandably reluctant to endanger the national unity reached during the battle for independence by embarking on serious economic and social reforms that carry with them dangers of division. He may proclaim revolutionary changes, but he is careful not to antagonize any vested interests. Conversely, he may decide to sacrifice unity for the sake of revolution. In the latter case, he singles out domestic and foreign enemies and accepts a considerable narrowing of his basis of support in order to gain disciplined cohesion. He may also use demagogic methods to obtain the illusion of popular support.

Few are the reformers who are capable of maintaining at the same time (1) the consensus of the educated elite, the only group capable of fully understanding the rationale for change, and (2) the support of the masses without which the reforms would have a dysfunctional effect and little impact on the economic growth they are supposed to stimulate. The support of elites and masses is only partially obtained through charismatic appeals; to endure it must largely be based on rational arguments and the ability to convince rather than to sway or coerce. This demands a carefully thought-out strategy of change, supported by an ideology that permits the insertion of innovation within a reassuring context of continuity and coherence. It demands also an efficient instrument to carry out the strategy.[2] The leader must be a good organizer and have at his disposal an efficient transmission belt made up of regional and local "cadres," capable not only of transmitting his message, but also of introducing notions of rationality, performance, and responsibility. The cadres must be able to stimulate a sense of participation without which the new structures will have no vitality. Finally, the successful leader must establish a high degree

339

of congruence between ideology, strategy, and organization in order to avoid discontinuities and contradictions and to allow for the insertion of innovations into a coherent whole. In the Tunisian experience this congruence has been the result of both fortunate timing and brilliant leadership. The Neo-Destour party was launched in the early thirties by a man who knew how to impose his vision of the good society to come, his sense of strategy, and his principles of organization. The components of successful leadership were present early enough to ensure undisputed legitimacy to the leader of the Party and then of the State. His charisma was an added source of recognition; but this would have been inoperant in the long run without more tangible qualities.

THE IDEOLOGY

Some form of ideology is necessary to legitimize development. As a system of explanation and promise, an ideological framework strengthens the legitimacy of a modernizing regime, for it helps clarify long term objectives and justify the methods used in their implementation. It establishes a system of norms on which to judge past, present, and future performances. It gives a sense of continuity and rationality to what would otherwise appear as unrelated and arbitrary innovations. It buttresses national unity and justifies the sacrifices that one generation is to make for the benefit of the next.

On the other hand, an ideology also establishes a set of high standards that may well endanger the political system if results lag too far behind goals. An ideology cannot remain purely mythical, nor can it be a foreign importation divorced from the indigenous political culture.

Unlike ideologies elsewhere in Africa, Destourian socialism is not a mere ritual but, rather, a reflection of actual policy. It is a guide to action in so far as it is translated into results through a realistic strategy and efficient party. The congruence between ideas and realizations stems from the pragmatic quality of Destourian ideology. This is stressed by the party propagandists who prefer to speak of Habib Bourguiba's "message" rather than use the term "ideology," fearing that the latter may be considered as a dogmatic blueprint of an ideal society that builds a screen between man and reality. They stress the fact that man is too complex to be offered a precise and immutable formula of social organization, that there is no ideal solution, that there are only imperfect ones. At best, the leader can only choose "revolutionary compromises" as the measure of man and social reality, but within "a dynamic perspective of progress" that gives direction to the strategy of change and is a realistic alternative to a dogmatic blueprint. Whether or not this dynamic perspective is too pragmatic to be considered an ideology, it serves the same purpose, since it is a legitimizing rationale for consensus building.

340

It is also a supple instrument for effective social change. Logically and ethically unassailable, it is at the same time vague and "unscientific." This vagueness is probably an asset, since the ideology can satisfy a wide range of opinion and can be adapted to changed conditions through reinterpretation. Thus, Destourian ideology has fitted equally well the liberal and socialist phases of the Bourguibist strategy of modernization. In 1961, the element of continuity was maintained when Bourguiba embarked on the Plan and the accompanying radical reforms of structure; "Destourian socialism" continued to be essentially an instrument to maintain social and political cohesion. It was enough to introduce a few innovations, such as the cooperative system and the "social function" of property, to pass from liberalism to socialism.

Bourguiba's message, whether ethics or ideology, includes three basic articles of faith. These are both assumptions concerning human nature and ideals to be forwarded. The first is a belief in human dignity and perfectibility. Human dignity, both individual and collective, calls for national self-determination, but is not satisfied with the winning and consolidation of independence. It calls also for the "promotion of man," the battle against underdevelopment, as well as for a continuous effort toward democracy. Democracy is the highest conquest of man, according to Bourguiba, but also the most difficult to realize.

The second principle, faith in human solidarity, further justifies nationalism, economic development, and the ultimate goal of democracy. National cohesion demands a fight against the centrifugal forces of regionalism and tribalism and all leftovers of the traditional structures of yesterday. It demands a strong and respected state transcending all vested interests. But, in the long run, the indestructible state must be anchored on a harmonious society of good citizens, conscious of their dignity, solidarity, and responsibility. Economic and social development is necessary, but, above all, to create the conditions of civic morality indispensable to the perpetuity of the state and to social and political harmony. In the final analysis, the goal is a psychic harmony in which man, well integrated in the society, reconciles in himself his social and individualistic tendencies.

The third article of faith is confidence in the supreme power of Reason. This means, first, a rational approach to problems, the full acceptance of the values underlying the rational and scientific approaches of Western culture, which are accepted in Tunisia without the reservations and ambivalence shown in other Arab countries. Reason also means realism and pragmatism, the objective appraisal of forces and problems and the realistic setting of objectives, or what Bourguiba has called the "politique des étapes," in which strategy is geared to the realization of what is attainable now, and yet concurrently contributes to the reach for long-range objectives. Realism is thus opposed to dogmatism, sentimentality, wishful thinking, and all forms of irrationality.

The combination of Bourguiba's three assumptions justifies the

341

preponderant role of pedagogy in the long struggle to transform man and society. Since man is rational, perfectible, and basically social, he can be educated toward modernity and good citizenship. The problem is to raise his intellectual and moral levels to make him understand the concordance between the general interest and his own interest. A national consensus, based on a rational acceptance of the common good, can be reached in regard both to goals and to methods of government. Once it is reached, genuine democracy becomes possible.

This is the broad and supple framework that made possible the transition from liberalism to socialism in 1961. The dignity of man was reinterpreted to demand a great effort at production and an insistence on better distribution of wealth, in order to ensure material conditions for moral and intellectual growth. Reason demanded the Plan, defined as the application of reason to economic problems. Solidarity demanded greater justice, a more equitable effort in sectorial and regional development, an emphasis on cooperatives as the highest form of economic and social organization, and the concept of property as "social function."

Thus, the coherence and continuity of the ideology are clearly kept with the introduction of Destourian socialism. The unitary ideology is left intact. No enemy, domestic or foreign, is singled out. The goals are still the promotion of man, social harmony, guided democracy. Destourian socialism is not an imported ideology nor a dogmatic one; it is pragmatic in its search for efficiency and in its adaptability to new conditions. It still claims to transform society through consent and not coercion. The state is not to be the great manager, but must only coordinate, harmonize, and regulate; the society itself should generate its own centers of decision-making, particularly decisions concerning management, so as to limit the role of the state. There is only a change in methods imposed by new conditions, since the hopes put in the liberal economy had not materialized. Thus, tribal and state lands that had been divided into individually-owned parcels to stimulate production are now regrouped into cooperatives for the same purpose, to maximize production.

Destourian socialism is also opposed to the generalization of the public ownership of the means of production demanded by the Marxists. Instead, it proposes the theory of the "social function of property," one of its main innovations. It is the negation of the right of "usus et abusus," traditionally considered the foundation of private property. It is also, and above all, the affirmation of the importance of sound management, a stimulus to production, an encouragement to greater effort and initiative.[3] In a sense, it is a device to make modern entrepreneurs out of the traditional bourgeois, generally merchants or owners of land, by giving them a strong incentive to modernize their methods or to move into more productive fields.

At the same time that Destourian socialism encourages efficient methods of production, it uses the concept of the social function of property as a useful weapon with which to make individuals adjust their production to collective needs. It can be used to discourage farmers from growing wheat if fruit trees are deemed more useful, to force them to use additional labor for intensive cultivation as a means to absorb unemployment, or to use fairer labor practices. It is, thus, the legitimizing concept for a whole gamut of reforms.

The other innovation of Destourian socialism is the emphasis given to cooperatives as a superior form of economic and social organization. The cooperative sector, however, is to coexist with the public and private sectors, this coexistence being proclaimed the source of social and political harmony. [4]

In the long run, the cooperative sector will prove its ability to reconcile conflicting interests by initiating a new framework for human relations, the power of decision being diffused among all economic and social agents. This democratic solution is applicable at a higher level than the enterprise. Through powerful and autonomous regional and national unions of cooperatives, the democratic ideal can spread from the bottom to the top and penetrate the state apparatus itself. The concept of joint participation in decisions is thus projected at the national level where all economic and social agents will participate in the decision-making process at the highest level. [5]

The ultimate goal is still to transform man by making him a truly social being, unselfish and cooperative. In the past, Bourguiba had emphasized civic education and "encadrement" as the means to create good citizenship; now he has added a third instrument, on the urging of his minister of Plan and National Economy, Ahmed Ben Salah. This third instrument, the cooperatives, in fact complements the first two, in that it is destined to create the proper structures for changing attitudes and behavior. Thus, "Bensalism" is not a heretical version of Bourguibism, as Jean Lacouture has put it. It is based on the same assumptions concerning human nature as Bourguibism, on the same goal of the harmonious society of good citizens, and largely on the same methods.

The coexistence of the three sectors justifies the continuation, and even the strengthening, of the unitary ideology. Until harmonious coexistence is ensured, the role of the party as the guardian of unity is more justified than ever. As it becomes responsible for the success of the Plan, it must call for efficiency, discipline, and solidarity; it must press for unity at all costs, particularly during the difficult period of adjustment to the new structures. The Plan creates a more important role for the party than it had immediately after independence. As the "motor of the economy," it is given definite functions of initiative, control, and mobilization. Planning also means a rejuvenation of the party, through the integration of the young and competent products of the University into the political system in such a way as to avoid a possible conflict of generations. The party is thus revitalized by being given new responsibilities and a new legitimacy. This illustrates the concordance of ideology, strategy, and organization, which needs to be made more explicit in this context.

343

THE STRATEGY

Speaking in Bucharest on July 12, 1968 (*L'Action*, 13 July 1968), Bourguiba explained to a Rumanian audience the essence of the Tunisian experiment. "Bourguibism," he said, is a method of dealing with problems, "a logic of action." "Truth for me is what is concrete. . . .If in the name of generous abstractions one risks creating new miseries, I say: 'this is wrong' and I turn my back to the theory to seek what is useful." What Tunisia has opted for is "an experimental socialism, an agreement daily negotiated with a changing reality . . . a socialism that makes one step forward only when society . . . is capable of absorbing what is being proposed."

Bourguiba's strategy stems from his existential view of man, considered as both the end and the means of progress. He is proud of the fact that he has succeeded in inculcating his sense of realism and efficiency into the Tunisian people. When he was asked, in an interview on French television, why he thought Tunisians were radically different from other Arabs, Bourguiba answered that the difference was due in large part to the Cartesian formation of the elite.[6] "We are concerned with logic as well as efficacy" he declared. Long before independence "we have impressed upon the Tunisian elite, the cadres, and the young people, the sense of efficacy, of political strategy." For the Arabs of the Middle East it is another story. "They have another mentality, they live in a world of sentiment, of passion, sometimes of unreality. Unfortunately, they have no leader courageous or honest enough to go at countercurrent . . . to bring cadres and youth to a more healthy concept of reality." He then gave a concise definition of a sound strategy for the Arab world that also defines his own strategy of development; "to create union through an efficient and coherent strategy at the service of precise objectives, taking into account what is feasible and preparing for each step."

Continuity and coherence must be maintained in a relatively fast tempo of change. What acts as a brake and cannot be legislated against is the limited capacity of the people to accept the new economic and social structures that cannot prove effective without their support. In the race toward progress the new economic structures are subordinated to the creation of new mental structures, since

all depends in the last analysis upon the degree of the mental evolution of man. . . . We can allow ourselves to accelerate the rhythm (of change) as fast as people's minds open themselves, and fortunately open minds are more and more numerous in Tunisia. This rhythm will become more rapid as the general level of the population is further raised.

The problem is thus to launch the maximum economic reforms compatible with the people's capacity to understand them and adjust to them. It is a see-saw process in which economic and mental structures have a reciprocal impact.

This concern with maintaining consensus by moving ahead cautiously explains Bourguiba's strategy in the first years of independence. The essential problem was to strengthen the new state and preserve at all costs the unity built during the long struggle for independence. Thus, he turned down the proposal for radical economic reforms urged by Ben Salah and the labor unions in 1955 and 1956, for he felt that they risked creating a clash between the conservative and radical wings of the modernist elite. Yet he dared to attack some of the strongholds of tradition by removing major obstacles to progress, such as the traditional type of education, the low status of the Moslem women, the "habous," since these basic reforms had the support of the modernist elite. An attack on traditionalism was thus a safe proposition as well as a way of reducing the position of those who had often collaborated with the French, or been the supporters of the Old Destour. At the same time, his attack consolidated the new values of nationalism and "democracy" by weakening the set of values that had kept the traditional society together and had justified acceptance of foreign domination.

Was the unitary ideology then discounted, when, in 1961, Bourguiba put into practice the ideas of Ben Salah, when the Plan was launched and structural reforms announced, together with the ideology of Destourian socialism? For there was a very real risk of antagonizing the conservative wing of the modernist elite, including large and small landlords and merchants and the rising group of entrepreneurs in the modern sector of the economy. The structural reforms threatened also to upset the equilibrium on which rested the economy of subsistence since they would offer no evident and immediate compensation for the income derived from a small piece of land or a small shop and they were even likely to increase, at least on the short run, the number of unemployed. The coalition of all victims, real and potential, of the structural reforms could therefore create an explosive situation, particularly since the policy of austerity would affect most Tunisians in one form or another.

On the other hand, the situation in 1961 was much more propitious than in 1956 for the Plan and for thorough economic and social reforms. There was real danger in 1956 of a clash between the bourgeoisie and the industrial proletariat. The latter was strongly organized in the UGTT (Union Générale des Travailleurs Tunisiens), a group that was as powerful as the Destour party and could become its rival. By 1961 the UGTT's strength had been curbed and its leadership was well in hand. A large segment of the modern bourgeoisie was now in power, forming a strong politico-administrative elite of technocrats, administrators, and party men. It was self-confident and thus willing to innovate within safe bounds.

The problems of development were also better understood in 1961 than in 1956. A good deal of experimentation, and of thinking about problems of economic growth, had resulted from the program of "economic and social promotion" that gave local party cells the initiative in formulating projects of development. The idea of planning and structural reforms had

345

made many converts. The younger elements of the elite had, in fact, become impatient and were pressing for a socialist solution, particularly of the nondogmatic type.

The problem then was to minimize the possible unpleasant consequences of the reforms while at the same time dramatizing the need for thorough reforms; i.e., to innovate while ensuring continuity. A great effort was made to convince owners of capital that the general interest corresponded in fact with their own individual interests and that they had nothing to fear from the State so long as they were productive and accepted a slight limitation of their freedom of choice, a limitation that was in fact to their own advantage. To the Sfaxians particularly, Bourguiba would, year after year, use the same arguments to incite them to give up old-fashioned practices of spending their money and to urge them to put their savings into productive channels. He would tell them that the State was there to protect their savings and make them fructify, not to seize them as in the old days. Their own enlightened self-interest demanded that they contribute money, effort, and initiative to help the country develop as fast as possible; for this was the price to pay to avoid social tensions and the possibility of class conflict. Destourian socialism was in fact protecting them, at a small cost, from the possibility of revolution.

For several years after the launching of the Plan, the scope and speed of change were relatively moderate. Starting with the Second Plan in 1964, the tempo of change became faster. Cooperative units of production multiplied in the North and South. Commercial reforms moved on at full speed. Was this increasing speed indicative of a new approach to social change? Would it indicate the success of Ben Salah's revolutionary approach as contrasted with Bourguiba's reformist stand and signify the abandonment of the unitary ideology and prudent strategy?

Critics of Ben Salah often accuse him of sacrificing the effectiveness of reforms for the sake of speed, a speed motivated by the need to reach the point of no return as quickly as possible, while he still has the backing of the President. Whether or not there is any truth in this accusation, it must be recognized that the basic strategy of change has not been abandoned; the speed of the reforms is not at the expense of the educational effort. Ben Salah has become the most active pedagogue of the regime, the indefatigable spokesman for the virtuous revolution. Week after week, in towns and villages, he keeps telling people of their own opportunities and responsibilities in economic development. They must count on themselves, not on the State. He keeps stressing that the precondition of economic growth is a systematic effort to open the minds of the people; they must rid themselves of the burdens of tradition, resignation, and isolation. His passion for pedagogy is a far cry from the radical position he took in 1956 when the UGTT Congress condemned "the error of trying to transform man and his morality, or society and its mores, through exhortation, advice and sermons. These are soporifics unworthy of a dynamic people. The individual and the collectivity can be reformed only within the framework of a profound revolution of economic structures, for it is on those structures that society rests in the final analysis."[7] Now he deems the reforms of mental structures as essential as the reforms of economic structures, and in fact the main condition for economic success.

He also stresses the pragmatic aspects of the reforms. Ready-made systems have proved their dangers, he says, for there is no magic formula for development. Since different methods are needed to fit different situations, intellectual honesty demands a constant search for better methods, a constant experimentation. His pragmatic approach is found in the relatively slow start in the program of structural reforms. At first, only some importers and wholesalers were affected by the commercial reforms and rather efficiently led from commercial activities to industrial entrepreneurship. Pragmatism is also found in the adoption of various types of cooperatives to fit regional conditions: service cooperatives, where private property is strongly anchored and agricultural methods relatively efficient; cooperative units of production in the wheat producing areas of the North where mechanization demands the regrouping of small parcels; cooperatives of polyculture in the Center and South where the key problem is water. Lastly, there is pragmatic experimentation with various types of economic organizations and various tempos of change in each of the 13 governorates.

The cooperative units of production that have multiplied in the Northwest could well be seen as products of realistic thinking rather than of ideological bias. They were established to introduce modern farming methods, to integrate the subsistence sector into the modern sector, to diversify production as well as to create a sound basis for community development. Small parcels, generally less than 20 acres, were regrouped around the nuclei of nationalized colon farms whenever possible, to benefit from collective mechanized farming methods. There were too many unskilled farmers to divide colon lands equitably and expect that they would not revert to traditional methods of cultivation; nor could these lands have been sold to a few individuals without maintaining, side by side, modern and traditional sectors, rich and poor farmers.

A good illustration of the practical approach of Ben Salah is found in the recent reform of commerce. After years of experimentation had led to wide differences in the nature and scope of the reform in the 13 governorates, the decision was reached in 1967 to establish a unified system applicable to the whole of Tunisia as a prelude to legislation. The governors met to discuss the problem; experts of Plan toured the country to gather information; a note of general orientation, distributed by Plan, established common approaches, criteria, and methods. It stated the objectives of the reforms; to shorten and rationalize the circuits of distribution and to reorient men and capital toward productive sectors. It was a question of increasing national production through better distribution and to facilitate planning through a more adequate determination of domestic markets. Even more important, it was a question of creating

347

maximum capital formation in commerce to allow for reinvestment in industry. This involved compressing the costs of distribution through a concentration of the units of distribution, shorter circuits, better management, and adequate capital. It also involved establishing efficient means of collecting profits for reinvestment purposes. The cooperative formula was adopted whenever possible but room was left for regrouping shopkeepers in private companies, a formula that was deemed more realistic in the cities. Different methods were worked out for the different sectors along lines that corresponded best to the assigned objectives. Thus, a highly pragmatic system was established on the basis of the experience required through experimentation. It attempted to reconcile the preference for the cooperative system as a factor of social harmony with the need to attract capital and use it in the most efficient way to produce sizeable savings for investment in industry. The "social function" of commerce was to serve both producers and consumers, but not at the expense of the general interest interpreted as the need for maximum capital formation for reinvestment. Commerce was only the most convenient instrument for the formation and collection of savings, thanks to its strategic position.

The only losers were those middle men who could not always see how their own interests coincided with the general interest; but presumably proper education would take care of that. Instead of using force, the state wanted to establish the reforms in collaboration with the people involved; hence, the experimental approach. Since persuasion and not force had to be employed, it was the role of the party, not of the administration, to initiate the kind of change that was likely to be objectionable. Ben Salah made it clear that the governors were given a free hand in experimenting with structural change as party leaders rather than as heads of the regional administration. For the party alone was in a position to convince people that they should accept some limitation to their freedom of choice, freedom to run their business or manage their farms as they always had. Through "dialogue" with the interested parties, it could explain and persuade.[8]

In conclusion, there seems to be a complete identity of view between Bourguiba and Ben Salah concerning timing, scope, speed, and methods of reform. Both agree on the danger of precipitate action and the need to subordinate the creation of new economic and social structures to the people's capacity for absorption. Their strategy of change is thus directly inspired by the Destourian ideology and the importance it gives to pedagogy. But the conservatism of peasants and shopkeepers would have delayed the reforms for many years if pedagogy alone had been used to change attitudes; and Tunisia could not afford to wait. Since 1964, at least, the solution seems to have been to act first and convince next. New cooperatives are planned and it is then the role of the party to explain to the people concerned the why and the how and to gain their support with a minimum of arm-twisting. The assumption is that they will sooner or later understand the concordance of their own interests with the general interest and will integrate themselves with the new structures and actively participate in their success. A second assumption is that the new structures themselves will have a strong pedagogical value, especially in combination with the continued educational effort of the party.

Both education and experimentation illustrate the all important role played by the party in facilitating the implantation of new structures. They illustrate, also, the interdependence of strategy and organization, the latter being the servant of the former, but also its guide, since the strategy needs to be subordinated to the ability of the party to carry it out with the minimum of constraint.

ORGANIZATION: REGIONAL
AND LOCAL LEADERSHIP

From the inception of the Neo-Destour party, Bourguiba has paid special heed to the problem of organization and leadership. His aim was to create an efficient instrument for carrying out his strategy of national liberation. After independence the problem was to adapt the party to its new tasks, to establish its proper relationship to the State, modify its organization, and renew its cadres. The party was to maintain an effective transmission belt for a two-way communication system between the political elite and the masses. It was also to bridge the gap between generations and thus ensure continued national cohesion.[9]

The concept of "encadrement," implying both organization and a "hierarchy of competence and responsibility," translates in organizational terms the pedagogical concern of the regime, itself anchored on basic assumptions concerning man and society. Encadrement is thus in accordance with the ideology and strategy, since it offers the methods best fitted for effective modernization, including the implementation of Bourguiba's vision of "guided democracy."

According to Bourguiba, democracy is "the highest manifestation of human dignity," since it gives man the feeling that he is governing himself. But he insists that it is also an objective most difficult to reach and that it is, in fact, the last stage in the process of development, since its preconditions are a strong and respected state, a homogeneous nation, and high enough standards of living and of education. Time and again he says that democracy demands of the people a rational approach to problems, the ability to make sound analyses and select the right leaders, and an acute sense of the general interest.

Until the citizens have acquired a clear awareness of the general interest and are able to master their impulses, participation in decision making must be gradual and follow the development of the citizens' sense of responsibility. Until people have acquired enough maturity, democracy has to be guided. This means that only a selected minority of citizens, the

349

"responsables" of the party, can play an active part in the elaboration of decisions and the choice of leaders. It is the role of the small minority to lead others in their apprenticeship for democracy. Thus, an elitist principle is made to serve a democratic goal.[10]

Bourguiba pointed out with pride in November 1962 that the strength of the party, built up after decades of struggle, derived from the quality of the leaders and an organization constantly adapted to changing conditions. From the beginning the party was organized "to become an efficient instrument for a well thought-out strategy, with a hierarchical structure, elections at all levels and organs of arbitration to give party workers a sense of organized action and of a hierarchy of responsibility." With independence came the difficult aftermath of victory; "for a fighting party victory may indeed be a factor of disintegration and death, just as it may commit it to dictatorship or the pursuit of wealth." He explained that most of the early party officials trained during the long struggle were now used for building the state, since few citizens had been prepared for public responsibilities. This left a large empty space in the party.[11] With the rush of new members to the party and a scarcity of competent leaders, there was a risk of imbalance between cadres and members. Hence arose the need to change the structure of the party in 1958 through replacing the elected leaders of the Federations by appointed delegates, whose task was to select and train local leaders. Once their mission was accomplished, it was possible in 1963 to go back to the principle of elections and to create the Coordination Committees, the members of which are again elected by the representatives of the cells.

With the advent of Plan and the structural reforms of the economy, the political formation of the cadres had become inadequate. Technical training was indispensable for them, said the President. They had to have some knowledge of agricultural problems, of finances and budgeting, of problems of equipment and investment, of cooperatives. Party cadres had to be well informed. But similarly administrators and technicians now needed "to adopt a militant spirit, widen their horizons, abandon their ivory tower. . . .They have to join in the discussions of the cells to improve their knowledge and to come into contact with the people."[12] A new type of *militant* was needed, and the old fighters had to be prevented from keeping the new people out "at the risk of pushing them toward other political formations, at the risk of sclerosis and of a conflict of generations."

Thus, with the establishment of the Plan, regional and local party leaders need not only to explain and convince but to assume quasi-managerial functions of initiative, control, and coordination. They must somehow combine technical efficiency with the ability to guide, coax, and inspire. Competent modernizers, they must understand both the technical and human aspects of development. Obviously, few leaders can come close to such high expectations. The surprising element is not so much the relative failure of cadres at the grass-roots level as the relative success of the regional leadership in handling both the technical and human aspects of the problems of development.

At the regional level the supreme instance of the party is the Coordination Committee, whose members are elected by the cells' representatives every two years. This is the essential link between the national elite and local cadres, as well as between the party and the administration. Its chairman, the Governor, and its vice-chairman, the Secretary General, can be considered the regional representatives of the national political elite, since most of them are young university graduates. The other members of the Coordination Committee represent the best of the local party cadres; they are elected but the party headquarters see to it that only the most dynamic and competent ones are chosen.[13]

An important function of the Coordination Committee is to oversee the implementation of reforms, while avoiding direct administrative involvement. Frequent contacts with the base are made to obtain a complete and objective picture of the problems involved. Not being directly involved in administrative matters, members of the Coordination Committee are in a position to look at a situation critically and to make suggestions for improving methods and procedures and for stimulating performances.

The main function of the Coordination Committee is, of course, educational. This involves the training of officers and members of cells through frequent visits, through seminars, conferences, and "journées d'études." Seminars are also organized to train the cadres of cooperatives in human relations and their members in the "cooperative spirit." The conferences of cadres at the local and regional level that coordinate the programs of the cells also allow several hundred "militants" in each governorate to educate themselves through the work they do in commissions and plenary sessions.

The commissions and subcommissions of the Coordination Committee, the most important of which are those responsible for economic and social development, are the meeting places between party militants, administors and technicians. This is where problems, both technical and human, are discussed and solutions are found. This is where the confrontation takes place between the political, social, and technical aspects of the reforms, in an open discussion among participants who feel on an equal footing and free to express their own views.

The most interesting by-product of the work of the commissions is the symbiosis that is taking place through teamwork; party militants become aware of technical problems and technicians of political, social, and psychological ones. The young technicians, fresh out of the University, used to look down on the ignorant and verbose politicians. The latter had no love for the young technocrats. Now, according to Governor Hédi Baccouche,[14] mutual respect is replacing old prejudices as each side has come to understand the importance of the other's role and to appreciate its contribution to the solution of a problem. Active participation and frequent disagreement have had great pedagogical value, he pointed out. A

351

cohesive regional elite is being created that has the feeling of actual participation in the reaching of important decisions, all the more so since the governor generally accepts the recommendations of various commissions. The concrete aspects of the problems have helped to avoid a clash of abstractions and have permitted great latitude in the adoption of means. Thus, old militants have acquired a taste for techniques and have come to specialize in some aspects of the economic reforms, while many technicians have become active militants.

A solidarity of the regional elite is being developed as all those concerned partake of the feeling of working toward the transformation of society around concrete problems. Political opposition thus tends to disappear, the governor said, since every competent person is called upon to participate in the work of a commission, whatever his political views. This feeling of solidarity, he insisted, is a direct result of the Plan. Communication and coordination have led to the awareness of interdependence among the various aspects of the economic and social life of the nation. The multiplicity of coordinating agencies is thus justified by their psychological usefulness as much as by their functional roles.

It is not surprising that the regional elite, most of them young people with secondary or higher education, should find their functions highly rewarding, and even exhilarating. They are the privileged few who are detached enough from the more prosaic aspects of the reforms to enjoy the excitement of innovation and control. A sense of self-importance combines with involvement and the certitude of playing a useful role in the development of their country. In close contacts with both the national political elite and the local cadres, they can appreciate the strategic importance of their functions.

If we pass now from the regional elite to the local cadres we find a less competent, less dynamic, and less homogeneous group of people. And yet it is here that efficient leadership matters most since the local leaders are those who directly transmit the message, who are most directly involved in the daily problems created by the reforms, and who are also the most directly responsible for their success. It is at the grass-roots level that the role of the party is both crucial and demanding. The cells have a direct responsibility in the field of economic and social development. Cell officers are responsible for various aspects of the reforms, including cooperatives. Commissions on economic and social development and on "orientation and training" are directly concerned with the many problems raised by the reforms. Cell officers are called upon to explain and convince, to "animate" and supervise. The cell prepares the ground for the establishment of a new cooperative through a lengthy campaign of explanation.[15] Once established, it acts as the cooperative's godfather. It is up to the cell's officers to broaden the civic education of the members of the cooperative and in cooperation with the URC (Regional Union of Cooperatives) to train them in their responsibilities and to incite participation in management.

The local cadres have all too often failed to create a sense of involvement and participation in decision making on the part of the peasants. The latter are all too likely to believe that they are employed by the State and that the State makes all decisions for them and is alone responsible for their welfare. Few are those who can succeed in coaxing the general assembly of the cooperatives to discuss problems and accept responsibilities. Yet, without active participation, the cooperative is in danger; when people consider themselves uninvolved, low morale results and this, in turn, breeds low productivity.

A comparison of the relative effectiveness of regional as against grass-root leadership suggests the limits inherent in the policy of encadrement. However intensely indoctrinated by the regional elite, the local cadres cannot be pulled out of their environment and made into effective innovators. They remain ambivalent in their new roles—of modern demeanor when dealing with the regional and local hierarchy and of traditional outlook in their relations with fellow peasants. They can hardly be expected to rise above their own limitations as uneducated peasants attached to their traditional ways, despite the efforts made by the regional elite to educate and motivate them. They are "transition cadres," bridging the gap until the next generation of leaders, now at school, can take over. They often think that their role is limited to making the other peasants respect a certain number of rules. Hardly comprehending the purposes of the reforms, they cannot adapt and innovate. They prefer to see in the cooperative only what is advantageous to them and in their functions the psychological rewards of bureaucratic prestige.[16]

The limitations of the "animateur," in a milieu hostile or indifferent to reform, suggest that the milieu itself need be receptive enough for a leader to have an impact as an agent of change. In the long run, receptivity to change will result from the new knowledge and values taught in schools, as well as from the impact of the new socioeconomic structures themselves. The sons and daughters of the cooperative farmers may then be ready for active participation and integration into the cooperative. Perhaps the role of the party now is less to convince than to hold the line until the impact of the school and the cooperative itself is fully felt. It can capitalize on its prestige, on its two-way communication system, and on the militancy of many of its members to discourage opposition, but it is not likely to be effective pedagogue as long as the people themselves are not able to absorb change.

The reforms of structures have perhaps been more successful in mobilizing elites than masses.[17] By making a few thousand people participate in decision making at the regional and local levels, the reforms have produced dedicated militants who have become the bulwark of the regime in which they feel integrated and vital; and this has occurred independently of their actual performance in convincing large numbers. This political asset is, however, temporary unless the gap between elite and masses is successfully bridged. This demands a large scale effort to improve

353

the quality of local cadres, an effort that is now being made. It demands, also, time to digest change and consolidate the new institutions.

In the long run, political encadrement may well be self-defeating unless the "hierarchy of competence and responsibility" can make room for genuine democratic rule, even at the cost of efficiency. The hierarchical pattern will have an inevitable tendency to perpetuate itself unless a conscious effort is soon made to allow the guided ones to learn through their own errors.

In the long run also, the political culture imparted by the one-party rule and the unitary ideology is likely to prove inadequate once people develop new needs through education and higher living standards and make new demands on the political system. Some form of political pluralism may then have to replace party hegemony under the rule of the man of destiny. In the meanwhile, the experience acquired in decentralization and teamwork at the regional and local levels may prove a strong incentive to adopt a decision making formula that involves large numbers of competent participants at all levels of the political system. In this sense the autocratic ruler will have prepared the way for democratic experimentation. By encouraging frequent discussion of problems and constructive criticism, he will have created the psychological preconditions for meaningful democratic structures.

The present-day autocratic ruler will have left strong assets to his successors: a coherent and nondogmatic ideology and a strategy adaptable either to rapid change or to cautious experimentation; an ethos of efficiency that has already permeated large sectors of the society and has acquired credibility through tangible accomplishments; a well-organized and disciplined party which, through renewing itself and remaining open, can probably ensure an orderly transfer of power and a new legitimacy and can perhaps even create the institutional base fitting the pluralistic society of tomorrow.

POSTSCRIPT

Shortly after the publication of this article, Ahmed Ben Salah was condemned to ten years of penal servitude and his economic and social policy was abruptly terminated. The return to laissez-faire was accompanied by a sharp inflation and a rapid deterioration of the living standards of the masses. On the other hand, the expected liberalization of the regime did not take place and its main champion, Ahmed Mestiri, resigned in September, 1971 (*Le Monde*, 7 September 1971). Deprived of its Socialist ideology and strategy, the Party is threatened with sclerosis and can probably no longer serve to prevent a dangerous polarization of opinion.

Several observations can now be made concerning this unexpected turn of events. The first is that Ben Salah's decision to extend the cooperative

354

system to the whole country was a grave political mistake that is difficult to account for. The second is that, under the appearance of unity, the political elite was highly heterogeneous and had powerful conservative elements ready to strike back when their vital interests were at stake. The third is that the health of the regime depended on the health of one man; physically diminished by his illness, the President apparently did not foresee the political consequences of Ben Salah's initiative and backed him up only to adandon him a few months later under the pressure of his entourage. Now that he has regained health and vigor, the President seems determined to continue to impose his will through the instrument of a Party that has lost its main asset—its appeal to youth. The last comment is that most foreign observers—and this writer in particular—entertained a number of illusions about the Tunisian experiment in social engineering, including the vital role played by the Party.

NOTES

1. The Neo-Destour party split from the Old Destour in 1934. Under the leadership of Habib Bourguiba, a young lawyer educated at the University of Paris and deeply influenced by French Cartesian thought and Jacobin political tradition, the Neo-Destour soon became a well organized and effective mass party, with no fewer than 300 cells by 1937. Unlike the Old Destour, which was a Tunis-based party appealing mainly to the traditional elite, most of the Neo-Destour leaders had a French university education and most of the party members were recruited in the coastal towns and villages of the Sahel. The new style of leadership combined political education and organization with a nationalist mystique and a positive program of economic and social reforms. Thanks to disciplined mass support, Bourguiba could carry out his strategy of liberation that led to the granting of internal autonomy in 1955 and to full independence in 1956.

2. Tactical and personal qualities of leadership are assumed. They include the ability to gather and weigh proper information, make rapid decisions, delegate responsibilities, inspire loyalty, control the execution of policies, etc. The line between strategy and tactics is, of course, somewhat arbitrary. The problems of scope and speed of change, of proper timing, of selection of major objectives and methods are considered here of strategic, rather than tactical, significance.

3. See the editorials of Mohamed Sayah, director of the PSD (Parti Socialiste Destourien), in L'Action, Tunis, 13-14 February 1968.

4. "Le Séminaire National sur la Coordination des Secteurs Economiques, Tunis, les 10 et 11 Septembre 1965" (Tunis, 1965).

5. See also Ahmed Ben Salah's speech on the first National Seminar on Cooperation, 15-20 July 1963 (La Voie Cooperative, Tunis, November-December 1963).

6. *L'Action*, 31 March 1968.
7. *Sixiéme Congrés National de l'U.G.T.T.*, 20-23 September 1956 (Rapport économique, Tunis, 1956).
8. *L'Action*, 13 February 1968. It is significant that the Minister of Defense, Mr. Mestiri, resigned his post in January 1968 over the issue of commercial reforms and the way in which governors were allowed to launch them without the benefit of previous legislation. He called this "arbitrary rule." To Mestiri's argument on behalf of legality and predictability, Bourguiba answered by stressing the concept of experimentation and dynamic evolution: "To those who ask where we are going I will answer that I could not say, for each step leads to the next in opening unforeseen perspectives and imposing new action." (*L'Action*, 28 January 1968). It is widely believed in Tunis that Mr. Mestiri will not long remain in the apolitical limbo which he courageously entered. This would fit the President's strategy of recuperating competent lieutenants as soon as it is politically feasible.
9. See Clement H. Moore, *Tunisia Since Independence, the Dynamics of One-Party Government* (Berkeley and Los Angeles, 1965) and Lars Rudebeck, *Party and People: A Study of Political Change in Tunisia* (Stockholm, 1967).
10. See (in *L'Action*) Bourguiba's speeches of 26 April 1966; 19 December 1967; 21 October 1964; 27 January 1968; 30 December 1968.
11. Speeches (in *L'Action*) of 22 November 1962; 19 October 1964.
12. Speech (in *L'Action*) of 22 November 1962.
13. At Djendouba the cell representatives elected four "wrong men" to the Committee of Coordination in 1967. The director of the party appointed four other men to sit with the duly elected members. The same thing happened at Gabés where one member of the Coordination Committee was appointed. Since the representatives of the people were not competent enough to exercise a sound choice, it was the duty of the party leadership to appoint proper leaders. This is what the director of the party told local "militants" at Djendouba, when he scolded them for their lack of maturity and sound judgment.
14. Interview with the author, 10 July 1967. Hedi Baccouche was then governor of Bizerte. Shortly afterward he was appointed governor of Sfax, where he proved as successful as in Bizerte in implementing the structural reforms.
15. This is not always the case. In a speech to the Central Committee of the PSD (*L'Action*, 23 March 1969), Bourguiba alluded to the bloody incident that had been caused by the creation of a production unit in the Sahel village of Ouardanine. This incident, he said, was due to the "unforgivable" incomprehension of the officers of the cell, who should have known how to handle the situation. He pointed out that lack of imformation about the state of mind of the people was the greatest danger that faced the party. On other occasions, the President made it clear that he was also aware of the shortcomings of local administrators who often ignore the legitimate grievances of the

people or have no sympathy for them. (See his speech of 7 October 1968.)

16. Lilia Ben Salem, "Les Cadres de l'économie localé en Tunisie." To be published in *Revue Tunisienne des Sciences Sociales.*

17. The assumption in this article of a broad consensus among the elites may seem to be contradicted by the dual opposition of conservatives and radicals. The latter was given great publicity by the September 1968 trial of students involved in the manifestation that took place at the University the previous March. Severe jail sentences seemed to most observers totally out of proportion to the gravity of the incidents. The official thesis of a plot against the security of the State was hardly convincing, even to many party militants who saw in the repression a grave political mistake. Then the director of the "Sureté nationale" was arrested in December for excess of zeal, and the extensive power of the director of the party was curtailed by the appointment of a liberal associate director. As a consequence, decisions that used to be made unilaterally by the party director are now made by the Political Bureau. The morale of the liberal party militants has greatly improved, as well as that of a number of left-wing intellectuals who, for the first time, are participating in the discussions of the party's ideological committee. Some of the imprisoned students were freed in March 1969, another indication of the new trend. All this is to suggest that the "broad consensus" has been reaffirmed despite swings of the pendulum, personal and regional rivalries, and disagreement about policies. Bourguiba's inimitable style contributes to keeping it alive; he not only sees to it that rival clans keep coexisting peacefully, but he carefully avoids creating lasting resentments among associates temporarily out of favor. The recent closing of the ranks of party leaders and their effort at collective decision making should also contribute to the maintenance of the consensus.

PATTERNS
OF ELITE SUCCESSION
IN THE PROCESS
OF DEVELOPMENT

John H. Kautsky

The following pages attempt to trace the various paths of political change that societies may follow in the process of economic development. Politics is conceived of as involving conflicts of interest, and we shall, therefore, emphasize not only change rather than stability, but also conflict rather than consensus. This requires first of all an analysis of those divisions in society that might give rise to conflicts. The lines of conflict differ greatly from society to society, but since we here generalize about all societies undergoing economic development, we must draw the lines very loosely and roughly. Thus, we are concerned with the politicization of broad socio-economic groupings, like peasants, industrial workers, and urban middle strata of artisans, traders, etc., without distinguishing between groups within them or paying attention to divisions cutting across them, like ethnic or religious ones.

Primarily, our focus is on various types of elites, not because we believe that any society as a whole is governed by some one power elite, but because in societies with limited political participation major decisions at the national governmental level, are made by a relatively few people. This does not mean, however, that others may not make decisions within the army or the church, within the village or the tribe, within the factory or the trade union. In underdeveloped countries, we distinguish broadly between two types of elites. One of these is the aristocrats, that is, those who control (but do not necessarily own) the land and the peasants, and who have retained the values appropriate to such an elite in the traditional society, notably those relating to the maintenance of their control of land and peasants. The other elite comprises the modernizers, that is, those who

From John H. Kautsky, "Patterns of Elite Succession in the Process of Development," *Journal of Politics* 31 (May 1969): 359-96. Reprinted by permission of the author and the publisher.

have received an education or training appropriate to an industrially advanced society, have adopted some of its values and seek to realize them in their own underdeveloped society. The concepts of aristocrats and modernizers must be broadly interpreted to be applicable to most underdeveloped societies and even then they will not fit all of them. Thus, where there were only tribal but no traditional societies (as defined below) in the past, as in large parts of Africa, one cannot speak of an aristocracy at all, and some of our generalizations may therefore not apply there. Furthermore, the aristocrats and the modernizers only relatively exceptionally appear as groups in politics, that is, as united by common interests and common political behavior. Sometimes, one can ignore divisions within each grouping and generalize broadly about them as groups. More often, however, we will stress conflict among groups within the aristocracy and among the modernizers as the principal form of the politics with which we will be concerned. Indeed, the diversification and proliferation of the elite groupings constitutes much, though by no means all, of the story here outlined, in terms of the major group conflicts, the various patterns of political change that may take shape in the course of economic development.

THE TRADITIONAL SOCIETY AND
DEVELOPMENT FROM WITHIN
AND FROM WITHOUT

Since any change is relative to the condition preceding it, a discussion of patterns of political change must begin with some reference to the politics of traditional society. By this term we mean an agrarian society composed of an aristocracy and a number of primitive peasant villages under its control, that has not been subject to any impact of economic development from within or without. If one seeks to generalize about the politics of traditional societies, one is struck by uniformities across the centuries and various cultures.[1] Since traditional societies are to be found in the past of most present-day societies, no matter how advanced—the United States being one of the few major exceptions—and since significant remnants of traditionalism, especially in the realm of ideology, are left in all of these, no sharp distinction between a Western and a non-Western political process can be drawn.

Traditional societies are frequently formed by the conquest of a number of primitive peasant villages by a nomadic tribe which then becomes an aristocracy generally intent on conquering more territory and peasants. Aristocrats and peasants remain sharply distinct, often ethnically and culturally, and always in terms of class position and functions. The aristocracy is, above all, concerned with warfare and government, the latter chiefly an extractive enterprise involving taxation, and with some auxiliary functions such as religious administration, the maintenance of

359

communications and of water works. Given these functions, aristocracies develop value systems stressing such concepts as honor and glory, service and duty, and contempt for manual labor and moneymaking. The peasantry on the other hand, which supports the aristocracy through its services or payment of taxes, tribute, or rent, carries on agricultural work and maintains a high degree of autonomy within its villages. In sharp contrast to that of the aristocracy, its value system tends to stress the benefits of frugality and of peace.[2]

Given their isolation and unchanging existence, the peasants cannot conceive of any fundamental change in their position and could, in any case, not organize to bring it about. Usually they rise up against aristocratic rule only in response to a short-run deterioration in their condition. Such peasant revolts are relatively rare and almost invariably futile as long as there is no economic development and no urban influence on the peasants. Apart from such revolts, there is no political interaction, that is, no conflict, between the two major classes. Politics, the conflict for scarce resources like power and prestige and material wealth, goes on within classes, within each village community among peasants, and, beyond the village level, within the aristocracy. Indeed, what history we learn of traditional societies consists mostly of intra-aristocratic politics—wars and conquests, changes in boundaries and in dynasties, marriages and deaths of rulers.

In addition to peasants and aristocrats, there are those in the towns and cities of traditional societies, who, directly or indirectly, serve the needs of the aristocracy, such as servants and clerks, entertainers, artists and early scientists and philosophers, and craftsmen and merchants.[3] We will loosely refer to these collectively as the old middle class. Generally these people are as incapable as peasants of making an effective revolution or of demanding reform, though in the guilds we find the first organizations that can acquire some concessions from the aristocracy.

In some places in Western Europe, in a slow process beginning in the late Middle Ages, some members of this old middle class did develop enough power to become independent of and eventually to challenge the predominance of the aristocracy. They thereby broke the uniform pattern of traditional politics that had until then prevailed throughout the world and thus initiated a process of change that is by now encompassing the entire world and is, for all we know, an endless one. Here we need not describe the process of modernization as it took place in Europe. What is important for us to stress is that if economic change develops from within a society, the process of accompanying political change is different than if the impact of economic change comes to a society from without. It must not, therefore, be assumed that the present-day underdeveloped countries must follow the Western European pattern of politics.

During the gradual emergence of a bourgeoisie out of the old middle class in Western Europe, the aristocracy had time to adapt itself to change. Monarchies grew more powerful and absolute, and the feudal aristocracy turned into a court aristocracy. Professional centralized bureaucracies, judiciaries, and armies developed and the Church, too, became attached to the court, while royalist policies of mercantilism strengthened the bourgeoisie. In contrast, in the now underdeveloped countries, where economic change has come, generally much more suddenly, from without, that is, from already advanced countries, the aristocracy, if there is one at all, does not have time to build such institutional defenses and the accompanying ideological ones of conservatism. Its demise tends to be much more abrupt and definitive therefore. A comparison of the fate of the Russian aristocracy or the Indian maharajahs with that of the British aristocracy or of such remnants of French aristocratic rule as the centralized bureaucracy or clericalism is instructive in this respect.

Once strong enough, the bourgeoisie in Western Europe could challenge the aristocracy, most openly in the French Revolution, and its ideology of liberalism began to assert itself. In other now industrially advanced countries, notably Germany and Japan, aristocrats themselves sponsored industrialization through and in alliance with native private capitalists who had never managed effectively to oppose the aristocracy. To neither of these two processes is there a parallel in underdeveloped countries, where initial industrialization generally rests on the investment of foreign rather than native capital and where private capitalists are rare or absent. On the other hand, modernizing intellectuals, operating through governments they control, may play a major role in the process of industrialization, while the chief function of their counterparts in Western Europe was merely to serve as ideologists for other groups.

Among the latter were radical—anarchist, syndicalist and socialist—labor movements which turned against the bourgeoisie and the remnants of the aristocracy in Western Europe and thus tended to bring these two former enemies together. Also reacting to industrialization, despairing strata of the old middle class along with some unemployed workers and peasants feeling threatened by modernization, were sometimes radicalized to form Fascist movements. These turned both against labor and against aristocracy and bourgeoisie—though where they came to power, it was in an uneasy alliance with aristocratic and bourgeoisie groups against labor and against political changes associated with industrialization.[4]

In so far as industrial workers and members of the old middle class and the peasantry become politicized by the impact of industrialization in underdeveloped countries, the immediate effect is not, as it was in Europe, deep and bitter conflict within the society. On the contrary, since industrialization comes from without, hostilities to it can be turned outward, and most of the politically involved groups can achieve unity under the banner of anti-colonialism or anti-imperialism. The resulting movement is often called a nationalistic one, though, unlike that of European nationalism, its focus of unity is not ethnic, linguistic, or cultural. The anti-colonial movement typically cuts across racial, language, and religious as well as social class lines.[5]

Economic development from without comes either through colonialism, which we generally define as the relationship between an industrially advanced country and an underdeveloped one serving as its source of raw materials, or through an attempt by a traditional regime to strengthen itself against advanced foreign countries by introducing some aspects of their societies or through both processes. Let us now look at how the impact of economic development from without affects the major social groupings in the traditional society as well as the new ones created by that impact.[6]

THE MODERNIZING MOVEMENT IN UNDERDEVELOPED COUNTRIES

One of the first consequences of contact between a traditional and a modern industrial society is likely to be the growth of a group of modernizers in the former. These are people, initially generally drawn from the aristocracy or the upper strata of the old middle class, who receive their higher education or at least live for some time in an advanced country (often having been sent there by the traditional or colonial authorities either as students or as exiles). Or they may be educated at home by the standards of an advanced country or trained in an institution imported or imitated from an industrial country, like a modern army, governmental or corporate bureaucracy or a trade union. Most of them can be regarded as intellectuals, if that term is broadly defined. In any case, they acquire professional skills and, above all, values appropriate to a modern society. In general, these involve a new relationship to time, to nature, and to their fellowmen[7] and, more specifically, they include a belief in the possibility and desirability of material progress, of greater wealth for all, of greater equality, and of mass participation in politics. No matter what advanced country comes to serve as their model of a proper political system and society and in what ideological form—liberal, democratic-socialist, or communist—they absorb their new values, the modernizers become revolutionaries in their own societies, dedicated to rapid modernization. Since economic backwardness and dependence on foreign powers are in their minds inextricably related, each one seeming to cause the other, their program demands generally both industrialization and independence.

The modernizers have no capital to invest, there is initially no wealthy bourgeoisie, the aristocracy is prevented from investing its wealth by its anti-business attitudes and its lack of interest in industrialization, and foreign enterprises are not trusted by the modernizers to establish the kind of industry that would produce wealth and consumer goods for the underdeveloped country. The government, then, becomes the only agency that can do the job of rapid industrializing through taxation and control of foreign investment and foreign aid and through its ability to mobilize and organize large numbers of people. Modernizers hence must capture control of the government to turn it into such an agency.

To obtain governmental power, modernizers must remove not only foreign colonialism but also the native aristocracy from power (unless, of course, there is none, as in parts of Africa). Since the power of the aristocracy generally rests on its control of the land and the peasants, the modernizers advocate land reform, which is to give the peasant control of the land and its products and thus to undermine the economic and political position of the aristocracy. Land reform is, no doubt, also advocated by the modernizers, because they want to raise the living standards and the status of the peasant, in line with their commitment to material abundance and equality, and because they want to secure the support of the peasantry for their programs, but land reform and its effects cannot be fully understood if it is not seen as an attack on the aristocracy too.

The modernizing movement may be composed almost exclusively of the modernizers, as we define them. In time, however, it may also be joined by segments of virtually all major social groupings in the underdeveloped country as the society becomes transformed under the impact of foreign industrial influence. Thus, what labor movements develop in the early, generally foreign-owned industrial enterprises—the mines and plantations, the railroads and ports, and the processing industries—often come under the leadership of the anti-colonial modernizers. In some countries, indeed, unions, under modernizing leadership, become the backbone of the entire modernizing movements, as, for example, in Tunisia, Guinea, and Kenya. In some countries, to be sure, both in Africa and the Near East, the thin stratum of workers that is organized constitutes a privileged elite tied closely to the colonial economy and thus champions the *status quo*.

As everywhere in the early stages of industrialization, workers generally are discontented, perhaps not so much because they live in abject poverty—they were just as poor and possibly even poorer when they were peasants—but because, as people totally unprepared for change by their unchanging peasant existence and value-system, they are suddenly subjected to very radical change, moving from the security of their family and village to the anonymity and loneliness of the urban slum, from a life regulated by customs and traditions regarded as natural to one subject to harsh industrial discipline. Since the boss against whom the worker directs his most immediate discontent is quite often a colonial foreigner and the government which he opposes may also be a foreign colonial one or a foreign-influenced aristocratic one, labor discontent can feed into the anti-colonial unity led by the modernizers.

With few exceptions, like the Russian Narodniks, modernizers prefer to seek their mass support among workers who are both physically and, having been uprooted from the traditional order, intellectually and psychologically more accessible to their appeals than peasants. However, where modernizers fail in the cities, which are also strongholds of colonial and aristocratic power, and are driven into the countryside, they may turn for support to the peasants. Though less so than the workers', the peasants' traditional way of life, too, has been disrupted by the intrusion of a money economy into the village community, sometimes the introduction of one-crop economies and dependence on the impersonal forces of the world market, often dependence on money-lenders, middle men, and merchants, and the evolution of "big peasants" on the one hand and landless ones on the other. Even if some of these changes have financially favorable effects, they all, simply because they are changes, produce discontent and frustration among the peasants.[8] These feelings can be turned into support for the modernizing movements by their anti-colonial and anti-aristocratic appeals and particularly their promises of land reform.

The modernizing movements come to power with peasant support only exceptionally, since it is difficult to mobilize, and modernizers can usually manage to gain power without it. In a few important instances, however, they have done so, notably in China, Algeria, and Cuba.[9] Since modernizers turn to the countryside only after they have failed to overcome their enemies by peaceful or violent means in the cities, that is, if they confront the determined opposition of the government, the modernizing movement resting on peasant support generally initiates a civil war, and, more specifically, a guerrilla war.[10]

The old and the new lower classes—peasants and workers—are not the only reservoir from which modernizers may draw support for their movements. Members of the old middle class, particularly its lower strata of small shopkeepers, traders, and artisans, facing the competition of cheap imports from industrialized countries, are threatened with unemployment or descent into the working class. Again, their discontent is a response not only—and not necessarily—to economic decline, but to change for which life in the traditional society had not prepared them. A change in their class position in a highly stratified society involves a loss of status, of prestige, and of self-respect. Change from the small shop, just as from the village, to the factory means the physical as well as the psychological separation of one's work and its products from one's personal life and hence what is often called the alienation of the worker. Since the source of the frustration of the old middle class may be perceived as foreign, people from this grouping, too, can be attracted to join the anti-colonial movement led by the modernizers. Lacking the organizations of industrial workers and the numbers of the peasantry (who, if sufficiently discontentedd, can also be organized by the modernizers for military purposes), the old middle class is not likely to add much strength to this movement, however. One overt form its participation may take is that of riots and mob action, especially against the persons and property representing the colonial power.

Even some members of the upper classes may join the modernizers' anti-colonial movement. The native bourgeoisie is generally small and politically weak, given the anti-business bias of traditional ideology, which on this point is shared by both aristocracy and modernizing intellectuals. Some of its members, like native plantation and mine owners, producing raw materials for export to industrialized countries, are so tied to the colonial economy that they are not likely to oppose it. But others produce consumer goods, like textiles, in competition with those of the advanced industrial countries or are engaged in industries, like steel manufacturing in India, that depend for their expansion on the expansion of other industries at home. Such businessmen may well share the desires of the modernizers for further industrialization, independence (which may bring protective tariffs), and land reform (which may improve their domestic market).

When a traditional society comes into contact with an industrial one, the aristocracy generally remains in control of the former. This is true not only where the traditional society remains an independent country, but even where it becomes a colony, for then some system of indirect rule is likely to prevail. The industrial power or its business enterprises operating in the underdeveloped country rely on the aristocracy to maintain so-called law and order. In return, the aristocracy receives a share of the proceeds of the colonial economy, whether in the form of royalties or export taxes, rent, subsidies, or bribes.[11] As this economy arouses the opposition of the modernizing movement, the aristocracy also becomes more and more dependent on the foreign industrial power or enterprises to keep it in control, until withdrawal of the colonial power becomes tantamount to the loss of power for the aristocracy, as it was, for example, for the maharajas of India, the Sultan of Zanzibar, the sheikhs of South Arabia and the native big land owners of Cuba.

Aristocrats in this position of mutual dependence on the foreign industrial power are likely to be implacable enemies of the modernizing movement. But not in all underdeveloped countries are aristocrats in this position. In a very few cases—Cambodia and Ethiopia may be examples— the modernizing movement may as yet be so weak that the aristocracy does not feel in need of foreign support to maintain itself and may even regard foreign influence as a limitation on its powers and perhaps a threat, because it is likely to give rise to a modernizing movement. The result may then be a traditional, rather than a modernizing, anti-colonial movement led by the aristocracy, though, such aristocracies are likely to take some modernizing measures as well.

However, even where the modernizing movement is a threat to the continuance of the traditional rule of the aristocracy in the country as a whole, it is by no means equally threatening to all aristocrats and all aristocratic institutions. Those occupying the top governmental positions in a country are almost certain to be removed if the modernizing movement is victorious and the colonial power or enterprises withdraw. Large landowners may feel similarly threatened depending on their

365

estimate of the likelihood of successful land reform. On the other hand, aristocrats still firmly in control of smaller areas within a country may, rightly or wrongly, expect to receive a larger share of power from a successful modernizing movement than from the colonial or foreign-influenced regime.

Among the institutions on which aristocratic power in the traditional society rests, religious ones are often most resistant to change, probably because, unlike most others, they have strong popular roots, especially in the peasantry. This is true not only in the West where the church had centuries to adjust to the slow process of modernization and had, like the military and bureaucracy, become one of the institutional and ideological bastions of absolutism, which it then survived to remain powerful to this day. It appears to be equally true in underdeveloped countries, even where the modernizing revolutions are carried on under the banner of thorough-going anti-clericalism. Thus, in Mexico, Russia, and Turkey, although the aristocratic governing class was effectively and permanently removed by the revolution, the new regimes failed in their efforts to do the same to the clergy.

Religious leaders, then, have less to fear of a modernizing movement than most of the aristocracy. Indeed, so powerfully may they be entrenched that the modernizers themselves may invoke religious symbolism on behalf of their own movements, as has been true of Sukarno in Indonesia, Nasser in Egypt, and Ayub Khan in Pakistan. This may further strengthen the religious officials, but it may also be an attempt of the modernizers to weaken and by-pass them by appealing directly to the religious population. Being dependent for their power on the preservation of traditional beliefs and values, the clergy has even more reason than other aristocratic groups to resent the foreign modern influences of colonialism that undermine the basis of its power. Thus its members may join the anti-colonial movement and constitute a traditional anti-modern wing within it, either under the leadership of modernizers or, to some extent, as rivals to them.

The anti-colonial movement can, then, draw some support from virtually all major social groupings, both the old and the new ones, in an underdeveloped country and can unite both modernizing and traditional elements. This unity may be preserved as long as colonialism, that is, the influence of the industrial power or powers on whom the underdeveloped country has been dependent, remains or appears to remain as a threat. No doubt this accounts in part for the tendency of the modernizing leadership to insist that their revolution must yet be completed in the future and that there is a continuing menace of colonialism or so-called neo-colonialism.

Almost invariably, the leadership of the anti-colonial movement is in the hands of modernizers, mostly of intellectuals.[12] It is they who initiated and, in its beginnings, virtually constituted the movement. It is they alone, who, given the nature of their education and experience, have the necessary imagination and vision to set a positive goal for the movement in addition to negative anti-colonialism and resentment of the *status quo*. It is they alone who feel the need to obtain mass support for their objectives and who have the necessary organizational, literary, and oratorical skills and also the free time to mobilize it. Aristocrats who do sympathize with anti-colonialism are likely to lack these skills and they are handicapped in obtaining mass support by their attitude of contempt for the lower classes, even if their ideal goal of returning to the precolonial traditional order has some mass appeal, as it well might, especially among the peasantry.

Given the relative weakness in anti-colonial movements of traditional elements, who may well be further weakened by divided loyalties, and given the leadership by modernizers, anti-colonial movements as a whole are modernizing movements. They are likely to become more so as modernization progresses, strengthening the modernizers and the labor movement within the society, further disintegrating the traditional way of life of the peasantry and old middle class and thus opening them to modernizing influences, and making the aristocracy more dependent for its survival on colonialism, thus weakening the aristocratic-traditional element within the anti-colonial movement.

No special mention has here been made of Communism as a modernizing movement, not because it is unimportant in a discussion of political change in the process of development, but because our generalizations about modernizing movements apply to Communism. The Russian Revolution itself may be seen as the victory of a modernizing movement. For a long time thereafter both the Communists and their enemies—and this is still true of many, especially among their enemies—were caught up in the myth, to some extent a self-fulfilling one, of the proletarian, world revolutionary character of Communism, which seemed to set Communism sharply apart from the so-called nationalist movements in underdeveloped countries. In the past two decades, however, Soviet and Communist party policies have gradually effected a convergence between the two movements, generally in terms of policy and even ideology and in a few cases even in terms of organization.[13]

THE TRANSITION FROM ARISTOCRATIC TO MODERNIZING RULE

Having briefly analyzed the impact of modernization from without on the traditional society and the reaction to it of both old and new groups in the form of an anticolonial movement, we can now trace some of the patterns of political change that have been and may yet be evolving in the large part of the world that has been subjected to the impact of economic change from without.

As ideal types, the traditional regime of an aristocracy maintaining the *status quo* and a regime of modernizers dedicated to rapid industrialization and radical land reform are sharply distinguishable and are useful analytical categories. However, while pure traditional regimes existed—until a few decades or a few centuries ago—in most parts of the world and while virtually pure regimes of modernizers have come to replace them in a few present-day or until recently underdeveloped countries, like Russia and China, and may yet in some others, the transition from one kind of regime to the other can never be an immediate one. Various intermediate stages, which may or may not lead to others and eventually to a pure modernizing regime, necessarily intervene.

A regime of a modernizing movement cannot immediately succeed a pure traditional one, because such a movement is itself a product of some modernization. In a pure traditional society there are no modernizers to found and lead such a movement and no workers to follow them nor have peasants and members of the old middle class nor any aristocrats been aroused to join them. The new groups themselves and the discontent of the old ones develop only in response to industrial influence from without. This influence may take the form of investment of foreign and domestic capital in factories and railroads to lay the basis for modern military strength for the aristocratic regime, as in Russia around the turn of the century, or the establishment of a colonial economy involving the development of extractive industry, like mining and oil drilling, of some industry processing raw materials, and of systems of transportation, as, for example, in Mexico and Iraq.

Sergei Witte, the Tsarist minister of finance, President Porfirio Diaz of Mexico, and Premier Nuri al-Said of Iraq were all modernizing aristocrats. They began the transformation of the economies and the societies of their countries without changing the aristocratic nature of their regimes. The aristocracy introduces this form of modernization or cooperates in its introduction by foreign business concerns in order to strengthen itself and not to grant concessions of power to other groups. It shares the profits of the new industry, as through taxes or royalties, with the foreign or domestic investors and it avoids such measures as land and tax reforms which would attack the sources of its wealth and power. Though in practice the difference may not always be clear, the modernizing aristocracy must, for all these reasons, be distinguished from the elite we have referred to as the modernizers, who represent an anti-aristocratic force.

While aristocrats may benefit from their type of modernization for some time, their modernizing efforts lead eventually to their overthrow, for they serve to create new discontented groups who can probably not be satisfied under aristocratic rule, like modernizers and workers, and to turn old and formerly passive ones into discontented ones, like sections of the peasantry and of the old middle class. However, revolution may be long postponed where modernization intrudes from abroad into a very backward society. For example, in Saudi Arabia or Kuwait, there are few peasants, the nature of the new industry (oil drilling) requires few workers, and there is as yet little contact with the outside world to create modernizers. Also, as has been true particularly in Kuwait, the new wealth going to the aristocracy is so immense and the population so small that, by distributing even a fraction of this wealth, the ruler can substantially raise popular welfare and thus presumably keep much of the population contented. Yet such measures as the building of hospitals, systems of communication, and especially of schools tend to create modernizers who are not likely to remain satisfied with existing conditions, and there is some question whether the demands of frustrated modernizers leading eventually discontented lower class groups will not outrun the concessions a ruling aristocracy can make without endangering its own power. Though aristocratic regimes introducing modernization and especially industry to enrich and strengthen themselves may maintain themselves in power for some time, it seems reasonable to expect that eventually they will be removed.

A similar fate probably awaits those rulers of traditional societies that have not been subject to the colonial type of industrialization and are not or not yet introducing industry themselves, like the emperor of Ethiopia, the kings of Jordan and Afghanistan and of Nepal and Bhutan and Prince Sihanouk of Cambodia. All of them are modernizing aristocrats. With aid from more advanced countries, they have been modernizing their systems of education, administration, public health and communications and their armies, first, no doubt, to strengthen their regimes in a world of more modern powers, but then also to meet the demands of the very people their reforms produced, students and teachers, physicians, bureaucrats, and army officers, in short, the modernizers. As the aristocracy seeks to maintain itself in power and avoids measures like land and tax reform and as the number and self-confidence and the impatience and frustration of the modernizers grow, a conflict between the two develops which is likely to lead eventually to the victory of the modernizers. In Ethiopia there was already a revolt (in 1960) against the Emperor which still bore some of the characteristics of traditional intra-aristocratic politics, but also prominently involved modernizers, especially students and army officers.

One form of modernization carried on by ruling aristocracies in hitherto traditional societies—that of the military—is worthy of special mention. As members or descendants of a warrior class, intent on preserving or expanding the territory under their control, ruling aristocrats tend to become aware of the relative backwardness of their military establishments as compared with those of more advanced neighbors far sooner than they become concerned with the underdevelopment of their societies in other areas. They seek to overcome this backwardness as quickly as possible and are likely to be more adept at doing so than at introducing "civilian" modernization, for example, industrialization or advanced education. Modern weapons and means of communication and transport are then supplied to the armed forces, and officers have to be

369

trained to operate these. Young men are therefore sent to the military academies of advanced industrialized countries or are trained by military instructors from such countries. Like other modernizers, this "intelligentsia-in-uniform"[14] acquires not only some of the skills but also some of the value orientations of an industrialized society and thus becomes revolutionary vis-à-vis the traditional rulers. The replacement of the Sultan by Kemal is a classical example of the process here described and that of the Imam of Yemen may be a more recent one.

Since the traditional rulers are quite often military men, too, their removal may easily be mistaken for just another coup d'etat in the common succession of military rulers of the traditional society. However, in principle at least, the distinction between the military man serving the aristocracy and preserving the *status quo* and the intellectual-in-uniform dedicated to rapid modernization is clear and is often indicated by their respective attitudes toward land reform. In practice, to be sure, the distinction may be blurred, and even a single military leader may at various times play one role and then the other or parts of both roles at the same time. Thus, Perón may have come to power as a traditional military ruler and then shifted his bases of support and his policies to those more typical of the modernizing intellectual-in-uniform. Conversely, Chiang Kai-shek may be said to have begun his career as an anticolonial modernizer who, unable to revolutionize his society or to compete with another modernizing movement, was forced to rely more and more on traditional war lords, on businessmen with foreign ties, and on foreign support. Batista could even, at the same time, base himself on trade unions, like Perón, and on the landed oligarchy and colonial interests, like the traditional *caudillo.*

In countries like Egypt, and the Sudan, Iraq and Pakistan, modern armies, and with them modernizing officers, were initially created not by the traditional regime, but by the colonial power in control of these countries. When that power, Britain, withdrew, it left behind both modern army officers and traditional regimes, relying on landlord, religious, and British support. Following the Turkish example, the former removed the latter, and the regimes of four modernizing officers—Nasser, Abboud, Kassem and Ayub Khan—were established.

In some Latin American countries a somewhat similar transformation from traditional to modernist military rule has taken place more gradually and less clearly than in the Moslem countries. Armies have been professionalized and modernized, and army officers have increasingly been drawn from the "middle sectors" rather than the landed oligarchy.[15] Different groups of officers may now have different relations to the landed interests, the Church, the foreign corporations, native business interests, the professional middle groups and different attitudes toward industrialization, foreign property, trade unions, land reform and tax reform. However, only rarely, notably in Mexico, have Latin American military rulers carried out a social revolution like some of their Middle Eastern counterparts.

Some other regimes intermediate between those of modernizing aristocrats and those of modernizers need to be mentioned before we pass on to a discussion of modernizing regimes. In Iran, the present Shah is the son of a modernizing army man who made a revolution much like Kemal in neighboring Turkey, but failed to revolutionize his society even as much as Kemal. Indeed, he evidently needed the symbolism of the traditional monarchy to try to carry through his reforms. His son has thus been dependent on both the traditional large landowners and the tribal chiefs and on urban modernizing elements and has sought to maintain a precarious balance between them. He has carried out land reform distributing his own crown lands to the peasants and in this manner has sought to please the peasants and especially the modernizing advocates of land reform without arousing the aristocracy. It may be anticipated that such policies will not fully satisfy either side very long, and, indeed, the Shah has already had to contend with riots and demonstrations led both by the traditionalist religious leaders and the modernizing students, as well as the more powerful opposition of landed interests on the one hand and the brief interlude of the modernizing regime of Mossadeq on the other. The Shah might be regarded as a modernizing aristocrat or as a modernizer, but there seems to be a good chance that at some point in the future he will be replaced by a less-modernizing aristocrat or, more probably, a more-modernizing modernizer.

Another phenomenon intermediate between aristocratic and modernizing rule may be some sort of cooperative or federal scheme permitting the continuance of aristocratic rule within or beside that of modernizers. Thus, Uganda, on becoming independent in 1962, came under a government of modernizers, but within the country there remained some traditional kingdoms, notably Buganda.[16] Although they maintained themselves longer after the end of colonial rule than the realms of the maharajas in India or the sheikhs in South Arabia, by 1966 a violent conflict between the Kabaka of Buganda and the Prime Minister of Uganda ended in a victory for the latter. In Ghana the Ashanti chiefs enjoyed some autonomy during the early Nkrumah regime[17] and similar arrangements no doubt prevailed with respect to many tribal authorities—though these may be regarded as primitive rather than traditional elements—in a number of African countries as well as in Asian ones like Iraq, India, and Pakistan.

In Nigeria, the North dominated by the traditional Hausa-Fulani emirs coexisted with the southern regions dominated by modernizers in a federal system in which the Northern traditional forces predominated at the national level. The army coup of January 1966 was, in part, a revolution by modern army officers against the traditional regime in the North, though it also overthrew the modernizing regimes in the South. The counter-coup of July 1966 by Northern army elements seems to have secured traditional rule in the North for the present but has also threatened the very existence of the Nigerian federation. The experience of both Uganda and Nigeria, then, demonstrated that coexistence of traditional and modernist rule within a single government is difficult, if not impossible, to maintain for long.

On the basis of the rather varied experience briefly reviewed here, it seems reasonable to generalize that once modernization has been introduced into a traditional society through the influence of foreign industrial societies—and there is today no traditional society where this has not to some extent been done—the rule of the aristocracy is doomed and one of modernizers is likely to replace it.[18] Attempts by the aristocracy to introduce some degree of modernization itself may serve a delaying function and thus be of crucial importance to the aristocrats involved, but eventually modernizers leading the anticolonial modernizing movement will come to power anyway.

MODERNIZERS IN POWER

Following some of the transitional processes we have outlined, modernizers—sometimes by themselves and sometimes with the aid of and even in conjunction with other groups—are likely to come to power. In order to analyze subsequent conflicts, we can no longer, as we have up to this point, operate with a category of "the modernizers." We could treat the modernizers as a single group in their conflict with the traditional-colonial order, for in relation to it they are united by common interests. Once the common enemy has been overcome, however, differences among the modernizers appear or those that have been present all along come to the fore.

When modernizers come to power, obviously not all of them achieve equal power. We can begin our analysis of conflicts among modernizers by drawing the simple distinction between those who come to occupy the positions of power, especially the very top positions of government, and those who obtain only subordinate positions or none at all. The line between the two is certainly not a sharp one. It may divide those enjoying the confidence of an outstanding leader from the other modernizers; it may run between modernizers educated abroad and those educated at home; it may be one between cliques or political parties—here the existence of a Communist Party distinct from the "nationalist" movement may be significant—or it may separate civilians from military men. Generational cleavages among those socialized at various stages of the transitional process from the traditional society to the post-revolutionary one, especially those who grew up before and those who matured after modernizers came to power, may produce conflict. In particular, those who fought in the revolutionary movement of the modernizers and those who did not are likely to resent each other. The former are bitter at the attempt of the latter to benefit from a struggle in which they did not participate; the latter soon tire of a situation in which past achievements and hardships which they cannot match are regarded as the only legitimate road to power. Generational conflict is often of particular importance in underdeveloped countries because of the growing number of young people who, in a rapidly changing political order, have not shared the experiences of the older ones.[19]

Modernizers come to power having aroused vast expectations among their followers with their promises and their own hopes for a society of abundance and equality at home and a powerful and equal state in the world of nations. The fulfillment of these promises depends on rapid industrialization which may be altogether impossible or extremely difficult, given lack of capital, of resources and of the required attitudes and skills in the population and often given rapid population growth that may outrun any growth in wealth. The hopes aroused by the modernizers can be fulfilled either not at all or certainly not very quickly and can be realized even in the long run only at heavy cost to some of the very people who expect to benefit. Bitter disappointment and frustration on the part of modernizers out of power or in subordinate positions is thus virtually inevitable and they are bound to be directed against the modernizers in power.

The modernizers in power remain dependent for capital and technical assistance on the aid of industrialized countries. They generally seek to gain a measure of independence in international affairs by diversifying their economic dependence among a number of advanced countries, preferably those in conflict with each other, a policy accounting in part for their frequent posture of neutralism. Still, the economic bonds with the former colonial power are strong, and, to the extent that they are maintained by the ruling modernizers, these are subject to the accusation of selling out to neocolonialism.

Similarly, the removal of the traditional aristocratic elites from all positions of power may be far more difficult to accomplish than the modernizers had hoped. Aristocrats can be pushed out of the central government relatively easily, but may be much more firmly entrenched on the local level in some areas, particularly the more backward ones, where the disintegrating effects of modernization on the village community had not yet arrived to revolutionize the peasantry. Traditional religious organizations may enjoy a good deal of support among the peasants and the old middle class and also among workers recently drawn from these classes and they may turn that support against the ruling modernizers. Land reform may well run into the passive resistance or active sabotage of the landed aristocracy, and it may be impossible to carry it out or to carry it out thoroughly as the modernizers had hoped. Here, too, those in power are compelled to compromise with forces they had set out to defeat and here, too, they are liable to be accused of betrayal.

It may well be that any revolution, in order to bring some of its leaders to power, must generate such high expectations and intense convictions on the part of some of its followers, that these can explain the "failure" of the revolution, that is, its failure to fulfill their expectations, only by the treason of the leadership. Certainly, this is true with respect to the anti-colonial and anti-aristocratic ideals of the modernizers. Paradoxically, some of the embittered and frustrated modernizers out of power, may, in their efforts to turn those in power out of office enter into alliances with

373

traditional or colonial interests also opposed to the new government. The modernizers in power, then, can, sometimes with equal justice, fling back at their opposition the accusation of betrayal of the revolution to the forces of reaction and neo-colonialism.

A number of additional factors may add to the tension and conflict between modernizers in power and those out of power. Having long been in opposition to colonial and aristocratic regimes, modernizers tend to be oppositional and negatively critical toward government, an attitude quite likely to be retained vis-à-vis a government of modernizers that does not fulfill their expectations.[20] This posture is bound to be resented by those in power, who feel they need cooperation in tackling the tremendous problems facing their new government. Again, each side can accuse the other of betraying the revolution and each feels misunderstood by the other.

Frequently, in societies whose government had been conducted by aristocrats as an extractive enterprise for their personal enrichment, their modernizing successors in power, too, may avail themselves of opportunities to acquire wealth and live pleasantly. But what was quite proper for a king, a raja, or a high priest becomes "corruption" for a modernizer, for he came to power with the modern-industrial conception of government as an institution serving the masses rather than the rulers. Much of the population may not know the difference and may forgive and even be impressed by the high living of their new rulers, but their fellow modernizers left out of power, who had often fought the old order inspired by puritanical zeal, are bound to resent this sacrifice of revolutionary principle, and, given their own poverty, may be a little envious, too.

Army officers take seriously their new role as guardians of national independence and honor. Accustomed to the relatively simple life of the barracks where the ability to command marks the leader, they are likely to be particularly impatient with what they perceive as the slow and bungling, compromising and corrupt policies of civilian modernizing rulers. Some, in staff positions, may be more skilled specialists than their civilian counterparts; others are even less equipped than the civilian modernizers to deal with the problems of rapid modernization, but both types may well feel that all that is required to translate the plans and dreams of the revolution into reality are more decisiveness, efficiency, order, and discipline, that is, military rule.[21]

If, finally, we add to all these elements of conflict that fact that modernizers often come to power at a relatively young age, leaving those out of power little hope that they will soon be able to succeed them if they but wait for sickness and old age to take its toll, it is readily apparent that rule by modernizers is likely to be anything but stable. Indeed, if the politics of the traditional society is chiefly conflict among aristocrats, politics in the period of modernizing predominance is conflict among the modernizers.

Since, on the one hand, the conflicts are bitter, and those on both sides are revolutionaries who think more of destroying their enemies than of compromising with them and, on the other hand, the conflicts arise long before any orderly, "constitutional," widely accepted methods for a transfer of power have evolved, such transfers are likely to take the form of coups d'état. For every successful coup, there may be several unsuccessful plots and conspiracies. As the modernizers constitute only a thin stratum in the population, usually little mass violence is involved in coups, whether successful or not, and at most only the top leaders themselves and perhaps some of their immediate entourage are killed.[22]

As traditional regimes are replaced by those of modernizers, coups of one group of modernizers against another become more frequent. Lenin's October Revolution against Kerensky's regime may be regarded as an early example. More recent successful cases may be mentioned—a list that will undoubtedly grow in the next few years: in 1954 Nasser removed General Neguib in Egypt, in 1958, General Ne Win replaced U Nu in Burma, In 1960 U Nu replaced Ne Win, and in 1962 Ne Win again replaced U Nu. At least since the union with Egypt in 1958 (and perhaps since the ascendency of the Baath party in 1954) the military coups in Syria, taking place at the rate of about one per year, can largely be characterized as conflicts among modernizers. In 1963, in Iraq, General Kassem, after numerous unsuccessful attempts ever since his own revolution in 1958, was overthrown and killed, to be followed by other military regimes in a long succession of plots down to the present. In 1964, General Abboud in Sudan was ousted by a civilian coalition which has itself since changed. Also in 1964, military leaders in Bolivia overthrew the government of Paz Estenssoro and subsequently with some peasant support suppressed resistance by mine workers led by modernizing intellectuals. In 1965, Colonel Boumedienne replaced Ben Bella in Algeria who had himself earlier eliminated his revolutionary rivals like Premier Ferhat Abbas. Also in 1965, army leaders in Indonesia upset the balance on which Sukarno's regime had rested. In 1966, the army chief of Ghana removed Nkrumah from power and was in turn replaced by another general in 1969. In 1968, modernizing officers ousted President Belaunde in Peru, and in 1969 Ayub Khan was ousted in Pakistan.

As one group of modernizers replaces another in power, the new group is likely to pursue more or less the same policies as the old one vis-à-vis the aristocracy and the colonial power. It will use the same symbols, commonly those of "socialism" and "anti-imperialism," and will insist that "the" revolution goes on. However, hidden by the same slogans, a policy shift with regard to industrialization *may*, in fact, occur. A new group of managerial modernizers, often distinguished by their technical, scientific, and administrative training, and by appropriately different attitudes from the revolutionary modernizers, may grow as a result of the commitment to industrialization of the latter.[23] The new group may demand more rapid and effective steps toward industrialization than revolutionary modernizers are able to take and thus threaten their regime. The latter are likely to defend themselves by insisting that the revolution must go on, that it is still menaced by enemies at home and abroad. Policies pursued in line with this attitude may serve to delay industrialization and thus to keep the revolutionary modernizers in power and the managerial ones out.

Still, distinctions between revolutionary and managerial modernizers tend to be obscured by both elites themselves. Even while they follow different policies, they employ the same symbols to justify them. The revolutionary modernizers advocate not only revolution, both before and after they come to power, but also industrialization which, with its promise of eventual abundance, serves to justify the revolution. The managerial modernizers advocate not only industrialization, but also insist that they will carry on the revolution, for it is only from it that they derive their legitimacy. Even Brezhnev and Kosygin claim to be merely Lennin's disciples and heirs and continue to employ revolutionary slogans. The symbols are used by both elites, but they serve different functions. To the revolutionary modernizers, the revolutionary symbols are calls to action, those calling for industrialization are symbols of reassurance; to the managerial modernizers, the demands for industrialization are calls to action, but the revolutionary symbols are designed to induce political quiescence.[24]

In the Soviet Union the revolutionary modernizers were replaced in power by managerial ones, most strikingly in the great purges of the thirties. In very different forms, a similar process seems to have taken place in Mexico and may now be going on in Eastern Europe, Israel, and, at least on the lower levels of government, in India. In China, the conflict between the two types of modernizers has been raging for some time, with the ruling revolutionaries insisting that the revolution must go on and its militant spirt be maintained and seeking to denigrate the managerial modernizers as revisionists and careerists and to downgrade the technicians' concerns as of secondary importance.[25]

PATTERNS OF FUTURE CHANGE

In seeking to find patterns of political change in the development process, we have so far been able to evolve broad generalizations from the experience of quite a few societies. On this basis we could predict with some confidence that the remaining traditional and/or colonial regimes would probably eventually be replaced by modernizing regimes. But beyond the period of modernizing rule we can only try to project present trends and learn from the experience of a very few societies. The few that emerged from the traditional-colonial society some time ago, either through a fairly sudden revolution as in Mexico, China, Russia and Turkey, or more gradually as did the now industrially more advanced countries of South America and also India, have each followed their own peculiar pattern of political change. It would be rash to assume that each of the dozens of underdeveloped countries would necessarily follow one of these patterns. So far, revolutionary modernizers have come to power in most underdeveloped countries, but there has not yet been enough time for managerial modernizers to emerge in great numbers, and they have come to rule only a few countries. We can by no means be sure that they must necessarily emerge or come to power at all or that, if they do, they will in fact succeed in industrializing.

Given the tremendous difficulties in the way of industrialization, it is certainly entirely possible—it may indeed be probable—that some now underdeveloped countries will not become industrialized at all. So far only a handful of countries that have followed the non-Western path of development are clearly on the way to industrialization, and only one, the Soviet Union, has become an advanced industrial power (and it did not confront a problem of overpopulation and was much more advanced industrially at the time of the Revolution than most underdeveloped countries are today).[26] On this basis, one can hardly assume that all underdeveloped countries will become highly industrialized. What, then, may be the political future of underdeveloped countries if they do not become industrialized?

Once the aristocracy has been pushed out of power and the myth that it cannot be challenged has been destroyed; once the primitive village community has begun to dissolve and its subsistence economy has been replaced by integration into the world economy; once the old middle class has been faced with the competition of modern factories and commercial organizations; and once the new groupings of revolutionary modernizers, of workers and perhaps of modern businessmen and even of some managerial modernizers have emerged, it is obvious that a return to the traditional society is out of the question. That, after all, would require ending all contact with the industrialized world and wiping out all the effects of such contacts in the past. Economically, then, a society may remain suspended—or stagnating—between the traditional agrarian and the modern industrial state, moving toward neither one nor the other; politically, it is likely to remain under the rule of the revolutionary modernizers.

For quite some time, revolutionary symbols can keep much of the population content even in the absence of the tangible benefits which successful industrialization would eventually provide.[27] However, even with little or no industrial progress, some aspects of modernization, particularly in the fields of education and mass communications, may well develop. The probable result will be steady or declining per capita wealth but rising expectations of a life more satisfying materially and physically. Widespread and growing discontent seems inevitable, which may revive ethnic and religious conflicts and produce unrest in urban areas among workers and members of the old middle class.[28]

In the absence of rapid economic development, no serious challenge to

377

the rule of modernizers is likely to arise from any other group. Modernizers out of power, however, and especially those in government and military positions below the top level, frustrated and disappointed with those in power, will seek to take their place. Thus, several generations of revolutionary modernizers seem possible, and an endless succession of coups and conspiracies, successful and unsuccessful, should be the result. In these conflicts among modernizers, contestants may well seek support from the discontented lower strata, leading workers and remnants of the old middle class in riots and demonstrations and perhaps even organizing peasants for guerrilla warfare. Generally fairly bloodless and brief, such struggles can therefore also involve bloody uprisings and even prolonged civil wars.

Since the modernizing leaders, both those in power and those out of power, are of the revolutionary type, they will continue to employ antitraditional and anticolonial symbolism. In search of scapegoats for their inability to meet the expectations both of the lower strata and of other modernizers, they will direct such activities as riots against remnants of traditionalism, like big landowners or religious institutions,[29] and especially (possibly even in alliance with such traditional remnants) against the visible symbols of "colonialism." If prophesies of colonial threats become self-fulfilling, as when attacks on foreign persons and property invite some kind of foreign intervention, the position of revolutionary modernizers both in and out of power finds further justification. Thus it seems not unreasonable to predict an indefinite period of widespread discontent, turmoil and governmental instability for societies that cannot move on to effective industrialization.

This picture, which, perhaps because it is so unattractive to many of us, has rarely been drawn,[30] may well depict the future of a good part of the underdeveloped world. However, other parts presumably will eventually undergo effective industrialization. What will the political concomitants of that process be? On the basis of the very few examples of underdeveloped countries that, after a modernizing revolution, have by now traveled very far on the road of industrialization, we can hardly hope to draw generalizations valid for others in the future. We shall simply outline two ideal types of development, one in which modernizers seek to maintain themselves in power during the process of industrialization and one in which they come to share their power with other groups. No country is likely to fit either of the two types completely—though Russia and China have approximated the first one, Mexico, Turkey, and India the second one—and most will no doubt fall in some intermediate or mixed category or, for all we can know, perhaps some rather different one.

In the conflicts among modernizers, revolutionary modernizers in power are likely, if they can, to use a measure of terror to intimidate their rivals and some mass propaganda to try to mobilize support of the lower classes for their own cause. These methods may find much more widespread use if and when managerial modernizers come to control the government. These will not only confront the hostility of various groups of revolutionary modernizers, but, if they succeed in advancing industrialization (which we now assume), they will also create and strengthen new groups, especially among industrial workers, that become organizable and could, at least potentially and at first perhaps under the leadership of some disgruntled revolutionary modernizers, become a threat to the managerial modernizers. The latter may respond with the use of mass terror, mass regimentation and mass propaganda to intimidate, suppress, and persuade any potential opposition and to organize the population on behalf of the objectives of the regime. Since regimes of managerial modernizers are interested in rapid industrialization, they use these methods for purposes not only of suppression but also of aiding industrialization.

Industrialization is always and everywhere a painful process, because it radically changes the lives of people, especially peasants, who are not prepared for change. The more rapidly the change occurs, the more painful it becomes. Modernizers intent on pushing industrialization forward will, then, confront a good deal of passive and even some active resistance from already politicized peasants and those peasants who have already been turned into workers—the very groups that supported the modernizers in their struggle against the traditional-colonial order—as well as indifference and apathy from those peasants not yet caught up in the process of change. On the basis of their understanding of Western history, the modernizers are fanatically convinced that industrialization is the key to their country's domestic and international problems, that it will, indeed, eventually bring contentment to the very groups that oppose it. They therefore use their control of the government to compel workers and peasants to cooperate in the industrialization effort. As they see it, they know the "true interests" of workers and peasants and must hence force them and persuade them to take a course which they resist taking on their own.

Terror, regimentation, and propaganda can all be employed to solve problems which must be solved if rapid industrialization is to succeed. They can help mobilize and control a supply of labor for industry and elicit a flow of food and raw materials from the remaining peasants in the countryside, and the modernizing rulers can hope that both can be accomplished with less expenditure of scarce capital than incentive wages or payments might require. Some forms of forced labor and control of workers and of government organization or agriculture are likely to be employed by managerial modernizers in power, then.

Terror, regimentation, and propaganda can also serve to compel those whose expectations of abundance have been aroused by promises of industrialization to accept postponement of their fulfillment. Trade unions which demand a larger share of the product of industry for consumption and thus tend to slow down the industrialization process by reducing capital left for investment, are suppressed and converted into government agencies seeking to make the worker work harder for less. Mass

379

propaganda is employed to convince everyone, especially those who cannot be made to work and accept deprivations by terror or regimentation, like professional and technical personnel, that industrialization will, indeed, bring abundance—but not for a while; in the meantime sacrifices are demanded. The ideology of managerial-modernizing regimes invariably combines the two elements of demands for present-day sacrifice and promises of future abundance.

If regimes of managerial modernizers industrialize their societies, they thereby, whether they desire and know it or not, change themselves. Since managerial modernizers are difficult to distinguish from the revolutionary modernizers and may replace them only gradually, they come to power with the support of some workers and perhaps some peasants. Their symbols being the same as those of the revolutionary modernizers, they continue to appear as champions of labor organizations and land reform and of the workers' and peasants' right to their product. As managerial modernizers turn to effective industrialization, however, it soon develops that strong trade unions and the individual peasant's control of his land and product are obstacles to rapid industrialization with scarce resources. The regime's policy toward workers and peasants changes, then, to one of regimentation and compulsion, though in form trade unions and peasant ownership, now called cooperative or collective, are maintained, for the managerial modernizers even now continue to hold the ideology of their revolutionary predecessors which makes them appear to themselves as well as others as the representatives of the "masses."

In fact, if managerial modernizers succeed in advancing industrialization, they lose the support of workers and peasants (as well as of the revolutionary modernizers). However, in the very process of industrialization, they build up new bases of support. These are the rapidly growing governmental hierarchies—the government and party bureaucracies, the military and the police, and the managerial, technical and scientific staffs directing industry—into which the multiplying managerial modernizers now divide and into which some workers, peasants and former revolutionary modernizers are recruited. In pursuit of their diverse functions, these hierarchies and their subdivisions come into conflicts with each other, which constitute the politics of this type of society, but they all share an interest in maintaining the regime in power.

If and as industry advances further, the functions of the regime of managerial modernizers and the relative strength of the various groups among them change. When opposing revolutionary modernizers have been eliminated, by being either purged or converted into managerial modernizers; when industry begins to produce consumer goods and the feverish pace of work begins to slacken so that worker and peasant discontent can be reduced; when, in time, mechanization and eventually automation shrink the numbers in these discontented strata and increase those in the white-collar and professional groups who tend to identify with the regime, then the threat of opposition to the government and of obstruction to industrialization decreases. Then the suppressive functions of the governmental, party and military hierarchies decline and the police apparatus loses some of its power. On the other hand, those directly in charge of industry—the managers and engineers and scientists—grow in power and the other bureaucracies come more to reflect their interests, such as those in greater autonomy of managerial and technical personnel and in regularized bureaucratic procedures to replace the arbitrariness associated both with the crash programs and the terror of the period of rapid industrialization. More generally, a consumer ethic comes to replace the producer ethic of the earlier period within the new upper class and eventually perhaps in the entire society.[31]

This process of change does not move in a straight line and need not necessarily continue. At each point there are groups within the regime that may slow it or stop it or even reverse it, because they have an interest in the *status quo* or the *status quo ante*. The process is also inhibited by the persistence of the old ideology of the revolutionary modernizers with its symbols of revolution and struggle against imperialism and its championship of the lower classes, an ideology from which the new upper classes still derive their legitimacy and some support at home and abroad. If the prophesies of the ideology are taken seriously by the regime and by its foreign enemies, they can become self-fulfilling and produce conflicts which may slow and even stop the development outlined here.[32]

So far, only the Soviet Union has traveled any considerable distance along the path we indicated and it has therefore inevitably served as our prototype of this line of development. Yugoslavia and other Eastern European countries have followed a similar road. Other underdeveloped countries may yet do so if managerial modernizing regimes replace their revolutionary modernizing ones and succeed in advancing industrialization. China and Indonesia, Burma and Pakistan, Iraq, Egypt, and Algeria, Ghana and Guinea, Bolivia and Cuba, and others might conceivably move more or less far in this direction.

However, some of the countries just named and others may also, if they advance toward industrialization at all, move in another direction politically. After the modernizers' antitraditional and anticolonial revolution, which, as we saw, may be gradual and may be incomplete, industrialization may proceed under political conditions different from those just discussed. As industry advances, managerial modernizers undoubtedly gain some influence both in private enterprise and in the governmental civilian and military bureaucracies (and the lines between the private and governmental spheres need not be very clear), but they need not come fully to control the government.

In the conflicts among groups of modernizers, both revolutionary and managerial, various modernizers, impelled by their Western ideologies to justify their claims on the basis of mass support, seek to mobilize and organize such support among workers, peasants and members of the old middle class. To do so, they must appeal to the newly developing needs of

381

these groupings. Thus, to workers under advancing industrialization, they must offer higher wages, shorter hours and better working conditions; to peasants, shaken out of their age-old torpor by better communications, they must promise the benefits of land reform and, if and when that has been achieved, higher prices for the food they sell to the cities; to artisans and shopkeepers, threatened by advancing industrialization, they must hold out hope for protection against its effects. As modernizers articulate and, in a sense, thus create these interests, they turn them into explicit, vocal, and even organized ones. Trade unions and peasant organizations are, then, likely to be created by modernizers rather than by workers or peasants, yet in time they cease to be mere tools of modernizers used for the political purposes of the latter. They tend to develop purposes of their own, and the modernizers become identified with these and become their representatives.

As some modernizers become absorbed in emerging mass movements, others, in their conflicts with them, turn for allies to the old and new upper classes. A few may come to the defense of what is left of the landed aristocracy. Others may influence and be influenced by remnants of the traditional society, among which, as we noted, religious ones are particularly persistent, resulting in such modern-traditional hybrids as the Christian-Democratic parties of some Latin-American countries, the peasant-based Democratic and Justice parties appealing to religious traditionalism in Turkey, and the Hindu resurgence movement of the Jan Sangh party as well as the caste associations in India.[33] Other modernizers ally themselves with private businessmen, who probably grew out of the old middle class or the extractive colonial economy, but may now develop an interest in building up heavy industry and eventually consumer goods production in their country. Like some intellectuals in eighteenth- and nineteenth-century Europe, such modernizers become ideologists of capitalism.[34] Finally, as opportunities for them in an increasingly industrial society multiply, more and more of the modernizers become absorbed in their chosen professions, the formerly revolutionary ones as lawyers, teachers, and journalists, the managerial ones as administrators, engineers, and scientists, and they withdraw from political activity.

It may, then, not always be possible for a group of managerial modernizers to gain control of the government and to use its instruments of suppression, organization and communication to advance industrialization. If industrialization proceeds nevertheless, the modernizers, in their conflicts, may become the leaders and ideologists of both new groups created by industry, like capitalists and workers, and of old groups politicized by their resistance to industry or by their attempts to come to terms with its effects, like aristocrats, peasants, and the old middle class. As these groups enter (or, in the case of the aristocracy, remain in or reenter) the political process, it changes from one involving modernizers only or also some aristocrats to one involving great masses of people with very divergent interests and policy positions. The result can be

382

a condition of balance among the major groups in which no one can dominate the others, but in which the relative strength of each is, of course, subject to change.

In that situation of balance, conflict is still intense, and no group sees any particular virtue in maintaining the balance. Each regards it as an unfortunate situation of deadlock, perhaps as an intolerable limitation on its pursuit of those policies which it regards as essential. The state of balance may nevertheless persist, because no one is strong enough to upset it, but it may not. In this early state of balance that goes with early industrialization, the lower classes—peasants, workers, the old middle class—and their organizations still are not likely to play a powerful independent role in politics. It is still among the modernizers and among what is left of the aristocracy that those most eager and able to upset the balance will probably be found.

The balance is likely to have arisen (as it did in Argentina after the fall of Perón) where the revolutionary modernizers had been unable altogether to wipe out the aristocracy or traditional institutions, especially religious ones or military ones dominated by aristocratic interests, and where these either maintained some positions of power beyond the antitraditional revolution or managed to regain them later. Frustrated by the resistance of these traditional forces to rapid modernization, modernizers committed to this goal may try to remove them from power and thus to upset the balance in what is, in effect, a second wave of the modernizers' revolution against traditionalism. The 1960 revolution in Turkey led by General Gursel against a regime relying heavily on peasant-based religious tradition-alism, was evidently such a second wave, based as it was on modernizing military men and students, the same forces that had backed Mustapha Kemal. In different ways the regime of Lázaro Cárdenas in Mexico and the Communist revolution in China could perhaps also be regarded as such second waves representing the impatience of modernizers with the slowness or failure of modernization to proceed in a state of balance that had developed after an antitraditional and anticolonialist revolution.

The "second wave" attempt to upset the balance may or may not succeed. Modernizers, having been disappointed after their first revolution, may this time use more vigorous methods of suppression against the remnants of traditionalism and, if managerial modernizers gain some influence, they may then proceed toward industrialization using their methods of suppression also to speed industrialization. China might serve as an example of a society that moved from the path of balance (or deadlock) to the path of industrialization under the rule of modernizers which we dealt with earlier.

It may also be, however, that the modernizers' second wave is too weak to upset the balance. In Turkey, the Democratic Party was dissolved and its leader Menderes was hanged, but within two months the Justice Party, its successor, entered the governing coalition and has since won a massive election victory. Attempts at third and fourth waves of modernizing

383

revolution may, of course, follow, as had already happened in Turkey, and they may yet be successful in reestablishing a regime led by modernizers. However, as the situation of balance persists, it would seem that the other groups should gain in strength and should become more and more difficult to suppress so that the chances of a regime led by modernizers probably wane in time.

There is also the possibility of the balance being upset by the remaining aristocrats. Comparing their position with that before the modernizing revolution, they feel deprived of the power they consider rightfully theirs. They, too, may be a frustrated, embittered group, then, and a reactionary one in the sense that they may wish to return to the traditional order. This, as we noted earlier, is not a realistic goal, nor are they likely to be able to regain power by themselves in the face of opposition not only by modernizers but also by workers, peasants, the old middle class and businessmen.

However, where in the state of balance, labor movements led by modernizers appear as a threat to private capitalists, too, the latter may become allies of the aristocracy. Such an alliance constituted one of the two foundations of Fascist regimes as they arose in inter-war Europe. The other foundation, however, the Fascist movements, which in Europe provided the mass bases for these regimes and thus enabled them to suppress their opposition, would probably be lacking. In Europe this mass base came chiefly from the old middle class and secondly from the propertied peasantry. In underdeveloped countries, the old middle class is likely to be less numerous and less politicized, and the peasantry is generally not propertied and is hence anti-aristocratic. Both groups, to the extent that they are politicized, are anti-colonialists and, in view of the frequent link between the aristocracy and colonialism, not likely to ally themselves with the aristocracy.

Thus an aristocratic-big business alliance is a possibility, but given the probable absence of the Fascist mass support it received in some countries in Europe it is not likely to be able to upset the condition of balance. That it could do so without mass support would seem possible only where a landed aristocracy and the traditional religious hierarchy have remained powerful even though there has also been enough modernization to create a strong native group of private capitalists, a combination of circumstances most closely approximated in the industrially more advanced countries of South America, but one that is generally quite rare in underdeveloped countries.

The state of balance is probably a relatively exceptional path of development for underdeveloped countries, but the longer it lasts the more firmly it may become established and the more likely it is to be perpetuated. If it is not accompanied by industrialization, it may assume the form of deadlock and will be akin to the stage of stagnation and perpetual instability mentioned earlier. But if industrialization does proceed, then the nature of the groups constituting the balance changes.

The old groups, like peasants and old middle class, tend to disappear altogether or become integrated into the industrial economy and modernized as farmers and small businessmen. Similarly, aristocrats may disappear or be converted into modern farmers or businessmen, while what is still left of the old aristocratic institutions of the military, the bureaucracy and the church are modernized and come to be manned and influenced by nonaristocrats. Workers and capitalists become content, feel less threatened by each other and by the weakening aristocracy and its institutions and ideology, and become diversified in their interests.

The intensity of conflict and of ideology declines as the major groups split up into many minor ones with overlapping membership and each group becomes satisfied with incremental changes in the balance of power. No group seeks to upset the balance among groups completely, partly because it could, in any case, not do so. Eventually, the maintenance of the balance might even become a positive value for some or possibly almost all groups. At that point, the society approaches that type of politics with which we have become familiar in the most industrialized countries of the West.

This point, if it is ever reached at all, is, of course, so distant for many underdeveloped countries that such a prediction is hardly more than speculative. It is based less on tendencies now visible in the underdeveloped countries than on recent trends in the present industrially advanced countries. Indeed, there is some reason to doubt that these trends will continue in the advanced countries themselves as new types of tensions and conflicts arise from factors that have been beyond the scope of our analysis here, such as those one can loosely refer to as automation and abundance, urban and suburban problems, racial and generational differences, and war and the threat of war.

NOTES

1. For my own attempt at generalization about the politics of traditional societies, see my forthcoming book, *The Politics of Traditional Societies* (New York: John Wiley & Sons).

2. For an insightful study of peasant life and attitudes, see Robert Redfield, *Peasant Society and Culture. An Anthropological Approach to Civilization* (Chicago: University of Chicago Press, 1956).

3. An outstanding work generalizing about urban life in traditional societies in many areas and periods of history is Gideon Sjoberg, *The Preindustrial City, Past and Present* (Glencoe, Ill.: Free Press, 1960).

4. On the middle class character of Fascist movements, see Seymour Martin Lipset, *Political Man* (Garden City: Doubleday & Co., 1960), pp. 131-76. On their relation to the upper classes see Alexander Groth, "The 'Ism' in Totalitarianism," *American Political Science Review* 58, no. 4 (December 1964): 888-901, and Alexander Groth,

Revolution and Elite Access: Some Hypotheses on Aspects of Political Change (Davis: Institute of Governmental Affairs, University of California, 1966).

5. I have sought to show that, due to differences like those mentioned here, the concepts derived from Western patterns of politics are not necessarily useful for an understanding of the politics of underdeveloped countries in "The Western World and the Non-Western World," *American Behavioral Scientist* 7, no. 8 (April 1964): 25-29.

6. Some of the points made in the following section and a few others in this article are summarized and revised from my "Essay in the Politics of Development," in *Political Change in Underdeveloped Countries*, ed. John H. Kautsky (New York: John Wiley & Sons, 1962), pp. 1-119.

7. This is how the changes implied by the word modernization are summarized by Dankwart A. Rustow, *A World of Nations: Problems of Political Modernization* (Washington: The Brookings Institution, 1967), pp. 3-5.

8. Resentment directed against money lenders and merchants is aggravated where these are ethnically and culturally distinct from the peasants, as was true of the Jews in Eastern Europe and is true of the Chinese in Southeast Asia, Indians in East Africa and Levantines in North and West Africa.

9. In Cuba, only a relatively few agrarian laborers were involved in Castro's guerrilla army. Theodore Draper, *Castroism: Theory and Practice* (New York: Praeger Publishers, 1965), pp. 70-76.

10. On guerrilla warfare, see Franklin Mark Osanka, ed., *Modern Guerrilla Warfare* (New York: Free Press of Glencoe, 1962); for varied attempts to apply social science concepts and theories to the subject of internal war, see Harry Eckstein, ed., *Internal War: Problems and Approaches* (New York: Free Press of Glencoe, 1964).

11. The role of government as a "base of economic power" is a major element in the highly suggestive theory of Merle Kling, "Toward a Theory of Power and Political Instability in Latin America," *Western Political Quarterly* 9, no. 1 (March 1956): 21-35.

12. On the leading role of intellectuals in modernizing movements, *see* Harry J. Benda, "Non-Western Intelligentsias as Political Elites," *Australian Journal of Politics and History* 6, no. 2 (November 1960): 205-18.

13. All the points hinted at in this paragraph are elaborated in my *Communism and the Politics of Development: Persistent Myths and Changing Behavior* (New York: John Wiley & Sons, 1968).

14. The term is that of Hugh Seton-Watson, *Neither War Nor Peace* (New York: Praeger Publishers, 1960). p. 176. On the military in underdeveloped countries, see Morris Janowitz, *The Military in the Political Development of New Nations* (Chicago: University of Chicago Press, 1964), and John J. Johnson, ed., *The Role of the Military in Underdeveloped Countries* (Princeton: Princeton University Press, 441-67. In it I present much evidence of conflict between the two

1962), and also my review article, "The Military in Underdeveloped Countries," *Economic Development and Cultural Change* 12, no. 4 (July 1964): 436-43.

15. John J. Johnson, *The Military and Society in Latin America* (Stanford: Stanford University Press, 1964).

16. To be sure, in terms of economic development, education and some prevailing values—but not those affecting the traditional authority of the Kabaka—this traditional kingdom was more modern than the rest of Uganda. David E. Apter, *The Political Kingdom in Uganda. A Study in Bureaucratic Nationalism* (Princeton: Princeton University Press, 1961).

17. The ability of the traditional societies of Ashanti and of Buganda to absorb modernization is compared by David E. Apter, "The Role of Traditionalism in the Political Modernization of Ghana and Uganda," *World Politics* 13, no. 1 (October 1960): 45-68.

18. In the industrially more advanced countries of South America, which are in this respect somewhat midway between the European pattern mentioned above and the one characteristic of underdeveloped countries, the aristocracy has maintained some power for so long that, by the time modernizers become influential, they may have to share power with other modern groups, such as businessmen, who have developed in the meantime.

19. Lucian W. Pye, "The Non-Western Political Process," *Journal of Politics* 20, no. 3 (August 1958): 476-77. For a highly relevant study based on intensive interviews, see Victory T. LeVine, *Political Leadership in Africa: Post-Independence Generational Conflict in Upper Volta, Senegal, Niger, Dahomey, and the Central African Republic* (Stanford: The Hoover Institution, 1967).

20. On the "oppositionalism" of modernizing intellectuals, see Edward Shils, "The Intellectuals in the Political Development of the New States," *World Politics* 12, no. 3 (April 1960): 329-68.

21. Lucian W. Pye, "Armies in the Process of Political Modernization," in *Aspects of Political Development*, ed. Pye (Boston: Little, Brown & Co., 1966), pp. 172-87; Janowitz, *The Military in Political Development*.

22. The purges of 1965-66 in Indonesia resulting in the deliberate killing of perhaps some 300,000 people are atypical. They were not carried on in the course of the coup, but in its aftermath, evidently as an attempt by the newly successful groups of modernizers—factions of the army and students—to weaken rival groups, chiefly organized by the Communist Party and also the air force.

23. A longer section on the distinctions and conflicts between revolutionary and managerial modernizers, reprinted from an earlier draft of this article in my *Communism and the Politics of Development*, pp. 165-67, has been sharply abbreviated here. I have since dealt at length with the subject in an article on "Revolutionary and Managerial Elites in Modernizing Regimes," *Comparative Politics* 1 (July 1969): types of elites in a number of underdeveloped countries, but I also

387

find several conceptual and practical difficulties in clearly distinguishing between them in terms of their training, their attitudes and their policies. I therefore cast some doubt on my earlier hypothesis that successful industrialization and the replacement of revolutionary by managerial modernizers are necessarily concomitant processes.

24. The concept of symbolic reassurance is developed by Murray Edelman, "Symbols and Political Quiescence," *American Political Science Review* 54, no. 3 (September 1960): 695-704.

25. This is one aspect of the Sino-Soviet conflict, for the Soviet Union, representing managerial modernizers, is seen as a threat by the Chinese revolutionary modernizing rulers, while the use of revolutionary symbols by the latter places restraints on the Soviet managerial rulers since it reminds them and their followers of their own revolutionary heritage.

26. According to Walt Rostow, the Russian economy had "taken off" as early as 1890-1914. Writing in 1960, Rostow listed only four other underdeveloped countries—Argentina, Turkey, India, and China—in which the take-off might by then have occurred and he was not sure of any but the first one. W. W. Rostow, *The Stages of Economic Growth* (Cambridge: Cambridge University Press, 1963), p. 38.

27. Almond and Verba found that in Mexico, unlike the four more advanced countries they studied, pride in one's government and a positive reaction to one's nation are not coupled with the expectation of performance from the government. They remark that "this may be the pattern one would expect to find associated with a revolutionary or aspirational orientation to politics" and they describe it as follows on the basis of their Mexican findings: ". . . the symbolic importance of the Revolution in Mexican politics has persisted to the present day. . . . A highly active sense of participation and patriotism coexists with a low evaluation of actual government performance. Participation exists on an aspirational level. The Mexican with a strong sense of participation is positively oriented to his nation as symbol and to his political system on the more general level. He does not expect any better performance from the actual government." Gabriel A. Almond and Sidney Verba, *The Civic Culture* (Princeton: Princeton University Press, 1963), p. 252. However, Almond and Verba do not tell us whether this pattern of attitudes is held equally by different groups in the population. Also, there has in fact been "performance," i.e., much industrial advance, in Mexico. One can only speculate on whether similar findings of widespread positive attitudes toward the government would be made in countries under regimes of revolutionary modernizers where there has been little or no industrialization.

28. The Feierabends have done some imaginative cross-national studies correlating frustration (a ratio of material "satisfaction indices" to indices of "want formation" as produced by exposure to modernity) and political instability, though they ascribe frustration to entire nations rather than groups within them and can hence not distinguish between different types of instability emanating from different groups. See especially Ivo K. Feierabend and Rosalind L. Feierabend,

"Aggressive Behaviors Within Polities, 1948-1962: A Cross-National Study," *Journal of Conflict Resolution* 10, no. 3 (September 1966): 249-71.

29. Where these are available, the ethnically distinct members of the old middle class referred to in footnote 8 above, also frequently serve as scapegoats.

30. Samuel P. Huntington *Political Order in Changing Societies* (New Haven: Yale University Press, 1968) has envisaged the possibility of "political decay." He, too, sees instability as resulting from demands outrunning the government's capacity to fulfill them, but assumes that capacity to fulfill demands is a function, not chiefly of growing wealth, but of growing institutionalization.

31. The growth of bureaucracy and bureaucratic interests in the Soviet Union is stressed by Zbigniew Brzezinski, "The Soviet Political System: Transformation or Degeneration?" *Problems of Communism* 15, no. 1 (Jan.-Feb. 1966): 1-15; for evidence pointing to the emergence of a consumer ethic even two decades ago, see Alex Inkeles and Raymond A. Bauer, *The Soviet Citizen: Daily Life in a Totalitarian Soceity* (Cambridge, Mass.: Harvard University Press, 1959).

32. See my article on "Myth, Self-Fulfilling Prophecy, and Symbolic Reassurance in the East-West Conflict," *Journal of Conflict Resolution* 9, no. 1 (March 1965): 1-17.

33. Lloyd I. Rudolph and Susanne Hoeber Rudolph, *The Modernity of Tradition. Political Development in India* (Chicago: University of Chicago Press, 1967), pp. 15-154.

34. Merle Kling, *A Mexican Interest Group in Action* (Englewood Cliffs, N.J.: Prentice-Hall, 1961).

REVOLUTIONARY AND MANAGERIAL ELITES IN MODERNIZING REGIMES

John H. Kautsky

INTRODUCTION

Among the underdeveloped countries that have experienced a modernizing revolution, the Soviet Union and Mexico are the most outstanding cases of successful economic development. The political concomitants of that development have differed widely in the two countries; but in each, the revolutionary leadership that had overthrown the old regime and established a new, modernizing one has in turn, as industrialization has proceeded, been replaced by a new elite of bureaucrats and technocrats. It is not surprising, therefore, that the hypothesis has been more or less explicitly advanced that in underdeveloped countries generally there is some link between industrialization, on the one hand, and, on the other hand, the replacement of the leadership of revolutionary modernizers by that of managerial modernizers.[1] Depending on which of the two variables one regards as the independent and which the dependent one, one may suggest either that if industrialization is to proceed, the replacement of elites must take place or that if and when industrialization does proceed, the replacement of elites will take place.

In favor of the first suggestion one can argue that it is possible, after all, that, apart from the obvious economic and cultural obstacles to successful, rapid industrialization, the leadership of revolutionary modernizers, committed though they are to the goal of industrialization, may itself stand in the way of reaching that goal. Lacking the requisite skills and attitudes, the revolutionary modernizers may have to be replaced if the

From John H. Kautsky, "Revolutionary and Managerial Elites in Modernizing Regimes," *Comparative Politics* 1 (July 1969): 441-67. Reprinted by permission of the author and the publisher.

goal is to be attained. And since they resist being replaced, they adopt attitudes and pursue policies which in fact serve the function of justifying their continuance in power and which may slow or prevent industrialization. In favor of the second suggestion, one can argue that an industrial economy not only requires leadership by people with administrative, managerial, and technical skills but also itself produces such leadership.

The hypothesis that the industrialization of underdeveloped countries and the replacement of their revolutionary modernizing leadership by managerial modernizers are linked seems to be in accord with common sense,[2] but sufficient evidence is not yet available to test this hypothesis, let alone to confirm it. In only four major countries—Mexico, China, Russia, and Turkey—did revolutionary modernizers come to power as much as a generation ago. One can hardly expect that many of the other countries that have experienced such a revolution much more recently would by now have progressed very far on the road to industrialization and, hence, to managerial and administrative rule. It is certainly striking that, in the only two of the four countries mentioned that have in fact undergone substantial industrialization, managerial modernizers have come to constitute a powerful—perhaps even the most powerful—elite group. Brezhnev and Kosygin in the Soviet Union and the successors to Mexico's last revolutionary leader, Cárdenas, particularly Avila Camacho, Alemán and Ruiz Cortines, may be regarded as representing managerial modernizers.

In China, too, industrialization has been progressing, and there, too, managerial modernizers seem to be rising and competing for power. We may also add that in Israel and in the Eastern European countries the transition from revolutionary to managerial modernizers seems to have been in progress for the past few years. In these countries, revolutionary modernizers came to power only about two decades ago, but much of the population and of the economy were, at the time of the revolution, no longer caught up in the traditional order, as they are in most underdeveloped countries.

The general hypothesis that, concomitant with industrialization, an elite of managerial modernizers rises to power does find support, then, in the experience of the few countries that have made substantial progress toward industrialization following a revolution of revolutionary modernizers. (This process of political change is quite different from that which accompanied the industrialization of Western countries and of Japan, with which we are not concerned here). However, evidence derived from the experience of these countries is too limited to be conclusive, and the hypothesis must remain tentative for the present. At best, it will be possible to establish its validity only if and when, perhaps in a few decades, some of the many underdeveloped countries that have in the past few years come under the control of revolutionary modernizers make substantial progress toward industrialization.

In the meantime, it is possible, of course, to look for bits and pieces of

391

relevant evidence to see to what extent processes that occurred in various ways in the Soviet Union and Eastern Europe, in Mexico and Israel, may be repeated in other underdeveloped countries. We furnish some such evidence in the following pages, though our purpose here is not to present newly discovered data but merely to organize some scattered well-known ones so that they might provide us with some insights into, though not with predictions of, the evolution of postrevolutionary societies in underdeveloped countries. However, even such inconclusive attempts to test the hypothesis of the replacement of revolutionary by managerial modernizers are premature. For, clearly, before we can hope to test it, we must be able to distinguish between the two types of elites. To try to do so is the principal task of this article.

It is commonly and reasonably assumed that revolutionary modernizers are distinguishable from managerial ones with respect to (1) their background, experience, and training, (2) their attitudes, and (3) their policies. In order to test that assumption, we shall attempt to distinguish between them in terms of these three categories. Under each, we shall try to draw the picture of an ideal type of revolutionary modernizer and an ideal type of managerial modernizer. Though we shall illustrate them with selective evidence drawn from the real world, these ideal types as such cannot be expected to be found in pure form in the real world. Rather, they are meant merely to provide us with the analytical categories of revolutionary and managerial modernizers that can help us organize the data of the real world and determine to what extent real leaders fit into one category or the other.

Without anticipating too much of what follows, it may be stated here that the most significant result of our efforts lies not in their success but in calling attention to the difficulties they encounter. Difficulties in "operationalizing" the distinction between the two types of modernizers, i.e., in finding data which will permit us to place real leaders into one or the other of the two categories, cast doubt on the validity of the distinction itself. And this, in turn, renders questionable the possibility of testing—and hence of ever confirming—a hypothesis which at the outset seems quite persuasive.

DIFFERENCES BETWEEN REVOLUTIONARY AND MANAGERIAL MODERNIZERS

Background, Experience, and Training

In underdeveloped countries, the leadership of movements pledged to rapid and thoroughgoing modernization can only come from individuals who have broken out of the framework of the traditional society and have adopted values that are appropriate to an industrial society and that are hence revolutionary in the traditional environment. Typical of these values is a belief in the possibility and the desirability of material progress and of a far higher degree of social and economic equality and political participation for the great mass of the population than is characteristic of traditional societies. Contacts between such societies and advanced industrial ones, as they develop under colonialism or under the sponsorship of the native aristocracy or under both provide the opportunity for some natives to acquire these alien values. They may do so in institutions imported or imitated from industrial countries, like modern armies and bureaucracies, industrial and commercial enterprises, or trade unions. Most often, however, modern values are transmitted to members of the traditional society either in their own countries or, even more effectively, in an advanced country, through the process of higher education. We designate the natives who are distinguished from all others by their modern values as "modernizers."

In a traditional society, especially before there has been much modernization, most people who receive a higher education are likely to be drawn from the aristocracy. In any case, responding to the prevailing aristocratic attitudes which regard work and money-making as contemptible, and responding as well to the lack of industry in their societies, most students choose to be educated not in such fields as the natural sciences, engineering, agronomy, or business administration, but rather in law and medicine, in the humanities and the more speculative and value-oriented of the social sciences, in journalism and teaching. Such choices are reinforced where the system of higher education in the advanced country, under whose influence the modernizer has come, is itself strongly shaped by aristocratic attitudes, as has been notably the case in Britain.

If modernizers want to put into effect in their own underdeveloped countries their newly acquired values of material progress and abundance, equality and participation, they must desire rapid industrialization and also, in many cases, land reform. To carry these out, they must control the government and must, therefore, wrest control from the traditional aristocracy or from the colonial power or from both. In the minds of the revolutionary modernizers, defeat of the aristocracy and colonialism may also appear as the end toward which they work, and industrialization and land reform as the means to that end; but in any case demands for industrialization, independence, and control of the government are inextricably intertwined in a program that implies the need for social, economic, and political revolution.

Because they are determined to carry out this program and because they are ideologically committed to a goal of popular participation in government and need to believe that they represent "the masses," the modernizers are likely to try to mobilize some mass support. This they can generally do among workers, who have lately been torn out of their traditional, and usually rural, environment and have thus become physically, psychologically, and intellectually accessible to the modernizers. They can do it less easily, and usually less successfully, among the

393

peasants and among the old middle class, who remain physically and ideologically more caught up in the traditional order.

By our definition, then, at least the first generation of modernizers are revolutionaries vis-à-vis the traditional-colonial society. Some of them may merely think revolutionary thoughts, but many will also come to express these thoughts, especially since the training and professions they chose tend to encourage the development of oratorical, polemical, and writing skills. These skills are employed in attacks on the old order, in argumentation and conflict among the revolutionaries themselves and, wherever possible, in their attempts to gain a mass following. The last task, however, also requires some development of organizational skills. Thus, the process of dreaming and talking about revolution, and then of preparing and finally making a revolution, selects out from among the modernizers those who come to lead the revolutionary movement. From this process there emerges, as the ideal type of revolutionary modernizing leader, a man who combines the qualities of a good thinker, writer, speaker, and mass organizer.

Different circumstances, no doubt, require these skills in different degrees. Thus, it may be hypothesized that, among revolutionaries functioning abroad, as students or as exiles, the most effective thinkers and writers, and perhaps speakers, would emerge as leaders. Among revolutionaries remaining at home, on the other hand, particularly if they must operate illegally, those adept at organizing conspiracies and recruiting mass support may become leaders. Whether at home or abroad, the life of the revolutionary is often a hard one, and those with certain personality traits and attitudes are most likely to survive it and to reach the top of their movements. To the values, the training, and the skills that we have ascribed to the revolutionary modernizers, we might then add such personal qualities as persistence, dedication, fanaticism, and dogmatism.

In order to determine to what extent the experience and training of real revolutionary leaders conform to those of the ideal type of revolutionary modernizer drawn here, some biographical data were obtained about the man who occupied the top position of governmental power immediately after the revolution (and, in Russia and China, also the man who led the second revolution, i.e., Lenin and Mao) in each of 30 societies that have pretty clearly passed through a revolution from a traditional or colonial regime to one pledged to rapid modernization. Only that one man, rather than also those surrounding him, was studied in order to avoid the question of who was, indeed, a revolutionary "leader." Also, data on top leaders are, in any case, more easily available than data on their subordinates. (These data on the top leaders are briefly presented in the Appendix.)

This quick survey reveals that of 32 revolutionary leaders:

> 8 (25 percent) received university or advanced professional training wholly or in part in an industrialized country (Ayub Khan, Banda, Bourguiba, Kenyatta, Madero, Nehru, Nkrumah, and Nyerere);

17 (53 percent) received such modern advanced training entirely in their own or some other underdeveloped country (Abboud, Arévalo, Ben Gurion, Betancourt, Castro, Kassem, Kemal, Kerensky, Lenin, Mao, Nasser, Obote, Paz Estenssoro, Sallal, Sukarno, Sun, and U Nu);

4 (13 percent) received no higher education, but spent considerable periods living or traveling in industrialized countries (Ben Bella, Ho Chi-Minh, Tito, and Touré);

2 (6 percent) received no higher education and did not live or travel extensively abroad, but spent considerable time in a modern institution at home, i.e., the schools (Kaunda), or the colonial bureaucracy (Lumumba);

1 (3 percent) fits into none of the above categories, but even he traveled abroad extensively as a seaman (Karume).

In addition to the 25 (78 percent) of the 32 revolutionary leaders who received a higher education at home or abroad, three (9 percent) attended Western-type secondary schools in their own country (Kaunda, Lumumba, Touré). Thus, a total of 28 (88 percent) received an education appropriate to an industrialized country. Of all the 32 revolutionary leaders, 18 (56 percent) lived or traveled extensively in industrialized countries, for purposes other than their education, before coming to power. Including stays abroad for educational purposes, 19 (59 percent) lived or traveled in industrialized countries.

Our data also disclose that, of all the 32 revolutionary leaders, 16 (50 percent) served in modern institutions, as follows:

7 (22 percent) in the army (Abboud, Ayub Khan, Ben Bella, Kassem, Kemal, Nasser, Sallal);

7 (22 percent) in schools or universities (Arévalo, Kaunda, Kenyatta, Mao, Nyerere, Paz Estenssoro, U Nu);

1 (3 percent) in trade unions (Touré);

1 (3 percent) in the bureaucracy (Lumumba).

11 (34 percent) served in modern professions, as follows:

4 (13 percent) as lawyers (Bourguiba, Kerensky, Lenin, Nehru);

2 (6 percent) as physicians (Banda and Sun);

2 (6 percent as journalists (Betancourt and Ho Chi-Minh);

2 (6 percent) in modern agriculture (Ben Gurion and Madero);

1 (3 percent) in commerce and industry (Obote).

(Some of the above were chiefly professional politicians and revolutionaries. This is even more true of the following three leaders.)

3 (9 percent) were trained in modern professions, but evidently did not practice them, as follows:

1 (3 percent) as a lawyer (Castro);

1 (3 percent) as an engineer (Sukarno);

1 (3 percent) in philosophy and education (Nkrumah).

2 (6 percent) were manual workers (Karume and Tito).

None was a peasant or craftsman.

It may therefore be claimed that, while only a very small fraction of the total population of underdeveloped countries has received a higher education, has lived or traveled extensively abroad, or has served in a modern institution or profession, all or virtually all of the top revolutionary leaders in such countries have done one or more of these things. There is thus ample evidence to show that actual revolutionary leaders are quite close to our ideal type of such a leader with respect to their experience and training.

Before we turn to a discussion of the origins and backgrounds of managerial modernizers, we must point, at least parenthetically, to the possibility of a succession of regimes of revolutionary modernizers. Otherwise, we might give the mistaken impression that the replacement of revolutionary modernizers by managerial ones is inevitable after one generation of revolutionaries or, for that matter, at some later point in time.

Revolutionary modernizers, especially since they tend to be highly doctrinaire, are likely to come into conflict with each other even before the revolution over questions involving its goals, strategies, and tactics. Once their common enemies, whose opposition held them together to some extent, have been defeated in the revolution, conflicts among the revolutionary modernizers become even more prevalent. There is a good deal of evidence, drawn from all parts of the underdeveloped world and from the experience of several decades, to support the generalization that modernizing revolutions are followed by such conflicts. One may predict that this will commonly be true of future modernizing revolutions as well. One can also conceive of conflicts among revolutionary modernizers going on well beyond the passing of the first generation of revolutionaries, especially if industrialization does not proceed successfully. Disappointment with the failure of industrialization may then give rise to further generations of revolutionary modernizers fed by growing communication with the industrial world and by an expanded system of education that produces growing numbers of nontechnically trained people.

In this context, we need not discuss the conflict among revolutionary modernizers any further,[3] though this conflict may constitute much of the politics of the postrevolutionary era for quite some time. Eventually, however, a new factor may enter the political arena in the form of the managerial modernizers. How do they develop?

Colonialism or a modernizing native aristocracy both generally (by opening up communications between the traditional society and an advanced industrial one) and specifically (by providing education and training to some natives of the traditional society) produce revolutionary modernizers who eventually turn against both the aristocracy and colonialism. Similarly, regimes of revolutionary modernizers, both generally (by popularizing the ideas of rapid industrialization) and specifically (by providing technical training to some individuals) produce managerial modernizers who may eventually turn against the revolutionary ones. One is almost tempted to describe these tendencies in the Hegelian terms of theses giving rise to their own antitheses or in Marxian ones of some elements in society sowing the seeds of their own destruction or producing their own gravediggers.

The victory of revolutionary modernizers arouses vast hopes and aspirations for rapid economic development. These may help overcome the widespread and deep-seated prejudices that prevail in the traditional society against technical and scientific work. Responding to the rhetoric—and to the convictions—of revolutionary modernizers, some students may then be inspired to enter the fields of science, technology, and administration in the hope of being able to contribute to the industrialization of their backward societies.

Committed as they are to the objective of industrialization, the revolutionary modernizers also frequently take more direct steps to create managerial modernizers. Indeed, the creation of such modernizers may be regarded as part of their commitment to create a modern society. Thus, students going abroad for their advanced education may be encouraged to study certain technical fields by the award of government scholarships (a policy practiced even by governments of countries such as Guinea, where very little industrialization has in fact taken place), and they may be prevented by government controls from studying any other subjects.

Similarly, the curricula of schools and universities at home may be changed so that, as Ayub Khan's regime in Pakistan reported: "Our educational system instead of producing clerks and 'babus' for Government offices turns out scientists, engineers, chemists, physicists, plant managers, Foreign Service personnel, and other professional people to shoulder the responsibilities of a modern, forward-looking society."[4] It may well be that such attempts to promote the development of managerial modernizers are not simply the outcome of the revolutionary modernizers' ideological commitments to modernization; they may also be more or less deliberate efforts to prevent the growth of a new generation of revolutionaries that might challenge the incumbents for power.

Where revolutionary modernizers take measures to advance industrialization, they must at first rely for the execution of these measures on technical experts who are either foreigners, quite often from the former colonial power, or persons closely linked to the prerevolutionary ruling groups. Since the revolutionaries see both of these groups as politically unreliable, they will wish to replace them as quickly as possible with newly trained managerial modernizers, who will be obligated to the revolutionaries and hence, they hope, controlled by them. Where industrialization is to proceed rapidly and on a large scale, as under Stalin's and Mao's first five-year plans, great numbers of administrators, managers, and engineers need to be quickly recruited and trained. They must, therefore, necessarily be drawn from the lower strata of the population, especially from the industrial working class. This situation accords nicely with the ideology of the revolutionary modernizers, which promises equal oppor-

397

tunities for the formerly disadvantaged. Where the process of early industrialization is accompanied by conflicts among the revolutionary modernizers, as it was under Stalin, purges create openings for managerial modernizers in the bureaucracy, too, and thus enhance the opportunities for the growth of this new group.

It is easy to differentiate between the ideal types of revolutionary and managerial modernizers by their background, training, and experience. To put real leaders into one category or the other is not always equally simple. There is usually not much difficulty in obtaining biographical data on leading figures, and those who were educated to be poets, philosophers, journalists, teachers, or physicians can be distinguished from those who were trained as scientists, engineers, economists, or administrators. However, some practical problems arise. For example, two of the most common professions held by the leaders of underdeveloped countries, the legal and the military, cannot easily be classified as "revolutionary" or "managerial"; lawyers may be akin to philosophers or to administrators, officers to agitators or engineers. Another problem may be the lack of biographical data on decision makers at the middle level of governmental and economic hierarchies. Yet it is precisely there that managerial modernizers are likely to appear first as industrialization proceeds. Only in countries where this process has gone on for some time can they be expected to reach the top level. Therefore, an analysis of the top leadership, on which biographical information is most easily available, will not reveal the presence of managerial modernizers who may be rising in the system. These, however, are problems that can be overcome by access to needed data. In principle, revolutionary modernizers can be clearly distinguished from managerial ones by their training and experience. But we cannot assume that a certain kind of training and experience necessarily leads to a certain kind of behavior; in short, we cannot define the two types of modernizers in terms of their training and experience. Clearly, we would not wish to classify Sukarno as a managerial modernizer because he was trained as an engineer. We turn, therefore, to the next indicator of our distinction, that of attitudes.

Attitudes

We have already met the ideal type of revolutionary modernizer—a man fanatically dedicated to the cause of revolution against traditionalism or colonialism or both. To say, however, that he is more idealistic and less pragmatic or realistic than the managerial modernizer is not quite correct. It is not the impractical dreamer who becomes a successful revolutionary but, rather, the highly realistic organizer and agitator.

The distinction between revolutionary and managerial modernizers is not one between idealism and realism but one between the ideals that are being realistically pursued. To the revolutionary modernizer, the revolution itself—that is, primarily, the seizure of political power by modernizers—is the ideal to be obtained. To the managerial modernizer, that revolution lies in the past; his operative ideal becomes the realization of industrialization, which he regards as the prime goal of the revolution. When the job of the modernizers is to stir up and organize masses of people to march and even to die, the manipulation of revolutionary symbols is by no means impractical. It only becomes so after the revolution, and it is only then that the revolutionary modernizer who, for reasons to be noted, continues to engage in this manipulation, appears impractical. By the same token, the managerial modernizer, if he existed in a revolutionary situation, would seem, with his insistence on building factories, a hopelessly unrealistic idealist. After the revolution, however, he emerges as the realist who prefers the computer to the "Thoughts of Chairman Mao Tse-tung" or its local equivalent.

Once the traditional or colonial regime has been replaced by one of modernizers, it turns out that "the" revolution really has two separable aspects. These are, on the one hand, the seizure of power and the destruction of the old regime and its supporters and, on the other hand, industrialization. The managerial modernizers, having been produced by the hopes of the revolutionary modernizers for rapid industrialization, become more and more impatient as these hopes are not realized. To them, the promise of the revolution remains unfulfilled as long as industrialization is not being carried out. That very attitude, however, constitutes a threat to the revolutionary modernizers in power, especially if what hold they had on the lower classes through the use of their revolutionary symbols has begun to weaken in the face of continued misery and rising expectations.

Revolutionary modernizers, lacking the necessary expertise, cannot themselves carry through the complex technical and scientific tasks of planning, organizing, and building industry. If these tasks are to be undertaken, they must turn over some power to managerial modernizers. Most regimes of revolutionary modernizers have in fact done so in order to take some steps toward economic development. However, whether or not they sense that thoroughgoing, effective industrialization would require the complete displacement of revolutionary by managerial modernizers and, indeed, whether or not this is true, the revolutionary modernizers act to maintain a maximum of power. To justify their retention of power, they naturally claim, and feel, that their particular expertise—that in revolution making—is still needed. Hence the almost universal assertion by revolutionary modernizers that the revolution is not yet complete, that it must go on.[5] To be sure, the managerial modernizers may also hold that the revolution must yet be completed, but to them the completion demands industrialization, while to the revolutionary modernizers it means that the revolution is still threatened by domestic and foreign enemies. Just as, in their conflicts with each other, revolutionary modernizers feel that there is *Not Yet Uhuru*[6] (the title of a recent book by one such modernizer engaged in a conflict of that kind), so in self-defense against managerial modernizers they may see their revolution menaced by betrayal, perversion, or at least stagnation if they do not remain in power or return to power to push it.

Revolutionary modernizers are always inclined to see threats and plots against their regimes by traditional and "neocolonial" forces at home, in exile, or in foreign governments. These threats may be real or imaginary— or imaginary ones may become real through the mechanism of the self-fulfilling prophecy—but, in any case, they serve to justify the continued role of revolutionary modernizers as defenders of the revolution.

Even where those against whom the revolution was directed have been completely routed, the revolutionary modernizers often perceive the threat of "reaction" when, with a sense of shock, they become aware that the generation growing up under their rule is no longer inspired by what they regard as the values and spirit of the revolution. To men who dedicated their lives to the cause of revolution, the revolution that brings them to power is necessarily the high point of their lives. What follows it is almost inevitably anticlimactic, disappointing, and frustrating. As they grow older, they watch with horror how the younger generation that did not participate in the revolutionary struggles fails to realize their own high ideals. They are seized by feelings of nostalgia for the "good old days" of the revolutionary past, which they now recall in some idealized form. The fears and uncertainties, the doubts and bickering, are forgotten, and the revolution is remembered as a time of selfless idealism and discipline, of courage, simplicity, and camaraderie, and of ennobling suffering. The further the revolution recedes into the past, the more desperately and urgently do the revolutionary modernizers seek to inspire the younger generation with their brand of revolutionary romanticism and puritanism.

The most striking example of what we have described is no doubt the movement that Mao significantly designated "the Great Proletarian Cultural 'Revolution'." It was a wholesale attempt to revive the spirit of Yenan.[7] Mao took his famous swim in the Yang-tse in July 1966 in order to symbolize revolutionary willingness to brave dangers and surmount difficulties. But Mao is not unique. His plain, austere uniform finds its counterpart in the open collar of Ben Gurion who, living in a desert settlement, yearns for the hard days of the courageous and idealistic Zionist pioneers, and for the glories of the struggles against the British and the Arabs that secured Israel's statehood. The parallel is even closer, and the terms "romantic" and "puritan" apply even better, to Castro, who wears a fatigue uniform to recall the excitement and hardships of his "Yenan" in the Sierra Maestra. And, while Sukarno's uniform was anything but plain, his pleas to return to the "spirit of 1945"[8] and to "live dangerously"[9] fit into the same tradition of revolutionary romanticism. Had Lenin lived longer, he might well have displayed symptoms of a similar attitude, as did Trotsky in exile and as Boumedienne may well do if he remains in power long enough. Even revolutionary modernizers who, unlike all the above-mentioned leaders, came to power relatively easily— either in a quick coup d'état or when they were put into office by a departing colonial power—now like to recall the days of "struggle" as both glorious and dangerous.

It appears, then, that attempts to maintain or revive the revolutionary spirit to which they are themselves wedded are common among revolutionary modernizers. (One striking exception is Tito, who seems to be reconciled to its decay.) Consequently, they want to continue the revolution. A continuing revolution, however, requires the continued existence of enemies. Revolutionary modernizers, therefore, tend to see their prerevolutionary and their postrevolutionary enemies in the same light. In fact, their enemies may be genuine counterrevolutionaries, i.e., people who wish to return to the *status quo ante;* they may be rival revolutionary modernizers of the sort we mentioned earlier; they may simply be persons who have lost interest in, or who never shared, the values of the revolutionaries. But they may also be managerial modernizers.

While, in our view, the emergence of managerial modernizers constitutes a step beyond the rule of revolutionary modernizers, to the latter it seems a backward step. Thus, their revolutionary exhortations against "reaction" may well be attempts to defend themselves against the managerial competitors they fear. This appears particularly evident in the case of the present turmoil in China. Mao Tse-tung identifies "revisionism," that is, the rise of managerial modernizers, both in Yugoslavia and the Soviet Union and in China, with the restoration of "capitalism," that is, the prerevolutionary regime, and insists that the proletarian class struggle and revolution will have to be fought for many decades to come lest future generations in China make their peace with imperialism and join the counterrevolution.[10]

An obvious way for revolutionaries already in power to support their conviction that the revolution is not yet complete and must go on is for them to assert that it must spread beyond the borders of the country. The belief in an international and even a world revolution is generally identified with Communism. In this, as in other respects, however, Lenin and the Bolsheviks of his generation are merely prototypes of the revolutionary modernizers, and the idea of world revolution is not peculiar to them. In the first place, though they saw and formulated it, like all their ideas, in terms of Marxian concepts, world revolution is not a Marxian idea. Marx, after all, was largely unconcerned with the underdeveloped world, and he linked revolution to a high level of industrialization. His advocacy of international solidarity, therefore, could extend only to the relatively few countries where there were industrial workers.

In the second place, the years since the Russian Revolution have seen numerous other revolutions that were led by modernizers who regarded them as international phenomena. Some of these, to be sure, were

401

Communist from the start or became Communist later on. Mao's and Castro's, for example, were seen by their leaders as merely the beginnings of continent-wide or even world-wide struggles against imperialism. However, non-Communist revolutionary modernizers also think of themselves as leaders of international movements and come to sound much like their Communist counterparts—especially since the latter have in recent decades exchanged the Marxian symbolism of proletarian anticapitalism for the anti-imperialism of the revolutionary modernizers of underdeveloped countries. Thus, Nkrumah, writing shortly after his ouster (which he blames on the "neocolonialists"), not only describes the "African revolution" as "incomplete" but speaks also of "the world-wide struggle ... between ... the independent developing states and ... the neo-colonialist, imperialist countries ..." and, more simply, of "the struggle taking place in Africa and the world between the forces of progress and those of reaction."[11] Quite similarly, Sukarno considered it his task not only first to liberate Western New Guinea and then to "crush Malaysia," those nearest outposts of neocolonialism, but also to lead all the "new emerging forces" throughout the world against the foe of "necolim" (neocolonialism, colonialism, and imperialism.)[12]

The vociferous identification of Ben Bella and Boumedienne with "liberation movements" everywhere; the pan-Arabism of Nasser and of other military and revolutionary modernizers in Iraq and Syria; the pan-Africanism of Touré and other African revolutionary modernizers; perhaps even the anticolonial posture of Nehru—all imply that the revolutions which brought these leaders to power are not yet really complete or secure. And all of these positions may thus serve to justify the continuance of revolutionary modernizers in power.

Revolutionary leaders commonly think of their own revolutions as the proper model for the revolutions they advocate elsewhere, thus again suggesting that their particular experience and skills in revolution making remain relevant for the future. Lenin insisted that all Communist parties throughout the world, regardless of their environment, be organized in the image of the Bolshevik party, which was preparing for urban-centered coups; Mao thinks of the world revolution as a process of rural guerrilla warfare surrounding the cities; Castro, too, conceives of revolution as spreading out from the backward rural areas by means of guerrilla warfare, and Boumedienne now advocates such warfare in Israel.

Evidence concerning the attitudes of managerial modernizers is far less obvious than that concerning the attitudes of revolutionary modernizers, no doubt because fewer of the former have reached positions of top leadership, and perhaps also because they are less vociferous. Nevertheless, the difference between the two types of modernizers appears to be clear. The managerial modernizers impatiently demand effective steps for industrialization, whereas the revolutionary modernizers feel that the revolution must go on. However, analyses of the writings and speeches of both types, and even interviews with them, may well fail to reveal this

402

difference, for each type of leader speaks, and probably thinks, in terms of the symbols both of revolution and of industrialization.

Thus, both the 1961 Program of the Communist Party of the Soviet Union and the Bolshevik Program of 1919 speak of the international revolutionary movement;[13] a Khrushchev and even a Brezhnev, as well as a Lenin, have advocated world revolution; and all of Lenin's successors have stressed that they are merely disciples of the great revolutionary modernizer. They have been able to do so, however, because Lenin stood not only for revolution, but also for industrialization. In his last article, "Better Fewer, But Better" (1923), he proposed that industrialization get under way and added: "In this, and in this alone, lies our hope."[14] And the Bolshevik Program of 1919 had called for "all possible increase of the productive forces" as "the fundamental and principal point" of Soviet economic policy.[15]

That revolutionary modernizers demand industrialization is not surprising. As we saw earlier, that demand is, from the very beginning, closely tied in their minds to their anticolonial and antitraditional demands for independence and revolution. In a sense, it is industrialization, with its promise of future abundance and of greater equality and popular participation in government, that serves as the justification for the revolution. Before revolutionary modernizers make revolutions, while they are making them, and even after they have achieved them, they must keep talking industrialization, as well as revolution, to reassure themselves and their followers that the promises of the revolution will be kept.

Since the symbols of industrialization have from the very beginning been closely associated with the revolution, the managerial modernizers, too, can regard themselves as being part of the revolutionary tradition. When they demand that industrialization be undertaken or speeded up, they see themselves as merely asking for the fulfillment of the promises of the revolution. Hence, though we distinguish them from revolutionary modernizers, managerial modernizers also employ both sets of symbols— those of revolution and those of industrialization. Moreover, as the children and, in their own minds, the executors of the revolution, they derive their legitimacy from it. While calling for industrialization, they must invoke the revolution to reassure both themselves and the mass support which their revolutionary predecessors mobilized that, in the process of industrialization, the ideals of the revolution will not be abandoned.

To be sure, although they employ similar symbols, revolutionary and managerial modernizers still can express their different attitudes by using these symbols with different degrees of emphasis and interest. The Brezhnevs and Kosygins speak and write at greater length, and with far greater expertise, on industrialization than on revolution. To Lenin, on the other hand, industrialization was an afterthought, however important, to the subject of revolution. His definition of Communism as "Soviet power plus electrification of the entire country" shows both his commitment to rapid industrialization as a goal and his vague and naive conception of the process.

Similarly, the two Soviet Communist party programs referred to above differ widely in their emphases. The Program of 1919 stresses, and rests upon, the assumption that in 1917 "there had begun the era of a world-wide proletarian communist revolution,"[16] but its section on "Economics" is relatively brief, vague, and visionary, and it contains nothing very specific on industrialization.[17] The 1961 Program, on the other hand, devotes many pages to "the Creation and Development of the Material and Technical Basis of Communism,"[18] employing terms like kilowatt-hours and tons of steel, machine tools and spare parts, chemical industry and telemechanic and electronic devices, which were hardly part of the vocabulary of Lenin and his revolutionary colleagues. On "the international revolutionary movement of the working class," however, the 1961 Program is vague and quite unrealistic, combining some now very threadbare myths about militant proletarian class struggles in capitalist countries with references to quite nonproletarian "anti-imperialist national-liberation revolutions, people's democratic revolutions, broad peasant movements, popular struggles to overthrow fascist and other despotic regimes, and general democratic movements against national oppression."[19]

Our examples of the use of both revolutionary and managerial symbols by both revolutionary and managerial modernizers have been taken from the Soviet Union, because there the change from the one type of elite to the other is the clearest and probably the most complete. But the advocacy of rapid industrialization is, as we stressed earlier, virtually universal among revolutionary modernizers, and the employment of revolutionary symbolism seems to be equally common among managerial modernizers no matter where they have come to the fore. Thus, in Mexico and in Yugoslavia, in Israel and in India, not only are the glories of past revolutionary or independence struggles constantly invoked, but even the current modernizing and industrializing efforts are somehow regarded as "revolutionary."

The word "socialism" may well be so popular with modernizers in underdeveloped countries in part because it has both "revolutionary" and "managerial-industrial" implications that blur the differences between the two types of modernizers. "Socialism" has revolutionary connotations from its history both in Western and Eastern Europe; and it acquired "industrial" connotations in the Russian Revolution, where it first became the label of a modernizing movement rather than of Western intellectual or labor movements. Since then, some very different types of existing and hoped-for regimes in underdeveloped countries have been described as "socialist," not only in Communist-ruled countries from Yugoslavia and Poland through Mongolia and China, to Cuba, but also in Africa ("African Socialism"), the Near East ("Arab Socialism")—not to mention such local varieties as the Mexican, the Algerian, the Israeli, the Indian, and the

Indonesian. Soviet, Yugoslav, Mexican, Israeli, and perhaps Indian managerial modernizers can be as "socialist" both as their own revolutionary predecessors and as the revolutionary leaders of China and Cuba, Algeria and Egypt, Ghana and Indonesia. Thus, managerial modernizers can imply that they are revolutionary, and revolutionaries can indicate their commitment to industrialization, by using a single term.

The blurring of the differences between the attitudes of revolutionary and managerial modernizers in their own words and their own thoughts appears, then, to be a common phenomenon. If we assume that the differences in attitudes are nevertheless real, we shall have to look for proof, not in the words, but in the deeds of the two types of modernizing leaders. We turn next, therefore, to a consideration of some of the differences between the policies of revolutionary and the policies of managerial leaders.

Policies

No sharp line can be drawn between attitudes, as we have now discussed them, and policies. For our purposes here, however, we mean by a policy a pattern of allocating scarce resources. The different attitudes we have described should give rise to alternative patterns of resource allocation.

Thus, if revolutionary modernizers seek to perpetuate the spirit of the revolution and to restore in the present and the future the momentum of a revolution already in the past, their efforts will necessarily be reflected in educational policy. Policy conflicts between revolutionary and managerial modernizers should emerge over such questions as the allocation of financial resources, of teaching personnel and of the students' time and effort, over emphasis on revolutionary doctrine and values as opposed to administrative, scientific, and engineering techniques—in short, to use Chinese terminology, over whether to train "reds" or "experts."[20]

In China, children receive military training less to produce military expertise (which can hardly be done at an early age) than to indoctrinate them with a spirit of sacrifice and a willingness to face dangers. Urban youngsters are sent to live among peasants not only to teach the peasants but to absorb what is held to be the revolutionary spirit of the rural poor. During the Great Proletarian Cultural Revolution, admission to college on the basis of competitive examinations or scholarly merit was replaced by admission on the basis of social origin and ideological purity. The college curriculum was cut from five years to two, with students spending three years doing manual labor with workers, peasants, or soldiers.[21] The goal of such reforms is said to be the obliteration of the distinction between intellectuals and manual laborers. Although one may doubt that the revolutionary spirit can be rekindled and maintained by measures such as these, it is clear that, whatever young students may learn from illiterate

405

peasants and workers, it will not be managerial and technical expertise. Even if some scientists and engineers continue, as is probable, to receive adequate training in China, there can be no question that the general educational reforms are antimanagerial in their intent and in their effect.

These changes in the field of education are themselves but a reflection of the Chinese revolutionary leaders' growing fear of the experts—the managerial modernizers—whose growth they had themselves fostered in the early 1950s, when they sought to follow the Stalinist model in their first Five Year Plan. During the late 1950s, in the period of the Great Leap Forward and the Commune movement, ideological purity was put ahead of expertise; the generalist, or the "red"—the revolutionary modernizer— was favored over the "expert." Thus, in his report to the Second Session of the Eighth Congress of the Chinese Communist Party, held in 1958, Liu Shao-chi (then still regarded as a good Maoist) demanded that the entire population take a hand in building up industry in order to "refute the mysticism of this supposedly being the monopoly of a few," and in order to "necessarily campaign firmly and steadfastly against the tendency of the one-sided bias towards the latest technology" and "against the tendency of the one-sided overemphasis on the role of the specialists."[22]

Representing the managerial response to such views, a Soviet pamphlet characterized them as showing a "snobbish-leftist attitude to technology and specialists."[23] It similarly commented on the statement in the article "Long Live Leninism!", which constituted the Chinese opening salvo in the Sino-Soviet conflict, that "Marxist-Leninists have always maintained that in world history it is not technique but man, the masses of people, that determine the fate of mankind."[24]

In the present Cultural Revolution, the revolutionary modernizers in China are once again placing the greatest emphasis on the power of sheer will and on the mass mobilization of labor to obtain their goals of industrialization. They evidently hope to achieve industrialization without, in the process, creating a powerful group of managerial modernizers, whom they regard as counterrevolutionaries, and, indeed, by weakening the managers they have already created. Putting "politics in command" of production, they hope that the zeal of revolutionary modernizers can be a substitute for the expertise of managerial modernizers.

The faith of the Chinese revolutionary leaders that will power and manpower can, as they say, perform miracles, if they are guided by the proper doctrine, has been applied not only in the area of production but also in military affairs. It has evidently led to policy conflicts here as well. Military officers who seek to keep the armed forces professional and demand advanced weapons have been opposed with the view, derived from the experience of revolutionary guerrilla warfare, that in war it is man who counts, not weapons and machines. As "Long Live Leninism!" stated, "an awakened people will always find new ways to counteract a reactionary superiority in arms and win victory for themselves."[25] The revolutionary modernizers seem to be inclined to do away with a specialized army, demanding, on the one hand, that military units be employed in agriculture, industry, and public works and, on the other, that civilians be turned into soldiers and that factories, rural communes, and government and party organizations all be turned into "revolutionary schools" like the army.[26]

The contrast between managerial attitudes and policies and the revolutionary downgrading of expertise and faith in will and, especially, in ideology is well illustrated by some informal remarks which Khrushchev made at a conference on productivity, in response to a question as to why machines, rather than party work, had been emphasized. Khrushchev said:

> My dear comrade, if at the factory where you are a party functionary, a defective article is put out while you are giving a lecture on the upbuilding of Communism in our country ... wouldn't it be more useful if you organized the people for work on a scientific basis and higher qualitative standard? This is precisely what party work is, when everyone does his job, when everyone knows his trade, produces good parts and assembles good machines. What you propose is to give primacy to the reading of lectures about how people will think a hundred years after the triumph of Communism. True, this is a wonderful subject for a lecture and don't you take it that I am against good lectures, but we can wait with such reports and lectures for some 50 or 80 years. But if we turn out defective machines and poor quality articles, we shall not go very far.[27]

At the present time, policy conflicts between revolutionary and managerial modernizers are being fought out most openly and, indeed, even violently, on the national level in China and, on the international level, in the Sino-Soviet dispute. It is, therefore, from China and the Soviet Union that we have drawn our illustrations. However, while the views of Chinese revolutionary modernizers may be extreme—and are certainly expressed in extreme language—they are probably not atypical. Lenin, who is virtually our model of the revolutionary modernizer, expressed views not dissimilar to Mao's. In his *State and Revolution* (which was, to be sure, written shortly before, rather than years after, his revolution), he displayed his faith in the ability of the masses, "all under the control and leadership of the armed proletariat,"[28] to organize and run the process of production. Mao's opposition to "material incentives" is paralleled by Lenin's insistence on the payment of "workmen's wages"[29] to administrators. The abolition of ranks in the Chinese People's Liberation Army is reminiscent of a similar measure in the Red Army. One may also note that a similar emphasis on equality prevailed during the early years of statehood in Israel, when the idealism of the pioneers was still dominant.[30]

Like Mao, Lenin showed his failure to appreciate the importance of technical expertise in the process of industrialization when he said (in *State and Revolution*) that the key "functions of control and accounting—becoming more and more simple—will be performed by each

407

in turn, will then become a habit and will finally die out as the special functions of a special stratum of the population."[31] He also described these functions as "already fully within the capacity of the average city dweller"[32] and as "the extraordinarily simple operations of checking, recording and issuing receipts, which anyone who can read and write and who knows the first four rules of arthmetic can perform."[33]

Present-day Chinese statements to the effect that "we will learn to swim by swimming"[34] are strikingly reminiscent of Trotsky's statement in 1920 of the Bolshevik view "that one learns to ride on horse-back only when sitting on the horse."[35] A parallel to Mao's impatience, which led to the Great Leap Forward, may be found in Lenin's 1923 article, "Our Revolution." There he exclaims:

> "Infinitely commonplace ... is the argument ... that ... the objective economic premises for socialism do not exist in our country. ... What if the complete hopelessness of the situation, by intensifying tenfold the energies of the workers and peasants, offered us the possibility of proceeding to create the fundamental requisites of civilization in a way different from that of West European countries?"[36]

Though directed against the Marxist-Menshevik argument that the "material conditions" in Russia were not ripe for the socialist revolution, does this not reflect, by implication, the antimanagerial, Maoist conviction that the "energies of the workers and peasants," properly led and indoctrinated, can bring about the industrialization, or the "fundamental requisites of civilization"—which, according to orthodox Marxian doctrine, were a prerequisite of the socialist revolution?

Trust in the power of a strong will to overcome obstacles is not confined to Communist revolutionaries. Ben Gurion, faithful to Herzl's motto, "if you will it, it is no legend," furnishes another good example of the belief that strong determination can transcend all difficulties and that such determination is superior to expertise.[37] Indeed, one might suggest that all revolutionary modernizers must share this faith to some degree, for without it they could hardly be revolutionaries; they could not hope to turn their backward countries into advanced ones in the course of a generation.

The romantic puritanism we discussed earlier as being characteristic of revolutionary modernizers idealizes a life of hardship, austerity, equality, and dedication to work; it denounces the display of material wealth, luxury, waste, and corruption. This attitude is opposed to what is now decried in China as the "concept of self" and "material incentives." It thus runs counter to such demands of managerial modernizers as those denounced as "careerism" and those represented by the Soviet economist Liberman's proposals for profit incentives.

Although the views of Chinese managerial modernizers do not reach us, they are probably similar to Soviet views that oppose the Maoist identification of revolutionary purity with poverty. Thus, Professor G.

Glezerman replied as follows to the "ultra-revolutionary" Chinese leaders (claiming to be revolutionaries themselves, managerial modernizers see revolutionary ones as "ultra-revolutionary") and their "slanderous accusations" of Soviet "bourgeoisification":

> . . . They see the mark of "bourgeoisification" simply in the growth of the working people's personal earnings and well-being, leading allegedly to loss of revolutionary spirit. To counterpose the growth of material welfare to the preservation of revolutionary purity, however, actually means branding as meaningless the working people's struggle for socialism and communism, the struggle they are waging to insure all the conditions for a prosperous and cultural existence for all, and by no means to perpetuate their poverty.[38]

That such differences in attitudes have policy consequences need hardly be repeated. While managerial modernizers are being denounced in China, in the Soviet Union industrial managers, who often still are opposed by bureaucratic managers (but not by revolutionary modernizers), are proposing and obtaining reforms whose main theme seems to be the increase of economic efficiency through the use of modern managerial techniques and through greater autonomy for the local managers.

In international affairs, too, the different attitudes of revolutionary and managerial modernizers lead to different policies or different patterns of allocating scarce resources. We noted earlier the very common tendency of revolutionary modernizers to think of their revolution as being incomplete and, consequently, international in nature. This attitude serves to justify their own retention of power and, furthermore, to inspire the post-revolutionary generation with revolutionary ideals.

Revolutionary modernizers, then, tend to look abroad for revolutions and revolutionary movements that they can consider allied to their own and for foreign forces that they can regard as their enemies. They usually find both, either because such movements and forces already exist, or because they develop in response to the revolutionary modernizers' self-fulfilling prophecy. The two possibilities are often so intertwined that they are difficult to distinguish. Moreover, it is often pointless to ask whether an enemy exists in reality or only in the minds of the revolutionary modernizers. In a sense, he who is regarded as an enemy *is* an enemy, and in any case the enemy existing in the revolutionary's mind will condition his behavior in directions that will probably make the enemy very real indeed. Similarly, though no doubt more rarely, a revolutionary movement abroad that is weak or only potential in character could, if revolutionary modernizers believe in its existence, be activated by their propaganda and material support.

We can cite many examples of foreign enemies who have served to prove that the revolution was threatened and that revolutionary modernizers were still needed at the helm. When the Bolsheviks came to power in Russia, both they and conservative forces in the West were so thoroughly caught up in the myth of the proletarian, anticapitalist nature of the

409

Bolshevik revolution that there was no question on either side that "capitalist" regimes were the natural enemy of the Soviet regime. Both sides acted on that assumption, and thus, through a process of the mutually self-fulfilling prophecy, the myth of inevitable Soviet-Western conflict came true.[39] While the Russian Revolution could hardly be described objectively as chiefly a proletarian, anticapitalist movement, the Chinese Revolution contained from its beginnings strong antiforeign, anti-imperialist elements. The foreign enemies of the Chinese Communists, first Japan and then the United States, were thus, in effect, given for the revolutionaries, and again their existence was confirmed by the reactions of each side to the other.

Although Castro's revolution was less anti-American in the beginning, here, too, the self-fulfilling prophecy produced the necessary foreign imperialist enemy. Sukarno's revolution was chiefly anticolonial, and specifically anti-Dutch, from its inception, and the presence of the Dutch in Western New Guinea constituted rather naturally the neocolonialist threat he needed. Only after the Dutch withdrawal from New Guinea did Sukarno discover that a similar threat emanated from the British in Northern Borneo; each side, then, in the usual fashion, reinforced the enmity of the other.

To Ben Gurion, the hostility of the surrounding Arab states provided a ready-made enemy to perpetuate the spirit of national mobilization in which revolutionary leaders thrive, and, into the early years of Israeli statehood, the Zionists could regard the hostility embodied in the Arab League as a creature of British imperialism. And to Nasser and the other revolutionary Arab leaders in Syria, Iraq, and even in far-away Algeria, Israel could be pictured as an outpost of Western imperialism, a prophecy that became self-fulfilling in the joint British-French-Israeli Suez venture in 1956 and in Israel's reliance on the United States in the 1967 war and thereafter. Thus, in the Arab-Israeli conflict, regimes of revolutionary modernizers on each side have provided the enemy needed by the other side.

But to support the claim and the belief that their revolution is an ongoing and an international phenomenon, revolutionary modernizers need not only foreign enemies but also revolutionary allies. They must, therefore, support revolutionary movements abroad. The Bolsheviks did so, first in Hungary and Germany and later, through the Comintern, in other countries, notably China. In turn, the Chinese Communists have supported a number of foreign revolutionary movements, not only Communist-led ones like the Vietminh but also non-Communist ones like the FLN (National Liberation Front) in Algeria and the UPC (Union of the Peoples of Cameroun) in the Cameroons. Touré and Nkrumah also supported the UPC, and Nkrumah gave aid to rebels in the Congo. Both Ben Bella and Nasser sent arms and money to the Congo rebels; Ben Bella also supported revolutionaries in Angola, while Nasser sent 50,000 troops to help maintain the republican revolution in Yemen. And Castro has been aiding and even stimulating guerrilla warfare in Venezuela and Bolivia.

It goes without saying that attempts by revolutionary modernizers already in power to identify themselves with revolutions still in progress require the allocation of resources that might otherwise be spent on industrialization at home. The same is true of other activities that occupy revolutionary modernizers in pursuit of an internationalist role. Most, like Sukarno and Nasser, spent huge amounts on their armed forces to fight their real or imaginary enemies, to support their revolutionary allies and, more generally, to gain international prestige. To further their prestige abroad, they have also typically spent scarce reserves of foreign currency on national airlines and on elaborate embassy buildings.[40]

In their attempts to appear as leaders of international revolutionary movements, revolutionary modernizers are under some compulsion to demonstrate the unity of the movements they lead. Where several governments of revolutionary modernizers are involved, the result may be "unions" of their countries, even if they are not geographically adjacent. The Ghana-Guinea and later Ghana-Guinea-Mali union, and the various schemes that have united, at one time or another, Egypt, Syria, Iraq, and Yemen, were attempts at such unions. All of them are likely to fail, however, since subordination of the revolutionary modernizing leaders of one country to those of another hardly serves the purposes of the former.

More common than governmental unions as demonstrations of international revolutionary unity and solidarity are congresses that represent governments, parties, trade unions, and even isolated revolutionary groups and individuals from various countries. They involve no loss of power for any participants, but, on the contrary, give the revolutionary leaders of each country an opportunity to present themselves, in their own eyes and in the eyes of their countrymen, as international revolutionary leaders. Here again the activities of the Bolsheviks, with their congresses of the Communist International, the Red Trade Union International, the Toilers of the East, and other "front" organizations, were but forerunners of similar ventures undertaken by later revolutionary modernizers. Into this category fall Nkrumah's and Touré's pan-African and Nasser's pan-Arab meetings; Sukarno's Afro-Asian Conference at Bandung, as well as the Conference of New Emerging Forces that he had planned before his downfall; a second Afro-Asian Conference prepared by Ben Bella before he was deposed; and the Tri-Continental and Latin American Solidarity Congresses held by Castro.

Such congresses also may involve the expenditure of scarce investment capital and may therefore be opposed by managerial modernizers. Indeed, the vast sums allocated to build assembly halls and luxury accommodations for foreign delegates seem to have figured in the downfall of both Sukarno and Ben Bella—though this is not to imply that they (especially the latter) were overthrown by managerial modernizers.

Although the international involvements sought by revolutionary modernizers are probably not intentionally designed to inhibit industrialization at home, in effect they serve that function, and hence also the function of preventing the revolutionary modernizers from being replaced

411

by managerial ones. International commitments do serve explicitly as an excuse for the failure of revolutionary modernizers to produce industrialization and, more generally, the material abundance they have promised. The argument, as familiar in modern Indonesia and Algeria as it was in Leninist Russia, is that these goals cannot be achieved until the revolution is safe, that is, until its foreign enemies have been defeated and it has triumphed internationally. To managerial modernizers growing up under the rule of revolutionary ones, however, expensive international involvements may well seem at least a contributory cause of that failure, and they may well blame their revolutionary leaders for it.

How such different attitudes can produce different policies, though they are expressed by similar symbols, is illustrated by the priorities Lenin and Stalin assigned to the building of industry and the spreading of revolution. Lenin could not envision the success of "socialism" (industrialization) in Soviet Russia until the revolution had been carried abroad, especially to Germany. Stalin, under whom managerial modernizers began their rise to power, reversed this order. He stood for "socialism in one country"—the industrialization of Russia—which only then could serve as the center of world revolution.

To argue that there may be a policy conflict between revolutionary and managerial modernizers over international involvements is not to imply that the latter will necessarily pursue more peaceful policies if and when they come to power. After all, the causes of international conflict are manifold, and many kinds of regimes may be involved in them. It is merely suggested that managerial modernizers are less likely to support revolutionary movements abroad than are revolutionary modernizers. Certainly as the Soviet government has come under the control of managerial modernizers, it has shifted its policy (and that of the Communist parties it can influence) from one of supporting revolutionary movements to one of supporting governments in power, so that it is now in sharp conflict with the revolutionary policies of Mao and especially Castro.[41]

Like their revolutionary predecessors, managerial modernizers are likely to favor governmental control and sponsorship of industry. For one thing, they often exercise their own power through the channels of the governmental bureaucracy and they will not want to yield it either to foreign or to native owners of private capital—which may well not be available in any case. For another, the managerial modernizers probably are themselves caught up in the same ideology and symbolism that motivates the revolutionaries. Even if they are not, they are anxious to establish their own "socialist" and "anti-imperialist" legitimacy, especially as long as they are still competing for power with revolutionary modernizers. To the latter, after all, a relatively friendly attitude toward foreign capital and native private enterprise constitutes a betrayal of the revolution. They are quick to levy such charges against their managerial rivals who may be quite vulnerable to them, particularly where, as is likely, they enjoy less mass support than the revolutionary modernizers.

Nevertheless, being more interested than the revolutionary modernizers in taking practical steps toward industrialization, managerial modernizers may be more willing to attract foreign capital to their countries and, also, to encourage industrialization under the auspices of native private businessmen. A change in policy toward foreign capital and private business has certainly taken place in Mexico between the regime of Cárdenas, the last of the revolutionary leaders, and those of his more managerial successors. There are indications of a similar change in India from Nehru's government to the governments of Shastri and Mrs. Gandhi. And a growing deemphasis on collectivism may also be noted in Israel with the replacement of the revolutionary Ben Gurion by the more managerially-inclined Eshkol and Dayan.[42]

However, similar policy changes had also occurred after the initial revolutionary regimes in Mexico and Turkey had been replaced respectively by those of Calles and his immediate successors and that of Menderes. All of these governments were more responsive to foreign and traditional pressures, but they could hardly be characterized as those of managerial modernizers. Greater friendliness to foreign investments and private business also came after the overthrow of the civilian revolutionary regimes of Paz Estenssoro, Nkrumah, and Sukarno by their respective military leaders, Barrientos, Ankrah, and Suharto. There may be some reasons—for example, Suharto's liquidation of Sukarno's "Crush Malaysia" campaign and the replacement by economists of a number of military men in the cabinet—to regard the Indonesian military regime, and perhaps those of Bolivia and Ghana as well, as somewhat more managerially inclined than those of their revolutionary predecessors, but they cannot, at least not yet, be adequately described as regimes of managerial modernizers. Rather, the civilian-military conflicts in these three countries, like the one in Algeria, can be treated as the kind of conflict among revolutionary modernizers that was mentioned earlier.

The difficulty we encountered in using policy differences toward foreign capital and native private business as a criterion to distinguish between the revolutionary and managerial modernizers is matched by many other such difficulties. Thus, it is not necessarily clear that policies of austerity and belt-tightening are an indication of Maoist revolutionary puritanism and attempts to revive the spirt of sacrifice; they may also be realistic, practical measures taken by managerial modernizers in order to fit goals to available means or, in Stalinist fashion, to squeeze as much capital and labor as possible out of the population for the purpose of rapid industrialization. On the other hand, one cannot simply assume that the building of a steel mill or an atomic reactor constitutes a triumph of managerial modernizers; such projects may be merely the revolutionary modernizers' symbols of their commitment to industrialization and national greatness. Similarly, increased budgetary allocations for the armed forces may be a demonstration that control is in the hands of revolutionary modernizers, who feel the need to fight enemies of their

413

revolution at home or abroad, or perhaps that the military leaders who are thereby strengthened are themselves managerial modernizers, using the armed forces to engage in tasks of economic development. Clearly, distinctions between alternative policies will have to be more finely drawn than those we have suggested above, if they are to serve as indicators of the predominance of revolutionary or managerial modernizers in a political system.

One might think that the ultimate distinction between the two types of modernizers, should simply be: Do they or do they not in fact industrialize their country? But, unfortunately, the matter cannot be that simple. We do not have sufficient historical evidence to say with certainty that revolutionary modernizers cannot industrialize. Indeed, the Soviet Union and Yugoslavia became industrialized under the top leadership of the revolutionary modernizers, Stalin and Tito. And China, like many other underdeveloped countries, has moved in some degree toward industrialization under similar leadership. All we can say is that no society can move very far in this direction without developing some managerial modernizers in some positions of power; but they do not by any means have to hold all the top positions. To be able to claim that necessity, one would have to define as managerial modernizers all modernizers under whose leadership industrialization takes place. Definition, rather than empirical evidence, would then validate the hypothesis that industrialization and the rise of managerial modernizers are concomitant processes.

Thus, just as successful industrialization does not prove that managerial modernizers are in power, so failure to industrialize a country does not prove that managerial modernizers are not in power. There are obviously many factors besides the absence of managers in power or the prevalence of revolutionary policies and attitudes that can effectively prevent successful industrialization. Surely, even regimes of managerial modernizers could be stymied by lack of capital or resources, lack of needed skills and attitudes in the population, or apathy and resistance on the part of various groups—unless, of course, we once again commit the tempting mistake of simply defining as managerial modernizers only those who do succeed in industrializing.

CONCLUSION

It would appear, then, that we cannot distinguish sharply between revolutionary and managerial modernizers in terms of their experience and training, their attitudes, or even their policies. This is true because there are not, or not yet, enough regimes that could reasonably be regarded as being controlled by managerial modernizers to provide us with sufficient data to support some distinguishing criteria. It may also be the case, however, that our two concepts, and particularly that of the managerial

414

modernizer, are not very useful. We have, of course, regarded them all along only as representing ideal types, and we have assumed that, in the real world, modernizers are ranged along some kind of continuum between the pure revolutionary and pure managerial types. It may turn out, however, that, especially after revolutionary modernizers have come to power in underdeveloped countries, different kinds of leaders will evolve who are not just more or less revolutionary and more or less managerial, but who simply cannot be classified along these lines.

Thus, it appears that in some countries, such as India, where politicians have to compete with each other for popular support, some of the emerging leadership, particularly at the local level, is closer to the traditional culture and hence perhaps less modernizing than the revolutionary leadership it succeeds. This, of course, need not prevent the concurrent emergence of managerial modernizers, particularly in those sections of government and society that are directly concerned with the development of the economy, but also in any others, such as health care and the military, that make extensive use of modern techniques. Quite possibly, the expectation that managerial modernizers will succeed the revolutionary ones in the course of economic development will turn out to be too simple, and what will in fact occur will be a diversification of elites. Managerial modernizers will be but one of the successor elites to the revolutionary modernizers, and managerial modernizers themselves will be subdivided from the beginning—and will later become more so—among various types of administrative, scientific, technical, and engineering personnel.

As we stated at the outset, we cannot test, much less validate, the hypothesis that industrialization and the replacement of revolutionary by managerial modernizers accompany each other if we cannot clearly distinguish between the two types of modernizers. Since this is precisely our position now, the hypothesis will have to remain no more than a hypothesis for some time to come.

It is also possible, however, that a hypothesis relating industrialization to the replacement of revolutionary by managerial modernizers cannot be tested at all, because the two variables—industrialization and elite replacement—are not clearly distinguishable. Whether there really are or are not two distinct sets of attitudes that characterize revolutionary modernizers and managerial modernizers is, as we have noted, difficult to determine and by no means clear. It may or may not be true that it takes one type of man to build a political movement and another to build a factory. But there is, in any case, reason to believe that it is not so much attitudes and values that shape policies (as was assumed above for the sake of argument) as it is the prevailing system characteristics and, especially, the availability of wealth.

Whether revolutionary and managerial modernizers are, or are not, different types of men we do not, and perhaps cannot, know. But we do know that there are different types of societies, especially more or less

415

industrialized ones. Perhaps all we can put forth with certainty is the commonplace that in industrial societies there are managers—since some people must manage industry—and that in societies with little or no industry modernizers cannot be managers. It may be merely the times and the types of societies that create the distinctions between the two kinds of modernizers, and it may therefore be hopeless to look for distinctions between them apart from the times and societies in which they live.

Appendix
Biographical Information on Revolutionary Leaders

Country	Revolutionary Leader	University or Professional Education in Industrialized Country	University or Professional Education in Underdeveloped Country	Other Travel or Stay in Industrialized Country	Experience at Home in Modern Institution or Profession
Algeria	Ben Bella	—	—	France	French army
Bolivia	Paz Estenssoro	—	Bolivia	—	Professor
Burma	U Nu	—	Burma	—	Teacher
China	Sun	(Hawaii school)	Hong Kong	US, England, Japan	Physician
	Mao	—	China	—	Teacher, Librarian
Congo	Lumumba	—	(Mission school)	—	Bureaucracy
Cuba	Castro	—	Cuba	—	—
Egypt	Nasser	—	Egypt	—	Army
Ghana	Nkrumah	US	Gold Coast	England	—
Guatemala	Arévalo	—	Argentina	Europe	Professor
Guinea	Touré	—	(French-type secondary school)	France	Trade unions
India	Nehru	England	—	England	Lawyer
Indonesia	Sukarno	—	Indonesia	Japan	—
Iraq	Kassem	—	Iraq	—	Army
Israel	Ben Gurion	—	Turkey	US	Kibbutz
Kenya	Kenyatta	England, USSR	—	England	School Principal
Malawi	Banda	US, England	—	England, US	Physician
Mexico	Madero	France, US	—	US	Modern Landowner
Pakistan	Ayub Khan	England	India	—	British-Indian army

Biographical Information on Revolutionary Leaders *(Continued)*

Country	Revolu- tionary Leader	University or Professional Education in Industri- alized Country	Underdeveloped Country	Other Travel or Stay in Indus- trialized Country	Experience at Home in Modern Institution or Profession
Russia	Kerensky	—	Russia	—	Lawyer
	Lenin	—	Russia	Europe	Lawyer
Sudan	Abboud	—	Sudan	—	British- Sudanese army
Tanganyika	Nyerere	England	Uganda	Europe	Teacher
Tunisia	Bourguiba	France	Tunisia	Europe, US	Lawyer
Turkey	Kemal	—	Turkey	—	Army
Uganda	Obote	—	Uganda	—	Business
Venezuela	Betancourt	—	Venezuela	US	Journalist
Vietnam	Ho Chi-Minh	—	—	France	Journalist
Yemen	Sallal	—	Iraq	?	Army
Yugoslavia	Tito	—	—	USSR	—
Zambia	Kaunda	—	(English- type secondary school)	England, US	Teacher
Zanzibar	Karume	—	—	(Sailor)	—

NOTES

1. The present article grew out of an attempt to test this hypothesis. I am grateful to some of my graduate students who, by trying to do the same thing with reference to a number of particular countries, have not only provided me with a few of the data I utilize here but have given me a greater awareness of the conceptual and practical difficulties involved in such an attempt.

2. James S. Coleman also distinguishes between, on the one hand, "the first wave of modern educated elites," or "the politically dominant leaders who carried out the revolution (nationalism or Communist)" and, on the other hand, "the second post-revolutionary generation of technicians and managers." But he and some of the literature he cites cast doubt on the hypothesis that the latter will replace the former. "Introduction to Part III," *Education and Political Development*, ed. James S. Coleman (Princeton, 1965), pp. 358-62.

3. I did this briefly in "Patterns of Elite Succession in the Process of Development," *Journal of Politics* 31 (May 1969).

4. *Pakistan News Digest* (Karachi), 1 July 1965.

417

5. "We may conclude then that the government's intensive concern with symbolic activity is a reflection of intra-elite politics as well as of power maintenance.... All such activity which underscores the doctrine of the unfinished Revolution justifies the retention of power by a larger group of politician-administrators (including some prominent army officers) who have political qualifications for the positions they hold but no technical ones." Herbert Feith, "Indonesia's Political Symbols and Their Wielders," *World Politics* 16 (October 1963): 95. Ben Gurion concluded a recent interview, "No, the state of Israel of which we dreamed has not yet come into being." *Le Monde*, Weekly Selection, 23 April 1969.

6. Oginga A. Odinga, *Not Yet Uhuru* (London, 1967).

7. On the Great Proletarian Cultural Revolution, see A. Doak Barnett, *China After Mao* (Princeton, 1967); Roderick MacFarquhar, ed. *China under Mao: Politics Takes Command* (Cambridge, Mass., 1966); and, for background, James R. Townsend, *Political Participation in Communist China* (Berkeley and Los Angeles, 1967). On the conflict in Israel, see Dan Avni-Segre, "Israel, A Society in Transition," *World Politics* 21 (April 1969): 343-65.

8. Feith, "Indonesia's Political Symbols," p. 81.

9. Sukarno introduced Mussolini's "vivere pericoloso" as a national slogan in his Independence Day address of 17 August 1964. Willard A. Hanna, "The Indonesia Crisis—Mid-1964 Phase," *American Universities Field Staff Report Service*, Southeast Asia Series 12, no. 7 (Indonesia): 1.

10. Edgar Snow, "Interview with Mao," *New Republic*, 27 February 1965, p. 23.

11. Kwame Nkrumah, *Challenge of the Congo* (London, 1967), pp. ix, xi.

12. One observer of Indonesian politics describes some of the "themes recurrent in the rhetoric of guided democracy" as follows: "The nation's aims cannot be achieved by compromise and calculation, but only by enthusiasm and faith; the goals themselves expand, become millenial: the revolution will not be completed until imperialism has been crushed and the just and prosperous society established over the entire world." Ruth McVey, "Indonesia," *Survey*, no. 54 (January 1965): 115.

13. Both programs are reprinted in *Soviet Communism: Programs and Rules*, ed. Jan F. Triska (San Francisco, 1962), pp. 23-153.

14. V. I. Lenin, "Better Fewer, But Better," *Selected Works* 9 (New York, 1937), p. 401.

15. Triska, *Soviet Communism*, p. 143.

16. *Ibid.*, p. 130.

17. *Ibid.*, pp. 143-46.

18. *Ibid.*, pp. 71-89.

19. *Ibid.*, p. 50.

20. On the conflict between the two, which seems to be at the heart of

present-day politics in China, see Franz Schurmann, *Ideology and Organization in Communist China* (Berkeley and Los Angeles, 1966).

21. Chu-yuan Cheng, "Power Struggle in Red China," *Asian Survey* 6 (September 1966): 482. More recently, it has been reported that, in line with Mao's statement that "the lowly are the most intelligent, the elite are the most ignorant," hundreds of thousands of high school and university students are being sent to do manual labor in factories and, especially, in the countryside and frontier regions, not for a few years but presumably for life. Peggy Durdin, "The Bitter Tea of Mao's Red Guards," *New York Times Magazine*, 19 January 1969, pp. 28-35.

22. Quoted in (no author), *Certain Aspects of the Inner Life of the Communist Party of China* (Moscow, n.d.), p. 15.

23. *Ibid.*

24. Translated from *Red Flag* (No. 8, 1960) in *The Sino-Soviet Dispute*, G. F. Hudson, Richard Lowenthal, and Roderick MacFarquhar (New York, 1961), p. 92.

25. *Ibid.*, p. 93.

26. A similar reliance on will power and manpower, as opposed to planning and expertise, and on the military and guerrilla warfare as "schools" for economic development is to be found in Castro's thought: "The school of war taught us how men can do many things, how they can accomplish many tasks when they apply themselves in a practical way. This was the school of war, where a small nucleus of combatants developed into an army without bureaucracy. . . Without bureaucracy! It went to war, waged war, and won the war without bureaucracy. . . . And war taught us what man can do when he dedicates himself to working with enthusiam, interest, and common sense." Quoted from Castro's speech of 20 February 1967, to farm-machine workers in "Cuban Communism," Irving Louis Horowitz, *Trans-action* 4 (October 1967): 9. See also Joseph A. Kahl, "The Moral Economy of a Revolutionary Society," *Trans-action* 6 (April 1969): 30-37.

27. Reported in *The New York Times*, 14 September 1960, p. 3.

28. V. I. Lenin, "The State and Revolution," *Selected Works* 7, p. 48.

29. *Ibid.*, pp. 41-42.

30. In the early 1950s, the ratio between the net incomes of the senior civil servants and those in the lowest grades was 1.3 to 1 (as compared to 12 to 1 in the United States). Edwin Samuel, *Problems of Government in the State of Israel* (Jerusalem, 1956), pp. 63-64. I owe this reference and the one cited in fn. 37 to Yael Ishai, "Transformation from Revolutionary to Managerial Leadership—Israel: A Case Study" (unpublished, 1967).

31. Lenin, *Selected Works* 7, p. 48.

32. *Ibid.*, p. 47.

33. *Ibid.*, pp. 92-93.

34. Quoted from *Jenmin Jih Pao* in *The New York Times*, 8 February 1967, p. 5.

35. Leon Trotsky, *Terrorism and Communism: A Reply to Karl Kautsky* (Ann Arbor, 1961), p. 101.

36. V. I. Lenin, "Our Revolution," *Selected Works* 6, pp. 510-11.

37. Among Zionists in the pre-State period, "there was a general belief that the strong determination of pioneers could overcome all difficulties predicted by experts and could build a country despite the warnings of scientific and professional knowledge." Benjamin Akzin and Yehezkel Dror, *Israel: High Pressure Planning* (Syracuse, N.Y., 1966), p. 12.

38. G. Glezerman, "Questions of Theory: Society, the Collective and the Individual," *Pravda*, 21 October 1966, in *Current Digest of the Soviet Press* 18 (23 November 1966): 15.

39. I dealt with this process at some length in "Myth, Self-Fulfilling Prophecy, and Symbolic Reassurance in the East-West Conflict," *Journal of Conflict Resolution* 9 (March 1965): 1-17.

40. For a listing of numerous other expensive prestige projects initiated by Sukarno, see Feith, "Indonesia's Political Symbols," p. 83.

41. See my *Communism and the Politics of Development: Persistent Myths and Changing Behavior* (New York, 1968).

42. Ishai, "Transformation." Dayan illustrates the point that managerial leaders are not necessarily more peaceable than revolutionary ones.

SOME REFLECTIONS ON THE ROLE OF A POLITICAL OPPOSITION IN NEW NATIONS

David E. Apter

THE ROLE OF A POLITICAL OPPOSITION

The role of a political opposition has proved ambiguous in most newly independent nations. New governments rarely see the necessity for a regular opposition party nor do they always accept the idea of opposition as a normal feature of government. There are many reasons why this is so. Most new nations have come into being after a prolonged period of struggle with colonial authorities which has caused nationalist leaders to monopolize loyalties. Also, opposition groups having themselves been associated with nationalism at some stage of their existence, often have an antigovernment reflex common to those whose political actions have been aimed at changing the fundamental character of a country rather than accepting well established rules of political life and working within them. Indeed, many opposition leaders in new nations regard the new government much as they did their colonial predecessors, i.e. as basically illegitimate.

Considering such factors as these, we shall seek to show that an opposition in new nations needs a more limited and specialized role in order to safeguard its position and gain widespread acceptance. A great deal of discretion and responsibility is required on the part of those in the community whose views differ substantially from the government's. The key features of this role will be the subject of this paper.

In order to understand why an opposition needs to find a limited but

From David E. Apter, "Some Reflections on the Role of a Political Opposition in New Nations," *Comparative Studies in Society and History* 4 (January 1962): 154-60. Reprinted by permission of the author and Cambridge University Press.

indispensable role, we must recognize the special difficulties facing political leaders after independence. New nations are plagued with almost the entire range of political problems known to man. They are beset by an accumulation of immediate and often mundane tasks such as building up adequate medical, health, educational, transport, and other services, as well as improvement of housing, food supplies and other basic necessities beyond the subsistence level. To state this more sharply, in most of these countries per capita calorie intake remains far below that considered necessary for ordinary labor. Vivid in the minds of many political leaders are memories of the days when, not so long ago, they slept on the verandah and suffered from want of food and shelter. Some political leaders rose from poverty and obscurity to power in a short time. Politics is their only profession. For them to go out of office is, in effect, to become unemployed.

Concern with the role of a political opposition thus appears to many such political leaders as an academic exercise, divorced from the realities of life, or at best suitable for wealthy countries where political life is less stern and the future more secure.

We shall seek to show that this evaluation of political opposition is short-sighted, even though understandable. In the day-to-day bread and butter politics of a nation, an opposition can help to determine the success or failure of a government wrestling with its problems. A political opposition is neither a luxury nor a danger. If it performs its functions well, an opposition can be of crucial service both to the government of the day, and to the people of a new nation.

In the West the idea of opposition is not often questioned. It is assumed to facilitate representation and channel diverse demands into constructive paths. This view is by no means common elsewhere. The Western view of democracy as the open competition of political parties catering to diverse public needs and thereby transforming demands into policy, is not wholly accepted in most new nations. Since theirs is rather a perspective of struggle, political leaders do not regard struggle as at an end when independence is achieved. Instead they ask the public to work together for the "higher" phase. This might be liberation of a continent from colonialism, as is the aim of Ghana, or integration of a single nation out of several autonomous states as is desired in the Middle East and in parts of former French West Africa.[1] In addition most new nations are anxious to industrialize. Whatever the obstacles, industrialization is attractive to political leaders. The urge is great to catch up with the West and modernize economic and social institutions. Whether cast in the role of crusader, or anxious to produce economic growth, political leaders easily accept the view that a political opposition is troublesome and dispensable, restricting the pace of development, at least in the early years following self-government.

Hence, when we look at many nations which attained independence since the war, the outlook for the opposition appears bleak. In Burma charges of party corruption and selfishness led to the army taking over government. It was the army rather than politicians who swept the squatters from the cities, and distributed food to the hungry. In its zeal and efficiency, the army made the politicians look like foolish men, more proficient at scrutinizing monastic texts than dealing with the problems of the day. Facing similar problems, Indonesia is riddled with factionalism. Political party conflict can be found in every organized sector of life; in the army, the trade unions, the civil service and even in clan and village organizations. The country is so divided by party conflict that even "guided democracy" is impossible to achieve. If anything, opposition there is all-pervasive. Even the government is a coalition of oppositions.[2]

In the Sudan, the independence of the nation was challenged by political groups retaining strong ties with Egypt. The army took over in part to safeguard newly won autonomy. Even in Ghana, where the opposition has certainly not been extinguished, the entire executive committee of the Accra branch of the opposition United Party was put under preventive detention.

Fear that opposition will produce factionalism, corruption, and separatism is pervasive in new nations. The opposition is often blamed for producing a situation which in fact is inherent in the postindependence period of a nation. When the cement of nationalism is weakened a new basis for social solidarity must be found. Independence is an act of parliament or a stroke of the pen. Then the real difficulties begin. There is far more to self-government than a simple administrative transfer of power. Power is left to the nationalists like gold dumped in the streets, and many are bruised in the hectic scramble to gather it up again to place it in the strong box of the nation where it can be used for public good.

New governments have a tendency to set impossible goals for themselves. To accomplish many of the objectives which they attempt to achieve, "human obstacles" have to be overcome. Some of these obstacles derive from the traditional conservatism of people who are loath to change familiar ways. But nationalist political leaders, fresh from their victory against the colonial powers, want to show the world what they can produce with freedom. They desperately desire to breathe a new vitality into their corner of the world. Hence no new nation is without its dramatic and expensive development plan. Set for five years or ten, emphasizing industry, or agriculture, or mining, each new nation seeks to fulfill the grand plan which will produce net growth, steady economic savings, high levels of investment, and material benefits for all.

Impatient of the men in the villages who push the soil with outmoded implements and cling to rural ways, the new emphasis is upon discipline, education, and innovation. Unity is the demand of the hour—and cooperation. Join the party and the nation can be free and prosperous. A house divided cannot stand.

About such matters there is no "wrong" or "right" view. At the moment of independence the need for unity is great. It is easy for responsible leaders in government to take the view that an opposition simply magnifies grievance and exploits differences. Those who won independence know that it was not granted because of the kindness of colonial officials. Fought for by those willing to risk and dare, power has been captured by the nationalists; and having won it they intend to hold it by almost any means. The result is known. Rare indeed is the responsible opposition which can prosper in such a political climate.

TYPICAL PATTERNS IN NEW NATIONS

New nations tend to have either a great many parties, or a single dominant party with the opposition purely nominal. The Sudan was an example of the first, with the two main parties divided over the issue of closer union with Egypt. Government was a shaky coalition between large and small parties. India and Ghana are examples of the second. They possess a large mass "Congress-type" party which grew out of the nationalist movement, while competing parties remain small and relatively helpless.

In the first instance, competition between the parties characteristically weakened the unity of the state. Indeed few examples of a successful post-independence multiparty system can be found among the new nations except Israel and Nigeria. Others show a growing public dislike of party government. There develops a characteristic desire for a strong man who will be powerful and pure, leading the nation to harmony and achievement.[3] Hence it becomes possible for a single well organized group to be popularly preferred to several political parties. This is particularly so when bitter rivalry between parties divides the public. The greater the rivalry, the more people with passionate political attachments wish for an end of party conflict; but they are less willing to accept the dominance of any party other than their own. Hence they may look to an outside force (army, civil service) to save them from themselves. Excessive fear of tyranny thus produces oligarchy.

Where there is a dominant party of the congress type and a nominal opposition, factionalism and intraparty intrigue become the prevailing political style. Politics then is similar to that in a bureacracy, where each party official builds up his own support inside the party and seeks to outmaneuver the others.

To avoid this, mass party leaders attempt to impose discipline under the guise of fraternalism. Effectively organized, the single mass party system can become the weapon of change and discipline in a society. For example, political leaders in Ghana were struck with the Liberian system where the True Whig Party has prevailed for many generations. Conflict occurs within the ranks, but the party presents a united front to outsiders. Hence conflict and difference do not appear to challenge the unity of the party. Loyalty to the party becomes loyalty to the state.[4]

Political leaders in single mass party nations often discover that political opposition has not disappeared but is latent and underground. If, in order to prevent this, government tries to control information, public opinion (or expression of it), voluntary associations like trade unions, etc., democracy itself becomes hopeless. Often using the phrases of democratic socialism to mask a power position, government becomes the "organizational weapon" and seeks to eliminate all groups which might challenge its power. To oppose then becomes identified as an act of treason. In such circumstances, opposition must, of course, go underground. When the government becomes alive to its presence, it declares that the opposition is engaged in treason, sabotage and other acts against the state.

THE FUNCTIONS OF AN OPPOSITION

The problems which we have discussed are not only of concern to the leaders of governments in new nations. They are also problems for the opposition. Both need to discover issues which are popular but which will not so divide the public as to generate mutual contempt between citizens. The opposition must oppose but not obstruct. Both must nourish and preserve society by helping to transform private demands into acceptable public policy. To enlarge on this theme it is necessary to discuss the functions of an opposition in more specific terms.

Interest Representation

The opposition has an important task in representing *interests* which have been overlooked by the majority party. Otherwise groups in the population whose interests have not been effectively represented, can become discontented. One feature of democratic government is that while it cannot appease all interests simultaneously, it will not, for long, continue to give advantage to one group over another. The long-run prospect of equal treatment for all thus kindles an interest in government on the part of the public, and creates a faith that government will deal, sooner or later, with the problems that plague them. Increasingly the public takes an interest in its government.

Still another factor enters here. Let us make a distinction between values and interests. Values are the basic beliefs and attachments held by the public. Interests are the immediate desires which they wish to satisfy. A belief in freedom or equality is a value. A demand for assistance to cocoa farmers, or for an irrigation system, or for a local council is an interest. Interests and values are, of course, related, and the ensemble of interests is one means of judging values. However, value conflict is a different matter from that of interest conflict. The latter is competition

425

between groups for getting their demands met. If, for example, a government is to engage in development planning, interest groups will try to indicate types of development of immediate concern and benefit to them. They may ask for a scheme to be sited at points most beneficial to them. Value conflict, on the other hand, involves fundamental beliefs about what is right and wrong. *Value conflict challenges the foundations of society as a moral order, because at the values level, such conflict cannot be reconciled except by victory in a power struggle.*[5]

The task of an opposition, then, is to express interests as the basis for the perpetuation of the values to which it adheres, rather than to oppose government on value grounds. It can do this by advocating the interests of those who feel themselves aggrieved, and by suggesting alternative polices to the government. If, for example, it is proposed to create a semi-industrial area by the use of forced savings, planned allocations of the labor force, and the commitment of resources which might otherwise be available for other schemes, opposition might arise from the population affected by the program. Ancestral land might be violated for example, or control over land hitherto vested in a particular group might be upset. Pursuing the original plan at the expense of the wishes of the local people might engender value conflict. Government, taking as its primary value the need to produce material benefit and equality for all people, might assume that the original plan is of critical importance in achieving this. If in its zeal it rides impatiently over the interests of the local population, the opposition might well charge that individual rights are being trampled underfoot, and that liberty is impaired. There develops value conflict. Value conflict produces rupture in social behavior between people who become scandalized at one another's behavior, impairing, often irreparably, the relations between them. Government can easily leap to a position of repairing the damage by eliminating the aggrieved group in the interests of harmony and progress.

Hence, the opposition has a fundamental role to play here. It needs to act as a mediator, formulating and representing diverse interests in such a way that tact and compromise become the style of political life, rather than strife and persecution. The reconciliation of interests is one important means to this end.

Provision of Information

Another important function of an opposition is to provide otherwise unavailable *information* to government about public reaction to a particular official policy. In this respect, the opposition keeps the government informed about the consequences of official policy.

This function is particularly important in those nations dominated by a single mass party. The assumption here is this. Where the leadership in control of government is aggressive, impatient and progress-minded, the government soon begins to lack information, because the party itself becomes identified with the state. People will not care to make known their opposition to government leaders or the local followers of the dominant party because the risks might be too great. For example, a farmer who wants a loan for developing his farm might well understand that an agricultural loans board is dominated by people from the majority party who would be less likely to give favorable judgment on his application if they knew he belonged to an opposition. The same is true for families with children seeking scholarships from the government, or jobs and sinecures. The majority party controls all the patronage and all the avenues of opportunity. Political cynicism begins to spread and the public becomes adept at producing "spontaneous support" for the leaders even if in their hearts they despise them. This is a kind of political corruption which is far more harmful than such characteristic forms of corruption as misappropriation of funds, because society is then based on delusion and deception.

Indeed, if dissatisfaction remains hidden, only to break forward in sporadic but bloody intervals, the government sits on a powder keg. Its own party gets information pleasing to the ears of government officials. The true state of affairs remains uncertain, and political leaders therefore seek to control the entire organized life of the community. To reduce the consequences of ignorance when they are denied information, government leaders use coercion. By this means they seek to avoid blame for mistakes, and so remain invulnerable at the polls.

An opposition which indicates important centers of controversy and dissatisfaction is thus performing a valuable task. If people can freely ventilate their grievances by allowing the opposition to voice them, government is thereby provided with a knowledge of sensitive changes in public opinion and can modify its policies accordingly. This helps to make political goals more realistic, and avoids that kind of political ignorance which produces coercion. Just as the fluctuations in the glass of a barometer indicate information about the weather, so the rise and fall of support to an opposition indicates to government the effectiveness of its policies.

Exercising Criticism and Provision of Alternatives

The opposition has the responsibility of providing *criticism* and posing useful alternatives to government policies. This function, properly performed, helps government to set goals best qualified to produce public satisfaction. On matters of budget, welfare and other major concerns, criticism keeps the government responsive to the public and aware of weaknesses in its program. This is a classic function of an opposition and does not require extended discussion here.

The three functions, representation of interests, provision of information, and constructive criticism, are the main contributions of an opposition. We shall see how these three functions relate to representative government.

OPPOSITION AND DEMOCRACY

An opposition capable of performing the functions we have listed is instrumental in preserving the structure and spirit of representative government if these functions operate within three important spheres. The first involves the *values of democracy* itself, the second refers to *conciliar or parliamentary control over the executive*, and the third *involves effective representation*.

Our conception of democracy is of a political system committed to democratic values, conciliar control, and representation, especially through universal adult suffrage.

All democratic systems possessing these characteristics are, in the actual practice of government, operated by a party system. Competing parties can make each of these spheres active and meaningful, or they can dull them and make them inoperative. Hence, in this sense, democracy depends upon the performances of political parties.

Israel, with a responsible multiparty system has been operating effectively in all these spheres. Ghana, for a time threatened with conflict over values, especially those pertaining to individual rights, seems now to be most effective in the first and third spheres, with conciliar control rather ambiguous. There was a time in 1957 when 27 members of the backbench of the Convention Peoples Party, the government party, threatened to bolt to the other side. Government took strong action to bolster up temporarily fading fortunes and has emerged triumphant. At the moment conciliar control would appear to be weak. Other nations as well, show a mixed picture. In few can it be said that democracy is flourishing—but there is no doubt that democratic values are the dominant mode of politics. Even in Pakistan or the Sudan, there remains a strong commitment to democratic values even if, for the moment, conciliar control is in abeyance. Indeed in both those countries there remains a strong possibility that the political parties, having been chastened by the unexpected intervention of the military, will be restored to life when the army considers the moment propitious.

Political parties play the key role in the way these three spheres of democracy can work.

THE PRESERVATION OF VALUES

Political values are a reflection of preferences and beliefs and therefore underlie the formal or constitutional appearances of government. Political values must be shared and accepted by the people who need to be willing to support them. Confusion over political values can destroy the consensual basis for a viable nation.

To breathe life into representative institutions requires genuine commitment to democratic values. These provide the rationale for this relatively complex political form. No system can survive on purely instrumental grounds. Values become the basis for emotional feeling about the society itself. Values are the symbolic expression of political right or wrong.

What are the values with which we are particularly concerned? Those most characteristic of democracy are the product of four hundred years of struggle in the West. First there was struggle against religious orthodoxy. Orthodoxy was identified as a form of repression and dogma. *Liberty* was viewed as freedom of thought. Next, the idea of liberty was extended to include *individualism*, and the political rights of men. This took the form of struggle against autocratic monarchs. *Political equality* subsequently led to demands for economic equality with an emphasis on opportunity, fair shares for all, and public education. Through socialist criticism along these lines, and through nineteenth-century notions of progress, democracy thus acquired an economic dimension distinct from private property. Today we have the notion "psychic inequality," a consequence of social inequality, and there are efforts to obliterate those characteristics of a social order which breed feelings of inferiority and shame.

Although it took the West centuries to identify and realize these values, new nations strive to achieve them simultaneously. Modern nationalism is a demand for their realization. The problem is, however, that effort to achieve one can controvert the others. A paradox emerges. Overwhelming emphasis upon any one set of the values which are characteristic of democracy leads to a denial of others. The historical experience of the West was largely a process of realizing, *in turn*, each of the values we have identified. To achieve them all simultaneously is immeasurably more difficult.

Ghana, for example, emphasizes expansion of opportunity. Political leaders wish to emancipate people from ignorance and to utilize their talents. By this means they seek to restore respect to Africans and give people of color in all nations, including South Africa and the United States, courage to fight discrimination. Ghana also wishes to demonstrate through her own achievements after independence that the colonial powers cannot presume to judge the welfare of others and decide when a country is ready for independence. Ghanaians know that the best way to achieve these objectives is by demonstrating progress in Ghana. There is concentration on economic growth while attacking tribalism, separatism, and rural backwardness. Conflict has been produced between those anxious to achieve "progress" and those whose ways are more set in favor of custom and tradition and who, if they are not bewildered, become antagonistic to government policy. Values are challenged because liberty and freedom have become practical questions of liberty and freedom for

429

whom. These are no longer regarded as inalienable rights. From a government point of view the question is whether or not a part of the population is free to jeopardize the development of the country as a whole. The opposition charges that the majority cannot be allowed to ignore the minority on such issues. Each side challenges the legitimacy of the other's acts. Value conflict, hitherto incipient, can easily become open and manifest.

However, if we consider the case of Ghana further, it turns out that in practice, most of the conflicts over value are directly derivable from inadequate reconciliation of interests. Rarely has it been the case that what the people want, and what the government seeks to accomplish are as far apart as it appears. In performing its function, i.e. indicating to government what the interests of disaffected groups might be, pointing out the most crucial demands, communicating to government the depth of feeling and emotion involved, and proposing some compromise suitable for both groups, value conflict can be avoided through actions of the opposition.

This is not simply a matter of niceties. If there is value conflict government endangers its own success. Nothing is more desperate for progress-minded political leaders than to find that the public becomes not an asset, a pool of talent, and a reservoir of strength, but a weight to be shifted from one shoulder to the next, finally crushing those who are attempting to march forward with the burden.

Local support, and the transformation of interest conflict into satisfactory cooperation thus is possible if the opposition represents, communicates, and criticizes government policy. The public begins to share the burden of government. Otherwise plans worked out in Accra or Lagos or Cairo or Delhi, have a way of being just enough out of perspective that they have unanticipated consequences which jeopardize their success and perplex leaders. No plans are perfect.[6]

It can be argued that all this requires considerable nobility from political party leaders. Opposition leaders commonly complain in new countries that the opposition can scarcely perform its functions if its very existence is being threatened. Indeed, many of the differences which arise between government and opposition bear little relationship to problems of national progress. Quite the contrary, it is often the case that the government and the opposition shared much the same objectives in the past, i.e. national liberation and independence, and continue to support much the same aims. Often what is involved is personal conflict between men who share an intimate social environment. They know all about one another. The vulnerability of each is exposed, and exploited. It is by no means rare that when one side becomes politically dominant, the leader who is personally an anathema to members of the opposition taunts them and goads them with displays of power. In such instances the surge of resentment and bitterness which comes over the opposition leads it into acts which play directly into the hands of government. Engaged in that kind of struggle, each side pre-empts the "public interest" as their party interest.

The problem is especially acute where the opposition is a combination of brilliant and educated men joined with embittered renegades from the dominant party and with a sprinkling of confused traditionalists. Characteristically, oppositions in new countries are a blend of traditionalists, renegades and sophisticates. They fail to discipline themselves, perform erratically and inconsistently (although at times brilliantly), and do not give the government assurance that they can be relied on for responsible action.

Where the mass party is overwhelmingly preponderant numerically, the opposition is not only small in numbers, but often composed of an elite antagonistic to popular and diverse membership of a mass party. Quite often a form of "class" conflict is built into the relationship between government and opposition in which the latter is alienated by being deprived of a share in power. Meanwhile the former may have leaders who take pleasure in humiliating the self-titled aristocrats who represent all that the mass parties dislike.

If an opposition party is to survive in such a situation, it requires unusual discipline and self-control. Normally, however, such oppositions are incapacitated by their membership. Rarely can they resist personalizing the issues and maligning the motives of government leaders.[7]

A delicate tread is thus required, the more so because mass political organizations are themselves riddled with factionalism and easily threatened. The more powerful the mass party, the more intense will become intraparty intrigue and fighting. It is here that the mechanism of conciliar government becomes so important because among other things, a legislature and an election system help to transform conflict between parties by putting them in a forum in which the performance is open to the public. The public makes the ultimate decisions about which side is preferred. If government and opposition carry their conflicts outside of the parliament and into all the other institutions of the country, public and private, a struggle for pure power soon emerges. Power then inheres in the dominant party, rather than in the institutions of government, to be won and lost, in turn, through the normal vagaries of electoral fortune. And if the power of the state inheres in the dominant party, then value conflict is profound and violence and coercion lurk on all political paths.

CONCILIAR CONTROL OVER THE EXECUTIVE

The most burdensome problem for an opposition is to respect the legitimacy of government, when that government is dominated by a party

431

which the opposition finds abhorrent. When the distinction between government and party breaks down, then representative government is at end, because embedded in the idea of democratic government is the concept that the party is a conveyer of the people's will through the institutions of government, but is not the repository of state power.[8] Here lies one of the fundamental differences between democratic and autocratic political belief. In the former, there is a respect for the limitations of office, a belief that such office is temporary for any occupant.

The opposition has an important responsibility for preserving these ideas through its action in parliament. It needs also to perform its functions in ways helpful to government, and by doing so to facilitate the system of political representation.

An opposition has to strike that difficult balance between being an enemy and a contender for the government. If it poses a threat to a majority party such that it serves as a potential center of gravity, pulling members away from the majority party to the extent of destroying it, the opposition may be viewed as an enemy. We indicated that factionalism characterizes the mass party in power. The opposition can sometimes attract enough factions to split the dominant party. This is undesirable, because it encourages mass party leaders (especially those trained in doctrine which assumes the party is "everything") to void such threats through punitive action. Majority party leaders may be propelled toward coercion under the guise of populism and discipline. And, since the mechanism of coercion is an application of state power, i.e., police or courts, the institutions of government are brought into contempt. Neither the government nor opposition parties can long have faith in their own government under such circumstances.

On the other hand, the opposition has to pose enough of an electoral threat to the dominant party so that both develop party discipline. Although we do not have space to discuss it adequately, an underlying feature of representative government is the coherence and discipline by which parties are organized so that they can represent the public, decide policy, and put it into practice.

Party discipline is important not only for representative purposes, but it is crucial also in the sphere of conciliar control over the executive. The opposition which finds the difficult point of balance between threats to the government party and ensuring party discipline, will be respected and be able to carry out its functions in a parliamentary setting. The opposition can do this by: (1) convincing the government backbench of the correctness of opposition views on particular policy so that backbenchers bring pressure on their own party leaders; and (2) in rare circumstances, it can threaten the life of the government by a potential antigovernment coalition with disgruntled government-backbenchers joining with the opposition to force a general election.

Parliamentary party discipline, however, has other effects. It promotes an atmosphere of constraint and propriety in the legislature so that reasonable discussion can prevail, despite moments when tempers become inflamed. Such a climate is necessary if the functions of an opposition are to be achieved. In such a climate issues can be more easily decided on the basis of general merit. Alternative policies can be more clearly phrased and made more comprehensible to the people themselves. In this way parliament itself can become more meaningful to the public, which expects so much from a new government and its leaders.

It takes a delicate combination of forces to produce a climate of respect for the institutions of government and a situation where issues can be made more clear, so that a concept of the public interest gradually can become identified.

If such a pattern begins to take root, a whole series of subtle constraints upon the arbitrary power of the executive can be exercised, even when there is a preponderant government majority in parliament. Instead of "cabinet dictatorship," responsible government can develop. And instead of multiparty factionalism arising (as is often the case where parties are evenly divided) the government has assurance of a strong enough majority to carry through its program.

Party discipline then gives rise to coherence. Coherence allows policy alternatives to be posed in clearer fashion. Alternatives can provide government with knowledge of the best policies to carry out, and indicate necessary modification, and in the forum of parliament, ministers can be made more responsive to legislators. In this fashion, the opposition can preserve the second sphere of representative government, i.e., conciliar control. At the same time, it can reflect, more adequately, those interests of which the government may not be cognizant, and help to prevent unforeseen political difficulties.

REPRESENTATION

Representation, the third sphere of democratic government, is as important as the other two. Political party competition, i.e., the struggle between the party in power and the opposition is the life blood of democracy. Indeed one observer argues that "the democratic method is that institutional arrangement for arriving at political decisions in which individuals acquire the power to decide by means of a competitive struggle for the people's vote."[9]

By electoral means leaders are selected, a mandate for a program provided, and the public participates in the process of government. It is in competing for elections that the three functions of an opposition are carried out at the public level. They must seek out interests which they think are popular and which reflect public feeling. They need to communicate this to the public by arranging their program and ideas in a package which shows the public at a glance what the contents are. Finally,

433

the opposition attempts to sharpen the responsibilities of the electorate by criticizing the program and policies of the government and pointing out weaknesses and failures.

Hence, the representative aspect of government, underwritten by electoral competition, requires an opposition which is allowed to perform freely. Under these conditions generalized factionalism in the country becomes crystallized into main groups. And one of the practical rules of politics which works out in normally functioning democracies is that *when there is open party competition and free elections, both parties, government and opposition, seek the support of the large middle spectrum of voters,* i.e., those who comprise the bulk of the voting population. Hence, gradually, both parties draw closer together in their ideology and their programs to the point where relatively minor differences become the issues on which elections are fought. This is the experience of every successful parliamentary system.[10]

Nor is it difficult to see why this is the case. If we take the simplest possible case, a government with a "radical" program, and an opposition with a "conservative" program, we find that in real terms, most people in the country conform to neither one extreme nor the other, but fall somewhere in the middle. That is, they are in favor of some "radical" policies and some "conservative" ones. On the other hand, the extremists on either end of the political spectrum have no hope of winning elections themselves.

The important electoral factor is the middle group and in making coherent appeals to them, neither the government nor the opposition can have an extreme program. Hence the importance of free party competition—*it does not divide where all political parties are responsible—but instead exerts a constant pull on the parties drawing them together.* It neutralizes the extremists.[11] Thus party competition is basically not divisive as is commonly thought, but most often unifying instead.

The forms of disunity which characterize governments in new nations are thus often premature. Equally, an opposition which fears and mistrusts the government of the day helps to magnify the fears of a majority party leadership that the opposition, in its efforts to achieve power is out to destroy all. In those first years of self-government both sides need to recognize how absolutely necessary each is to the other.

CONCLUSION

We have indicated the challenge to opposition which has appeared in almost every new nation. Opposition, we have tried to show, is essential if the problems of governing new nations are not to engulf those in public office and impel them to coercive solutions. In representing interests, providing information, criticism and alternative policies to government, the opposition can aid government in the three critical spheres of a democratic system, namely, preservation of a belief and acceptance of democratic values, helping to control the acts of the executive by conciliar control and advice, and giving coherence and meaning to the representative system.

In addition, by serving as a rallying ground and focal point for grievance, a responsible opposition can transform potential disenchantment with government into positive channels, preventing apathy, and avoiding cynicism about democracy.

New nations need more than bargaining power to gain the respect of the world. They need to demonstrate positive achievement. A responsible opposition can help win the struggle for unity, freedom, social betterment, and racial equality.

NOTES

1. Such as the Sahel-Benin Entente.

2. See Herbert Feith, *The Wilopo Cabinet, 1952-53; a Turning Point in Post-Revolutionary Indonesia (Ithaca: Modern Indonesia Project,* 1958), pp. 165-93.

3. See E. Shils, "The Concentration and Dispersion of Charisma," *World Politics* 11, no. 1 (October 1958).

4. This view is shared by other observers. For example, Pye indicates that "the fact that the ruling party in most non-western countries identifies itself with an effort to bring about total change in the society makes it difficult to limit the sphere of political controversy." See Lucian W. Pye, "The Non-Western Political Process," *Journal of Politics* 20 (1958): 473.

5. See Bertrand de Jouvenel, *Sovereignty,* trans. J. F. Huntington (Chicago, 1957), pp. 265-66.

6. See the discussion on planning by W. Arthur Lewis, "On Assessing a Development Plan," *Economic Bulletin, Journal of the Economic Society of Ghana* (June-July 1959).

7. The question has been raised whether or not an opposition could survive at all. The assumption here is that such opposition members have the choice of nominal opposition or oblivion. The benefits of opposition are preferable to oblivion. Hence recruits to the opposition can be found, especially where they do have an impact on government policy.

8. See D. E. Apter, and R. A. Lystad, "Bureaucracy, Party, and Democracy," in *Transition in Africa,* ed. G. E. Carter and W. M. Brown (Boston, 1958), pp. 42-43.

9. See J. A. Schumpeter, *Capitalism, Socialism and Democracy* (New York, 1942), p. 269.

10. There are, of course, exceptions. Where the middle spectrum does not show an identity of interest or is very small, political parties

435

exacerbate differences. The Third and Fourth French Republics are good examples of what can happen.

11. Where government is composed of the extremists these generalizations are of course inoperable. Rarely is it the case in new nations that extremists do in fact run the government.

MASS PARTIES AND NATIONAL INTEGRATION: THE CASE OF THE IVORY COAST

Aristide R. Zolberg

Public concern with Africa and Asia in recent years has focused on the evolution of many countries from dependent to independent status through a series of constitutional steps taken by colonial rulers in response to pressures exerted by local leaders within the context of a secular trend toward self-determination. Decolonization is indeed intrinsically important from a historical point of view. Moreover, the appearance of a bevy of new actors has deeply altered the nature of the international political system. How will they act on the international stage? How can they be influenced to behave in a manner compatible with Western interests? Faced with unusual problems, political decision makers in the West have often turned to students of politics to obtain some guidance.

However relevant the study of these phenomena may be, it should not lead us to neglect other aspects of the politics of new nations. From the point of view of the analysis of political change in general, for example, the juridical birth of the new states is significant mainly because it provides the institutional cocoon in which the metamorphosis of traditional societies into modern nations has begun to occur. Although in order to understand the complexities of nation-building no aspect of culture and society should remain unexplored, the examination of the contributions of political parties and movements to this process is particularly relevant because it is related to one of the oldest problems of politics, namely man's ability to direct social change toward selected goals through volitional action.

Scholarly observers of the African scene have often reported the positive contributions of political organizations to national integration. In

From Aristide R. Zolberg, "Mass Parties and National Integration: The Case of the Ivory Coast," *Journal of Politics* 25 (February 1963): 36-48. Reprinted by permission of the author and the publisher.

West Africa, nationalist movements are usually ranked foremost among the many factors which transform agglomerates of tribes and ethnic groups into societies coextensive with arbitrarily defined national boundaries. This is by no means an accidental consequence of their activities because such organizations, although they arose primarily in protest against alien rule and were directed toward its rapid elimination, often had also as their explicit goal the modernization of the social structure. This is particularly true of those that took the form of mass parties.[1] In his study of the Convention People's Party of Ghana, for example, Apter concluded that it "formed a major element in the societalization of what was a predominantly localized and fragmented set of tribal and regional purview, excepting in municipalities and excepting a small educated minority of the population."[2] This began to occur even before the organization had an opportunity to act as a lawful political party, from the very moment it was successful in obtaining a mass following. Wallerstein, generalizing from the experience of many additional parties and movements, has suggested even more forcefully that "the most important mechanism to reduce the conflict between ethnicity and national integration is the nationalist party."[3]

The pattern of development of the Ivory Coast does not deviate significantly from that of the region as a whole. As a review of the growth of the *Parti Démocratique de Côte d'Ivoire* (PDCI) will indicate, here too, the dominant mass organization has contributed to national integration. The relevance of this case study lies in that it suggests that the consequences of the party's activities cannot all be entered on the credit side of the ledger, even though its leaders repeatedly asserted that nation-building was one of their major goals. In the process of adjusting to what they perceived as being necessary to develop and to maintain their organization, Ivory Coast leaders designed a structure which reinforced some of the obstacles to national integration. It might even be argued, on the basis of available evidence, that some elements of party structure have even become additional obstacles to the achievements of the goals specified by party leaders after they assumed responsibility for government of the new state.

* * *

Shortly after World War II, the *PDCI* developed, with the help of experienced French Communist organizers, a highly structured party apparatus which it has maintained to this day through major changes of ideological orientation.[4] The party itself is a *section* of the interterritorial *Rassemblement Démocratique Africain*, of which the Ivory Coast's paramount leader, Félix Houphouet-Boigny, has always been President. Territorial organization may be summarized as follows:

a. *Basic Units:* Throughout most of the country, the smallest party organization is the village subcommittee. In small urban centers, there is a subcommittee in each *quartier* (ward). In the two African districts of Abidjan, the capital city, the party is divided into ethnic subcommittees. The basic units are headed by a *bureau* elected by card-bearing party members; the bureau itself selects a secretary-general from its midst.

b. *Middle level:* The subcommittees are organized into *sous-sections* at the level of the administrative *subdivisions* into which the Ivory Coast is divided. There are approximately 55 *sous-sections* headed by a bureau composed usually of selected secretaries-general of subcommittees. Again, the bureau selects a secretary-general from among its members.

c. *National level:* Prior to the 1959 Party Congress, the secretaries-general of the *sous-sections* formed a General Committee which elected the National Executive Committee. At the apex was the Secretary-General of the PDCI. Members of this executive body were selected to work with the interterritorial *RDA* Coordinating Committee.

Although the party's constitution provides for regular renewal of the bureaus at all levels, no elections were held between 1948 and 1959 at the national level. The few changes which occurred were due to deaths, jailings, and occasional resignations when leaders withdrew from active political life or disagreed with party policies. The remaining members then usually co-opted a secretary-general of a *sous-section* to fill the gap.

The career patterns of some of the national leaders indicate how the *PDCI* structure contributed to the formation of a national elite. An illustration is provided by the case of one member of the national executive who described his start in politics as follows:

Before the RDA was created, around 1944, I was displeased with the attitudes of the people in Abidjan who considered the Bété, the ethnic group to which I belong, as inferiors. This was due to the fact that the Bété had contact with the French later than people of the coastal areas and especially of the East. They were despised and called man-eating savages. Therefore, I founded a Bété mutual-aid society in Abidjan in 1944.[5]

In 1947, the Bété mutual-aid society became a subcommittee of the *PDCI*, following a pattern which will be discussed below. The Bété leader was then elected to the national executive, where he has remained ever since. Together with eight other members of this body, he was jailed by the French in 1949. As a "martyr" during the period of repression, he became a hero known and respected throughout the country. His political activities were not limited to Bété regions of the Ivory Coast: he travelled throughout the country to organize *sous-sections* and to prepare electoral campaigns. As a member of the RDA Coordinating Committee, he worked in other territories as well. Other top leaders followed similar career patterns. Some of them were elected to office in France or in Dakar, the seat of the *Grand Conseil* of the former federation of French West Africa, where they defended Ivory Coasts interests. From 1957 on, many filled newly-created executive positions at the territorial level.

Thus, at the uppermost level of party organization, the established structures encouraged the transformation of local ethnic leaders into

439

national leaders. They learned to work and plan for the success of a countrywide organization during a period of 12 years. Control of the central organs of government in the Ivory Coast by the *PDCI* has given these individuals the opportunity of occupying governmental posts in which they must make decisions for the country as a whole. The support they retained among their followers on the basis of ethnic solidarity has been to some extent transferred to the level of national institutions, which have thus been endowed with legitimacy. It is at this level that the positive effects of the structure of a mass party upon national integration are most clearly visible and that the generalizations cited earlier are verified.

* * *

In a country like the Ivory Coast, which is characterized by a high degree of ethnic diversity and many traditional hostilities between ethnic groups, it is not sufficient to study the consequences of the nationalist movement upon national integration at the level of the leadership alone. It is among the masses, where primordial solidarities are most intense, that the effects of the nationalist organization must be studied if its contributions to national integration are to be properly evaluated. We must ask, indeed, not only whether the party promoted political transformation in the direction desired by the advocates of nationalism, but furthermore whether it is not possible that the party's activities had negative as well as positive effects, i.e., whether they did not reinforce particularisms or even create an ethnic consciousness where it did not previously exist. The Ivory Coast experience suggests that these negative consequences did appear and that when nationalist leaders took over the reins of government they were faced with the necessity of undoing their own creations in order to achieve their explicitly stated goals. This problem, not yet resolved two years after independence, is a significant illustration of some of the difficulties that new nations in general may face.

The case of the Treichville *sous-section* provides a useful test of this hypothesis, since this major borough of Abidjan, the capital city of the Ivory Coast, is one in which other factors of social change tended to diminish the importance of purely traditional ties. A recent census distributes its 70,000 inhabitants among 108 ethnic groups.[6] This enumeration includes native-born Ivory Coasters as well as individuals born elsewhere in Africa. Unlike some other African cities, Treichville is not divided into well-differentiated neighborhoods, in part because of the control exercised by the French administration over its settlement.[7] Thus, face-to-face contacts among neighbors occur across ethnic groups rather than within them. The active population is engaged in secondary and tertiary economic activities and is thus subjected to modern rather than traditional external influences. Finally, the colonial authorities eliminated traditional political leaders from the administration of urban affairs several years ago.

Immediately after World War II, a large number of ethnic associations sprang up in the city, as in the case of the Bété mutual-aid society mentioned above. These associations. " ... remained closed to other Africans ... and thus rested on a racist foundation. ..."[8] In its first organizational drive, the *PDCI* utilized many of them as nuclei for local subcommittees. One observer, critical of the *PDCI*, confirms that "certain politicians exploited these associations for electoral ends."[9] Party leaders, however, justify this procedure on the grounds that it answered immediate organizational needs.[10] During the early days of illegal activity and resistance, the basic unit of the party had to be a fighting unit. In addition, it was necessary to develop efficient means for the downward communication of party directives to a mass which spoke a great variety of dialects. It was important also to devise tightly knit units which could sell membership cards, collect party dues, and above all, utilize social pressures to keep straying individuals within the party fold. Ethnic associations which existed in the city met these needs. Once this pattern was established, it persisted throughout the life of the party.

According to party leaders, there were 117 ethnic subcommittees in Treichville in 1959.[11] These units often include only members of a tribe who are also natives of a particular group of villages. For example, the *Baoulé*—who constitute about one-fifth of the population of the Ivory Coast and about one-eighth of the population of Treichville[12]—are distributed among 23 subcommittees in Treichville. They have created a *Baoulé* Central Committee which has no official existence within the party structure. This was done, according to one informant, in order to assert *Baoulé* strength in the face of attempts on the part of other ethnic groups to assert their supremacy in the local party organization.

Meetings of the subcommittees were held once a week until 1956. Since then *PDCI* supremacy on the national scene has resulted in a relaxation of activity, and meetings are held about once a month, except during electoral periods when they revert to the earlier schedule. These get-togethers are intended to expose the members to communications from the higher echelons of the party. Elections of the bureau of the subcommittees are normally held once yearly. In many of the units, however, leadership has become traditional rather than bureaucratic. There is some evidence that brother follows brother, son follows father, or nephew follows uncle in a given bureau post, according to the pattern of transmission of authority that prevails within the particular ethnic group under consideration.

Each bureau includes several offices known as "propagandists" which are filled by individuals belonging to major clans within the tribe who can communicate directives to the different extended families to which the members belong. The subcommittees are repositories of party membership cards which they issue to members; they are allowed to retain ten per cent of the proceeds from sales for their own activities. They are entitled to two votes in the yearly elections of the bureau of the Treichville *sous-section* of 20 members. The latter have developed an informal

441

division of labor: each individual is responsible for contact with a few ethnic subcommittees.[13]

Thus, except at the uppermost echelons, the party organization in Treichville provides little or no opportunity for horizontal communication between members of different ethnic groups. Face-to-face meetings which result from party activities take place within the confines of an ethnic group or subgroup. The organization utilized ethnic solidarity 12 years ago as a base to build party solidarity. The latter has in turn helped to maintain and to reinforce ethnic solidarity by providing a series of tightly knit cell-type basic units. It cannot be said, in this case, that "new types of membership units, such as branches of the nationalist movement, slowly cut across the traditional units."[14]

In the remainder of the country the activities of basic party units have had similar consequences. Villages are usually ethnically homogeneous; subcommittees may thus at the most further village solidarity. Concerning ward subcommittees in urban centers, it is necessary to indicate that human ecology reflects ethnic affiliations of the kinship system itself.[15] In one town in which there has been a great deal of conflict between the original inhabitants of the area and immigrants from other parts of the Ivory Coast, one observer reports the following:

> Public reunions and in general all political activity takes place separately, each [sub] committee chairman minding his own ward There is no liaison at the base among the various wards. In this sense the party, which might constitute an integrative factor for the immigrant population, provides absolutely nothing of the kind. The separateness of each of the ethnic groups is a fact acknowledged and admitted by the Africans themselves.[16]

* * *

A crucial consequence of party structure was revealed during the campaign preceding the elections of 1959. In Treichville, ethnic subcommittees were reactivated in order to help the *sous-section* in the selection of candidates to the national legislature. This was tantamount to election, since the Ivory Coast is a one-party state. Treichville, then a part of a larger electoral district, was allocated three seats by the party's National Executive. After several weeks of consultation and compromise, the *sous-section* drew up a list of 18 names from which the party's top leaders made the final selection.

The mode of consultation—regardless of whether it was intended as a genuine step to consult local committees, or whether it was engineered to give the appearance of consultation—encouraged selection based on ethnic representativeness. It raised the hopes of each of 117 ethnic subgroups of having one of their own represent them in the Assembly. It legitimized expectations that a *député* must be a defender of his ethnic group before anything else. It encouraged candidates to consider themselves the ambassadors of the ethnic groups to which they owed their selection. Finally, competition between the groups renewed ethnic solidarity among the party rank-and-file.

Party leaders who participated in the process of selection report that they tried to reduce the list of candidates below 18 but were unable to do so. It is clear, of course, that you cannot take a common denominator among incommensurables, whether they be apples, pears and oranges, or Baoulé, Agni, Mossi, Dioula and Bété. The national executive's final selection of three individuals belonging necessarily to specific ethnic groups could be interpreted by all other groups as depriving them of representation. As one member of the Treichville *sous-section* bureau put it, "After all we went through, we don't know whom these people represent, nor even whether they represent Treichville at all."

* * *

National party leaders are fully aware of the dangers inherent in the continued existence of ethnic groupings within and without the party. In a declaration to the constitutional drafting committee prior to the 1959 elections, M. Auguste Denise, then Secretary-General of the *PDCI* and Prime Minister of the Ivory Coast, summarized the problem as follows:

> We are not a territory lucky enough to have a limited number of ethnic groups. We have over 62 tribes. In the ten or thirteen years since we were born to political life, we have had as our ambition—in the fold of a party known to all of you and in which the majority of us are militants—to fuse these tribes in order to develop, little by little, a sort of single race. Instead, we see the opposite taking place. . . .[17]

In dealing with ethnic associations outside the party, which have often formed nuclei for the organization of opposition parties, the government has attempted to use legitimate coercion.[18] In dealing with particularism which results from party organization itself, the proposed solution has been party reorganization at the base.

A proposal to eliminate ethnic subcommittees in Treichville was put to the national executive during 1958 but was abandoned in fear of weakening the party immediately before an electoral period.[19] In June 1959, the *Bureau Politique* decided to go ahead with this proposed reorganization. Concerned mostly with Treichville, it would divide the borough into ward units and further into block organizations. While blocks tend to be ethnically homogeneous, the wards into which the city would be divided are not.[20]

If our hypothesis is reasonable, the implementation of such a proposal should have encountered serious difficulties. Ethnic group leaders have entrenched positions in the party hierarchy, which they have occupied for many years. They may interpret attempts to disband their subcommittees as threats upon their own power and prestige. Since they command support from their tribal brothers they may put forth the view that the national leadership is attacking ethnic groups themselves.[21] If the threat is deemed sufficiently great, ethnic subcommittees might become the nuclei for the organization of dissident groups. While the existence of an opposition might offset the omnivorous tendencies of a one-party state,

443

the ethnic character of such an opposition might accentuate centrifugal tendencies and lead to the increased use of coercive methods by the government to overcome them. The extermination of all opposition might then be legitimized by appealing to the value of national integration.

Recent developments have confirmed this reasoning, and the obstacles the party has encountered testify to the continued importance of the problem under consideration. The committee of high-level party leaders appointed to implement the reorganization of Treichville reported a few months later that it had been unable to carry out its assignment because "there were no natural neighborhoods in Treichville."[22] They had encountered serious resistance among the subcommittee leaders who form the backbone of the party and whom they dared not antagonize. In 1960, it was announced once again that ward committees would soon be created. But these turned out to be special units for civil servants who already live in government projects and who for the most part had not been previously active in the government party.[23] Moreover, party resolutions to the contrary notwithstanding, new ethnic subcommittees continue to appear. The Bakoué, a small ethnic group from the western part of the country, complaining that until now they had been scattered among the Bété, the Yacouba, and other subcommittees, called a meeting of all the residents of Treichville who considered themselves Bakoué in September, 1960. The general secretary of the PDCI *sous-section* attended this gathering and warmly welcomed the new ethnic unit to the party fold.[24]

Even where the party does not have to eliminate existing units but can start from the very beginning on a nonethnic foundation, the obstacles it has encountered are very great. In 1958, the party authorized the creation of a youth branch of the movement, with a status somewhere between that of an ancillary organization and that of a full-fledged political party.[25] Younger men with secondary or university education, highly critical of the ethnic structure of the PDCI and impatient with particularism in all its forms, attempted to organize the Treichville branch of their movement on a ward basis at the beginning of 1959. Shortly afterwards, however, they reverted to the organization of ethnic subcommittees. Questioned on this switch, members of the youth executive explained that there was at first very little response to calls for meetings and much difficulty in communicating with potential followers. A return to organization based on ethnic groups enabled the youth movement to round up an impressive number of members and ultimately to achieve a good bargaining position in dealing with the senior party. Youth leaders, while touring the country in order to organize branches of the JR. DACI throughout the hinterland, found that local initiators had usually excluded "foreigners" from their midst, i.e., for the most part Ivory Coast civil servants assigned to administrative posts outside their native region. While urging their followers to overcome racism and family squabbles, the visitors did not attempt to rectify the situation, lest their new-born organization be jeopardized.

* * *

The hope of reconstructing the PDCI in order to enable the party to shoulder the burdens of government in the Ivory Coast has by no means been abandoned. But it is apparent, from the above analysis, that in the course of dealing with threats to the maintenance of the organization, the party, like any other organization, often engages in activities that are detrimental to one of its explicit goals, national integration.

Is the situation discussed here peculiar to the Ivory Coast? An adequate answer would require the analysis of other situations based on comparable data. Various hints suggest that intensive research would uncover similarities elsewhere. Addressing the interterritorial congress of the *RDA* at Bamako in 1957 Modibo Keita, later President of the Mali Republic, suggested that the pattern analyzed here prevailed in many territorial sections and that the movement as a whole must make an effort to eliminate ethnic units "in order to avoid future difficulties due to the crystallization of militants on positions based on ethnic affiliations."[26] In general, as Coleman has indicated, the growth of territorial nationalism in Africa has been accompanied by the rise of subnationalisms based on primordial ties.[27] Although this has been revealed in dramatic fashion in multiparty states such as Nigeria, the Congo (Leopoldville), and Kenya, where political alignments tend to follow lines of ethnic cleavage, the case of the Ivory Coast suggests the appearance of this phenomenon in one-party states, where there is no apparent competition, as well.

It is evidently impossible to establish a quantitative balance sheet of the "positive" and "negative" consequences of the activities of a political party from the point of view of a country's national integration. On the basis of the data presented here, we cannot determine whether the PDCI's contributions to the development of a new society in the Ivory Coast outweigh the obstacles it has placed in the path its leaders want to follow. In the long run, it is likely that its integrative functions will overshadow the others. Nevertheless, it is clear that the political forces visible in contemporary Africa do not all lead in the same direction. Although mass parties can channel social change, their ability to exert leverage upon social processes is limited by their maintenance needs which force them to come to terms with elements in the social structure which party leaders consider undesirable.

In order to achieve a balanced appraisal of the contributions of a political organization to the process of social change, it is therefore necessary to specify the sphere in which its effects are studied and to be aware of the discrepancies between the wishes of its leaders and political realities. In particular, it is imperative to analyze the structures of political organizations in action, as distinguished from their formal structures described in constitutional documents and from ideological statements. Generalizations concerning the functions of political organizations in the new states are most useful as guides to direct further observation. But the accumulation of empirical process-oriented case studies in hitherto

445

unexplored countries remains a task of high priority for political scientists lest general theories of political development be erected on a base of fragile hypotheses.

NOTES

1. For the distinction in structure, orientation, and ideology between "mass" and "patron" parties, inspired from Maurice Duverger's classification, see: Ruth Schachter, "Single-Party Systems in West Africa," *American Political Science Review* 40 no. 2 (June 1961): 294-307; and Thomas Hodgkin, *African Political Parties* (Baltimore: Penguin Books, 1961).

2. David E. Apter, *The Gold Coast in Transition* (Princeton: Princeton University Press, 1955), p. 212.

3. Immanuel Wallerstein, "Ethnicity and National Integration," *Cahiers d'Etudes Africaines* 2, no. 3 (1960): 138.

4. For the political development in the Ivory Coast, see: Aristide R. Zolberg, "One-Party Government in the Ivory Coast" (Ph.D. diss., University of Chicago, 1961).

5. Interview, 18 May 1959.

6. Ivory Coast, Ministère du Plan, Service de la Statistique, *Inventaire Economique de la Côte d'Ivoire 1947-1956* (1958), pp. 29-30.

7. Evidence for this statement was gathered from communications with researchers engaged in a study of urbanization in Abidjan for the Ministry of Public Works of the Ivory Coast.

8. F. J. Amon d'Aby, *La Côte d'Ivoire dans la cité africaine* (Paris: Larose, 1951), p. 37. My translation.

9. *Ibid.*

10. All facts contained in the discussion on Treichville, and opinions attributed to Treichville politicians, unless otherwise mentioned, were gathered in interviews with party leaders in April and May 1959.

11. A count of party subcommittees gathered from meeting notices appearing in *Abidjan-Matin* from January to June 1959, adds up to 93 different subcommittees only.

12. Ivory Coast, *Inventaire*, pp. 26, 29, 30.

13. *Abidjan-Matin*, 19 February 1959, p. 2.

14. Apter, *Gold Coast in Transition*, p. 127.

15. See for example, R. Grivot, "Agboville: Esquisse d'une cité d'Afrique noire," *Etudes Ebournénnes* 4 (1955): 84-107.

16. Henri Raulin, "Problemes Fonciers dans les regions de Gagnoa et Daloa," *Mission d'Etude des Groupements Immigrés en Côte d'Ivoire*, Fascicule 3 (1957), p. 126. My translation.

17. Ivory Coast, *Procés-Verbal des Travaux de la commission spéciale* (1959), mimeo. stenotyped record.

446

18. The government has succeeded in including in the Constitution an article making "any particularistic propaganda, of an ethnic or racial nature," punishable by law. In addition, several leaders of ethnic associations were jailed in 1959 on a charge of endangering the security of the state.

19. Interview with a member of the National Executive, 19 April 1959.

20. The decision was announced in *Abidjan-Matin*, 18 June 1959. Information on wards and blocks was gathered from the same source as in (9), above.

21. In informal conversations on this subject, informants reported that subcommittee leaders expressed this view soon after the announcement of reorganization was made public.

22. Interview with a member of the *Bureau Politique*, 1959.

23. *Abidjan-Matin*, 25 February 1960.

24. *Ibid.*, 3 October 1960.

25. Information concerning the RDA Youth Movement was gathered from interviews with its leaders and personal observation at meetings and during a tour of the country.

26. "Rapport d'Organisation: Comptes-Rendus du troisiéme Congrés interterritorial du RDA," Bamako, 1957 (mimeo.).

27. James S. Coleman, *Nigeria: Background to Nationalism* (Berkeley and Los Angeles: University of California Press, 1958).

THE MILITARY
AND MODERNIZATION
IN THE MIDDLE EAST

James A. Bill

The purpose of this article is to analyze the role played by the military in the socio-political changes taking place in the Middle East. The analysis approaches the difficult task of relating the military to the processes of modernization first by evaluating and classifying the bewildering array of military coups that have occurred in the area. The patterns of cooperation and conflict within various military establishments as well as between military and civilian forces will also be viewed in the context of modernization. Finally, through documenting certain similarities and identifying related characteristics among the various military elites, it is hoped that useful insights will be provided into the background and development of the military role in the processes of modernization.

Empirical support for the generalizations presented in this article has been drawn from the experiences of particular Middle Eastern societies and military establishments. The key societies referred to herein are those of Egypt, Iran, and Iraq. Evidence will also be drawn from the experiences of the military in Turkey and Syria. The "military" refers to all armed forces, including the army, navy, and air force, but excluding particular police forces and gendarmeries. Because the army comprises the overwhelming bulk of the military in these countries, the words "military," "armed forces," and "army" are used interchangeably.

TWO IMAGES OF THE MILITARY

The role of the military in instituting or thwarting processes of social change is a factor that has recently become most relevant in regard to the

From James A. Bill, "The Military and Modernization in the Middle East," *Comparative Politics* 2 (October 1969): 41-62. Reprinted by permission of the author and the publisher.

less-developed areas of the world. In the limited discussion that has touched this point, two quite contradictory positions have usually been taken. The first considers the military in these areas as the central pillar buttressing the status quo. The army is viewed as a conserving force that steadfastly thwarts all attempts to introduce significant change. Edward Shils supplies several reasons for such a stance by the military:

> Yet it probably remains a fact that the military have a feeling of sympathy for tradition, not only for their own military tradition but for the traditional style of society as well. Hierarchic dignity, respect for superiors, solicitude for subordinates, solidarity, and conventionality produce in professional soldiers an attachment to the same phenomena in civilian society. Their humble origins and their separation from urbane pleasures and indulgences sustain this sympathy. The result is distrust of those who derogate traditional life and rush to overturn it.[1]

The second school of thought views the military in the less-developed areas as the champion of change. The army is portrayed as a dynamic force that uproots stifling traditions and replaces them with new patterns. In his study of social change in the Middle East, Manfred Halpern emphasizes "the transformation of the army from an instrument of repression in its own interests or that of kings into the vanguard of nationalism and social reform. . . ."[2]

Because it maintains a virtual monopoly on the instruments of force and coercion in these societies, the military is in the best position to carry out either type of program. The fact that it is also relatively well-organized and well-disciplined renders it even more powerful in relation to the rest of the groups in the society.

Role of the Military—To Conserve

There are several reasons why the military is considered, and in some cases rightly so, to be a force that impedes change. It is a fact of history that within military forces there has always been intense sympathy for tradition and the traditional way of life. As Shils indicates in the passage quoted, the very structure and function of the military reinforce such feelings and inculcate such values in military personnel.[3]

It is also true that the armed forces are to a certain degree isolated from civilian society. As such, they often tend to be distrustful of civilian elements. This suspicion is heightened by the inefficiency, compromise, and ascriptive practices that are so common among Middle East civilian governmental institutions. This distrust becomes directed toward the more progressive as well as toward the conservative civilian groups. Thus, the army often views civilian innovators with hostility and opposes their programs.

In certain Middle Eastern countries the highest echelons of the military

449

elite are composed of men who are opposed to any kind of fundamental change. They believe that such changes would jeopardize their positions of power and influence. The senior officers who control the organization and who make the vital decisions are seldom interested in seeing the status quo altered. This vested interest is intensified by the fact that these senior army officers are wealthy landowners and members of parliament in many of these societies. It is also significant to note that Middle Eastern monarchs have traditionally attempted to ensure that the military elite's stake in the status quo remain strong.

Even when the military conspicuously introduces such change as vast improvements in the fields of transportation and communication, it does so within the given socio-political context. Technological advancement here, for example, directly serves to buttress traditional political patterns. Scarce and valuable resources are often channelled to military priorities rather than to social and educational developmental programs. As J. C. Hurewitz convincingly argues, there is an important difference between "military modernization" and social, economic, and political modernization. The former often impedes the latter.[4]

In expressing his dissatisfaction with the military as a modernizing force, Professor Shils points out that this is complicated by the fact that the armed forces in these areas cannot even satisfactorily guarantee order. In his words, the military which "promises to maintain order and—as an afterthought—to modernize, does so only by sweeping the disorder temporarily into a box from which it recurrently springs in full strength."[5]

Role of the Military—To Modernize

Several scholars have argued that the military is a force that propels social change and political modernization in many of the less-developed societies of the world.[6] A major influence that has led certain military bureaucracies to assume such a role has been the impact of the West. Western achievements and advancement, in general, and Western military technology, in particular, have implanted in the minds of many Middle Eastern army officers the pressing need to improve and modernize their own military forces. In order to carry out military reform, it became evident that other changes had to be introduced into the society. Industries had to be established to provide equipment, while men had to be educated and trained to manufacture and use that equipment. As Morroe Berger points out, it is especially meaningful to notice that the Muhammad Ali period in Egypt was preceded by the Napoleonic invasion. In a similar but more recent vein, it is significant that Nasser's Egypt was preceded by many years of British occupation. There is little doubt that both the Napoleonic invasion and the British occupation alerted the Egyptian military to the drastic need for change.[7]

As it attempts to modernize its own organization, the Middle Eastern army is forced to raise the level of education of its personnel. While the lowest echelons are being cleansed of illiteracy, the officer corps are acquiring more specialized skills. At the same time, they are introduced to a broader scope of subjects and are sometimes taught courses in political science, psychology, and sociology. Such strides in education contribute to the trend that is moving certain Middle Eastern armies toward the support of general social transformation by alerting the personnel to highly advanced trends and techniques in the West. Another important effect of increased education in the army is that its members often acquire the extremely scarce technical skills which are essential to modernization and economic development.

The fact that the armed forces stand some distance from civilian society also can be used to explain their role as an innovating force. Lucian Pye has argued that the acculturative process in the army is especially thorough. This provides a higher degree of psychological security in the army than that which may prevail among inhabitants of a city, for example. Because of the intense nature of the acculturative process within the military, there is a much more definite break with family circles and other groups that are bound especially close to tradition. The factors of separateness and psychological security make the member of the army less vulnerable to the pressures of conservative civilian elite forces. This distinction, intertwined with the greater possibilities for vertical mobility within the army, contributes further to the weakening of any sense of identity between the army officer and the civilian politicians and industrialists.[8]

Finally, the bulk of the middle-ranking army officers are now being drawn from the middle and lower-middle classes in society. These men are usually well-educated and have been imbued with values that condemn foreign influence in their homelands. They decry the old domestic social structures that have so often frustrated their own hopes and aspirations. This type of army officer has taken power in some areas of the Middle East, while in others he is controlled and suspiciously watched by those opposed to fundamental social change. In both cases, however, this type of officer can be generally recognized as an advocate of modernization.

Thus, there are many reasons behind the military coups that are so common in the Middle East. The military may act to preserve traditional values or to introduce new ones. Its action may be spurred by its dissatisfaction with the corruption and inefficiency that pervade the old regime or with the old social structure in general. It may move to modernize due to its exposure to foreign influences and techniques or it may act to destroy what it considers subjection to foreign forces and control. It may attempt to preserve or improve its own integrity and standing in the society. It may find itself involved in conflicts that are ideologically based or it may take action under the control of certain individuals or groups who seek to further their own ambitions. In the end, any one of the above reasons, or any combination thereof, may do much to explain a particular military action in the Middle East.

THE MIDDLE EASTERN MILITARY COUP

The kind of military coup that occurs in the Middle East is a key in determining whether or not fundamental change will be instituted. By creating general classifications for the coups, one is better able to understand the individual coup as well as its consequences upon the society. The military coup may fall into four general categories:[9]

1. One tradition-oriented ruler or elite may replace another tradition-oriented ruler or elite, with the result that there is no transformation of the existing system.
2. Tradition-conserving forces may overthrow a modern-oriented regime, resulting in a halt to further transformations of the system.
3. One modernizing ruler or elite may replace another modernizing ruler or elite, an event which may or may not result in transformations of the existing system.
4. Modernizing forces may overthrow a tradition-oriented regime resulting in transformations of the existing system.

In this analysis, modernization is not synonymous with economic development or industrialization. Although substantial increases in production, greatly expanded transportation systems, sharp rises in national per capita income, and burgeoning urban construction surely are involved in modernization, they do not necessarily imply that socio-political systems are being transformed.[10] Much of this type of change may occur without the introduction of any basic changes whatsoever in the social structure of the country. Thus, the rewards of such development may be channeled into the hands of a very small group or class. A rigid traditional social structure may very well exist and still allow much of this type of change to occur. Labelling such a society "modernizing" seems a bit premature at best. A more dynamic analysis would perhaps indicate that this type of society is soon to pay an extremely high price for its program. Because such a policy maximizes the benefits of a limited group, it deprives the society of the skills and cooperation of the rest of the population and thus lessens the opportunities for introducing and institutionalizing change. Ironically, the more the tradition-oriented elite attempts to introduce this kind of change, the more it accelerates the alienation of the rest of society as expectations are heightened and aspirations sharpened. Thus, not only is the process of change limited, but the result is often a violent upheaval or internal war.

Modernization, then, as referred to in this paper, is a process in which new elites drawn from different classes and entertaining entirely new values come into power and initiate their programs. Genuine social and political participation is accorded to all groups and classes as they appear in society. Comprehensive advances in such fields as industrialization, education, and living standards are usually, but not necessarily, indicators that such a process is in motion. The military coup is of prime importance within this framework of analysis because it always results in a change of individual elites whose stance concerning modernization becomes crucial. It is in these terms that the coups are classified.

In the first type of military coup, military intervention results in one tradition-oriented elite losing its position to another such elite. A prime example of this occurred in Iraq in 1936 when the army, under General Bakr Sidqi, suddenly seized power. Despite profound disagreements that split its own ranks, the new military regime was unified in turning against the reform-minded civilian groups that had supported the coup. The new regime was no more interested in introducing fundamental changes than its predecessors had been. This same kind of coup took place six more times within the next five years in Iraq, with the military always playing a key role.

There are innumerable examples where this type of change has occurred without *active* military intervention. In these cases, the military has remained in the background where it has tacitly given its blessing to the changeover. All cabinet changes in Iran, Iraq, and Egypt during their periods as twentieth-century monarchies were of this variety.[11] During one 28-year stretch in Iraq, for example, Nuri el-Said was Prime Minister 14 different times. In Iran, military support for the Pahlavi monarchs resulted in a situation where majlis (national assembly) membership was dominated for years by the same groups of men. A 35-year analysis of majlis representation, encompassing the sixth through the nineteenth majlises (1925-1960), indicates that 52 different individuals were present in at least every other majlis (represented in seven majlises or more), while 68 others sat in at least one out of every three majlises (represented in five or six majlises).[12]

Examples of the second category of coup are relatively scarce. A prime instance in recent Middle Eastern history when traditional forces have overthrown a modern-oriented regime occurred in Iran in August 1953. The army intervened to overthrow the harassed, but modern-oriented, regime of Muhammad Musaddiq and to reestablish the traditional government under the effective aegis of the Shah. The Iranian army officer primarily responsible for the coup, General Fazlollah Zahedi, immediately became Prime Minister.[13] The reinstated old regime then continued the policy it had been forced to abandon in 1951. This included a policy of repression and discrimination against the burgeoning middle classes—a sector whose cooperation and commitment is essential for modernization.

A second example of this type of military coup occurred in November 1961 when Syria broke from the United Arab Republic. The new Syrian elite that came to power with military support was the same tradition-oriented group that had ruled Syria prior to 1956. There is an extraordinary similarity between the elite that came to power in September 1954 and the one that came to rule as a result of the coup in 1961. The parliaments that were elected in September 1954 and December 1961 possessed an almost identical alignment of parties and party seats.

453

Fifty-nine of the same men who sat in the 1954 parliament were again elected following the coup in 1961. Also, the same powerful men (el-Azm, Dawalibi, Kuzbari, Assali, Hourani) were present in the ruling elites of both periods.[14]

An extension of this category might include the instances of military intervention where the army has acted in support of the traditional regime by suppressing popular uprisings. Thus, after the Iranian army, with the aid of planes, bombs, and tanks, had reportedly crushed a tribal uprising in 1963, former Prime Minister Alam warned the nation, "It is no joke to come to grips with the Army."[15] In January 1962, the army sent commandos into Tehran Univeristy where they violently put down antigovernment student demonstrations. Dramatic examples of this type of military activity occurred in Iraq in 1948. 1952, and 1956. The Jordanian and Moroccan monarchies have also consistently used the military to buttress and maintain their political ascendance.

The third type of coup is one in which a particular modernizing elite replaces another such elite. This is what has been occurring in Iraq, for example, since the key coup of 1958. On 8 February 1963, a group of young officers, many of whom were lieutenants and a few of whom were influential colonels and generals, engineered a successful coup against the government of General Abdul Karim el-Kassem. Nine months later, another coup took place. This coup saw the military forces once again divide as another group of officers took power. It is significant that after seizing power the leaders of both of these coups emphasized the point that they were merely continuing the revolution of 1958. All parties involved recognized the momentous nature of the 1958 coup but rationalized their own seizure of power by pointing to the fact that their predecessors had deviated from carrying out the necessary transformations.[16] In situations where this type of coup occurs, there is usually very little implementation of basic reforms since the modern-oriented elites expend their energies upon the struggles that go on within their own ranks.[17] Besides Iraq, this kind of situation also prevails in contemporary Syria.

The final class of military coup is the one in which a traditional regime is overthrown by forces that subsequently begin to implement fundamental changes in the society. The outstanding example of this, of course, was the coup which the army carried out in Egypt in 1952. The same type of coup occurred in Iraq in 1958, but the new Egyptian elite was much more successful in stabilizing its own position. Hence, it has been better able to implement its policies. Thus, in Egypt the entire socio-political structure has been transformed, while a social class whose policies had long suppressed basic change has been destroyed. As Morroe Berger describes the new elite in Egypt, "The present military elite is itself the human engine of change, pushing the community onward seeking modernization in all realms as an end in itself."[18]

The foregoing analysis of Middle Eastern military coups indicates that these coups do not necessarily lead to modernization. Even when a coup brings to power an elite willing to modernize, the means for it to realize this goal may not exist. On the other hand, it is extremely rare for a modernizing regime to be overthrown by a tradition-oriented force able to reestablish the old social structure. It is also true that those societies in the Middle East that are most successful in modernizing are such because of revolutionary acts in which the military has been the prime actor.

Thus, the military has played highly diverse roles in relation to the processes of modernization in the Middle East. Much of the reason for the particular stance that the military has assumed in this regard resides in the patterns that mark its external and internal relationships of cooperation and conflict. As the coup typology indicates, military-civilian interactions, for example, take on special significance when viewed in light of the challenge of modernization.

MILITARY-CIVILIAN POWER RELATIONS

Relationships between the military and certain civilian groups and organizations have fallen into various patterns in the Middle East. For purposes of analysis, key examples of military-civilian group interaction will be classified into two general categories, according to whether or not the interaction occurred in the immediate seizure or in the maintenance of power. There are, of course, numerous examples of military-civilian group cooperation and conflict in the Middle East. The cases outlined below have been chosen because they are among the most dramatic examples of such relations as they have developed during especially crucial periods.

Military-Civilian Group Interaction and the Seizure of Power

In the early 1920s, Mustafa Kemal and his military followers relied heavily upon civilian groups as they won the War of Independence and established the Turkish Republic. In the War of Independence, religious-conservative groups provided important support; but in the actual seizure of power, Kemal was backed by the Defense of Rights movement which denounced the Sultan's government in Istanbul. Teachers, lawyers, and intellectuals provided the bulk of the support for this movement and their societies spread throughout Anatolia. This civilian support was extremely important to Kemal, since it was instrumental in his military victories over the Greeks as well as in his triumph over the central government.[19]

Another example of this type of cooperation occurred in Iraq during the 1936 military coup. A group of progressive civilians allied themselves with a group of army officers forming a coalition that was able to plan and carry out the successful coup. The civilian organization in this case was known as the *Ahali* group. It was composed largely of reform-minded young men who had been plotting changes for several years.

455

In the fast-moving events in Iran during 1951-1952, civilian groups played extremely important roles. These roles were continued in the coup of August 1953 which saw the Musaddiq government overthrown and the Shah's regime reinstated. Although the military was responsible for the coup, civilian mobs poured through the streets of Tehran and supported the army. This civilian support, which consisted largely of hired elements from south Tehran, was implemented in a direct manner at the time of the coup itself.

Despite the importance that military-civilian cooperation meant to the success of the coups briefly described above, the military at the same time maintained especially hostile relations with other civilian groups. In Turkey, Kemal's forces were steadfastly opposed by the royalists in Istanbul. It may also be noted that, while supporting him in the War of Independence, most religious and conservative civilian groups opposed his seizure of power and the establishment of a republic. In Iraq, the supporters of the beleaguered regime fiercely contested the move by the army. Landlords, tribal shaykhs, and religious leaders denounced the coup. In Iran in 1953, the Communists were the most powerful civilian group to oppose the coup. After two previous days of victorious street fighting, however, they did not enter into physical combat with the forces that carried out the August 19 coup.

In these three examples of military-civilian group interaction, it is evident that the cooperation of particular civilian elements has been vital to the success of particular coups. There are other cases, however, where the coups have been carried out almost entirely from within the military itself. Such was the case in Egypt in 1952 and, to a lesser extent, in Iraq in 1958 and in Syria in March 1949. In these cases, however, it was not long following the initial coup before military-civilian relationships became extremely important.

Military-Civilian Group Interaction and the Maintenance of Power

After gaining power in July 1952, the Egyptian military elite soon realized that it needed the support and cooperation of civilian organizations and groups throughout the land. Thus, a little more than a month after taking power, the Free Officers instituted the Agrarian Reform Law. This was designed to move the peasant masses behind the new military regime. The "Liberation Rally" and "National Union," as well as the "Arab Socialist Union" of today, stand as proof of subsequent attempts by the regime to gain grass roots support among the civilian population. In March 1954, the Egyptian military elite was able to maintain and solidify its position through the direct assistance of a civilian group. In a showdown period which found the military itself internally fissured as well as confronted by hostile civilian organizations, the elite that controlled the army was able to enlist the support of the trade unions. It was this alliance with labor that enabled the military to survive the crisis and to secure the day.

General Kassem and the military officers who seized power in Iraq in 1958 came to rely very heavily upon the support of Communist groups. Opposed by certain elements in the army as well as elsewhere, Kassem and his following in the armed forces were forced to rely again and again upon Communist support. The outstanding example of this cooperation occurred in March 1959 when the Mosul Brigade of the Second Division revolted and set up its own government. The Kassem forces, in alliance with the Communists, finally were able to put down the revolt in a violent encounter. It was the Communist "People's Militia" that was largely responsible for quelling the uprising.

Although the military regimes referred to above have relied heavily upon certain civilian groups, it is also evident that they have met determined opposition from other civilian groups. In Egypt, the elite found itself pitted against the Wafd, the Communists, and the Muslim Brotherhood. The struggle that ensued was one in which the very existence of the participants was at stake. By the end of 1954, the military had won a clear victory over all three organizations. The Wafd organization disintegrated most easily since the army simply demolished its base of economic support. The Communist movement was attacked through mid-1956 and then again beginning in 1959. The powerful and dangerous Muslim Brotherhood was destroyed in the fall of 1954 after one of its members fired eight shots at President Nasser.

In Iraq, General Kassem and his military supporters were opposed by pro-Nasser and pro-Baathist civilian groups as well as by certain landlord and ultra-conservative elements. Because large numbers of men within the military came to share the same values as these opposition civilian groups and because Kassem was forced to move against his own main base of civilian support (the Communists) in order to maintain his independence, he did not fare as well as his counterparts in Egypt. In early 1963, the Kassem military regime was overthrown by another military group that enjoyed the full support of the Baath Party.

The success or failure of a military elite to maintain its position depends a great deal upon its relations with the civilian groups in the society. In terms of a successful program of modernization, these relationships are more crucial at the post-coup stage than at the time of the actual seizure of power. The important mass participation and commitment cannot be attained by a small group of army officers no matter how powerful they may be. National institutions and political parties must be built throughout the society in order to link the leaders and the masses, the ministers and the villagers. In this sense, the military elite must do more than maintain a tenuous hold upon the formal levers of power by balancing civilian supporter against civilian opponent. It must gain mass support for progressive programs. This has been the fundamental difference between the Nassers and the Kassems.

INTRAMILITARY POWER RELATIONS

In the Middle East, the army has been continually rent by internal cleavage and conflict. Because of the key position the military holds in the society, such strife is felt throughout the entire country. Conflicts that spring from within the army also tend to result in a relatively high amount of violence, since the instruments of physical destruction are concentrated here.

There are two noticeable trends concerning intramilitary politics in the Middle East. First, there has often been a significant gap in the thought and actions of the military personnel, reflecting differences in social background, rank, and age. This gap becomes especially conspicuous during times of unrest and upheaval when the army is deeply split into conflicting groups. Secondly, successful military coups in the Middle East are followed by tense power struggles within the army that often result in a series of subsequent coups.

Significant Fissures in Middle Eastern Officer Corps

Certain tradition-oriented Middle Eastern regimes have been overthrown by military elements (Military Coup Type 4). Upon examining these elements, one is immediately struck by the great similarity of age, rank, and social background. These similarities are not confined to separate countries or armies, but extend across national boundaries and relate the personnel responsible for the coups to one another. The men who engineered the coup in Egypt in 1952 were much the same type as the men who took control in Iraq in 1958. Such men have also made their appearance in Turkey and Syria. A recognition of these important similarities can assist in the formulation of cautious hypotheses regarding the behavior of Middle Eastern army officers.[20]

In Egypt, with the exception of General Naguib, who "never belonged to the Free Officers movement,"[21] the members of the Revolutionary Command Council following the coup presented the following picture. All eleven men were between 30 and 35 years of age. Eight of the eleven entered the military academy in 1936 and graduated from there in 1938. At the time of their successful coup, four were lieutenant colonels, four were majors, two were wing commanders, and one was a squadron leader. Nonvoting members of the Council included four more colonels and two captains.[22] The overwhelming majority of the free officers were drawn from the middle and lower-middle classes in the society. As Keith Wheelock has written, "Their movement was not based on the masses; yet, inarticulately perhaps, it expressed the revolt of the suppressed middle class."[23]

Young, progressive army officers also sprang into prominence in Turkey in the 1920s, in Iraq in 1958, and in Syria in the late 1950s. The nationalist officers who surrounded Mustafa Kemal in Turkey were in their early forties, while those that remained loyal to the traditional Istanbul government were much older.[24] In the Iraqi coup of 1958, 44-year-old Kassem was surrounded by colonels such as Abdul Salam Aref, Fadhil Abbas el-Mahdawi, and Nadhim Kamel Tabakchali. These Iraqi officers "were representative of the class from which they sprang, middle and lower-middle class."[25] This type of leader began to make his presence felt in Syria in the late 1950s when colonels like Abdul Hamid Sarraj, Amin el-Nafuri, and Jamal Faysal and captains like Mustafa Hamdun and Ahmad el-Hunaydi moved into positions of power. One of the best examples of the different stances taken by the junior and senior grade army officers in the Middle East concerns the 431 officers convicted for membership in the Communist Tudeh Party in Iran in 1954. The list included 23 colonels, 64 majors, 100 captains, 197 lieutenants, 32 air cadets, and 15 warrant officers. The 23 colonels were the highest ranking officers involved.[26]

The personnel that compose the armed forces of a country are drawn from the population at large. They are recruited from different groups and classes in the society and often continue to entertain the values and ways of these groups. As time passes the actors become imbued with values that are peculiarly military, yet it is doubtful that they ever become totally detached from the bonds of their premilitary life.[27] In the Middle East, a special relationship has existed between the young middle-ranking officer and the striving, burgeoning middle classes in these societies.[28] Many were raised in middle class surroundings. These officers, like the middle classes in general, were violently opposed to the "triple enemy: imperialism, the monarchy and feudalism."[29] Extremely nationalistic, these elements deplored the traditional regimes which allowed their homelands to be humbled and exploited by foreign powers. It is no accident that the Iraqi coup in 1936 occurred but four years after Iraq was released from mandate status, that the Syrian coups in 1949 closely followed the withdrawal of French troops in 1945, and that the Egyptian coup in 1952 followed within five years of the discontinuation of British occupation of Egypt proper.[30] The middle-ranking officers shared many of the same frustrations that plagued the middle classes in general. They felt that their skills and talents were not being put to the best use and that the organization and society of which they were a part were inefficient and corrupt partly because of this.

One important reason why the coups in these Middle Eastern societies have sprung from within the ranks of the junior grade officers is that the senior officers have been much more firmly committed to the traditional order.[31] The generals have been large landholders and have held influential positions in the parliaments and cabinets. The ruling elements in the old regimes have always recognized the value of possessing the loyalty of these senior officers and have thus showered favors upon them. Nuri el-Said "knew them all personally, and . . . treated senior officers with a friendly familiarity."[32] In today's Iran, this technique is vividly evident. The Shah

459

provides the generals in the Iranian Army with material and political benefits that become greater as years pass. Not only does the monarch see that these officers are handsomely rewarded, but he also handpicks them and replaces them when he feels it is expedient to do so. Although special care is taken to see that the middle-ranking officers are well rewarded also, it is not insignificant to note that within these ranks there is an extraordinarily high rate of attrition. Since 1954, over 1,000 middle-ranking Iranian army officers have been arrested or dismissed.[33]

The type of intramilitary tension analyzed above takes place prior to and during the seizure of power by the young officers described. This does not imply, however, that major struggles within the military cease once this new group has attained power. Quite to the contrary, the period following the takeover is the scene of an even more violent and complex conflict.

CONTINUING CHARACTER OF THE MIDDLE EASTERN COUP

The newly-installed military elite in Iraq in 1936 enjoyed power for less than nine months. Following its short rule, six more military coups took place in Iraq in rapid succession. One year following the Iraqi coup of 1958, two large-scale military uprisings were put down by the harassed forces of Kassem. In February 1963, a successful military coup overthrew General Kassem. This regime itself was overturned nine months later and a new military government took power. The Syrian military that seized power in March 1949 governed for only four and a half months. Its overthrow in August 1949 was followed by a series of coups that extend to the present day. The elite that engineered the Egyptian coup in 1952 has had a better future, although it also became involved in a bitter power struggle. Bakr Sidqi, Abdul Karim el-Kassem, and Husni Za'im, the leaders of the coups in Iraq in 1936 and 1958 and in Syria in March 1949, all lost their lives at the hands of their own armies.

Once having achieved power, the military is suddenly confronted with deep dissension and dramatic division. Its members had moved together against a foe despised by all. Now confronted with the need to consolidate their position, to enact positive programs, and to establish an operating government, the members of the military suddenly discover the depth of the differences that mark their political orientations. These fissures widen and take on the character of ideological disagreements as the new regime endeavors to implement constructive programs. The leaders of the new elites realize this difficulty best of all. Thus, they continually warn their armies to remain united. On 16 June 1959, General Kassem, sensing the unrest and divisions appearing in his army, delivered a stirring speech to his officers in which he asked them to remain united. In one of many similar statements, he said, "The Army is the base on which the people depend.

The people always think of depending on the Army. The Army must therefore remain a united force incapable of being disunited. It must remain a united force...."[34] One month later to the very day, the rebelling Second Division of the Iraqi Army took power in Kirkuk.

The values and beliefs of civilian opposition groups come to be championed in the army; thus, Communists, Baathists, landlord groups, and Muslim Brotherhood sympathizers were in evidence in the officer corps of the armies of Egypt and Iraq. Recognizing the dangers of this situation, General Kassem pleaded with his army to steer clear of any civilian group affiliations. He warned his officers: "We do not like that the trends and leanings of these parties should get into the ranks of the Army under any circumstances."[35] Three months following the November 1963 coup in Iraq, the new president and commander of the army, Colonel Abdul Salam Aref, repeatedly warned his armed forces "to keep clear of party politics."[36]

Despite the leaders' calls to unity, disunity has prevailed. In Iraq in 1936-1937, the officers that supported Bakr Sidqi lost out in the power struggle to a group of nationalist officers who gained more strength within the army and took control of the government. The Bakr group had hoped to unite the Arabs and Kurds, while the nationalist officers stressed Pan-Arabism.

Following the Iraqi coup in 1958, Kassem and his followers were opposed by at least three different groups of army officers: (1) those who stressed Arab unity and were sympathetic to Egyptian President Nasser; (2) those who feared reforms which would undermine their socioeconomic position; and (3) those who were sympathetic to the Communists. Kassem moved against all three groups. Initially, he acted against the first group when he demoted and then arrested his deputy premier and minister of interior, Colonel Aref. When Aref's regiment resisted, the members were forcefully disarmed. In March 1959, the Mosul revolt led by Colonel Abdul Wahab Shawaf and Brigadier Nadim Kamel Tabakchali was violently put down. Shawaf and Tabakchali were both classmates of Colonel Aref and the revolt was pro-Aref and anti-Communist. In December 1958, Kassem arrested a group of high army officers who belonged to the extreme right and who opposed the entire reform program. Finally, General Kassem also moved against those in the military who were sympathetic to the Communists. In July 1959, he put down the Kirkuk revolt which was Communist-inspired and directed. Thus, the Iraqi military elite headed by Kassem was in constant conflict with other military groups. Many times the General had to rely upon one rival group in order to put down another. It is reported that during his four-and-a-half-year rule, Kassem retired about 2,000 officers from the army.[37]

After the coup in 1952, the Egyptian military elite moved against dissenting elements within its own ranks. Two months after its successful coup, the new regime retired 450 army officers of all ranks.[38] Similar to the action of Kassem in Iraq, Nasser and his supporters moved against both the extreme right and the extreme left within the army. In the campaign against the right, Nasser took quick action against influential military men who were Muslim Brotherhood partisans. In the spring of 1953, Colonel Rashad Muhanna and a number of other officers were tried, found guilty, and sentenced to life imprisonment by a Revolutionary Tribunal headed by Nasser himself.

Stern measures were also carried out against military leaders who were suspected of Communist leanings. Such influential officers as Khalid Muhieddine, Abdul Moneim Amin, and Yussef Sadik Mansour—all members of the Free Officers' executive council—were dropped from their positions because of alleged Communist proclivities. In May and June 1954, 16 army officers were arrested for plotting with the Communists. These particular officers were led by Captain Ahmad Ali Hassan el-Masry and had been influential in the cavalry which had defied Nasser in February 1954.[39]

These intramilitary struggles vary in intensity and direction from society to society. They have, however, been omnipresent in the Middle East. They take place before and after as well as during the actual coups. They cannot fail to have an important impact upon the society in which they occur. If a certain element gains a relatively firm hold, its policies are likely to be implemented and will affect the society accordingly. If competing forces within the military elite are closely matched in power, it is unlikely that there will be any fundamental changes brought about. Thus, Ataturk's Turkey and Nasser's Egypt have been able to see definite measures acted upon. Recent events in Iraq and Syria, however, illustrate quite clearly the case where continual and intense intramilitary power struggles have arrested the process of modernization.

THE MILITARY AND MODERNIZATION
IN MIDDLE EASTERN SOCIETY

Certain military coups in the Middle East have brought to power new elites drawn from progressive social classes and dedicated to revolutionary change in traditional social and political patterns. Thus, societies led by men like Ataturk and Nasser differ greatly from societies led by Nuri el-Said and King Farouk. They also differ substantially from societies led by the Young Turks, by Reza Shah and his son, and by Muhammad Ali. Although the latter witnessed a certain break with the past and also saw improvements made in the fields of education and industry, the social structures of the societies were scarcely altered. The values of the traditional elite predominated in the thinking of the new ones.

The experience of the Middle Eastern military forces in the process of modernization reveals that the aspirations for modernization must be present.[40] This condition has certainly not been present in all ascendant military groups in the twentieth-century Middle East. In two of the four categories of military coup, there has been no intention to modernize. The engineers of these coups are similar in that they desire to conserve and protect the traditional structure of society. As time has passed, however, these types of coup have begun to be supplanted more and more by other types.

In 1952 in Egypt and in 1958 in Iraq, coups took place which destroyed the tradition-oriented elite and installed leaders with radically different values. In Egypt, the new elite has maintained itself in power and has been able to implement its policies and to begin institutionalizing change. In Iraq, the initial coup in 1958 was followed by two more in 1963 and another in 1968. Meanwhile, little has been done to carry out fundamental reform. In order to modernize it is necessary that more than the will to do so be present. It is also essential that the means be available.[41]

The military elite desiring to modernize must first stabilize its own position. As has been indicated, the elites in Iraq and Syria have been unable to do this. Besides the military and civilian groups who oppose modernization itself, the new elite is opposed also by groups that entertain different ideas and ideologies on what methods should be used in modernizing. The struggle is such that the elite is forced to use authoritarian methods to maintain its position and to carry out its program. Because the opposition forces coalesce and temporarily overlook their own conflicts of interest, the ruling elite is forced to resort to increasing coercion. At the same time, it attempts to lay a base of popular support and to rally groups in the society to its side.

A certain amount of authoritarianism is necessary if the military elite is going to meet the challenge of modernization. If it is not able to consolidate its position, it cannot carry out its programs. If it should decide to introduce genuine constitutional democracy immediately, its opponents would join hands and easily turn it out of office. As a result, upon achieving power the new governing forces would split and divide and traditional forces would regain control.

The greatest problem that confronts the modernizing military elites in the Middle East is how to marshall the support of their societies behind them in order to meet the challenge of modernization. Unfortunately, as Gamal Abdul Nasser realized only too well, the nation does not move in serried ranks behind the modernizers. A dangerous situation arises when the authoritarian means being used to maintain power and to spearhead reform become so overbearing that they destroy all freedoms in the society and the elite is driven to rely on harsh physical and mental sanctions. Besides the many general arguments that denounce such a regime, it might be pointed out in the context of this article that such authoritarianism may also act as a brake upon modernization. Such measures alienate and hinder exactly those groups and classes in the society whose talents and skills are needed most in any attempt to modernize. Thus it is, that those Middle Eastern military elites that have chosen to modernize must somehow gain the support of the society in general without becoming the easy prey of their enemies and without resorting to a stifling and overbearing authoritarianism.

NOTES

1. Edward Shils, "The Military in the Political Development of the New States," in *The Role of the Military in Underdeveloped Countries,* ed. John J. Johnson (Princeton, 1962), p. 31.

2. Manfred Halpern, *The Politics of Social Change in the Middle East and North Africa* (Princeton, 1963), p. 253.

3. Drawing on a study of the United States armed forces, Morris Janowitz makes this general point concerning the military. See Janowitz, *The Professional Soldier: A Social and Political Portrait* (New York, 1960), pp. 175-256.

4. J. C. Hurewitz, *Middle East Politics: The Military Dimension* (New York, 1969), pp. 426-28.

5. Shils, "The Military in Political Development," pp. 65-66.

6. See Lucian W. Pye, "Armies in the Process of Political Modernization," in *The Role of the Military,* ed. Johnson, pp. 68-89; and Halpern, *The Politics of Social Change,* esp. pp. 253-80. John J. Johnson argues this point concerning Latin America; Guy J. Pauker agrees in regard to Southeast Asia; and Morroe Berger and P. J. Vatikiotis posit it with regard to Egypt. See Johnson, "New Armies Take Over in Latin America," *New York Times Magazine,* 8 March 1964, pp. 14, 97-99; Pauker, "Southeast Asia as a Problem Area in the Next Decade," *World Politics* 11 (April 1959): 339-45; Berger, *Military Elite and Social Change: Egypt Since Napoleon* (Princeton: Center of International Studies, Research Monograph no. 6, 1960), pp. 1, 20, 24, 29-30; and Vatikiotis, *The Egyptian Army in Politics: Pattern For New Nations* (Bloomington, 1961), esp. pp. xv, 211, 233.

7. For the effective elaboration of this point, see Berger, *Military Elite and Social Change.*

8. See Pye, "Armies in the Process of Political Modernization," pp. 80-82.

9. Two cursory schemes concerning the military and social change have been briefly introduced by Bernard E. Brown and Samuel P. Huntington. See Brown, *New Directions in Comparative Politics* (London, 1962), p. 60; and Huntington, "Patterns of Violence in World Politics," in *Changing Patterns of Military Politics,* ed. Huntington, (New York, 1962), pp. 32-37.

10. This argument has been best presented by Manfred Halpern and Samuel P. Huntington. See Halpern, "The Revolution of Modernization in National and International Society," in *Revolution,* ed. Carl J. Friedrich (New York, 1966), pp. 178-214; and Huntington, *Political Order in Changing Societies* (New Haven, 1968), pp. 22-59.

11. The only two exceptions were the Musaddiq cabinets in Iran.

12. During this period, the average size of the majlis was 128 deputies. These figures have been calculated on the basis of statistics provided in Zuhrah Shaji'i, *Nimayandigan-i Majlis-i Shawra-yi Milli dar Bistuyik Dawrah-yi Qanunguzari* [The Representatives of the National Consultative Assembly during the Twenty-One Legislative Periods] (Tehran, 1965), pp. 291-381.

13. It has become common knowledge that United States financial assistance and planning contributed to the success of this coup. Yet, it is a gross over-simplification to argue that the United States overthrew the Musaddiq government since the attitudes, divisions, and stances of Iranian domestic forces were the crucial factors. For a balanced analysis of this incident, see Richard W. Cottam, *Nationalism in Iran* (Pittsburgh, 1964), pp. 226-30.

14. Claud R. Sutcliffe has called my attention to these conspicuous parallels. See *Bulletin de la Presse Syrienne*, no. 662 (October 6-8, 1954); and *Bulletin de la Presse Arabe*, no. 1367 (December 4-5, 1961). For a useful and comprehensive examination of the social backgrounds and characteristics of Syrian parliamentary deputies and cabinet ministers through 1959, see R. Bayly Winder, "Syrian Deputies and Cabinet Ministers, 1919-1959," *Middle East Journal* 16 and 17 (Autumn 1962; Winter-Spring 1963): 407-29; 35-54.

15. *Kayhan International* (Tehran), 24 July 1963.

16. *Iraq Times* (Baghdad), 8 January 1964.

17. Another profoundly relevant factor here has to be the Arab-Israeli conflict. The Egyptian and Syrian military organizations, for example, have been so absorbed in this issue that there is little time or energy left for the fundamental business of modernization.

18. Berger, *Military Elite and Social Change*, p. 30.

19. For an especially fine account of the key role civilian organizations played in Mustafa Kemal's seizure of power, see Dankwart A. Rustow, "The Army and the Founding of the Turkish Republic," *World Politics* 11 (July 1959): 539-42.

20. As Dankwart Rustow points out, one must proceed very carefully when relating political behavior to social background. The latter does not necessarily determine the former, although it certainly influences it. We have attempted to avoid some of the difficulties involved by following Rustow's own suggestions. For example, analysis is herein applied to groups rather than to specific individuals (e.g., middle-ranking army officers) and factors other than class background are considered (e.g., rank and age). See Rustow, "The Study of Elites: Who's Who, When, and How," *World Politics* 18 (July 1966): 690-717. After warning that "there are many steps between the impact of social origin and the political perspectives of a professional group," Morris Janowitz points out that "in shaping the political perspectives of the military, however, social origin seems to be of greater consequence in the new nations than in contemporary Western industrialized countries." See Janowitz, *The Military in the Political*

465

Development of New Nations (Chicago, 1964), p. 56. For analyses relating social background and military activity in Latin America, see Gino Germani and Kalman Silvert, "Politics, Social Structure and Military Intervention in Latin America," *European Journal of Sociology* 2 (Spring 1961): 62-81, as reprinted in *Garrisons and Government: Politics and the Military in New States*, ed. Wilson C. McWilliams (San Francisco, 1967), pp. 227-48; John J. Johnson, *The Military and Society in Latin America* (Stanford, 1964), esp pp. 93-133; and Jose Luis de Imaz, *Los Que Mandan* [Those Who Command] (Buenos Aires, 1964), pp. 45-84. In his comprehensive and well-researched study of the military in the Middle East, J. C. Hurewitz chooses to place more emphasis upon ethnic-religious social divisions than on social class distinctions. See his *Middle East Politics*, esp. pp. 103-4, 428-29.

21. Vatikiotis, *The Egyptian Army in Politics*, p. 89.

22. This information has been drawn largely from data provided by P. J. Vatikiotis. See *ibid.*, pp. 48-49, 74.

23. Keith Wheelock, *Nasser's New Egypt: A Critical Analysis* (New York, 1960), p. 10.

24. Rustow, "The Army and the Founding of the Turkish Republic," pp. 526-36.

25. Caractacus (pseud.), *Revolution in Iraq: An Essay in Comparative Public Opinion* (London, 1959), p. 124.

26. These figures have been tabulated on the basis of a comprehensive government list of the names, ranks, and positions of all the officers involved. See Military Governorship of Tehran, *Kitab-i Siyah* [The Black Book] (Tehran, 1955), pp. 345-72.

27. For a comprehensive discussion supporting this point, see Janowitz, *The Professional Soldier*, pp. 79-103.

28. The earliest systematic formulation of the relationship between the Middle Eastern military and the middle class was that of Manfred Halpern, "Middle Eastern Armies and the New Middle Class," in *The Role of the Military*, ed. Johnson, pp. 277-315.

29. Gamal Abdul Nasser, "Forward," in Colonel Anwar El Sadat, *Revolt on the Nile* (London, 1957), p. ix.

30. See Dankwart A. Rustow, "The Military in Middle Eastern Society and Politics," in *The Military in the Middle East: Problems in Society and Government*, ed. Sydney Nettleton Fisher (Columbus, 1963), pp. 10-11.

31. Notable exceptions here include Major General Muhammad Naguib in Egypt in 1952, General Bakr Sidqi in Iraq in 1936, and Brigadier Abdul Karim el-Kassem in Iraq in 1958. In all three cases, however, these men stood virtually alone among scores of colonels and majors.

32. Caractacus, *Revolution in Iraq*, p. 120.

33. See James A. Bill, "The Social and Economic Foundations of Power in Contemporary Iran," *Middle East Journal* 17 (Autumn 1963): 411.

34. Major General Abdul Karim el-Kassem, "Speech at Officers' Club on June 16, 1959," in *Principles of 14th July Revolution* (Collection of Kassem's Speeches, Princeton University Library), p. 19.

35. *Ibid.*, p. 21.

36. See, for example, *Iraq Times* (Baghdad), 23 December 1963; 8 January 1964; and 6 February 1964, p. 1.

37. *New York Times*, 17 February 1963, p. 1.

38. *New York Times*, 26 September 1952, p. 4.

39. Much of the information in this paragraph has been drawn from Wheelock, *Nasser's New Egypt*, esp. pp. 16, 19-24, 38-39.

40. See, for example, Huntington, *Political Order in Changing Societies*, p. 34.

41. Manfred Halpern writes that modernization is defined in terms of an enduring *capacity* to generate and absorb persistent transformation. See Halpern, "The Rate and Costs of Political Development," *Annals* 358 (March 1965): 20-28.

POLITICAL DEVELOPMENT AND MILITARY INTERVENTION IN LATIN AMERICA

Martin C. Needler

It is noteworthy that the recent spate of writings in the field of "political development" has shown a pronounced tendency to omit consideration of Latin America. Thus the "communications" and "bureaucracy" volumes in the SSRC political development series[1] are totally innocent of Latin American data, as is an excellent recent treatment of—of all things!—the political behavior of the military in developing areas.[2]

The Latin Americanists, for their part, have largely stressed those key features of the area's politics which have long remained constant—executive predominance, military intervention, and the influence of the peculiarities of Hispanic culture. At the same time, it is clear that the social changes usually collectively termed "modernization"—urbanization, technological borrowing, and the development of mass communications grids—together with their political correlate, the expansion of the political community to include hitherto excluded social elements, are proceeding in Latin America too. Accordingly, it becomes desirable to reexamine the "statics" of Latin American politics in the light of the "dynamics" of the processes of political development and social mobilization.

The present article attempts this reexamination with respect to the most characteristic feature of Latin American politics, the coup d'etat and the establishment of a de facto military government.

A priori, mutually contradictory theses about the relations of the military coup to social development can be constructed—and indeed the literature on the subject abounds in such contradictory theses, evidence to support each of which is always available.[3] These hypotheses focus on

From Martin C. Needler, "Political Development and Military Intervention in Latin America," *American Political Science Review* 60 (September 1966): 616-26. Reprinted by permission of the author and the American Political Science Association.

whether military intervention in politics, represented most typically by the extra-constitutional seizure of power, is (a) increasing or decreasing, and (b) occurring primarily with the object of promoting socio-economic change or of resisting it. Their starting points are the changes assumed to be going forward in the armed forces—the growth of professionalism, recruitment from a wider range of the population, greater influence from the United States, etc.

Now if evidence can be cited on either side of a proposition about developmental tendencies, it is clearly necessary to quantify these items of evidence along a time dimension; what is needed, accordingly, are empirical data giving the change in the frequencies of the occurrence of each of the contrasting possibilities over time.

The empirical questions we want answered, therefore, are:

1. Since the breakdown of early twentieth-century stability began the current period of change in Latin America, have coups d'etat become more or less frequent?
2. What changes have been occurring in the function of the coup in relation to changes taking place in the larger society?
3. What are the effects of changes in the Latin American military on the form, structure, and timing of the coup d'etat, and what political significance do these effects have?

INCIDENCE OF COUPS D'ETAT

One must first eschew the hopeless task of trying to account for coups d'etat that were not successful. The categories of coups that were aborted, suppressed, or abandoned melt into each other and into a host of other non-coup phenomena so as to defy accounting. At the same time, of course, since coups are after all illegal, they are matured under conditions of secrecy which make it inevitable that the unsuccessful projects for coups which become known about represent a highly biased sample. At the same time, an unsuccessful coup attempt may be the work of one or two atypical people; its occurrence does not necessarily say anything about the state of the polity as a whole, as does a successful coup.

During the 30-year period 1935-1964, there were 56 successful changes of government by extra-constitutional means in the 20 independent countries of Latin America. The frequency of their occurrence was as shown in Table 1.

That is, the number of successful coups normally fluctuates between one and three per year. The clearly exceptional period was that from 1938 to 1942, during which only a single coup took place.

The first explanation which suggests itself is that these were years of recuperation from depression in which economic conditions were improving and the performance of government was likely to be regarded as

469

satisfactory.[4] One would then hypothesize that a successful coup or revolt is less likely when economic conditions are improving.

TABLE 1. FREQUENCY OF SUCCESSFUL COUPS
D'ETAT IN LATIN AMERICA,
BY YEAR, 1935-1964

1935	1	1945	2	1955	2
1936	3	1946	2	1956	2
1937	3	1947	1	1957	1
1938	0	1948	4	1958	1
1939	0	1949	4	1959	1
1940	0	1950	1	1960	1
1941	1	1951	2	1961	2
1942	0	1952	2	1962	2
1943	2	1953	1	1963	4
1944	6	1954	3	1964	2

A very rough test of this hypothesis can be made on the basis of figures for annual changes in real per capita product given in the UN Statistical Yearbooks for the 1947-1963 period.

It should be borne in mind, here and at subsequent points, that statistical data from Latin America leave much to be desired. It should also be noted that the data are not complete. However, data are available, for most of the years during that period, for ten countries in which coups d'etat occurred.

During 1947-63, it is possible to assert, real per capita income figures for these countries showed a rise over the previous year's figure 87 times, a drop 39 times, and remained the same ten times. (These figures cannot be assumed to be typical of Latin America as a whole, it should be noted, since it is precisely the countries whose economies are likely not to be improving which do not report reliable economic statistics.) If coups d'etat occurred without relation to the state of the economy, one would then expect at least twice as many coups to have occurred in years which showed improvement as in those which showed deterioration, since there were more than twice as many "improvement years" as "deterioration years." However, that is not the case. Of the 15 coups occurring during years for which the economic data are available, seven took place during years which showed an improvement, seven during years of deterioration, and one when no change was reported. The incomplete nature of the evidence should be stressed; in future years more complete calculations will doubtless be possible; other factors, not now identifiable, may be partly responsible; but the available data are consistent with the hypothesis postulated, that the overthrow of a government is more likely when economic conditions worsen.[5]

470   It seems reasonable, accordingly, to regard the years of low coup

activity from 1938 to 1942 as due to the economic recovery of that period. Since 1949, a very slight secular trend in the reduction of the frequency of coups may be discernible. Since economic conditons are generally improving, although irregularly, this too might be expected on the basis of the same premise. Yet it should be remembered that variation in economic conditions can be held responsible for only a part of the variation in the frequency of coups as, the data discussed above also show.

COUPS D'ETAT AND SOCIAL AND POLITICAL CHANGE

We turn now to the question of changes in the function of the coup in relation to social and political change. This question is extremey awkward to get at, since the origins of coups are often obscure, and the intentions of those staging them mixed. The author nevertheless believes it sound to explain the coup functionally rather then genetically, or in terms of factors external to the military rather than of internal characteristics of the military establishment, because of several considerations.

First, a military coup is not made by the military alone. Almost invariably, the conspirators are in touch with civilian politicians and respond to their advice, counting on their assistance in justifying the coup to public opinion and helping to run the country afterwards. This relationship not infrequently takes the form of a coup only reluctantly staged by the military at the insistence of civilian politicians, who appeal to the officers' patriotism, the historic role of the army in saving the country at its hour of need—of which national history doubtless affords many examples—and so on.[6] The chairman of one military junta which had outstayed its welcome spoke bitterly of some of its latter-day detractors "who used to cry at the doors of the barracks asking that the constitutional government be removed and even used to complain about the apathy of the military who did not want to act."[7]

Second, among the various conspirators, with their varying orientations and objectives, the position of those who can most count on outside support, whose own objectives are most in harmony with the aims of major outside forces, will be strengthened.

Third, the autonomy of the military decision to intervene may further be reduced by the fact that the political situation to which the military respond has been "engineered" by outside groups desiring intervention so as to trigger military predispositions in that direction. It is not unknown, for example, for Right-wing activists to fake "Communist" terrorist attempts in order to help create an atmosphere conducive to military intervention.[8]

If the military coup is thus frequently called into play by the workings of the political system, what is its function in relation to social and

471

economic change? Clearly, its purpose must increasingly be to thwart such change. This is so because the point of the coup is to prevent from happening what, it is assumed, would happen in its absence.[9]

Since social mobilization is proceeding, that is, constitutional presidents are likely to be responsive to social classes of progressively lower status, as these enter the political arena by moving to the city or otherwise become mobilized. The policies of each successive constitutional president are thus likely, on balance, to constitute a greater threat to the status quo than those of his predecessor. This may be interpreted to the military by those trying to secure their intervention as a threat to the personal interests of military officers in the economy at large, as a challenge to the military in its role of preserver of domestic order, or, most likely, as a long-term threat to the special status and privileges, and even the continued existence, of the military institution.[10]

It thus seems probable that as social and economic development take place:

1. military intervention increasingly takes the form of an attempt by the possessing classes to maintain the status quo;
2. military intervention is increasingly directed against legally elected presidents heading constitutional regimes;
3. interventions increasingly occur to forestall the election and inauguration of reforming presidents; and
4. popular resistance to military intervention increases, resulting in greater likelihood that a military coup will lead to open fighting.

An analysis of the 56 successful insurrections[11] which occurred in the 20 countries of Latin America during the 30-year period 1935-1964 appears to confirm each of these hypotheses, and thus to substantiate the argument made above. Table 2 gives the numbers and percentages of insurrections during each of the three decades of the period in which:

1. The reformation of the social and economic status quo was clearly a goal of the conspiratorial group; this shows a decrease.
2. A low level of violence (essentially a bloodless coup without street-fighting or other popular involvement) was maintained; this also decreases.
3. Constitutional, rather than de facto governments were overthrown; this shows an increase.
4. The insurrection occurred during the 12 months prior to a scheduled presidential election, or in the four months immediately following; this likewise increased.

DYNAMICS OF COUPS D'ETAT

Even if it be granted that the major determinants of the occurrence of a successful coup lie in the functioning of the total political system rather than in the internal dynamics of the military institution, those dynamics are of significance in such questions as the timing of the coup, and become especially important in determining the directions followed after the coup is successful and its leaders installed in government positions.

An examination of this problem must start from an appreciation of the fact that officers of the armed forces are not dominated by a single political viewpoint, but hold a variety of political orientations. The correlates of these political orientations in personal characteristics have not as yet been systematically evaluated and weighed for the Latin American military, along the lines of Morris Janowitz's *The Professional Soldier.*[12] However, available evidence suggests that on top of a primary set of conditioning factors such as those which the American voting studies indicate are significant in party preference—that is, family tradition, social and economic level, and ethnic or other particularistic identification—is imposed a second set of factors peculiar to the military profession: rank, branch of service, occupational specialty, and career pattern. In a situation in which a coup d'etat becomes a possibility, ranking military officers are called on to develop policy positions on the question of the continuance in office of the president. The position each officer assumes will have two components, one based on attitudes towards the president's personal abilities, his programs, and the arrangements he is making for the succession; the other, partially independent of the first, reflecting the officer's views on the question of military intervention in politics in general.

TABLE 2. STATISTICS OF SUCCESSFUL INSURRECTIONS, BY DECADES, 1935-1964

	1935-1944		1945-1954		1955-1964	
	No.	Percent	No.	Percent	No.	Percent
Total	16	100	22	100	18	100
(1) Reformist	8	50	5	23	3	17
(2) Low in Violence	13	81	15	68	6	33
(3) Overthrew Constitutional Governments	2	12	7	32	9	50
(4) Around Election Time	2	12	7	32	10	56

The changes which have been taking place in Latin American armed forces in recent years suggest that the variety of political views represented within the military services has been on the increase, as the social origins from which officers are drawn have become less upper-class,[13] as the range of military technical specialties has been extended, and as the sheer size of military establishments has increased.[14] At the same time the increasing complexity of the governmental apparatus and the steady expansion of the proportion of the population which participates in politics, together with the technical improvement in the means of communication, have meant

473

that a military coup needs itself to be more complex, to be more carefully planned, and to involve more people if it is to be successful. Because of heightened popular involvement in politics, a coup is also more likely to lead to open fighting, rather than being accepted passively by an indifferent population. Given the range of political orientations within the military services, then, the task of the organizer of a successful coup d'etat is thus to build up a coalition of officers of a size and character adequate to execute the successful coup. The prime mover or movers in organizing the coup must therefore be engaged over a period of time in the process of building a coalition which will eventually exceed, in size and "weight,"[15] the minimum necessary to insure success.

The originators of the conspiracy and the first to join it are those most opposed to the president and his policies, while other officers of different political orientations and a greater commitment to constitutional procedures have higher thresholds to interventionism. However, as time goes on, these thresholds will be reached for many officers as the tendency of the president's policies becomes clearer, as the country's situation, seen from their point of view, worsens, or as the succession problem becomes more acute with the approach of the end of the president's term.

It is of course possible that as time goes on the changes which take place in the situation are such as to reduce the degree of hostility to the president on the part of the organizers of the conspiracy, which may then disintegrate. It seems clear, however, that a successful coup would show a curve of support within the ranks of the military, rising over time and beginning with the original instigator of the plot, who represents the most extreme opposition to the president. The development of the curve of military support for the coup is likely to be exponential as the end of the president's term approaches. Under normal conditions the president prepares to hand over power to a successor of his own party or orientation, sometimes using not only his personal influence but also extra-legal techniques to guarantee the succession. This raises the prospect of another four or six years of the same policies; yet the trepidation of those who oppose them necessarily increases. The heir-apparent is in part an unknown quantity, which is disquieting; his previous public service will normally have taken place as a member of the president's cabinet, in which his own views necessarily had to be subordinated to those of his chief.

If there is a chance that the heir-apparent would be defeated in the elections, the conspirators may await their outcome before striking. If he is indeed defeated, the need for conspiracy disappears; if he is elected, it then becomes necessary to strike before his inauguration, since his actual occupancy of the presidency would enable him to consolidate his power. Yet it is risky to wait until after the elections, which will mobilize his supporters and which may give him a strong mandate and thus strengthen his position with domestic and foreign opinion.

Thus, for these reasons also, the likelihood of a coup d'etat could be expected to increase as a president's term wears on, reaching its high point prior to a scheduled election but remaining high until the inauguration of a new president, this tendency becoming more marked over time, in response not only to the accelerating social mobilization of the masses but also to the increases in the size, technical differentiation, and range of social origins of the officer corps.

Within the group of conspirators, then, a series of thresholds to interventionism is present, the lowest being that of the instigator (or group of instigators) of the plot, the highest being that of the last man (or group) to join in the coup before it is launched. The position of this hypothetical last adherent to the conspiracy is interesting to consider. If one recalls that the success of the coup is predicated on the formation of a decisive coalition to support it, then it is clear that the last adherent or set of adherents to the movement provided the critical margin of support, not just in its size, but especially in its "weight."

The importance of this hypothetical "swing man" in the situation, that is, may be due to any one of a series of factors—his personal influence within the armed forces; his prestige among the public; and/or his critical position in the command structure of the armed forces. It then becomes probable that because of his higher rank, greater prestige, and crucial importance for the coup, the "swing man" is placed at the head of the provisional government that emerges after the revolt is successful—as provisional president, as chairman of the ruling military junta, or as minister of the armed forces behind the facade of a civilian provisional government.[16]

An interesting and paradoxical situation is thus created. The "swing man" becomes the leading figure in the new government; yet he is the person who was least committed to the objectives of the coup, whose threshold to intervention was the highest of all the conspirators, and who was a last-minute addition to the conspiracy perhaps out of sympathy with, or not even aware of, the more fundamental aims of the group that hatched the original plan. Indeed, a situation can actually be created in which the head of the new government actually sympathized with the aims of the conspiracy not at all, but joined it at the last minute only to avoid pitting brother officers against each other, possibly precipitating a civil war.

These characteristics of the "swing man" can perhaps be made clearer by an illustration. A classical occupant of the role of "swing man" has been Marshal Castelo Branco of Brazil. A *New York Times* reporter described his position in the 1964 coup as follows:

> General Humberto de Alencar Castelo Branco has been called a "general's general." He rose to his present post of Army Chief of Staff after a long professional career in which he gained the high respect of his fellow officers but remained virtually unknown to the general public. . . .
>
> In the present crisis, the soft-spoken general first played the role of the reluctant dragon in refusing to join the developing movement

475

against President Joao Goulart. His scruples were the same as those of many other Brazilian officers: The Brazilian Army has a tradition of protecting legality and the Constitution, and General Castelo Branco was not eager to become involved in a coup against a constitutional President.

But the general became convinced that the continuation of the Goulart regime would lead Brazil to chaos and possibly a sharp shift toward the extreme left. He then drafted a position paper, the "Castelo Branco analysis" that became the justification for the army's support of last week's rebellion.

Such is the respect enjoyed by the short, stocky, bull-necked general, that his analysis served as the turning point in the hesitations of many commanders in the crisis over Mr. Goulart.[17]

Clearly, in this kind of situation ample material exists for a conflict to emerge within the new provisional government. The conflict develops along the following lines. The erstwhile "swing man," now, let us say, president of the provisional junta, regards the objectives of the coup as realized with the overthrow of the former president and begins to make preparations to return the country to constitutional normality and to hold elections. The original instigator of the coup and the group around him, on the other hand, resist this tendency and instead urge the necessity for the military to keep power for a longer period, to purge all sympathizers with the deposed president completely from public life, to outlaw his party indefinitely, and to restructure political life to make it impossible for the tendency which he represents again to come to power.

During the recent period the basic situation described above has been reproduced in reality most faithfully in Argentina, Brazil, and Peru, and with local variations in Guatemala, Ecuador, the Dominican Republic, and Honduras.

In Argentina this basic set of dynamics has played itself out again and again since the overthrow of Perón in 1955, the irreconcilable anti-Perón forces being known as the *colorados*, or "reds," whose most characteristic figure is Admiral Isaac Rojas.[18]

Due to the more amorphous character of politics in Brazil, the same basic situation crystallized more slowly. The opposition between the military irreconcilables and the heirs of Getúlio Vargas has nevertheless been waged intermittently for 10 years. The coup staged to prevent the inauguration of Kubitschek and Goulart in 1955 was unsuccessful; the coup designed to prevent the inauguration of Goulart as President in 1962 succeeded merely in having the powers of the presidency temporarily curtailed; only with the overthrow of Goulart in 1964 was the military anti-Getulista movement fully successful. After the successful revolt of 1964, the pattern described above became operative in its purest form, with conflict developing between the prestigious "swing man," Marshal Castelo Branco, metamorphosed into Provisional President, and the *linha dura*, the "hard line" of the irreconcilable military opposition to the heirs of Vargas.[19]

A similar process took place in Peru following the coup d'etat of 1962. For 30 years the commanding officers of the armed forces had resisted the assumption of power by the revolutionary APRA movement, despite the fact that it commanded a majority, or at least a plurality, of the votes during the entire period. The party had begun in the twenties and thirties as a revolutionary Marxoid group, strongly anti-Yankee and prepared to use violence. During the 30-odd years of its sojourn in the wilderness, however, the party leadership, and especially the party's founder, Víctor Raúl Haya de la Torre, had "evolved" to a more moderate position of which anti-communism was the central principle. At the same time, in the search for a respectability which would allay the misgivings of the military about the party, APRA's major tactician, Ramiro Prialé, led the party into alliance with increasingly more conservative forces, culminating shortly after the 1962 presidential election in an entente with the forces of General Manuel Odría. This was clearly the ultimate stage of the party's evolution, since Odría was a former military dictator who had outlawed and persecuted the party during his period of office, and who had run his election campaign in 1962 on a militantly anti-APRA platform. Haya had gathered more votes than any of the other candidates in the presidential elections of 1962, although only a handful more than Fernando Belaúnde and fewer than the one-third of the vote necessary to prevent the election's being decided by Congress. However, the new Congress, due to the vagaries of the electoral system, heavily over-represented the APRA. Immediately following the election, the coup was staged, the leaders of the armed forces implausibly charging that the electoral results were vitiated by widespread fraud. In an unsuccessful last-minute attempt to avert the coup, the APRA leadership announced that its congressional votes would go to General Odria in a self-sacrificing attempt to break the impasse and avert the breakdown of constitutional procedures.

This situation made possible the emergence of a more muted version of the split which occurred in the Argentine and Brazilian cases. The ranking officer of the military junta, General Ricardo Pérez Godoy, was willing to return the country to constitutionality on the basis of the APRA offer to have its congressmen vote for Odría. The two key younger members of the junta, Generals Lindley López and Vargas Prada, who had personal and family ties to Belaúnde, opposed this solution, which would enable the APRA to exact concessions, for example in the shape of posts in an Odría administration. Pérez Godoy was accordingly forced to resign and the reconstituted junta presided, during 1963, over elections in which, because of the withdrawal of two minor candidates, Belaúnde was successful.[20]

It appears overwhelmingly likely that as time goes on and popular participation in the processes of politics becomes greater, the Peruvian type of situation, in which over as long a period as necessary the popular choice is kept out of the presidency by repeated military intervention, will

477

become increasingly common. As was suggested above, the pattern has extended itself to Argentina and Brazil already. Honduran politics seem to be moving in the same direction as the army has become increasingly committed against the Liberal party; the Guatemalan military staged their coup in 1964 to prevent the return to power of Juan José Arévalo; and the Dominican armed forces have clearly attempted to assume a similar position relative to Juan Bosch and the Dominican Revolutionary Party.

The logic of this type of situation suggests that the conflict between the most popular individual or party on the one hand, and the military irreconcilables on the other, tends to go on for some time, rather than being resolved by a single coup. This occurs for two reasons. In the military junta which forms after a coup, first of all, the irreconcilables normally are in a superior strategic position. The more moderate "swing man," whose prestige has entitled him to the chairmanship of the junta, may wish to restore constitutional processes as soon as possible. If this is likely to lead to the coming to power of the individual or tendency originally vetoed by the coup, however, the position of the junta president becomes untenable. Although he occupies the position with most authority and he may have placed close associates in the cabinet, theirs are not the key posts under showdown conditions: the key posts belong to those in direct command of troops, that is, the minister of the armed forces, the three service commanders, and even the commanders in the field. Because of this lack of congruence between the positions of authority when affairs are moving smoothly and the positions of power when a split develops, it is normally easier in such a situation to stage a coup d'etat than to prevent one.[21] The odds are therefore that the irreconcilables will be able to prevent the return to constitutionality for an extended period if this should seem likely to favor the archenemy.

Once military elements have vetoed the popular leader and his party, moreover, the hostility between the two becomes self-perpetuating and self-reinforcing, since those who participated in the original coup have reason to believe they will forfeit at least their careers, and perhaps more, if the outlawed party should ever gain power. As one Dominican colonel put it after the coup of 1963 when he was asked his attitude towards a return of Juan Bosch: "If Bosch ever comes back, he will throw me into jail so deep I will never find my way out." Because of this set of circumstances the restoration of constitutional procedures becomes extremely difficult: unless the distribution of voter sentiment changes drastically it is only too likely that the person or party which secured a majority in the last election would do as well in the next one. A temporary return to constitutionality may be possible on the basis of rigged or restricted elections, as has been the case in Argentina. Nevertheless, the Argentine political problem is not permanently solved. Given the persistence of the military irreconcilables and their point of view, the only permanent resolution of the problem lies in: (1) the definitive removal from the political scene of the vetoed leader by death or his renunciation

478

of politics; (2) a shift in the distribution of popular opinion to the disadvantage of the vetoed party; or (3) the party's gaining respectability by drastic modification of its program or tactics. In Latin America, the third alternative seems a formal possibility only, since the irreconcilables may simply refuse to believe that the shift towards respectability is genuine. Thus the military veto against the APRA was still applied in 1962, despite the party's evolution to a moderate Center or even Right-of-Center position. If the political problem has in fact been resolved in Peru—and this is not yet clear—it has been by way of the second alternative, in that the APRA may have been driven permanently below a third of the vote by a combination of disaffection from the Left as the party's leadership has grown more conservative, and the permanent establishment in popular favor of Belaúnde's *Acción Popular*. Elsewhere a similar result may be achieved, at least temporarily, by the expansion or contraction of the electorate to shift the balance of forces against the vetoed political movement—by giving the vote to resident aliens, for example, or by taking it away from illiterates.

CONCLUSIONS

This examination of the internal logic of the Latin American coup d'etat in the circumstances of the current phase of history has so far led to three conclusions. First: the overthrow of a government is more likely when economic conditions are deteriorating. Second: as the military services have become larger and more various in the social origins of their officers, as military occupational specializations have become more differentiated and more highly professionalized, and as elections have become representative of the sentiments of a wider range of the population, coups d'etat have tended increasingly to occur in the period immediately prior to a presidential election and the subsequent inauguration, to be conservative in policy orientation, to be directed against constitutional governments, and to be accompanied by violence. Third: the tendency has emerged for conflict to develop, following a coup d'etat, between a more fundamentalist "hard line," and a "soft line" that shows greater readiness to restore constitutional procedures and is normally represented by officers of higher rank, occupying positions of greater prestige in the provisional government.

It is possible to draw a further conclusion, with policy implications for the United States, from this analysis. There has long existed a difference of opinion among students of U.S. foreign policy as to both the desirability and the feasibility of attempting to discourage military seizures of power in Latin America. The desirability argument is outside our present province,[22] but it is possible for us now to add something on the feasibility question—that is, how successful United States attempts to discourage military coups can be.

The failure of the United States to recognize a provisional government issuing from an extra-constitutional seizure of power, plus the imposition of other mild sanctions such as the suspension of military and economic aid, is of different effect to countries differently situated. The smaller countries whose economies are more dependent on actions of the United States—Bolivia, plus the countries of Central America and the Caribbean— are more susceptible to United States pressures than the larger South American countries. Nevertheless, examples can be cited of military coups which have taken place despite clear United States opposition, even in countries in the Caribbean area. These have been regarded as indicating that American opposition to such coups is ineffectual. The coup which took place in Peru in 1962, and the 1963 coups in Honduras and the Dominican Republic, for example, took place in the face of strong and explicit American opposition.

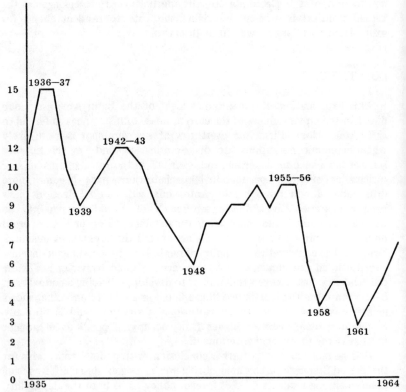

FIGURE 1. Number of dictatorial governments in power in Latin America, by year, 1935-1964.

It still seems premature to conclude that American opposition to the military seizure of power is bound to be ineffectual, however. One problem here is methodological, since it is not possible to enumerate the coups d'etat that did *not* take place (although in two countries where American influence is heavy and which have known a history of military seizures of power, Venezuela and Panama, the constitutional succession has in recent years been unbroken while other countries of the area were experiencing violent changes of government). If the analysis made above is correct, however, the success of a coup d'etat depends, especially where the military services are large and highly differentiated, on the adherence to the coup in its later stages of officers least committed to its goals, less inclined to military intervention, and with more prestige and a higher position at stake. Since the success of the coup thus may well depend on its being joined by relatively few officers with a relatively weak commitment to its goals, it seems overwhelmingly likely that *any* deterrent to intervention—such as the suspension of military aid, or a credible threat not to recognize the new government—while not sufficient to deter the hard-core organizers of the coup, may nevertheless be sufficient to tip the scales against intervention for the crucial "swing man," or for the small group occupying the same tactical position, and thus may cause the coup to be abandoned, or to be launched without adequate support and thus to prove abortive.

In the coup situation, accordingly, even the mildest deterrent threat, such as a firmly stated nonrecognition policy on the part of the United States, may still be effective, because of the pre-coup balance of forces.

Light can also be thrown on the general problem raised in the opening section of the article, that of the relation between the constant features of Latin American politics and developmental trends, by an examination of the varying incidence over time of the characteristic military dictatorship in the area.

Here observers have tended to divide into the optimists, who perceive the evolutionary forces at work in the area as tending in a democratic direction, and the cynics, who take an attitude of "plus ça change . . ." The incidence of military dictatorships in the area seems to support the views first of one group, then of the other. A few years after Tad Szulc published his *Twilight of the Tyrants*,[23] which celebrates the replacement of dictators by democratic regimes, Edwin Lieuwen can write a *Generals vs. Presidents*, which analyzes the reverse phenomenon.

The relation of cyclical and evolutionary patterns on this point can best be demonstrated by a graph. Figure 1 plots the number of unequivocally dictatorial regimes[24] in power during at least six months of each year over the period of the last 30 years during which evolutionary changes have clearly been occurring.[25]

Conclusions of great interest can be drawn. Clearly, the factors which produce military dictatorships seem in part cyclical. At the same time, the cyclical pattern reproduces itself around a clearly descending trend line, so that each successive peak in the number of dictatorships existing contemporaneously is lower than the last: in 1936-37, there were 15

481

dictatorships; in 1942-43, there were 12; in 1955-56, there were 10. Similarly, successively lower levels of dictatorship are reached at each low point of the cycle: in 1939, nine dictatorships; in 1948, six; in 1961, three.

The conclusion seems inescapable that, in this respect as in the others examined, while Latin American politics has certain abiding characteristics which produce its distinctive features, these are being progressively modified under the influence of forces of an evolutionary character.

NOTES

1. Lucian W. Pye, ed., *Communications and Political Development* (Princeton: Princeton University Press, 1963); and Joseph LaPalombara, ed., *Bureaucracy and Political Development* (Princeton: Princeton University Press, 1963).

2. Morris Janowitz, *The Military in the Political Development of New Nations* (Chicago: University of Chicago Press, 1964).

3. A series of such pairs of mutually contradictory hypotheses drawn from the literature is neatly formulated by Lyle N. McAlister in his contribution to *Continuity and Change in Latin America*, ed. John J. Johnson (Stanford: Stanford University Press, 1964), pp. 158-59. Some authors point out the evidence that various mutually opposed tendencies exist, without attempting to subsume them in some general formulation. This is Johnson's own approach: see his *The Military and Society in Latin America* (Stanford: Stanford University Press, 1964), Introduction and Chapter 9; and also that of Irving Horowitz, "United States Policy and the Latin American Military Establishment," *Correspondent* (Autumn 1964). Edwin Lieuwen reconciles opposing tendencies by means of positing cycles in which a set of trends in one direction is succeeded by a countervailing set; see his *Arms and Politics in Latin America*, rev. ed. (New York: Praeger Publishers, 1961), esp. Chapter 5.

4. Edwin Lieuwen discusses the relation between the depression and military intervention in "Militarism and Politics in Latin America," in *The Role of the Military in Underdeveloped Countries*, ed. John J. Johnson (Princeton: Princeton University Press, 1962).

5. It should not be thought that economic conditions always worsen as a result of a coup. At least as commonly, in the writer's experience, conditions improve as business confidence shows an upsurge after a coup, which normally occurs without appreciable economic disloca-tion and typically removes a government regarded as incompetent.

6. McAlister argues in favor of this "revisionist" approach, which regards military intervention as chiefly a response to functional imperatives rather than as an expression of willful selfishness, in "Changing Concepts of the Role of the Military in Latin America," *Annals* (July 1965): 90-92.

7. Admiral Ramón Castro Jijón, quoted in the *Diario Las Américas* (Miami), 28 May 1964. For a detailed account of the creation of an interventionist frame of mind on the part of the military, see Chapter 5 of my *Anatomy of a Coup d'Etat: Ecuador, 1963*. John J. Johnson gives an example from Brazil of public incitement of the military to revolt by civilians on p. 124 of his *The Role of the Military in Developing Societies* (Princeton: Princeton University Press, 1962). S. E. Finer discusses the interventionist mood in Chapter 5 of *The Man on Horseback* (New York: Praeger Publishers, 1962).

8. For one such case of which the author has personal knowledge, see *Anatomy of a Coup d'Etat: Ecuador, 1963*, p. 19.

9. This is also Lieuwen's view: "On the balance, the armed forces have been a force for the preservation of the *status quo;* their political intervention has generally signified, as it does today, a conservative action. ..." Edwin Lieuwen, "The Military: A Force for Continuity or Change," in *Explosive Forces in Latin America*, ed. John Te Paske and Sydney N. Fisher (Columbus: Ohio State University Press, 1964), p. 77.

10. It is the conclusion of Edwin Lieuwen's insightful *Generals vs. Presidents* (New York: Praeger Publishers, 1964), pp. 101-7, that the last factor mentioned has been the crucial one in the recent coups.

11. Successful insurrections took place during the period in Argentina: June 1943, February 1944, September 1955, and March 1962; Bolivia: May 1936, July 1937, December 1943, July 1946, May 1951, April 1952, and November 1964; Brazil: October 1945, August 1954, November 1955, and April 1964; Colombia: June 1953 and May 1957; Costa Rica: March 1948; Cuba: March 1952 and January 1959; Dominican Republic: September 1963; Ecuador: August 1935, October 1937, May 1944, August 1947, November 1961, and July 1963; El Salvador: May 1944, October 1944, December 1948, October 1960, and January 1961; Guatemala: July 1944, October 1944, June 1954, and March 1963; Haiti: January 1946, May 1950, and December 1956; Honduras: October 1956 and October 1963; Nicaragua: June 1936; Panama: October 1941, November 1949, and May 1951; Paraguay: February 1936, August 1937, June 1948, January 1949, September 1949, and May 1954; Peru: October 1949 and July 1962; Venezuela: October 1945, November 1948, and January 1958.

12. Morris Janowitz, *The Professional Soldier* (New York: Free Press, 1964).

13. Medina Echevarría states flatly that the officers seizing power today "come, practically without exception, from hard-working middle-class families"; José Medina Echevarría and Benjamin Higgins, *Social*

Aspects of Economic Development in Latin America, Vol. II (UNESCO: Paris, 1963), p. 88.

14. The evidence for these developments is summarized by Edwin Lieuwen in Chapter 5 of *Arms and Politics in Latin America*, rev. ed. (New York: Praeger Publishers, 1961), pp. 122-53. If one thought solely in terms of these factors, as some authors do, regarding military political activity exclusively as being "pushed" by pressures internal to the military, rather than being also "pulled" by the demands of the total political situation, then it would be logical to expect these changes to result in greater professionalism and technicism, reducing military involvement in politics, and in greater sympathy with the lower classes, rendering such involvement more progressive in orientation. Although several authors have assumed viewpoints of this type, they do not appear substantiated by the evidence cited above.

15. The concept of "weight" is discussed below.

16. This set of dynamics is of course not peculiar to Latin America. Classic occupants of the role of "swing man," with local variations, have been Naguib in Egypt, Gürsel in Turkey, Aguiyi-Ironsi in Nigeria—or even de Gaulle in France.

17. "Man in the News," *New York Times*, 6 April 1964. Typographic errors in the original have been corrected.

18. See Arthur Whitaker, *Argentine Upheaval* (New York: Praeger Publishers, 1956); Lieuwen, *Generals vs. Presidents*, pp. 10-25; James W. Rowe, *The Argentine Elections of 1963: An Analysis* (Washington: Institute for the Comparative Study of Political Systems, n.d.), pp. 11-18; Peter G. Snow, "Parties and Politics in Argentina: The Elections of 1962 and 1963," *Midwest Journal of Political Science* 9 (February 1965): 1-36.

19. See *Generals vs. Presidents*, pp. 69-85; and Phyllis Peterson, "Brazil: Institutionalized Confusion," in *Political Systems of Latin America*, ed. Martin C. Needler (Princeton: Van Nostrand Reinhold, 1964), pp. 473-77.

20. See *Generals vs. Presidents*, pp. 26-36; and M.C. Needler, "Peru Since the *Coup d'Etat*," *World Today* (February 1963).

21. In one variant of this situation, the provisional president may save his own personal position by switching sides at the last minute and adopting the program of the "hard liners," if the forces they can marshal seem decisive. This tactic was adopted by Castelo Branco in early 1966.

22. I have discussed it in "United States Recognition Policy and the Peruvian Case," *Inter-American Economic Affairs* (Spring 1963).

23. Tad Szulc, *Twilight of the Tyrants* (New York: Holt, Rinehart & Winston, 1959).

24. To be considered "dictatorial," a government:
1. Had to be not an avowedly provisional regime holding office for 36 months or less;
2. Had to come to power, or remain in power after the conclusion of

the constitutionally prescribed **term** of office, by means other than a free and competitive election; **or** rule in clear disregard of constitutionally guranteed liberties.

25. The idea of approaching the problem in this fashion was suggested to the author by Ronald Schneider's article "The U.S. in Latin America," in *Current History* for January 1965.

CIVIL-MILITARY RELATIONS IN DEVELOPING COUNTRIES

Keith Hopkins

The purpose of this paper is to review some of the structural determinants of the interaction between the civilian government and military organizations in developing countries. Perhaps the most obvious expressions of this interaction are *coups d'état*. Both their frequency in recent years and their dramatic quality have ensured their study, mostly by historians and political scientists, rarely by sociologists. According to Finer, coups have occurred in 32 of the 51 states existing in 1917, and in at least 20 of the states founded since 1945.[1] Each year, if not each month, increases that number. Many writers (notably Finer, Goodspeed, Johnson, Lieuwen[2]) have caught what I take to be the atmosphere of coups:

> The date: 11 July 1963. The time: 12 noon. The place: the War Ministry in Quito, Ecuador. The orders: a tank battalion will surround the presidential palace and neutralize the presidential guard while troops rush in to arrest the President. As the soldiers entered, President Arosemena fled upstairs to his private apartments and phoned nearby Army barracks for help. It was too late: they had already made commitments to the newly formed military junta.
>
> Aroused mobs congregated in front of the presidential palace, and demonstrations against the armed forces took place in the port city of Guayaquil. Vice-President Varea tried to summon Congress. The resistance came too late and proved ineffective. The mobs were dispersed with a few rifle shots. Troops battered down the palace door and seized President Arosemena. That evening he was put aboard an Air Force plane and deposited in Panama City. Vice-President Varea was also flown into exile.[3]

From Keith Hopkins, "Civil-Military Relations in Developing Countries," *British Journal of Sociology* 17 (June 1966): 165-82. Reprinted by permission of Routledge & Kegan Paul Ltd.

But neither the frequency of coups nor their dramatic character justifies their being used as a universe for the analysis of civil-military relations. One reason why they may not be a good index is that failed coups and alleged "coups," that is those nipped in the bud, are not easily aggregated to successful coups; nor can they be ignored. Finer, for instance, suggested that more coups fail than succeed.[4] Secondly, military organizations may exert a strong influence on governmental policy or on budgetary allocations to the military, without recourse to a coup. In this sense coups are like convicted criminals to the criminologist, the visible part of an iceberg, but an iceberg of unknown size; they provide a useful set of statistics but they may not be a fair sample of crime, let alone of deviance. Besides there are so many opportunities for exerting pressure within the framework of legality, even to the extent that the pressure is legally condemned (e.g. blackmail).

TABLE 1   MIDDLE EAST AND NORTH AFRICA[5]

States and population '000s	Mil. exp. as % of nat. budget	Mil. exp. as % of G.N.P.	Size of mil.	Size of police	Annual % growth of G.N.P. per capita	G.N.P. per capita 1957 U.S. $	% pop. in cities over 20,000	% pop. over 15 lit-erate	Coups and failed coups F
Pakistan 101,000	50	3.3	253,000		0.3 (1953-60)	70	8.0	13.0	1958
Syria 5,500	45	11.0	61,000	98,900	-2.2 (1954-60)	173	38.8	27.5	1961
Jordan 1,900	40	16.3	55,000			129	25.5	17.5	
Iran 22,523	38	4.1	180,000	26,000		108	21.0	15.0	
Iraq 7,000	37		82,000			156	23.6	10.0	1958/63 F 1959
Israel 2,500	34	10.3	75,000		5.8 (1952-60)	726	60.9	93.7	
Afghanistan 13,800	31	6.8	87,500	21,000		50	7.5	2.5	
Turkey 30,256	25	5.2	480,000		1.8 (1952-60)	220	18.2	39.0	1960
Egypt 28,000	17.4	8.6	180,000			142	29.1	19.9	(1952)
Lebanon 1,900	19	4.2	11,000	2,750		362	23.0	47.5	1962
Saudi-Arabia 3,500	18	10.8	55,000			170	9.5	2.5	
Algeria 12,000	11.1	4.2	48,000	44,000	4.7 (1950-58)	178	14.1	19.0	F 1963 1965

TABLE 1   MIDDLE EAST AND NORTH AFRICA[5] (Continued)

States and population '000s	Mil. exp. as % of nat. budget	Mil. exp. as % of G.N.P.	Size of mil.	Size of police	Annual % growth of G.N.P. per capita	G.N.P. per capita 1957 U.S. $	% pop. in cities over 20,000	% pop. over 15 lit- erate	Coups and failed coups F
Morocco					-1.9				
13,118	10.5	4.7	44,800	14,000	(1952-60)	142	24.2	12.5	
Yemen									
5,500			25,000			50	0.1	2.5	1962
Tunisia					2.0				
4,500	10	1.5	17,000		(1950-58)	173	19.9	17.5	
Libya									
1,559	5.8	3.5	7,000	11,000		60	18.4	13.0	

For obviou. reasons, therefore, some significant modes of interaction between the civilian government and military organizations are beyond our knowledge. We have to resort to external indices, which are likely to be inadequate. This applies to coups for the reasons outlined above, but also, for example, to the size of armies, or to the size of the military budget as a percentage of the national budget. It may be, for example, that the civilian government identifies with military expansion; indeed it may be that civilian politicians are the prime movers in such expansion; there may be a real threat of war. Nevertheless I thought it worthwhile to tabulate some factors (Tables 1-3): the size of armies and of police forces, the size of the military budget as a percentage of the national budget and as a percentage of G.N.P., as well as other rough indices of economic and social development in developing countries in three areas of the world.[5] Not only are these indices rough, the information on which they are based is of varying inaccuracy. Moreover, except by arbitrary scaling, the different indices cannot be reduced to a single dimension. Nonetheless, such tabulation has advantages over selective illustration.

TABLE 2   WEST AFRICA[5]

States and population '000s	Mil. exp. as % of nat. budget	Mil. exp. as % of G.N.P.	Size of mil.	Size of police	G.N.P. per capita 1957 U.S. $	% pop. in cities over 20,000	% pop. over 15 lit- erate	Coups and failed coups F
Mali								
4,500	21.2	3.2	3,500	1,250		1.8		
Upper Volta								
5,000	14.1	6.1	1,500	1,400		2.3		
Togo								
1,500	13.5	4.1	1,450	300	50	4.5	7.5	1963
Chad								
2,750	13.5	1.8	900	2,000		1.0		

TABLE 2 WEST AFRICA[5] (Continued)

States and population '000s	Mil. exp. as % of nat. budget	Mil. exp. as % of G.N.P.	Size of mil.	Size of police	G.N.P. per capital 1957 U.S. $	% pop. in cities over 20,000	% pop. over 15 literate	Coups and failed coups F
Dahomey 2,250	12.0	2.0	1,800	2,000		5.5		1965
Senegal 3,500	11.6	7.6	5,500	4,000		10.0		F 1962
Niger 3,100	10.8	1.2	1,200	1,350				
Nigeria 55,654	9.9	0.9	11,500	23,000	78	10.5	10.0	1966
Guinea 3,000	8.1	3.1	5,000	3,300		5.1		
Ghana 7,100	7.4	2.5	17,000	9,000	172	6.4	22.5	1966
Ivory Coast 3,600	6.9	2.4	4,000	2,300		6.8		
Liberia 1,400	6.7	1.8	3,200	700	100	0.0	7.5	
Sierra Leone 2,500	4.9	1.3	1,360	2,000		3.1	7.5	

TABLE 3 LATIN AMERICA

States and population '000s	Mil. exp. as % of nat. budget 1964-5	Mil. exp. as % of G.N.P.	Size of mil.	Size of police	Annual % growth of G.N.P. per capita	G.N.P. capita 1957 U.S. $	% pop. in cities over 20,000	% pop. over 15 literate	Coups and failed coups F
Colombia 15,097	23	1.2	24,000	10,000	2.2 (1950-59)	263	22.4	62.0	
Paraguay 1,817	19	4.5	18,000		-1.0 (1950-60)	114	15.2	65.8	
Dominican R. 3,452	19	3.2	19,000		0.9 (1945-59)	239	12.2	59.9	1963
Peru 10,365	17	3.0	37,000	18,000	1.5 (1950-58)	179	13.9	47.5	1963
Argentina 21,247	14	2.6	120,000 (inc. 80,000 NS)		-0.4 (1950-60)	490	48.3	86.4	
Bolivia 3,520	13	2.1	9,000		-0.2 (1950-55)	99	19.4	32.1	1963
Ecuador 4,650	12	1.96			1.8 (1950-60)	189	17.8	55.7	1961/3
El Salvador 2,723	11				1.8 (1953-59)	219		39.4	1960
Brazil 70,967	11	2.5	273,000		3.1 (1948-60)	293	28.1	49.4	F 1961 / 1964

TABLE 3   LATIN AMERICA (Continued)

States and population '000s	Mil. exp. as % of nat. budget 1964-5	Mil. exp. as % of G.N.P.	Size of mil.	Size of police	Annual % growth of G.N.P. per capita	G.N.P. per capita 1957 U.S. $	% pop. in cities over 20,000	% pop. over 15 literate	Coups and failed coups F
Venezuela					4.4				1958
8,573	10	2.6	21,000		(1950-60)	648	47.2	52.2	F 1962
Mexico					2.3				
34,923	10	0.7	62,000		(1948-59)	262	24.0	50.0	
Honduras					0.4				
2,008	10	1.3	2,500		(1952-59)	194	11.5	44.0	1963
Chile					1.3				
7,374	9	2.8	47,000		(1950-60)	379	46.3	80.1	
Nicaragua					4.2				
1,593		2.8	5,000		(1945-59)	T 160	20.1	38.4	
Haiti					0.3				
4,000		2.9			(1945-59)	T 105	5.1	10.5	
Uruguay					2.3				
2,590	7	1.0			(1945-59)	T 478		80.9	
Guatemala					1.2				
4,278		1.5	7,500	2,500	(1948-60)	189	11.2	29.4	1963
Panama					1.6				
1,075		0.27		3,400	(1950-58)	329	33.1	65.7	
Costa Rica					3.4				
1,370		0.5		1,200	(1945-59)	T 357	15.4	79.4	

Yet another qualification has to be made. I am concerned with the interaction of the institutionally separate civilian government and the military. Yet quite often there is symbolic identification of both institutions in the head of state. The President or King is in command of the armed forces and dresses up in the uniform of general or admiral, even though he himself plays no specifically military role. Historically there have been societies in which political and military roles were fused or interwoven at several levels of the hierarchy (e.g. Prussia, feudal Europe). Such a fusion does not solve the problem of how to control soldiers, but it may require a different kind of analysis from one which treats the civilian and military institutions as separate. In highly industrialized countries also, the military has in some respects become civilianized.[6] For example, there may be a fusion of military and civilian technology, or military personnel may be used as diplomatic advisers. At some levels then roles may have become sufficiently fused and the skills so transferable as to make the distinction civil-military conceptual rather than existential. And the same problem arises in different guise where the military has for a prolonged period taken over civilian government (e.g. Egypt); at what level are such rulers military or civil?

THE EXTERNAL REFERENTS
OF THE MILITARY

Presumably the rationale of an institutionally separate military is that technical standards of fighting require both training and specialization which can most conveniently and *"efficiently"* be carried out by professionals. Even if some military tasks can be carried out by part-timers or by short-service volunteers (full or selective national service), a permanent cadre is needed. Even more these professionals are needed to defend the nation state against the threat, real or imagined, of external enemies. I say rationale without any suggestion that this is the real or whole reason. There are many other reasons: e.g. cultural traditions, institutional inertia, past wars and the maintenance of internal order. But let us first look at external defense.

We are not here concerned with the great powers, but rather with those nations who in varying postures of deference or defiance shelter beneath their wings. The size of the armies in these nations (cf. Tables 1-3) correlates reasonably with their population, but how does it correspond with the needs of defense? Of course there can be little objective measure of that. It may be that these countries are caught in an international system of alliances and suspicion, which they cannot control. What can be said is that military costs are sufficiently high to form an obstacle to economic development. There are, however, considerable regional variations. In Africa most countries are recently independent; previously defense was chiefly the concern of the colonizing powers. Now, however, the armies and the money spent on them are growing. In Southeast Asia and in the Middle East the armies are very large and could perhaps be justified by pointing to the degree of disturbance in the former and the fear of Israel in the latter. But in Latin America, in spite of U.S. guarantees of peace and the absence of wars, the military continues to be a substantial expense. Of course it is possible to argue that wars are infrequent because there are armies; historically this is not valid; *a priori* the argument looks as good inverted.

By the same token that the ostensible rationale of the military is external defense, the referents of its equipment and training are also external and competitive. It has been argued that whereas local business can be technologically backward because it has only local business to compete with, armies judge their equipment by the standard of technically advanced countries. For this reason the military, it is said, forms the most forward-looking and technologically advanced element in many developing countries. This is the case all the more because military officers, keenly aware as they are of foreign military competition, come into contact with their counterparts in technically advanced countries and learn from these contacts to see their country in all its corrupt inefficiency.[7] Hence the modernizing fervor of the military and its willingness to intervene and take over from politicians who lack or neglect such a perspective.

It is true that a significant proportion of officers from some developing

491

countries have training abroad, and that technically advanced countries do send military advisers (and salesmen) to developing countries.[8] It is also true that the armed forces of developing countries are equipped with some weapons which are technically in advance of the manufacturing standards of the native industries. But the question remains as to whether the use and maintenance, as opposed to the manufacture of technically advanced weapons, plus the contact of training and trade with technically advanced countries and their representatives are sufficient to imbue the military in developing countries with a passionate mission for the modernization of their countries.

It may be the case that the military in developing countries contains the most technically accomplished men in elite positions and it may be that these or others are the most forward-looking and modernizing of all elite groups. Evidence on this point would be better than assertion, and evidence is noticeable by its absence. After all politicians, too, have contact with technically advanced countries, and it is worth remembering that infantry rather than highly mechanized units predominate in most military forces of developing countries. Indeed the air forces which may have the greatest concentration of advanced equipment are politically negligible. Nor does it seem very profitable to talk of a desire to modernize, in the abstract. Such a desire may be widespread, like the desire to consume Western goods. What matters more is the order of priorities and of sacrifices. Who is going to be deprived of what in order that others should consume what goods?

Since such problems are not easily soluble within the framework of traditional institutions, they exacerbate social dissensus. The political intervention of the military seems to me to proceed not so much from its prior attitudes to social change but from its strategic position within the arena of social dissensus, for its relatively large size and hierarchic organization facilitate a cohesion which no other elite group can match.

THE MILITARY IMAGE

Before we look at the structural determinants of military cohesion it is opportune to examine the range of military stereotypes which have been implicit in the previous discussion. On an analytical plane these may be subdivided into the images the military have of themselves, the images of the military held by different groups within the society, and the image as contrasted with the reality.

One major stereotype common to most cultures is that of the hero/warrior, the courageous individualistic leader of men. In our own culture this has survived the onslaught of both technical revolution and mass armies. Colonels are given medals for the bravery of their regiments, pilots are much more culture heroes than machine makers. Generals use their military-hero cachet as a springboard for political election. In its role as defender of the nation, then, the army may see itself and be seen by others as standing above the self-interested vagaries of political polemic; and this image may serve as a legitimation of its interference in politics "in the national interest." This may be particularly so when the state has been liberated from colonial oppression by a revolutionary army, which then forms the core of the official military.

Set against this image is the hostile stereotype of the rigid, doctrinaire, status-conscious prig of blinkered conservative views, pilloried for example in the Captain of Köpenick, or our own Colonel Blimp.[9] Somewhat in between these extremes is Janowitz' idealization of the modern American military officer, a specialist in violence, technically oriented yet prepared to meet the unexpected and death in the service of his country. In this context the dominant mode of integration is not the barked ritualized word of command from superior to subordinate but skill-oriented discussion and diplomatic manipulation between managers. And it is this image which Janowitz qualifies (middle-range managers caught in heroic posture), personifies and extrapolates on to developing countries.[10]

It is difficult if not impossible to know how widespread these images are, or how well they match reality. Suffice it to say that the military's self image as disinterested modernizers or protectors of law and order seems very common. Contrarily, Finer, for example, stresses the frequency with which military coups are precipitated by threats to military self interest and are followed by increases in military pay and budgetary allocations.[11] The main danger seems to be an acceptance of a stereotype as coextensive with reality.[12]

There is, I think, one particular characteristic of the military which facilitates the survival of the image of the military as efficient. This is the infrequency of wars. The efficiency of the military is therefore, in terms of its primary rationale, untested. This may be one reason why the military in developing countries can be the prototype or only example of the large formal hierarchic organization, typical of highly industrialized nations. It is a formal organization with more than the usual amount of formality, as typified by the routinized ritual of drill.[13] Given the infrequency of wars, calls upon its initiative or skill at *all* command levels are low. Quite unlike other large-scale organizations (e.g. governmental bureaucracy, manufacturing organizations) the military does not have to mesh with other elements of the social structure, except in terms of consumption and communication. The military is thus enabled to maintain a complex and large structure in pre-industrial society precisely because only low efficiency demands are made upon it and because its formal hierarchic image can be preserved by strict discipline and constricted initiative.

MILITARY COHESION

In spite of the integrative power of strict hierarchy and discipline, cohesion is, as Andreski has underlined, variable.[14] It is impossible to analyze all the determinants of this variability or to put them on any single

493

scale of measurement. Let us assume the superiority of military fire-power over the civilian population, with only a brief reminder that civilian enthusiasm (e.g. the Hungarian revolution, 1956) or military inertia may belie this technical superiority.[15]

This raises the problem of the identification of enlisted men with overall military objectives, and especially with the policy or interests of senior officers. Why do common soldiers risk their lives by fighting for the political ambitions of leaders, when their own interests are neither threatened nor likely to be improved? Several partial and tentative answers are possible. The relative frequency of death and high levels of poverty may induce a fatalism among those "who have nothing to lose." Conventional military discipline might hold so long as there is no risk of fighting (coups are often bloodless) and if the military formations used are tight and large. There may be a chance of plunder and the hope of a rise in pay. The soldiers, under cover of "obeying orders," may choose to ignore the political implications of their actions. But the chances of such obedience are likely to be diminished if the soldiers are not professionals but national servicemen, who do not identify with the army system and maintain civilian and political associations different from the officers organizing the coup (e.g. France, 1961). In general, the more isolated the soldiers are (for example, if they live in barracks and have restricted leisure time and are isolated from their families) the more susceptible they are likely to be to political intervention. If they live freely with the civilian population their attitude to military intervention in politics is likely to be civilianized.

It is often argued that similar social origins produce cohesion among the officers. On this basis Janowitz explains military cohesion and the identification of military officers with aristocratic rulers in Absolutist Europe, just as he and other commentators impute an identity of interest of upwardly mobile officers in developing countries and their opposition to the traditional elite.[16] But surely this is a crudely Marxist position to take; social equals are not always allies, they do not always agree on the division of spoils. Moreover, it is reasonable to suppose that professional education and career experience, combined with the pervasiveness of military life inculcate in the military officer of whatever social origin a sense of professional identity. Indeed these career experiences may be of more importance than social origins themselves.

Ideally the prospects of promotion by criteria acceptable to officers (whether by ascription, achievement or both) help officers identify with the military system. Military hierarchies are pyramidic like other formal organizations, but differ from them in one important respect. Their age structure is seriously imbalanced.[17] In the U.K. and the U.S.A. middle-ranking officers are compulsorily retired in middle-age, and this system is facilitated by pensions, the availability of alternative employment with a reasonable chance of maintaining status and attractive rates of pay during short terms of service. In pre-industrial Europe and other traditional societies recruitment of officers from a land-owning class gave them both an additional source of income and an alternative occupation in the event of being maimed or retired. In so far as developing countries have small middle classes the recruitment of officers from non-propertied families must create considerable tensions about retirement if the youthful age structure of the military is maintained. The leadership of coups by relatively junior ranks (typically colonels or majors) may be symptomatic of the narrowing of career prospects at this rank; but support from other officers may be more readily forthcoming since political involvement secures alternative employment or at least income for aging officers, which they otherwise might not get.

The cohesion of the military is also affected by the specialization of the armed forces. The navies and air forces of developing countries where they exist usually employ far fewer men than the armies, which consist predominantly of infantry, but their equipment is often much more expensive. In any case all three are often in competition with each other for budgetary allocations, and can occasionally be found on opposite sides attacking or supporting a civilian government. In such cases *esprit de corps* may increase the fierceness of fighting and the risk of bloodshed, if only by bomber attacks.

Military cohesion may vary at yet two more levels. Geographically the military is dispersed throughout the country, which may be an obstacle to unanimity. Units near to the capital are more likely to be politically involved or at least, successful in their interventions. Secondly, day to day internal order is usually catered for by specialized units, which are often paramilitary, but institutionally separate from the military. In some cases these police forces imitate military formations and equipment and live in barracks, but they are usually under a separate and nonmilitary command (e.g. the Minister of the Interior). Their necessary dispersion throughout all towns and villages generally robs them of the cohesion which contributes to the success of coups. Their daily involvement with the general public and their corruptible image robs them of the above-politics and national unity symbolism which occasionally, if only temporarily, legitimates military intervention. This said, the existence of the police, sometimes in considerable numbers, as a possible counterweight to the military cannot be neglected. Their armed existence remains as a caution against simplistic utopians who might urge the disbandment of the army as a nostrum against military intervention.

Thanks to modern weapons the military can easily dominate the civilian population or government. But I have tried to show that the military is not as cohesive as the single word, military, might imply. The degree of disunity might affect the chances of a coup's success, or its stability if successful. Finer has argued that divisions among the military may stimulate coups, even though the chances of success are reduced. But surely the perceived chances of success would be a major, though not overriding determinant of action.

495

THE INCIDENCE OF COUPS

Although coups alone may form a biased sample of civil-military relations for the reasons which I have already discussed, information about them is at hand and may prove helpful. I shall therefore present Finer's typology of civil-military relations and both his and von der Mehden's tabulation of the distribution of recent coups.[18] Finer perceives a continuum of civil-military relations ranging from legitimate pressure groups, by way of blackmail and the displacement of one civilian government by another, to the complete supplantment of civilian government by the military. He claims a second parallel continuum of political maturity as measured by three potentially overlapping variables:

a. the strength and extent of popular approval of constitutional means of transferring power (e.g. elections) as the exclusive source of political legitimation;

b. the strength and extent of popular recognition of the legitimate political authority;

c. the variety and power of differentiated institutions (e.g. trade unions, industrial groups, the Church).

TABLE 4 DISTRIBUTION OF COUPS AND ATTEMPTED COUPS 1957-64
IN STATES BY STAGE OF ECONOMIC DEVELOPMENT[18]

A	B	C	D	E	
		Urbanization % population		Total of states suffering	
	G.N.P. per capita 1957 in dollars	living in places of over 20,000	Total of states in world	military intervention 1958-65	Col. E as % of col. D
Stage of development					
I	45-64	0-18	12 } 30	9 } 19	75
II	70-105	0-19	18	10	55
III	108-239	6-72	31	13	42
IV	262-794	7-82	36	5	13
V	836-2,577	30-70	14	1	6

TABLE 5 DISTRIBUTION OF COUPS AND COUP ATTEMPTS IN
MODERNIZING COUNTRIES SINCE INDEPENDENCE[18]

Type of political system	Number of countries	Countries with coups	
		Number	Percent
Communist	3	0	0
One-party	18	2	11
One-party dominant	12	3	25

TABLE 5   DISTRIBUTION OF COUPS AND COUP ATTEMPTS IN
MODERNIZING COUNTRIES SINCE INDEPENDENCE[18] (Continued)

Type of political system	Number of countries	Countries with coups	
		Number	Percent
Two-party	11	5	45
Multiparty	22	15	68
No effective parties	17	14	83

He claims that military coups are more likely in two types of society: (1) where these factors are relatively weak or small, (2) where even though these are relatively strong there is a high degree of dissensus among competing groups in the society, which brings about an overt crisis of disorder.

In addition Finer has recently analyzed successful and attempted coups in the period 1958-June 1965 and has related these to levels of economic development, as measured by per capita income and urbanization. He has thus convincingly documented the more frequent occurrence of coups in countries of low economic development (Table 4). But there are two difficulties. Firstly this does not help explain why some countries of low economic development have coups and not others. Secondly, the correlation of low economic development and military coups does not help validate the attractive hypothesis on the relation between levels of political maturity and military intervention. In this regard the evidence of von der Mehden may be useful (Table 5). He shows a cumulative correlation between political fragmentation or open dissensus (as expressed by two or more political parties) and military coups.

THE SOCIAL STRUCTURE OF
DEVELOPING COUNTRIES

Military intervention in politics may be seen as the product of two forces, the organization and attitudes of the military on the one hand and the configuration of social and political institutions on the other. We have examined the military and its relation to some other elements of the social structure. Of course there is nothing wrong with treating the military as an independent variable for the purpose of analysis; but there is no suggestion that the military is actually autonomous. Far from it; it is enmeshed with the international systems of military alliance, and is also a part and product of the social structure of each country. We shall now try to analyze the effect of some common elements of the social structure of developing countries on military relations with civilian governments.

Developing countries typically have small elites, of whom an important section bases its wealth and status on its traditional rights as landowners. Probably only one part of the elite is dedicated to modernization, at least if this involves the diminution of traditional privileges. Nevertheless the incubus of modernization, the concentration of spending power in the

497

hands of the government, the ideology of democracy, and the rise of a professional, technically-minded and achievement-oriented elite section act as a partial solvent of some of the traditionally embedded processes. Typically the institutions of political succession (e.g. elections) are weak, revenge is more common than compromise; the desires for consumption are stronger than the ability to pay; the demand for economic growth cannot be met without frustration, mismanagement and corruption, real or imputed. Some sectors advance too rapidly or disproportionately, others too slowly. For example, there may be more educated people than opportunities for their employment. Population growth cancels out increases in G.N.P. Rural overpopulation leads to rapid urbanization with all its associated problems. The frustrations are immense, the problems barely soluble. Agreement as to goals may exist, though even that is probably not universal. The means are disputed with a mutual distrust which stems from regionalism and other particularistic modes of thought.[19]

Merle Kling has argued that military intervention in Latin America is a function of the great profitability of governmental positions and the rigidity of ownership and control over other sources of wealth, primarily because of economic colonialism. Hence a bitter struggle for power over the government, the one sector left vacant for native competition.[20] This argument can be presented in a more generalized form.

Given a certain degree of bureaucratic centralization and legitimate and effective means of raising taxes, control over the government will give high prestige both symbolically and financially. Moreover, many developing countries are rapidly increasing public revenue and governmental control of private wealth. The masses are often apolitical or badly organized and there is no firm tradition of alternating political power, with the executive restraint that such alternation implies. Competition for office takes place within a small elite, within which personal contact may be frequent.

Janowitz thinks that the politician is typically possessed of a developed negotiatory skill, that he is adept at persuasion and compromise. By contrast the traditional soldier is inclined to dogmatism and dictate, and has a trained incapacity for diplomacy.[21] This may be so; it seems dangerously close to a stereotype. Certainly the political profession in U.K., U.S.A. and France, for example, seems far less specialized than most other professions. Where the scope of governmental tasks is relatively limited, military officers may have some rational grounds for considering themselves as competent as politicians who have few obvious professional qualifications. Compared with industrialized countries the conflicts are exacerbated by a combination of factors: the intransigent problems of modernization and its impact upon traditional privileges, the consequent frustration, the apolitical masses, the prestige and power of government, the weak institutions for the transfer of political power, the small elite, the low professionalization of politics and politicians and the mobilizing inadequacies of government by negotiation and compromise.

In such a situation it is not surprising that the intervention of the military is often what Janowitz terms *reactive* rather than *designed*,[22] a gesture of self-interested or public-spirited despair against the obvious inadequacies of professional politicians. In other countries, especially Latin America, military intervention is sufficiently common for politicians ever to be aware of its possibility. Indeed the military may be invited, cozened or blackmailed to intervene, just as it may act on its own initiative whether to obstruct the corrosion of traditional elite privileges, to speed modernization or to improve its own position. One principle remains constant. The military intervenes in a power vacuum where physical coercive potential is viewed as more applicable than other means of social control. Such coercive power may be imagined as well as real. Interventions are facilitated by the relative weakness of the masses and the restricted sphere of governmental activity. The government should be sufficiently concentrated for the military to have something to take over, but neither so dispersed or complex that it is ostensibly beyond the competence of the military to control, or at least capture.

THE EXECUTION OF THE COUP

The essence of a successful coup is surprise; the nation, the political elite and other centres of power, especially the rest of the military, should be presented with a *fait accompli* or at least a bandwagon which it is easier to mount than to rock. The next desideratum is internal and external legitimacy. Internally, the military is helped by its image as the protector of the nation. Externally, it is helped by the current competition between the great powers so that the violence of a coup is readily condoned if some tendentious hope of future democracy is proffered. If necessary a civilian figurehead can be propped up to preserve the flow of foreign aid. Mostly coups cost few lives, or only the accidental death of a few civilians. Sometimes, perhaps in the hope of reciprocal immunity, the outgoing president is sent abroad to enjoy the fortune he has accumulated against just such an emergency. The price of failure in a coup ranges from loss of a military career to an unpleasant death for the leader and his actual, supposed or even potential colleagues.

THE SYNDROME OF MILITARY GOVERNMENT

No sooner is a military government established than a fresh series of problems begin. The military is able to preserve its public image of disinterest and uncorruptibility so long as its isolation (typically in barracks) has limited its involvement with the populace. Its confrontation with the intractable problems of government tests its organizational capacity in a way to which it is not used. It has been claimed that the initial impact of the military on civilian government is the best; for it

499

cleans up some corruption and in the short term may cut some gordian knots of red tape.

A lot may depend upon the complexity of governmental tasks. Where governmental functions are minimal, the elite very small and the masses apolitical or fragmented, there is no need for careful symbolic manipulation of the masses, or for means of aggregating political support, unless some revolution in the distribution of power or wealth is intended. Nor need the military fear its own incompetence. Governmental tasks at this level either do not require high intelligence and skill (though they may profit from them), or are customarily performed *inefficiently* by the standards of industrialized nations. The actors themselves might justify the *inefficiency* in terms of their fulfilling traditional ascriptive and particularistic obligations.

As the complexity of government increases, so do the difficulties of the military. Yet both Finer and Janowitz make too much of the military's negotiatory or political incapacity. Some or even most officers may see social problems as soluble by discipline or they may regard social inferiors (e.g. trade-union leaders) as subordinates who should obey rather than negotiate. There is probably a certain element of this trained incapacity. But on the other hand both Finer and Janowitz argue that the military attracts the able, ambitious and socially mobile; surely among these there are some who can equal the skills of some politicians and bureaucrats. Besides, the more complex the government, the more likely it is that the coup involves an alliance between the military and some bureaucratic and political elements.

The structural weakness of military government seems more important than the imputed shortcomings of its personnel. A coup is not always based on universal agreement among the military, and even if this is gained it is more likely to be agreement to overthrow the civilian government than agreement on the ends to pursue or the means to implement them afterwards. A frequent initial step is to move military officers into high government posts, and to raise military budgetary allocations and pay. In both steps there are dangers, over and above the requirements of efficiency. The secondment of senior officers, presumably members of the junta or their supporters, separates them from the basis of their power, the military.[23] Increases in budgetary allocations diminish the likelihood that the military government will be able to solve the problems of development over which the civilian government failed. A rise in pay underlines the government's illegitimacy; for where one coup has succeeded, might not another?

Thus in addition to the normal tasks of government, the military government is faced with the problem of legitimation at home and abroad, and of its security against counter-coups. It is torn between the Scylla of delegation and the Charybdis of civilizing itself which raises the problem of controlling the military. If elections are promised, they have to be controlled. The military *modus operandi* is normally more restrictive than the civilian; under the pressure of its dilemma it easily becomes oppressive. The initial success in cleaning up the bureaucracy or in public works is offset by the resistant inertia of an oppressed populace or resentful pressure groups. In general, there is no evidence that military regimes promote faster rates of economic growth than civilian governments (Egypt and Pakistan may prove exceptions); large military budgets do not help.

The military image of uncorruptibility may become tarnished, and the military may well feel like retreating into its professional role. The difficulties of military government are symptomized in the recurrent legislation exempting the junta from judicial reprisals for having participated in the coup. Finer epitomizes the dilemma in the saying: Who rides the tiger can never dismount.[24] A military coup and regime antagonize opponents and make the military fear revenge. It may then waver between continuing control and retirement, or stick at some half measure, such as limiting the choice of the electorate to a middle of the road party which will not upset military privileges. As a last alternative the military junta may realize that the safe prolongation of its power may lie in the manipulation, aggregation or creation of power forces outside the traditional centres of power. One notable example of this development is Peron's mobilization of the trade unions.

The distribution of alternate sources of power and the need to exploit them may be two important determinants of the political direction of military government. For one of the problems in this field is to explain the reactionary, conservative or reformative zeal of military governments. It cannot be explained in terms of the social origins of military leaders, and it is unnecessarily restrictive to understand political action along a single dimension of left-right. There may be some military governments which are fervently reformative and seized power to that end. But occasionally there is information which reveals an amazing naivety on the part of the coup leaders. Nasser, for example, seems to have thought that all he had to do was to depose Farouk, and a grateful nation would of itself unite to modernize. Instead the populace was slow to be grateful and the politicians came only with suggestions of rivals to execute. To its own surprise the military found itself supplanting civilian government.[25] I suggest therefore that much can be understood not in terms of ideology but in terms of the problems of keeping power by seeking the support of uncommitted power groups. And it may be that as some countries industrialize, the trade unions or peasantry are a sturdier prop than landowners. To return to Egypt, in what sense can Nasser's government now be called military?

CONCLUSION

There is no rational or objective measurement of the needs of external defense; societies are anyhow caught up in an international system which they cannot individually control. This said, the amount of money spent on the military seems large and incompatible with declared aims of economic development. Against this it is argued that the military carries out many programs of education and construction which contribute to national unity and development. But surely teachers are better educators and engineers better builders; why put them into military uniform? Secondly, the military consumes a large amount of skill and imported equipment whose only visible product is shell smoke and craters in training areas. National service, away from home and traditional relationships, may do something to create labour mobility and national consciousness. It may be that some military leaders are filled with a genuine altruism and determination to modernize their countries, but their self-justifying statements should be examined with detachment. By further research it should be possible to scale military power over, and interpenetration with, civilian government and assess its effect upon growth rates. The record of military power in Latin America is not impressive.

Complex industrial societies have differentiated the civil and military, but it is presumably a prejudice that only politicians can or should rule. It is a democratic belief that industrial resources are best mobilized through the grass-roots growth of individual initiative and enterprise. It is a common sociological belief that central bureaucratic control is a precondition of modernization. A military government provides such control; yet it may be that it sweeps from sight but does not solve the problems an industrializing country must face, namely the tolerance of the flexible interaction and interrelation of manifold power elements within the society.

Societies always have difficulty in adapting themselves to change, especially where the change undermines the power of existing elites. Military involvement in politics is symptomatic of the centripetality of conflict; the more the dissensus, the more alternative sources of power become involved in the dispute. Military power, by virtue of its organization and equipment, is usually supreme. At first sight it may seem an ideal solution for the management of conflict. But its very supremacy prevents the independent growth of other mechanisms of tension management, and limits further change.[26]

NOTES

1. S. E. Finer, *The Man on Horseback* (London, 1962); *New Society* (November 1965).

2. Finer, *The Man on Horseback*; D. J. Goodspeed, *The Conspirators: A Study of the Coup d'Etat* (London, 1962); J. J. Johnson, *The Military and Society in Latin America* (Stanford, 1964), and in J. J. Johnson, ed., *The Role of the Military in Underdeveloped Countries* (Princeton,

1962), pp. 91-129; E. Lieuwen, *ibid.*, pp. 131-63; *Generals v. Presidents: Neo-militarism in Latin America* (New York, 1964).

3. Lieuwen, *ibid.*, p. 45.

4. *The Man on Horseback*, p. 160.

5. The sources of the tables are: B. M. Russett, *et al.*, *World Handbook of Political and Social Indicators* (Yale, 1964); *The Statesman's Year-Book 1965-6* (London, 1965); N. Brown and W. F. Gutteridge, *The African Military Balance*, Adelphi Paper 12 (London, 1964); D. Wood, *The Middle East and the Arab World: the Military Context*, Adelphi Paper 20 (London, 1965); *The Military Balance 1965-6* (London: The Institute of Strategic Studies, 1965); D. Wood, *The Armed Forces of African States*, Adelphi Paper 27 (London, 1966). I also made some corrections to the above data from the files of the Institute of Strategic Studies.

6. Cf. M. Janowitz, *Sociology and the Military Establishment*, rev. ed. (New York, 1965).

7. M. Janowitz, *The Military in the Political Development of New Nations* (Chicago, 1964), esp. pp. 42 ff.

8. W. Gutteridge, *Armed Forces in New States* (London, 1962), pp. 17-19; M. J. V. Bell, *Military Assistance to Independent African States*, Adelphi Paper 15 (London, 1964), addendum 1965: "Over 2,500 Africans have been trained in French military schools between 1960 and 1964."

9. Cf. A. Vagts, *A History of Militarism* (New York, 1937).

10. Janowitz, *The Military in Political Development*, and *The Professional Soldier* (Glencoe, Ill. Free Press: 1960).

11. Finer, *The Man on Horseback*, pp. 47 ff.

12. As do, for example, S. P. Huntington, *The Soldier and the State* (Harvard, 1957), and M. Halpern, "The New Middle Class," in *The Role of the Military*, ed. Johnson, pp. 277 ff.

13. Cf. L. Pye, "Armies in the Process of Political Modernization," in *The Role of the Military*, ed. Johnson, pp. 73 ff.

14. S. Andrzejewski, *Military Organizations and Society* (London, 1954).

15. According to one study, made during World War II, less than one-quarter of American infantrymen, themselves under fire, fired their rifles; cf. Janowitz, *Sociology and the Military Establishment*, p. 12.

16. Janowitz, *The Military in Political Development*, pp. 3 and 49 ff., but see the qualifications on p. 56; M. Berger, *Military Elite and Social Change* (Princeton, 1960), p. 22. This problem is discussed by S. Andreski, "Conservatism and Radicalism of the Military," *European Journal of Sociology* 2 (1961): 53-61; G. Germani and K. Silvert, "Politics, Social Structure and Military Intervention in Latin America," *ibid.*, pp. 62-81.

17. I have no specific information about the age structure of officer corps in developing countries, but I tentatively assume it to be more often

503

true of them than not. See also A. D. Biderman, "Sequels to a Military Career," in *The New Military*, ed. M. Janowitz (New York, 1964), pp. 287-336.

18. Finer, *The Man on Horseback*, p. 139, and in *New Society*. R. von der Mehden, *Politics of the Developing Nations* (Englewood Cliffs, N.J., 1964), p. 65, as adapted by S. P. Huntington, "Political Development and Decay," *World Politics* 17 (1965): 427.

19. Cf. E. Shils, "The Military in the Political Development of the New States," in *The Role of the Military*, ed. Johnson, pp. 7-67.

20. "Towards a Theory of Power and Political Stability in Latin America," in *Two Worlds of Change*, ed. O. Feinstein (New York, 1964), pp. 183 ff.

21. Janowitz, *The Military in Political Development*, pp. 40 ff. See also Finer, *The Man on Horseback*, p. 196.

22. Janowitz, *The Military in Political Development*, p. 85.

23. Cf. Finer, *The Man on Horseback*, esp. pp. 190 ff.

24. *Ibid.*, p. 120.

25. G. A. Nasser, *Egypt's Liberation: a Philosophy of the Revolution* (Washington, 1955), pp. 32 ff.

26. Cf. Shils, "The Military in the Political Development of the New States," pp. 60 ff.

BUREAUCRACY AND NATION BUILDING IN TRANSITIONAL SOCIETIES

S.C. Dube

Bureaucracy forms an important element of the modernizing elite in many of the economically less developed countries which have attained national independence during the last two decades. Trained in the colonial tradition, this organized and articulate segment of the native society functioned as a bridge between the dependent indigenous people and the ruling power from the West. Although it had to work under the direction of the imperial power and had largely to carry out its policies, it was not without nationalist sentiments and aspirations. Held suspect during the days of the struggle for freedom, both by politically-oriented fellow-countrymen and by the alien rulers, members of this class had, by and large, acquired a progressive orientation and the more sophisticated among them had definite ideas regarding the programs of economic and social growth to be adopted by their country at the attainment of national independence. In many countries they were the only organized body of natives with considerable training and experience in administration; they naturally found themselves called upon to assume major responsibilities in the formulation and implementation of national plans for economic development and social change.

The general change in political climate, the assumption of power by the political elite, the changing alignments of power and pressure groups, and the emergence of new institutional and administrative patterns raised in their wake a series of complex problems for the bureaucracy. In consequence, it had to make some significant adjustments in its thought-and work-ways and to adapt itself to the new ethos. On the other hand, in many sensitive areas it found itself either openly resisting or accepting some of the new elements only theoretically. Thus, with or

From S. C. Dube, "Bureaucracy and Nation Building in Transitional Societies," from the *International Social Science Journal,* Volume 16, no. 2, 1964. Reproduced with the permission of UNESCO.

without the overt acceptance of the new patterns, it stood for continuity of some of the established norms. In meeting these intricate problems of adjustment and value-conflict, the character of bureaucracy in transitional societies is undergoing a rapid change. Since it occupies a pivotal position in these societies, and will possibly continue to do so in the foreseeable future, an understanding of the character and culture of bureaucracy is essential for those concerned with the programs of economic growth and social change in the economically less developed countries.

Planning for economic growth is an extremely complicated business which involves highly specialized knowledge and developed manipulative skills; the implementation of these plans presupposes deep administrative insights and a keen evaluative perspective. In the context of the program of community development, it is common these days to emphasize the ideal of planning by the people, but the crucial fact that this stage must necessarily be preceded by the stages of planning for the people and planning with the people is not given sufficient emphasis. The acceptance of these three stages means successively diminishing functions for the bureaucracy in matters of local and regional planning and in developmental administration, but it is essential to bear in mind that the gap between the first and the third stage is very considerable and that the transition to the final stage depends largely upon the manner in which the process is initiated and the first two stages are carried out. Both these stages involve considerable direct participation by the bureaucracy; the second stage particularly—which requires the initiation of a process of withdrawal—has critical significance. Optimism, bordering on wishful thinking, cannot alone diminish the importance of bureaucracy; its role in the process of planning and developmental administration is bound to figure prominently for several decades. The problem of the integration of local, regional and national plans demands knowledge and skills which perhaps only the bureaucracy possesses. Of course, as the process acquires greater complexity the technocrat is drawn into it more deeply, for without the utilization of his specialized knowledge planning for successive stages would become increasingly difficult. Nevertheless, much maligned and distrusted as it is, bureaucracy is not without a vital role to play in the process of planning for economic and social development. Modifications in its structure, values and work-ways are necessary to adapt it to the idiom of the fast changing situation, but the fact remains that it cannot be done away with. An understanding of its character and the initiation of imaginative plans for changing its structure and values so as to make it a more effective instrument for development must therefore be considered an essential prerequisite to planned change in these countries.

Discriminatingly recruited on the basis of specified criteria and carefully trained according to established and time-tested plans, bureaucracies in most of the former colonies and dependencies became efficient instruments of administration. Although they were oriented more to functions of law and order and the collection of revenues, they were also entrusted from time to time with some nation-building responsibilities. In discharging their responsibilities they showed all the classical characteristics of bureaucracies: they were formally organized with unambiguous demarcation of roles and statuses and were articulated to clearly defined goals; they were efficient and equipped with the required knowledge; they were well-versed in formal rules of procedure and recognized their predominance; and finally they were trained to function in an impersonal manner under conditions of near anonymity.

In addition to the above, bureaucracies in these societies had certain special characteristics. In their respective countries they were perhaps the first large and organized group to enter the transitional phase between tradition and modernity—the twilight zone lying between societal types described variously in continua such as communal-associational, sacred-secular, status-contract, and *gemeinschaft-gesellschaft.* In other words, they were among the pioneers who sought to break away from the traditionally affective and emotion-based communal society and to set in motion the forces that were to contribute towards the emergence of a different type of society—a society characterized by affective neutrality and based on rational ends-means calculations for individual goals. As a distinct subcultural entity within the larger framework of their society, they were at least partly absolved from the traditional obligation of having to share communal attitudes, sentiments and repressive authority, and were among the first to constitute a group characterized by specialized division of labor, by different but complementary interests and sentiments, and by restrictive authority. It is not suggested here that they could break away completely from tradition to adopt the ideals and values of modernity; in the critical areas of choice making they had before them a wide zone of fluid values in which were present the elements of both tradition and modernity. The logic and rationale of selectivity in the process of choice making has not been analyzed in depth, but the fact that, gradually and in an increasing measure, bureaucracy adopted several elements of modernity is not without significance.

It might be useful to describe here some special features of these bureaucracies, as they emerged and crystallized during the colonial phase.

1. Bureaucracy constituted a special subcultural sement—the high prestige strata of the society. Entrance to it was theoretically not barred to any section of the community, although in actual practice only the traditionally privileged could provide the necessary general background and the expensive education required for success in the stiff tests prescribed for entry into its higher echelons. In limited numbers others also gained entrance into the relatively closed group of higher civil servants. Middle-level and lower positions in it attracted the less privileged. Bureaucracy had a class bias and it tended to have a stratification of its own; its upper crust functioned as a privileged class. On the whole it symbolized achievement rather than ascription. Over time, it came to have distinct vested interests, and was sensitive to all threats to its position and

507

privilege which it guarded jealously against encroachment from any quarter.

2. It existed largely in the twilight zone of cultures. Partly traditional and partly modern, it could and did in fact choose from the elements of both. In several ways it was alienated from the masses and uprooted from the native cultural traditions; significant differences in styles of living and in modes of thought separated the two. The Western rulers, on the other hand, never conceded equality to it. In consequence, bureaucracy maintained dual identification and was characterized by a dual ambivalence.

3. Besides offering security of tenure and relatively higher emoluments, bureaucratic positions carried vast powers which made them additionally attractive and important. The powers vested in a minor functionary gave him prestige, perquisites and privileges far beyond those justified by his emoluments and position in the hierarchy. Formally the role and status of functionaries at different levels were defined, but in actual practice the system of expectation and obligation between them tended to be diffused rather than specific.

4. Within the framework of the over-all policy laid down by the imperial power, in day-to-day administration the bureaucratic machine enjoyed considerable freedom from interference. Thus there were few hindrances to its exercise of power, which was often authoritarian in tone and content. Bureaucracy had, in general, a paternalistic attitude to the masses. The masses, on their part, accepted the position and looked to the administration for a wide variety of small favors.

5. Administration was concerned mainly with collection of land revenue and with maintenance of law and order. The general administrator under these conditions enjoyed supremacy. Subject matter specialists of welfare and nation-building departments were relegated to secondary positions and functioned under the guidance and control of the generalist.

6. Bureaucracy was carefully trained in formal administrative procedure and routine. Stereotypes in this sphere were well-developed and were scrupulously observed.

7. In the limited framework of its functions and set procedures bureaucracy found a self-contained system. It resented and resisted innovations.

8. Its attitude to the nationalist forces within was most ambivalent. Few within the bureaucracy were devoid of patriotic sentiments and aspirations, but only in rare exceptions could they openly side with the forces of nationalism. Requirements of their official position made them an instrument for the execution of imperialist policies. This naturally aroused in the nationalist leadership feelings of anger and distrust against them. This rejection by the leaders of the nationalist forces as well as by the politically-conscious masses was largely at the root of their ambivalent attitude towards the nationalist forces.

Bureaucracy welcomed the advent of independence as much as any other group in the former colonies and dependencies, but the first years of freedom were for it a period of great stress and strain. It had covertly resented Western domination, but in the first decade of independence it remained under the shadow of suspicion because of its former association and identification with the alien power. While its power and prestige were decreasing, its burdens and responsibilities were increasing. Attacked from several sides simultaneously and with mounting pressures, bureaucracy found itself in a difficult and uncomfortable position.

The more important areas in which it had to work for a redefinition and consequent readjustment of its position and responsibilities were (a) the culture of politics, (b) the emerging ethos, and (c) the expanding sphere of State activity and the new institutional arrangements.

THE CULTURE OF POLITICS

In the new order the supremacy of administration was replaced largely by the sovereignty of politics. Politics became the most important activity and the politician came to occupy a position of unquestionable supremacy in matters of decision making. Within the framework of this culture of politics, there was an unmistakable tendency towards the merging of political roles with personal and social roles; the expectations of the politician from his followers and administrative subordinates were diffused. Politics centred round individuals; informal factions or groups formed around key personalities were thus more meaningful units of political organization than the formal structure of political parties. Personal loyalty to politicians, under these conditions, played an important part in the process of political identification and decision making. Administration under such leadership could not remain wholly impersonal. The political elite was nurtured more in the politics of agitation than in the politics of nation-building, and as a hangover from the past it persisted in its agitational approach. Nucleated around individuals, political processes lacked organic unity; communication was not adequately articulated. In general, political parties represented some kind of a revolutionary world view and philosophy, and on larger international and national issues they stood for an unlimited Utopia. On specific issues, especially of a regional or local character, the position was significantly different; political opinion on them was often narrow, sectarian and parochial. Thus political thinking regarding issues at different levels lacked cohesion and integration. The attitude of the political elite was characterized by ambivalence. They sought to work for modernization, without giving up their love for tradition; attempts to harmonize, synthesize and integrate the elements of the two, even on a conceptual level, were neither systematic nor serious.

In many countries the bureaucracy was trained well enough to accept political direction, and only in a few exceptional cases did it try to gain the upper hand. Adjustment and adaptation to this political culture, 509 however, was not without problems and difficulties. The new order posed a definite threat to bureaucracy's structure, values and interests. While its formal structure reamined intact, the definition of roles and statuses within the hierarchy was disturbed by the emergence of the politician as the focal point of decision making. The personal nature of political decision making was another unsettling factor. It not only affected the internal status system of the bureaucracy, but also sometimes bypassed its special knowledge and side-tracked its procedural routine. In many specific contexts administration could not function in an impersonal manner. Interpersonal relations between the politician and the administrator tended to be uneasy. The politician recognized the value and importance of the bureaucracy, but he continued to have a definite antagonism towards it, to exhort and admonish it to change its ways, and to ridicule it for some of its modes of thought and action that were out of tune in the new order. Much of this criticism was valid, but the manner in which it was made was often irritating to the bureaucrats. Many members of the bureaucracy had silently admired the self-sacrificing patriots as heroes, but in close proximity they saw them without the halo that surrounded them during the days of the national struggle. Often, the gap between their profession and their practice particularly annoyed the perceptive members of the bureaucracy. The politician was himself adopting many of the ways which he criticized in the bureaucrat. Some members of the administration were all too willing to adapt, but their over-readiness to do so was viewed by the discerning administrator as a dangerous departure that could in the long run undermine the very character and role of the bureaucracy.

THE EMERGING ETHOS

The emerging ethos also presented bureaucracy with a series of problems. In the new setting it could not maintain its image of power, nor could it continue to exist as a high-prestige class enjoying exceptional privileges. A closer identification with the masses was called for; the paternalistic and authoritarian tone of administration had also inevitably to change. On a theoretical and emotional level the desirability of this basic change was conceded, but a system of rationalization was developed at the same time to justify the maintenance of the *status quo*. Today a great contradiction persists between emotional awareness of the desirable and willingness to accept it in practice.

THE EXPANDING SPHERE OF STATE ACTIVITY AND NEW INSTITUTIONAL ARRANGEMENTS

The structure, values, and work-ways of the bureaucracy in almost all former colonies and dependencies were geared to law and order and to revenue administration for which it was efficiently trained. Administration for nation building necessitated a different approach involving a new value attitude orientation and a modified institutional set-up. It is in these spheres that the failures of the bureaucracy are perhaps the most pronounced.

By and large the bureaucracy resists innovations in its structural arrangement. It appears to have a firm faith in the superiority of the pyramidal structure of administration and in the infallibility of the generalist. Efforts to nuclearize the administration for nation building are resented, and there is great resentment if any attempt is made to dislodge the general administrator from his high pedestal. Concepts of inner-democratization, of administrative decentralization, and of delegation of authority and responsibility at best receive only lip servie. Coordination becomes difficult because of faulty communication between the general administrator and the technical specialist. Effective utilization of the specialist is blocked by the accepted or assumed supremacy of the general administrator whose self-confidence borders almost on arrogance. The latter perhaps realizes that he is not trained for certain jobs, but he rarely concedes this publicly. Innovations have been made in these spheres, but the marks of bureaucratic resistance are still evident.

Subconsciously the bureaucrat still perhaps believes in the efficacy of the traditional approach to administration. New approaches are discussed and half-heartedly accepted, but only in rare cases do they receive a fair trial. Extension and community development approaches, for instance, have encountered considerable resistance from the bureaucracy. Indeed, many members of the administration would be glad to revert to type, and would willingly reverse the process that has gained partial acceptance for these approaches after years of experimentation and persuasion.

It is generally recognized that the cumbrous administrative routine, good in its time, today practically immobilizes developmental administration. Yet, all attempts to change the rules of procedure result invariably in the formulation of rules that are as complex as those they seek to replace, if not more so.

Efforts at deconcentration of power, such as the experiment of democratic decentralization for development in India, meet with even greater resistance. Doubtless the infant "grass-roots democracy" is not without shortcomings, but its threats to the perpetuation of bureaucratic vested interests have alerted the administrator, whose approach to the experiment is extremely guarded, wooden and unimaginative.

Attempts have been made at reorienting the bureaucracy to the new philosophy of administration, but they have often been viewed as mere short-lived fads and fancies. Indirectly the new approach has made some headway, but there is little evidence to suggest that its utility has been generally accepted.

In the tasks of nation building in transitional societies bureaucracy has a vital role to play. It consists, by and large, of people with progressive motivation, wide administrative experience, and a rich store of pooled

511

knowledge. Far from being written off, it cannot be ignored. It must also be conceded that it has played an important part in the process of economic and social growth and has been willing to go part of the way at least to adjust to the new situation. It has functioned both as a model and as an instrument for modernization. But its effective utilization has been blocked by some of the paradoxes of the new political culture and by the inner contradictions within its own structure and ordering of values. In several respects the hard core of the bureaucratic culture has been unyielding, and has offered great resistance to innovation. The blame does not lie entirely as its own door, but at the same time the present state of uncertainty cannot be allowed to continue indefinitely. Lack of adequate understanding of its culture and values and of a balanced assessment of its past and future roles has been an important factor in the failure to utilize bureaucracy more effectively in programs of economic growth and planned change.

BUREAUCRACY
AND ENVIRONMENT IN CEYLON

Robert N. Kearney & Richard L. Harris

For many of the newly independent states of Asia and Africa one of the most significant legacies of Western colonial rule is the existence of a public bureaucracy organized according to Western administrative concepts and incorporating to some degree Western notions of rationality, efficiency, and impersonality. The colonial period was predominantly a period of bureaucratic rule in which the bureaucrats were often seen as constituting an elite of talent and wisdom, and in the areas under British control the colonial bureaucracies sometimes built admirable records of integrity and ability. Following independence, the bureaucracies have been forced to make occasionally painful adjustments to altered political conditions. At the same time the almost universal commitment to rapid economic development and the frequent desire to weld into national societies diverse ethnic and religious communities have greatly expanded the tasks of the bureaucracies. In these circumstances, the characteristics and effectiveness of the former colonial bureaucracies and their problems in adapting to the conditions of independence have become of critical importance to the future of most, if not all, newly independent states.

In the present study, an attempt is made to trace the impact of the social, cultural, and political environment on the contemporary bureaucracy of Ceylon.[1] The discussion of bureaucracy and environment in Ceylon, it is hoped, will contribute to the comparative analysis of the characteristics, problems, and prospects of non-Western, ex-colonial bureaucracies, particularly in those states which have emerged from British rule. Although parts of Ceylon were controlled in turn by the Portuguese

From Robert N. Kearney and Richard L. Harris, "Bureaucracy and Environment in Ceylon," *Journal of Commonwealth Political Studies* 2 (November 1964): 253-66. Copyright © 1964 by Leicester University Press. Reprinted by permission of the publisher.

and Dutch for three centuries, the modern bureaucracy was a product of British rule from the beginning of the nineteenth century to the grant of independence in 1948 and shared much of the heritage of the vastly larger and more famous bureaucracy of British India. While this paper is primarily concerned with the weight of external factors on the bureaucracy, it should be noted that the bureaucracy has simultaneously exerted a strong influence on its environment and played a major role in the process of modernization in Ceylon.

THE PRESTIGE OF THE PUBLIC SERVICE

As in many newly independent and economically underdeveloped nations, government employment in Ceylon has an enormous attraction for the educated and skilled members of the nation's labour force. Studies of occupational preference consistently show that government employment is rated higher than any other occupation in Ceylon.[2] For the educated Ceylonese the public service is almost the only source of secure employment since the government dominates the small nonagricultural segment of the economy and has a virtual monopoly of white-collar employment. More than 20 percent of all Ceylonese wage and salary earners are in the public service.[3] Pensions, employment security, and fairly high salary rates sharply distinguish government employment from the uncertainty and insecurity of private employment.

The great prestige enjoyed by the public servant has, however, probably contributed at least as much as material advantage or employment security to the attractiveness of a bureaucratic career. The social prestige of the modern bureaucrat is in large measure a heritage of Ceylon's feudal and colonial past. Traditional Sinhalese society was rigidly stratified by class and caste on the basis of status prescribed by birth. In this hierarchical society, government officials were drawn exclusively from families of the highest rank.[4] Hence, the belief developed that officialdom represented the "best" families. This traditional outlook on officialdom was reinforced by the experience of European colonial rule. By their social exclusiveness and supreme confidence in the superiority of their own civilization, the European colonial administrators helped to perpetuate the popular association of governmental position with superior social status.[5] The notions of tutelage and paternalism inherent in colonial rule reinforced the elitist conception of the colonial bureaucracy.

The first Ceylonese to enter the colonial service were recruited from among the Sinhalese low-country *Mudaliyars* (chiefs), and authority over the peasantry was exercised through feudal aristocratic *Mudaliyars* and Kandyan *Ratemahattayas* by the colonial regime until 1946. Headmen forming the base of the regional administration until 1963 were selected from the venerated, high-caste, landowning families of the locality. The presence of these feudal elements in modern administration has helped to establish a link in the mind of the Ceylonese villager between the contemporary bureaucrats and the exalted feudal nobility.

SOCIAL STRATIFICATION AND THE
BUREAUCRATIC HIERARCHY

Social and economic developments of the past century have significantly modified traditional Ceylonese social organization, leaving in contemporary Ceylon a transitional society in which elements of the traditional exist alongside elements of the modern. While the rigid stratification of traditional society has been altered in a number of respects, social classes tend to be sharply differentiated on the basis of education, language, and manner of living, which are closely related to wealth and birth. For several generations, the island has been dominated socially and economically by those who were able to obtain an education taught in the English language. A wide chasm of social status and culture has separated the English-educated Ceylonese, commonly called the English-speaking elite, from the vernacular-educated, producing one of the most profound divisions of Ceylonese society.[6] The members of this westernized elite enjoyed exclusive access to the higher positions in the colonial bureaucracy. They held political power at independence in 1948, but their political domination was broken in 1956, when resentment of the privileges conferred by education in English helped propel a more popularly based and nationalist Government into power.

In the highly status-conscious environment of Ceylon, it is not surprising that the bureaucracy reflects the basic inequalities and sharp divisions of the social hierarchy. Like the society, the bureaucracy is stratified into highly differentiated classes or status groups. At the apex of this bureaucratic hierarchy is the administrative and professional officer class, constituting less than one percent of the entire bureaucracy. The members of this group, called staff officers, are drawn from Ceylon's small number of university graduates and represent the narrow social stratum of the English-speaking elite.

Below the class of administrative and professional officers lies the middle segment of the bureaucratic hierarchy, the clerical class. Individuals in this class are also English-speaking but are socially inferior to the staff officers and have received English-language education only to the secondary level. The social distance which separates members of these two groups is much greater and more obvious than that which commonly exists in Western bureaucracies.

The base of the bureaucratic pyramid consists of a class of bureaucrats known in Ceylon as "minor employees." Eight out of ten public servants are members of this group of unskilled and semiskilled maintenance and

515

service employees.[7] The social and cultural gulf separating the top from the bottom of the bureaucratic hierarchy is suggested by the contrast between the sarong-clad and barefoot semiliterate minor employee and the university-educated staff officer attired in a western business suit. The distance is similarly visible in the obvious relationships between the two groups, characterized by obsequiousness on the part of the minor employee and haughtiness on the part of the staff officer.

The salaries paid to individuals in the different bureaucratic classes reveal the disparity between them in terms of standard of living and economic status. In contrast to the United States and Canada where the salary received by the highest paid public servant is about six times that received by the lowest paid public servant, in Ceylon the salary of the highest paid public servant is approximately 40 times that of the lowest.[8] The economic gaps that exist between the different classes are further illustrated by the fact that the average starting salary of a government clerk is roughly twice that of a minor employee, while the average starting salary of a staff officer is five times that of a clerk.[9]

In some ways the clerical class has the least desirable position in this highly stratified bureaucratic hierarchy. Promotion from the clerical level to the administrative level is severely limited by the class structure of the bureaucracy. The educational and social distinctions maintained between the two levels impose a status barrier which few ever cross. Besides the bleak opportunity for advancement, the salaries of government clerks fall drastically short of supporting the urban standard of living to which they aspire. Frustrations arising from this dissimilarity between aspirations and economic and social status seemingly have caused the government clerks to be one of the principal sources of support for the left-wing political parties in Ceylon.[10]

Slightly more than 1,000 persons hold administrative positions in the entire public service of over 245,000 members.[11] However, until very recently this small cadre of administrative officers contained an even smaller administrative elite known as the Ceylon Civil Service, which enjoyed special prerogatives and immense prestige. The C.C.S., the Ceylonese counterpart of the Indian Civil Service, was formed in 1803 as the first overseas civil service responsible to the British Crown. Originally the Service included the highest British administrators sent to govern the island, and as late as 1927 two-thirds of the positions in the C.C.S. were filled by Englishmen. After 1948, the number of Civil Service officers remained around 200, although the public service doubled in size and the number of non-Civil Service administrative officers increased by more than 50 percent.[12]

After independence, the C.C.S. continued to exist as a class apart from the rest of the administrative service. Civil Servants had different salary grades and promotion prospects from non-Civil Servants and a number of the top administrative posts in the government were reserved for Civil Service officers. In 1959, while the C.C.S. comprised only about 13 percent of all administrative personnel, its members held 40 percent of the top administrative positions and an even greater number of the next highest administrative positions.[13] The existence of this small and privileged group, which was felt to be a relic of colonial rule without purpose in an independent nation, was widely resented within, as well as outside, the bureaucracy. A government commission studying the public service referred to the C.C.S. as an administrative "caste" which because of the special privileges and snobbishness of its members caused constant friction and discontent in the administrative level of the public service.[14] On 1 May 1963, the C.C.S. officially was abolished and the former Civil Service officers were incorporated into a Unified Administrative Service of 1,030 officers grouped in five grades.[15]

INFLUENCES OF THE EDUCATIONAL SYSTEM

Until recently, the prerequisite for securing a position in the government bureaucracy was an education taught in the English language. In fact, a primary purpose of the educational system in Ceylon in colonial times was to provide a supply of English-educated recruits for the public service. For most of the nineteenth century British colonial officers assisted by Ceylonese clerical employees formed the combination which governed the island.

The colonial system of education, geared to educating students for positions in the government service, exhibited the strong bias in favor of the humanities and neglect of technical studies which was characteristic of the "generalist" preferences of the British colonial services.[16] This emphasis continues today and the educational system remains to a large extent committed to dispensing the same liberal education formerly required of recruits to the colonial bureaucracy. The public service officers of the Department of Motor Vehicles or the Irrigation Department today frequently hold degrees in Buddhist civilization or English literature. Although the Government has repeatedly charged that the educational system inadequately supplies the nation's technical and scientific needs, the underproduction of graduates in technical subjects has been encouraged by the bureaucracy's practice of paying higher salaries and offering better promotion prospects to administrative officers than to technical and professional experts. This practice seriously discourages students from studying in the technical fields and forces technically trained individuals in the public service to seek administrative posts in order to improve their financial position and obtain higher status.

Education is commonly sought in Ceylon as a means of securing a bureaucratic job and the dowry and status public employment commands.[17] The entire educational process reflects this orientation in that it

517

is basically designed to prepare the student for passing the national educational examinations required for entrance into the different levels of the public service. Indeed, the key examinations in the school system are looked upon as stepping stones to positions in the public service. The present General Certificate of Education examination, for example, is generally regarded as the stepping stone to a post in the clerical grades, just as the University degree is thought of as the key to a post in the administrative and professional officer grades.[18]

THE IMPACT OF ETHNIC AND RELIGIOUS COMMUNITIES

Although westernizing influences appear to have made considerably greater headway in the bureaucracy than in the society as a whole, the barriers separating Ceylon's ethnic and religious communities remain of considerable significance to the public service. Where strong consciousness of communal group membership lingers, the ethnic and religious composition of the bureaucracy becomes a matter of public concern. Almost inevitably, communal competition for the prized public employment develops and appeals are made to communal loyalties to support claims on public service positions.

The advantages of early establishment in the bureaucracy and access to English-language education have given certain ethnic and religious minorities a disproportionate share of public service posts. Among the first Ceylonese to enter the colonial bureaucracy were members of the small Burgher (Eurasian) community, whose swift mastery of English and recruitment to the public services was facilitated by their familiarity with European culture and concentration in Colombo near the first schools. The Tamils of Jaffna, faced with harsh economic conditions in the North, were quick to benefit from English-language educations made available by American missionaries and early entered the colonial bureaucracy in large numbers. In contrast, except for members of the Sinhalese low-country aristocracy, the Sinhalese of the majority community were slow to gain admission to the public service. Kandyan Sinhalese of the interior seldom acquired the requisite command of the English language and were almost totally absent from the colonial service. The share of bureaucratic posts held by the Burgher and Tamil minorities declined gradually and the Sinhalese, particularly from the coastal areas, improved their relative position in the later years of colonial rule. However, the Sinhalese, who comprise more than two-thirds of the Ceylonese population, have continued to be underrepresented in the public service.[19]

Smoldering resentment over disproportionate minority representation in the bureaucracy has been fundamental to the communal strife which has plagued Ceylon since independence. A rapid expansion of vernacular education through the secondary level commencing in the 1930s led to demands for entry of the Sinhalese-educated into the public service, which remained the preserve of the English-educated following independence. At the same time, developing Sinhalese nationalism awakened mass Sinhalese political consciousness and sharpened awareness of communal differences. Communal loyalty was soon enlisted to utilize the political strength of the majority community in the competition for government employment.[20] To the Sinhalese, minority entrenchment in the public service has meant that "the Tamil man is sleeping on the Sinhalese man's mat."[21] The official language issue, originally designed to break the hold of the English-educated on the public service, developed into a demand by the Sinhalese for preferential access to the bureaucracy. The demand for *swabhasha* or the Ceylonese people's "own language" was transformed into the call for "Sinhalese only" as the official language of government.[22]

A new Government, brought to power in 1956 by the emergent nationalism and communal self-consciousness of the Sinhalese rural masses, immediately enacted legislation changing the official language from English to Sinhalese. After the passing of the Official Language Act, communal tensions exploded into violent riots in 1956 and 1958. A Tamil *satyagraha* campaign, intended to prevent implementation of the Official Language Act in the Tamil areas, paralyzed administration in the North for three months in 1961.

The language changeover in the bureaucracy has been accompanied by considerable administrative confusion and bureaucratic demoralization, since few public servants were proficient in Sinhalese. Despite incentive bonuses and threatened loss of regular salary increases unless an examination in Sinhalese was passed, at least half the public servants were believed to be unable to perform their duties in the new official language by 1961, five years after the enactment of the Official Language Act.[23] The requirement that entrants into the public service should develop a working knowledge of Sinhalese within three years of their appointment will presumably constitute a major obstacle to the securing of public employment by Tamil- and English-speaking Ceylonese and may be expected to alter the future ethnic composition of the bureaucracy to the advantage of the Sinhalese.

Parallel to clashes between ethnic communities for positions within the bureaucracy has been a rising concern for the religious composition of the public service. Ceylon's Hindu population is Tamil-speaking and the question of Hindu representation in the bureaucracy is indistinguishable from the question of Tamil representation. The Muslims commonly have turned to trade and have displayed slight interest in public employment. The sharp conflict is between the Buddhist majority, who are ethnically Sinhalese, and the Christian minority, composed of Sinhalese, Tamils, and Burghers. While the exact proportion of Christians in the public service is unknown, it almost certainly far exceeds the Christian proportion of the population.

519

Most English-language education was formerly in the hands of Christian missionaries, and Christian denominational schools dominated the field of education in English from the latter part of the nineteenth century until they were taken over by the government in 1960. The educational advantage of Christians is reflected in enrollments in the University of Ceylon. Until 1946 Christian students actually outnumbered Buddhists at the University, although the Buddhists constitute 64 percent of the island population and the Christians only 9 percent. Although the proportion of Christians in the student body has since declined, it has remained well above the Christian proportion of the population.[24]

Buddhist resentment at the large number of Christians in the public service and the relative underrepresentation of Buddhists, intensified by the belief that the Christians benefited from favoritism in selection during the colonial period, have prompted repeated demands that the religious composition of the bureaucracy should more nearly reflect the religious composition of the society. In 1962, the influential All-Ceylon Buddhist Congress proposed that recruitment to the public service and army should be based on proportional representation of the island's various religious groups.[25] This suggestion was incorporated in the recommendations of the National Education Commission. The final report of the Commission urged that admission to the University and public service be regulated by quotas assigned to religious groups on the basis of their relative size.[26]

CASTE AND FAMILY
INFLUENCES

Caste attitudes and loyalties continue to influence the bureaucracy although for many years the government has formally opposed continuation of caste distinctions. Caste enters the bureaucratic recruitment and promotion processes through the preference higher officers grant members of their own caste. Although caste distinctions may be of declining significance in the society, caste members are still united by a strong sense of solidarity, based on caste endogamy, which suggests the possibility of kinship or of future family connections. Membership of the same caste, thus, is a convenient lever for evoking preference in the selection or promotion of public servants.[27] Although the magnitude of caste preference in the bureaucracy cannot be determined, privately made references to caste favoritism, particularly in the upper grades, are fairly common. Occasionally, charges of caste preference appear more openly. For example, the Permanent Secretary to the Ministry of Defense and External Affairs was recently charged in Parliament with favoring members of the *Karava* caste in his ministry.[28] Caste lines are alleged to emerge in the present Cabinet when it considers projects which would create new government jobs, because of the fear that these new posts will be filled disproportionately by members of one caste. Ministers of the same caste as the Minister who is to have charge of the project frequently support the proposal, apparently expecting favoritism in employment to be shown to members of their caste. Similarly, Ministers of other castes may oppose the project because they fear that "their people" will not receive adequate recognition in the distribution of jobs.[29]

Caste more openly influences bureaucratic assignments to posts exercising direct authority over the public. Popular reaction to low-caste persons in positions of authority over them apparently has not greatly changed in the hundred years since Emerson Tennent lamented: "A reluctant conformity is exhibited on the part of high-caste persons placed officially under the orders of low-caste headmen; but their obedience is constrained, with no effort to conceal impatience. . . ."[30] The low popular esteem of public servants of lower caste has seriously undermined their authority and imperilled the performance of their duties.[31] A colonial practice of tailoring certain appointments to local caste sentiments in the interest of tranquillity in administration is still evident. It is common knowledge in Ceylon that caste has been decisive in the appointment of headmen and teachers. Except for low-caste villages, headmen consistently were selected from among the high-caste landowners. Assignment of a low-caste schoolteacher to a predominantly high-caste village has commonly aroused the villagers to appeal to the local Member of Parliament to secure the teacher's transfer.

Widespread nepotism is not uncommon in Asia, where the family frequently holds the first loyalty of the individual and family welfare is accorded priority over such a shadowy concept as the public interest. In contemporary Ceylon, family ties have retained considerable strength. The effects of family bonds are patently obvious in the private business practice of employing sons, brothers, cousins, and in-laws. In this environment, it is surprising that nepotism does not appear to be rampant in the bureaucracy. This may be explained by the persistence of strong colonial traditions of bureaucratic integrity and the wide acceptance of western values and attitudes among the senior Ceylonese public servants, resulting in less willingness to condone nepotism. Undoubtedly, however, individual public servants occasionally manage to give unsanctioned advantage to relatives.

Most of the charges of nepotism appearing in the nation's press relate to the semicommercial government corporations, which are of recent origin and lack some of the formalism and integrity of the regular government departments. That nepotism does exist was revealed at a recent hearing conducted by the commissioners of the Salt Corporation. Among several examples of nepotism uncovered was the case of a typist who confessed that if her uncle had not been secretary of the Corporation she would neither have obtained nor been able to keep her position. The young lady was incensed at having been reprimanded during her employment for making errors in every line of letters she typed.[32]

THE BUREAUCRACY AND THE
POLITICAL ENVIRONMENT

Rapid and profound political changes in Ceylon have had an impact of as yet uncertain magnitude on the Ceylonese bureaucracy. In the first decade after independence, resurgent Sinhalese nationalism, Buddhist discontents, and the language issue led to the political mobilization of large sections of the formerly inert rural Sinhalese masses. The election of 1956 ended the political domination of the conservative, highly western-ized, and affluent English-speaking elite and brought to power a political leadership more attuned to the aspirations of the Sinhalese villagers. The following years were turbulent. Communal violence flared, the governing coalition was plagued by instability, and in 1959 Prime Minister S. W. R. D. Bandaranaike was assassinated. After nearly a year of confusion and caretaker Governments, Bandaranaike's party, the Sri Lanka Freedom Party, scored an election victory and the nationalist and populist leadership headed by Bandaranaike's widow was confirmed in power, apparently with increased determination to effect fundamental social and economic reforms.[33]

Political interference in the public service, a common feature of Ceylonese public life at least since the Donoughmore Constitution of 1931-1947, appears to have increased considerably in recent years.[34] This rapid growth of interference seems closely related to the new political trends of the island. With the popular political awakening have come rising demands for and expectations of governmental action to alleviate social and economic discontents, particularly those of the rural villagers, who form 85 percent of the island's population. The Ceylonese bureaucrat accustomed to the role of "officer of the Crown" from the colonial era, has seemed little inclined to regard himself as a "public servant" and has commonly been indifferent to the needs and convenience of the public. There is little notion within the bureaucracy that it exists to serve the society. Indeed, it is not improbable that a major portion of the public service believes that society exists primarily to support the bureaucracy. Poorly equipped by education, sophistication, or status to deal with the officers of the public service, the Ceylonese villagers have turned progressively to the politicians for assistance.

As a result of shifts in political power since 1956, the parliamentary candidate is no longer assured of election by the backing of the larger landowners and leading families in his constituency. He has become dependent for election on the support of the rural masses. Many politicians have concluded that this support can best be won by the performance of innumerable individual services for constituents, their families, or their villages. Thus, increasingly the villagers have sought political intercession with the bureaucracy and the politicians have been receptive to these requests as a way of obtaining necessary electoral support. The result has been a striking shift in the role of the M.P. to that of an agent for his constituents in their dealings with the bureaucracy. M.P.s now accept as a matter of course that a constituent with a problem concerning the government will come first to his representative in Parliament. M.P.s are involved daily in such tasks as expediting pensions, securing rice ration books, arranging entrance into schools or hospitals, obtaining approval for the construction of village roads, and locating public employment for constituents.[35]

Political intervention is particularly prevalent in the transfer of government teachers. The M.P.'s aid is solicited to transfer from the village school a teacher who has run afoul of village opinion for personal, caste, or educational reasons. Teachers or their relatives ask M.P.s to intervene to halt impending transfers or secure transfers to desired schools. When a quorum cannot be found in Parliament, it is a standing joke that the majority of M.P.s are at the Education Department. In denouncing one instance of political interference in teacher transfers, an irate M.P. declared it to be "disgraceful that the whole might and political power of the Government has been brought to bear on routine administrative transfers of the Department of Education." The M.P. was enraged because other politicians had intervened to prevent transfers he had supported.[36] Service to local interests and responsiveness to constituents' desires were stressed in a defense of political intervention offered by one M.P.: "We interfere in teachers transfers not to obtain any personal benefit but in the interest of the people in our areas."[37]

The recent expansion of political interference is not, as has been said, simply a sign of degenerating public morals. While corruption and personal gain are not absent,[38] basically this expansion represents the search for a new channel of popular access to the bureaucracy. Political interference has grown in response to public demand.

The political changes which marked the election of 1956 created the conditions for a clash of interests between the upper levels of the bureaucracy and the new political leadership. The higher public servants are largely drawn from the affluent, urban, upper-middle class. Because of their westernization and identification with the former colonial regime, they appeared, to many spokesmen for the growing Sinhalese nationalism to be an alienated group which had turned its back on traditional Sinhalese culture. The new political leaders won power with the support of the rural villagers, particularly members of the Sinhalese-educated rural lower-middle class.[39] The "Sinhalese-only" official language issue which was instrumental in bringing the new leadership to power was a direct attack on the exclusiveness of the English-educated public servants, whose position and status depended on their command of the English language. The victorious politicians directed some appeals to the lower levels of the public service, but in their self-professed concern for the rural villagers and traditional culture there was little to attract the urban and westernized members of the upper levels of the bureaucracy. In addition, Government

523

policies aimed at compensating for past disadvantages suffered by the Sinhalese and Buddhists alienated some of the numerous Tamil and Christian members of the public service.

Although conditions for a clash of interests seem to have existed since 1956, tensions between the higher public servants and the political leadership were not apparent until 1960, possibly because the entire country was preoccupied with the communal strife and political instability. After the elections of 1960, increasing evidence of tensions appeared.[40] Bureaucrats came under attack by Government M.P.s for disloyalty to the Government and openly aiding the political opposition.[41] The 1960 election manifesto of the Government party threatened a thorough reorganization of the public service.[42] A resolution at the party's 1961 annual conference urged the Prime Minister to eliminate "sabotage" of the Government's programs by the bureaucracy.[43] An article in a party publication claimed that the dismissal of all public servants who were disloyal to the Government was the most serious task facing the Government and asserted that "our country can prosper only if we completely destroy the lazy, disloyal or corrupt public servant. . . ."[44]

The response of the bureaucrats to the political interference in administration and mounting attacks by politicians has remained somewhat ambiguous. Many have attempted to placate the apparently hostile political environment and embrace the emergent nationalist and populist movement. Some have sought refuge in the glorification of the period of British colonial rule. A few of the most embittered have expressed regret over the failure of an attempted coup d'etat staged by a group of military and police officers in January 1962.[45] The most common reaction, however, has been what the Salaries and Cadre Commission called a "general deterioration in the output and efficiency of the public service," evident in "absenteeism and unpunctuality, lack of interest, and indifference towards work."[46] The present state of the public service led the Governor-General to speak in bewilderment of the decline in bureaucratic integrity and morale from colonial standards.[47]

CONCLUSION

Political animosity and interference appear to have damaged bureaucratic morale and impaired the effectiveness of the public service, although the depth of the effects is difficult to gauge. While lingering influences of caste, communal, or family loyalties have probably reduced the rationality and impartiality of the bureaucracy, adjustment to changing circumstances in the aftermath of independence has been the principal source of stress in the contemporary bureaucracy. Such adjustment has been made difficult because of the wide separation of the bureaucracy, at least at the higher levels, from the rest of the society.

Although traditional influences are observable in the bureaucracy, the extent to which public servants above the bottom levels adopted Western habits and the English language, discarding the outward manifestations of indigenous culture in the process, made the bureaucracy vulnerable to the force of growing nationalist and populist political currents. The official language issue, an attack against the exclusive hold on the bureaucracy of the English-educated, was both the first major manifestation of aroused Sinhalese nationalism and the first challenge to the privileged position of the westernized elite. The disproportionate representation within the bureaucracy of ethnic and religious minorities made the bureaucracy and the incumbent bureaucrats a natural target of the newly awakened demands for recognition of the Sinhalese majority. The isolation of the westernized bureaucratic elite was increased by the sharp horizontal cleavages within the bureaucratic hierarchy.

The exclusive and elitist tendencies of the bureaucracy have roots in traditional society and the colonial era. Traditional concepts of status and privilege combined with colonial notions of an elite possessing a superior wisdom to open a wide gulf between the higher bureaucrats and the masses of their countrymen. The necessity for a knowledge of English for public employment served to reinforce the idea of exclusiveness, and westernization in language and manner of living became a symbol of elite status. It has been this exclusiveness and alienation which has, at least for the present, made difficult the adjustment of the Ceylonese bureaucracy to the political trends arising after independence.

NOTES

1. For the importance of indigenous social and cultural values and habits in influencing behavior within non-Western bureaucracies, despite formal acceptance of Western administrative organization and practices, see R. V. Presthus, "The Social Bases of Bureaucratic Organization," *Social Forces 38* (1959): 103-9; and R. W. Gable, "Culture and Administration in Iran," *Middle East Journal 8* (1959): 407-21.

2. Of the many indications of this preference, see M. A. Straus, "Mental Ability and Cultural Needs: A Psychological Interpretation of the Intelligence Test Performance of Ceylon University Entrants," *American Sociological Review 16* (1951):371-75; and B. Ryan, "Status, Achievement, and Education in Ceylon," *Journal of Asian Studies 20* (1961): 463-76.

3. *Report of the Salaries and Cadre Commission: 1961*, Part 1 (Sessional Paper 3—1961), p. 30.

4. R. Pieris, *Sinhalese Social Organization* (Colombo, 1956), pp. 169-79. See also R. Knox, *An Historical Relation of Ceylon* (first publ. 1681; Glasgow: James MacLehose, 1911), p. 106.

5. See Ryan, "Status, Achievement, and Education," pp. 467-69.

6. On westernization and English-language education as a source of class division, see *Sinhalese and Tamil as Official Languages*, Report of a Select Committee of the State Council (Sessional Paper 22—1946); *First Interim Report of the Official Languages Commission* (Sessional Paper 21—1951); G. C. Mendis, "Adult Franchise and Educational Reform," *University of Ceylon Review 2* (1944): 37-44; H. A. Passé, "The English Language in Ceylon," *University of Ceylon Review 1* (1943): 50-65; and Hector Abhayavardhana, et al., *The Role of the Western-Educated Elite* (Colombo, 1962). It should be noted that what is usually called the "English-speaking elite" does not include all persons with some command of English.

7. *Statistical Abstract of Ceylon:* 1960, p. 143.

8. *Report of the Salaries and Cadre Commission:* 1961, Part 1, pp. 49-50.

9. *Ibid.*, p. 50.

10. Ryan, "Status, Achievement, and Education," p. 473.

11. *Statistical Abstract of Ceylon:* 1960, p. 143.

12. Based on data from the *Ceylon Civil List* for the years 1948, 1952, 1955, 1957, and 1959.

13. *Ceylon Civil List,* 1959.

14. *Report of the Salaries and Cadre Commission:* 1961, Part 1, p. 161.

15. *Ceylon News,* 9 May 1963.

16. A useful history of education in Ceylon during the British period which frequently mentions the connection between public employment and education is contained in H. A. Wyndham, *Native Education* (London, 1933), pp. 33-36.

17. Ryan, "Status, Achievement, and Education."

18. See C. R. Hensman, ed., *The Public Services and the People* (Colombo, 1963), p. 40.

19. This discussion is based on S. J. Tambiah, "Ethnic Representation in Ceylon's Higher Administrative Services, 1870-1946," *University of Ceylon Review 13* (1955): 113-34.

20. For a perceptive discussion of communalism as a product of competition for public service employment, see G. C. Mendis, *Ceylon Today and Yesterday* (Colombo, 1957), pp. 97-107.

21. Ceylon Senate, *Parliamentary Debates,* vol. 10, p. 608.

22. See I. D. S. Weerawardana, *Ceylon General Election:* 1956 (Colombo, 1960), pp. 1-15, 98-109; W. H. Wriggins, *Ceylon: Dilemmas of a New Nation* (Princeton, 1960), pp. 228-70, 337-42.

23. *Report of the Salaries and Cadre Commission:* 1961, Part 2 (Sessional Paper 4—1961), p. 11.

24. Sir Ivor Jennings, "Race, Religion and Economic Opportunity in the University of Ceylon," *University of Ceylon Review 2* (1944): 2-4; *Statistical Abstract of Ceylon:* 1954, p. 142.

25. *Ceylon Daily News,* 28 May 1962.

26. *Final Report of the National Education Commission:* 1961 (Sessional Paper 17—1962), pp. 152-53.

27. This phenomenon was noted in the *Report of the Kandyan Peasantry Commission* (Sessional Paper 18—1951), p. 37. A discussion of the impact of caste on administration is contained in B. Ryan, *Caste in Modern Ceylon* (New Brunswick, N.J., 1953), pp. 323-29.

28. *Ceylon News,* 13 September 1962.

29. This is based on the report of a well-informed and reliable informant, but by its nature cannot be confirmed.

30. E. Tennent, *Ceylon: An Account of the Island, 2,* 3d ed. (London, 1859), p. 157.

31. E.g. the plight of a low-caste Colonization Officer is described in B. H. Farmer, *Pioneer Peasant Colonization in Ceylon* (London, 1957), p. 303.

32. *Ceylon Observer,* 31 January 1962.

33. On political trends through the 1956 election, see Wriggins, *Ceylon.* Recent political change is treated at length in R. N. Kearney, "Ceylon: A Study in Political Change" (Ph.D. diss., University of California, Los Angeles, 1963).

34. See *Report of the Salaries and Cadre Commission:* 1961, Part 2, pp. 101-2.

35. These views of the changing role of the M.P. represent conclusions from lengthy conversations with several dozen M.P.s, confirmed by observation of contacts between M.P.s and their constituents in the lobby of the Parliament Building, government administrative offices, and the homes of M.P.s.

36. *Ceylon News,* 10 January 1963.

37. *Ibid.,* 8 November 1962.

38. E.g. see *Reports of the Parliamentary Bribery Commission,* 1959-60 (Parliamentary Series no. 1, Fifth Parliament).

39. See Wriggins, *Ceylon* pp. 326-69; Mendis, *Ceylon Today and Yesterday,* pp. 117-24.

40. In addition to the indications noted below, see Hensman, ed., *Public Services and the People.* An episode related in Parliament by one M.P. suggests an attitude toward the politicians which is not uncommon in the higher levels of the public service. When the M.P. demanded of a public servant the reason for a shortage of water buffaloes, he was told the shortage existed because "the buffaloes are now in Parliament." Ceylon House of Representatives, *Parliamentary Debates, 48,* p. 2,738.

41. *Ceylon Observer,* 5 November 1961; Ceylon House of Representatives, *Parliamentary Debates, 39,* p. 375.

42. *Srī Lankā Nidahas Pakshayē Mäthivarana Prakāsanaya:* 1960 [Sri Lanka Freedom Party's Election Manifesto: 1960] (Colombo, 1960), p. 18.

43. Resolutions Presented to the Sri Lanka Freedom Party Annual

Conference on 2 December 1961, at Ratnapura (mimeo.).

44. *Srī Lankā Nidahas Pakshayā Dasavāni Sānvathsarika Kalāpaya:* 1961 [Sri Lanka Freedom Party Tenth Anniversary Number: 1961] (Colombo, 1961), p. 174.

45. These varied reactions were encountered among public servants during 1961 and 1962. See also Hensman, ed., *Public Services and the People*; and Abhayavardhana, *Western-Educated Elite*, pp. 3-46.

46. *Report of the Salaries and Cadre Commission:* 1961, Part 2, p. 100.

47. *Ceylon Observer,* 17 May 1962.

SUGGESTIONS FOR FURTHER READING
PART SEVEN: THE ELITES, PARTIES, MILITARY, AND BUREAUCRACY AND POLITICAL DEVELOPMENT

Ashford, Douglas E. *The Elusiveness of Power: The African Single-Party State.* Cornell Research Papers in International Studies, no. 3. Ithaca: Cornell University Press, 1965.

Bienen, Henry. *The Military Intervenes: Case Studies in Political Development.* New York: Russell Sage Foundation, 1968.

Carter, Gwendolen, ed. *African One-Party States.* Ithaca: Cornell University Press, 1962.

Finer, S. E. *The Man on Horseback: The Role of the Military in Politics.* New York: Praeger Publishers, 1962.

Fisher, Sydney N., ed. *The Military in Middle Eastern Society and Politics.* Columbus: Ohio State University Press, 1963.

Gutteridge, William. *Armed Forces in New States.* New York: Oxford University Press, 1962.

Hodgkin, T. *African Political Parties.* Baltimore: Penguin Books, 1961.

Huntington, Samuel P. *The Soldier and the State: The Theory and Politics of Civil-Military Relations.* New York: Vintage Books, 1957.

Hurewitz, J. C. *Middle East Politics: The Military Dimension.* New York: Praeger Publishers, 1969.

Janowitz, Morris. *The Military in the Political Development of New Nations: An Essay in Comparative Analysis.* Chicago: University of Chicago Press, 1964.

Johnson, John J. *The Military and Society in Latin America.* Stanford: Stanford University Press, 1964.

Johnson, John J., ed. *The Role of the Military in Underdeveloped Countries.* Princeton: Princeton University Press, 1962.

LaPalombara, Joseph, ed. *Bureaucracy and Political Development.* Princeton: Princeton University Press, 1963.

LaPalombara, Joseph, and Weiner, Myron, eds. *Political Parties and Political Development.* Princeton: Princeton University Press, 1966.

Mackenzie, W. J. M., and Robinson, Kenneth, eds. *Five Elections in Africa.* New York: Oxford University Press, 1960.

McWilliams, Wilson C., ed. *Garrisons and Government: Politics and the Military in New States.* San Francisco: Chandler Publishing Co., 1967.

Riggs, Fred W. *Administration in Developing Countries: The Theory of the Prismatic Society.* Boston: Houghton Mifflin, 1964.

Vatikiotis, P. J. *The Egyptian Army in Politics: Pattern for New Nations?* Bloomington: Indiana University Press, 1961.

Welch, Claude E., Jr., ed. *Soldier and State in Africa: A Comparative Analysis of Military Intervention and Political Change.* Evanston: Northwestern University Press, 1970.

Zolberg, Aristide R. *Creating Political Order: The Party-States of West Africa.* Chicago: Rand McNally, 1966.

Zonis, Marvin. *The Political Elite of Iran.* Princeton: Princeton University Press, 1971.